JAPANESE
WOMEN WRITERS

Japanese
Women Writers

A BIO-CRITICAL
SOURCEBOOK

Edited by
Chieko I. Mulhern

GREENWOOD PRESS
Westport, Connecticut
London

Library of Congress Cataloging-in-Publication Data

Japanese women writers : a bio-critical sourcebook / edited by Chieko
  I. Mulhern.
      p.   cm.
    Includes bibliographical references and index.
    ISBN 0–313–25486–9
    1. Women authors, Japanese—Biography.   2. Japanese literature—
  Women authors—History and criticism.   I. Mulhern, Chieko Irie.
  PL725.J37   1994
  895.6'099287—dc20   94–617

British Library Cataloguing in Publication Data is available.

Library of Congress Catalog Card Number: 94–617
ISBN: 0–313–25486–9

First published in 1994

Greenwood Press, 88 Post Road West, Westport, CT 06881
An imprint of Greenwood Publishing Group, Inc.

Printed in the United States of America

The paper used in this book complies with the
Permanent Paper Standard issued by the National
Information Standards Organization (Z39.48–1984).

10 9 8 7 6 5 4 3 2 1

CONTENTS

PREFACE

This volume aims to serve a tandem purpose: first, as a bio-critical reference book to provide cultural and literary insights into the lives and works of major Japanese women writers; and second, as a guide to comparative studies of Japanese women from various perspectives, focusing, for example, on life course, career pattern, social mobility, historical evolution, gender myth, cultural paradigms, feminine ideology, familial roles, and self-image.

The wide-ranging, in-depth coverage encompasses fifty-eight women writers from the 9th century to the present. All of them fall into the category of ''mainstream'' writers in that they occupy prominent places in Japan's literary history rather than reigning in a subgenre of ''women's literature,'' as female writers of other countries have been obliged to do in the past. In fact, all but a few recently rediscovered premodern diarists and possibly one modern writer are well known to the Japanese general public, if not exactly widely read today.

The following criteria were applied in selecting each writer: (1) her work was already available in English as a translation or an original writing, including partial publications and quotes in dissertations; (2) she was a subject of study by Western scholarship, or a willing scholar was found to do original research on her and write an entry in English; (3) her works seemed quite likely to appear in translation before long; and (4) her works were deemed potentially of great interest to Western scholars and general readers.

The Chronology, listing the fifty-eight writers in order of their birth dates, shows inevitable gaps. The Japanese writing system is generally traced back to the reign of Suiko, Japan's first female *tennō* (emperor, sovereign: thirty-third in the imperial genealogy, reign 592–628), when the imported Chinese characters came into practical use under official endorsement. Major literary works are extant from the Nara period (710–94), but they consist of imperial histories, local gazeteers, and a massive collection of poetry known as *Manyōshū*. A sizable number of women, ranging from sovereigns and empresses to housewives and rural maidens, have extant poems, including some superb ones, attributed to them, but there is not enough bio-critical material on any single woman poet to corroborate the attribution or to make up an entry in this reference volume.

Japan's literature came to its first full bloom in the aristocratic Heian period (794–1192), centering on the imperial court in Kyoto. Fiction in the form of long narratives and poetic tales attained a consummate form culminating in *The Tale of Genji* by Murasaki Shikibu. Unfortunately, all other Heian narratives are anonymous, and bio-data on women, even the female members of the aristocracy, are nearly nonexistent. Just recently some Japanese scholars began to apply Western methods of stylistic analysis in an effort to determine the gender of the authors of important Heian narratives, but so far with no decisive results. Fortunately, however, the importance of the nonfiction works known to be by women belies their small numbers and the paucity of their biographical sources.

Women serving or presiding in the higher circles at court in Kyoto or in the households of samurai nobles sustained the traditional arts of poetry and diary-memoirs well into the medieval Kamakura period (1192–1333) under the shogunate, located in Kamakura, not far from today's Tokyo. The Muromachi period (1336–1573), however, provided few opportunities for women to participate in literary activities. The urbanized samurai aristocrats ruling from the Muromachi shogunate in Kyoto patronized the male-only troupes of the newly matured Noh theater; Zen monks produced Chinese poems and ink paintings; and male intellectuals wrote essays that would become known as the "recluse literature." Itinerant nuns, as well as street entertainers and monks, are known to have created the narrative genre called *otogizōshi* (richly illustrated short stories). Some four hundred of these popular tales are extant in picture scroll or printed booklet forms, but few bear the names of the author or the painter.

The feudal Edo period (1600–1868) saw commercial publishing houses build great fortunes and professional writers emerge to make a living by the pen (actually, brush) for the first time in Japan's history. But the repressive Tokugawa shogunate severely restricted the personal conduct and geographical movement of the populace so that women were, in effect, excluded from participating in poetic gatherings at which haiku poems were composed. It was also beyond women's means to author works in the explosively popular new genres, such as the business fiction depicting the successes and failures of commercial enterprises, short stories set in the pleasure quarters, the multivolume adventure romances, and plays for the sophisticated puppet theater or the all-male Kabuki theater.

Then, at the long last, in the Meiji period (1868–1912), following the Meiji Restoration of 1868, which launched Japan into the modern age, women with the benefit of advanced education beyond the newly implemented compulsory elementary school found fiction writing to be one of a few means to earn money or assert social opinions. In the Taishō period (1912–26), flooded with Western ideas ranging from democracy, socialism, and liberalism to pessimism and anarchism, women founded schools, published women's magazines, went abroad to study or work, formed literary societies, allied with international organizations, and joined radical movements. Many went on to win fiction awards for works incorporating such life experiences.

The early part of the Shōwa period (1926–89), particularly the prewar and wartime years leading to Japan's defeat in 1945, suffers from the ravages of the physical and mental persecution by the thought-control police, extreme censorship, and coerced cooperation with war efforts. While male writers were forced to suspend literary activities in military service, in prison, or in war propaganda media, some women writers honed their realistic techniques by observing the social conditions and depicting them in what would become the classics of proletarian literature, even as they worked for wages and carried on radical underground programs for class and gender equality, in the absence of their male comrades.

During the first two postwar decades, many women born in the Shōwa period made highly acclaimed literary debuts and heralded the onset of a neo-Heian phenomenon, with female authors' prominent presence in the mainstream of Japanese literature becoming a norm again. The rate of their success has been accelerating ever since to the extent that women have won fully a half, if not more, of the leading literary awards in the last twenty years. Their numbers are swelling fast, with ever younger members joining the ranks to contribute new popular trends, fresh subject matter, ethnic perspectives, and cross-genre techniques. Some of them, such as the three youngest writers covered by this volume, are all but revolutionizing the concept of literature itself, each in her ingenious way.

The majority of the fifty-eight included here are poets and novelists or authors of classical narrative fiction, but the list includes premodern diarists as well as modern dramatists, television scriptwriters, and movie scenario writers. Twenty-four were living as of 1994 and publishing works in numerous monthly fiction magazines, newspapers, weekly news journals, and other national media. This volume aims to be as comprehensive as possible under the circumstances but does not attempt to be inclusive.

More and more works by Japanese women have been coming out in English translations in recent years, and the number of doctoral dissertations on Japanese women writers is notably increasing—welcome trends indeed for specialists and Western general readers. By now there are more potential subjects than one reference book can hope to accommodate with substantial coverage. Enough major writers to fill another volume had to be left out of our list mainly for logistical reasons, such as the absence of a scholar willing and able to take on the particular writer or lack of accessible primary sources and research material at the present time.

Each writer is listed under her full name, given in the Japanese order, with surname first wherever possible. Exceptions are nearly all of the fifteen premodern women, who are historically identified only by pseudonyms, sobriquets,

titles of their kinsmen, or their relationship to male family members, with confusing versions of their appellations in existence. The name used in the entry
heading here represents the contributor's informed choice or the one deemed
easiest for future researchers to locate in Japanese encyclopedic sources. Modern
writers are referred to by their pen names or real names most often used in their
published works, regardless of changes in their legal names through adoption,
marriage, and divorce.

Each entry is article-length, packing much more substantial information and
analysis than a simple enumeration of key dates and facts. Detailed discussion
of the subject's life and works illuminates relevant historical backgrounds, the
literary climate of her time, and reevaluation of her accomplishments in the light
of multidiscipline insights gained from the latest literary, gender-related, cross-
cultural, and comparative studies.

Entries generally consist of five sections. "Life" chronicles the writer's life
course, focusing on factors formative to her character, personality, familial roles,
interpersonal relationships, aspirations, and literary training. In the least-
documented premodern cases, this section considers genealogies, official records, and ongoing controversies among scholars over the interpretation of
whatever few extant sources there are. "Career" traces the evolution of the
writer's career course, touching also on sociohistorical forces conducive to her
emergence and success. For some of the premodern women, this section examines the legends that have grown around their life or famous works and that
exerted lasting influences on Japan's literary history and popular imagination
through the ages.

The "Major Works" section introduces publications judged to be representative or most significant of the opus in terms of such measures as artistic originality, literary and social honors won, possible interest for Western scholars in
other disciplines, and feasibility for translation. Each work is analyzed in depth
and in the broader perspectives of literary history, native and foreign influences,
impact on society, and artistic merits. Extensive quotations are provided where
no published translations are available as yet, or where the contributor needed
her/his own versions for specific analytical approaches. Most of the whole poems
and narrative passages from novels, for which few venues of publication exist
at this time, are appearing in English for the first time here, constituting precious
primary sources.

"Translated Works" covers the English editions, whether minor works or
part of an acclaimed work. This section can serve as a guide in classroom
teaching and also enhance reading enjoyment with poignant explication of issues
and the work's significance.

"Bibliography" lists the subject's works in foreign language publications,
followed by critical writings on her in English. Some of the entries cite few
items or older references only, but they represent all that exist at this time or
that have been found through the best effort of the contributor and the editor.
Earlier in the sections within the text, each work under discussion is identified

by its original Japanese title in romanization and its literal translation, but in the Bibliography, multiple titles of the same work may appear as given in the published editions, sometimes bearing little resemblance to the original.

As major additions and reassignments of entries became necessary during preparation of this book, some contributors generously took on extra assignments on short notice and produced amazing results far beyond my expectations. Many of the entries were completed as early as 1987, and some as recently as 1992. The bio-data and bibliographies have since been updated to the best of our abilities and knowledge.

I have been greatly impressed and encouraged by the interest in this reference book project shown by scholars and students over the years. No other volume of its kind exists to date in English or in Japanese. Japan specialists researching modern writers can benefit, as I have, from a timely Japanese publication, *Gendai josei bungaku jiten* (Dictionary of Modern Women Writers, ed. Sadataka Muramatsu and Sumiko Watanabe, Tokyo: Tokyo-dō, 1990). But I have found no Japanese compendium on premodern women, writers or otherwise.

I wish to express my profound respect and gratitude to the authors of the entries, whose tireless, high-caliber endeavors have brought this project to completion.

Chieko I. MULHERN

BIO-CRITICAL ENTRIES

A/B ──────────────────────

ABUTSU-NI (1222?–83), poet, memoirist. Real name: unknown.

Life: The biological parents of Abutsu-ni (the Nun Abutsu) are unknown, but she was adopted at an early age by Taira no Norishige, who served as the governor of the provinces of Tōtōmi and Sado, held the post of Commander of the Right Gate Guards (*Uemon no kami*) and rose to Junior Fifth Rank Lower Grade. In her youth she was known as Ankamon-in Echizen, Ankamon-in Uemon no Suke, and Ankamon-in Shijō, indicating that she served as a lady-in-waiting to Empress Ankamon-in (1209–83). Other sobriquets with place name associations, such as Saga Zenni (the Saga Nun) and Hokurin Zenni (the Hok-urin Nun), were used in referring to her, even after she acquired the pseudonym Abutsu-ni, by which she is known today.

It is not clear when Abutsu entered court service, but she was probably quite young, perhaps in her teens. Her reputation as a poet may have been instrumental in securing a court appointment. While Abutsu was at court, she was involved in love affairs that resulted in the birth of three children. Her eldest and second sons, known as Ajari and Rishi, both became members of the Buddhist clergy. Her daughter, known as Ki Naishi, was a lady-in-waiting to Shin'yōmeimon-in (1262–96), the consort of Emperor Kameyama (1249–1305; r. 1259–74). Ki Naishi bore a child to then Retired Emperor Kameyama while in service.

It is believed that Abutsu met Fujiwara Tameie (1198–1275), the son of poet-critic Fujiwara Teika (1162–1241) and heir to the Nijō school of poetry, when she was commissioned to make a copy of *The Tale of Genji*. Abutsu's reputation as a *Genji* scholar is believed to have led to her inclusion in the ambitious project, and it is likely that Abutsu became intimate with Tameie at this time, when she was still in her thirties and he already in his fifties. According to the diary *Saga no kayoi* (The Saga Road) by scholar-poet Asukai Masaari (fl. ca. 13th c.), Abutsu had earned a reputation as a scholar among her contemporaries and was living in Saga with Tameie and presenting a series of learned lectures on *The Tale of Genji* during the Bun'ei era (1264–75).

Abutsu is best remembered for her artistically fruitful relationship with Tameie, but no evidence survives to ascertain if she ever became Tameie's principal wife. It is clear that she played a vital role in his twilight years by bearing Tameie two sons: Tamesuke (1263–1328), the founder of the Reizei school of poetry, and Tamemori (1265–1328).

Abutsu capitalized on Tameie's affection for her and her sons in an attempt to secure for her offspring a place in the poetic hierarchy after his death. She took possession of some critical texts that had been handed down to Tameie from Teika and used them to teach the five-year-old Tamesuke. Further, Abutsu tried to convince Tameie to revise his will to bequeath to Tamesuke the Hosokawa estate, the most lucrative of his holdings, which had formerly been promised to Tameuji (1222–86), Tameie's eldest son, some forty years older than Tamesuke and by a different mother. Although Tameie died without having named an heir to the Hosokawa estate, Abutsu appealed to the authorities to mediate the settlement of the inheritance dispute.

On her son's behalf, Abutsu filed her appeal first to the imperial court and then to the Kamakura shogunate. In 1279, she journeyed to Kamakura to personally present her case to the shogunate; the trip and her stay in Kamakura yielded her best-known work, *Izayoi nikki* (The Journal of the Sixteenth-Night Moon). After enduring the hardships of the journey, she was to wait for years for a decision, but all in vain, for the shogunate was fighting for its own survival against repeated Mongol invasions of 1274 and 1281. She died in Kamakura in 1283 without learning the outcome of her suit.

Career: Ankamon-in (1209–83), whom Abutsu-ni served in her youth, was the granddaughter of Emperor Takakura (1161–81; r. 1168–80), the elder sister of Emperor Go-Horikawa (1212–34; r. 1221–32), and one of a few women in Japan's history to be granted the rank of Empress. Like many women writers of the Heian period (794–1185), Abutsu-ni graced the empress's salon and proceeded to advance in rank, for by all indications she was an educated and beautiful young woman whose poetic reputation had preceded her service at court.

Imperial anthologies include forty-eight of Abutsu's poems, the first three of which were selected by Tameie in his capacity as compiler of *Shokukokin wakashū* (Collection of Ancient and Modern Japanese Poetry Continued, 1265). Fifty-nine poems are found in the large private anthology *Fubokushō*, compiled in the years 1308–10 by a disciple of Tamesuke, Fujiwara Nagakiyo. Although today Abutsu is prominent more as a diarist-memoirist, her association with Tameie certainly elevated her status as a poet among her contemporaries. In addition to the approximately three hundred extant poems by Abutsu, the Matsudaira library has a recently discovered manuscript, *Ankamon-in no Shijō gohyakushū* (The Five Hundred Poem Sequence by Ankamon-in no Shijō), which has yet to be studied.

Abutsu was responsible for establishing the Reizei school of poetry on behalf of her son Tamesuke, who was only thirteen years old at the death of his father in 1275. From her travel diary, *Izayoi nikki,* it is clear that Abutsu was on friendly terms with members of the Kyōgoku branch of the family. During her stay in Kamakura, she frequently corresponded with the poet Kyōgoku Tameko (d. 1316?), the younger sister of the head of the Kyōgoku school of poetry, Kyōgoku Tamekane (1254–1332). Five exchanges of correspondence between Abutsu and Tameko are on record, and also a poetic exchange is recorded in her diary. They reveal a deep friendship between Abutsu and Tameko based on their mutual love of poetry.

Although Abutsu's career at court was short-lived, she led a rather controversial life. In *Utatane* (Dozing, ca. 1238), ostensibly written in retrospect by the young Abutsu, she cuts her own hair to take the tonsure after being jilted by her high-ranking lover. However, the symbolical renouncement of the world did not prevent Abutsu from bearing five children. An actual change in lifestyle more in keeping with that of a nun is more likely to have occurred after the death of Tameie in 1275.

Abutsu proved herself a nurturing mother in writing a poetic treatise, *Yoru no tsuru* (The Night Crane), to Tamesuke and an advisory letter, *Niwa no oshie* (Garden Instructions), to her daughter, Ki Naishi. As a protective mother, Abutsu also implored both the court and the shogunal government in Kamakura for a favorable ruling on the inheritance dispute on behalf of her son by Tameie. Besides being considered a competent scholar of the *Genji,* she was an independent woman referred to as *onna aruji* (female head of the household) after Tameie had taken Buddhist vows. Following Tameie in taking holy orders, she was called Abutsu.

Works in Translation: Utatane (Dozing, ca. 1238), memoir. There is some question about the authorship and the compositional time frame of *Utatane,* but it is generally agreed that it was written by Abutsu in retrospect at a time considerably earlier than the composition of *Izayoi nikki. Utatane* is a fairly short work with an intense focus on the psychological state of the narrator soon after she was abandoned by her lover, a high-ranking noble who was already married. Internal information regarding a trip to Tōtōmi in *Izayoi nikki* supports the attribution of *Utatane* to Abutsu's hand. One of Abutsu's first three poems to be represented in imperial anthologies appears in *Utatane* with a variant first line. Further, Abutsu records how touched she was when she returned to the Hamamatsu area in Tōtōmi and met the descendants of those she knew in her youth. Thus, it seems fairly safe to assume that Abutsu was the author of *Utatane.*

The work can be divided into two parts: the first part, resembling a memoir (*nikki*), deals with the lover and the immediate aftermath of their breakup in Kyoto in autumn; the second part, essentially a travelogue (*kikō*), describes the narrator's attempts to cope with her situation and begins with the narrator's abruptly cutting her own hair and setting out on foot from Kitayama (North Mountain) to a nunnery in Nishiyama (West). The narrator moves on to Higashiyama (East) and then back to Kitayama before accompanying her father to his post in Tōtōmi. However, after being in residence there for only one month, the narrator returns abruptly to Kyoto after hearing about the failing health of her nurse.

Threading through both parts of *Utatane* is the narrator's grief of having been jilted by her lover. The exploration into the devastation of the narrator's psyche is the unifying theme. *Utatane* contains a total of twenty-two poems interspersed throughout the prose text. Although the scale of the work is limited, *Utatane* has often been accorded more literary merit than *Izayoi nikki*.

Utatane lies well within the diary (*nikki bungaku*) tradition. Woven through the theme of the lonely lady are conventional images associated with a plaintive lover, such as the autumn moon, autumn dew, the inability to distinguish fantasy and reality, and the comparison of love to a dream, all familiar items in Heian *nikki*. This work defies convention and tradition, however, in its intense concentration on the narrator's unrestrained passion, which seems to border on obsession.

The composition date of *Utatane* is in dispute. Some scholars are convinced that it was written directly after the events described by the narrator. Others propose that the blending of disparate styles (i.e., lyrical, allusive passages in combination with plain descriptive styles) may indicate that the work was written at a time far removed from the events but with conscious effort to reproduce the psychological state of the narrator as closely as possible.

Immediacy is effected by the narrative mode's resembling an interior monologue that takes the reader inside the narrator's mind. Although retrospection and reflection may be detected in the work, judgmental statements are kept at a minimum to preserve this sense of immediacy, which is bolstered by the consonant narrative, showing that the narrator has no inkling of what will occur to her after the described events.

Izayoi nikki (The Journal of the Sixteenth-Night Moon, 1279–80), travelogue. With eighty-six poems, this work chronicles Abutsu's attempt to secure for her son the rights to the Hosokawa estate by appealing to the shogunal government. Hers was not the only succession dispute among the descendants of Teika: Tameie's two other sons, Tameuji (1222–86) and Tamenori (1226–79), and their respective offspring, Tameyo (1250–1338) and Tamekane (1254–1332), were struggling for primacy in the poetic hierarchy. Tameuji and Tameyo safeguarded the Nijō school, while Tamenori and Tamekane broke away to establish the rival Kyōgoku school of poetry. Abutsu's friendship with Tamekane's younger sister, Tameko, probably helped motivate her to set up the Reizei school of poetry for her son.

Izayoi nikki can be divided into four parts. An introductory section explaining Abutsu's intention for traveling from the capital to Kamakura features poetic exchanges with all five of her children and expresses sorrow at parting. The second part on her two-week trip to Kamakura contains fifty-five poems in highlights of her daily entries. Some vague references to dates and titles in this section led scholars to speculate that the work was written in retrospect rather than concurrently. The third part consists of Abutsu's correspondences with people in the capital while she was in Kamakura, an epistolary section dotted with poetic exchanges with no unifying structure. The final part, with no relation to the first three parts, is made up of a long poem (*chōka*), the antiquarian form popular in the *Man'yōshū* period (Collection of Ten Thousand Leaves, ca. 759), most unusual to be employed in the 13th century.

During the Kamakura period, it became common practice for authors to give literary titles to their own creations, rather than leaving them to be called, say, the Abutsu-ni Collection, as had been the case in the past. Presumably Abutsu chose the titles for both *Utatane* and *Izayoi nikki,* in which several times the title word appears within the respective text. In the manner of *Tosa nikki* (The Tosa Journal, ca. 935), which may have served as a poetry handbook, *Izayoi nikki* could have been intended as a handbook to guide her children in poetic composition. Aside from possible pedagogical functions, the *Izayoi nikki* is by no means a great literary work, with no unifying theme or focus to hold the attention of the reader for any great length of time.

Nevertheless, *Izayoi nikki* is important to modern readers on several fronts. In literary history, the work provides an inside account of the dispute that shook the hereditary school of poetry (Mikosa, Mikohidari, later Nijō) established by Fujiwara Teika (1162–1241). Second, *Izayoi nikki* is one of the few travel diaries written by a woman in the Kamakura period. (The earliest example of a woman's travel diary is *Sarashina nikki,* written by Takasue's Daughter in the Heian period.) Third, the life of this unorthodox individual provides a fascinating look at the state of women in a period when men held hereditary headships in literary schools at court as well as in administrative posts in the shogunate. One of the last women to take up the tradition of autobiographical writing established in the 10th century with Michitsuna's Mother, Abutsu-ni fills a niche in literary history as an inheritor of a genre who faithfully adhered to its conventions yet managed to produce a work all her own befitting a new age.

BIBLIOGRAPHY

Translations and Critical Works

Aston, W. G. *A History of Japanese Literature.* Rutland, VT: Charles E. Tuttle, 1972.
Biographical Dictionary of Japanese Literature, S. V. "Abutsu-ni."
Brower, Robert, and Earl Miner. *Japanese Court Poetry.* Stanford, CA: Stanford University Press, 1961.
Carter, Steven D. *Waiting for the Wind: Thirty-Six Poets of Japan's Late Medieval Age.* New York: Columbia University Press, 1989.
Huey, Robert N. *Kyōgoku Tamekane: Poetry and Politics in Late Kamakura Japan.* Stanford, CA: Stanford University Press, 1989.
Keene, Donald. "Diaries of the Kamakura Period." *Japan Quarterly* 32.3 (1985): 286–89.

————. "Izayoi nikki" and "Utatane" in *Travelers of a Hundred Ages*. New York: Henry Holt, 1989.

Kōdansha Encyclopedia of Japan, S. V. "Abutsu-ni."

Konishi, Jin'ichi. *A History of Japanese Literature, Volume Three: The High Middle Ages*. Trans. Aileen Gatten. Ed. Earl Miner. Princeton, NJ: Princeton University Press, 1991.

McCullough, Helen Craig. *Classical Japanese Prose: An Anthology*. Stanford, CA: Stanford University Press, 1990.

Mamola, Claire Zebroski. "Abutsu Ni." In *Japanese Women Writers in English Translation: An Annotated Bibliography*. New York: Garland, 1989.

Miner, Earl. *An Introduction to Japanese Court Poetry*. Stanford, CA: Stanford University Press, 1968.

Miner, Earl, Hiroko Odagiri, and Robert E. Morrell. *The Princeton Companion to Classical Japanese Literature*. Princeton, NJ: Princeton University Press, 1985.

Putzar, Edward. *Japanese Literature: A Historical Outline*. Tuscon: University of Arizona Press, 1973.

Reischauer, Edwin O. "The Izayoi Nikki." *Translations from Japanese Literature*. Cambridge: Harvard University Press. 1951.

Wallace, John R. "Fitful Slumbers: Nun Abutsu's *Utatane*." *Monumenta Nipponica* 43.4 (1988): 391–416.

S. Yumiko HULVEY

ARIYOSHI Sawako (1931–84) novelist, playwright, play director, translator. Real name: Ariyoshi Sawako.

Life: Ariyoshi was born into an old family of landed gentry in Wakayama City that had enjoyed prestige and power for generations. When she was four years old, her father, a bank employee, was transferred to Tokyo and then to Java. Ariyoshi was consequently enrolled in a Japanese elementary school in Batavia. She was a sickly child, and, since Japanese children's books were not easily available in Batavia, she spent her time in bed reading the collections of fiction by Natsume Sōseki (1867–1916) and Arishima Takeo (1878–1923) that belonged to her father. Returning to Japan in 1940, she entered an elementary school in Tokyo. The capital was to become her home for the rest of her life, except for a few years of wartime evacuation in Wakayama. Though her exposure to the tradition and culture of rural Wakayama was quite limited, this particular region came to play an important role in her career: some of her major novels are set in rural Wakayama. Another important formative influence was her mother, an enthusiastic supporter of the Seitō-sha (the Bluestocking Society), a feminist literary group that began to advocate women's liberation in 1911. The majority of Ariyoshi's protagonists are women who face adversities but ultimately succeed in winning emotional and financial independence from men. The love-hate relations between mother and daughter are a common theme threading her works.

Ariyoshi majored in English literature at Tokyo Christian Women's University. At the same time she read many works by Japanese proletarian writers such as Kobayashi Takiji (1903–33) and Miyamoto Yuriko (1899–1951). The influence of proletarian literature can be detected in the wide range of Ariyoshi's protagonists, who include poverty-stricken weavers and tangerine growers, inhabitants of "forgotten islands" dotting Japan's sea-lanes, geisha, and other performers of traditional arts who, by adhering to their age-honored ways of living, are forced to occupy only marginal places in highly modernized contemporary Japan. Ariyoshi was never an overtly political writer, but her sympathy for the socially oppressed and her objection to wars are explicit in her works. More significant, however, was her encounter with Kabuki theater and other forms of traditional Japanese performing arts. She later wrote: "What motivated me to write . . . was my encounter with Kabuki. After returning from a colony— beautiful on surface only—to spend the days of disillusionment in Japan in the state of 'national emergency' and in its aftermath, I was saved by Kabuki, that greatly stimulated my aesthetic sense." She subsequently joined a Kabuki study group at the university and published in *Engekikai* (Theater World) a series of prizewinning essays on Kabuki actors. She eventually became a consultant for the magazine and began to study other forms of traditional Japanese arts such as the 14th-century *Nō,* the 18th-century puppet theater called Bunraku, the tea ceremony, and haiku.

Upon graduation in 1952, Ariyoshi went to work for a publishing company. She also joined the literary group Shin-shisō (New Ideology) and wrote her first short story, "Rakuyō no fu" (The Song of the Setting Sun, 1954) for a journal, *Hakuchigun* (A Horde of Idiots). During the same year, she took a job as secretary for Azuma Tokuho (b. 1909), a prominent Kabuki-style woman dancer, and assisted her with dance recitals of the Azuma Kabuki Troupe. In 1956, Ariyoshi made a sensational professional debut with a short story, "Jiuta" (Ballad), by earning the Bungakkai New Writers' Award and a nomination for the prestigious Akutagawa Award, which launched her on her literary career to become one of the most prolific and versatile writers in postwar Japan. She also wrote stage adaptations of her own fiction works and directed them herself.

In her busy schedule, she managed to find time for travel abroad. In 1960, she spent a year at Sarah Lawrence College as a Rockefeller scholar and traveled to Europe and the Middle East before returning to Japan. Her experience in the United States yielded two lengthy novels dealing with social issues such as racism and imperialism. She revisited the United States for research in 1965 and again in 1971. During the last visit, she was a guest lecturer at the University of Hawaii, where she taught a semester course on late Tokugawa literature. She spent five months in New York, Paris, and London before returning to Japan. Ariyoshi was also a frequent visitor to China. She was invited by the Chinese government in 1961, along with critics Hirano Ken (1907–78) and Kamei Katsuichirō (1907–66) and novelist Inouye Yasushi (1907–91). She revisited Peking for six months in 1962 and again in 1965, this time to study Chinese Catholicism. Accepting another invitation from the Chinese government, she flew to the country in 1974 as well but, seeing the sad effects of the cultural revolution on Chinese writers, hurried back to Japan after only four days. She returned to China in 1987, however, and lived in communes, sharing with young Chinese farmers her concerns regarding the use of chemical fertilizers. Moreover, she visited Cambodia and Indonesia, as well as New Guinea, where she spent a month with her woman friend, an anthropologist who was studying aborigines. Ariyoshi's interest in women's issues also took her in 1978 to France, where she met the French writer Benoite Groult, whose work she later translated into Japanese and published under the title *Saigo no shokuminchi* (The Last Colony).

In 1961, Ariyoshi married Jin Akira, impresario running the Friends of the Arts Enterprise, and gave birth to a daughter, Tamao. The marriage, however, ended in divorce after a mere two years. The cause of their split was never made public, but the difficulty of holding a career while living with her in-laws is considered to have played a significant part.

Ariyoshi's intense lifestyle unfortunately exacerbated the health problems she had suffered since childhood. Particularly after a lengthy hospitalization for the treatment of malaria contracted in New Guinea in 1968, she was plagued by chronic insomnia, among other illnesses. She tried to overcome the problem by exerting herself in physical exercise but, by 1978, her work had slowed down considerably due largely to her poor health. She never recovered from the slump until her death in 1984 at the age of fifty-three. The official cause of death was cardiac arrest, but many years of dependency on sedatives and alcohol to ease the problem of insomnia undoubtedly contributed to her untimely death. It is indeed ironical if Ariyoshi, who had fought adamantly against chemical pollutants, did indeed succumb to chemical dependency.

Career: Ariyoshi was incredibly prolific. Suffice it here to list only the works of greatest significance. She was little known until her debut with "Ballad" in 1956 at the age of twenty-five. Encouraged by its enormous success, she followed it up with a flood of works in the same year: a dance drama—*Aya no tsuzumi* (A Damask Drum; adapted into a play); a *jōruri* play for the puppet theater—*Yukiya konkon sugata mizuumi* (Crossing Over a Snowy Lake; performed in the same year); and four short stories—"Kirikubi" (A Severed Head); "Shiro no aitō" (A White Requiem); "Masshiroke no ke" (White All Over); and "Buchiinu" (A Spotted Dog). Her pace picked up, if anything, through the 1950s: in 1957 two novels—*Shojo rentō* (Maiden's Prayers) and *Dangen* (A Broken Koto String); six short stories, including "Akachoko monogatari" (The Story of a Red Sake Cup); "Shiroi ōgi" (A White Fan; later retitled "Hakusenshō"), nominated for the Naoki Award; and a television drama, "Ishi no niwa" (A Stone Garden; later adapted into a stage play), written for NHK (the powerful national television network), which received the Fine Arts Festival Award. In 1958, she demonstrated her versatility by publishing a weekly-magazine serial novel, *Geisha warutsu Itariāno* (Geisha Waltz Italian-Style); "Eguchi no sato" (The Village of Eguchi), featuring a French priest and a Japanese courtesan; "Uminari" (The Sound of the Sea), which captures the sad life of an aged ex-politician; "Ka to chō" (A Mosquito and a Butterfly), a love-hate story of a blind masseur and his wife; "Yakusha haigyō" (No Longer an Actor), about a Kabuki actor whose career and relationship with a woman were destroyed by his manipulative master; and eight other short stories. In 1959, she earned the Ministry of Education Fine Art Festival Award for *Homura* (Flames), a *Gidayū* play broadcast on NHK Radio. For these brilliant accomplishments in both literature and theater, she was hailed as a "true genius." Ariyoshi rounded out her first productive half-decade that year with one of her major novels, *Kinokawa* (The River Ki; made into a film in 1966), in addition to "Namayoi" (Half-Drunk); "Watashi wa wasurenai" (I Will Never Forget), the first of her "social issues" stories about Japan's "forgotten islands" and their inhabitants struggling for survival in premodern living conditions; and six other short stories. While at Sarah Lawrence College, she wrote "Kitō" (A Prayer) and "Shin onna daigaku" (The New Great Learning for Women), a contemporary version of the neo-Confucian precepts for women in feudal Japan.

In 1961, Ariyoshi published a short story, "Tomoshibi" (The Light), and began to write a novel, *Kōge* (Incense and Flowers; made into a play in 1963 and into a film in 1964), serialized in *Fujin Kōron* (Women's Forum) for one year. She earned both the *Fujin Kōron* Readers' Award and the *Shōsetsu Shinchō* Award. She also serialized "Heiten jikan" (The Closing Time) in the *Yomiuri Newspaper* for eight months. In addition, she published eight short stories, two of which are particularly outstanding: "Sambaba" (Three Old Women; later produced as a play) tells a sad, yet humorously bittersweet rivalry of three women, the wife, the mistress, and the sister of a prosperous businessman long since dead, forced to live together and care for each other during and after World War II, and "Onna-deshi" (Woman Disciples), on the other hand, portrays three women deeply in love with their Ikebana mentor, a master of modern flower arrangement. In 1962, a play, *Kōmyō Kōgō* (Empress Kōmyō), was produced on stage. The enormous success of *Sukezaemon yondaiki* (The Four Sukezaemons) was followed by two significant novels in 1963, *Aritagawa* (The River Arita) and *Hishoku* (Not Because of Color).

With the birth of her daughter and a divorce only six months later, 1964 proved a difficult year for Ariyoshi, but she nonetheless managed to publish two excellent novels, *Puerutoriko nikki* (Puerto Rican Diary) and *Ichi no ito* (The First String), which traces the life of a woman who adheres to her unchanging love for a man through drastic social changes and eventually helps him become one of the foremost *jōruri* artists. Of exceptionally high aesthetic quality, this work reveals Ariyoshi's profound knowledge of the world of traditional performing arts and her deep respect for, and criticism of, the rigid, uncompromising spirit of the artists.

The latter half of the 1960s was another busy, but highly productive, period, starting with "Hidakagawa" (The River Hidaka) and "Nyokan" (Women's House) in 1965 and crowned by *Hanaoka Seishū no tsuma* (Hanaoka Seishū's Wife; translated as *The Doctor's Wife* in English and *Kae* in French; made into a stage play and a film), which earned the prestigious Woman Writers' Award.

Ariyoshi herself adapted this 1966 novel into a four-act play and successfully directed its performances the following year; 1967 proved just as fertile. *Izumo no okuni* (Okuni of Izumo), about a 16th-century woman dancer, brought her both the *Fujin Kōron* Readers' Award and the Fine Art Award. *Fushin no toki* (The Time of Distrust; made into a film in 1968 and a play in 1969) exposes the dark side of contemporary life dictated by greed and deception. For *Umikura* (The Dark Sea), dealing with a planned U.S. missile base in Japan, Ariyoshi earned the *Bungei Shunjū* Readers' Award. *Akachoko* (A Red Sake Cup), written for Azuma Tokuho's stage production, won another Ministry of Education Fine Art Festival Award. Despite illness, Ariyoshi also managed to write *Onna futari no Nyūginia* (Two Women in New Guinea, 1968), a humorous reportage of her experiences in New Guinea; and *Mōkyōjo-kō* (On Lady Mōkyō, 1969), a memoirlike story about a legendary Chinese woman about whom she heard during her visit to China.

Ariyoshi's output in the 1970s was more unusual and ambitious, ranging from a collection of children's stories, *Kaminagahime* (The Long-Haired Princess, 1970), and a reportage, *Chūgoku tenshukyō 1965-nen no chōsa yori* (Catholicism in China: From My 1965 Research), to *Yūhigaoka sangōkan* (Yūhigaoka Building, Number Three), which depicts intricate relationships among housewives living in company housing, and *Furu Amerika ni sode wa nurasaji* (Never with Americans, 1970), a play depicting a prostitute who chooses death rather than entertaining the American sailors from Commodore Perry's "black ships" on the eve of Japan's modernization. Ariyoshi adapted *Narayamabushi-kō* (On the Ballad of Narayma, 1956), a novella about the ancient custom of abandoning old women in the mountains, into a play and directed it herself in 1971. The next year, she made great social and political impact with a best-seller novel, *Kōkotsu no hito* (The Twilight Years, 1972), which exposed the problems of the aged. She also translated with Elizabeth Miller *The Trial of the Catonsville Nine* (1970) by Daniel Berrigan (b. 1912), rewrote it into a play, and directed its performance.

After *Managoya Omine* (Omine of the Managoya Shop, 1973), a tale of a housewife who defies a life dictated by the feudal code of behavior, came *Boshi henyō* (The Mother-Daughter Transformation, 1973); *Ōgon densetsu* (The Golden Legend, 1974; the title later changed to *Kidogawa* [The River Kido], 1974), the best-selling "nonfiction novels," *Fukugō osen* (Compound Pollution, 1975) and "Fukugō osen sonogo" (Compound Pollution: A Follow-Up, 1977); and a play, *Nihonjin banzai* (Hurrah to the Japanese People, 1977). Despite poor health, she also managed to write *Ariyoshi Sawako no Chūgoku repōto* (Ariyoshi Sawako's Report on China, 1978) and serialized the novels *Akujo ni tsuite* (On an Evil Woman, 1978); *Kazunomiyasama otome* (Her Highness Kazunomiya, 1978), which won the Mainichi Cultural Prize; and *Kaimaku beru wa hanay-akani* (Merrily Sounds the Curtain-Time Bell, 1978), a mystery about the murder of an actress. Thereafter, Ariyoshi produced only two nonfiction works—*Nihon no shimajima: ima to mukashi* (Japanese Islands: Their Past and Present, 1981) and *Ariyoshi Sawaka to shichinin no spōtsuman* (Ariyoshi Sawako and Seven Sportsmen, 1984)—before her death in August 1984.

Major Works: 1. On Kishū women: *Kōge* (Incense and Flowers, 1961); *Sukezaemon yondai-ki* (The Four Sukezaemons, 1962); *Aritagawa* (The River Arita, 1963). The most representative of Ariyoshi's works are these novels, set in her birthplace of Wakayama, formerly the feudal domain of Kishū. Women in those stories are often metaphorized as rivers for their quiet but unlimited potential power for enrichment and destruction of life. Like the protagonists of *The River Ki* and *The Doctor's Wife* (see "Translated Works"), these women are bound to *Ie* (patriarchal families) and their traditions. The *Four Sukezaemons,* for instance, depicts contributions made by the wives of Sukezaemon I to IV to the unprecedented prosperity of their *Ie,* of their marital family that carries a curse to last for seven generations. With their wisdom and hard work, the women quietly lead their husbands to play major roles in achieving peace with neighboring provinces, developing an irrigation system, and pioneering in a new field of modern nutrition. They are the foundation of *Ie,* holding up their husbands, who are revered successively as its main pillar. The bond to *Ie* is also emphasized in *Incense and Flowers.* A major character leaves her *Ie* for the glamour of life in Tokyo. Her daughter is consequently forced to leave Kishū and becomes a geisha, while her mother works as a prostitute. With empathic eyes and a mature style, Ariyoshi captures in this work the love-hate relationship between the two women and their struggles for survival through the hardships of World War II and its aftermath. The daughter eventually succeeds in becoming a proprietress of a small but prosperous inn, but her dreams of marriage and a family remain unrealized. The heroine of *The River Arita,* on the other hand, begins her life with no link to *Ie.* As an infant and again as a child, she is twice washed away by the river and is raised by two families of tangerine growers in the region. She devotes herself to the trade, finds a happy marriage, and establishes the *Ie* of her own.

2. On career women: *Tsuremai* (Duet, 1963); *Midaremai* (Discordant Dance, 1966); *Shibazakura* (The Flocks, 1970); *Boke no hana* (The Quince, 1973). Many of Ariyoshi's protagonists are career women. The heroine of *Duet* and its sequel, *Discordant Dance,* for instance, is an artist of classical Japanese dance. She competes fiercely with her talented stepsister, and with leading disciples of her deceased husband, before emerging as the head of a large, prestigious school of dance. Demonstrating Ariyoshi's thorough knowledge not only of the performing art itself but also of complex human relations in this closed society, this work brings out the best of her aesthetic sensibility and storytelling ability. Another example that belongs to this category is a two-part novel, *The Flocks* and *The Quince.* The story traces the lives of two women from their teenage years as apprentice geishas to postwar years during which they become successful entrepreneurs. Ariyoshi places them at polar opposites; one, for instance, is an orphan, while the other is emotionally tied to her mother, who had sold her into the house of geisha. Similarly, the former is reserved and enduring,

while the latter is extroverted and exploitive. Yet they are bound together by love and resentment throughout the many years of hardship and triumph. The tension between the two and the detailed descriptions of the customs of this little-known society create in this work an aesthetic of superb quality.

3. On victimized women: *Boshi henyō* (The Mother-Daughter Transformation, 1973); *Akujo ni tsuite* (On an Evil Woman, 1978). Unlike the women previously described, some of Ariyoshi's heroines are victims of exploitation. *The Mother-Daughter Transformation,* for instance, portrays a young movie actress relentlessly exploited by the film industry. Although she is given leading roles in serious works, she is recognized not as an individual but as the replica of her actress mother in her youth. Moreover, she is overworked and deprived of freedom to socialize with young men. The intricate emotions of love, respect, resentment, and jealousy that link the mother and the daughter become dominated by profound fear and hatred when the daughter discovers that her screen partner, with whom she has fallen in love, is her mother's lover. She undergoes plastic surgery to erase all traces of resemblance to her mother and consequently comes to be considered an actress of no particular merit. Another woman in this category is the heroine of *On an Evil Woman,* an enormously successful entrepreneur who ends her life in a mysterious death. The accounts of her life given by twenty-seven persons drastically contradict each other, but the majority picture her as a deceptive, "evil" woman driven by greed, a victim of the materialism that characterizes contemporary Japan.

4. "Social-issue" novels: *Puerutoriko nikki* (Puerto Rican Diary, 1964); *Umikura* (The Dark Sea, 1968). An enthusiastic reader of proletarian literature in her youth, Ariyoshi wrote several stories that concern contemporary social issues, particularly after her first visit to the United States. Among them is *Puerto Rican Diary,* the protagonist of which is a Japanese student studying in a private American college for women. While on a field research trip to Puerto Rico with her classmates, she becomes keenly aware of racial prejudice among them, as well as of their imperialist attitude toward the economically deprived people of the island. Moreover, she witnesses the discriminations of the islanders by elite Puerto Ricans of Spanish origin. She leaves the island with a sad realization that democracy fails to function as long as economic exploitations exist among the peoples of the world. In *Umikura,* the eighty-year-old heroine represents Mikurajima, one of Japan's "forgotten islands," and its tradition. While younger inhabitants leave their island home because of the lack of job opportunities, she remains convinced that the entire population—some two hundred—can sustain their lives on the island by planting and selling trees, as their ancestors have done for generations. She adamantly refuses to consider a proposal that the island be made into a U.S. missile base. The reactions of other islanders, however, are more complex; many are attracted by the prospect of large monetary compensation. At the end, the authorities conclude that the island is worthless for the proposed use, leaving the islanders deeply disappointed and concerned

for other islands that may become the alternate targets of the military development.

Translated Works: 1. Short stories. "Jiuta" (Ballad, 1956). Featuring an aged *Jiuta* master who disowns his beloved daughter for marrying a Japanese American, this work presages Ariyoshi's representative works: it deals with the little-known society of artists working in the traditional Japanese theater; it relies on the literary device of dichotomies commonly found in "serious" literature; yet its style is that of "popular" literature. It demonstrates the author's empathy for people who are suffering, as well as her aesthetic sensibility and exceptional talent in storytelling. The dichotomies—for instance, of the old and the new, a man and a woman, love and hatred, and despair and joy—result in a fascinating tension.

"Eguchi no sato" (The Village of Eguchi, 1958). This is a rare story in which Ariyoshi exposes the hypocrisy of the conservative, elitist values held by Japanese Catholics. A beautiful geisha, Satoko, who comes to the church is their polar opposite, and a French priest defends her against the protests of his parishioners. Here, too, dichotomies—between the mundane and the beautiful, the arrogant and the innocent, the rich and the poor, and spirituality and flesh—play the key role in characterization and in the development of the main theme. Moreover, by creating a scene in which Satoko's dance enacts the story of a 12th-century courtesan of Eguchi who allows a night's lodging to the poet-priest Saigyō in his distress, Ariyoshi cleverly juxtaposes their relationship with that of the Catholic priest and Satoko. This literary device in particular gives the disturbing story a touch of exquisite beauty.

"Kitō" (Prayer, 1959). In the late 1950s, the Japanese people, who had become desensitized about the atomic bombing of Hiroshima and Nagasaki, were confronted with the new terror of the survivors' giving birth to babies with severe physical and mental defects. "Prayer" is a moving story that places this tragedy in its thematic center. It realistically captures the profound anxiety of a young survivor-mother and her extended family concerning the health of her son. He is a healthy, happy child but, like his mother, carries within him a susceptibility to radiation illness. A prayer for a nuclear-free world, this work should be of interest to those concerned about contemporary world issues, peace studies, psychology, and literature.

"Tomoshibi" (The Light, 1961). This pastoral work portrays the proprietress of a quiet little bar, an oasis, or *tomoshibi* (the light) in the darkness, on a busy street of the Ginza. Her thoughtfulness communicates to her clients, all ordinary office workers who enjoy moments of relaxation at her bar before returning home after a long day, and brings about a "miracle" to one of her employees who is self-conscious of her minor facial deformity. Revealing Ariyoshi's sensitivity to, and empathy for, working women and those who suffer, this is an enjoyable story.

"Sumi" (The Ink Stick, 1961). Featured in this work are two perfectionists, a woman artist of classic Japanese dance and an old male artisan who paints exquisite patterns on her costumes. Like the father and the daughter in "Ballad," they are bound together through their devotion to beauty. The man's device is india ink, and the woman gives life to his final products by means of her dance. Ariyoshi convincingly glorifies the power of art that transcends the dichotomies of the old and the young, male and female. With her painstakingly detailed description of the brilliant kimono material against the dark backdrop of the man's quiet passion for his dying art and his eventual death, Ariyoshi creates an aesthetic quality akin to *yūgen* (profound or mystic beauty).

2. Novels. *Kinokawa* (The River Ki, 1959). Spanning over sixty years from 1897 to 1958, this novel probes the meaning of *Ie* (the family) for the four generations of women living on the edge of the River Ki in Wakayama prefecture. The eldest woman is a personification of tradition, the core of which is the patriarchal family system. She is also the symbol of life instinct metaphorized by the river. Here Ariyoshi equates life with tradition. She also suggests that women are the major force in transmitting and refining the tradition. In order to substantiate this main theme, she creates the other three women. The heroine Hana is a faithful successor of her mother's generation, but inevitable changes in time and tradition are suggested in her quiet enthusiasm for the 1911 women's liberation movement. Her daughter, Fumio, raised in the era of Taishō democracy, on the other hand, openly rebels against the tradition represented by her mother. Yet it is to the old *Ie* that she returns for assurance and comfort in crises. Appreciating her mother's past effort to eradicate the dehumanizing aspects of tradition and thus to strengthen its positive effects, her daughter, Hanako, the youngest of the four generations, happily accepts the tradition that she has inherited from her matrilineal predecessors. Ariyoshi dichotomizes tradition and modernization only to close the story with the synthesis of the two, on an optimistic note of anticipation that Japan's tradition will continue to flow, like the River Ki, and that women dictated by their inner "nature" will continue to play the role of its refiner and transmitter. The use of the Wakayama dialect in the first half of the story and the Tokyo dialect in its latter half is particularly effective, not only in highlighting the continuation and the changes but also in demonstrating the author's exceptional technique in storytelling and in creating vivid images of the women and a pleasing aesthetic quality.

Hanaoka Seishū no tsuma (The Doctor's Wife, 1966). Set in a Wakayama village, this story, too, concerns the meaning of *Ie* and the role of women as its supporting pillar. Unlike *The River Ki,* however, the focal points here concern the conflict between tradition and change and the latter's eventual victory over the former. The story is based on the life of Hanaoka Seishū (1760–1835), who developed an anesthetic and performed the world's first successful surgery under general anesthetic in 1805, on breast cancer, as duly acknowledged at the Museum of Medical History in Chicago. Ariyoshi skillfully weaves factual information with fictional elements to create a rich tapestry of exceptionally high aesthetic quality. The focus of her attention, however, is not on Seishū but on two women, his mother and his wife, who compete fiercely for Seishū's affection while maintaining the surface appearance of an ideal traditional relationship between a mother and a daughter-in-law. While the mother sacrifices herself only for the sake of *Ie* and for the undivided affection of its patriarch, his wife, Kae, actively collaborates with him out of genuine concern for his work and patients' well-being and consequently emerges victorious in the competition. Yet Ariyoshi makes one spinster sister declare on her deathbed that women's happiness is not to be found in marriage and that men are much more privileged than women in this life. While these subplots contradictory to the main theme of this story are disturbing, they are nonetheless effective in illuminating the extent of the wife's struggle to share in her husband's work and her contribution to modern medicine as well as the enlightened view that Seishū exhibits in making it possible. (The French translation is entitled *Kae*.)

Hishoku (Not Because of Color, 1964). Based on Ariyoshi's observations while in the United States, this story considers racial prejudice. Through the eyes of the protagonist, a Japanese war bride married to an American black man, she exposes the complex problem of prejudice and discrimination directed not only against Afro-Americans and Asians but also against Latinos and Jews in the United States. Living in Harlem and working with other Japanese war brides of blacks and Puerto Ricans, the heroine begins to understand that her misery is not because of the color of her husband and children but because of racism that manifests itself in the vicious circle of economic deprivation and chronic apathy of all minorities. With deep empathy for the oppressed, she comes to identify with the oppressed and decides to pursue her life not as a Japanese woman, but as a black wife and mother. This is a significant work that informs readers on the complexity of the problem of prejudice and its devastating psychological and economic effects.

Kōkotsu no hito (The Twilight Years, 1972). This social-issue novel probes the problem of the elderly, seldom dealt with before in Japanese literature. The setting is contemporary Tokyo, and the protagonist is a working woman burdened with the difficult task of caring for her father-in-law, whose physical and mental faculties deteriorate rapidly after his wife's sudden death. Using the finding of her own research that exposed the inadequacy of governmental support for the elderly, Ariyoshi forces readers to confront this serious social problem.

Fukugō osen (Compound Pollution, 1975). This semidocumentary novel is Ariyoshi's version of *Silent Spring* (1962) by Rachel Carson (1907–1964), a scientific study of the harmful effects of chemical fertilizers and insecticides on the human body. Like Carson, Ariyoshi is outspoken in warning about the immeasurable harm caused by the chain reactions triggered by the use of chemical products. Her approach, however, is not purely scientific; by means of anecdotes, she relates the problem in terms of everyday life and thus succeeds in convincing the reader of the immediacy and the seriousness of the threat.

Izumo no Okuni (Okuni of Izumo, 1969). A fictional biography of Okuni, a street entertainer whose dancing is believed to have inspired the development of the Kabuki theater, this novel re-creates Japanese life in the late 16th to the early 17th centuries. Ariyoshi's skillful use of semiclassical diction and local dialects, her flowing narrative style and vivid images, and her incorporation of historical events into the fictional plot make for informative and enjoyable reading.

Kazunomiyasama otome (Her Highness Kazunomiya, 1978). In this controversial novel, Ariyoshi posits that the imperial princess Kazunomiya (1846–1877), who married the fourteenth shogun, Tokugawa Iemochi (1846–1866), was actually a fifteen-year-old maidservant substituted for her. Exceedingly self-conscious of a physical handicap, the princess in Ariyoshi's story refuses the marriage arranged by the court and the shogunate officials, escapes to a temple, and spends the rest of her life as a nun. Trained to act like the princess, the first substitute is transported to Edo (the present-day Tokyo) to be wed. Under severe stress, however, she becomes crazed on the way, is replaced by yet another impostor, and commits suicide. The new impostor marries the shogun and outlives him through the turbulent period, until the warrior regime is toppled and Japan emerges a modern monarchy after the Meiji Restoration (of the imperial power) of 1868. With extensive research, Ariyoshi succeeds in illuminating the tragic lives of the young women involved, as well as in introducing the intriguing details of life in the imperial court.

BIBLIOGRAPHY

Translations

"Ballad." Trans. Yukio Suwa and Herbert Glazer. *Japan Quarterly* 22. (1975): 40–58.

Compound Pollution Currently being translated by Y. Kim.

The Doctor's Wife. Trans. Wakako Hironaka and Ann Siller Konstant. Tokyo: Kodansha International, 1978.

Her Highness Kazunomiya Trans. Mildred Tahara. Forthcoming.

"The Ink Stick." Trans. Mildred Tahara. *Japan Quarterly* 22. 4 (1975): 348–69.

Mulhern, Chieko. "Japanese Business Fiction: Women Writers with Clout." In Arai Shinya. *Shoshaman: A Tale of Corporate Japan,* Berkeley: University of California Press, 1991, i–xxv.

Okuni of Izumo. Trans. James Brandon. Forthcoming.

"Prayer." Trans. John Bester. *Japan Quarterly* 7. 4 (1960): 448–81.

The River Ki. Trans. Mildred Tahara. Tokyo: Kodansha International, 1980.

Tahara, Mildred. "Ariyoshi Sawako." In *Heroic with Grace: Legendary Women of Japan,* ed. Chieko Mulhern. Armonk, NY: M. E. Sharpe, 1991, 297, 323.

"The Tomoshibi." Trans. Keiko Nakamura. In *The Mother of Dreams.* Ed. Makoto Ueda. Tokyo: Kodansha International, 1986, 241–57.

The Twilight Years. Trans. Mildred Tahara. Tokyo: Kodansha International, 1984.

"The Village of Eguchi," Trans. Yukio Suwa and Herbert Glazer. *Japan Quarterly* 18.4 (1971): 427–42.

Yoshiko Yokochi SAMUEL

BEN NO NAISHI (1220s?–ca. 1270?), poet, memoirist. Real name: unknown.

Life: Although Ben no Naishi is known only by this sobriquet meaning "Controller-Handmaid," she belonged to a distinguished literary branch of the Fujiwara family that traced its lineage back to the scholar-statesman Fuyutsugu (775–826). Her father, Fujiwara Nobuzane (1176/77?–1266/70?), was a respected court poet and an eminent portrait painter who authored a miscellany, *Ima monogatari* (Tales of the Present, after 1239?), and his own Poetry Collection (ca. 1247). Her grandfather, Takanobu (1142–1205), also a famous court poet and an accomplished artist, has a poetry collection and two nonextant works to his name, a fictional tale, *Ukinami* (Floating Waves), and a historical tale, *Iya Yotsugi* (Still More Yotsugi). Her great-grandfather, Tametsune (also called Tametaka and Jakuchō; fl. ca. 12th c.), was one of the poets known as the "Three Jaku of Ōhara" and compiled a twenty-scroll poetic anthology, *Goyōwakashū* (The Later Collection of Leaves), and authored a historical tale, *Imakagami* (The Mirror of the Present, 1170).

When Ben no Naishi's great-grandfather Tametsune renounced the world to join his brothers at Ōhara, his wife, Bifukumon-in no Kaga (d. 1193?), embarked upon a second marriage with the influential poet Fujiwara Shunzei (1114–1205). They had several children, including the outstanding 13th-century poet Fujiwara Teika (1162–1241) and a woman known as Kengozen (b. 1157), who wrote a journal, *Kenshunmon-in no Chūnagon nikki* (also called *Tamakiharu,* ca. 1219). Although Ben no Naishi's grandfather Takanobu was the elder half-brother of Teika, their twenty-year age difference seems to have inhibited the growth of brotherly affection between them.

Of Ben no Naishi's five brothers, the profile of Tametsugu (1206–65) emerges the most clearly. Although not distinguished as a poet, Tametsugu followed in the footsteps of his father and grandfather as a portrait painter. He also became the first male member of his family to rise as high as Junior Third Rank, a promotion granted him in 1258 by Emperor Go-Fukakusa. It is believed that he was the artist who painted a portrait of Konoe Kanetsune (1210–59) in 1247 to commemorate Kanetsune's appointment as regent. His descendants remained prominent in artistic circles until the 15th century.

Ben no Naishi also had three elder sisters. Sōhekimon-in Shōshō no Naishi (d. 1266–70?) was a noted poet in the service of Sōhekimon-in (1209–33; consort of Emperor Go-Horikawa [1212–42; r. 1221–32]; and the mother of Emperor Shijō [1231–42; r. 1232–42]). Shijō-in Shōshō no Naishi (dates unknown) was in the service of Retired Emperor Shijō, but nothing else is known of her life. The eldest sister was known as the wife of the war minister, Ariuji. A younger sister, Shōshō no Naishi (d. 1265), served the eighty-ninth emperor Go-Fukakusa (1243–1304; r. 1246–59) alongside Ben no Naishi.

Born and raised in the capital of Kyoto, Ben no Naishi was trained in the polite accomplishments necessary for court service. Nothing is known about her until 1243, when her name appears for the first time in the *Record of The Kawai Shrine Poetry Contest* as Tōgū no Ben (Crown Prince's Controller), accompanying her father, Nobuzane, and her elder sister, Sōhekimon-in no Shōshō. She probably entered court service soon after Go-Fukakusa's birth in the Sixth Moon of 1243. Shortly thereafter, in 1246, she was joined at court by her younger sister, Shōshō no Naishi (Lesser Captain-Handmaid).

Ben no Naishi and Shōshō no Naishi remained in Go-Fukakusa's service for the duration of his thirteen-year reign. Not much is known about Ben no Naishi's life after Go-Fukakusa's abdication in 1259 in favor of his younger brother Kameyama (1249–1305; r. 1259–74). She took Buddhist vows in 1265, following the deaths of Shōshō no Naishi and her elder brother Tametsugu, and sometime prior, Ben no Naishi bore a daughter to Fujiwara (Hosshōji) Masahira (1229–78). Known as Shin'yōmeimon-in no Shōshō (dates unknown), the daughter served Shin'yōmeimon-in (1262–96), the consort of Emperor Kameyama.

Ben no Naishi spent the final years of her life living as a nun-recluse at a place called Ogi, near the foothills of Mt. Hiei north of Kyoto. Although the exact date of Ben no Naishi's death is unknown, she outlived her father and her elder sister, Sōhekimon-in Shōshō no Naishi, both of whom died between the years 1266 and 1270.

Career: When Ben no Naishi went into service in 1243 at the court of the crown prince who would later reign as Go-Fukakusa, she was presumably around the age of fifteen. Retired Emperor Go-Saga (1222–72; r. 1242–46), father of Go-Fukakusa and an avid patron of *waka* (thirty-one-syllable classical poetry) and *renga* (linked verse), took notice of Ben no Naishi because of her competent performance at various poetry contests. Under his order two imperial poetic anthologies, *Shokugosen wakashū* (Later Collection Continued, 1251) and *Shokukokin wakashū* (Collection of Ancient and Modern Japanese Poetry Continued, 1265), were compiled. Go-Saga himself has twenty-two compositions preserved in the linked-verse anthology *Tsukubashū* (Tsukuba Collection). Ben no Naishi's reputation as a poet and the high regard the court bestowed upon her father and grandfather were probably the major catalyst for launching her career at court.

Forty-four of her *waka* are included in imperial anthologies from the tenth *Shokugosen wakashū* through the twenty-first *Shinshokukokin wakashū* (The New Collection of Ancient and Modern Japanese Poetry, 1439). In addition, her memoir contains about two hundred *waka,* along with about sixty poems by her sister, Shōshō no Naishi.

Ben no Naishi was a member of the active mid-Kamakura *renga* coterie prominently represented in *Tsukubashū.* Ben no Naishi and Shōshō no Naishi were the most visible women in this *renga* collection, with thirteen and fifteen poems, respectively. Often referred to as *nyōbō rengashi* (lady *renga* masters), they enjoyed a literary status no doubt enhanced by the reputation of their father, Nobuzane. For Nobuzane to have eleven poems included in the *Tsuku-*

bashū despite his modest fourth rank is a sure testament to his high status as a *renga* poet. The *renga* connoisseur Ton'a (1289–1372) heaps lavish praise on Nobuzane and his daughters and quotes directly from *Ben no Naishi nikki* in his miscellany, *Suia ganmoku* (The Water Frog Essence; also *Suia shō*, 1360–64).

Although court life in the Kamakura period (1185–1333) differed in many respects from that of the Heian period (794–1185), the literary tradition of aristocratic women blessed with abundant leisure time and trained in cultivated pastimes allowed them to continue writing into the 14th century. There were, however, some distinct changes to be noted in the works of Kamakura women. Their memoir literature tended, on the whole, to reflect a public perspective as compared with the private one seen in Heian works. Further, in aesthetics, the Heian preference for the "new, fresh and modern" was replaced by one that sought to preserve the minutiae of aristocratic culture on the verge of extinction. It is only natural that Ben no Naishi's memoir exhibits these characteristics.

Translated Work: Ben no Naishi nikki (The Poetic Memoir of Ben no Naishi, 1246–52), poetic journal. Adopting a public stance and shifting from first- to third-person narration, the work focuses on the minutiae of court life experienced by the author during the reign of a child emperor in the mid-Kamakura period. It consists of fairly short, dated entries that set up the court events or occasions that inspired poetic composition, with poems serving as the emotional highlights. Of the approximately three hundred poems in the work, two hundred are by Ben no Naishi, sixty by her sister Shōshō no Naishi, and the rest by court acquaintances.

All extant manuscripts are severely damaged toward the end of the second scroll, leading many scholars to conclude that about half the original work has been lost. Although the extant text covers seven years abruptly ending in 1252, definite references in later works indicate that the original full text covered the entire thirteen-year reign of Go-Fukakusa until his forced abdication in 1259. Ton'a's *Suia ganmoku* contains quotations from what seem to be nonextant portions of *Ben no Naishi nikki,* and the imperial poetic anthology, *Gyokuyō wakashū* (Collection of Jeweled Leaves, ca. 1313 or 1314), also preserves poems taken from the missing part of the memoir, obviously composed while Ben no Naishi was still at Go-Fukakusa's court. Even more explicit evidence that Ben no Naishi was still in court service in 1259 is found in the two entries in Chapter 6 of the historical tale *Masukagami* (The Clear Mirror, 1338–76). The chapter title, "Oriiru kumo" (Descending Clouds), is based on a line from the second of Ben no Naishi's poems quoted by the author of *Masukagami* in the following sections:

On the twenty-eighth day of the Eighth Moon of this year 1259, the eleven-year-old crown prince (Kameyama) performed the coming-of-age ceremony. His former name was Tsunehito. The rumors that were circulating made Emperor Go-Fukakusa indignant and unhappy. Late one night, while people were quietly telling tales, His Majesty calculated that 5,074 days had passed while he had made obeisance at the Naishidokoro. Ben no Naishi composed this poem:

Surely the gods will not forget:	chiyo to ieba
a reign endures a thousand years.	itsutsu kasanete
The days of his reign	nanasoji ni
number a little over five	amaru hikazu o
thousand and seventy.	kami wa wasureji

On the night of the twenty-sixth of the Eleventh Moon, His Majesty abdicated the throne. Even the sky looked sad; it began to rain, and everything was terribly depressing. It was as though Lady Ise had been speaking of this occasion when she said, "With no thought of returning to the Hundred-Stones Palace." Although His Majesty had prepared himself mentally for the transferral of the Sacred Sword and Necklace, he was deeply distressed when the time came to bid farewell to the regalia, his constant companion for the past thirteen years. Seeing him unable to hide his sorrow, Ben no Naishi composed this poem:

Darkness spreads like a shadow	ima wa tote
within this heart of mine,	ORIIRU KUMO NO
when rain pours down	shigurureba
from the DESCENDING CLOUDS	kokoro no uchi zo
because "Now is the time."	kakikurashikeru

These two entries in *Masukagami* are especially illuminating in terms of the relationship between the *Masukagami* and the *Ben no Naishi nikki* text. Scholar Tamai Kōsuke points out in his book *Ben no Naishi nikki shinchū* that Chapter 5, "Uchino no yuki" (Palace Snow), of *Masukagami* quotes verbatim the opening paragraph of Section 121 in the extant *Ben no Naishi nikki,* duplicating the style of presentation in the original—a brief introduction followed by her name and poem. Medieval authors of historical tales relied heavily on diaries and similar materials, often incorporating passages with little or no revision. Since it seems fairly safe to conclude that Ben no Naishi's memoir was the source for *Masukagami,* her lament over Go-Fukakusa's abdication can be taken as compelling evidence that the memoir originally extended to that point and that the text for the seven years between 1252 and 1259 has been lost.

It is interesting to further speculate that these entries indeed come from the closing section of the original memoir, for then it follows that Ben no Naishi opened the memoir with the abdication of Go-Saga, making way for Go-Fukakusa, and closed it after the latter's abdication, with a narrative structure or a unity of sort in mind. In contrast to the melancholy tone at the end of the work, the opening entry sparkles with optimism:

[Section 1] The Abdication
On the twenty-ninth day of the First Month in the fourth year of Kangen (1246),

Emperor Go-Saga abdicated at the Tominokōji Palace. It is impossible to write of everything that happened at that time. It was all so very splendid that I composed this poem.

From this day forth,	kyō yori wa
how can I help thinking	waga kimi no yo to
when I look up at	nazuketsutsu
the sun or moon in the sky,	tsukihi shi sora ni
"This is my lord's world"?	augazarame ya

An optimistic tone prevails for much of the work, despite the few occasions tinged by melancholy. Hints of Ben no Naishi's buoyant personality are revealed in entries such as the following:

[Section 120] The Cowardly Demon
During a time when Shintō services were being performed and there were few people in attendance at court, His Majesty grew bored and told me to put on a demon mask and try to scare people. Standing at the door to the Table Room with my divided skirt drawn up to my chest and my brown chemise draped over my head, I startled the Oban guards, and they began taking up their bows. I took fright at this unexpected development and fell down into the courtyard stream, evoking peals of laughter from the onlookers, who called out, "You cowardly demon!"

Always one with a ready wit, Ben no Naishi enjoyed challenging others not quite as quick as she:

[Section 30] The Koga Chancellor's Banquet
On the twenty-fourth, there was a banquet held at the residence of the Koga Chancellor. Late at night the Chancellor came to where Shōnagon no Naishi and I were on duty, our hair formally dressed, in the Table Room. The Chancellor said, "Is it very late? Is it around the time for the Ox Card to be posted?" When no one replied, Shōnagaon no Naishi whispered in my ear, "You've probably thought up a clever reply. Please answer him." I composed this poem.

Since you do not seem	utatane ni
quite aware that time has	ne ya suginamashi
advanced to the Ox Card,	sayonaka no
I wonder if you did not doze	ushi no kui to mo
through the Hour of the Rat.	sashite shirazu wa

Her clever verbal play on *Ne no koku sugite* (past the Hour of the Rat [11 P.M.– 1 A.M.) and *nesugi* (oversleep), insinuating that the man had slept through the Hour of the Rat, waking up two hours later during the Hour of the Ox [1 A.M.– 3 A.M.], characterizes the intellectual nature of her poetry and the vivacity of her personality.

A loosely strung, episodic work, *Ben no Naishi nikki* offers no clearly discernible theme. Apparent throughout the work is the desire to record minutiae about court life for posterity. To achieve this end, Ben no Naishi evokes the moon, one of the most potent images in classical Japanese literature, to provide an aesthetic setting and to reflect the emotive qualities of a particular event. Although the image of the moon that Heian and Kamakura memoirists call up most often leads to solitary, pensive thoughts of lost loves, times past, and the like, at times Ben no Naishi's moon is something to be viewed by a group of sensitive people at court.

[Section 54] The Appointments Ceremony

On the sixteenth, there was an appointments ceremony. His Lordship the Regent arrived; Tsunetoshi, Mitsukuni and some others also came. Tsunetoshi told the Handmaids to wait in the Table Room for the announcement to His Majesty. The Handmaids gazed at the moon, saying such things as, "When one is waiting for something, it seems to take forever. In the past, we have often stayed up all night to see the moon without feeling impatient. But now I feel unsettled because an official function is involved." I composed this poem.

This, too, is a	kore mo mata
kind of waiting:	matsu to shi nareba
I look at the moon,	aki no yo no
thinking, "Let it happen	fukenu saki ni to
before the autumn night deepens."	tsuki o miru ka na

I had a serving woman take the poem to Shōshō no Naishi who was in the Hot Water Room. This was her reply.

I wonder for whom	kokoro ni mo
you wait as you gaze	arade koyoi no
absently at the moon,	tsuki o mite
thinking, " . . . before	fukenu saki ni to
the night deepens."	tare o matsuran

For her, a bright, clear moon means auspicious times at court and a clouded moon denotes sad occasions marred by ill fortune such as death, abdication, or resignation.

[Section 34] The Change of Regents

On the nineteenth, there was a meeting of Senior Nobles in connection with the change in Regents. The Presiding Official was the Middle Counselor Junior Second Rank Yoshinori and the Chamberlain-in-Charge was the Head Chamberlain-Controller Akitomo.

At the moment Akitomo came to inform the Emperor of the Retired Emperor's decree, the moon clouded over and without knowing why, I was saddened. I composed this poem.

Can anyone think of this	haruru yo no
as a moon on a clear night?	tsuki to wa tare ka
There seems to be haze	nagamuran
clouding over part of the	kata e kasumeru
sky on this spring eve.	haru no sora ka na

Upon occasion Ben no Naishi follows convention, viewing the moon with nostalgic longing for court life of the past:

[Section 26] The Dawn Moon

When the Flushed Faces banquet, the pages' performances, the platform dancing and the command performances had ended, we all found the light of the dawn moon on the Seisōdō deeply moving. I composed this poem.

Could I ever forget	kokonoe ni
the dawn moon floating	yo o kasanetsuru
above the snow during	yuki no ue no
these manifold nights	ariake no tsuki no
at the nine-fold palace.	itsuka wasuremu

Thus, His Majesty repaired to the Kan-in Town Palace. I recalled things at the Greater Imperial Palace and composed this:

That in the abode of clouds	kumoi nite
I long for the ancient	arishi kumoi no
abode of clouds must be	koishiki wa
due to a heart that	furuki o shinobu
yearns for the past.	kokoro narikeri

Ben no Naishi nikki merits attention on several levels. First, as a source in cultural history the work provides much insider information on mid-Kamakura court life not found in the writings of her near-contemporaries, such as Abutsu-ni, author of *Izayoi nikki* (The Diary of the Waning Moon), which concentrates on the delineation of her travel to Kamakura and her cause—to secure her son Tamesuke's inheritance rights. Second, as a guardian of the Heian tradition, she perpetuates the genre while adapting it to fit the needs of her time and society. Third, as a member of a distinguished literary family, Ben no Naishi makes her own contribution to the list of meritorious works penned by her male ancestors. Lastly, she deserves to be lauded for her ambitious attempt to incorporate three literary forms: she combines *rekishi monogatari* (historical tale) in her intention to chronicle public events at court; *nikki bungaku* (diary literature) in her autobiographical prose headnotes; and *kashū* (personal poetry collection) in the abundant infusion of poems. These elements are mixed skillfully to create an authentic record of her life and her times.

BIBLIOGRAPHY

Translations and Critical Works

Biographical Dictionary of Japanese Literature, S. V. "Ben no Naishi."

Huey, Robert N. "An Analysis of Seven Poems." In *Kyōgoku Tamekane: Poetry and Politics in Late Kamakura Japan.* Stanford, CA: Stanford University Press, 1989.

Hulvey, Shirley Yumiko. "The Nocturnal Muse: Ben no Naishi nikki." *Monumenta Nipponica* (1989) 44.4: 391–413.

———. "The Nocturnal Muse: A Study and Partial Translation of *Ben no Naishi nikki, a Thirteenth-Century Poetic Memoir.*" Diss., University of California, Berkeley, 1989. Ann Arbor: UMI, 1990. 9006365.

Keene, Donald. "Ben no Naishi." In *Travelers of a Hundred Ages.* New York: Henry Holt, 1989.

———. "A Neglected Chapter: Courtly Fiction of the Kamakura Period." *Monumenta Nipponica* (1989) 44.1: 1–30.

Konishi, Jin'ichi. *A History of Japanese Literature, Volume Three: The High Middle Ages.* Trans. Aileen Gatten. Ed. Earl Miner. Princeton, NJ: Princeton University Press, 1991.

Niwa, Tamako. "Introduction." In *Nakatsukasa Naishi nikki.* Diss., Radcliffe College, 1955.

Perkins, George W. "A Study and Partial Translation of *Masukagami.*" Diss., Stanford University, 1977.

Putzar, Edward. *Japanese Literature: A Historical Outline.* Tuscon: University of Arizona Press, 1973.

S. Yumiko HULVEY

E

EIFUKU MON'IN, or Ex-empress Eifuku (1271–1342), poet. Real name: Saionji Kyōko.

Life: Born into the prominent Saionji family and married to Emperor Fushimi (1265–1317; r. 1287–98), Eifuku Mon'in or Ex-empress Eifuku (also pronounced Yōfuku) became one of the most influential cultural patrons of the late Kamakura (1185–1333) and early Muromachi (1336–1573) periods through the combined forces of her own family and of the imperial household. Eifuku had great cultural power and the highest prestige in a tumultuous period dominated by competition between rival lines of the imperial clan for sociocultural preeminence in the ancient capital of Kyoto, yet all lived under the de facto control of the warrior government from their distant capital of Kamakura. The life and literature of this important woman poet illustrate some of the ways in which the private and public spheres of cultural production were inextricably entangled with events in the public realm of male-dominated formal political institutions.

Eifuku's natal family, the Saionji, achieved their power through cultivation of relations with the Kamakura shogunate together with alliances with both of the competing lines of the imperial household that had, in the mid-13th century, split between two rival sons of Emperior Go-Saga (1220–72; r. 1242–46). Emperor Go-Fukakusa (1243–1304; r. 1246–59) headed the senior line affiliated with Jimyōin villa and also fathered Eifuku's future husband; his younger brother Emperor Kameyama (1249–1305; r. 1259–74) led the junior line associated with Daikakuji Temple. The rivalry between these two lines was generally caused by and intensified over the appointment of crown princes by the warrior government in faraway Kamakura. By the end of the 13th century Eifuku's father, Saionji Sanekane (1249–1322), had consolidated his power enough to be designated the official mediator between the Kamakura government and the imperial court, a position of considerable influence in the ongoing rivalry. The Saionji family successfully maintained ties with both imperial lines through the

well-established tradition known as marriage politics. Modern scholars have refrained from discussing the roles women may have played in what they describe
as a male means of political maneuvering, but Saionji success in this practice
can be measured by the extent of royal marriages in the mid-1280s: Sanekane's
paternal aunts had become empresses to Emperors Go-Saga and Go-Fukakusa
of the senior line, while Sanekane's sister was empress to Emperor Kameyama
of the junior line, and one of Sanekane's daughters would become empress to
the ambitious Emperor Go-Daigo (1288–1338; r. 1318–33) in the junior line.
In the context of this growing web of marriage relations, a first daughter, Eifuku,
was born in 1271 to Saionji Sanekane and his wife, Minamoto Akiko (known
to history by her very high-ranking title Akiko of the Junior First Rank), the
daughter of Minamoto Michinari, the Minister of the Center since 1269.

Little is known of Eifuku's life until she became principal consort to Emperor
Fushimi in the sixth moon of 1288, only a few months after he was enthroned.
Fushimi had been designated crown prince at the relatively late age of twelve
because of complications in the imperial succession disputes. Moreover, at the
relatively late age of twenty-four, he already had children by his other consorts.
Eifuku's father, Sanekane, moved quickly to ensure his daughter's position: he
had Eifuku adopt a son who had been born in early 1287 to a lower-ranking
consort named Fujiwara Tsuneko (d.u.), and managed to have the adopted son
the new crown prince the following year at the age of fourteen months. Adoption
was an effective tactic in the marriage politics of Japanese court society, and
all of Eifuku's known children seem to have been adopted in the same manner.
One important type of relationship that grew out of this practice is typified by
the close relationship that developed between Eifuku and the true mother of the
boy. More significantly for Eifuku's future position within court society, however, was that this arrangement secured her place as the designated mother of
the future emperor and thus her position as empress and one of the most influential people in the country.

Tension between the two lines of the imperial family flared into violence
directly threatening Fushimi in the third moon of 1290. A courtier associated
with the rival junior line burst into the emperor's quarters in an assassination
attempt. Fushimi, who happened to be in Eifuku's apartments nearby, successfully fled his attacker, who then committed suicide. The attempted assassination,
which was recorded in detail in the diary of Lady Nakatsukasa (fl. ca. 1250–
92) in the service of Fushimi's court, led to the implication of the head of the
junior line, Emperor Kameyama, who denied the allegations in a letter to the
Kamakura warrior government. While the attempted violence was not without
precedent in Japanese court politics, it caused quite a stir and must have been
quite frightening for the young Eifuku.

Eifuku received the name Eifuku and the title of ex-empress (mon'in), the
title by which she has come to be known to modern readers of classical poetry,
at the youthful age of twenty-eight, when her husband, Fushimi, abdicated in
1298. Her adopted son succeeded Fushimi as Emperor Go-Fushimi (1288–1336;

r. 1298–1301), and as a result Fushimi became the most powerful person in the imperial court as the *jisei no kimi,* or the most senior member who has not taken Buddhist vows in the line of the imperial family to which the current emperor belongs. Although Fushimi lost his powerful position of *jisei no kimi* briefly between 1301 and 1308, he regained it when his second son (by a mother other than Eifuku) was enthroned as Emperor Hanazono (1297–1348; r. 1308–18), and Fushimi played out his role as the most influential cultural patron and political figure at the court until his death in 1317. During the decade of Hanazono's rule, the Kyōgoku school of poetry first came to truly dominate Japanese court poetry.

Eifuku became head of the household at the Jimyōin palace at Fushimi's death to find herself in a position of safeguarding her own interests, as many of the senior members died in the Jimyōin imperial line, her natal Saionji clan, and the Kyōgoku poetry school. For the next decade Eifuku would remain the most senior member in the palace, where resided many young but important individuals, including two retired emperors, Go-Fushimi in his thirties and Hanazono in his twenties; another ex-empress; Go-Fushimi's empress, Kōgi Mon'in; and the future first emperor of the Northern Court, Go-Fushimi's crown prince and future emperor Kōgon (1313–64; r. 1331–33). As head of this illustrious household Eifuku supervised and arranged the many ceremonial and seasonal events and entertainments of such a family, including the births of children to Kōgi Mon'in, the coming-of-age ceremonies of the crown prince, and the memorial services of Fushimi, in addition to more lighthearted events like flower-and-moon-viewing excursions and the performances of popular entertainers. Eifuku also mediated between her and Fushimi's two sons, the ex-emperors, due to the complex relations between them that had been negotiated with the military government designating the succession of Go-Fushimi's children, rather than Hanazono's, to the throne.

While the appointment in 1326 of Eifuku's grandson as crown prince had seemed to secure certain influence for Jimyōin faction, Emperor Go-Daigo coveted the throne for his own children to retain power for himself. In 1331 Go-Daigo launched a clumsy rebellion against the Kamakura shogunate in an effort to assert full control over national politics but was quickly put down by the Kamakura authorities. In the aftermath, with Go-Daigo in exile, Eifuku's grandson was promptly installed by the shogunate as the new emperor Kōgon. At this point Eifuku seems to have retired from the Jimyōin palace in deference to the new emperor and moved back to her family mansion in Kitayama, near the site where Kinkaku-ji would be built in 1397. There she lived as the effective head of the Saionji family, despite the strict male primogeniture customs of Kamakura Japan that had replaced the female inheritance rights of the Heian period and earlier.

This period of happiness was not to last long. Emperor Go-Daigo recaptured the capital in 1333 to begin his restoration reign, plunging the Jimyōin line into great difficulties. The greatest tragedy for Eifuku during these years of misfortune was the execution by Go-Daigo in 1335 of the new head of the Saionji family, Kinmune (1310–35), for his involvement in a plot to assassinate Go-Daigo and restore the Kamakura government. Under the shadow of this great humiliation, Hanazono took Buddhist tonsure later that year, and Eifuku's other son, Go-Fushimi, died the following year. This period was perhaps the darkest and unhappiest of Eifuku's entire life.

Having already lost her mother in 1318 and her father in 1322, she suffered the loss of her most faithful supporter and younger brother in 1339. The fortunes of Eifuku's family began to revive in late 1336, however, when the warrior Ashikaga Takauji (1305–58), who had left the capital under Emperor Kōgon's orders earlier, returned to recapture the capital in 1336 and eventually to chase Go-Daigo's forces southward and establish a new era, now known as the Ashikaga or Muromachi era (1336–1573). Kōgon's rule had ended with the return of Go-Daigo to the capital in 1333, but Takauji installed Go-Fushimi's second son and another grandson of Eifuku as Emperor Kōmyō (1321–80; r. 1336–48).

At the Kitayama mansion Eifuku struggled to preserve Kinmune's heritage by fighting Kinmune's younger brother for the inheritance rights of Kinmune's son, born to a consort after Kinmune's execution. Eifuku's health had begun to fail by 1342, when she witnessed the court promotion of Kinmune's son and Ex-Emperor Kōgon visited the Kitayama mansion. On the seventh day of the fifth moon of 1342, Eifuku passed away at the age of seventy-two.

Career: Literary developments that led to Eifuku's importance as a poet also occurred within the context of the rivalry in the imperial household. Eifuku's husband, Emperor Fushimi, had been deeply interested in poetry since his designation as crown prince in 1275. The decade of the 1270s also saw the rise in importance of two young poets who became his official poetry teachers in 1280, the sister and brother Kyōgoku Tameko (ca. 1250–52–after 1315) and Kyōgoku Tamekane (1254–1332). With Fushimi's patronage and full participation as an important poet in his own right, these two siblings would prove to be the leaders of a new and innovative school of poetry, to be known as the Kyōgoku school. In its early years this school struggled against its already established rival, the Nijō school of poetry, which together with the Kyōgoku school and the Reizei school descended from the three sons of the poet Fujiwara no Tameie (1198–1275), a son of the enormously influential poet Fujiwara no Teika (1162–1241). The Kyōgoku school became inextricably involved with the rise and fall of the Jimyōin imperial line in the 1280s, when Tameko and Tamekane were taken in as Fushimi's tutor, and then Fushimi sponsored the first poetry meeting of the Kyōgoku school in 1285. Its first and only major treatise on aesthetics was written by Tamekane, now known as *Lord Tamekane's Poetic Notes,* in 1285–87.

Eifuku entered Fushimi's court in mid-1288 and played an unusual role in the next important event in the history of Kyōgoku poetry: Fushimi's ultimately unsuccessful attempt to commemorate the school in the long-established literary institution of the imperial poetry anthology. Before formally requesting that the anthology be compiled, Fushimi sent Tamekane to Ise Shrine, dedicated to Japan's central Shinto goddess, Amaterasu, where he was commanded to offer thirty poems at the shrine after delivering an imperial request for protection from a repeat of the Mongol invasions of 1274 and 1281, as well as from a drought and earthquake that had occurred earlier in the year. While Tamekane was on his journey, the emperor took the unusual step of praying fervently each night in the Hand Maiden's Office (Naishidokoro) in his palace, where a divine mirror was kept as a symbol of Amaterasu herself. Then one evening, Eifuku had a dream in which she received a talisman of the Naishidokoro from a court lady wearing a white robe. The emperor took this as a sign that Amaterasu had accepted his request and was further persuaded when the drought soon ended and the Mongol ruler Kublai Khan (r. 1260–94) died the following year.

Whatever the significance of Eifuku's dream for literary as well as military history, this incident represents a vestige of the great respect Japanese women commanded as shamanic mediums. In accepting her dream as a divine omen, Fushimi followed the customs of his ancient predecessors who had the empress serve as a medium for communicating with divinities to determine political and military policy, as recorded in the first imperial histories, the *Kojiki* (Records of Ancient Matters, 712) and the *Nihongi* (Chronicles of Japan, 720). Eifuku's dream is a vestige of this role of women, still found at the imperial court long after the importation of Buddhism in the 6th and 7th centuries. Shamanesses continued to play central roles at the village, as seen in religious tales, from such late Heian and Kamakura period collections as *Konjaku Monogatari* (Tales of Times Now Past) to the *otogizō-shi* short narratives of the Muromachi and Edo (1603–1868), up into the modern period.

Fushimi ordered in 1293 that plans for an imperial anthology be submitted, but he was forced to compromise with the Nijō school poets in selecting an editorial committee. With Tamekane and Tamekane's bitter rival, the senior Nijō school poet Nijō Tameyo (1250–1338), the editorial committee was unable to make any progress on selecting poems for the anthology, and it was ultimately abandoned. One reason for the failure of Fushimi's attempt to compile the first Kyōgoku school anthology of poetry included the political intrigues surrounding his favorite poet, Tamekane, which led to Tamekane's resignation of his court post in 1296 and his arrest and exile from the capital in 1298. This marked the end of the first attempt by the Kyōgoku school of poetry to dominate the poetic circles in the imperial court.

Eifuku began to come into her own as a poet and member of the Kyōgoku school of poetry during this first period of limited success. While in her teens and early twenties Eifuku does not seem to have participated in the early, experimental poetry meetings of the school in the 1280s, when some of the earliest poets of the school, such as Fushimi, Tamekane, and Tameko, were first establishing themselves as important figures in contemporary cultural circles at court. Her increasing recognition as a court poet is apparent in her participation in the important August moon poetry meeting of 1297, when the Kyōgoku school established itself as a separate school of court poetry and rival to the dominant Nijō school. In her poems from this meeting Eifuku's writing seems still immature and clumsy, for she writes timid poems that often simply explain natural scenery. But Eifuku establishes herself as both a mature poet and one of the leading poets of the new school at the age of thirty-three with her poems written for a poetry contest of 1303, which was called to celebrate the return from exile of Tamekane and recorded in *Sentō Gojūban Utaawase,* or Fifty Matches of Poetry at Sentō. This event marked the first flowering of the Kyōgoku school, as well as Eifuku's coming of age as a poet.

Among the poets important in this formative period of the school were, in addition to such important male poets as Fushimi, Tamekane, and Eifuku's father, Sanekane, such important early female poets as Tameko and a large number of other women poets active either in Eifuku's service or in Fushimi's quarters. Chikako (Minamoto no Shinshi; fl. 1287–d. 1317) was a handmaiden to Emperor Fushimi and the third most important female poet in the Kyōgoku school. At a poetry contest in 1303, for example, Eifuku, Tameko, and Chikako lined up on one side to oppose Fushimi, his son Go-Fushimi, and Tamekane on the other side. Another woman, now known only as "Ex-empress Eifuku's Handmaiden" (ca.1264–1347), was one of the ten poets with the most works included in the two Kyōgoku school imperial anthologies and was, of course, a close associate in Eifuku's social as well as literary life. With this large number of important women poets active in this period, women's determination of aesthetic taste moved out of the private women's quarters in households of the aristocrats and the imperial family and into the traditional male domain of the public literary world.

Younger women joined the ranks of court poets in Eifuku's time, for the poet known as "Ex-empress Eifuku's Handmaiden" raised another woman poet, Princess Shinshi (ca. 1302–10–ca. 1376), who by the middle of the century would be counted among the most talented members of the younger generation of Kyōgoku school. A large number of highly talented women poets were all active in Eifuku and Fushimi's court side by side with the important diarist Nakatsukasa no Naishi (fl. ca. 1250–92), providing a lively and stimulating literary environment, with the women's quarters and poetry meetings and contests serving as the primary social institution for the composition of some of the greatest literature of the 13th and 14th centuries. The literary talents of these women assembled in Eifuku and Fushimi's court re-created the great peak of Japanese women's cultural activity during the mid-Heian period, when an unsurpassed group of great novelists, diarists, and poets gathered at the court of two empresses: the author of *The Tale of Genji,* Murasaki Shikibu (ca. 978–1016?), the poet and diarist Izumi Shikibu (ca. 970s to after 1027), and the two poets Akazome Emon (d.u.) and Ise no Tayū (ca. 987–1063?), who were in the service of Empress Akiko, the primary consort to Emperor Ichijō (980–1011; r. 986–1011), competing in literary accomplishment with Sei Shōnagon (964?–ca.

1024–27) and others serving Empress Teishi (976–1001), the concurrent principal consort of Emperor Ichijō (980–1011; r. 986–1011).

In 1311 Fushimi requested an imperial anthology, and Tamekane completed what in 1313 was titled the *Gyokuyōshū*. The first of only two imperial anthologies to include a significant number of Kyōgoku school poems, it demonstrated the predominance of the Kyōgoku school poets in capital literary circles during the reign of Fushimi's second son, Hanazono. Eifuku's nature poems in this anthology followed the Kyōgoku characteristics of strong, dynamic images, contrasting with the carefully controlled imagery of Nijō school poets, and her love poems are characterized by a distinctive freshness and gentleness that distinguished these poems from her later work.

Eifuku's forty-nine poems are outnumbered only by those of Fushimi (ninety-three), Tameko (sixty), and their important patron and Eifuku's father, Sanekane (sixty-two), among poets living at the time of the anthology. Because of his controversial political reputation, Tamekane, who many modern historians would argue today was the most important poet of the school, had only thirty-six poems included. Through the canonical authority of the imperial anthologies, Eifuku at the age of forty-four secured a position in the history of Japanese court poetry.

The literary fortunes of the Kyōgoku school rose and fell with the political influence of Fushimi's imperial lineage, and by 1316 both took a sharp downturn that would lead to major changes in the school and place Eifuku in the position of the leader of the school. In 1313, the year that the *Gyokuyōshū* was completed, Fushimi took Buddhist orders along with his favorite court poet, Tamekane. Three years later Eifuku also "retired from the world" by taking the tonsure and took the Buddhist name Shinnyogen. Meanwhile, Tamekane was arrested in 1315 and exiled in 1316; he would never return to the capital after this exile, for he died in 1332, still banished from the court. The banishment seriously impaired his ability to contribute to the stylistic development and activities of the Kyōgoku school. Tameko, who had been a major formative influence in the early decades of the school, seems to have died sometime after 1315. Finally, in 1317 the Kyōgoku school suffered a very serious blow when Eifuku lost her husband, Fushimi, a founding member and the most powerful patron of the school. Eifuku, who had been the youngest and the last of the major first-generation poets to establish a reputation, survived all of the others to become the senior and leading member of the school.

During the next two decades Eifuku was to lead the Kyōgoku school through its most difficult period, when it was threatened in turn by their rivals in the Nijō school of poetry, by the continued decline in influence through the deaths of the most important political figures in Eifuku's own family, the Saionji, and also by their political and even military opponents during the upheaval accompanying the Kemmu Restoration of 1333, the fall of the Kamakura government, and the founding of the Muromachi shogunate (1336–1573). Eifuku's commitment to furthering the Kyōgoku school heritage seems to have deepened as the rival Daikakuji line of emperors pressed their advantage in the literary sphere through the compilation of two imperial anthologies of poetry. Eifuku realized the depth of rivalry between her school and the Nijō poets when a poem she submitted for inclusion was rewritten without her permission, and the new version was included in the *Shokusenzaishū* of 1320 despite her repeated attempts to withdraw it from consideration.

To make sure that the Kyōgoku poets did not submit poems for the second Nijō-controlled anthology, Eifuku reported an admonition she received in a dream visit from Fushimi. Thus Eifuku reinvoked the same shamanistic role described earlier after the Mongol invasions, but this time to bolster her efforts to vigorously oppose the Nijō poets. The unwillingness of the Kyōgoku poets to submit their poems for the next anthology resulted in exceptionally low Kyōgoku representation and reduced its canonical status by making it all but a Nijō school anthology.

By taking such a firm stand against the Nijō school, Eifuku was following in the footsteps of such strong women contemporaries as Abutsu (d. ca. 1283), whose *Izayoi nikki* (Diary of the Waning Moon) records her trip to Kamakura to argue with the military government in an effort to safeguard the literary inheritance of her eldest son. Unlike Abutsu, who did not fight in her own interests but in those of her son, Eifuku engaged in the Nijō school conflict, with her own literary career and the future of the Kyōgoku school itself in jeopardy. Eifuku's disputes with the Nijō school in the 1320s served to sharpen the differences between rival poetic styles and philosophies and ultimately resulted in strengthening the distinctive Kyōgoku poetic features.

Eifuku worked during the 1320s and 1330s with whatever means possible to train the new leaders of the school. By acting as judge at a number of poetry contests at the Jimyōin palace, she was able to deepen the younger poets' familiarity with the Kyōgoku style. They included important poets who would prove to be major Kyōgoku school patrons: her son Go-Fushimi; his two sons who would later serve as the emperors Kōgon and Kōmyō; and, most significantly for the school, Hanazono, who would compile between 1344 and 1346 the seventeenth and largest imperial anthology, the *Fūgashū,* which was also the second and final Kyōgoku school imperial anthology.

The *Fūgashū* constituted the ultimate fruit of the careful groundwork Eifuku had laid during the preceding decades. Unfortunately Eifuku was not to live to see the completion of the second major monument of the Kyōgoku school. Her last poem, addressed to ''Ex-empress Eifuku's Handmaiden,'' who was living at the time in the provinces, recalls the wonderful days of the early poetry meetings of the Kyōgoku poets at Fushimi's court. After her death in 1342, Eifuku was memorialized by her grandson Ex-emperor Kōgon at the Jimyōin palace, and also her son Ex-emperor Hanazono honored her a few years later by the inclusion of the second largest number of poems in the *Fūgashū*. Her later works show dramatic growth and improvement over her early love poetry, as well as a maturity and a subtle depth of feeling in a number of masterful nature poems.

Major Works: Several of Eifuku's poems are counted among the best of the corpus of the Kyōgoku school, generally acknowledged as the most outstanding innovator and contributor to the development of late classical Japanese *waka* poetry. Her poetry has been preserved primarily in the two imperial anthologies, the *Gyokuyōshū* and the *Fūgashū,* and also in *Eifuku Mon'in Utaawase,* which some scholars believe to be self-edited.

Like virtually all poets of the middle and late classical eras, Eifuku wrote almost exclusively in the *waka* form, traditionally consisting of five "lines" of five, seven, five, seven, and seven syllables, respectively. However, one distinctive Kyōgoku school practice was to violate the traditional syllable counts, creating an effect of tension, emphasis, or other types of emotional stress. Many of the Kyōgoku poets also experimented with a variety of new uses of language, including repeated words, parallel syntactic structures, and, most significantly for their contrast with the Nijō school poets, prosaic and even conversational diction. Eifuku employed these techniques in her own writings.

Like much of Japanese court poetry, Eifuku's poems center on two subjects: love and the natural world. The heterosexual love affair, like the predictable course of the four seasons, had a conventionalized treatment in the Japanese court literary tradition: affairs often began with a man's advances, which the woman rebuffed initially, only to give in to his love for a brief period of happiness; the affair, which was often read as being extramarital, then declined toward its end as the woman began to spend longer and longer periods of solitary misery as she received visits from her lover less and less frequently. Compared with court traditions in many other cultures, classical Japanese literature is distinctive in the unusually important roles a large number of women authors played in virtually all periods, and yet the conventionally defined course taken by two lovers in literature reflects the power of the male to define the course and the ultimate outcome of personal relations. Men enjoyed a monopoly on crucial aspects of the affair, including the decision of when and how often to pay a visit: first frequently in ardent pursuit as his interest was aroused and then less and less often as his devotion waned. The woman's position in the affair was defined largely by resistance, then, to the man's advances early in the affair, by the degree of passion as their ardor flourished and finally by the despondency and bitterness she felt in response to the man's failing interest as love turned to other emotions late in the relationship.

One of the best sites for identification of the woman's voice in such a male-defined conventionalized treatment of love is at the points of transition in the affair, when the female poetic subjects may be heard resisting the course of events leading inexorably to solitary despair. The female subject both knows that the love affair is doomed and yet must, by poetic convention, continue to waste away in her solitary devotion to the male. One important example of this theme in Eifuku's love poetry was written in 1303, very early in her career, as

part of a sequence written on the topic of bitter love given her by her husband,
Emperor Fushimi:

When, even now,	Kaku bakari
after such heartlessness,	uki ga ue dani
I long for him,	aware nari
if he came to long for me,	aware nari seba
how would it be?	ikaga aramashi

(*Gyokuyōshū*, 1696)

Eifuku's narrator here defies the conventional response to disappointment in love
by asking how this affair might proceed if her lover were to break tradition and
actually show some feeling for her, even if it were only a sense of nostalgia for
their days of happiness together. A sense of resistance to the course of love
affairs can be seen in the irony that the woman has difficulty even imagining
that her lover might show any indication that he shares the emotions of regret
and longing in which her world is completely absorbed. In many other of her
love poems, Eifuku is much less ambiguous, evoking a sense closer to bitterness
as well as warning against feelings of resentment.

One distinguishing feature of Eifuku's love poetry is her treatment of the late
stages of an affair. In some of her best work Eifuku successfully captures a
sense of impending doom generated by the inevitable downward spiral of the
relationship and the unrequited longing and despair for the woman. One distinctive characteristic of Kyōgoku school poetry is the careful attention to the
details of ordinary experience, especially for Eifuku, the most subtle changes in
the natural world and in the realm of human affairs. Eifuku was a master at
presenting in her love poems the faintest intimations of the passing of a lover's
interest, as well as finding the universal in its most concrete expression, as in
the following love poem:

Disheartened,	Yowarihatsuru
"Now [love] has ended,"	Ima wa noki wa no
I feel, and	Omoi ni wa
even misery into longing	Usa mo aware ni
has changed.	Naru ni zo arikeru

(*Gyokuyōshū*, 1707)

At the very moment that she finally gives up completely on a love affair, Eifuku's feminine narrator also observes the transformation of the very misery she
has endured through the last phase of the relationship into feelings that may be
less negative, yet perhaps not less painful. This careful observation of subtle yet
quite important shifts in nuance of feeling and significance is one of the most
distinctive contributions of the Kyōgoku school to the Japanese poetic tradition.

Another dimension to Eifuku is also evident in the poems previously quoted
where she uses the term *aware* (translated here as "longing") to show what

love means to a woman at this stage in an affair. In her use of the term Eifuku is distinguished from many of her contemporaries, most notably Yoshida no Kenkō (c. 1283–c. 1350), who uses the term to mean "sorrow" or "the pity of things" less than three decades later in his *Essays in Idleness*. Even within the very limited vocabulary acceptable in the court poetic tradition, the term *aware* is one of the good range of terms for different subjective states, for classical Japanese is a language especially strong in identifying the various complex feelings often associated with love. While in the Kamakura and early Muromachi periods this term was often used to mean bittersweet, melancholy, intense sorrow or even misery, Eifuku here means something very close to "love" with a significance nearly equating love with deep sorrow. Yet her use betrays fine gradations of feelings in its association with, and echoing of, feelings of unhappiness and distress, for, as in the first poem (*Gyokuyōshū* 1696), *aware* results from a lover's cruelty (*uki*), while in the second work (*Gyokuyōshū* 1707), misery (*usa*) is transformed into *aware*. In remembering that the female subjects of her love poems (and their readers) were fully aware of the unhappy emotional states into which their love affairs would inevitably lead them, it is clear why Eifuku defines love in such unhappy terms while preserving the rich complexities of feeling that they may arouse.

Nature poetry is the second major subject in Eifuku's literary legacy, and the unusual stress on imagery represents a second major innovation of Eifuku and other Kyōgoku poets. Nature poetry in earlier periods had shown some disjunction in a break in the very brief *waka* poems of only thirty-one syllables between two sharply distinguished sections, one on a natural subject and one on a human, often deeply subjective element. The very best of these poems traditionally achieved its depth from the subtle, or even elusive, implicit associations between the two different subjects that the reader was expected to develop. The Kyōgoku school poets developed this technique in new directions, and an early, representative example of Eifuku's experiment in this style is found in this poem:

River plovers	Kawa chidori
in the cold moonlit evening:	tsukiyo o samumi
are they sleepless?	inezu are ya
Each time I awaken	nezamuru goto ni
I hear voices.	koe no kikoyuru

(*Gyokuyōshū*, 925)

The first few lines describe a freezing winter night too cold for the river birds to sleep, where the sleeplessness of the birds could equally refer to the narrator herself, who becomes the central focus in the final section of the poem. The reader must use imagination to determine what the possible reasons for shared absence of sleep might be and how the subject's restlessness might somehow be linked to the unhappy plovers. Eifuku builds in this poem on her poetic heritage, alluding to a much earlier *waka* by the prominent poet Ki no Tsurayuki

(868 or 872–945), one of the compilers of the first imperial anthology, *Kokinshū*
(905) and author of *Tosa Diary:*

Yearning unbearably	omoikane
I go to find her;	imogari yukeba
this winter evening	fuyu no yo no
river wind, so cold	kawakaze samumi
the plovers cry.	chidori naku nari

(Shūishū 224)

While Tsurayuki introduces first the subjective mood of the narrator before
turning to an objective description of the frozen, wintry scene, Eifuku reverses
his conceit and gives priority to the objective scene before she allows the questioning voice to lead the reader to the subjective dimension in the poem. Both
poems, however, leave it to the reader to discern the lines along which the poetic
subject's sorrow and the cries of the plovers may find each other, although
Eifuku's work, in typical Kyōgoku fashion, gives more room to the imagination
through sharper disjunction and more ambiguous associative links.

A major innovation in the nature poetry of the Kyōgoku school poets, however, was to seemingly eliminate the subjective voice from the poem entirely.
Having been trained in a poetic tradition in which the subject is ever-present,
Kamakura Japanese readers and writers of *waka* poetry had learned to expect
substantial subjective signification from their literature. Unlike previous periods
in the history of classical Japanese poetry, however, the *Gyokuyōshū-Fūgashū*
era is characterized by poems, often on natural objects, with no obvious human
subject whatsoever. In this way the Kyōgoku poets left their readers to develop
the inescapable, expected subjective human significance of the natural scene in
new and, when successful, quite fruitful ways. One of Eifuku's masterpieces,
and indeed one of the very best poems of the entire Kyōgoku school corpus,
was composed in this manner on the topic of ''Evening Blossoms'':

On the [cherry] blossoms	hana no ue ni
briefly shines	shibashi utsurou
the setting sun;	yuzuku hi
vanishing suddenly,	iru to mo nashi ni
the light has faded.	kage kienikeri

(Fūgashū, 189)

The poetic subject is present only implicitly, and even then only in the perception of the ''suddenly'' vanishing sun, which seems to unexpectedly interrupt
some pleasant spring reverie. Yet the reader has been trained by conventional
usage that the cherry blossoms will quickly fall after an all-too-brief flowering
and that the falling blossoms are not objective descriptions of a spring scene
but invariably signify the impermanence both of human feelings in love and of
life itself. Behind the descriptive lines lurks a vague or even ominous sense of
decline or impending disaster in the natural world.

Compared with the poems of earlier periods, however, the subjective significance of Eifuku's nature poetry looms in a more pervasive, yet more subtle
way through the absence of any explicit mention of subjective referents. Implicit
still is the pervasive subjectivity of earlier nature poetry, but this subjectivity is
completely submerged beneath the surface, imperceptible to all but those trained
in the classical tradition. The subjectivity of nature imagery is certainly not new
in Japanese literary history, for this subjectivity has in fact characterized much
of Japanese (and Chinese) poetry and prose from their conception. What is
significant about the Kyōgoku school innovation is this erasure of the subjective
voice from the poem, leaving only the images to speak "for themselves." This
type of nature poetry gives the impression of presenting a "pure" image of the
natural world without apparent reference to any abstract realm of symbolic
meaning "beyond" the material and seemingly without expression of any subjective truth "within" the physical. Here, the premise that poetry has meaning
by reference to something outside the natural world or through association to
something internal to the writer or reader seems on the surface to be contro-
verted. Yet this poetry is clearly not a naive nature poetry and is by no means
an imagism of the sort with which readers of early 20th-century English poetry
may be familiar, the kind that renders nature poems conducive to interpretations
based on some abstract, universal human significance or a "hidden" meaning
that Western readers may search for when they encounter such poems.

One consequence is that these Kyōgoku poems have been criticized by some
modern Japanese and Western scholars for their overly attentive focus on details
of experience and intellectual poverty. Such a reading assumes that intellectual
or philosophical value depends on reference to abstract truths and cannot be
found in concrete experiences, an assumption that has been increasingly challenged by feminist readings of literature. Absence of any reference in these
poems to something "more" than the natural world, something "other" than
the physical world, turns the reader's attention back to the presence of the natural
world as it is. What is found in the poem does not mean something else, something other than the images themselves, but is meaningful somehow in and of
itself. To some feminist critics willing to characterize a cross-cultural women's
aesthetic in terms of such qualities as a resistance to transcendence or movement
away from abstraction, then the Kyōgoku school poetics might exemplify such
an approach to literary meaning and seem more representative of feminine literary values than of those aesthetics more completely identified with masculine
traditions in Japanese and world literature. Only time and the gradual accumu-
lation of feminist readings of classical Japanese poetry will tell whether this is
true, but the Kyōgoku school of poetry suggests one fruitful area for such further
research.

BIBLIOGRAPHY

Translations and Critical Works

Brower, Robert H., and Earl Miner. "The Late Classical Period." In *Japanese Court
    Poetry*. Stanford, CA: Stanford University Press, 1961, 338–423 passim.

Carter, Steven D. *Waiting for the Wind: Thirty-Six Poets of Japan's Late Medieval Age.* New York: Columbia University Press, 1989, 140–50.

Huey, Robert N. *Kyōgoku Tamekane: Poetry and Politics in Late Kamakura Japan.* Stanford, CA: Stanford University Press, 1989.

Iwasa, Miyoko. *Eifuku Mon'in: Sono Sei to Uta.* Tokyo: Kasama Shoin, 1976.

Joseph D. PARKER

ENCHI Fumiko (1905–86), novelist. Real name: Enchi Fumi (Mrs. Enchi Yoshimatsu); née Ueda Fumi.

Life: Enchi Fumiko was born Ueda Fumi, the youngest child of Tokyo University linguistics professor Ueda Kazutoshi (1867–1937), who studied with pioneer Japanologist and British philologist Basil Hall Chamberlain (1850–1935). Ueda promoted the systematic study of linguistics in Japan, participated in the compilation of the influential dictionary *Dai Nihon kokugo jiten* (Greater Japanese Dictionary), and served on the Committee for the Investigation of the Japanese Language, established in 1902. He is known today as the proponent of the theory of phonology that proposed that syllables beginning with ''h'' in modern Japanese had originally been pronounced with the initial consonant ''p'' in the archaic period. Although this theory met with fierce opposition when first introduced in the Meiji period (1868–1912), it is now *the* accepted theory in historical phonology.

The Ueda household consisted of Enchi's father, her mother, Tsuruko, her eldest brother, Kotobuki, her elder sister, Chiyo, and her paternal grandmother, Ine, who introduced Enchi to the world of Kabuki and *Nō* theaters and the popular fiction of the Edo period (1600–1867). Born in Asakusa, Tokyo, on October 2, 1905, Enchi enjoyed frequent outings to the theater with her family, reading Japanese classics from her father's library, and living a pampered life in prosperous surroundings filled with erudite books. When one considers her background, it is little wonder that she developed a love of literature and chose writing as her career.

Despite Enchi's privileged upbringing, her educational career was lackluster. Her education began in 1912 at a grade school affiliated with the Tokyo Ōtsuka Normal High School, unusual for being coeducational through the sixth grade level and for boasting a homogeneous student population whose families' backgrounds were either academic or bureaucratic. She was shy, introverted, and frail in health, which caused her to spend much of her early school days at home.

Enchi later attended the Women's High School, an affiliate of the Japan Women's University, but she was not an avid student and preferred instead to read the works of Tanizaki Jun'ichirō (1886–1965), Izumi Kyōka (1873–1939), and Nagai Kafū (1879–1959), along with foreign writers such as Oscar Wilde and Edgar Allan Poe, before gradually turning toward *The Tale of Genji,* the masterpiece of the traditional canon. Her interest in the Japanese classics seems to have taken root in her elementary school days and to have reached fruition during her days at the Japan Women's University.

Although Enchi advanced to the Japan Women's University and studied for four years, she left without receiving her degree, choosing instead to pursue an independent course of study in English, French, classical Chinese, and the like. This continued from age seventeen until she married at the age of twenty-four.

During this time Enchi decided to become a playwright and began a daily commute to Ueno Library to read Western plays in translation and to attend performances at the Tsukiji Little Theater, founded by Osanai Kaoru (1881–1928), a leading force in the *shingeki* (modern drama-theater) movement. She was the only woman to attend lectures by Osanai and was one of the first women to have three successful plays staged at his theater. About the time of Osanai's death in 1928, she became acquainted with novelists of the proletariat movement such as Hirabayashi Taiko (1905–72), Hayashi Fumiko (1903–51), and Kataoka Teppei (1894–1944), although she did not become passionately involved in left-wing activities due to her concern for her father's position. However, she was sufficiently impressed with the heroics of Kataoka Teppei to begin a clandestine affair with him despite the fact that he was married and under government surveillance for his left-wing affiliations.

In 1930, Enchi married newspaper columnist Enchi Yoshimatsu, ten years her senior, to distance herself from the proletarian movement, whose adherents were being persecuted by the government, and to find a safer haven for her to continue the affair with writer Kataoka Teppei. After her marriage to Yoshimatsu, she found herself unable to write for two years, an indication that she was not adjusting well to married life. Although she hoped to continue the affair with Teppei, she was loath to violate the sanctity of her marriage vows and may have been further hindered by the birth of her daughter, Motoko, in 1932. Even though the marriage was loveless, she remained married to her husband until his death.

Although Enchi broke off the affair with Teppei after her marriage, her interest in him was rekindled during the years 1935–37, when Teppei introduced her to the Nichireki group of novelists. But in 1938 Enchi broke with him permanently when Teppei failed to visit her during her convalescence from surgery. When Teppei died in Japan in 1944 after having served in central China as part of the writers' "Pen Corps," their relationship had been distant for a number of years.

By 1935, Enchi felt that she had reached an impasse in writing for the theater and joined a group of novelists known as the Nichireki in order to learn more about writing and became better acquainted with novelist Hirabayashi Taiko (1905–72), who proved to be a supportive, lifelong friend. Shortly afterward, they traveled together to Hokkaidō on a lecture tour with a few other women writers, but when Enchi returned to Tokyo, she was faced with the death of her father, who at seventy years of age had succumbed to cancer. She survived her loss by immersing herself in writing and succeeded in getting short works published in various journals. In 1938, she faced the first of many maladies she would encounter in her life: she developed breast cancer, endured mastectomy surgery, and then fought tuberculosis for half a year during the recovery period from surgery.

During the war in 1945, Enchi was displaced when her Tokyo home was destroyed during an air raid, making her move to her mother's house in Karuizawa, Nagano prefecture, until the end of the war. After the war, Enchi returned to Tokyo. Then in 1946, she was diagnosed with uterine cancer, had hysterectomy surgery at Tokyo University Hospital, and remained hospitalized for five months due to complications from pneumonia, during which she battled death on many occasions. As she was recovering her health in 1947, economic necessity prompted her to write juvenile fiction and literature introducing the Japanese classics to young girls. Although she continued to write fiction during this time, she received many rejections from editors of magazines and journals, but, supported by the encouragement of her close friend Hirabayashi Taiko, she continued to submit material to publishers.

Finally, during the late 1940s and early 1950s, Enchi's works found their way into print again and gradually gained notice. During the 1950s her career as a writer was established and her works awarded literary prizes. In 1956, Enchi lost her mother, Tsuruko, who died at the age of eighty-one, and three years later in 1959, her daughter, Motoko, married. In 1962, she went to Hawaii for a one-week vacation. In 1964, she and Hirabayashi went to Oslo to attend the annual meeting for the Japan Pen Club and later traveled around Europe for approximately forty days. In 1967, when she began translating *The Tale of Genji* into modern Japanese, she rented an apartment in Bunkyō-ku to devote her entire attention to the endeavor, which occupied six years of her life. Only a year after beginning the translation, Enchi was dealt a setback when she was diagnosed with a detached retina, had surgery performed, and endured darkness for over a month during the recovery period.

In 1970, Enchi gave lectures on Japanese women writers at the University of Hawaii during the summer session. Then in 1972, she lost three people close to her: her friend of over forty years, Hirabayashi Taiko, died of pneumonia in February; her friend of thirty years, Tsuda Tomoko (?) (Tokiko?), died on November 10; and her husband of over forty years, Yoshimatsu, died of pneumonia on November 26.

In 1973, she had surgery again for a detached retina at the age of sixty-eight but never fully recovered her sight. Thereafter, she continued writing by dictating to an amanuensis. By 1974, however, she was well enough to visit Europe again for about twenty days during the summer. In 1976, she was hospitalized for a heart malfunction and ordered to rest quietly for two months. In 1977, she again went to Europe and toured the region for about eighteen days. Until Enchi died at the age of eighty-one in 1986, she maintained an active life, publishing both fictional and scholarly works.

Career: Enchi's career as a writer can be divided into three contiguous areas: as dramatist, as novelist and short story writer, and as classical scholar. She began writing for the theater, but today she is known as a novelist whose works feature intertextual references to classical works written in the Heian (794–1185) and Edo periods (1600–1867). References to works from the traditional canon reflect Enchi's labors to render into modern Japanese premodern works from a wide range of genres and time periods, attesting to her avocation as classical scholar.

While Enchi was writing drama during 1926–34, her works were published in journals such as *Geki to hyōron* (Drama and Criticism), *Nyōnin geijutsu* (Women's Arts), *Hi no tori* (Sun Bird), *Shinchō* (New Tide), *Bungei shunjū* (Literary Spring and Autumn), *Bungakukai* (Literary World), and *Bungei* (Literary Arts), some of which remain leading literary journals today. The success she met during her early attempts to get her works published began to elude her in the mid-1930s, causing her to switch to novel writing rather than to continue writing drama without a publishing outlet. Thus, her career as a dramatist was cast aside when she was thirty, with the publication in 1935 of a collection of plays, *Seishun* (Passionate Spring), to commemorate the closure of one aspect of her career. Among the plays from this period are *Furusato* (Hometown, 1926), *Banshun sōya* (A Turbulent Night in Late Spring, 1928), *Kanojo no jigoku* (Her Hell, 1931), and *Arashi* (Storm, 1934). Although Enchi stopped creating drama of her own, her interest in drama never waned, though it became channeled into publishing criticism.

After deciding to become a novelist, Enchi did not appear overnight as an award-winning writer; in fact, she gained fame late in life (in her late forties) but continued to publish works until she was in her eighties. In the latter half of the 1930s, Enchi published short works in a number of reputable journals: *Murasaki* (Lavender, edited by classical scholar Ikeda Kikan), *Jinmin bunkō* (The People's Library, published by a left-wing literary group), *Nihon hyōron* (Japanese Criticism), *Shin nyoen* (New Woman's Garden), *Chūō kōron* (Central Review, still one of the leading intellectual journals today), and *Bungakukai* (The Literary World), among others. Among her earliest published works of this era are "Sanbun ren'ai" (Prose Love, 1936), "Genzai" (Original Sin, 1938), "Rengoku no ryō" (Spirits of Purgatory, 1938), and "Onna no fuyu" (A Woman's Winter, 1939).

During the early part of the 1940s, Enchi began experiencing difficulty getting her work into print. After the publication of a short story in 1942, she was unable to get her fictional works published for five years. In fact, during the years 1943–48, the only item published was a scholarly work for juvenile audiences, a study of *Otogizōshi monogatari* (Companion Booklet Tales). With the encouragement of longtime friend Hirabayashi Taiko, Enchi continued to submit works for publication amid many rejections until finally she was successful in getting approval for installments to journals once again.

The latter part of the 1940s proved to be the basis for the success Enchi would reap in the 1950s. In 1949, the first part of Chapter 1 ("Ajisai": Hydrangeas; later as "Hatsuhana"; Eng., First Bloom) of the novel *Onnazaka* (Female Slope, 1949–57; Eng. tr., The Waiting Years, 1971) was published in the journal *Shōsetsu Sanmyaku*. In 1951, "Kōmyō kōgō no e" (Empress Kō-myō's Painting) was published in the journal *Shōsetsu shinchō*. In 1952, the journal *Shōsetsu shinchō* inherited the responsibility of publishing the second part of Chapter 1, "Hatsuhana reki" (First Bloom Calendar; later as "Aoi budō"; Eng., Green Grapes) of *Onnazaka* from the earlier journal and by the year 1957 finished publishing the work in a special issue.

In 1953, Enchi first received public acclaim when her work "Himojii tsukihi" (Days of Hunger, 1953), which appeared in the journal *Chūō kōron,* was awarded the sixth Woman Writer's Prize (Joryū Bungakushashō). Further installments of *Onnazaka* continued to be published in the journal *Shōsetsu shinchō:* in 1953, the third part of Chapter 1, "Saihishō" (Colorful Maidservant Selection; Eng., Handmaid), and the first part of Chapter 2, "Nijūroku ya no tsuki" (Moon of the Twenty-Sixth Night), and in 1954, the second part of Chapter 2, "Murasaki tegara" (Purple Hair Ornament; Eng., Purple Ribbon).

In the mid- to latter part of the 1950s, Enchi wrapped up tales she had begun earlier and began new ones she would weave to conclusion a few years later. *Shōsetsu shinchō* continued to publish subsequent portions of *Onnazaka:* in 1955, the third part of Chapter 2, "Aoi ume shō" (Unripe Plum Selection; Eng., Unripe Damsons), and in 1956, the first part of Chapter 3, "Ibomai" (Half-Sister; Eng., The Stepsisters). On the other hand, the earliest chapters of a new novel, *Ake o ubau mono* (That Which Steals Red), "Ake o ubau mono," and "Waga koi no iro" (The Color of My Love) were published in *Bungei* in 1955, with the three concluding chapters, "Futatsu no gekijō de" (At Two Theaters), "Onna no dōke" (A Woman's Antics), and "Zoku Onna no dōke" (A Woman's Antics, Continued), appearing in 1956. A couple of short stories, "Yō" (Enchantress) and "Otoko no hone" (A Man's Bones), which have been translated into English, were also published in 1956.

The final and concluding chapter of *Onnazaka,* "Onnazaka" (Female Slope, Eng., The Waiting Years), was published in a special volume of *Shōsetsu shinchō* in 1957 and awarded the Noma Literary Prize (Noma Bungeishō) soon after it was printed as a book in the latter part of 1957. When the nine-year task of publishing *Onnazaka* concluded in 1957, the first installment of a new novel, *Hanachirusato* (The Village of Scattering Blossoms), appeared in a 1957 special issue of the journal *Bungei shunjū* with intervening and concluding chapters appearing in subsequent special issues of the same journal through 1960, with the exception of the third chapter, published in the journal *Bungakukai* in 1959. Further, a short story called "Mimiyōraku" (Earring) appeared in the journal *Gunzō* in 1957 as well, and another novella, *Aki no nezame* (Autumn Awakening), was published in the newspaper *Mainichi shinbun*. Finally, a short story, "Nise no en: shūi" (Karma Through Two Lives: Gleanings; tr., Love in Two Lives: The Remnant, 1983; Two Lifetimes—Gleanings, 1983), was also published in 1957.

Although Enchi's most prolific production of novels and short stories was in the 1950s, "Himojii tsukihi" (1954) and *Onnazaka* (1957) were the only works to receive public acclaim through the Woman Writer's Prize and the Noma Literary Prize. Enchi's major literary contribution of 1958 was *Onnamen* (Female Mask; tr., Masks, 1983), which appeared in serial form in the journal *Gunzō* and eventually found its way to English audiences when it was translated in 1983. In 1959, Enchi elected to continue with the theme of masks for a short story entitled, "Futaomote" (A Pair of Masks), which also appeared in the journal *Gunzō*.

Journal installments continued to be a venue for Enchi's works. Beginning in 1959 and ending in January 1961, *Koe* featured nine installments of *Namamiko monogatari* (The Tale of the False Shamaness, 1965), which remained unfinished when the journal ceased publication in 1961. After a four-year hiatus, Enchi rewrote some of the existing sections, provided a conclusion, and had the novel published in 1965. Shortly thereafter in 1966, it was awarded the fifth Women's Literature Prize (Joryū Bungakushō) and has been suggested by some scholars as her literary masterpiece.

In 1960, the novella *Kizu aru tsubasa* (Injured Wing) appeared in the journal *Chūō kōron,* and *Yasashiki yoru no monogatari* (Tale of a Gentle Night) was printed in installments from January through December in the journal *Fujin no tomo* (Woman's Friend) and released as a book in 1962. The conclusion of the novel *Hanachirusato* appeared in a special issue of *Bungei shunjū* in December after having made its debut in a similar volume in 1957, and several other works, such as "Hatsukoi no yukikata" (The Way of First Love), the novel *Watashi mo moeteiru* (I, Too, Am Burning), "Otoko to iu mono" (A Thing Called Man), and the like, were also published in 1960. In this year, too, a collection of Enchi's earlier works appeared in the series *Nihon bungaku zenshū* (A Complete Collection of Japanese Literature), published by Shinchōsha.

During the first half of the 1960s, Enchi's literary contributions were numerous: short stories, "Onna no mayu" (A Woman's Cocoon), "Yuki ori" (A Sprig of Snow), "Adashino" (Adashino), "Onna o ikiru" (Living as a Woman), "Mekura oni" (Blind Devil), "Hokuro no onna" (Woman with a Mole), "Utsukushii Shojo" (Beautiful Maiden), "Shitamachi no onna" (Woman of the Lower City), "Kekkon sōdan" (Marriage Discussions), "Keshō" (Changing Disposition), "Yume no naka no kotoba" (Words in a Dream), "Ningyō shimai" (Doll Sisters), and "Miyako no onna" (Woman of the Capital), and the novellas *Komachi hensō* (Komachi in Disguise), *Onna obi* (Female Sash), *Yuki moe* (Snow Burning), and *Shishijima kidan* (Strange Story of Shishijima), among others, for the years 1961–66. Despite her absorption with the classics during the late 1960s and early 1970s, Enchi produced several interesting fictional works in this period: *Niji to shura* (The Rainbow and Asura, 1968), *Yūkon* (Wandering Spirit, 1970), and *Saimu* (Glowing Mist; original title, *Karuizawa,* 1975).

However, when Enchi began translating the classical novel *Genji monogatari* (The Tale of Genji, ca. 1000) into modern Japanese in 1967, a task that occupied six years of her life, the lure of the classics proved pervasive enough to increase the production of her critical writing at the expense of her creative fiction. For example, Enchi continued to write a few fictional and scholarly works during the years 1968–71, but these were the least productive times on record for her and reveal the depth of her immersion in the translation effort. Upon finishing the translation of the *Genji* in 1972, with revisions extending into 1973, the greatest period of production for her critical writing extended from 1972 to 1978. Among the nonfictional works she produced were eulogies for her best friend, Hirabayashi Taiko, and reminiscences about Nobel Prize recipient Kawabata Yasunari in Oslo, Norway, in addition to numerous scholarly articles on the *Genji* and women writers of the Heian period.

Other nonfictional works by Enchi were translations, introductions, and commentaries on the Japanese classics produced throughout her life. Examples of some of the modern Japanese commentaries and translations produced by Enchi are Heian literary classics *Taketori monogatari* (Tale of the Bamboo Cutter, 1954), *Kagerō nikki* (The Gossamer Journal, 1960), *Izumi Shikibu nikki* (The Izumi Shikibu Journal, 1960), *Yowa no Nezame* (Midnight Awakening, 1968), and *Tsutsumi Chūnagon monogatari* (The Tale of the Riverside Middle Counselor, 1968), medieval tales *Otogizōshi monogatari* (Companion Booklet Tales, 1961), *Gikeiki* (The Yoshitsune Chronicle, 1961), and *Soga monogatari* (The Tale of the Soga, 1961), and Edo period masterpieces *Ugetsu monogatari* (Tales of Rain and Moonlight, 1956), *Harusame monogatari* (Tales of Spring Rain, 1956), and selected pieces of Nō, Jōruri and Kabuki plays.

Enchi Fumiko made an enormous contribution to the literary tradition she inherited from the premodern writers and established a modern tradition of excellence that will be hard to surpass. The level of her erudition is formidable, the scope of her research is extensive, and the force of her imagination is Herculean. Although her literary creations are difficult to decipher, it is indeed a worthy venture to invest time in divining the true meaning behind the surface story she weaves so skillfully. One of her most significant accomplishments is that she found a literary voice of her own, one that pays conscious tribute to the pioneer voices of women writers of the Heian period. In exploring their works for artistic inspiration, she played the role of medium conjuring up their memory for modern readers, but often universalized (or subverted, as the case may be) the original message to fit the needs of a woman of the 20th century. Enchi Fumiko is a rare genius, one of the most memorable writers of modern Japan. *Enchi Fumiko Zenshū* (Shinchōsha, 1977–78) in sixteen volumes contains many works that sketch the plight of women in various time frames, including the word *onna* (woman) in numerous titles, focusing on the inequity suffered by a woman in a patriarchal society, and offering budding feminist views.

In 1969, Enchi was awarded the fifth Tanizaki Prize (Tanizaki Jun'ichirō shō) for her autobiographical trilogy *Ake o ubau mono* (1956), *Kizu aru tsubasa* (Injured Wings, 1962), and *Niji to shura* (1968). In the following year, 1970, Enchi was selected as a member of the Academy of Art (Bungei-in), and in 1972 *Yūkon* was awarded the fourth Japanese Literature Grand Prize (Nihon bungaku taishō). Finally, in 1985, to culminate a sixty-year career, she received the Order of Culture (Bunka kunshō)—one of only two female authors (the other was Nogami Yaeko in 1971) to be honored with postwar Japan's highest award.

Major Works: "Himojii tsukihi" (Days of Hunger, 1953), short story. While many modern Japanese authors often display an array of Western influences, Enchi thrived on those from the Japanese classical canon. Like Tanizaki Jun'i-chirō (1886–1965) and Akutagawa Ryūnosuke (1892–1927), who are honored by the prestigious literary prizes named after them, Enchi delighted in finding a traditional work or historical fact to serve as a springboard for her literary creations. Further, like Tanizaki and Akutagawa, Enchi was an independent writer who did not belong to any particular school of literature, especially the "I"-novelist group, whose adherents relied heavily on raw autobiographical material as stuff of their "fiction." Tanizaki, Akutagawa, and Enchi did occasionally use life experiences in their fictional creations, but their inclusion was primarily motivated by literary concerns rather than by penchant for confession or narrative veracity. It is apparent that Enchi frequently used her own life experiences as sources for her novels, but even when critics discovered some striking factual similarities between her life and fiction, they found her emphasis to be always on creative concerns. After Enchi's marriage in 1930, for example, there followed a two-year period of silence, suggesting maladjustment and unhappiness in her marital relationship. When she finally began to write again, her main theme was unhappy marriages, and her works exuded an ambivalence toward men, but elevating it to a gender-role issue.

Winner of the Woman Writer's Prize (Joryū bungakushō) in 1954, "Himojii tsukihi" describes the oppressed life of a woman whose husband is unfaithful, is unable to financially provide for his family, and finally becomes an invalid requiring constant care. Ultimately, she is approached by her husband's son, who wants her to join in a conspiracy to murder him, but ironically, she decides to care for him, hoping one day to leave him. However, she dies of exhaustion before achieving her dream of escape. The depiction of abject hopelessness in the life of a woman won for Enchi the status of a serious writer.

Namamiko monogatari (The Tale of the False Shamaness, 1965), novel. Of the few works by Enchi in which most of the action takes place in the premodern period, the most notable is this fiction set in the heyday of the Heian period ruled by Regent Fujiwara Michinaga (966–1027) at the court of Emperor Ichijō (r. 986–1011) and his empress, Fujiwara Teishi (977–1000). Enchi acknowledges her debt to the *Eiga monogatari* (Eng., A Tale of Flowering Fortunes, ca. 1028) by Akazome Emon in a subtitle, "Gleanings from *A Tale of Flowering Fortunes*," but she departs from the original for the different perspective she provides and for the different purpose she seeks to accomplish.

After achieving recognition as a major author, Enchi felt confident to develop themes that were of vital importance to her but that may not have been considered marketable. Readers of Enchi's fiction may feel a sense of familiarity with themes found in the 11th-century classic, *Genji monogatari* (The Tale of Genji), where male-female relationships are doomed to unhappiness, where jealous spirits take possession of others, and where strong-willed women endure life in a polygynous and patriarchal society. Most of her female characters are outwardly calm and collected while inside they are burning with anger, passion, and unfulfilled desire. Even though most of her fiction is set in the modern period, there are frequent allusions to the literature and events of the premodern period, so that the flow of time is distorted, obscuring the usual distinction between the past and the present.

Namamiko monogatari is unique on a number of levels, but foremost is the narrative structure Enchi creates. She employs three voices to tell the tale: in the first, Enchi narrates in her own voice, seeking to establish herself as an unassailable authority on the tale she is resuscitating; in the second, she utilizes her own voice but limits it to paraphrasing in modern Japanese events of the original text; and, in the third, she speaks in the voice of the Heian-period narrator as she presumably recites from memory passages from the original text. The structure centers on a modern-day frame introduced by Enchi in her own voice, which serves as a prelude to a tale set in the Heian period that she ostensibly reconstructs from memory. Enchi's purpose in narrating in her own voice was to establish herself as a privileged narrator in the frame surrounding the interior story of *Namamiko monogatari,* set in the Heian period, rather than being motivated by a need to "confess" or "reveal" secrets about her personal past. She provides only details about herself that support her literary and technical needs without providing extraneous facts. She supports her claim of being privy to "inside" information by revealing that she is the daughter of scholar Ueda Kazutoshi, who inherited the library of Basil Hall Chamberlain, and quotes an excerpt from the literary dictionary, *Nihon bungaku daijiten* (Greater Dictionary of Japanese Literature), to substantiate her position.

Following that, Enchi immediately challenges the dictionary's authority by correcting the *katakana* transliteration of the name of Basil Hall Chamberlain from "Cham *bu* ren" to "Cham *ba* ren," stating that at home her father always pronounced the name that way. She then undermines her own authority by revealing uncertainty about the provenance of the *Namamiko* text (she cannot recall whether it was a part of Chamberlain's collection or her father's), then further declares that the text is now lost and that she must recount from memory a text she read forty years ago! The narrative framework creates the need for the reader to always remain alert and to constantly gauge and recalculate the reliability of the narrator.

Some literary critics consider *Namamiko monogatari* Enchi's masterpiece. In "The Medium of Fiction: Enchi Fumiko as Narrator" (1988), Van C. Gessel divines Enchi's purpose in depicting an atypically happy marital relationship in *Namamiko monogatari*. He claims Enchi herself is the false "narratorial medium": she weaves a tale of purported happiness in the marital relationship between Ichijō and Teishi but intends the complicated narrative structure to undermine the very surface story she has related. The ending suggests that truth is not absolute but is relative to the point of view from which a narrative is cast. Thus, Gessel concludes that the only truth that can be divined is that "no form of narrative can be regarded as the final word." He also maintains that the "false," unreliable text launches a major attack against the male-dominated genre of "I-novels," whose raison d'être is completely dependent upon the "truthfulness" of narrated events. The brilliant reading by Gessel of this difficult work ferrets out the subversive purposes of the author and renders the message it conveys consistent with those in other works in Enchi's oeuvre. A translation of this intriguing novel would enhance our ability to access a bit more of her vast, untranslated oeuvre.

Yasashiki yoru no monogatari (Tale of a Gentle Night, 1961), fiction. Another work with a premodern setting, this story was fiction written by Enchi as a conjecture of events preceding the extant portion of the manuscript of the late Heian *monogatari, Yowa no nezame* (also *Yoru no nezame* and *Nezame,* Night Awakening, ca. 1060; Eng., The Tale of Nezame, 1973), soon after she had completed a modern Japanese translation of this classical tale earlier in 1961. Enchi was aware of novelist Nakamura Shin'ichirō's fictional attempt to re-create events in the nonextant Part 2 of *Yowa no nezame,* but her interest was in the relationship that existed between the youthful female protagonist Nezame (aged sixteen through twenty-seven) and her husband, the old regent. Like many classical scholars, she held high regard for *Nezame* as a worthy successor to the spirit of the *Genji* and felt compelled to introduce it to a wider audience. It, too, would be a worthy translation project, benefiting modernists, feminists, and those interested in the traditional canon.

Yūkon (Wandering Spirit, 1970), novel. Spirit possession and *miko* (priestess-medium) assume major roles here, emphasizing Enchi's foray into the world of the supernatural and sensuality. Many of Enchi's themes have a precedent in premodern literature, but often she injects erotic and sensual aspects of the female psyche that are not present in Heian *monogatari* (narrative fiction). In "Eroticism and the Writings of Enchi Fumiko," Yoko McClain reports that Enchi stated that some women write about sex from a deep-seated need while others write for sensational or commercial reasons. McClain concludes that Enchi belonged to the first category and attributed some of the motivation to write about sex to the physical deprivation she experienced in her own life. Moreover, some of the eroticism in Enchi's work may be traced back to the literature and theater of the Edo period, which seems to have exerted considerable influence during her youth concerning sensuality and love.

Often, as in *Yūkon,* Enchi finds the embodiment of eroticism and sensuality in the figure of the *miko,* which was traditionally associated with young maidens who served at Shintō shrines. They performed a number of sacerdotal functions, among them the divination of oracles, acting as mediums during spirit possession exorcism rites, and playing ceremonial roles at various Shintō festivals. In other sources, *miko* has been labeled shamans (female equivalent to priests who act as mediums to summon good or evil spirits).

Classical literature is replete with accounts of royal princesses, who while serving in the capacity of *Saiin* (vestal virgins or high priestess) at Ise Shrine or Kamo Shrines, kept clandestine assignations while supposedly in seclusion for purification rites. For example, *Ise monogatari* (Tales of Ise, ca. 950) preserves a famous poetic exchange between Ariwara Narihira (825–880) and an incumbent *Saiin* in which sexual ecstasy is credited for the confusion between the world of reality (waking) and dreams (sleeping), the relevant factor being the sexual encounter bordering on the divine because of the official post held by the *Saiin.* Significantly, the assignation exacted no retribution for either party.

Yūkon pays quiet tribute to the classical tradition by bringing an innovative twist to the traditional concept of spirit possession. There is no explicit reference made to Lady Rokujō, who unsuccessfully tried to suppress her emotions and learned that her vengeful spirit attacked several female rivals in *The Tale of Genji.* The implied reference to Lady Rokujō in *Yūkon* takes the form of the middle-aged female protagonist, Suo, who similarly tries to suppress her emotions but finds her spirit wandering off to men who are objects of her sexual desire. Not only is this a twist on the concept of spirit possession per se with its usual object of inflicting bodily harm, but it is also an imaginative method of fulfilling sexual desire. Curiously, the men who share her fantasy retain total recollection of the encounter, thereby creating the familiar indistinction between the world of dreams and reality found in many of Enchi's works.

Saimu (Glowing Mist, 1975), novel. This story shares with *Yūkon* concerns for women past their prime; however, *Saimu* moves the clock forward to the sixties and seventies for the ages of the female protagonists. It examines female sensuality that lingers into old age, coupled with a venture into the world of *miko,* inspired by Enchi's research on the topic. In *Saimu,* Kawai Yukiko, a female descendant of the chief priests of the Kamo Shrine who possesses an erotic picture scroll, ''The Maiden in Service of the Kamo Shrine,'' is the promiscuous focal point of the novel. The other woman, Sano, is a sixty-nine-year-old writer who is a neighbor of Yukiko in Karuizawa.

Men who have had intercourse with Yukiko describe the experience in ecstatic, religious terms but subsequently succumb to unnatural deaths. After Yukiko dies toward the end of the work, Sano inherits the picture scroll from her. Shortly thereafter, Sano begins to physically resemble Yukiko and to enact Yukiko's erotic behavior, suggesting that Yukiko's spirit has ''possessed'' Sano. Enchi suggests a relationship between sex and the divine in the figure of the *miko,* albeit in the form of an old woman instead of the virginal maidens of antiquity. In *Saimu,* the traditional image of *miko* (shaman, medium) as Shintō shrine maidens and their relationship to the historical role of sex in that capacity is given a new and modern turn by Enchi's imagination.

Ake o ubau mono (That Which Steals Red, 1955–56), novel. Enchi's penchant for describing sexual desire occasionally leans toward the macabre and seems to be based partially upon her loss of female organs due to mastectomy and hysterectomy. *Ake o ubau mono* opens with the removal of all the female protagonist's teeth, calling to mind two former operations in which she first lost a breast, then her uterus. The protagonist continues by recalling the fate of the famous Chinese historian, Ssu-ma Ch'ien (145–ca. 90 B.C.), who was sentenced to castration for attempting to plead clemency for General Li Ling, defeated in battle in the Han dynasty (Former Han, 206 B.C.–A.D.25; Later Han, 25–189). Ssu-ma Ch'ien contemplated suicide after his sentence was carried out but later threw himself into writing the conclusion to his *Grand History* as sublimation for lost sexual ability. Evidently Enchi equated sexual drive with sexual organs and, because she, too, had suffered a loss, seems to have immersed herself in writing to deal with the psychological damages that resulted from it. Just as physical deprivation creates a reaction, societal injustices turn some women into political activists who strive to "right wrongs." But when reality offers little hope for change, some women elect to "write wrongs" in the world of literature. Enchi was never politically active, but she put her creative imagination to work in a number of fruitful endeavors to "write wrongs" on paper. In "Enchantress," Enchi created a female protagonist in a stale marriage exacting a type of revenge on her husband by having an imaginary affair with a younger man and writing a romance about it as an outlet for an overactive mind. In *Masks,* she empathized with women scorned in love as she wove alluring tales of intelligent women who harbored resentment against men and manipulated her characters to devise a revenge that could be enacted only by women.

Translated Works: The Waiting Years (*Onnazaka*, 1949–57), novel. This work helped establish Enchi as a serious writer but is in many ways regarded as "atypical" and criticized for exhibiting "fundamental weaknesses in its structure and mode of narration." Structurally, the novel is divided into three parts— the first chapter with three subtitles, "First Bloom," "Green Grapes," and "Handmaid," the second also with three subtitles, "Moon of the Twenty-Sixth Night," "Purple Ribbon," and "Unripe Damsons," and the third with only two subtitles, "The Stepsisters" and "The Waiting Years"—roughly a period of thirty years spanning the end of the Edo period (1600–1867) to the Meiji period (1868–1912). Leaps in the chronology of the narrative are often accompanied by shifts in point of view and levels of accessibility to the interior thoughts of characters.

The perceived flaws in the mode of narration may refer to the shifts in emphasis that occur as the novel progresses—from the wife, Tomo, to the mistress, Suga, and then back again to the wife at the conclusion. Swings in the emotional and sympathetic level of the narrative are bound to leave readers frustrated. The stoicism expressed by Tomo as she sets out to search for a young mistress for her husband, Yukitomo, greets readers who ready themselves to "see" the story from her point of view. Yet as the story proceeds, readers are given more interior views of the mistress, Suga, and are denied those of Tomo, thereby creating a distance between the reader and the character of Tomo. Just at the height of sympathy for Suga, the entire narrative turns away from both of these women and converges on a new generation of youngsters, returning only at the conclusion to the figure of the wife, Tomo. For all its inconsistencies, the focal point of the novel is the psychological damage inflicted upon women living in a polygynous household.

The Waiting Years deals primarily with the oppression and suppression of women, a theme portrayed in "Himojii tsukihi," by Saku, the hardworking wife who dies without ever having uttered a word of reproof to her unfaithful husband, and in "Boxcar of Chrysanthemums" (Kikuguruma, 1967; Eng., 1982) in the character Ichige Rie, who remained married to a retarded man without outwardly expressing the slightest resentment or objection. But even in this atypical work, there are typical elements. For example, there are germinal signs of Enchi's pet images and themes in the making, such as the phrase "the utterance of medium" in the first chapter, which betrays her fascination for this topic, and descriptions of the masklike faces of women who strive to conceal inner emotions, which foretell Enchi's literary endeavor, *Masks*.

Despite its technical problems, some scholars have noted an affinity between the 11th-century masterpiece *The Tale of Genji* (Genji monogatari) and *The Waiting Years*. In "The Medium of Fiction: Fumiko Enchi as Narrator," Van C. Gessel suggests that *The Waiting Years, Masks* (Onnamen, 1958), and *The Tale of the False Shamaness* (Namamiko monogatari, 1965) form a trilogy written by Enchi in tribute to *The Tale of Genji*. Gessel interprets *The Waiting Years* as "a view of a modern fallen *Genji* world as seen through the eyes of a long-suffering Lady Aoi" (Genji's first principal wife), *Masks* as a "shift to the perspective of Lady Rokujō" (a lover scorned by Genji), and *The Tale of the False Shamaness* as to a "certain degree a re-creation of the ideal, a reenshrinement of the Shining Prince as seen through the eyes of the faithful, loving Murasaki" (Genji's second principal wife).

Other scholars have suggested that *The Waiting Years* may be the closest Enchi ever came to writing in a semiautobiographical vein—the story of a woman oppressed by patriarchal society may have reflected, in part, the life experiences of her beloved grandmother, Ine, who lived in the Meiji period and endured a polygynous marriage with a man from a samurai family. The jealousy, insecurity, and mental anguish caused by polygyny receive central focus in this novel and reverberate like a familiar refrain in some of her other works. The similarity in polygynous marriage situations between the Heian and Meiji periods has caught the attention of those who study Enchi's works.

Yukiko Tanaka and Elizabeth Hanson, in an introduction to Enchi's "Boxcar of Chrysanthemums," allude to "subtle influences from *The Tale of Genji*" in *The Waiting Years*. But what exactly is the nature of the suggested affinity between the two? Is it in the similarity of topics, that polygamy is detrimental to the female psyche? Or is it the episodic nature in the structure of the two works? In light of the suggested affinity of the classical work and Enchi's *The*

Waiting Years, a study of its publication record reveals some hesitation on the part of Enchi to conclude the novel she had been writing for a number of years. Before concluding it, Enchi produced the following short story.

"Otoko no hone" (Skeletons of Men, 1956; Eng., 1988), short story. This story may have been written as an experimental conclusion to the novel *The Waiting Years.* It has an almost identical plot for the inner level of the two-layer story and takes advantage of the focus on the mistress, which had been developed extensively in the second chapter of the novel. Written in 1956, it preceded the conclusion to the novel by almost a year and may have provided Enchi with a chance to conclude the work focusing on the mistress instead of the wife.

"Skeletons of Men" displays Enchi's preference for using a frame of a story within a story. The exterior frame, related by an anonymous first-person narrator, involves two women, one of whom tells the narrator a story of an anonymous "blood-letter" found within the folds of her grandmother's antique *obi* (sash). The interior story introduces the scant remnants of the life of a married woman who was scorned by a man who was involved in polygynous relationships with a wife and several mistresses. The events of the interior story very closely parallel those found in *The Waiting Years* but provide the poignant fate of the mistress after the death of both the wife and husband.

"Skeletons of Men" shows a greater freedom to play with the themes with which Enchi was later associated than *The Waiting Years.* The addition of the exterior story piques the reader's interest when one of the protagonists, Shizuko, claims that she is "being manipulated by the spirit of the sash." The ending to this short story leans more decidedly toward the supernatural than the novel, which only hints at spirit possession in the final scene, announcing the last will and testament of the wife, Tomo, whereas in the former, specters and apparitions of the deceased float into view at the conclusion. Jealousy and resentment form the core of both works, but it is clear that Enchi, struggling for public recognition at the time, wanted the novel to be free from controversial topics that may have inhibited the novel's reception with the public.

"*Yō*" (Enchantress, 1956; Eng., 1958), short story. Narrated in the third person from the point of view of the female protagonist, Chigako, this work contains elements more representative of a story by Enchi: a world peopled by classical Japanese scholars, a couple enduring a loveless marriage, a connoisseur of Japanese antiquities, a woman attempting to regain her lost youth, an obscuring of the distinction between the past and the present, and hints of the supernatural. Chigako, a middle-aged translator of classical Japanese works into English, proclaims that the spirit of women writers of the Heian period have begun to influence her into producing "romances" of her own. The reference Chigako makes to Episode 99 of *Tales of Ise* (Ise monogatari, ca. 950) concerning the description of an old woman's thinning hair being like her own stuns the male specialist of Heian literature who never guessed the hidden passion of an intellectual woman who made her living using her mind.

The narrative centers on the unhappy twenty-year marriage between Chigako and Keisaku, commenting on factors such as the physical loss of teeth, hair, and youth and on the psychological deprivations due to misunderstandings, mistrust, and ennui. In contrast to the pessimistic conclusions of *The Waiting Years* and "Days of Hunger," Enchi injected a touch of humor into the startling conclusion, in which a story from her dreams suddenly becomes reality. The contrast between the amusing image of toothless mouths of the married couple and the melding between the world of fantasy and reality makes for one of the most unusual and memorable conclusions on record for Enchi.

"Nise no en—shūi" (Bond for Two Lifetimes—Gleanings, 1957), short story. An obscuring of the distinction between the world of reality and dreams occurs with a vengeance in this brilliant short story, displaying once again a frame of a story within a story. The interior story features a modern translation of a fragment of the *Harusame monogatari* (*Tales of Spring Rain,* 1809) by Edo period writer Ueda Akinari (1734–1809), noted for his tales of ghosts and the macabre. The exterior story is related in the first person by a war widow acting as an amanuensis to her old professor, an expert in Edo period literature, who is in the process of translating Ueda's tale. The story that Enchi chose to translate was that of Jōsuke, a Buddhist priest who was interred in a state of trance and whose desiccated body was exhumed when a man heard the sound of bells coming from beneath the ground. The priest is reverently revived but has no memory of his previous life and becomes involved sexually with the female village idiot and proves, at least to the family who rescued him, the futility of living piously. The agility with which the two stories are woven together, blending the past and the present, brings a delightful surreal quality to the conclusion, when reality and dreams mingle, creating the necessity for readers to contemplate what has actually occurred.

In "Bond for Two Lifetimes—Gleanings," an investigation of the existence of sexual drive without the guiding hand of intelligence is set into motion in the guise of the resuscitated priest, Jōsuke. Enchi's penchant for this topic is clearly apparent in the staging of similar scenarios portraying mentally deficient characters with normal sexual drives in other works—Harume in *Masks* and Ichige Masutoshi in a "Boxcar of Chrysanthemums." Enchi was evidently intrigued by the idea of the persistence of the sexual drive devoid of intelligence as an opportunity for exploring the psyche, especially since she had already investigated the antithetical position of the existence of the sexual drive without sexual organs in the course of writing other works.

"Kikuguruma" (Boxcar of Chrysanthemums, 1965), short story. Here the narrator speaks in a voice that is self-consciously close to Enchi's own to relate a story about a woman, Ichige Rie, who married a mentally retarded man. The focal point of the narration seems to lie in discovering the motivation behind Ichige Rie's acquiescence to the marriage and how the progression of years has changed the narrator's initial reaction to hearing the story. The narrator's original reaction of anger evolves into speculations about the possibility of a physical handicap concerning the woman that might have limited her opportunities for marriage with a "normal" man. Toward the end of the short story, the narrator, as if thinking aloud, reaches a resolution that the woman was not physically handicapped, yet chose a life that the narrator could not imagine for herself. The narrator had reached a level of maturity where she could finally accept the behavior of some people as beyond comprehension, without reacting with anger or demanding an explanation.

Onnamen (Masks, 1958), novel. In the novel *The Waiting Years* and several of the short stories previously discussed, female characters have been predictably well delineated, in contrast with unsympathetic or apathetic male characters. In *The Waiting Years,* the husband, Yukitomo, is depicted as a callous polygamist who cruelly condemns the women in his household to mental anguish. Especially reprehensible is Yukitomo's completely ignoring the sexual and emotional needs of his wife, Tomo, because he was so immersed in pursuing new conquests as to be unaware of the damages he had perpetrated until the end. In "A Bond for Two Lifetimes—Gleanings," the narrator reveals Professor Nunokawa's disgusting behavior in sexually harassing young female students while he was middle-aged and then contrasts it with the image of him in his declining years as a pitiful, physically debilitated old man who cannot even urinate without assistance. In "Enchantress," Chigako's husband, Keisaku, who is drawn not so much as a culprit as a man insensitive to his wife's needs and desires, comes off a bit better than other male characters for the humorous touch Enchi adds to their relationship. Male characterizations in "Skeletons of Men" are almost identical to those in the novel and do not require embellishment here. While Enchi's men exhibit few admirable qualities, the female protagonist of *Masks* is one of the most bewitching characters created by Enchi.

Toganō Mieko, the protagonist of *Masks,* comes closest to fulfilling the ideal of a strong, enigmatic woman who manipulates a host of minor players on a stage choreographed to create a surreal atmosphere. Mieko, a widow in her fifties, is an accomplished poet who is also interested in classical Japanese literature, especially *The Tale of Genji,* the masterpiece of the Heian period. The members of Mieko's entourage are Toganō Yasuko, the widow of Mieko's son, Akio, who died in a mountaineering accident; Harume, the retarded twin sister of Akio, sent away by Mieko to be raised in the country; Ibuki Tsuneo, a married Heian literature professor; and Mikame Toyoki, a bachelor psychologist and amateur folklorist. The characters are bound by their shared interest in the study of spirit possession and by the acquaintance of Toganō Akio, who before his death had been conducting research in Heian spirit possession as a professor of literature. When Akio died, Mieko persuaded Yasuko to continue Akio's research on spirit possession, thereby continuing the association with Ibuki and Mikame. Harume did not, of course, interact with the intellectual group in their study of spirit possession.

The theme of spirit possession is intertwined with images of female masks worn in the Nō theater. Masks appears in the title of this novel, *Onnamen*

(Female Mask), and is further embellished by three chapter titles bearing the names of specific female Nō masks—the first chapter, ''Ryō no onna'' (lit., spirit woman), for the vengeful spirit of a woman tormented beyond the grave by unrequited love; the second chapter, ''Masugami'' (lit., length of hair), for young women plagued by madness; and the third chapter, ''Fukai'' (lit., deep well or deep woman), for middle-aged women beyond the age of sensuality. Masks of the Nō theater occupy a substantial role in the novel with direct correlation to the three female characters: the mask for Ryō no onna refers to Yasuko, the one for Masugami to Harume, and the one for Fukai to Mieko. Images of ghosts who roam the world telling woeful tales full of tormented memories are de rigueur for Nō performances and find resonance in the novel in the form of malign spirits who, during exorcism rites, reveal causes for lingering in the world.

Ghosts and spirits are not the only things to cloud readers' vision of the novel—the lack of narrational guidance in *Masks* makes it a difficult work to comprehend. In ''Twin Blossoms on a Single Branch: The Cycle of Retribution in *Onnamen*,'' Doris G. Bargen states that a simple process such as recapitulating the plot in a chronological fashion becomes, in the case of *Masks*, an interpretation of the work. Bargen's twenty-four-page analysis is the most extensive work done on the interpretation of *Masks* to date and reveals a good deal of thought extracted from clues imbedded in the text. Without guidance from the narrator, there is little readers can do but seek clues along the way to make sense of the narrative and grope to divine the purpose it seeks to accomplish.

A further complication in reading *Masks* arises from the lack of a central point of view from which the narrative unfolds. The reader is allowed little access to the interior thoughts of the major characters, and when glimpses are made available, readers may be advised upon occasion to suspect their reliability. Enchi was much enamored of Tanizaki Jun'ichirō's and Akutagawa Ryūnosuke's works, which played with unreliable narration, and Enchi seems to have adopted their attempts and fashioned them into an elevated art form. She conceals everything from us and only hints at things she wishes us to grasp, never approaching us directly but always proceeding obliquely with hidden motives and veiled purposes. Even Enchi's intertextual references to the Heian classics are replete with mystery.

Masks contains significant references to *The Tale of Genji, The Tale of Nezame*, and *Tales of Ise. The Tale of Genji* occupies so central a role in the work that one ponders the significance of reading the modern work without having read the 11th-century masterpiece beforehand. The inclusion of an essay in *Masks* by Mieko on the significance of Lady Rokujō depends heavily on the intertextual knowledge of her role in *The Tale of Genji*. Lady Rokujō, an accomplished, highborn woman scorned in love by the hero, Genji, found that the repression of her emotions caused her spirit to leave her body to torment her rivals. The essay reflects Enchi's extensive research on the topics of spirit possession and *miko,* reveals the depth of the attraction the character held for her, and attempts to reevaluate the importance of the character of Lady Rokujō. The empathy Mieko displays for the character of Lady Rokujō in the essay is reflected in turn by Enchi for the characters of Mieko and her classical predecessor, Lady Rokujō.

Intertextual references to *The Tale of Nezame* and the *Tales of Ise* are limited to cases that directly support either the topic of spirit possession or *miko. The Tale of Nezame* is cited for the express purpose of bringing to light a case of spirit possession used for political purposes. In *The Tale of Nezame,* the heroine, Nezame, is falsely accused of a spirit possession in which a highborn female rival was involved. Nezame's political rivals hired a false medium and instructed the medium to implicate her as the malign spirit possessing the lady and causing her illness. The idea of employing false mediums for political ends must have caught Enchi's attention, for she created the novel *Namamiko monogatari* (The Tale of the False Shamaness, 1965), which specifically addresses this issue—spiritual mediums may have had worldly motivations to divine the origin of a malign possession to effect political and societal change.

Reference to the *Tales of Ise* delineates the relationship between *miko* (mediums, shamanesses) and sex and further suggests that some shamanesses in a heightened state of sensuality during trances were especially susceptible to sexual advances, placing them in the vulnerable position of falling prey to bribes on the promise of sexual or material favors. Continuing this train of thought, *Masks* makes direct reference to Narihira's sexual encounter with his younger cousin, serving as the Saiin (high priestess) of Ise, who of her own accord goes to Narihira's bedchamber, confirming the idea that shamanesses view sex as sinless and reinforcing the idea of divinely inspired sex proposed in *Saimu.*

Other sexual issues at stake in *Masks* are the concepts of twins (similarity), androgyny, and homosexuality, attacking the system of patriarchy that supports the concept of difference. The twins, embodied by Akio (autumn male) and Harume (spring female), foster the concept of androgyny, the male and female counterparts of one being. While still in the womb, Akio kicks his sister in the head, causing mental retardation and signifying brutalization of the female by the male, or woman as victim. Homosexuality is suggested in the relationship between Mieko and Yasuko, is complemented in the androgynous nature of different-sex twins, and is read as an alternative route to patriarchy. Masks from the Nō theater are another element suggesting androgyny in that the all-male cast don female masks to portray women on stage. Twins, androgyny, and homosexuality are combined with masks from the Nō theater to further obscure the traditional distinctions between male and female. Further references to the *Kojiki* (A Record of Ancient Matters, 712) hint at the affinity of twins to the legend of the incestuous mating ritual of the brother Izanagi and his sister Izanami, suggesting the mythical rebirth of the ancestral soul.

Enchi's love of triangular relationships finds plentiful occasions to make their inexhaustible appearance—Mieko, Yasuko, and Harume make a female triangle;

Yasuko, Ibuki, and Mikame make a traditional romantic triangle; and Yasuko, Ibuki, and Harume make a duplicitous triangle. These are just the most major ones to come to mind and could easily be appended by many more. Triangles and the number three, from the division of chapters to the literal meaning of Mieko's name (threefold child), all combine to weave an intricate web of conspiracy to cloak the true purpose of the major player, Mieko.

An infinitely intriguing tale such as *Masks* deserves a more thorough analysis than can be provided here; however, there are excellent, lengthy accounts available in English by literary critics who have plumbed the depths of Enchi's literary purpose, as listed in the bibliographic entries.

"Mekura oni" (Blind Man's Bluff, 1962), short story. It holds that true love is a frightening phenomenon. Narrated in the first person from the perspective of an older half-sister of the middle-aged female protagonist, Kinu, the story unfolds in a series of flashbacklike segments revealing, bit by bit, fragments of the protagonist's life. Pieces of the narrator's life are included when they enhance the reader's understanding of Kinu's life. The driving force behind the narrative is to relate the message that once in Kinu's life her passion won over her intellect and that the second time that occurred, she would take her own life rather than succumb to it again. Indeed, the narrative strongly suggests its occurrence as the rationale behind her suicide at the age of fifty-two, an age that one would imagine to be beyond passion.

Most familiar themes are missing in "Blind Man's Bluff," but those that this story does have are love affairs with younger men, sensual women who do not make a living using their minds, and connoisseurs of Japanese art. Absent are the more macabre elements such as *miko,* spirit possession, and intertextual references to the classical canon as a backdrop for modern interpretation of traditional themes and concerns of women.

BIBLIOGRAPHY

Translations

"Blind Man's Bluff" (Mekura oni). Trans. Beth Cary. *The Mother of Dreams and Other Stories.* Ed. Makoto Ueda. Tokyo: Kōdansha, 1986.

"A Bond for Two Lifetimes—Gleanings" (Nise no en shūi). Trans. Phyllis Birnbaum. *Rabbits, Crabs, Etc.* Ed. Phyllis Birnbaum. Honolulu: University of Hawaii Press, 1983.

"Boxcar of Chrysanthemums" (Kikuguruma). Trans. Yukiko Tanaka and Elizabeth Hanson. *This Kind of Woman: Ten Stories by Japanese Women Writers 1960–1976.* New York: Putnam, 1982.

"Enchantress" (Yō). Trans. John Bester. *Japan Quarterly* 5.3 (1958):339–57.

"Enchantress" (Yō). Trans. John Bester. *Modern Japanese Short Stories.* Tokyo: Japan Publications Trading Co., 1960.

"Enchantress" (Yō). Trans. John Bester. *Rice Bowl Women: Writings by and About the Women of China and Japan.* Ed. Dorothy Blair Shimer. New York: Mentor, 1982.

"Love in Two Lives: The Remnant" (Nise no en shūi). Trans. Noriko Lippit. *Stories by*

Contemporary Japanese Women Writers. Ed. Lippit and Kyoko Selden. New York: M. E. Sharpe, 1983.

Masks (Onnamen). Trans. Juliet Winters Carpenter. New York: Knopf, 1983. Tokyo: Tuttle, 1984.

"Metamorphosis" (Keshō). Trans. S. Yumiko Hulvey (forthcoming).

"The Old Woman Who Eats Flowers" (Hana kui uba). Trans. S. Yumiko Hulvey (forthcoming).

"Skeletons of Men" (Otoko no hone). Trans. Susan Matisoff. *Japan Quarterly* 35.4 (1988):417–26.

The Waiting Years (Onnazaka). Trans. John Bester. Tokyo: Kodansha International, 1971.

Critical Writings

Bargen, Doris G. "Spirit Possession in the Context of Dramatic Expressions of Gender Conflict: The Aoi Episode of the *Genji monogatari.*" *Harvard Journal of Asiatic Studies* 48.1 (1988): 95–130.

———. "Twin Blossoms on a Single Branch: The Cycle of Retribution in *Onnamen.*" *Monumenta Nipponica* 46.2 (1991): 147–71.

Burnham, Jonathan. "Review of *Masks,* by Fumiko Enchi." *The Times Literary Supplement,* June 14, 1985.

Carpenter, Juliet Winters. "Enchi Fumiko: A Writer of Tales." *Japan Quarterly* 37.3 (1990):343–55.

"Enchi Fumiko." *Contemporary Authors.* Ed. Anne Evory. 25 Vols. Detroit: Gale Research, 1981.

Encyclopedia of World Literature in the Twentieth Century, 1982 ed., S. V. "Enchi Fumiko."

Forestier, Lisa. "Review of Masks by Fumiko Enchi." *Book Forum* 7 (1988): 31–32.

Gessel, Van. C. "Due Time: Modern Japanese Women Writers." *Journal of Japanese Studies* 15.2 (1989): 439–47.

———. "Echoes of Feminine Sensibility in Literature." *Japan Quarterly* 35.4 (1988): 410–16.

———. "The 'Medium' of Fiction: Fumiko Enchi as Narrator." *World Literature Today: A Literary Quarterly of the University of Oklahoma* (1988): 380–85.

Heinrich, Amy V. "Double Weave: The Fabric of Women's Writing." *World Literature Today: A Literary Quarterly of the University of Oklahoma* (1988): 408–14.

Hisamatsu, Sen'ichi. *Biographical Dictionary of Japanese Literature,* S. V.

Hulvey, S. Yumiko. "Intertextuality and Narrative Subversion in the Works of Enchi Fumiko." In *Japan in Traditional and Postmodern Perspectives,* ed. Steven Heine and Charles W. Fu. University Park: Pennsylvania State Press, forthcoming.

Knapp, Bettina L. *Women in Twentieth-Century Literature: A Jungian View.* University Park: Pennsylvania State University Press, 1987.

Kodansha Encyclopedia of Japan, S.V. "Enchi Fumiko."

Kokusai Bunka Shinkōkai (Japan Cultural Society). *Introduction to Contemporary Japanese Literature: Synopses of Major Works, 1956–70.* Tokyo: Kokusai Bunka Shinkōkai, 1972.

McClain, Yōko. "Eroticism and the Writings of Enchi Fumiko." *Journal of the Association of Teachers of Japanese* 15.1 (1980): 32–46.

Mamola, Claire Zebroski. *Japanese Women Writers in English Translation: An Annotated Bibliography.* New York: Garland, 1989.

Mulhern, Chieko Irie. "Japan." In *Longman Anthology of World Literature by Women, 1875–1975,* ed. Marian Arkin and Barbara Shollar. New York: Longman, 1989.

———. "Women Writers Past and Present: Murasaki Shikibu and Enchi Fumiko." *Review of National Literatures* 18 (1993): 137–64.

Pounds, Wayne. "Enchi Fumiko and the Hidden Energy of the Supernatural." *Journal of the Association of Teachers of Japanese* 24.2 (1990): 167–83.

Thurow, Shari L. "Enchi Fumiko's Literature in Translation." *International Association of Orientalist Librarians* 34–35 (1989): 37–43.

Vernon, Victoria V. *Daughters of the Moon: Wish, Will and Social Constraint in Fiction by Modern Japanese Women.* Berkeley: Institute of East Asian Studies, University of California Press, 1988.

S. Yumiko HULVEY

F/G ──────────────

FUJIWARA Michitsuna's Mother (Michitsuna no haha, ca. 936–95), poet, memoirist. Real name: undetermined.

Life: The woman known simply as Michitsuna's Mother was born to Fujiwara Tomoyasu (d. 977), a minor official who served variously as governor of the provinces of Mutsu, Kawachi, Tamba, and Ise. Though directly descended from Fuyutsugu (775–826), one of the early architects of Fujiwara political hegemony, the family had settled permanently into the middle-level *zuryō* class during the career of Tomoyasu's grandfather Takatsune (fl. mid- to late 9th century). Two of Takatsune's siblings had achieved great heights as the adopted children of their ambitious uncle Yoshifusa (804–72). A brother, Mototsune (836–91), was appointed imperial regent and later chancellor, while a half-sister, Kōshi (842–910), became senior consort to Emperor Seiwa (850–80; r. 858–76) and mother of the future emperor Yōzei (868–949; r. 876–84). But Takatsune's own fortunes meanwhile gradually declined. He and his sons were noted neither as poets nor as politicians, though a daughter, known as Hyōe no Myōbu, found minor but lasting renown as a lady-in-waiting to Fujiwara Onshi (872–907), consort to Emperor Uda (867–931; r. 887–97). A glimpse of Onshi's brilliant poetic salon and Hyōe no Myōbu's participation in it appears in episode 147 of *Yamato monogatari* (Tales of Yamato, extant from the mid-10th century).

Though Tomoyasu thus found his family more or less fixed in the middle class, he seems to have made the most of the situation. He spent part of his career as governor of Mutsu and Kawachi, two of the largest provinces in the realm and great producers of rice (as well as horses, in the case of Mutsu). As Masuda Shigeo points out (*Udaishō Michitsuna no haha* [Shintensha, 1983] 26ff.), these were lucrative, if unglamorous, posts. More important, Tomoyasu married his poetically talented daughter (Michitsuna's Mother) to Fujiwara Kaneie (929–90), the man who was to set the stage for the zenith of Fujiwara fortunes in the early 11th century. Michitsuna's Mother was nineteen or twenty in 954 when she was married to Kaneie. Though at the time merely an assistant commander in the palace guards (*uhyōe no suke*), Kaneie already ranked well above her in social standing. His glory days as the father of imperial consorts and empresses were still some fourteen years in the future, but he was nonetheless a member of the powerful Kujō house and son of Fujiwara Morosuke (908–60), then Minister of the Right to Emperor Murakami. It is possible that Tomoyasu's appointment as governor of Mutsu the following year had something to do with the ties he had established through his daughter's marriage.

We will probably never know whether Tomoyasu expected further career advancement to come of his daughter's match. She, however, at least on the showing of her lengthy *nikki* (memoir; lit., "record of days"), seems to have fiercely desired more status than she ultimately got. In the mid-10th century, marriage was still a viable avenue for upward mobility among daughters of the *zuryō* class and their families. A case in point is that of Kaneie's principal wife, Tokihime (d. 980). Like Michitsuna's Mother, Tokihime was the daughter of a provincial governor but lived to see her own daughters married to emperors. Her eldest, Chōshi (d. 982), bore to Ex-Emperor Reizei a son who became Emperor Sanjō. A second daughter, Senshi (962–1002), bore to Emperor En'yū a son who became Emperor Ichijō. Each of Tokihime's three sons—Michitaka (953–95), Michikane (961–95), and Michinaga (966–1028)—held in succession the supreme title of Imperial Regent. Michinaga went on to become Chancellor and the most powerful political figure of his day. But Michitsuna's Mother was no rival for Tokihime in the sphere of childbearing. In some twenty years of marriage, she produced only one child—"and that a boy," as she puts the matter in her memoir. The boy was Fujiwara Michitsuna (955–1020). Sometime around the age of forty, she seems to have adopted one of Kaneie's daughters by a minor rival (the girl's real mother was the daughter of Minamoto Kanetada), but there is little evidence to suggest the foster daughter won for her adoptive mother any heightened recognition or higher social status through marriage. Thus, unlike many important Heian writers before and after her, Michitsuna's Mother lived in relative isolation from the highest levels of court society.

Career: Despite her apparent disappointment with her secondary position among Kaneie's wives, Michitsuna's Mother made through her marriage the right sort of connections for a woman of literary talent. Her memoir, *Kagerō nikki* (The Gossamer Memoir, after 974), records instances of her poetic correspondence with some of the most elegant and powerful figures of the day, among them Fujiwara Tōshi (d. 975, sister to both Empress Anshi [927–64] and Kaneie), a woman whose romantic liaison with Emperor Murakami (926–67; r. 946–67) had begun to create something of a scandal even before Anshi's death. Evidence of the reputation of Michitsuna's Mother as a respected poet can be found in a number of documents dating from the late 10th century. In 969, she was among an elect few asked to compose *byōbu uta* (screen poems) for the fiftieth birthday celebration held for Minister of the Left Fujiwara Morotada (920–69; Kaneie's uncle). Especially in her later years, she seems to have made her voice heard among the best poetic circles. Poems composed by her were delivered at an *utaawase* (poetry contest, Kazan-in no ontoki no utaawase) sponsored by Emperor Kazan (968–1008; r. 984–86) in 986; and in 993 she herself seems to have participated in Tōgū Okisada Shinnō tachihaki no jin no utaawase, or "the contest sponsored by the guards of Crown Prince Okisada (later, Emperor Sanjō)."

A number of her *waka* (thirty-one-syllable poems) survive in the *shū* (personal poetry collection) appended to the last volume of some copies of her *nikki*. The collection, variously titled *Michitsuna no haha shū, Kagerō nikki kanmatsu shū,* and *Fu no Dainagon-dono no haha ue no shū,* was probably not compiled by Michitsuna's Mother herself. Some speculate her younger half-brother, the colorful poet Fujiwara Nagayoshi (946?–between 1012 and 1017?), compiled it not long after her death, carefully culling for the collection nearly fifty *waka* that do not appear in her *nikki*.

Major Works: Like a number of other gifted female poets and writers of the Heian period, Michitsuna's Mother has long had a place in the canon of Japanese poetry. This means, among other things, that our image of her has been filtered by a long history of the reading and reception of her *waka*. Well known as an accomplished poet in her own day, Michitsuna's Mother established a literary reputation that survived her for generations. Over thirty-seven of her *waka* appear in twelve of the imperially commissioned *waka* anthologies *(chokusenshū),* beginning with the third of these, *Shūishū* (between 1005 and 1011), and continuing through the eighteenth, *Shinsenzaishū* (1359). Down through the centuries, selections of her *waka* consistently reappear in privately compiled anthologies and exemplary collections. Just as telling as her perennial status in the anthologies is the stature of the poet-critics who continued to read, anthologize, and comment upon her works. Within some twelve years of her death, Fujiwara Kintō (966–1041), the arbiter of poetic taste in Murasaki Shikibu's day, was including *waka* by Michitsuna's Mother in his exemplary collections and imaginary poetry contests. Her *waka* also appear in *Fukuro zōshi* (Book of Folded Pages) by the poet-critic Fujiwara Kiyosuke (1104–1177), in *Korai Fūteishō* (Poetic Styles Past and Present, 1197) by Fujiwara Shunzei (ca. 1114–1204), and, most impressively, in two of the collections of exemplary poems made by the great early Kamakura poet and scholar Fujiwara Teika (1162–1241): *Hyakunin shūka* (Exemplary Poems by a Hundred Poets, 1229–36) and *Hyakunin isshu* (One Hundred Poems by a Hundred Poets, 1235).

Michitsuna's Mother was especially admired for her love poetry. Of the thirty-seven *waka* included in the imperial anthologies, fifteen fall under the category of "love" or "longing" (*koi*), while many of the twelve included in the next largest category, "miscellaneous poems" (*za*), also concern "longing" as a topic. The frequency with which the following poem was anthologized has made of it a kind of signature text, exemplifying both the rhetorically conservative style as well as the themes for which Michitsuna's Mother has been remembered for a thousand years:

On and on I grieve   Nagekitsutsu
through the nights I lie alone   hitori nuru yo no
awaiting the light   akuru ma ha
so endless my vigils—   ika ni hisashiki
of such things—what do you know?   mono to ka ha shiru
                                      (Nihon Koten Bungaku Zenshū 9,
                                          136; all translations in this article
                                                          by Edith Sarra)

The phrase *akuru ma* is a pun or pivot word (*kakekotoba*) that plays on the conflation of two kinds of intervals (*ma*): the time before the night "brightens" and gives way to dawn (*yo no akuru ma*) and the time before the door opens. The context in which the poem appears in the *nikki* highlights the sarcasm and resentment at once disclosed and undercut by the witty elegance of the pun. In the *nikki* the poem is preceded by a prose description of how her husband's attentions to a certain "woman of the alley" had begun to trouble her. After an absence of several nights, he pays her a belated call just before dawn. Maintaining her silence, she keeps him waiting outside the gate until he gives up and goes away ("presumably to that place he had been thinking about so much"). She sends the poem to him next morning. Rhetorically restrained, the *waka* voices an oblique complaint that is made direct and forceful by its unsolicited appearance at her husband's residence on the morning following her refusal to receive him. Edward Seidensticker has characterized it as a "rather daring poem" (*The Gossamer Years,* Tuttle, 1964), but it is not so much the poem that renders the utterance "daring" as its context—a poetic exchange that a wife initiates in protest against her husband's faithlessness. The pattern is typical of the author's persona as heroine of the memoir, particularly in the first volume of that work. Of the twenty-one poetic exchanges recorded between the heroine and her husband in that volume, she initiates an immodest fourteen.

As author-heroine of the memoir, Michitsuna's Mother is renowned for frank delineations of her own jealousy, anger, and frustrated desire. Daring such a heroine may be, but her *waka* are not. The way in which her poems have been contextualized in the prose of the memoir spells out the image of a proud and off-putting, yet scandalously demanding and unruly, wife. Taken on their own merits, her *waka,* which to many suggest a fierce subordination of emotion to rhetorical convention, project a less romantic figure. In fact, the image of Michitsuna's Mother as a tense, disciplined master of poetic language and precedent was central to the legends surrounding her memory, at least among her medieval readers. *Guhishō* (1314?), a late Kamakura poetic treatise of unknown authorship, conjures up such a vision of her in the act of *waka* composition: "It is as though she practiced composing in a dark place, turning things over and over in her mind, with her back to the lamplight, and her eyes shut" (quoted by Uemura Etsuko, "Michitsuna no haha," in Ichimura Kō et al., eds., *Ōchō no kajin* [Ofūsha, 1970] 223).

Translated Works: Kagerō Nikki (The Gossamer Memoir, after 974), diary. Though she was read for centuries on the strength of her reputation as a poet, Michitsuna's Mother is best remembered today for this three-volume memoir of mixed prose and poetry that commemorates a twenty-year span of her marriage to Kaneie. It was among the first female-authored Heian *nikki* to be taken up for study and annotation by *kokugakusha* (scholars of national learning) in the Edo period (1600–1867), but their, and consequently our, understanding of the work has been hampered by the lack of early manuscript copies. All of the approximately sixty surviving manuscript copies of the memoir are late versions, the earliest reliable text dating only as far back as the reign of Emperor Reigen (1654–1732; r. 1663–87).

The memoir includes a total of over 250 poems, among them three *chōka* (long songs) and two *renga* (linked poems), with a little more than half of these poems (126) concentrated in the brief first volume. The final volume encompasses some eighty *waka,* or about a third of the total number of poems in the work as a whole. With their high ratio of poetry to prose, the first and third volumes share some of the generic characteristics of poetic narrative (*uta monogatari*), though the impulse toward historicity in *The Gossamer Years* (its use of dates throughout and, in the third volume, official titles rendering the characters identifiable as historical figures) distinguishes the style of this *nikki* from the more allusive, anonymous fictional style of *uta monogatari* such as *Ise monogatari* (Tales of Ise, extant from the early 10th century). The second volume, containing only fifty-five *waka,* is dominated by the prose account of the heroine's seclusion at a temple near Narutaki, in the hills bordering the western edge of the capital. In both style and themes, it involves a number of important departures from the *uta monogatari* influences apparent in the other two volumes. Its stylistic innovations center around the technique of *hikiuta* (allusions to, or quoted lines from, old poems embedded within prose passages). The following excerpt includes a famous example of this technique.

In the closing moments of the heroine's rebellious period of reclusion at Narutaki, the three relationships that define the sequence of a woman's life according to Confucian societal ideals (obedience to one's father, husband, and son) close in upon her and seem to determine the outcome of events. Glimmering just beneath the surface of the narrator-heroine's description of these final moments is an implicit critique of Heian marriage as a romanticized exchange of women among fathers, sons-in-law, and sons. Yet the narrator of this episode remains complicit with the paradigms that so oppress her as heroine. The passage is laced with superbly controlled images of helpless entanglement, the overdetermination of the event in the narrative undercutting somewhat the frustrating lack of control the heroine will continue to experience in her relations with the three significant men in her life throughout the rest of the memoir. In the final pages of the Narutaki sequence, the actions of all three of these men conspire to render the heroine's deliberations about nunhood and her own status as wife of a powerful man utterly—even ludicrously—futile. At significant junctures in this sequence, poetic allusions embedded in the prose passages (*hikiuta*) inscribe a new level of interiority in the characterization of the heroine. Her father ("the one person whose opinion I cannot ignore" [NKBZ 9, 272]), hurries to Narutaki the very day of his return from the provinces. In the capital, his daughter's scandalous seclusion is the talk of the town. Confronted with the prospect of public humiliation (*hitowarae*), the specter of "what people will say" (*tenge no koto*), and his grandson Michitsuna's "despondence" (*kono kimi ito kuchioshō nari tamainikeri* [NKBZ 9, 282]), he orders her to return to the capital. Her response:

I was being told that there would be no protests, and I felt powerless and confused. Without thinking I responded, "If that's how it must be, then let it be tomorrow." *Tossed about like a fisherman's float,* my mind was completely at sea, and then there was a clamor—someone had arrived. It seemed to be my husband—and now I was completely frantic (NKBZ 9, 282; emphasis mine).

"Fisherman" (*ama*) doubles homophonously with "nun" (*ama*). The fisherman's float (*tsuri suru ama no uke*), an image of restless movement within fixity, functions as a metaphor for the heroine's inability to decide between married life and nunhood. The metaphor alludes to a famous anonymous poem (*Kokinshū* no. 509):

Impossible to settle	Ise no umi ni
this heart	tsuri suru ama no
as though it were a float	uke nare ya
the fishermen cast	kokoro hitotsu o
into the sea at Ise	sadamekanetsuru

In a now classic essay on Heian women's literature, Akiyama Ken cites this passage as an illustration of its author's skillful use of *hikiuta* to establish a kind of "magnetic field" that foreshadows and motivates subsequent events in the narrative (*Ōchō joryū bungaku no sekai* [Tokyo Daigaku shuppankai, 1972, 9]). In other words (though Akiyama does not extend his argument this far), the allusion suggests that because the heroine cannot or will not leave Narutaki of her own volition, the next scene, in which Kaneie arrives to take her back to the capital himself, accords perfectly with both the heroine's utter indecisiveness and lack of control and the narrating voice's masterful rhetorical control. The helpless motions of her own desires, ambivalently tied both to herself and to the men in her life, nun and fishermen, captive and captors, are part of a role of her own devising, while her father and Kaneie oblige her by playing the role of fisherman. The narrator-heroine thus dictates the terms of their actions (and her own restless inaction) within the frame of her own narrative.

Akiyama goes on to argue that the technique of foregrounding narrative events with lyric utterances and allusions forms one of the notable differences between earlier prose narratives (*monogatari*) and what he terms the "feminine prose spirit," which begins to emerge in writings by women in the mid-10th century. He cites this technique in *The Gossamer Years* as one of the innovations in prose style forefiguring the achievements of *Genji monogatari* (the Tale of Genji, early 11th c.). His call for an exploration of the history of this development stimulated a surge of scholarly inquiries into stylistic connections between *The Gossamer Years* and other 10th-century writings by women writers who had been hitherto overlooked or scanted as innovators in prose literature, among them, the poet Ise (875–no earlier than 938), Ise's daughter Nakatsukasa (ca. 910–no earlier than 989), and the daughter of Kamo Yasunori (fl. last half of 10th c.).

While Akiyama Ken and others have suggested links between *The Gossamer Years* and the *Tale of Genji* at the rhetorical level, still others note thematic connections. There is a long passage in the famous "Conversation on a Rainy Night" section of the "Broom Tree" chapter in *Genji* that contains what some consider to be a kind of parody, from an (insensitive) male perspective, of the account of the heroine's seclusion at Narutaki in *The Gossamer Years.* This apparent reprise of the Narutaki sequence forms part of a network of passages and incidents in *Genji* interrogating the precarious balance between a culturally inscribed imperative for the suppression of female jealousy (and male guilt) in Heian court society and the bizarre forms such suppression generates.

No matter how much classical readers may have admired Michitsuna's Mother as an impeccable poet and prose innovator, her readers in this century have responded most significantly to the complex image *The Gossamer Years* inscribes of a poetically articulate, yet socially and erotically frustrated, woman. Proud of the recognition her literary merits win her, yet ultimately relegated to a secondary position among her husband's numerous wives and lovers, she seems like someone who was always teetering on the brink of doing something rash, of doing anything to stop her obsession with her own disappointments. Yet, shut up in her own house, straining her ears in the darkness for the noise of her husband's outrunners at the gates, there seems very little she can do. If an air of scandal hangs about her memory, it is not the conventionally attractive sort of scandalousness that makes figures like Izumi Shikibu (ca. 970–?) appealing to some modern readers. Her anger finds a target not simply in her husband but, more disturbingly, in herself and in the other women in her husband's orbit. She castigates herself for her acquiescence to the common pathos of neglected wives who "end up telling over beads and reading sutras" (NKBZ 9, 255). She gloats unabashedly over the death of the only child of one of her low-ranking rivals (NKBZ 9, 149–50) and the fact that another rival's house ("that place that I hate," NKBZ 9, 319) has caught fire. Such passages have often been interpreted in terms of their author's astonishing—sometimes the adjective used is "admirable"—candor. But how can we gauge the norms of behavior and self-expression (much less the probable value judgments that would have been attached to them) in an age so distant from our own? Literary history and the proclivities and needs of generations of readers have continuously altered the significance and interpretation of such texts. The evidence suggests that later Heian readers read *The Gossamer Years* primarily as a showcase for its author-heroine's exemplary skill in *waka* composition. In the 20th century, literary scholars as well as novelists have appropriated it as a classical forebear of the modern genre of *shishōsetsu* or *watakushi shōsetsu* ("I-novels"). Writing in 1905, the Meiji scholar Fujioka Sakutarō discussed *The Gossamer Years* as an example of the literature of self-reflection, a discussion elaborated and given greater currency in mid-20th century by the eminent classicist Ikeda Kikan.

Unlike the poetry of Michitsuna's Mother, *The Gossamer Years* continues to attract readers from outside academe. Some of them have come away from their reading with the distinct impression that not very far beneath the veneer of elegant restraint (apparent in the poems the memoir includes), there is something radically uncivilized about this text, something not at all in keeping with the cultural historians' lovely but pale image of the Heian period as an age when a "rule of taste" dominated. The novelist Enchi Fumiko (1905–86) identified this something boldly (and with more than a hint of the implicit self-loathing the narrator-heroine of *The Gossamer Years* seems to project) as the "raw, female odor of blood," characterizing the memoir as "decidedly not a work in which only beautiful things are recorded." Though Enchi singles it out as the fountainhead of the long tradition of autobiographical literature by Japanese women writers, "it is not," she confesses, "a work I can read with pleasure. I do not feel that I could make another novel out of it, nor yet is it the sort of work I want to read over and over again" ("Ōchō josei bungaku to gendai bungaku" [Heian Women's Literature and Contemporary Literature], *Kokubungaku* 10 [December 1965]: 209–10). She goes on, interestingly enough, to touch on the works two contemporary male authors have succeeded in making out of their readings of *The Gossamer Years:* Hori Tatsuo's *Kagerō no nikki* (The Gossamer Journal, 1939), and Murō Saisei's *Kagerō no nikki ibun* (The Gossamer Journal—Literary Remains), serialized in the journal *Fujin no tomo* (July 1958–June 1959).

Like other well-placed married women of her time, Michitsuna's Mother lived out most of her days as the occupant of one of several points in a web of static, but powerfully attractive, female rivals and their families. Her husband traverses this web at will (and all too willfully for her peace of mind), yet the memoir suggests she is embittered not so much by the system itself as by her own peculiar position in it. While rhetorically and thematically the *nikki* presages the *Tale of Genji* and its profound concern with the ramifications of Heian marriage systems and the various fates women were subject to in the upper echelons of court society, it does so by means of the depth, not the breadth, of its vision. The focus of *The Gossamer Years* is fixed upon one woman's personal circumstances, not those of upper-class men and women in general. But the intensity of its dark versions of events lays the groundwork for a more critical perspective on upper-class Heian marriage as a system designed to contain and limit feminine desire, one that labels transgressions of those limits as scandal, evidence of the blind disorder to which women will run if not constrained by marriage ties, familial order, and poetic conventions. Its minute interrogations of episodes from a marriage shed light upon the lineaments of situations that have taken center stage in contemporary women's studies. As one of the writers who did the most to bring these issues into the forum of literary prose in Japanese prior to the *Tale of Genji,* Michitsuna's Mother continues to command a special quality of attention from students of literature by and about Japanese women in general.

BIBLIOGRAPHY

Translations

The Gossamer Diary (excerpts). Trans. Arthur Waley. In *The Sacred Tree.* London: Allen and Unwin, 1926.
"The Gossamer Journal." Trans. Helen McCullough. In *Classical Japanese Prose: An Anthology.* Stanford, CA: Stanford University Press, 1990. Translation of Book 1 of *Kagerō Nikki.*
The Gossamer Years: The Diary of a Noblewoman of Heian Japan. Trans. Edward Seidensticker. Tokyo: Tuttle, 1964. Revision of 1955 translation, but minus the *waka* collection.
"The *Kagerō Nikki:* Journal of a 10th Century Noblewoman." Trans. Edward Seidensticker. *Transactions of the Asiatic Society of Japan.* Third Series (June 1955): 1–243. Contains a translation of the author's *waka* collection.

Critical Works

Keene, Donald. "The Gossamer Years." In *Travelers of a Hundred Ages.* New York: Henry Holt, 1989.
Konishi, Jin'ichi. *The Early Middle Ages.* Chapter 8. Vol. 2 of *A History of Japanese Literature.* Princeton, NJ: Princeton University Press, 1986.
Sarra, Edith. "*Kagerō nikki:* A Record of Many Unpleasant Things." In "The Art of Remembrance, the Poetics of Destiny: Self-Writings by Three Women of Heian Japan." Ph.D. diss., Harvard University, 1988.
Watanabe, Minoru. "Style and Point of View in the *Kagerō nikki.*" *Journal of Japanese Studies* 10 (Summer 1984): 365–84.

Edith Lorraine SARRA

FUJIWARA Shunzei's Daughter (Shunzeikyō no musume, 1171?–after 1252), poet, critic. Real name: undetermined.

Life: The most celebrated female poet of her age, the woman known as Shunzei's Daughter lived from ca. 1171 until sometime after 1252. She grew up in an era of great unrest owing to the struggle between the Taira and Minamoto clans (referred to as the Gempei wars) during the latter decades of the 12th century. She was particularly well known as a master of the technique of *honkadori* ("intertextual variation," i.e., a poem that provides a new twist on an

earlier composition while clearly evoking its precedent) and is widely believed
to be the author of a valuable text of feminine criticism, *Mumyōzōshi* (Text
Without a Name). One hundred sixteen of her poems are included in imperial
collections. Commenting on her historical status, the author of the famous *Hōjōki* (An Account of My Hut), Kamo no Chōmei (1155?–1216), for example,
ranks her together with another woman, Kunaikyō (d. ca. 1204), as the two
poets of the day able to withstand comparison with the great poets of old.

Shunzei's Daughter, however, was not, in fact the daughter, but the granddaughter, of the important poet and scholar Fujiwara Shunzei (1114–1204), ancestor of the Mikohidari family. Her mother was Hachijō-in Sanjō, one of
Shunzei's many daughters and sisters of the greatest poet-scholar, Fujiwara no
Sadaie (Teika) (1162–1241). Her father was Fujiwara no Moriyori, the son of
Ienari, the Nakamikado middle counselor and younger brother of the major
counselor Fujiwara no Narichika. Moriyori was a lesser captain and a member
of the Left Imperial Guards and also served as governor of Owari province.
Shunzei's Daughter acquired her name in part because she was actually raised
by her grandparents, Shunzei and his wife, who was the daughter of Fujiwara
no Chikatada. It is thought that the arrangement was necessitated after her father,
a member of an alleged anti-Taira faction, was stripped of his office and unable
to regain his former status even after the Taira were eventually defeated. Scholars also reason that the appellation derives from the fact that her poetry carries
forth the style of her illustrious grandfather. Teika is said to have felt tremendous
affection for Shunzei's Daughter, and the two were quite close, a relationship
that derived in part from his fondness for her mother, his sister. Teika helped
to look after her after the mother's death. Other names by which Shunzei's
Daughter was called are Saga no zenni, Koshibe no zenni, and the mother of
the Jijū Tomosada, the latter name appearing in *Shin chokusen shū.*

Around 1190, Shunzei's Daughter married Minamoto no Michitomo, the second son of the soon-to-be Tsuchimikado palace minister (Naidaijin) Michichika
(who was at the time a middle counselor), and bore him a boy and a girl. The
marriage effectively linked the Tsuchimikado and Mikohidari houses and indicates the closeness of the relations between Shunzei and Michichika, a relationship that arose largely as a result of their mutual poetic interest.

After her grandmother's death in 1193, a change in political climate began
to have drastic consequences for the married life of Shunzei's Daughter. In 1196,
the Chancellor (*kampaku*), Kujō Kanezane, retired (in favor of Motomichi). Two
years later, the son of Michichika's adopted daughter (Zaishi) became emperor
at the age of four. Michichika, as the new emperor's maternal grandfather (*gai-
sofu*), leapt ahead of those above him and gained promotion to the position of
Naidaijin after having been only a provisional major counselor. When Michi-
mune, the older brother of Shunzei's Daughter's husband (Michitomo), died in
1198, Michitomo's position in the family became of crucial importance. In 1199
he attained the rank of Tō no chūjō and the following year was appointed
consultant (*sangi*). To further guarantee his future and the fortunes of his family,

he married during the winter of 1199 Azechi no Tsubone, younger sister of Zaishi and wet nurse to the child emperor. In 1200, Shunzei's Daughter gave birth to a son, Tomosada, who, had it not been for his father's new marriage, would have taken his place as Michitomo's rightful successor.

In 1202, Shunzei's Daughter was invited by the cloistered emperor Go-Toba (1180–1239; r. 1183–98), who is impressed by her superior poetic talents, to enter his service and become a member of a poetry group known as the *Sendō kadan*. Due to the recent change in her marital situation, said to have brought her great sorrow and loneliness, it was a move encouraged by Shunzei and especially desired by Michitomo, even though Teika himself initially had reservations. Teika eventually acceded to the plan, knowing full well that royal service would bring glory to the family.

Shunzei died in 1204, and his death was followed in close succession by the death of two other people close to Shunzei's Daughter: the talented poet Takanobu (Teika's half-brother and Shunzei's Daughter's uncle) and the regent Yoshitsune, a staunch supporter of Shunzei's family and benefactor of the *Shinkokin* poets.

Shunzei's Daughter took Buddhist vows in 1213 but continued to play an active role in the poetry group (*kadan*) at the court of the cloistered emperor Juntoku (who abdicated in 1210), with whom she seems to have been on especially cordial terms. Scholars have surmised that Go-Toba had put Shunzei's Daughter in charge of Juntoku's childhood poetic training. She also became an active participant in the *waka* activities of the Kujō *sekkan* (regent) family and composed the *Tōin sesshōke hyakushu* (Hundred Poems at the Regent Family Estate). She later went into retreat at Saga, where she lived from about 1228, the year after Michitomo's death. Scholars feel that although they had lived apart for many years, his death was a decisive factor in her resolve to remove herself from worldly affairs. At this time she was referred to as Saga no Zenni and Chūin no ama. Her uncle, Teika, died in 1241. Ex-emperor Go-Toba had died on the island of Oki the previous year, and ex-emperor Juntoku died on Sado Island in 1242. With her close associates and sponsors gone, Shunzei's Daughter moved to land in Harima province (in Koshibe) that had belonged to Shunzei and lived out her life continuing to follow the dual paths of Buddhism and poetry.

Career: Shunzei's Daughter was held in high esteem by her contemporaries. The nun Abutsu (d. 1283), for example, in a text called *Yoru no tsuru* (Night Crane), cites a *waka* by Shunzei's Daughter as a skillful example of *honkadori:*

they scatter as they bloom,	sakeba chiru
the blossoms of this gloomy world,	hana no ukiyo to
possessed as I am by such thoughts	omofu ni mo
what are impossible to resent	naho utomarenu
are, alas, the mountain cherries	yamazakura kana

The poem, also found in *Shoku gosenshū,* is a "variation" on the following, from *The Tale of Genji:*

its affinity to the dew	sode nururu
that dampens sleeves in sadness,	tsuyu no yukari to
weighs heavily on my mind;	omohedomo
yet it is impossible to resent	naho utomarenu
the wild pinks of Yamato	yamato nadeshiko

The nun comments on the effortlessness of a master's handiwork and on the impossibility of its imitation. Another writer, Kamo no Chōmei (1155–1216), in his *Mumyōshō,* describes her poetic method this way:

When Shunzei's Daughter had to compose public (*hare*) poems, she would, some days before the event, pour over poems in all the various collections, and when she was satisfied with her perusal, she would put them all aside and, turning down the light and making sure that no one else was around, would begin forming verses in her mind.

The first time that Shunzei's Daughter's compositions caught the eye of Go-Toba was in 1201 at a poetry contest held at the residence of her father-in-law, Michichika. The participants, including the ex-emperor, were amazed when out of the six poems she presented, four won their individual rounds. At another contest that same year sponsored by the ex-emperor himself, twenty-five contestants submitted ten poems each. Out of the total, one hundred of the poems were then selected and arranged into fifty rounds. Shunzei's Daughter was among six of the poets who had six or more poems selected, and her winning percentage ranked her third in a tie with Kunaikyō.

During the summer of 1201, hundred-poem collections were composed by thirty poets. The poems were later put together as part of the monumental collection, *Sengohyakuban utaawase* (poetry contest of fifteen hundred rounds), which served as a major source for the compilation of the imperial anthology, *Shinkokinshū.* She was one of only two newcomers to the group (Yoshihira, son of Kanezane, is the other), and her poems won thirty-eight rounds, were involved in twenty-five draws, and lost twenty-seven rounds. Her total number of wins placed her, with two other poets, in sixth place. Here are a few examples from the contest, said to represent her best work:

no visitor appears,	tofu hito mo
only the storm accompanying	arashi fukisofu
the coming of fall,	
a time of falling out of favor;	aki ha kite
buried beneath old leaves:	konoha ni udumu
roadside grasses to mark this dwelling	yado no michishiba

(Autumn, 752)

asleep, deep in fiery thoughts	omohi ne no
the floating bridge of dreams	yume no ukihashi
is blocked to human passage;	todae shite
on my pillow as I awake, the fire cooled,	samuru makura ni
only the trace of your vanishing visage	kiyuru omokage

(Love 1, 1188)

while we are together:	miru hodo zo
comfort for a time;	shibashi nagusamu
assailed by sorrowful thoughts,	nagekitsutsu
on sleepless nights—in the sky,	nenu yo no sora no
only the clear moon at dawn	ariake no tsuki

(Love 3, 1287)

Probably her most famous *waka* is the poem that appears in *Shinkokinshū* (Love 2, 1081), noted as "On the occasion of the presentation of fifty poems":

love expressed through clouds,	shitamoe ni
beneath the smoldering fire	omohikienan
my ardent thoughts die away;	kemuri dani
there yet remains the smoke	ato naki kumo no
that rises into formless clouds to form a truly sorrowful end	hate zo kanashiki

The poem was originally composed for the "Sendō kudai gojusshu" (Fifty Poems Presented at the Sendō Palace) and is the source of Shunzei's Daughter's nickname, "Smoldering Lesser Captain" (Shitamoe no shōshō).

Major Works: Shunzeikyō no musume shū (Shunzei's Daughter's Collection), poems, 1233. During her stay in Saga, she compiled this private poetry collection of her own, as part of the source material for an imperial poetry anthology that Teika had been ordered to compile (*Shin chokusenshū*, 1235). In arranging the poems, she made a conscious effort to juxtapose her early compositions with those of more recent vintage, thereby configuring the collection in the mode of the *Shinkokinshū*, which also depended on an old-new structural pattern. Teika ultimately included only eight of her *waka* in *Shin chokusenshū* (only five of which are taken from her private collection), a slight, scholars feel, that was the result of his growing critical attitude toward Shunzei's Daughter's (and his father, Shunzei's) style. About 750 of her poems remain in various collections. Twenty-nine of her poems are included in the *Shinkokinshū*, a major source for which was *Sengohyakuban utaawase*.

Koshibe zenni shōsoku (the Nun Koshibe Letter), epistle. Besides composing the *Hōji gyohakushū* poems, Shunzei's Daughter wrote this letter to Fujiwara no Tameie (Teika's son), who was the compiler of the *Shoku Gosenshū*. In the epistle, which came to be read as an important document on *waka* poetics, she offers an evaluation of imperial anthologies, gives special praise to the *Shoku Gosenshū,* and critically compares the three, *Shinkokin, Shin Chokusen,* and *Shoku Gosen,* focusing especially on Go-Toba's royal lineage.

Mumyōzōshi (A Nameless Text), critique. Shunzei's Daughter is the candidate most often cited as the possible author of this important text, generally regarded as the first substantial example of prose criticism in the Japanese literary tradition, though actually some brief passages that would constitute "prose critiques" had appeared earlier in Heian texts.

In premodern Japan certain classes of learned and talented women, born into respected scholarly families, found themselves in a position to write with relative freedom and ease. In the Heian period (794–1185), for example, discourse in the native *hiragana* scripts even came to be termed the "Woman's hand" (*onnade*). While it is true that men also wrote in *hiragana,* in addition to a Japanized variety of Chinese characters that was their regular and official scriptive mode, women employed the mostly phonetic and therefore flexible native writing system to their advantage. Not only did they make it their own medium, but they produced prose works that have come to be treasured by later generations as being among the greatest of Japan's literary heritage. The Heian women's narratives, moreover, often contain passages that cast a cool eye of criticism upon the world out of which they emerged. They thus address such issues as relations between gender and writing, and empowerment and representation, which have been the focus of much feminist and literary criticism in recent decades; hence, dealing with this non-Western tradition cannot but prove beneficial in adjusting largely a Eurocentric handling of the problems in the Western scholarship. Even though men were beginning to dominate the writing of *hiragana* during the Kamakura period (1185–1333), women like Shunzei's Daughter and her court colleagues were still able to make important contributions to the culture of their particular time.

Written sometime during the 13th century, *Mumyōzōshi* presents a feminine perspective, thoroughly infused with Buddhist elements and concerns, on the most important figures, texts, and poems of the *hiragana* tradition. The authorial attribution cannot be unimpeachably verified, but the perspectives and attitudes strongly point to feminine authorship. The following discussion is based on the general assumption that this text was written by a woman, Shunzei's Daughter.

The text itself, ostensibly devoted to a critique of women by women, begins with the words of the narrator, who is an old woman: "It is sad when I think back on the springs and autumns of the eighty-three years that have now passed." Wandering about the eastern hills, the old woman first happens to seek shelter at a temple where the senior consort of Emperor Go-Shirakawa had regularly prayed. Next she comes upon a house with a thatched roof where she encounters a group of young women, who, after listening to the old woman's past experiences, engage in an all-night conversation on all sorts of matters, which the woman presumably records. The mode of conversation and its recording by a scribe place the text within a situation of reception typical of earlier Heian tales. The women begin with brief comments on topics such as things of this world that are difficult to give up—the sight of the moon, letters, epistles, dreams, tears, Amida Buddha, and the *Lotus Sutra*—and then launch into a discussion of *The Tale of Genji,* liberally illustrating their points as they do so with citations of *waka.* After enumerating the most interesting *Genji* chapters, they turn their attention to the different types of women who appear in the tale. The characters are categorized under topics such as remarkable (*medetashi*), enchanting (*imiji*), congenial (*konomoshi*), and frail (*itōshi*).

A section on male characters then follows. Almost every critique, revealingly, is framed in terms of how the men treat or respond to the women they encounter. The speakers are especially critical of Genji, who comes off less than grand, certainly not heroic, as a result of the way he treats women, while others, like the straitlaced Yūgiri, are generally admired for their steadfastness. The brooding ''Uji'' figure Kaoru is praised by one speaker as exemplifying the height of perfection.

The women then move on to elucidate moments that inspire emotional responses, which are grouped under the following emotive categories: moving (*aware,* the longest section), striking (*imiji*), pathetic (*itōshi*), distasteful (*kokoro yamashi*), and astonishing (*asamashi*). Next come evaluations of the three most important post-*Genji* tales: *Sagoromo, Nezame,* and *Hamamatsu.* The women discuss each tale in terms of the major figures that appear and what they consider to be their compositional defects. After adding brief remarks on other texts, many of which are no longer extant, and on the celebrated poem-tales *Ise monogatari* and *Yamato monogatari,* the speakers end with a series of discussions of real-life women poets: Ono no Komachi, Sei Shōnagon, Koshikibu no Naishi, Izumi Shikibu, Miya no Senji, Ise no Miyasudokoro (Lady Ise), Hyōe no Naishi, Murasaki Shikibu, Empress Teishi, Empress Shōshi, the Grand Ise Virgin (Senshi), and the Ono Empress Kanshi. The text ends as one speaker is about to discuss real-life male writers.

The discussions are often marked by copious poetic citations. For example, in the section on emotional responses where the women talk of those things that inspire *aware* (i.e., when one feels deeply moved by events, an emotion valorized by the great Edo scholar Motoori Norinaga as the predominant one in *Genji*), we find the death of the Kiritsubo Kōi and the grief of the Kiritsubo Emperor, the deaths of Yūgao, the Aoi Lady (Genji's principal wife), Kashiwagi, Murasaki, and Ōigimi, the visits to women that mark the eve of Genji's departure for Suma, and the ''Wizard'' (Maboroshi) chapter all punctuated with a poetic citation.

In the section on the different women, a speaker cites several *waka* compositions (six, in a short passage) to show Izumi Shikibu's superb poetic skill. Interestingly, no poems appear in the discussion of Sei Shōnagon, a situation that suggests her lack of poetic talent (a perspective that her *Pillow Book* itself substantiates) despite her being the daughter of the great poet-scholar Kiyohara no Motosuke. The speaker also notes the decline in the family fortunes of Sei Shōnagon's mistress, Empress Teishi, contrasts the real-world situation with the absence of any mention of such bleak matters in the *Pillow Book,* and ends by describing the poverty of her final days lived in a region far from the capital. In the case of the *Genji* author, a speaker relates an anecdote found in many sources that the *Genji* tale was begun by Murasaki Shikibu in response to a request for interesting tales by her mistress, Empress Shōshi, who had been approached earlier by the Great Kamo Virgin, Princess Senshi. To this another speaker offers a counterversion that says that Murasaki Shikibu began writing the tale before entering Shōshi's service. Her renown having in fact already spread, the story goes, the other women attending Shōshi were uncomfortable with the presence of such a potentially splendid figure. To their relief they discovered her to be an absent-minded, immature person bashful about even writing the character for the number ''one'' in front of others.

In conjunction with the critiques of women, the following comment on the marginalization of women to the act of compiling imperial collections provides another example of feminine self-awareness: ''There is nothing as unfortunate as the position of women; since ancient times there have been many of our sisters who have been inclined to modish behavior and who learned the ways of the poetic arts; yet it is deeply regrettable that a woman still has not compiled a poetry collection.'' Another speaker counters with the narrative examples of Murasaki Shikibu and Sei Shōnagon, upon which the conversation turns to the difficulty of achieving lasting fame and getting one's compositions selected for poetry collections. The passage resonates with the fact, as suggested above, that Shunzei's Daughter seems at one point to have been scorned by both Emperor Go-Toba and Teika, her former allies.

The *Mumyōzōshi* text, then, in its feminine stance of critique, its mode of narration, and its expression of self-awareness shows itself to be as valuable as the famous texts of the past included in Japanese canon. The following poem by Shunzei's Daughter collected in *Shinkokinshū* (Love 5, 1390) sums up such feminine sentiments:

truly a dream,	yume ka to yo
your visage I beheld,	mishi omokage mo
the vows that we exchanged;	chigirishi mo
though they remain with me	wasurezunagara
they cannot be of this world	utsutsunaraneba

Of course, the ''dream'' of the poet can be only a dreamy gesture, never the ''dream'' itself. In the same way, the power Japanese women had in the world to represent, to gesture, must be correlated with critical assertions of the ostensible victimization of the bearers of that power. The negative irony of the poem then participates in a reversal that turns it into a positive statement of the scriptive performance.

BIBLIOGRAPHY

Translations and Critical Works

Brower, Robert, and Earl Miner. *Japanese Court Poetry*. Stanford, CA: Stanford University Press, 1961.
Carter, Steven D., Trans. *Traditional Japanese Poetry: An Anthology*. Stanford, CA: Stanford University Press, 1991.
Encyclopedia of Japan, S. V. "Fujiwara Toshinari no Musume."
Honda, H. H., Trans. *The Shin Kokinshū.* Tokyo: Hokuseido, 1970.
"Mumyōzōshi." Trans. Michele Marra. *Monumenta Nipponica* 39. 2–4 (1984).

H. Richard OKADA

GOFUKAKUSA'IN Nijō (Lady Nijō; 1258–after 1306), memoirist. Real name: undetermined.

Life and Career: Little is known about Nijō's life, though scholars have inferred much from the account given in the single surviving work attributed to her, the (auto)biographical narrative *Towazugatari* (An Unsolicited Tale, 1307?). Because we have few sources of biographical information independent of *Towazugatari,* any discussion of her life will also be to some extent a discussion of that work.

Both of Nijō's parents had close ties to the imperial family. Her father, Koga Masatada (1228–72), was a major counselor and active in poetic circles at the court of Emperor GoSaga (1220–72; r. 1242–46). Before her marriage to Masatada, Nijō's mother, known as Dainagon no suke or Sukedai (d. 1259), had served at the court of Emperor GoFukakusa (1243–1304; r. 1246–59), Emperor GoSaga's son. Sukedai was, according to the account in *Towazugatari,* his first lover. Sukedai died when her daughter was only about two years old, and Nijō, as her only daughter, was destined for GoFukakusa's entourage from her birth, as solace for the woman he lost to Masatada. In highlighting Nijō's mother's relationship to GoFukakusa, *Towazugatari* evokes the tradition of Heian literary heroines who play the role of erotic substitute (*yukari*) for an idealized former love. The idea of the *yukari,* a woman sought by the hero because she resembles an earlier lover lost to him through death or forced separation, serves as one of the several intertextual structures against which the figure of Nijō emerges in *Towazugatari.* As in Heian fictional *monogatari* (tales), the *yukari* theme in this memoir functions ironically. In the two instances where the notion that Nijō was destined to be a replacement for her own mother is voiced (both times in speeches made by GoFukakusa himself), it is apparent that the idea has been little more than a wishful, unfulfilled projection of GoFukakusa's imagination. From Nijō's point of view, the intelligence that GoFukakusa had hoped she would replace her own mother in his affections serves as a negative reminder of what she has failed to become in her relationship with him. Yet, ironically, it is precisely because her relationship with GoFukakusa fails that their relationship duplicates and amplifies the pathos of Sukedai and GoFukakusa.

In 1272, at the age of fourteen, Nijō became one of GoFukakusa's ladies-in-waiting (*nyōbō*) and, given her family background, might have aspired to become the mother of a crown prince. Nijō took obvious pride in her family's political connections and literary reputation. The memoir is studded with passionate speeches by politically important figures like the dowager empress Ōmiya (1225–92, GoFukakusa's mother), and the regent Takatsukasa Kanehira (1228–95), who defended her on several occasions against the criticism of her detractors. While these passages testify to her pedigree and to the imperial family's esteem for her and her family, Nijō's very insistence upon them serves ironically to underscore the actual uncertainty of her political and material circumstances. For many reasons her position at court was from the beginning a precarious one. Her father died within a year of her official entrance into GoFukakusa's household, leaving her (as her memoir repeatedly emphasizes) an orphan with no reliable backers in court society. Though she was formally adopted by her maternal grandfather (the palace minister, Shijō Takachika, 1203–79), the memoir suggests that this was largely a bond of duty rather than affection on her grandfather's part. Expressions of anxiety about one's patrons (or lack thereof) are a conventional theme in Japanese court women's autobiographical writings, but in Nijō's case, her complaints seem to have been grounded in actual circumstances as well. She bore GoFukakusa only one child, a son, who died at an early age. Yet the possibility that she would bear others was probably one source of the ill will initially borne her by GoFukakusa's empress Higashi Nijō (1232–1304). Nijō early became the object of Higashi Nijō's complaints, and ostensibly the latter's long-standing grudge against her forced Nijō to withdraw from court service in 1283, at the relatively young age of twenty-six.

But other factors contributed to the disappointing turn of her political and romantic fortunes, and, as the author-narrator of the memoir, she is at some pains to convey the complex background and ironies of her fate. Bereft of her parents at an early age, she presents herself as one who depended ultimately on the continued patronage and goodwill of GoFukakusa to secure her position at court. She also seems to have received some material backing from Saionji Sanekane (1249–1322), the liaison officer between the imperial family and the Kamakura shogunate and one of the leading political figures of the day. But the memoir makes it appear that her political and economic reliance on GoFukakusa and Sanekane was complicated by the fact that both of them were her lovers. Still other lovers figured in her years at court, not all of them entirely welcome. She seems to have been involved briefly, and against her own wishes, with Kanehira. A fourth lover, with whom she was much preoccupied during her final years at court, was a Buddhist priest whose identity remains open to debate. For years scholars believed him to be Shōjō (d. 1281?), an abbot at Ninna-ji and half-brother to GoFukakusa. More recently, Matsumoto Yasushi has suggested it was not Shōjō, but rather his teacher Hōjo (*Chūsei kyūtei josei no nikki: "Towazugatari" no sekai* [Chūō Kōron sha, 1986] 94–98). Finally, Ex-emperor Kameyama (1249–1305), GoFukakusa's brother and chief political rival, seems to have all but forced sexual attentions upon her. Nijō suggests that her involvement with Kameyama was exaggerated by malicious rumors of which she, preoccupied at the time by her relationship with the Buddhist priest, was initially unaware. Her memoir implies that this gossip finally cost her Go-Fukakusa's continued patronage and left her vulnerable to Empress Higashi Nijō's machinations.

The security of her position was further undermined by her multiple pregnancies and the necessity of hiding her condition from the emperor. In addition to the son she bore GoFukakusa, Nijō describes the birth of three other children during the decade or so she spent at court: a daughter to Sanekane and two boys to the Buddhist priest. All three of the children were taken from her shortly after their birth and raised by others. While this was not an uncommon arrangement for women of Nijō's position, her account is unique for its detailing of the lengths to which she went to conceal the circumstances of some of her pregnancies and the paternity of her surviving children.

After her forced resignation from court service in 1283, Nijō reappeared briefly in court circles on at least two formal occasions. In 1285, she was summoned to serve at the ninetieth birthday celebration for her great-aunt, Lady Kitayama (1196–1302; the mother of Empresses Ōmiya and Higashi Nijō). In 1288, she participated in the presentation at court of Sanekane's daughter, the future empress Eifuku Mon'in (1271–1342). Nijō's presence as a member of Eifuku Mon'in's entourage on this date is attested to by one of the few other documents that touch on her career: a couple of lines in *Masukagami* (The Clear Mirror, or The Mirror of Increase, completed ca. 1370). The text, probably compiled from a number of different sources, is of unknown authorship, and the lines in question may themselves be based on one of Nijō's own writings, now lost. *Masukagami* records that Nijō was referred to as Sanjō on this occasion, her prior claims to the sobriquet "Nijō" having been disregarded or forgotten, an affront she seems to have resented. A shadowy reflection of the proud, articulate narrator-heroine of the memoir glimmers momentarily beneath the dispassionate inventory of women and carriages in the *Masukagami* account: "And in the second carriage on the left rode the daughter of the late Major Counselor Masatada, taking the name Lady Sanjō, though she lamented it bitterly" (*Nihon koten bungaku taikei* 87, 380–81; all translations in this entry are by Edith Sarra). Notably, the incident is not described in the extant texts of Nijō's memoir.

Nijō would have been about thirty at the time of Eifuku Mon'in's entrance into Emperor Fushimi's court. Shortly thereafter she took Buddhist vows and began the series of pilgrimages described in Books 4 and 5 of her memoir. During these later years, she traveled to Kamakura and to temples and shrines in both eastern and western Japan, where she seems to have been in some demand as a participant in *waka* and *renga* parties held by various priests and regional lords. The last datable events in the memoir occur around the year 1306.

Translated Works: Towazuoatari (An Unsolicited Tale, 1307?), memoir. The best-known English translation of this work is Karen Brazell's *The Confessions of Lady Nijō,* which won a national book award in the United States. We know of no other surviving literary works by Nijō, though some scholars speculate that she was also an accomplished painter. A black and white *emaki* (narrative picture scroll) on the theme of a Buddhist tale, *Toyo no Akari ezōshi* (The Illustrated Book of Toyo no Akari) has been attributed to her by some.

The manuscript of the memoir lay lost and unread for centuries until it was accidentally rediscovered in 1940. A complete, annotated, scholarly edition of the work did not appear until 1966. Translations into English and German were published in 1973. Nijō thus had little impact upon writers of the intervening generations, but the connections between her work and the literature of the preceding centuries are rich and complex. The text inscribes itself, as do so many works now classified as *nikki bungaku* (diary literature), somewhere between the genre of *monogatari* (largely prose narratives concerning real or imaginary characters) and *nikki* (memoir, lit., "records of days").

"*Towazugatari,*" a word comprising the title by which this work is known in Japanese, means literally "unsolicited tale(s)," a term that has a long and suggestive history in the tradition of *waka* and court women's writings. It appears in various Heian texts, including *Genji monogatari* (The Tale of Genji, early 11th century), to describe the irrepressible outbursts and reminiscing of former wet nurses and aged ladies-in-waiting. In *The Tale of Genji,* it is frequently coupled with adjectives like *ayashi* (strange) and *itazura* (troublesome), words that hint at the term's origins in older traditions of native shamanism. Messages from the gods and the dead, believed to be manifested in the involuntary speech of shrine priestesses and female mediums, were also strange, unasked-for tales, and something of this shadowy heritage lives on in the *Genji,* where the term is intimately connected with the disclosure of family secrets and hidden fates. The melodramatic, unsolicited tête-à-tête in which Bennokimi, the aged daughter of Kashiwagi's old nurse, reveals to Kaoru the secret of his paternity, is described as a "*towazugatari*" by the *Genji* narrator. By Nijō's time, the word seems to have come full circle from its sources in sacred discourse. "*Towazugatari*" also connotes the stale gossip of old ladies, and a writer (particularly if she was writing her own memoirs) might use it self-deprecatingly, to refer to the ostensible triviality of her own text. But the sense of the tale as a mass of old secrets the teller could not bear to leave untold, stories that forced themselves out despite her own better judgment, remained latent in the term, making it doubly appropriate for a writer who wished, for whatever reasons, to underscore the emotional authenticity of her account.

It is not certain that Nijō ever intended her text to be named "*towazugatari.*" The title may be the contribution of one of her early readers or copyists. But regardless of whether or not Nijō so titled her memoir, the name "A Tale No One Asked For" resonates with important thematic preoccupations apparent in the narrative itself, preoccupations that invite comparison not only with the explicitly named *towazugatari* scenes in the *Genji* but more broadly with the underlying claims and impulses of confessional narratives in other literary traditions. Nijō seems to have struggled with the contradictory impulse to claim innocence for herself at the same time that she sought absolution for a past life that she also implicitly recognized as sinful. As in many of the confessional narratives of Anglo-European traditions, Nijō's concern with past misdeeds and the assigning of blame, her implicit claims to authenticity and unpremeditated self-presentation, and, corollary to these, her apparent need to justify or defend herself against imagined or real accusations figure like recurrent master patterns in the weave of her text. Questions of guilt and blame continually rise to the surface of her account, even in passages that do not deal directly with the issue of serious transgressions. Consider the anecdotes Nijō chooses to tell about the amusements of life at court. In the early pages of Book 2, she recalls how she once conspired with Genkimon'in (fl. mid- to late 13th c.; daughter of Tōin Saneo and mother of Emperor Fushimi) to seek revenge on GoFukakusa for his treatment of them on the day of the Full-Moon Gruel Ceremony. The women plot their vengeance half in jest, and the account of the playful reparations demanded of Nijō and her relatives in retribution for the ladies' counteraffronts is presented as typical of the elaborately elegant diversions of court society. But Nijō notes with some disgruntlement that Genkimon'in got off without being blamed at all and, in the end, reports with satisfaction that GoFukakusa himself was required to make reparations, since he is ultimately held responsible for the behavior of the women in his service. In a gesture of closure that echoes the conventions of Buddhist *setsuwa* (didactic and/or diversionary tales of famous figures, events, and poems), Nijō sums up the anecdote as though it were an exemplum. Having cited the gist of the argument against GoFukakusa, she ends her account of the episode with a warning against the risks a superior runs when he presumes to judge the guilt of his inferiors.

The characterizations employed in the first three books of the memoir draw extensively and creatively upon the poetic motifs and heroines of fictional *monogatari* (especially *The Tale of Genji*) and *uta monogatari* (poem-tales, often centering on the sexual or romantic exploits of historical men and women). In Books 4 and 5, the narrative swerves away from the world of the court and the thematic preoccupations of courtly *monogatari* to incorporate elements of the *kikō* (records of travel) tradition. In these last two books, the image of the exiled lover Ariwara Narihira or the aged beauty Ono no Komachi and the figure of the poet-Priest Saigyō provide important thematic structures and sources of literary allusion and characterization. The relation between these two segments of the narrative is not, however, a noticeably oppositional one—as it is, say, in the pre- and postconversion chapters of St. Augustine's *Confessions.*

Nijō employed highly ambivalent, sometimes comically deflationary tech-

niques in her handling of classical models. She had discovered the energy inherent in tragicomedy, and many of the most allusive scenes in the narrative
are governed by its dynamism. The passage in which GoFukakusa suddenly
removes her from her father's house to his own residence on the third night of
their "wedding" recalls Genji's romantic abduction of Yūgao—a tale that ended
in tragedy for the heroine, who dies during the first night in the deserted mansion
where she and Genji are ensconced. Yūgao becomes a victim of a jealous spirit
that seems to emanate from Lady Rokujō, one of Genji's other lovers, a crown
prince's widow, much higher in rank than Yūgao. Nijō's mock abduction scene,
on the other hand, ends on a self-deprecatingly comic note, with GoFukakusa
himself behaving like a very un-Genji-esque antihero. After their arrival at his
residence, he retires to his own quarters without his heroine Nijō, explaining he
had merely brought her with him because "it was hard to just leave her behind
when she acts like an impossible child" (*Shinchō nihon koten shūsei* 20, 22).
Shades of the young Murasaki, Genji's ideal child bride, haunt the text here.
Though she is fourteen years old at the time, GoFukakusa refers to her here as
a *midori-ko,* a term usually reserved for children of four or five years of age.
As it turns out, the fate Nijō eventually meets in her long relationship with
GoFukakusa has little in common with the pathetically ephemeral career of
Yūgao (and even less with the long-lived stability of Murasaki's ties to Genji).
Yet when Nijō is finally forced to withdraw from court service by GoFukakusa's
empress, her medieval readers may well have recalled the relentlessly vengeful
spirit of Yūgao's haunter.

Medieval readers of the narrative would have also recalled that Yūgao was
beloved by two men: both Genji and his friend and rival Tō no Chūjō. It should
come as no surprise then, that allusions to Yūgao crop up again in one of Nijō's
most elaborate descriptions of her early encounters with Sanekane, the second
patron and lover to appear in the memoir. Once more, Nijō replays the *Genji*
precedents to great comic effect. Genji had been both amused and repelled to
overhear, after his first night with Yūgao, homely noises coming from lower-
class neighbors in the alley behind her run-down lodgings. Recalling this scene
from *The Tale of Genji,* Nijō describes the mortifying racket her own relatives
raise in the next room during one of Sanekane's secret visits to her house. Her
people stay up most of the night playing the *go* game and begging her loudly
to come out and join them.

The *Genji* allusions in this memoir also seem to work as a technique for
recuperating and exposing the perspective of the youthful self who persisted in
seeing herself in terms of the heroines of Heian literature, despite mounting
evidence denying or comically exaggerating the similarities between her own
life and scenes from the romances. One might read in them the irony of the
older woman who remembers and commemorates—with tenderness and humor—the language and imagery by which she understood the world and herself
as a girl. Other *Genji* and *uta monogatari* references, especially those in the last
two books, strike this reader as unequivocally melancholy, even angry in tone.

In some instances, particularly in certain of the travel narrative sections, Nijō outstrips her predecessors in conveying the intensely elegiac mood of tales about exiled lovers and wandering nobles.

Though many Japanese scholars do not consider *Towazugatari* to be stylistically as fine a work as some of the principal Heian *nikki,* for sheer variety of content, the memoir is generally ranked as the most interesting female-authored *nikki* that survives from the Kamakura period (1185–1333). Passages in which the narrator recounts having to act as the go-between (*michishiba*), escorting other women to GoFukakusa's bed, provide rare, de-romanticized glimpses of some of the more humiliating aspects of life as an emperor's lady-in-waiting. No one who reads the work in the context of earlier court women's writings will fail to notice that it contains some of the frankest descriptions of sexual relationships in the courtly tradition. The memoir demonstrates an unusual versatility of tone in its depictions of these relationships, ranging from the off-handed account given of the heroine's first sexual encounter with Sanekane ("although I had not intended to go so far as to give myself to him" [SNKS 20, 51]) to the intensely melancholy, brooding images of her tortured affair with the priest (complete with references to poetic legends about Ono no Komachi and Princess Somedono). The work is relatively explicit, not only about the extent of Nijō's sexual involvement but also regarding the anger, jealousy, victimization, and betrayal these involvements frequently generated.

The theme of sexual victimization is clearly illustrated in the claustrophobic, almost panicky descriptions of Nijō's relations with her various lovers and male pursuers, which reach a crisis of frequency and intensity toward the end of Book 2 and the beginning of Book 3. The narrator recalls a succession of scenes in which several of these men are present within almost the same physical space, each demanding her attention. Consider, for example, the passage in which Kanehira invites GoFukakusa to his villa at Fushimi and then insists, seemingly with GoFukakusa's consent, on having Nijō in his bed. Kanehira waylays Nijō as she is slipping back to GoFukakusa's quarters after a clandestine tryst of her own devising (apparently with Sanekane). Before dawn the next morning the party returns to the capital, with Nijō surprised to find both GoFukakusa and Sanekane riding in the same carriage with her. Kanehira's carriage follows close behind theirs. Exhaustion and repressed anger at her patrons breed in her what can only be described as a kind of alienation: "One could say," she remembers, "that what remained was just the sad shell (or shadow) of my past self" (SNKS 20, 153). Yet in spite of her outrage at Kanehira's behavior the evening before (or perhaps because of the discomfiting proximity of the other two men in the carriage?), she finds herself gazing longingly toward Kanehira's carriage when it turns away from GoFukakusa's party at a fork in the road. As narrator, Nijō is all too clearly attuned to the possibility that she will be seen simply as a sexual adventurer, a kind of adept at the ways of love at this juncture—a reading she preempts and complicates by underscoring her own sense of self-estrangement: "Since when," she asks, "had these things become such a habit

with me? Though these were my own feelings, they were incomprehensible to
me'' (ibid.). At another point in the narrative she recounts fleeing the presence
of both GoFukakusa and the priest in one room, only to find Sanekane in the
next, glumly complaining about her neglect of him: "There was no place for
me to hide anywhere, and so I listened to him" (SNKS 20, 174). A few pages
later, GoFukakusa's brother and rival Kameyama (or is it GoFukakusa after all?
the text is ambiguous here—perhaps deliberately so) takes her to bed while
GoFukakusa slumbers drunkenly just the other side of a folding screen.

Throughout the three volumes concerning her life at court, Nijō presents herself as a woman who had things to hide and in doing so draws on one of the
most subtle strategies that writers of fictional or (auto)biographical prose can
use for creating a sense of a character's psychological depth. Her desire, while
still a member of court society, was to keep her various affairs and transgressions
secret. Yet she portrays herself as having been repeatedly shaken by the realization that the things she had assumed to be secrets between herself and one or
another of her patrons were in fact already known to the others. Her uncle Shijō
Takaaki (b. 1243) seems to know of her liaisons with Sanekane from a very
early stage in the affair. He not only knows of the priest's passion for her but
actually connives with him to lure her into an encounter the two men have
prearranged. GoFukakusa is similarly aware of Sanekane's interest in her and
apparently takes a kind of voyeuristic pleasure in the attentions forced upon her
by Kanehira. After overhearing the priest's tormented, though suspiciously in-
cautious, confession of passion for her, GoFukakusa actively abets him in his
obsessive pursuit of Nijō, initially without the priest's awareness of it, but finally
(after confronting him with his knowledge, again, to Nijō's mortification) in
cooperation with him. Nijō's periodic discoveries that her secrets are in fact not
secrets at all, but part of a common currency of gossip and conspiratorial fra-
ternity between her various patrons, have a curiously deflationary effect. Her
depictions suggest that she felt the men around her trivialized her secrecy and,
by extension, her anguished interiority, in a way that was in some senses more
invasive than their sexual and material manipulation of her. The result is a
remarkably self-ironic, almost self-effacing mode of self-portrayal. Nijō conjures
up depths and secrets in herself that she later finds (and reveals to her reader)
to be merely the small change of court gossip.

Though her attitude toward her past is a complicated one, involving at different times various degrees of nostalgia and humor as well as resignation and
raw anger, Nijō seldom translates her mixed tenderness and resentment into the
kind of well-mannered irony for which *The Tale of Genji* is admired. The un-
romantic descriptions of Nijō's life at court come closer than most earlier court
literature to unmasking courtly love for what it often was, a politically motivated
exchange of women among powerful men. Seen in this light, Nijō's decision to
take the tonsure appears inextricably linked to her experiences at court. It is a
positive act by which she chooses one of the few modes of independence available to women of the day and thereby escapes not romantic love itself (she

makes it clear that her affection for GoFukakusa deepens during her exile from court), but the economy of bedroom politics, according to which aristocratic women were circulated among fathers, patrons, and sons-in-law as eroticized political commodities.

BIBLIOGRAPHY

Translations

The Confessions of Lady Nijō. Trans. Karen Brazell. Stanford, CA: Stanford University Press, 1973.
"The Confessions of Lady Nijō." Trans. Helen McCullough. In *Classical Japanese Prose: An Anthology.* Stanford, CA: Stanford University Press, 1990 (trans. of Book 1).
Lady Nijō's Own Story: "Towazugatari": The Candid Diary of a Thirteenth-Century Japanese Imperial Concubine. Trans. Wilfrid Whitehouse and Eizo Yanagisawa. Tokyo: Tuttle, 1974.

Critical Works

Brazell, Karen. "*Towazugatari:* Autobiography of a Kamakura Court Lady." *Harvard Journal of Asiatic Studies* 31 (1971): 220–33.
Keene, Donald. "The Confessions of Lady Nijō." In *Travelers of a Hundred Ages.* New York: Henry Holt, 1989.
Marra, Michele. "Images from the Past: The Politics of Intertextuality." In *The Aesthetics of Discontent: Politics and Reclusion in Medieval Japanese Literature.* Honolulu: University of Hawaii Press, 1991.

Edith Lorraine SARRA

H ─────────────────────────────────

HARADA Yasuko (1928–), novelist, short story writer. Real name: Sasaki Yasuko (Mrs. Sasaki Yoshio); née Harada Yasuko.

Life: Harada was born in Tokyo on January 12, 1928, the oldest of four sisters and two brothers, the fourth generation of Hokkaido pioneers. Soon after her birth, her parents left for Kushiro, Hokkaido, where she was raised and is still living. Her maternal grandfather, a native of Nagasaki, was one of the pioneers who led a group of roughnecks to Hokkaido to tame the wilderness of the Kushiro Plain. In her grandfather's days, the Haradas were quite an influential family in the area, owner of a "beautiful palatial red-brick house." Her father, who married the Haradas' only daughter, Tetsu, became their adopted son and heir, according to a practice still common among the Japanese. He and Tetsu, an understanding, gentle, yet determined woman, were as different as night and day. Harada Yasuko received none of the loving, tender care a young father often showers upon the first baby girl. She tried to rationalize his cold indifference by attributing it to his status as an adopted son. He displayed no willingness or competitive drive to manage the enormous fortune accumulated by his wife's grandfather and great-grandfather. The family fortunes quickly dwindled, and before long he had lost everything. This lack of a business sense combined with his passivity and indifference did not help enhance his fatherhood. He showed no interest in the development and welfare of his six children. The only time "he looked somewhat concerned was when I got sick," Harada recalled. Ever since she could remember, she had been sickly, spending more time in bed than at school. She often suffered from stomach and intestinal ailments, and once she even had acute pneumonia and nephritis. Other illnesses of all kinds came and went.

Despite her many physical woes, or because of them, from early on she found solace in the escape literature provided. Life was bearable when she read the fairy tales of foreign countries. Her favorite subjects at school were geography and history, rather unusual for a girl in Japan in the 1930s. Learning about alien lands reinforced her imagination, and, during the war that coincided with her schooling at Kushiro City Girls' High School, she began to write her own *Märchen*. In February 1945, six months before the end of the war, she was mobilized along with other students to work at an airplane factory in Kitami City. Torn out of her solitary world as a *bungaku shōjo* (a literary girl), she was "miserable, because I knew I couldn't survive a regimented life or communal living. In early August, I was hospitalized for a pulmonary complication, in a town where I knew no one, away from my family. . . . I knew Japan would lose the war . . . I thought I would succumb to the disease, everything would come crumbling down. At that moment I felt calm for the first time."

Between 1949 and 1953 she worked for the Eastern Hokkaido newspaper as a reporter, while she actively participated in a theater group and wrote short stories for local magazines. She married Sasaki Yoshio, also a newspaper reporter, in 1951. It was a "love marriage" in the true sense of the word. When she asked him if they could postpone their wedding because she wanted to write a novel first, he maintained his composure and replied, "You'll feel more settled and can write better when you're married, don't you think?"

Career: "Sabita no kioku" (Sabita's Memories, 1954), Harada's first short story, received national recognition in *Shinchō* as one of the best pieces of the year. "Yuki no su" (A Snow Nest, 1954) appeared in *Kindai bungaku* (Modern Literature Journal). After this brief "apprenticeship" in the boondocks of Hokkaido, her metamorphosis from an obscure local writer to an overnight celebrity is legendary. Her one and only best-seller and a winner of the Women's Literature Prize, *Banka* (An Elegy, 1956) held the postwar Japanese public spellbound. It stayed on the best-seller list throughout 1957. By the end of the year, 720,000 copies had been sold. The popularity of the book and its film version by director Gosho Heinosuke was phenomenal, as unprecedented as that of *Gone with the Wind* by Margaret Mitchell (1900–49). At the same time, the young author's sudden emergence was touted as "just as meteoric as that of the eighteen-year-old Françoise Sagan (1935–) with her *Bonjour Tristesse*," and the publisher's attempts at aggressive pictorial advertisement of Harada's book created the so-called "Banka Boom."

Tōto Shobō, which published *Banka,* had been in operation only six months, and nobody had heard of it before. In 1956 Japan was undergoing the pressure of the austere "Dodge Line" economic policy. Small publishers went bankrupt in great numbers. Even large presses had to brace themselves for the advent of the television age. Kōdansha, one of the largest publishers, was determined to survive the tough times and decided to create a small, independent, more flexible publisher that would pioneer new areas of interest and appeal to a different readership. Yamaguchi Hiroshi, Kōdansha's chief editor, who first took interest in the short story "Sabita's Memories," wrote Harada, asking her to send him a new work if she had one. By the time she mailed *Banka,* which was originally serialized in a local literary magazine in Kushiro, *Hokkai Bungaku* (North Sea

Literature), Yamaguchi had become ill. The manuscript remained unread. In the meantime, Harada, with no knowledge of his illness (or his transfer to a new post at Tōto Shobō), wrote to him twice. The two special delivery letters sat on his desk unopened. Finally, one of his colleagues, who sensed some urgency about Harada's correspondence, although he did not know anything about its content, had the foresight to inform her of Yamaguchi's condition.

Paralleling the Kōdansha-Tōto development was the film director Gosho Heinosuke's feverish search for some fresh, sentimental story to work on. He already liked Harada's "Sabita's Memories." As soon as he found out about the serialized novel, *Banka,* he moved in to acquire the film rights for the book. In October 1956 the final decision for publication had been left to Takahashi Kiyoji, the chief editor of Tōto Shobō. He wrote: "With a promise to my men that I would read the entire novel that Sunday, I took it home. My family has a fun ritual: every time I come home, my children rummage through my briefcase hoping to find some new books to read. That night was no exception. My lovable hunters were at the game again. After the foraging, my daughter, a student at Japan Women's College, picked out the manuscript of *Banka.*" The following morning, her eyes swollen from lack of sleep, she "reported" to her father that the female protagonist was one of a kind, nothing like anything she had ever encountered before, and the style was appealing. On that Sunday Takahashi sat down with the manuscript and, eleven hours later, made the decision to print it. As an unknown publisher printing a work by an unknown woman writer, he undertook a tremendous risk for Tōto Shobō. However, Takahashi instinctively knew the book would sell.

As was the case with the spectacular debut of *Banka,* Harada's subsequent works have continued to capture the interest of young women in their twenties and thirties. Because of this kind of readership and the fact that her narratives do not belong to the autobiographical "I-novel" tradition, still an enormous favorite of the Japanese public, critics basically regard her as a popular writer even today. She weaves her literary world out of imagination, rather than raw experiences that automatically tempt the Japanese reader to closely identify the protagonist with the author.

Major Works: Nichiyōbi no shiroi kumo (The White Clouds on a Sunday, 1979), novel. This work, first serialized in four different newspapers, is representative of Harada the entertainer at work. The novel follows Honjō Yuri, the only daughter of a doctor, who has failed in marriage and also finds herself losing her touch as a professional violinist; she by chance meets a young Self-Defense Corps fighter pilot, Konaka Chihiro. Love at first sight for Chihiro, he relentlessly pursues the broken-hearted young divorcée until she more or less gives in. With the Chitose Air Force Base as a backdrop and with the passionate love affair between a Japanese "top gun" and a beautiful, melancholy divorcée who has attempted suicide, Harada re-creates for contemporary Japanse women readers a clean and extremely entertaining romance novel. Unlike formulaic romance fiction, however, *The White Clouds on a Sunday* ends not with Yuri and Chihiro happily united in matrimony but with Yuri's discovering a new self-identity and starting a life on her own as she joins the Sapporo Symphony Orchestra.

Kaze no toride (The Fortress in the Wind, 1972), historical romance novel. In February 1971 Harada started serializing it in the *Hokkaido* newspaper. The serialization ended in April 1972, and eleven years later a revised edition was published by Shinchōsha. In the early 1960s Harada visited Wakkanai for the first time on an assignment for a magazine and extended her journey to Sōya City, the northern tip of Hokkaido. While on one of her solitary excursions, she came upon a cluster of gravestones in the heavy snow. They belonged to clansmen of the Tohoku region (the underdeveloped northern part of Honshu) who were sent by the Tokugawa shogunate in the early 1800s to defend Soya against Russia. From this came Harada's idea for a major novel, *The Fortress in the Wind*. Despite the fact that she always draws upon Hokkaido for the geographical settings of her stories, she had no interest in the history of Ezo (the former name of Hokkaido) and the Ainu people (the aborigines), no knowledge of what the Tohoku clansmen had contributed as pioneers in that godforsaken land, until she stumbled upon the Sōya graveyard.

The novel opens with a brief history of how the Russians came into contact with the Japanese on the island of Sakhalin, which faces the Sea of Okhotsk. According to the earliest written record, the Matsumae fief (at the southern tip of Ezo) dispatched an expedition to Sakhalin in 1635. It was not until 1783 that the first Russians set foot on the island. The Matsumae fief opened a trading post at Shiranushi, the southernmost village of Sakhalin, in 1790. In the fall of 1792 a Russian envoy led by Laxman landed at Nemuro, Ezo, with three Japanese castaways, and in 1803 another Russian representative, Rezanov, came to Nagasaki, Kyūshū. At this time, the rest of Japan was in turmoil as the 250-year-old *sakoku* (closed-door policy) was about to end. Between 1803 and 1804, in retaliation for Japan's refusal to open trade with Russia, some Russians set fire on Rezanov's order to the Japanese settlements among the Ainus at Kushunkotan and destroyed four Japanese vessels near the entrance to Sōya Harbor. In May 1853 the American Commodore Perry came to Uraga in central Japan; in June the Russian Rear Admiral Putiatin came to Nagasaki, and in August another Russian envoy, Nevelskoi, appeared in Aniwa Bay at Sakhalin to colonize the island. Alarmed by the rapid succession of Russian threats, the Matsumae fief dispatched troops to Sakhalin in 1854 and demanded the withdrawal of the Russians. To their surprise, the Russians immediately evacuated the island without bloodshed. What the Japanese did not know then was that the outbreak of the Crimean War forced the Russians to return to their homeland. From 1855 on, the Tokugawa shogunate, in anticipation of a dispute over the sovereignty of Sakhalin, ordered the four Tōhoku fiefs of Sendai, Akita, Hirosaki, and Morioka to jointly guard Ezo and Sakhalin.

The public awareness of Ezo history being minimal and Harada being one of the very few Hokkaidoite writers, *The Fortress in the Wind* serves a twofold purpose: to educate the reader and to provide an emotional outlet for the author. The story focuses on two sets of love triangle relationships: two women and a man, two men and a woman. Kojima Kaori, a twenty-six-year-old samurai of the Akita fief, volunteers to go to Ezo as a guard to escape an unconsummated marriage to a beautiful but spoiled eighteen-year-old, Kiku, who insists she is in love with another man with whom she has never exchanged a word. Dispatched to the Sōya station in Ezo, Kaori falls in love with Yū, the wife of his superior, Sukegawa Sōzaburō. Kaori sees the image of an ideal Kiku in Yū. Parallel to the Kaori-Kiku-Yū relationship is that of Watari Umpei, Kaori's schoolmate, who has been enlisted in the Ezo expedition, his Ainu love, Shorura, and a young outcast Ainu, Shiseku, who loves her.

There are three stories layered one atop the other in this historical fiction. The first one is an adventure-romance story of the two young samurais, Kaori and Umpei, and the second is the history of those committed pioneers who paved the way for a new land, Hokkaido. The third, the central focus of the novel, deals with a sad, devastating history of the Ainu people, whose nation once belonged to their *kamui* (gods) but now has been conquered by the *shamo* (*wagin* = Japanese). Through the relationship of Kaori and Umpei, Harada attempts to create a dream nation where *shamo* and Ainu can coexist. Her romanticism provides a respite from the brutal history of a doomed people.

Translated Works: An Elegy (Banka, 1956), novel. Before she began to serialize it, Harada explained the basic theme of the novel in a letter to one of her friends: "I'm thinking of writing a story about a girl. A girl who is drawn to the beauty of what in the end must perish, and for that reason she must also perish. This is an important theme for me, one of the songs I am compelled to sing." (Translation in this article is by Michiko Wilson.) The novel portrays the twenty-three-year-old Hyōdō Reiko, whose left elbow and hand are partially paralyzed. During one of her solitary strolls on a nearby hill, she meets Katsuragi Sadao, an architect, walking a dog with his three-year-old daughter. Later on, by chance she learns that Mrs. Katsuragi is having an affair with a young man. Out of curiosity she begins to visit Katsuragi at his office. When she calls him a "cuckold," instead of indignation, he displays affection, and they spend two nights together at a hot spring resort. While he is away on business, Reiko secretly makes friends with his wife and on impulse goes to see him in Sapporo. While he begins to love Reiko more deeply and is prepared to marry her, she realizes she is also in love with his beautiful wife. In the end Mrs. Katsuragi, who is the last one to know about Katsuragi and Reiko's relationship and is unable to bear the truth, commits suicide. Despite the sincerity of Katsuragi's love, Reiko tells herself that she does not deserve the love.

Behind the phenomenal popularity of *An Elegy* in postwar Japan lies the almost fifteen hundred years of subjugation of Japanese women, which lasted till 1945. Reiko is a model "new woman" for the postwar generation. She breaks taboos on all fronts, destroys every conventional image of Japanese women so far depicted in Japanese literature. Like the seventeen-year-old Cécile in *Bonjour Tristesse,* Reiko is purposeless, innocent, irresponsible, and cruel, caught between the dream world of an adolescent and the reality of the adult world. Reiko uses this neither-nor, betwixt-and-between, liminal realm to her advantage. Although her constant enemy is anxiety (*fuan*), the ulterior motive that dictates her capricious behavior is the desire for fun, to have a good time (*tanoshiku naru*). She tirelessly seeks out *tanoshisa,* the ultimate enjoyment and amusement.

All the major incidents surrounding Reiko stem from the anticipation of *tanoshiku naru.* Indeed, the narrative movement of the story continues as long as *tanoshisa* and *fuan* replace one another. When this pendulum motion ceases, she is no longer the innocent, liminal girl. As the title suggests, the author laments the end of this stage of youth, with its cruelty and impulsiveness. During the first encounter between Reiko and Katsuragi, her initial *reaction* (she never actually initiates anything) is: "I didn't stand up. Nor did I bother to look at my bitten hand. It was too late. I had picked up the ball at a whim [and let the dog bite my hand]. If I hadn't tried to pick it up, I could have avoided this bothersome obligation to speak to a stranger." However, by the time the man with the dog helps bandage her wounded hand with a handkerchief, she begins to find their brief conversation amusing and says: "I felt too embarrassed to call him *anata* [lit., "you," which indicates intimacy], and said, *ojisan* [lit., "uncle," which refers to any older male vis-à-vis the speaker]. I began to feel a little happy." She visits with Katsuragi in his office to look at some of his architecture books "because it made me feel happy." This light, spontaneous feeling is also the key to her desire to know Mrs. Katsuragi: "I wanted to approach Mrs. Katsuragi as much as possible. To have fun I was already with her and Kose Tatsuo [her lover] at their table. I was beginning to feel animated. But I wanted a joy that would make me breathless. For that, I must grab every possible chance, create every possible opportunity."

Watching Mrs. Katsuragi and her young lover together at a coffee shop, Reiko experiences a whole gamut of emotions, which is repeated throughout the novel: "It is *absurd* that I felt bad about prying into whether Mr. Katsuragi is happy in the house he has designed and built, now that I have witnessed his wife having a secret affair; I want to *show* him how erotic his wife looks now; it is rather *fun* to watch the two lovers; I must tell Mr. Katsuragi about his wife's infidelity but I feel *restrained;* I feel *pain* and *pleasure* at the same time; I no longer feel like visiting with Mr. Katsuragi and that makes me *anxious* and *irritated* as if I have been deprived of *some great fun.*" [The emphasis mine.] Even after Katsuragi kisses her on the mouth and several days later takes her to a hotel at a hot spring, she undergoes her usual emotional roller coaster: first, pain, love, and then a suspicion that he is just pitying her; a feeling of security and the fun of being with Katsuragi; back to a suspicion that his real love is his wife and she is someone he has just picked up along the way; and then hatred, fear leading into sorrow and passion spent.

Reiko the *amanojaku* (a contrary person) gets herself locked into an emotional loop like a spoiled child. Harada's creation of Reiko is one of those fascinating literary coincidences that delight the readers of the world's literature. Sagan's Cécile shares many of the same attributes with Reiko in her conniving, conspiratory manner. Witness, for example, how this French girl takes it upon herself to let her father know Anne is not for him or to snub Anne for her air of superiority: "When I left my conspirators at the end of an hour, I was rather perturbed. However, there were still grounds for reassurance; my plan might well misfire because my father's real passion for Anne would keep him faithful to her. In addition, neither Cyril nor Elsa could do much without my connivance. If my father showed any signs of falling into the trap, I could find some means of putting an end to the whole thing. But still it was amusing to try the plan out, and see whether my psychological judgment proved right or wrong" (*Bonjour Tristesse* by Françoise Sagan. Trans. Irene Ash. New York: E. P. Dutton, 1955, 77). However, Harada makes it very clear toward the end of *The Elegy* that Reiko is attracted to the mature, calm, understanding, soft-spoken Katsuragi because he plays the ultimate surrogate father in her mind. For the same reason, she cannot tear herself away from the beautiful, maternal Mrs. Katsuragi because she can potentially replace Reiko's long-dead mother. To accept Katsuragi in marriage is to commit incest with her own father. This is the reason Reiko must leave him and start anew.

After the initial rave reviews, many critics began to find fault with *An Elegy*, complaining that the protagonist has "no purpose in life," "is just a prankster and a spoiled girl." One critic went so far as to denounce Reiko, saying to the effect that she could never love a man; she has no principle or morality, and has the mentality of a thirteen- or fourteen-year-old. All her problems stem from the fact that she does not know how to make a living. She is an egoist to the core. These rather emotional and comical comments illustrate the kind of impact the work had on male readers in Japan in 1957. First of all, it was insulting for a Japanese male to read about a carefree, independent-minded, rather devilish young woman manipulating, deceiving, and prying into the privacy of a financially established man in his late thirties. To make things worse, she has the impertinence to reject the economical and emotional stability this perfect gentleman is willing to offer her. It took Dorothy Sayer's (1893–1957) Harriet Vane five years to accept Lord Peter Whimsy's sincere love, and that was bad enough from a man's point of view. Harada dared to offend the pride of conventional Japanese men and offered nothing in return. Furthermore, it is not just Reiko who irritates them. How about Mr. Katsuragi? He is the first postwar liberated man created by a woman writer. He offers Reiko a choice, lets her make up her own mind. For example, when he invites her to come with him to a hot spring resort, he says to her: "I don't want to push you. After all, we'll be staying overnight at a strange place. You'll have to decide for yourself whether you want to come with me or not." Indeed, it never occurred to the critics that Reiko is no worse than the cynical egocentric Shimamura in Kawabata's (1899–1972) *Snow Country,* who essentially makes a plaything out of the local geisha girl, Komako.

Second, *An Elegy* has nothing whatsoever to do with the private life of Harada. The work does not prove the authenticity of the author's genuine spiritual battle in life. The purely fictional narrative did not sit well with many of the male critics of that time. In terms of style, she cannot escape altogether the potboiler effect of her verbosity. There is very little subtlety or room for imagination for the reader to fill in as is the case with *jun bungaku* (pure literature). Nothing is ambiguous; everything is explained to the point of redundancy. Also, Harada's constant use of *watashi,* the first-person pronoun "I" (which is understood and assumed in Japanese sentences) breaks with the convention practiced by traditional writers. While they avoid *watashi* to de-emphasize individuality or persona, Harada establishes, in the manner of a Western novel, the strong presence of Reiko, the person, the woman, and the narrator, from the very beginning of the novel to the end. In the following short paragraph, Harada uses *watashi* seven times, where an ordinary Japanese writer would try to get by with two or three: "As *I* [unnecessary] watched the man's [Katsuragi] warm hand which touched mine, I was convinced that he regarded *me* [unnecessary] as something of a juvenile delinquent. My heart was already hardened. . . . *I* [unnecessary] said to myself that it did not really matter what he thought of *me* [unnecessary], that *I* [unnecessary] may really be a juvenile delinquent" (emphasis mine). All these stylistic "transgressions," however, turned out to be the true assets of the book because the public saw something Western about Harada's style, as though they were reading a foreign novel in translation. It was a refreshing diversion from the standard literary fare.

"Evening Bells" (Banshō, 1960), short story. It tells, in the first person, of a young woman who lives with her widowered father in a desperate attempt to open communication with him. She is atypical of Japanese women because marriage never enters her mind. She is still obsessed with what she witnessed as a young girl: strange, half-romantic, half-tragic relationships between her mother and her young piano teacher and between her father and a young daughter of one of his business associates. The story describes the narrator's rite of passage and her yearning for the affectionate father, which Harada was denied.

BIBLIOGRAPHY

Translations

An Elegy. Boston: Beacon Press, 1957.
"Evening Bells." Trans. Chia-ning Chang and Sara Dillion. In *The Mother of Dreams and Other Short Stories: Portrayals of Women in Modern Japanese Fiction,* ed. Makoto Ueda. Tokyo: Kodansha International, 1986.

Michiko N. WILSON

HASHIDA Sugako (1925–) television dramatist, essayist. Real name: Iwasaki Sugako (Mrs. Iwasaki Hisaichi); née Hashida Sugako.

Life: Hashida Sugako was born in an upper-middle-class family in Seoul, Korea, during the period of Japanese annexation. While still a child, she returned to Sakai City, Japan, with her mother, leaving the father behind in Korea.

In 1942 she enrolled in the Department of Japanese Literature at the Japan Women's College in Tokyo. When the college was closed for the duration of the war, Hashida found work in the payroll department of the navy near Osaka. When the war ended, she was twenty and forced to continue working, since the family house and savings had been destroyed. Then in October 1945 she lost her job. Even though her mother was destitute and forced to live with relatives, she encouraged Hashida to return to college. This she did, by using what little compensation she had received from the navy. She later transferred to the Department of Art at Waseda University. Her father, who had lost everything in Korea, was forced to turn black marketeer to support the family in Japan. Then Hashida's mother died.

Yet even this period of hardship and personal loss helped prepare Hashida for her career as television dramatist. In college, she fell under the influence of the work of Kikuchi Kan (1888–1948), a noted novelist and dramatist. Like his acclaimed 1919 stories *Tōjūrō no Koi* (Tojuro's Love) and *Onshū no Kanata ni* (Beyond Vengeance), many of his works were adapted for screen. Hashida acknowledges her debt to these and other Kikuchi masterpieces. Another important influence was the courageous response of her parents to the extraordinary conditions they were forced to live through. Her most popular television serial drama, *Oshin* (1983–84), attests to this influence, as the heroine's unrelenting struggle against extreme circumstances offers a strong thematic constant.

After graduating from Waseda University, Hashida went to work in the Script Department of the Shochiku Film Company, one of five major cinema enterprises in Japan. This company had a long history of melodramas and "home dramas" aimed at female audiences. Hashida learned much from her decade of involvement with Shochiku. After a golden age of Japanese cinema in the 1950s, an industrywide decline set in. Hashida was one of the casualties of a studio layoff in 1960. She spent the next five years as a struggling free-lance dramatist, selling few scripts and forced to yield to frequent rewrite demands. She survived in part by writing short fiction for girls' magazines.

In 1965 she married Iwasaki Hiroshi, a producer for Tokyo Broadcasting Station (TBS). Though somewhat slow to develop a career in television scriptwriting, she did find herself free to pursue her own literary interests. Hashida is now considered one of Japan's foremost and most prolific female television dramatists.

Career: Hashida's first big success came with the domestic drama *Ai to Shi o Mitsumete* (Watching Love and Death, 1973). Written for the TBS Sunday Theater, this play received rave reviews. Since then, almost all of Hashida's scripts aimed at female and family audiences have enjoyed enormous popularity. Examples include *Tonari no Shibafu* (The Grass Is Greener on the Other Side, 1976–77), *Fūfu* (Husband and Wife, 1979), and the broadcast sensation *Oshin* (1983–84), all written for NHK, the prestigious national network. Acclaimed works written for TBS, her husband's television company noted for drama series, include *Michi* (Road, 1980), *Onnatachi no Chūshingura* (Chushingura for Women, 1981), and *Daikazoku* (Big Family, 1983).

As might be expected, Hashida's outstanding achievement has been in the category of domestic drama. She herself has this to say about it: "The reason for my steadfast pursuit of domestic drama is that I want to treat family problems—problems of the greatest importance—in my own way. I cannot write about murder, juvenile delinquency, or adultery—all fashionable topics today. Domestic drama is the genre I feel comfortable with."

Hashida may be considered the television industry counterpart of Ozu Yasujirō (1903–63), a giant filmmaker who himself happened to be a scenarist. Ozu established the *shomingeki,* or drama about common people, in the early 1930s and remained faithful to it throughout his career as a director. His favorite subject was the middle-class family; Ozu illustrates how the relationships of its members are affected by events in their daily lives. Hashida's favorite characters also tend to be middle-class. Her dramas typically concern a white-collar family facing a series of everyday problems. Her material, however, is more immediately topical and contemporary, as she values direct communication with her enormous audience. Hence the problems her families face reflect not just the immediacy of their experience but also some pressing issue of the day as seen in the mass media. Her dramas have no villains in the true sense of the word.

Hashida's work has earned her the profession's highest awards: in 1979 she received the Broadcasting Culture Award; the Golden Arrow; and the Most Distinguished Individual Achievement Award; in 1983, the Cultural Achievement Award in Broadcasting; and in 1984, the Kikuchi Kan Award, given in memory of the novelist-dramatist Hashida most admires.

Major Works: Daikazoku (Big Family, 1984), television drama. This is a somewhat idealized case history of a family whose four generations live under one roof, a topic of considerable interest in a nation that ranks highest in the world for average life expectancy. The drama arises out of conflict among family members—especially a grandmother, daughter-in-law, and granddaughter-in-law. Hisahida makes their interpersonal friction spark visions of the wisdom, bond, and dream of the extended family—something the nuclear family does not offer.

Otoko ga Uchi o Deru Toki (When Men Leave Their Homes, 1985), television drama. Here Hashida works with one particular family problem getting its share of media attention in Japan, namely, married white-collar workers transferred to jobs away from their families. The resulting strain on family structure focuses on the father-son relationship. In this and all her domestic dramas, Hashida offers a narrative pattern consisting of crisis, character change, and happy ending. The given crisis creates tension, conflict, and ultimately some degree of accommodation among family members. Reconciliations based on newly gained awareness of roles within the family structure restore harmony among family members.

Translated Works: The Grass Is Greener on the Other Side (Tonari no Shibafu, 1976–77), television drama. Hashida's script of this drama has not been published in English, but an English-dubbed version was shown on U.S. cable television in the early 1980s. The original thirty-part series has also been edited for use as instructional material in conjunction with a textbook for advanced Japanese language study in English-speaking countries.

The core of this drama concerns the Japanese white-collar worker's dream fulfilled: owning a new house. Hashida had this to say about the dream and its significant nightmare potential in the 1970s (and in present-day Japan as well): ''I have long wanted to write a domestic drama that is in effect a satirical tragedy on the subject of people whose sacrifices made for the sake of a new house lead to the destruction of their family.''

The family in this case consists of a typical middle-class, white-collar worker, Kaname, his wife, Tomoko, and two children, who move into their new suburban house. Hashida offers a familiar narrative pattern of crisis, character change, and happy ending. Money is tight, the children have trouble adjusting to their new surroundings, and Tomoko clashes with her mother-in-law, Shino, who later moves in with them. Easing the money problem exacerbates the other two problems. Through a former classmate, Tokie, she finds a job in an elite businessmen's club run by her friend's boss, Tonomura. The idea is to earn extra family income and give herself time away from her mother-in-law. But Shino alienates her grandchildren by accusing Tomoko of coming home late and other unmotherly behavior. The older woman takes over the house and begins acting the nagging wife to her son, drawing him to her side in an atmosphere of confrontation, with Tomoko and the children as opponents.

To this basic familial conflict Hashida adds another form of discord: the husband-wife relationship also suffers the strain caused by Tomoko's success at her work. Her salary turns out to be higher than Kaname's. Worse yet, Kaname brings a prospective business associate to Tomoko's club and sees his wife's boss being too attentive. His jealousy is fanned by Tokie, who has designs on Tonomura. Meantime, the children at home feel neglected by their mother. Tomoko's own mother, herself a working woman, serves as counselor in all this. Torn between values of female independence and traditional demands of wife and mother, Tomoko decides to resign from work. But when she faces Tonomura, she changes her mind.

As might be expected, the climax offers a crescendo of these discords. Kaname's business is deadlocked by the interference of Tonomura, but what Kaname does not know is that his wife's boss is acting to protect him from involvement in a bad deal. Encouraged by his mother to think the worst of Tomoko, Kaname decides to give infidelity a try and yields to Tokie's blandishments. Tokie's motive is actually jealousy—she is in love with Tonomura, who appears to be too kind to Tomoko. So it happens that Tokie and Kaname are discovered unconscious together, due to a gas leak in her apartment. Feeling betrayed in every way, Tomoko goes to live with her mother. The final confrontation of Tomoko and Tokie, however, takes place on a different plane. Tokie claims that one of the reasons she seduced her best friend's husband was to teach her a moral lesson, namely, that "a housewife's place is in the home."

The drama ends with family restored. As so often happens in Hashida melodramas, reconciliation owes much to the heroine's new level of self-awareness. A prodigal husband's repentance and loving children's presence also help mend the breach. Tomoko returns to good housekeeping, studying bookkeeping in order to be able to work part-time at home. Now it is her mother-in-law's turn to spend more time away from home—as instructor of flower arrangement and tea ceremony.

Hashida is too determined a moralist to let the matter rest there. Tomoko's experience is shared by many Japanese women. In order to establish this sense of collective moral crisis, Hashida closes her play by coming full circle. In the final scene, Tomoko is entertaining her old classmate Mineko, who looks around at Tomoko's home and complains about the tiny house she and her family share with the mother-in-law. She longs for some privacy and is quite determined to have a new house. She asks Tomoko's advice: should she work as a hostess in a small bar near her house? Tomoko has nothing to say. In the final shot, the camera invites the audience to study Tomoko's bemused expression.

Oshin (Oshin, 1983–84), television drama. One of the most popular family melodramas ever aired on NHK, *Oshin* was also shown on cable television in America. This broadcasting sensation, which recorded a Japanese Nielsen rating of 65 percent, shows that Hashida's creative expression is not limited to cozy domestic drama. *Oshin* is an ambitious attempt to study the problems of contemporary Japanese women in a much wider sociohistorical perspective.

Oshin is the story of one woman's long, eventful life set against a backdrop of Japanese modern history through the turbulent eras: Meiji (1868–1912), Taishō (1912–25), and Shōwa (1925–88). The drama is devoted to the four phases of her life: childhood and youth; married life; widowhood; and old age. Since, as always, Hashida aims to reach the widest possible audience, she must revive the distant and unfamiliar Meiji and Taishō eras for younger generations of viewers. She does this by using a present-day college student, Kei, as chief witness to the long look backward into the life of his adoptive grandmother, Oshin (born 1900). He is the grandson of her former mistress, a wealthy woman in whose household she once served and whose friendship Oshin cherishes most in memory. Oshin loves Kei more than her own grandchildren. The strength of this tie with her past reinforces the educational theme, as young Kei responds to his grandmother's reminiscences and relates the past to his own sense of present-day values and understanding of past history.

The drama opens in 1983 in a small town on the Shima Peninsula. Oshin's second son is about to open the seventeenth store in a chain of supermarkets owned by the family. Yet suddenly, on the opening day, the eighty-three-year-old Oshin vanishes. Kei's search for her takes him to a hot spring in the Tohoku area, a place rich in associations with Oshin's childhood. The two of them visit various locales as Oshin relives her life for her grandson's benefit, revealing along the way much that is unknown to him.

In Part 1, "Servitude," Oshin, the third daughter of an impoverished tenant farmer, is sold at seven years of age to be maid-of-all-work for a merchant family. This means hard labor sixteen hours a day baby-sitting, cleaning, and doing laundry, all on a very poor-quality diet—rice mixed with chopped radish (one of the major metaphors in the drama)—and little enough of that. Wrongly accused of theft, she runs away and collapses in a snowstorm on a mountain. From this point on, her fate is changed by a series of father figures and mentors. The first is a pacifist-deserter from the Japanese army. Not only does he rescue her on the mountain path, but he also teaches her how to read and write and even introduces her to poetry. After he is hunted down and killed by soldiers, Oshin finds her way back to her family briefly; then, at eight years old, she enters service in the household of a rice dealer in the northern region. The business is run by a powerful grandmother-matriarch, Okuni, another father-mentor figure. This formidable woman educates Oshin over the next eight years. Oshin learns the skills expected of a Japanese merchant's wife of the time: the abacus, calligraphy, and tea ceremony, along with the female virtues of fortitude and loyalty.

Elements of melodrama are also at work in this section. One subplot concerns the increasingly desperate poverty of Oshin's family combined with her yearning for her mother, who is forced by hardship to seek work outside the home. Oshin is also subject to cruel persecution at the hands of Kayo, her employer's granddaughter. Crises on both fronts are resolved, however. Kayo experiences a change of heart, and she and Oshin become lifelong best friends. Oshin, now sixteen, is wooed by a wealthy merchant's son. Yet a spirit of independence prevents her from entering into a loveless marriage, even one that would bring security to herself and her family. To make matters worse, she is also pursued by Kōta, a student political activist from a wealthy family in Tokyo, the man Oshin's friend, Kayo, is determined to wed. A strange mixture of motifs—female independence and self-sacrifice—creeps in at the end of Part 1. Even though Kayo is sole heir to the family fortune, she risks losing all by leaving home to pursue the stubbornly indifferent Kōta. Avoiding yet another unwanted marriage and wanting to remove herself as an obstacle to Kayo's happiness, Oshin leaves for Tokyo to look for work.

Part 2, titled "Marriage," develops the melodramatic theme of character change brought about by response to experience. Here, this means trials of apprenticeship, jealousy of coworkers, reunion with a long-lost friend, marriage into a different social class, and persecution by a malicious mother-in-law. Yet Oshin's story is more than a tearful saga of personal hardship. Hashida enriches her script with much larger forces at work: economic depression, the great Kantō earthquake of 1923, and the social upheaval of the proletarian movement. Thus Oshin faces the double jeopardy of personal and collective tragedy.

Oshin is a heroine on a scale heroic enough to deal with a fate like hers. Each stage of personal suffering brings with it renewed moral strength, courage, and perseverance. Her apprenticeship as a hairdresser brings her another father figure and mentor, the strict mistress Taka. Her appreciation of Oshin's personal qualities and professional skill provokes the usual jealousy and ill treatment from fellow apprentices. Taka, however, encourages Oshin to go into business for herself, taking advantage of the vogue for Western coiffure. Then Oshin meets and marries Ryūzō Tanokura and encounters the obstacle of social prejudice; his family is landed gentry in Kyushu and sternly disapproving of this misalliance. Ultimately, however, Oshin's virtues win over even her husband's snobbish guardian. Another virtue Hashida is careful to develop in Oshin is woman's adaptive strength. Oshin has acquired from Taka an instinct for spotting new trends. When her husband's clothing business starts to fail, she saves the day by suggesting a new venture in ready-to-wear for children and working women.

Success is short-lived, however. The great earthquake in the Tokyo area destroys Ryūzō's new factory, forcing his wife and infant son to live like poor relations with his family in Kyushu. Oshin's mother-in-law, a Japanese archetype, bullies her, even stinting her food and demanding hard labor in the fields. Ryūzō becomes his mother's ally, and Oshin finds herself ostracized by the family. Like a typical melodrama, Part 2 is replete with misfortunes befalling the heroine one after another. Oshin tries to escape to Tokyo and fails. Her right hand is paralyzed. She gives birth to a stillborn child. Hashida makes Oshin a mouthpiece for a host of captive wives when she says to her husband: "Every single day I work until I become too exhausted to speak . . . I am poorly fed but endure in silence because I am told that every wife must endure her lot . . . yet when I think about the stillborn child. . . ."

Part 3, "Roaming," covers the years 1929–46, a traumatic period in Japanese history. Hashida concentrates less on Oshin's personal suffering and more on her decisive and courageous responses to the violent social and political changes under the clouds of war. Oshin is motivated to adapt and survive partly for the sake of her son, Yū, who accompanies her. Her struggle in trying to make a living takes her from one city to another until she settles in Ise, where she is later joined by her husband. They have another son and daughter and adopt two other children. The family is portrayed as building a bulwark against external forces victimizing individuals. After a number of false starts, Oshin establishes herself as a fishmonger, and the story moves gradually in the direction of prosperity and happiness as the family business guarantees livelihood and security.

Typical of the melodrama, however, misfortune reasserts its claims soon enough—this time on a much larger scale—as the world at large moves toward the catastrophe of World War II. Individual misery is seen against the background of economic depression, the rise and decline of socialism, and Japan's military expansion and ultimate defeat. Oshin's eldest son, Yū, is killed in action. Her dearest friend, Kayo, and her husband commit suicide when the family fortune is lost. Her own Ryūzō, a steadfast believer in Japanese militarism, also kills himself at the end of the war. Poverty, not patriotism, forces Oshin's brother to enlist in a defeated army.

Part 4, "Postwar Period," brings the story from 1946 to the drama's present 1983. Again, Oshin leads a family effort to establish a chain of supermarkets. Familiar trials and tribulations work out themes of family discord as new and old values conflict. Oshin stands for traditional values of the extended family supported by a small but honest business. Her surviving son, Hitoshi, prefers the nuclear, individualist family. He is an impersonal, calculating merchant, ambitious to propel himself and the family chain into territorial ventures backed up by a modern management system. Even his marriage is a shrewd investment, connecting him with a wealthy financier. Oshin's elder daughter, Tei, and her husband are equally determined and heartless materialists. In contrast to them, Oshin's adopted son Nozomi follows his heart in choice of profession and wife. He marries for love and lives in the country, content with the simple life and his sculptor's art.

By the middle of Part 4, Nozomi's son Kei has completed his "education." Thanks to his adoptive grandmother, he has gained some insight into the values of the past and discovered his own true identity as the grandson of her cherished friend, Kayo. Kei brings Oshin home to deal with the final crisis: imminent failure of the seventeenth store in the family chain—a loss that will lead to bankruptcy. Ironically, the family pulls apart, not together, in this crisis. Clearly, Hashida intends to teach a lesson learned the hard way as the younger generation of Oshin's family learn about life. The threat comes from a rival company's planning to buy land from Kōta, Oshin's first sweetheart of so many years before. Kōta's decision will make or break the Tanokura family. Hitoshi and the other materialistic members of her family expect Oshin to put pressure on Kōta. She, however, tends to think it might be better to start all over again from scratch.

Of course, Hashida cannot break with melodramatic convention by providing a tragic ending. The audience for this saga of unending struggle cannot be expected to relish seeing the heroine preside over a business and family failure that will compromise mother-child relationships as well. Clearly, by this time Oshin deserves to experience the peace and tranquility of old age on behalf of so many faithful viewers. At long last, Hashida's heroine is given a hero she deserves. Kōta understands Oshin's feelings about the family business. He not only refuses to sell his land to their competitor but finds a buyer for their troubled store as well, thereby saving Oshin's family. Toward the end of this saga, the narrator's voice underlines the importance of restored family solidarity and other traditional values as accepted by the younger generation. For the first time, the sons, Hitoshi especially, express respect for Oshin's perseverance and wisdom in old age.

The final scene of this drama of 250 installments aired over fifty weeks shows the old sweethearts reunited: Oshin, now eighty-three, and Kōta, eighty-eight, walk side by side on a hilltop overlooking the sea. This is Hashida's idyllic celebration of the friendship of a man and a woman who have lived through so much of Japanese history in such a troubled century. It also expresses the author's dedicated admiration for many a Japanese woman who, like Oshin, "has lived every moment of her life to the fullest" and now has no regrets.

BIBLIOGRAPHY

Critical Works

"Japan's O' Syndrome," *Time,* February 13, 1984.
Mulhern, Chieko. *Japanese TV Drama for, by, and About Women.* Women-in-Development Forum, Michigan State University, 85-III (February 1985).
————."Semblance of Reality," *Japan Update* (February 1992), 12–13.

Keiko McDONALD

HAYASHI Fumiko (1903–51), novelist, poet, children's story writer, reporter; (Mrs. Hayashi Rokutoshi).

Life: Hayashi Fumiko was born in Shimonoseki, Yamaguchi prefecture, daughter of Hayashi Kiku, a medicine maker's daughter from Kagoshima, and Miyata Assatarō, a peddler of sundry goods and lacquer ware. After her parents' common-law marriage ended with her natural father's infidelity, Fumiko traveled around the coast towns of Kyushu between the ages of seven and thirteen with her mother and her new peddler husband, Sawai Kisaburo. Fumiko's formal education started in 1910 in Nagasaki, but her schooling was often interrupted by her parents' transcient life-style, causing her to change elementary school as many as a dozen times. In 1916, the family settled in Onomichi, Hiroshima prefecture. This maritime city provided Hayashi Fumiko with what she needed to grow into a prolific writer: her elementary school teacher Kobayashi Masao became her literary mentor and encouraged her to go on to Onomichi Girls High School. She passed the entrance examination and worked her way through the four-year curriculum as a night laborer at a canvas-sail factory. An avid reader and a quick study, she was soon contributing her poems to the local newspapers.

Upon graduation in 1922, Fumiko went to Tokyo to live with her fiancé, a college senior, and took on whatever odd jobs were available to women. But a year later, when he found a good job, he proved not committed enough to marry her in the face of his family's objection. This betrayal was such a blow to the young Fumiko that she lost confidence in man's nature, as her friend and novelist-to-be Hirabayashi Taiko (1905–72) observed later. Nevertheless, it marked the beginning of Fumiko's odyssey. She spent unsettling years between 1923 and 1926, hopping jobs from housemaid to factory worker, waitress, cashier at a public bathhouse, saleswoman, office clerk, and barmaid. Such work experience nonetheless provided great creative stimuli and valuable subject matter for Fumiko, who found solace in keeping copious diaries that were to become the principal source for her acclaimed book, *Vagabond's Song* (*Hōrōki*, 1928, 30, trans. 1951 and 1987).

Between 1924 and 1925, she had a traumatic, though brief, marriage to an actor and then lived with a proclaimed anarchist poet, both of whom seemed, according to the descriptions in her work, to know nothing but how to abuse the goodness and naïveté in women. Fumiko was finally able to settle down in 1926 with her new mate, Tezuka Rokutoshi, an art student who would give her spiritual happiness for life, if not material luxury. Their blissful union amid dire poverty inspired a successful short story, "Seihin no sho" (Records of Honest Poverty, 1931). When they finally legalized their marriage in 1944, Tezuka consented to take on Fumiko's surname by giving up his own. They had one adopted boy child.

Vagabond's Song, which established her as a full-fledged writer, also made it possible for her to satisfy her wanderlust. Her overseas travels extended to China, England, France, and Southeast Asia; but domestic trips were suspended until the end of World War II in 1945. The postwar period saw Hayashi Fumiko emerge as a popular writer churning out a great number of stories. Responding good-naturedly to the flood of requests from editors, she overworked herself to the point of damaging her health. Two months after finishing her longest novel, *The Drifting Clouds* (Ukigumo, 1949–51), she died of a heart attack. Her funeral service was held with novelist Kawabata Yasunari (a friend and a future Nobel Prize winner) presiding.

Career: Of the many factors formative to Fumiko's growth as a writer, the most significant are the events of 1923 following the great Kanto earthquake, which devastated the city of Tokyo and forced her to return to Onomichi, the town where she had spent her adolescence. There she sought counsel once again from her high school teacher of Japanese literature, who had been a source of continuous moral support for her literary ambitions. When she returned to Tokyo in 1924, her sole purpose in life was to write. Most women writers of the day started their careers as writers of juvenile literature. Even as her own children's stories were rejected one after another, Fumiko managed to get her poems published in *Bungei Sensen* (Literary Front, a proletarian journal, 1923–32). This helped Fumiko keep in contact with a group of ideological poets, such as Hagiwara Kyōjirō (1899–1938), Tsuboi Shigeji (1897–1975), and Takahashi Shinkichi (1901–), who styled themselves as anarchists at the time. Through her association with these poets, Fumiko became acquainted with such novelists as Uno Kōji (1891–1961), Tokuda Shūsei (1871–1943), and Hirabayashi Taiko (1905–72). When Hirabayashi and her associates formed the Women Writers' Group in 1926, Fumiko joined them and published her poem "Kibibatake"

(Cornfield, 1928) in their new magazine, *Nyonin Geijutsu* (Women's Arts, 1928–32), the first noncommercial journal providing public forum for women artists, edited and published by Hasegawa Shigure (1879–1941), herself a dramatist and novelist. The subsequent serialization in the same journal of Fumiko's lyrical diary, "Aki ga kitanda" (Autumn Has Come, 1928), proved a stepping-stone to success. It drew the attention of a commercial publisher and of a benefactor who went on to subsidize the publication of her first private collection of poetry, *Aouma o mitari* (or, Ao o mitari: I Saw a Blue Horse, 1929). When her diary was published in book form with the comprehensive title *Vagabond's Song,* in 1930, it became a best-seller, though critical reaction was mixed.

With her autobiographical short stories, "Fūkin to uo no machi" (The Town with the Hand Organ and the Fish, 1931) and "Seihin no sho" (Records of Honest Poverty, 1931), Hayashi Fumiko established herself as an accomplished prose writer. Royalties from a collection of her short autobiographical pieces, *Kanojo no Rireki* (Her Vita, 1931), enabled her to fulfill her dream of going to Paris. Returning home in 1932, she found herself besieged with invitations to give speeches and write essays on her travel experiences. At this juncture Fumiko turned to nonautobiographical fiction, producing such works as *Nakimushi Kozō* (Crybaby, 1934) and *Kaki* (Oyster, 1935).

The outbreak of the Sino-Japanese incident in July 1937 affected Fumiko's life directly, for her husband was drafted into the army and sent to China. When the press asked her to go to the continent as a special correspondent, she accepted the offer and became one of the first reporters to witness the fall of Nanking in December 1937. From then on, Fumiko's activities fell in with Japan's war effort. Assigned to give speeches to the soldiers at the front and to file reports from such areas as Hankow, northern Manchuria, and French Indochina, Fumiko found the experience, especially in Indochina, to be a major inspiration for her last and longest novel, *Ukigumo* (Drifting Clouds, 1949–51, trans. 1965). The postwar period marked the peak of her literary career, during which she wrote numerous short stories, essays, and novels. Counted among the best are "Fubuki" (Blizzard, 1946), *Bangiku* (Late Chrysanthemum, 1948), "Hone" (Bones, 1949), and "Shitamachi" (Downtown, 1949, trans. 1961). A prolific writer with superb skill to convey human emotions, Hayashi Fumiko encompasses in her works the lives of ordinary people who try to live with remarkable tenacity under adverse conditions without losing their sense of humor or, most important, their moral integrity.

Major Works: "Seihin no sho" (Records of Honest Poverty, 1931), short story. This work, which earned the warmest praises from Uno Kōji, who was Fumiko's early mentor, depicts the spiritual happiness experienced by a wife of a newly wed couple. The husband, Komatsu Yoichi, has yet to establish his name as a painter and makes a living by doing odd jobs. The narrator, who has been twice divorced, feels secure in this marriage for the first time. A poem by her second husband that the narrator introduces summarizes her unhappiness and apprehension about the state of that past marriage. But in her life with a new husband, who is full of youthful goodness, hope, and genuine kindness, the narrator finally sheds her memories of the unhappy past. Focusing on the process of woman's awakening to the goodness in man, "Seihin no sho" is a hymn to people who live in material privation but do not lose pride and integrity, always retaining the capacity to endure hardship in good humor.

"Kaki" (Oyster, 1935), short story. Fumiko's trip to Europe in 1931–32 provided an opportunity to enlarge her perspective in seeing the world from the observer's vantage point. Until this time, her works had been largely autobiographical, but now she began to write about the lives of others, not entirely without empathy with the subject, but with studied detachment. The highly acclaimed "Kaki" earned Fumiko a reputation as a realist. Here she delineates the life of a quiet, honest, but somewhat monophobic craftsman whose skills are becoming obsolete in a rapidly changing society. Using a contemporary craze for raising goldfish as a device to develop the plot, the author lets the protagonist, Morita Shukichi, marry a country girl, Tama, whose sole goal in life is to improve her financial status in order to help her family. By presenting unreconcilable conflicts of values and personalities between the two, the author creates a convincing atmosphere in a tragic marriage at the end of which the man goes insane. Shukichi's single-minded devotion to his wife and his insanity after her desertion strike a sympathetic chord, much as does Prince Myshkin's state of mind after Natasha's death in Dostoevsky's *The Idiot,* a masterpiece that Fumiko admired. Fumiko's own work can also be read as a study of what loneliness does to man.

Translated Works: Hōrōki (Vagabond's Song, 1928–30), autobiographical fiction. Hayashi Fumiko's name is inseparable from this narrative, which is a lyrical rendition of her early life. It earned immediate recognition from general readers before literary critics reacted. Timing of the publication in book form in 1930 could not have been better, for it was in the middle of the worldwide depression, which did not spare the working class of Japan. The first-person narrator leads a hand-to-mouth existence, spending nights in cheap lodging houses. Her dream of becoming a writer, however, is always intact, though it drives her to occasional despair. Seeking jobs at one place after another, the narrator complains and mildly criticizes a social system that exploits the poor, yet she never loses her basic optimism and good humor. The narrative is interwoven with a rich vein of poetry, which was later published separately in an anthology, *Aouma o mitari.* The subject matter and the theme are realistic, but the style is highly impressionistic. This clinical study of men's behavior toward women is accepted by many as a faithful depiction of Fumiko's life before her success as a writer. Discernible, nonetheless, are influences from Northern European literature, especially from Knut Hansen's *The Hunger,* as Fumiko herself acknowledged.

Some elements of this work were to be further developed and elaborated in *Ukigumo* decades later. But in the meantime, in response to popular demand for her to write more about the lives of underprivileged women, Fumiko published

Zoku Hōrōki (Vagabond's Song, Part 2) in the same year, 1930. It shows the nature of a supplement to the first part, for example, in offering an episode involving the narrator's visits to her former lover and fiancé. Influenced by proletarian literature, prevalent at the time, the sequel contains more radical statements on social inequity than the first volume.

Vagabond's Song was made into a stage play and a film. After World War II, Fumiko responded again to ever-increasing demand by coming out with Part 3 in 1947. It is more or less a repeat of the earlier parts. Most notable here are the narrator's recollections of her life with her second husband, anarchist-poet Nomura Yoshiya, and the domestic problems between a friend, novelist Hirabayashi Taiko, and anarchist-artist Iida Tokutarō. Recalled a score of years after the actual events, the narrative of Part 3 shows mellowness and restraint in expression, demonstrating Fumiko's maturity as a writer.

"Bangiku" (Late Chrysanthemum, 1948), short story. A winner of the third Women Writers Award in 1949, Bangiku deals with the psychology of a man and woman who were once passionately in love with each other. Aizawa Kin, fifty-six years old, is a retired geisha whose beauty is now legendary. Still enjoying occasional visits from her admirers, she leads a comfortable life with her needs satisfied, both sexually and materially. When the man from a wartime affair, Tabe, telephones to announce his intention to pay her a visit, ripples stir on the quiet surface of her heart. Kin's fantasy, however, is abruptly checked when she meets him and learns of the real motive for his visit. He has come to ask for money. Involved in questionable business deals, Tabe has no other means to raise funds to extricate himself from legal trouble. He tries seduction, but Kin is adamant in her refusal. Outraged, Tabe shows signs of violent behavior, but is calmed by Kin's conciliatory words. The words, however, are only to avert violence. Later, she burns his photograph, which she has cherished over the years, signifying the death of the man in her mind—erasure of a fond memory. In a strictly nonemotive, detached, and concise style, Hayashi Fumiko weaves a tapestry of intense human drama, the struggle between man and woman. The actual setting is deceptively calm. The only action that suggests violence is Tabe's grabbing the charcoal tongs in the brazier. It is a far cry from the violence of the second husband described by the narrator in *Vagabond's Song*. Often compared with realist Tokuda Shūsei's masterful stories, "Bangiku" stands as one of the best among Hayashi Fumiko's short stories.

Ukigumo (Drifting Clouds, 1949–51), novel. Set a few years after World War II, this tale analyzes the behavior patterns and social attitudes of men and women in an unprecedented period of Japanese history. As in many others of Fumiko's works, the theme of *Ukigumo* is nonideological. Tinged with a strong conviction that man's fate is as fragile as floating clouds, the author's view of the world is decidedly dark and chaotic, yet strangely buoyant, perhaps reflecting an inherent optimism of the Japanese of the day. Two distinct and conflicting motifs—man's instinct for survival and man's despair under adverse conditions—are personified by two principal characters, one female and the other male.

A moderately educated woman, Kōda Yukiko typifies ordinary Japanese with a strong instinct to survive. Abused by her relatives while young, she has come to reject the conventional code of conduct as unworkable. She knows that men of higher station hide their egotism behind the facade of acceptable social behavior. She does not hesitate to utilize men's hidden motives to her advantage. A better-educated man, Tomioka, is a womanizer to whom Yukiko is, not uncritically but fatally, attached. They had once been lovers in an unreal world at an unreal time, the forest land of French Indochina between 1943 and 1945, while the region was controlled by the Japanese under an agreement with the French colonial government. In Dalat in southern Vietnam, Tomioka was a forestry engineer, and Yukiko a typist in a research institute named after Louis Pasteur. Utilizing her travel impressions of the area over 1943 and 1944, Hayashi Fumiko attained a narrative style at her best in describing the beautiful, heavily wooded landscape of southern Vietnam.

The story begins when Yukiko is released from the refugee camp in Tsuruga, one of the port towns on the Japan Sea coast at which Japanese returnees from overseas were processed. Yukiko delays taking a homebound train and rests at a small inn near the station. As she relaxes in a bath, her eye focuses on a large scar on her forearm. It is a flashback device to conjure up her triangular affair with Tomioka and his colleague, Kano. Younger than Tomioka and still single, Kano believed that he had the right to love Yukiko. What he did not know then was that Yukiko had already been deeply involved with Tomioka, a married man. When the truth came to light, Kano rushed to kill Tomioka but accidentally injured Yukiko instead. The scar that remains on her forearm serves in the novel as an effective sign to trigger her memories of the short-lived happiness that lasted till their repatriation to the war-torn homeland.

At their reunion in Tokyo, Yukiko finds Tomioka a broken man. He confesses that he has not the courage to tell his wife about what happened in Indochina. Filled with remorse and a deep sense of guilt, he cannot make up his mind whether to leave his wife or to terminate his relationship with Yukiko. The author pictures him as a lost soul, a real-life equivalents of which abounded in postwar Japan. Time and again, Yukiko plans to leave him, yet her decision is deterred by either her own desire to see him or his need for her. The unsavory relationship continues until Yukiko dies of an illness in Yakushima, an island at the southern border of Japan. By tenaciously delving into the complex psychology and behaviors of her protagonists, Hayashi Fumiko successfully delineates an unsettling panorama of the times, including men's deep sense of failure upon being confined in the small island chain that is Japan.

Of many minor characters, particularly notable are Kano, who represents the archetype of Japanese male candor and recklessness, and Mukai Seikichi, a middle-aged man who kills his young wife, Osei, who shows no regard for social protocol in pursuing her love affair with Tomioka. Tomioka can be viewed as a modern stereotype of indecisive males, as typified by the superfluous hero, Utsumi Bunzo, created by Futabatei Shimei (1864–1909) in his novel

Ukigumo (Drifting Clouds, 1887–91; trans. 1965). The supporting figures in Hayashi Fumiko's own *Ukigumo* may well be comparable to some of Ihara Saikaku's (1642–93) characters "who loved love" and died without much meaning. The creation of Yukiko's relative, Iba Sugio, is highly effective in developing the otherwise tedious chronicle of a love-hate relationship between Yukiko and Tomioka. The black market dealers, followers of newly risen religious organizations, and the women who cater to men's licentious needs all participate in conveying a sense of chaos. In all, minor characters who represent the values and life-styles of ordinary people make this saga of the times more convincing for their single-minded desire to survive.

BIBLIOGRAPHY

Translations

"Bones." Trans. Ted Takaya. In *The Shadow of Sunrise,* ed. Shoichi Saeki. Tokyo: Kodansha International, 1966.
The Floating Clouds. Trans. Yoshiyuki Koitabashi and Martin C. Collcott. Tokyo: Hara Shobo, 1965.
"Homecoming." Trans. Hisakazu Kaneko. *Orient West* 8.1 (May–June 1963).
"Late Chrysanthemum." Trans. John Bester. *Japan Quarterly* 3.4 (October–December. 1956).
"The Lord Buddha." Trans. Kenneth Rextroth and Ikuko Atsumi. In *The Burning Heart,* ed. Kenneth Rextroth and Ikuko Atsumi. New York: Seabury Press, 1977.
"Narcissus." Trans. Kyoko Selden. In *Stories by Contemporary Japanese Women Writers,* ed. Noriko Lippit and Kyoko Selden. New York: M. E. Sharpe, 1982.
"Song in Despair." Trans. Ichiro Kono and Rikutaro Fukuda. In *An Anthology of Modern Japanese Poetry.* Tokyo: Kenkyusha, 1957.
"Splendid Carrion." Trans. Shioya Saeki. *Eigo Seinen* 99.9, 12 (1953).
"Tokyo." Trans. Ivan Morris. In *Modern Japanese Literature,* ed. Donald Keene. New York: Grove Press, 1956.
"Vagabond's Song." Trans. Elizabeth Hanson. In *To Live and to Write: Selections by Japanese Women Writers 1913–1938,* ed. Yukiko Tanaka. Seattle: Seal Press, 1987.

Critical Works

Tanaka, Yukiko. "Hayashi Fumiko." In *To Live and To Write: Selections by Japanese Women Writers 1913–1938,* ed. Yukiko Tanaka. Seattle: Seal Press, 1987, 97–104.

Michiko AOKI

HAYASHI Kyōko(1930–), novelist, essayist. Real name: Hayashi Kyōko (formerly, Mrs. Hayashi Toshio); née Miyazaki Kyōko.

Life: Hayashi Kyōko was born in Nagasaki. Before her first birthday, her father, a Mitsui Trading Company employee, was assigned to a post in Shanghai, and there the family stayed until the spring of 1945, with occasional short visits to Japan. Her experiences in the first fourteen years of her life in Shanghai were to form a crucial foundation for her future and to provide rich materials for her writing career. In these years, Japanese living in China enjoyed the privileges denied to most Chinese citizens. When a military clash was imminent, such as the Shanghai incidents (the first in January 1932 and the second in August 1937), Chinese people had to flee the city as refugees within their own country, carrying their household goods with them. The Japanese, on the other hand, could go back to Japan to avoid danger and return to Shanghai when it was safe to do so, as Hayashi's family did. By the time Hayashi entered Japanese Girls High School in Shanghai in 1943, anti-Japanese movements were gathering momentum. Numerous incidents against Japanese people and establishments took place, some of which are covered in Hayashi's stories in *Missheru no Kuchibeni* (Michelle Lipstick, 1980). As World War II grew in intensity, Japanese forces suffered many losses in the Pacific, especially after the surrender of Italy in 1943. By early 1945, Shanghai became too dangerous for Japanese, and, in private, some business executives predicted Japan's defeat. In February 1945, Hayashi's father was ordered by his employer to send his family back to Japan. Late in that month, Hayashi, in the company of her mother and three sisters, left Shanghai on a hazardous trip back to Japan, as described in "Tanima no Ie" (Home in the Valley, 1981), a story collected in *Sangai no Ie* (Home in Three Worlds, 1984). They made their way back to Nagasaki in March 1945. Her father remained in Shanghai until after the end of the war. Hayashi lived in a boardinghouse to attend Nagasaki Girls High School, while her mother and three sisters evacuated to Isahaya, some twenty-five kilometers east. As part of the wartime student mobilization program, she and her 323 classmates were assigned to work at Mitsubishi munitions factory. She was inside the factory when the atomic bomb exploded in Nagasaki on August 9, 1945. She escaped from the debris with no apparent external wounds but suffered from severe radiation sickness for two months. Nursed by her mother, she recovered enough to return to the school when it reopened in October 1945 and graduated two years later. After a brief enrollment in a school of nursing, Hayashi went to Tokyo and in 1951 married a newspaper reporter twenty years her senior. They were divorced twenty years later.

As revealed in her writing, the experience of August 9 changed her life completely. Like most *hibakusha* (surviving victims of the atomic bombing), she began to live with the dread of radiation sickness, which was taking the lives of many of her friends. When she became pregnant, she was concerned about possible birth defects of her unborn child. After the son was born in apparent good health, she was obsessed with the fear of his early death. She and other *hibakusha* mothers shared a sense of responsibility in bringing their children to life but were concerned about their health and future. The realization that August 6 and 9 have created profound problems for the human race prompted Hayashi to write about the subject.

Career: In 1962 she joined a coterie magazine, *Bungei Shuto* (Literary Capital) and began writing. Her story based on her experience of August 9, entitled

"Matsuri no Ba" (Ritual of Death, 1975), won the *Gunzō* New Writer's Prize as well as the prestigious Akutagawa Award. Since then she has continued to write primarily on the subject of the bombing, deliberately choosing to be the reciter of the Nagasaki experience. In her works, the atomic bombing of Nagasaki with all its implications is often referred to as the "August 9th."

Her Shanghai years also play an important part in Hayashi's writing. Although many of her works may be divided into two categories—one dealing with Nagasaki and the other with Shanghai—a number of her stories intimate that the two subjects are ultimately interconnected through a fundamental concern for individual human beings. Further, these two subjects, forming undercurrents for most of Hayashi's works, provide the essential feature of her writing—a strong sense of continuity. With an awareness that the past continues to live in the present, Hayashi assumes her role as the uniter of the past and the present. Hayashi received the Woman Writer's Award for *Shanghai* (1983) and the Kawabata Yasunari Literary Award for "Home in Three Worlds."

All of her published works first appeared in leading literary journals, and many were later collected in separate single volumes.

Major Works: *Giyaman Biidoro* (Cut Glass and Blown Glass, 1978), collection. Two of the twelve stories in this volume have been translated into English and are discussed under "Translated Works." All the stories use a first-person narrator who is a *hibakusha* and mother of a son and relate the personal experiences of the narrator, her friends, and close associates. The subject is the impact of the atomic bombing on the lives of people (*hibakusha,* their children, and non-*hibakusha*) ten, twenty, and thirty years later. The past is closely connected to the present; in fact, the past is very much part of the present lives of the characters. "August 9 is linked to our children through our bodies," says the narrator in "Kage" (The Shadow). A strong sense of continuity is pervasive throughout the collection. In the title story, "Cut Glass and Blown Glass," the narrator visits antique shops in Nagasaki to look at glass artifacts. Later, she goes to the atomic bomb exhibit, where she finds a melted glass piece in which grains of lime, probably the remains of some dead creature, are "frozen" forever, symbolic of the indelible memories of the devastation of August 9 with which the Nagasaki *hibakusha* must live.

In "Hibiki" (Reverberations), the narrator's experiences in Shanghai on December 8, 1941 (Pearl Harbor day), and in Nagasaki on August 13, 1945 (two days before Japan's surrender), are presented as a reversed parallel. In Shanghai, the narrator and other Japanese were victors in war, watching the Chinese people fleeing the city for their lives. In Nagasaki, the narrator was among the refugees, the victims of the atomic bombing. Both events are associated in the narrator's consciousness through the reverberations from the past, which "stick to the soft membrane of her internal organs." The last story, "No ni" (In the Field), presents Hayashi's basic belief that the problems of the nuclear age are man-made and that any solution must be sought in human efforts.

Missheru no Kuchibeni (Michelle Lipstick, 1980), collection. All seven stories in this book deal with the subject and events of the Shanghai years, except for the last one. Told from a young girl's point of view, these stories present various aspects of life in Shanghai as experienced by the narrator and her family from the late 1930s till a few months before the defeat of Japan in 1945. "Rotabo no Roji" (The Rotabo's Alley) and "Muragaru Machi" (The Swarming Town) depict a tension mounting among the residents caused by the intensifying anti-Japanese movements and the repressive measures taken by the Japanese authorities to counter them. In "Hana no naka no Michi" (The Path Among the Flowers), frictions within the Japanese community are shown in the rumors of infighting between the Japanese army and navy. In "Kohoko" (The Huangpu River), the Japanese firm for which the narrator's sister works is searched, and four of its employees are arrested for alleged subversive activities. The title story is discussed in "Translated Works."

Translated Works: The last story, "Eishamaku" (The Screen), is set in a movie theater in Isahaya near Nagasaki in October 1945. The narrator, who survived the atomic blast, is now afraid to attend the school where many of her classmates are absent, suffering from radiation sickness. Her mother takes the narrator to a show to cheer her up. In the theater they recognize Mrs. Tsuda and her son, who were their neighbors in Shanghai. His appearance suggests that the young man, who joined the Japanese air force as a high school student in Shanghai, has just been released from prison. Although the four leave the theater together, no probing questions are asked, no explanations offered. Clearly the war transformed the lives of many: the young man now seems indifferent to everything around him, while the narrator lives with constant fear of death.

Naki ga Gotoki (As If Nonexistent, 1981), novel. Based on the direct, personal experience of atomic bomb victims, this work expresses greater concerns for the present condition and for the future, if any, of humankind in the nuclear age. This novel reveals very clearly the author's sense of mission. "As the days go by, August 9 goes deeper and deeper into my consciousness," says Hayashi. "The flash of August 9 is rekindled in my brain at every opportunity. It momentarily burns out my thought and senses and scalds my brain blank." The main action is set on the eve of another anniversary of August 9, some thirty years after the blast. At the home of Haruko and her American husband, visitors engage in conversation on the current social and political conditions, war and the threat of nuclear annihilation, and the lasting effects of the atomic bombing. The presence of both *hibakusha* and non-*hibakusha* as well as an American accords this work wider perspectives. The essential message is clear: the devastation of Nagasaki should be understood in relation to the present time and, more important, as the experience of individual human beings. After all, the death and destruction of August 6 and 9 in Hiroshima and Nagasaki are human acts; the suffering and pain are human experiences; and, ultimately, individual human beings must stand up for the survival of the human race and peace on earth. One must not act "as if nonexistent."

Shanghai (1983), nonfiction. Here Hayashi combines the memories of her

Shanghai years with the descriptions and observations of the city that she re-visited after thirty-six years' absence. Hayashi took the tour ''to reaffirm the place of the past where I spend my girlhood'' but realized in the end that the past was no longer as it had been. What stands between the past and the present is the experience of World War II: the atomic bombing changed her life forever, and her father died a broken man because of the war. This journey evokes two images of the city: the old Shanghai, which she calls her girlhood home, and the new Shanghai, which she is now visiting. Throughout this book, Hayashi approaches the people of the new China basically with affection, understanding, and appreciation.

Sangai no Ie (Home in Three Worlds, 1984), collection. Three of the eight stories contained in this volume, ''Chichi no Iru Tani'' (My Father's Valley), ''Ie'' (The Home), and ''Kemuri'' (The Smoke), focus on the narrator's father, revealing her affection and sympathetic understanding for him. She sees him as a victim of war. On his return from Shanghai he nearly lost his life as his ship struck a mine and sank. He never really recovered from this traumatic experi-ence. ''He died an exhausted death, having spent all his energy in living,'' she says in ''The Home.'' Three stories deal with the recurring theme of the effect of August 9 on the *hibakusha*.

''Shakumei'' (Apology) presents a moving episode of a *hibakusha* woman, Hata. Seriously wounded by the blast, Hata nevertheless is able to walk, seeking a refuge. Soon she comes upon her classmate Hirano, who is critically injured, too weak to walk. Hata gives her handkerchief and scarf to cover Hirano's wounds and moves on. For the next three decades Hata lives with a sense of remorse for not staying with her dying friend. At the class reunion thirty-two years later, Hata makes her apology to Hirano's twin sister, who in turn reveals that she and her family have been searching for the kind soul who looked after her twin before her death. In ''Buji'' (Alive and Well), a Nagasaki *hibakusha* narrator visits Hiroshima, where she reflects on the subject of the bombing and the problem of the nuclear age as the concern for all humanity on earth. She asks what is the meaning of ''being alive and well'' in the face of possible nuclear annihilation.

The award-winning title story, ''Home in Three Worlds,'' is a reflective piece with a Buddhist undertone, dwelling ultimately on the questions of how to live and how to die. The title may be derived from the proverb ''Women have no home in all three worlds.'' The three worlds may refer to the past, present, and future but may also be a Buddhist allusion to the world of sensuous desires, the world of matter free of desires, and the world of pure spirit. A visit to the ''locker-style vault'' in the Buddhist temple ossuary purchased by her mother for the family prompts the narrator to reexamine her own life. She is a woman in her early fifties who longs to be rid of all desires and attachments of flesh. She pictures her father now resting in the vault as a sexless being in death's timeless and sleepless world. If her body has no home in the past, present, or future as implied in the title, then the locker-style vault with its triple-tiered interior may be the only home for her when she attains her desired state of sexlessness at the end of her life.

Michi (The Road, 1985), seven stories and a play. This collection deals with the subject of the atomic bombing and its lasting effects on *hibakusha.* "Do-kikai" (Class Reunion), "Omowaku" (Speculation), and "Zansho" (Afterglow) show how the *hibakusha* must live not only with the memory of August 9 but with the deep-rooted concern for their own health and for the health and future of their children, the so-called second-generation *hibakusha.* "Afterglow" is about Hayashi's only son—his boyhood, his coming of age, his engagement and marriage, and his business assignment to the United States. In the title story, a female *hibakusha* narrator visits Nagasaki in December 1975 to ascertain the details of the deaths of her three teachers in a futile effort to "settle" the matter of August 9 in her mind and to be free of it. Clearly, the story reinforces the sense of continuity, a notable feature of Hayashi's writing. The memories of Nagasaki not only are kept alive in the minds of characters but continue to affect their lives even thirty years later. *Hareta Hi ni* (On a Sunny Day), the only play Hayashi has written, represents perhaps the most explicit pronouncement of the author's convictions on the subject of the bombing, its ultimate significance to the life and integrity of every human being on earth. The setting is a public health center, on the day of the semiannual medical examination for *hibakusha.* The principal character identified as The Woman asserts that she is a *hibakusha,* a victim but, more important, a human being who is living *now,* who desires to live. Her message is that August 6 and 9 have become the subject of concern for the entire human race for its continuing existence.

Translated Works: "Ritual of Death" (Matsuri no Ba, 1975), short story. This autobiographical work presents detailed accounts of August 9, 1945, and the subsequent two months by the first-person narrator who was working at a munitions factory, 1.4 kilometers from the hypocenter. Hayashi gives graphic descriptions of the devastation within the factory as a microcosm of the disaster unfolding in the entire city. The Japanese title, which literally means "the ritual ground," refers to the open ground in the factory site used for a daily ritual to send off the student-soldiers called to the front. At the moment of the blast, one was in progress. But at this last ritual, those going to the front and those staying behind were all killed. The pathos of the story is made explicit by the English title, "Ritual of Death." The narrative is marked by frequent shifts in time from August 1945 to later periods into which the characters survived, thus giving a strong sense of continuity. Hayashi maintains a remarkable degree of objectivity, even detachment, as well as a pervasive sense of irony, as evidenced by the ending: "At the conclusion of the atomic bomb documentary film edited in the U.S. appears a fine line—'Thus the destruction ended.' "

"Two Grave Markers" (Futari no bohyo, 1975), short story. Hours after the atomic bombing, a fourteen-year-old girl is forced to choose between friendship and survival. Two girls from the same village were in a factory when the bomb was dropped. Yoko is severely wounded while Wakako sustains no external injury. Both manage to flee to a mountain slope, but Yoko is too weak to move any farther. Wakako decides to leave, despite Yoko's plea to stay with her. Wakako eventually returns home and is questioned about Yoko, whose body is recovered later. Tormented by a gnawing sense of guilt, Wakako dies of radiation sickness the day after Yoko's forty-ninth-day memorial service. Two grave markers now stand side by side on the mountain slope. This is a poignant story of a young girl's psychological trauma in her efforts to justify her actions in the aftermath of the atomic bombing.

"The Empty Can" (Akikan), short story. Thirty years after the bombing, five women, four of them *hibakusha,* gather to reminisce about their past and to bid farewell to their old high school, soon to be closed. This is a moving piece, representing notable characteristics of Hayashi's work on the subject of bombing. Her role as the uniter of the past and the present is clearly marked. She presents the *hibakusha* who grow older, carrying intangible yet never-fading memories of the bombing in their minds as well as visible reminders on their bodies. Oki had a piece of glass removed from her back almost a quarter of a century after the blast and discovered that the glass had been wrapped in a silky, flosslike fat in the flesh as a pearl would be inside its shell. Another *hibakusha,* Kinuko, is scheduled to have a similar operation the next day. Though physically absent, she provides a poignant episode reinforcing a sense of continuity. She is remembered by the other women as the orphan who brought to school every day an empty, lidless can seared red by the flames, in which she kept the bones of her mother and father.

"Yellow Sand" (Kosa), short story. It is based on Hayashi's experience in Shanghai, where she spent most of the first fourteen years of her life. The yellow sand that causes a brown haze in the Japanese sky brings back the memory of Shanghai. The main focus is on an incident involving Okiyo, a Japanese prostitute living in Shanghai, seen through the eyes of a seven-year-old girl. This young narrator is friendly with Okiyo, who is ostracized from the Japanese community because she takes Chinese customers. The girl once witnesses a public "union of bodies" between Okiyo and a Chinese male in the open view of spectators. The girl's friendship continues until one afternoon Okiyo hangs herself. The story presents a sympathetic portrayal of a Japanese prostitute who has no hope of returning to Japan, condemned to remain in loneliness and isolation in China.

"Michelle Lipstick" (Missheru no kuchibeni, 1980), short story. Through a young Japanese girl narrator, this autobiographical story portrays the condition of the Japanese sector in Shanghai in the final years of World War II and gives an intimate look at the lives of her Chinese neighbors, such as the morning ritual of cleaning the *modon,* a portable wooden chamber pot, which is a fixture in every Chinese household. This seemingly peaceful activity signaling the beginning of the daily routine in the community is followed by an unsuccessful search by the Japanese police for Chinese youth suspected of anti-Japanese activities. In Japanese high schools in Shanghai, which the narrator and her sister attend, girls are encouraged to volunteer for nurses corps and boys for the armed forces, a reflection of intensifying war efforts by the Japanese military. Two days before Italy's surrender, despite the dangerous situation in and beyond Shanghai, the narrator's sister goes on a school excursion to Peking under heavy military guards. The sister brings home a French-made lipstick called "Michelle" as a souvenir from Peking. Historically, the sister's school excursion is probably the last such event undertaken by Japanese schools in Shanghai, hence signifying the end of an era, the end of Japan's supremacy in China. On a personal level, the trip may signify for the sister the end of innocence of childhood, and the French lipstick she brings home may be symbolic of her reaching adolescence.

BIBLIOGRAPHY

Translations

"The Empty Can." Trans. Margaret Mitsutani. In *Atomic Aftermath: Short Stories About Hiroshima and Nagasaki,* ed. Kenzaburo Oe. Tokyo: Shueisha, 1984, 135–51.
"Michelle Lipstick." Trans. Margaret Mitsutani. In preparation.
"Ritual of Death." Trans. Kyoko Selden. *The Japan Interpreter* 12.1 (1978): 54–93.
"Rotabo's Alley." Trans. Margaret Mitsutani. *Tokyo Kōgyō Daigaku Jinbun Ronsō,* no. 13 (1988) and no. 14 (1989): 131–50 and 83–90.
"Two Grave Markers." Trans. Kyoko Selden. *Bulletin of Concerned Asian Scholars* 1.1 (January–March 1986): 23–35.
"Yellow Sand." Trans. Kyoko Iriye Selden. In *Stories by Contemporary Japanese Women Writers,* ed. Noriko Mizuta Lippit and Kyoko Selden. New York: M. E. Sharpe, 1982, 197–207.

Critical Works

Tsukui, Nobuko. *The Atomic Bomb Literature of Japan: An Introduction.* In preparation.
                                                                                      Nobuko TSUKUI

HIGUCHI Ichiyō (1872–96), poet, novelist. Real name: Higuchi Natsu (commonly, Natsuko).

Life: Higuchi Ichiyō's life was short. She died at age twenty-four. Living during the formative years of modern Japan and its literature, Ichiyō may be said to have lived life to its fullest. Some literary historians mourn her too brief life and conjecture that she might have changed the literary map of 20th-century Japan, had she lived longer.

Born the second daughter of an ex-farmer turned samurai, then a minor official of the Tokyo city government, Ichiyō managed to finish an elementary education. Bright as she was, she wanted to continue her schooling, an idea her father supported. But her mother was of the opinion that women did not need higher education. Therefore, beginning in 1884, Ichiyō took sewing lessons—a skill that later helped her earn a meager living. At the sewing teacher's house she met Shibuya Saburō, a man with whom Ichiyō's parents apparently arranged for her to be married. Meanwhile, her father bought her some poetry books and introduced her to an acquaintance, Wada Shigeo, from whom Ichiyō learned *tanka,* short poems consisting of thirty-one Japanese syllables. In 1886, Ichiyō became a student of the Haginoya (lit., "house of bush clover"), a private school of poetry run by *tanka* poet Nakajima Utako (1844–1903). Her fellow students included the future novelist Miyake Kaho (Mrs. Miyake Setsurei, née Tanabe Tatsuko, 1868–1943), who proved to be Ichiyō's lifetime rival and inspirational friend. She would compete with Kaho and others at school poetry contests and excel.

But in 1887 her eldest brother died after expending much of the family's funds for medical treatment. Despite the fact that the Confucian order prevailed in society and she had another brother, Ichiyō was made heir apparent, because the surviving brother was at odds with her father and was not living with the family. In 1889, her father died. He had retired from his government job and had failed in a business venture. Ichiyō, her mother, and her younger sister had to move in with Ichiyō's brother. Life with the brother was everything but peaceful, so Ichiyō often chose to stay at the Haginoya. In September 1890, she moved to a small house in the Hongō district in Tokyo, and with her mother and sister, she made a meager living by sewing and doing laundry. To further depress the family and hurt Ichiyō's pride, Shibuya Saburō canceled their engagement.

In 1888, Miyake Kaho had successfully published her first novel, aided by the noted writer Tsubouchi Shōyō (1859–1935), and reportedly earned a considerable sum of money. Trying to emulate her friend, Ichiyō sought tutelage with Nakarai Tōsui (Nakarai Kiyoshi, 1860–1926), a writer of popular novels for the daily paper *Tokyo Asahi,* through the help of her sister's friend. She began visiting the Ueno Public Library frequently to study and write. Ichiyō was to produce some four thousand *tanka* poems and twenty-one stories in all. Overworked before long, she contracted tuberculosis. Mori Ōgai, a medical doctor as well as a writer, sent her a physician. But it was too late. Ichiyō died on November 23, 1896, in the presence of only her mother and sister. Mourners included a nearby pawnshop owner who said that he did not know Ichiyō was an accomplished writer. Ichiyō never married. Throughout most of her life, she had kept diaries, penetratingly detailed and as lyrical as her *tanka* and prose works.

Career: Her first short story, "Yamizakura" (Cherry Flowers in the Darkness), appeared in 1892 in the first issue of a literary magazine, *Musashino* (The Musashi Plain), which Nakarai Tōsui launched. Ichiyō used her pen name, Ichiyō, in this work for the first time. By "Ichiyō" she meant that she did not have *ashi* (feet), a pun for *ashi* (money), like Bodhidharma, who had lost his feet and traveled by *ichiyō* (a "leaf" boat). Ichiyō had more short stories published in the second and third numbers of Tōsui's magazine. Thus *Musashino* did launch Ichiyō as a writer, but, with limited circulation, it did not help her financially. She continued associating with the Haginoya *tanka* school, but rumors and slander spread among the students; her platonic relationship with Tōsui, then a widower, was scandalized. Ichiyō was admonished by Utako. Devastated, she decided to stop seeing Tōsui, only to internalize her feelings for him. By that time, Ichiyō had finished a draft of ''Umoregi'' (Buried Wood), and she was recognized by some of the established novelists and critics of the day, including Hoshino Tenchi (1862–1950), Hirata Tokuboku (1873–1943) and Baba Kochō (1869–1940).

Ichiyō wrote more short stories, some depicting her imaginary relationship with Tōsui, and wanted to sell them. Kaho introduced Ichiyō's ''Umoregi'' to a popular journal, *Miyako no hana* (Flowers of the Capital), and had it published. She also informed Ichiyō of a new magazine called *Bungakkai* (Literary World) being prepared for publication by Tenchi, Tokuboku, and others. Ichiyō and Tokuboku met, and her short stories appeared in *Bungakkai*. Ichiyō began to receive remuneration for her manuscripts, but that was not enough to support her family. In 1893, she moved to a small shop/house near the famous licensed pleasure quarters of Yoshiwara and decided to open a sundry and candy shop in hopes of supplementing her income. The shop was soon found to be unprofitable. Ichiyō could not even pay interest on the money borrowed to open the shop. Incognito, she visited twice a fortune-teller by the name of Kusaka Yoshitaka and tried to borrow money from him, only to be propositioned to become his mistress.

Inopportunely, she learned that Kaho, married to an influential man, paid a good sum of money to the Haginoya in order to be licensed as an independent *tanka* teacher. Roused by a spirit of competition, Ichiyō made up her mind to write enough novels to live on the manuscript fees. She wrote ''Yamiyo'' (Dark Night) and drafted ''Ōtsugomori'' (Last Day of the Year). She also made an arrangement with Utako to serve as her assistant at the Haginoya.

The Sino-Japanese War had started, and the economy of some sectors of the country was said to be very good. Ichiyō had to solicit old friends at the Haginoya and newly acquired writer friends alike for financial assistance. One day in May 1895, she recorded in her diary: ''We have not a grain of rice left after this supper today. Mother's lament is endless, and my sister's complaints are incessant.'' One of her *tanka* read:

My lodging is	Waga yado wa
without bush cover or pampus grass,	hagi mo susuki mo
yet autumn comes	aranakuni
clearly announced	aki kuto shiruki
by the sound of the wind.	kaze no oto kana

''Yamiyo'' was published in *Bungakkai* in July 1894. It dealt with the corruption of a merchant and a politician, as if to suggest that the author was critical of contemporary social systems and their conditions. ''Ōtsugomori,'' also appearing in *Bungakkai* that year, was a wry drama of a maid's money problems. The renowned novella, *Takekurabe* (lit. Comparison of Heights), was published only a few months later. A team of respected critics, including Mori Ōgai (1862–1922), Kōda Rohan (1867–1947), and Saito Ryokuu (1867–1904), praised it highly, when *Bungei Kurabu* (Literary Club) republished it in 1896.

Ichiyō's rise to being a recognized writer was quick. The editors of journals, such as *Kokumin no tomo* (Nation's Friends) and *Shinbundan* (New Literary Platform), sought her work. Young writers, mostly from the *Bungakkai* group, visited her. Tōsui also visited. Some showed Ichiyō affection as well as respect, while some criticized other authors in front of her. The Ichiyō house was like a literary salon.

Poetic Works: Ichiyō started her literary career with *tanka* and continued to write it throughout her career. The *tanka* school Haginoya did not allow students to venture into new styles or ideas. The subjects given to students were conventional, and the students were instructed to use old techniques, such as *makura kotoba,* or the ''pillow words,'' to open poetry and the classical, interjective particles to close it. When the teacher assigned a composition subject, the students would carefully observe and contemplate the given subject until they came up with ideas or statements on the subject, and then they would express them within prosodic rules and linguistic limitations. Artistic polish was achieved as the teacher and the students read their works, criticized them among themselves, and compared them with the numerous old and new works on the same subject. For them, a wide knowledge of classical and contemporary poetry was more necessary than originality. Through such training by Wada Yoshio and Nakajima Utako, Ichiyō nurtured her writing ability.

One of her earliest *tanka,* about *ume,* or ''plum,'' written when Ichiyō was twelve, read:

In a mountain hamlet,	Yamashizu no
rustic as the fence may be,	aware kakine mo
people stop in their tracks	hito tomaru
at the scent from the garden	niwa no ume ga ka
since the plum began to blossom.	sakisomeshi yori

The *tanka* for which the sixteen-year-old Ichiyō won the highest points at a competition was:

As I watch	Uchinabiku
the swaying willow,	yanagi o mireba
halcyon is the scene.	nodokanaru
even under a misty moon	oborozukiyo mo
there goes a breeze but softly.	kaze wa arikeri

The subject given at the contest was *Tsukimae no yanagi* (willow before the moon), an old, standard one. In handling this and other traditional subjects in these early poems, Ichiyō showed her precociousness as well as her mastery of *tanka* techniques. However, rooted in old practices in terms of both technique and diction, they showed little to suggest that they were products of the rapidly changing new age.

The Haginoya school, attended by daughters and wives of the aristocrats, the high-ranking government officials, and the rich, also functioned as a place of social gatherings. Both appropriate clothing and artistic skills were needed for *tanka*. Ichiyō would wear her mother's old kimono to school, and there were subtle discriminations that bothered her. Yet, the Haginoya was a gateway to literature for Ichiyō. There she learned classical poetry and gathered useful information on literary aspirants, writers and editors, such as Tōsui, and their connections. She also learned of Kaho's and other friends' marriages there, each time becoming a bit more depressed. The single Ichiyō continued to attend the Haginoya.

Ichiyō wrote that her early *tanka* were "merely arranged words" (*kotoba o tsuranetaru nomi*) or "imitations of hackneyed expressions" (*iifurushitaru kuchimane*) and that it was difficult for her to express true feelings in them. "As I came to know *mono no aware* [deep feelings for things] in the world," she continued to write, "my feelings towards such objects as the moon and flowers were deepened and various things that I could not contain within my heart began to overflow as poetry." Not surprisingly, this understanding of poetry was essentially the same as that of the ancient Japanese poets, whose works she studied at the Haginoya. At the same time, her view was not much different from that of the Japanese romantics, who, inspired by the romanticists in the West, were soon to exalt the freedom of their youthful spirits in the literary world.

Whether it can be called "merely arranged words" or "imitations of hackneyed expressions," the following *tanka* of 1890 is precise in form and technically flawless. The last "line" of the poem, with its appropriate interjective particle, is elegant while giving the poem a stabilizing force.

Loneliness was	Sabishiki wa
only for the twilight,	yūgure nomi to
I thought.	omoishini
But the morning breeze	asa fuku kaze mo
proves just as sad.	kanashikari kere

The emotions expressed, however, may be termed too ideological or intellectual. As Ichiyō learned more of *mono no aware,* that is, after she realized that she was in love with Tōsui, her *tanka* became more unabashed to express her feelings, but only occasionally. For example:

Exhausted from laments,	Nagekiwabi
unable to succumb	shinan kusuri mo
even to a death portion,	kainakuba

| I long to melt away | yuki no yama niya |
| in the snowy mountains. | ato toke namashi |

I am one	Ware wa sawa
so much in love,	koisuru mi nari
just as deeply	hitogoto ni
immersed in thoughts	kikeruga gotoki
as others I used to hear about.	mono-omoi sou

The first *tanka* was preceded by a pun-filled prefatory note that included Tōsui's name: Nakarai-sama, ushiya kuruma no hiki-meiritsutsu (As master Nakarai's ox and cart are pulling away, my mood sinks lower). The second one is the most expressive of love among all of Ichiyō's *tanka*. Except in these few *tanka*, Ichiyō never clearly expressed her love for Tōsui, even in her intimate diaries. However, these poems are rather poorly written, engrossed with ambiguous wordplay.

Ichiyō once admitted that the *tanka* was like a "slow ox cart," not in keeping with "the age of steam engines and ships." Her writing of December 1, 1893, contained a remark somewhat critical of *tanka*, saying that it was "easy to learn [how to write], but difficult to make it poetry." The fact remains that her *tanka* was mediocre at best. After she began associating with the members of the Bungakkai, she had opportunities to read some *shintaishi* (new-style poetry), but she did not write any new, long, freestyle poetry.

Her diary, titled *Mizu no e nikki* (Daily Records on Water), recorded in April 1895: "There are many people whom I think I like. Which one of them should I choose and love? But should I die for one particular person, I would be rumored that I was crazed in love. How would it be if I died for all of them? No one would know the truth, yet they would think I was queer. Will it not be all right?" The entry continued:

People of the world	Yo no hito wa
may never suspect	yo mo shirashi kasi
that I am following	yo no hito no
the path quite unknown	shiranu michi o mo
to the people of the world.	tadoru mi nare ba.

Putting aside the poem, which is full of double entendre built on a slim frame of weak logic, *Mizu no e nikki* revealed Ichiyō's naïveté or lack of experience in life. Longing for someone unattainable, she feared that she might be "buried," after having been abused and not understood by anyone, like some of the heroines of her stories.

Prose Works: Ichiyō's observations and contemplations upon given subjects soon moved into the world of imagination. That is, she added *kotobagaki*, or prefatory explanation, to her *tanka*—the same process by which the ancient *uta-*

monogatari (tales around poems) were produced. Also, her diaries contained many *tanka* interwoven with prose. Like some of the ancient poet-novelists, she incorporated her experiences into *tanka*esque expressions. She began writing prose fiction, reflecting events in her life. The events were many—her brother's death, her father's death, impoverishment, borrowing money, feeling jealousy, hurting from slander, losing love, and so on—and the outcome was prose fiction of lasting lament in elegant classical style. It was lyrical beauty, like *tanka,* usually devoid of a grandiose conflict or a stunning solution. Tōsui advised Ichiyō to try to appeal to the masses by emphasizing the plot—not entirely useless advice for Ichiyō. Ichiyō's intuition and training in classical literature told her that exciting plots alone would not make good stories, and she noted in her diary that she would not write the kind that would be thrown into the reader's wastebasket once it was read.

As much as she was aware of *tanka*'s limitations, Ichiyō knew Tōsui's lack of sufficient ability to guide her as a writer. But for Tōsui, there was her love. She suffered from love's anguish and fought it with a pen. Finding it both vindictive and satisfying, she published her first work in Tōsui's magazine and continued to do so until the magazine met its demise, while grabbing every possible chance to increase her personal and publishing connections. She took advantage of Kaho's influence and, through her, approached other authors and editors. She tried to sell her stories, while trying to borrow money even from people whom she had never met.

What she learned from Tōsui, from her parents, who had eloped from their native Yamanashi village, from her brother, who was disowned by the parents, from Shibuya Saburo, who unilaterally broke their marriage engagement, from Kaho's friendship and success, from the Haginoya school students, and from the moneylenders and others was a sort of fatalism, resembling resignation as in Buddhism. It was the realization of life's irrationality, so to speak, and her being awakened in it. She pondered life and her place in it, often fighting against her own envy, and wrote as a release. Her stories were revelatory of such things as family tradition and social convention, desire and love, rivalry and jealousy, betrayal and disappointment, failure and early death, and doubts about writing. Almost totally indifferent to politics and social thoughts and to religion, she did not seek solutions to the problems she depicted. Nor did she let anything or anybody supernatural play a compassionate role in her stories. In her stories, there is repression, a sorrow of someone—usually an unmarried female—drifting through the flow of time fraught with irrationality. Of her twenty-one stories, eighteen deal with unhappy heroines, committing suicide, becoming insane, becoming a concubine, being divorced, or just enduring.

Ichiyō was independent of the various movements and phenomena of Westernization. She acted ignorant not only of such things as short hair and Western clothes for women but also of the knowledge of Western thoughts being introduced by the members of the coterie *Bungakkai* (which was originally a branch of an early women's education/liberation magazine). One of the founding members of *Bungakkai* and its editor, Hirata Tokuboku, wrote that Ichiyō did not read European literature, having only indirectly heard of Western literary trends and activities. She was also indifferent to the movement of *gembun-itchi*, or the unification of the literary and colloquial styles. Having been interested in *tanka* and versed in Japanese classics, including *The Tale of Genji* and works of the 17th-century writer Ihara Saikaku (1642–93), she felt she had enough at hand upon which to base her work. Besides, she was constantly bogged down by poverty. Irrationality was plentiful around her. Even after her stories gained respect by contemporary men of letters and she began entertaining their visits, Ichiyō apparently kept her association with them mostly on a personal level. The stories she contributed to the magazine *Bunqakkai*, including "Takekurabe," were different from theirs in content and style, conception and execution. The temperament shown in her works was sorrowful, with a tint of cynicism or sometimes humor, and only latently critical of what caused the sorrow.

According to Ichiyō, contemporary novelists "looked all the same." She was apparently skeptical of writers who belonged to a literary clique and who insisted upon their own creedlike religion. Stating that she would favor "all different," rather than "all the same," she wrote, "It is all right . . . to reveal the hidden, to shed light on the buried, and like the sun and the moon in the sky, to wish to be fair to all, and to write as though there is intention when in fact there is none and as though there is no intention when in fact there is one." Ichiyō revealed "the buried," but she was perhaps too modest in showing her "intention." Her realism was based on her resigned view of life, like a Buddhist's. In essence, it was *tanka*esque. Ichiyō's preference for "all different" did not necessarily mean that she particularly supported individuality. Little was evidenced that she possessed a strong self.

Within about a month after Ichiyō was buried at a Buddhist temple in Tsukiji, her first *zenshū*, or complete works, was published, almost immediately followed by a revised version. In both, Saitō Ryokuu, one of the critics who earlier praised Ichiyō and who visited Ichiyō frequently in her final years, played a part in publishing them. Ichiyō was fortunate in this regard, for these two *zenshū* were followed by a great number of studies of Ichiyō. Many studies minutely detailed Ichiyō's daily life, and they induced more *zenshū*. Should Ichiyō have stayed healthy, she would have had to wait longer for her *zenshū*. Ichiyō then would have sought, probably with considerable difficulties, a new writing style, as classical language was soon proven to be decisively less appealing to the general readership. More fundamental, she would have had to face the problem of the self. She would have asked why it was that men were placed as they were and if there were ways to break the fatalism that appeared to her to control the world. Moreover, she would have had to question Confucian morality and reexamine her feelings for, and attitude toward, Tōsui. However, she would have continued to care for her mother as a faithful Confucian daughter should have.

The motif common in Ichiyō's stories was a sorrow of unfortunate women:

a young girl becoming a prostitute, a prostitute killed by her former customer, and the like. "Misfortune is caused by heaven," Ichiyō wrote in 1894 for the characters in "An' ya" (Murky Night); "Misfortune is not a punishment we caused to ourselves. Yet they despise us as orphans; do they have demons or serpents in their hearts?" Ichiyō leaked the voice of protest, but too often the protest was like a whine. Her characters merely endured adversity. In general, Ichiyō's stories did not point to a society that some contemporary writers considered the cause of personal misfortune. They are distinguishable from the genres known as "serious novels" (shinkoku shōsetsu) or "social novels" (shakai shōsetsu) that were being written by issue-conscious writers.

The language of the stories is luxuriant, almost a prose equivalent of classical love poems. It contains skillful wordplays, such as puns and allusions, and crisp, noun-ending phrases are connected together to form run-on sentences. There are rhythm and, as in some poems, a certain degree of vagueness. The dialogue is sometimes tinted with colloquialism, and it is blended in the narrative part in classical language. In fact, the dialogue occupies a large part of Ichiyō's stories and functions more to forward the plot or to explain the situation than to characterize the persona—the method that she maintained throughout her career. Her stories are characterized by relatively thin plots. Overall, her writing style is intricate, rich, and beautiful. It provides the stories with a lyrical mood.

Translated Works: "Yamizakura" (Flowers at Dusk) is a lyrical piece that hardly has a plot. There is vagueness that suggests that the heroine is in love. However, neither the heroine nor the boy next door, to whom she is apparently attracted, is well drawn. The story ends inconclusively.

"Wakarejimo" (Parting on Frost) has a more complex plot, probably Tōsui's influence. That plot, however, obscures other novelistic techniques in this work. The device that the heroine's father employs is unnatural, the subsequent meeting of the heroine with her former love is too coincidental, and the motivation for the lovers' double suicide is unconvincing.

"Kyō-zukue" (Sutra Table), published also under a different pen name, as was "Wakarejimo," again presents a woman who is slow to admit that she is in love; when she finally does, the man with whom she thinks she is in love moves away and dies. With a heroine in search of herself and her conviction, *Kyō-zukue* reflects the anguish of the author's own love.

"Umoregi" (Buried Wood) was said to have been inspired by Kōda Rohan's novel *Goju no to* (The Five-Storied Pagoda). Its main character, a potter, does try to uphold his ideals, as did the stern, artistic hero of Rohan's novel. The work was perhaps Ichiyō's attempt to break with Tōsui's guidance by instilling some ideals in her literature. However, "Umoregi's" potter character has a devoted sister, whose sole desire is to see her brother succeed. The author's real concern, a young, dedicated woman as a suppressed heroine, surfaces. Despite the obvious importance of the heroine's role in the story, her character is not developed. She commits suicide, when the deception of their old acquaintance-turned-professional benefactor of art is disclosed. The anger that the potter displays at the end does not have a specific aim, and what prevails in the story seems to be the fatalistic idea that man's lot cannot be changed after all.

"Ōtsugomori" (Last Day of the Year) shows the author's immaturity in creating a workable plot and cohesively developed characters, contrary to the praise it received from the *Bungakkai* members. An orphan becomes a maid and is driven to steal a small amount of money from a drawer—a situation perhaps resembling situations in the novels by Ihara Saikaku (1642–93). The maid's master is rich and a stereotype villain. The maid is good-natured, hardworking, but typically poor. The story twists so that a dissolute son of the same household takes the rest of the money from the drawer, and no one else knows the maid's theft. In this work, there seems to be something more than fate at work. With its suggestive, grim tone, *Ōtsugomori* advanced the author into a new kind of realism.

"Takekurabe" (Growing Up or Child's Play) is a mature work, realistically portraying characters, each with a different temperament and mood. The world in which the characters live is a small downtown section near Yoshiwara, the famous licensed pleasure quarters. That unique, shadowy world is also portrayed as well as the psychology of the lively characters. Time passes in the demimonde, and the characters—playful children—inevitably age, all coming to grips with their lot and adolescent pains. In the end, they part, one by one moving into only a slightly larger world where their courses of life are predetermined. The work possesses beauty and sadness deriving from the sense of fate each of the young characters faces. "Takekurabe" stands out not only among Ichiyō's prose works, but in the literary corpus of the last half of 19th-century Japan.

"Nigorie" (Turbid Stream), like earlier works, depicts the spite and sorrow of the women who are destined to live in the lower strata of society. Some rate it higher in quality than "Takekurabe," seeing it as a development of the realism the author cultivated in "Ōtsugomori."

Diaries: Considered by some to be very artistic, Ichiyō's diaries are often compared with an autobiographical fiction, or *watakushi shōsetsu* (the "I-novels") that were produced in abundance after Ichiyō's time. Stylistically, her diaries are like her novels, written entirely in classical Japanese, and do not include any punctuation marks. They are punctuated, so to speak, by the numerous *tanka* and revealing notes on facts, people, and events. The segments covering Ichiyō's association with the fortune-teller Kusaka Yoshitaka, for example, offer a mysterious side of the grim writer and may be read as a fiction that deals with the plight of a young, attractive woman. What makes these diaries more valuable is their tally of activities of Ichiyō's contemporary writers, some of whom, perhaps thinking that they were the mainstream of literature, visited Ichiyō's poverty-stricken house to give her advice and encouragement. The literary output of those who outlived Ichiyō is curiously small, with a few exceptions. The exceptional writers were those who, holding editorial jobs or some means to support themselves, underwent changes in writing style and strengthened their descriptive power while deepening both their introspection and their observation of the kind of misfortune and fate that Ichiyō observed. The fact remains, however, that Ichiyō was the first female writer in a very long while in Japan's history.

Ichiyō's major prose works were translated quite early. "Takekurabe" appeared in 1930 as "They Compare Heights," translated by W. M Brickerton, in *The Transactions of Asiatic Society of Japan*. What made "Takekurabe" really known to the West was Edward Seidensticker's translation, "Growing Up," included in Donald Keene's *Modern Japanese Literature*, 1956. Later, Robert Danly translated it as "Child's Play" and included, along with eight other translated stories, in his dissertation, *In the Shade of Spring Leaves: The Life and Writings of Higuchi Ichiyō. A Woman of Letters in Meiji Japan*, New Haven, CT: Yale University Press, 1981. Danly's book includes a bibliography. Among the notable translated works before Danly's book were Hisako Tanaka's translations of "Nigorie" (Muddy Bay) and "Jūsanya" (The Thirteenth Night), both appearing in *Monumenta Nipponica* in 1958 and 1961, respectively.

While Danly's study of Ichiyō, Part 1 of *In the Shade of Spring Leaves*, gives necessary information on the life and works of Ichiyō, it is important to refer to the book's notes. They explain in detail the texture of Ichiyō's writing style, which is dense with untranslatable literary allusions.

BIBLIOGRAPHY

Translations

"Flowers at Dusk," "A Snowy Day," "The Sound of Koto," "Encounters on a Dark Night," "On the Last Day of the Year," "Troubled Waters," "The Thirteenth Night," "Child's Play," and "Separate Ways." Trans. Robert Lyons Danly. In *In the Shade of Spring Leaves: The Life and Writings of Higuchi Ichiyō, a Woman of Letters in Meiji Japan*. New Haven, CT: Yale University Press, 1981.

"Growing Up." Trans. Edward Seidensticker. In *Modern Japanese Literature*, ed. Donald Keene. New York: Grove Press, 1959.

"The Last Day of the Year." Trans. Tei Fujiu. In *Hanakatsura*. Tokyo: Ikuseikai, 1903.

"Muddy Bay." Trans. Hisako Tanaka. *Monumenta Nipponica*, 1958.

"Teenagers Vying for Tops" and "In the Gutter." Trans. Seizo Nobunaga. In *Takekurabe*. Tokyo: Information Publications, 1960.

"They Compare Heights" and "Parting of the Ways." Trans. W. M. Bickerton. In *Transactions of the Asiatic Society of Japan*, 1930.

"The Thirteenth Night." Trans. Hisako Tanaka. *Monumenta Nipponica*, 1960 and 1961.

Critical Works

Danly, Robert Lyons. *In the Shade of Spring Leaves: The Life and Writings of Higuchi Ichiyō, a Woman of Letters in Meiji Japan*. New Haven, CT: Yale University Press, 1981.

Keene, Donald. *Dawn to the West: Japanese Literature of the Modern Era.* New York: Holt, Rinehart and Winston, 1984.

Lyons, Phyllis. "Higuchi Ichiyō." In *Longman Anthology of World Literature by Women: 1875–1975,* ed. Marian Arkin and Barbara Schollar. New York: Longman, 1989, 137–38.

Ueda, Makoto. "Growing Up." In *Approaches to the Modern Japanese Short Story,* ed. Thomas E. Swann and Kinya Tsuruta. Tokyo: Waseda University Press, 1982.

James R. MORITA

HIRABAYASHI Taiko (1905–72), novelist, biographer, social and literary critic, political activist, writer of detective stories and children's literature. Real name: Hirabayashi Tai.

Life: Hirabayashi was born in Suwa, Nagano prefecture, into an impoverished family. Formerly a local gentry, a sizable fortune had been built by her grandfather, who had been a leading member of the Liberal party, but he lost it when he failed as an entrepreneur in the spinning industry. His adopted son-in-law, Hirabayashi's father, went to Korea to make money with a vain hope of rebuilding the family fortune, and her mother made a living by farming and running a small general store. Young Hirabayashi helped with attending on customers and bookkeeping, even as she avidly read Tolstoy and Dostoevski from her brother-in-law's collection. In 1918 she entered Suwa Women's Higher School at the top of the class, taking what turned out to be the first step in her growth into a prolific writer. Suwa was noted for prominent poets of the Araragi School of *tanka* (thirty-one-syllable poem), such as Shimaki Akahiko (1876–1926) and Tsuchiya Fumiaki (or Bunmei, b. 1890). Hirabayashi was fortunate enough to have Tsuchiya, then assistant principal of her school, to initiate her into the realistic Araragi style and techniques. There she was exposed also to the works of realist writers such as Shiga Naoya, Kunikida Doppo, and Zola. Awakened to the issue of social inequity, she contributed "Aru yo" (A Certain Night) to *Bunshō Kurabu,* which was printed in February 1922.

In the spring, on graduation day, she went to Tokyo and became a telephone operator trainee, but within a month she was fired for having made a personal call on the job to Sakai Toshihiko (1870–1933), a radical socialist who would be chairman of the Japan Communist party upon its formation in July. Sakai found her a job at Japan-Germany Book Company, where she met anarchist Yamamoto Toshio. While living with Yamamoto, she was arrested along with him in the precautionary mass roundup of radicals under martial law immediately after the great earthquake of 1923. Banished from Tokyo upon release, Yamamoto and Hirabayashi went to Manchuria, where she, suffering from beriberi and night blindness, lost a newborn baby girl due to malnutrition. Upon returning to Japan alone, she joined various groups of anarchist artists and lived with a number of painters and poets, wandering from one man to another, from one place to the next. Looking back on this period of her life, she wrote later, "I had a devil in my heart who was not satisfied with vicarious experience and insisted on going through the vicissitudes of life with this very body'' (*Sabaku no hana* [Desert Flowers], 1955–57).

Counted among more lasting influences is the friendship formed with two activist couples who lived nearby: Tsuboi Shigeji (1897–1975) and his wife Tsuboi Sakae (1899–1967), and anarchist poet Nomura Yoshiya (b. 1903) and Hayashi Fumiko (1903–1951). After Hayashi broke up with Nomura, Hirabayashi shared an apartment with Hayashi for a while, both working at odd jobs and making rounds of publishers to sell their writings. "Azakeru" (Self-Mockery, 1927) is a testimony to her tempestuous life between 1923 and 1926, describing her experience of living with exploitive, egotistic, and dependent men.

In early 1927, she entered into an arranged marriage with Kobori Jinji (1901–59), a Marxist member of the journal, *Bungei Sensen* (Literary Battle Front, 1924–32). Involved in a political incident of 1937, Kobori was hunted by the police and went into hiding. Hirabayashi was detained supposedly for questioning, but even after Kobori turned himself in, she was kept in detention for eight months, released only when she was literally on the brink of death from pleurisy complicated by peritonitis. She miraculously recovered, thanks to desperate nursing by Kobori, who lost his sight for a time from exhaustion. This marriage of ideological comrades ended in 1955, when Kobori's unfaithfulness for the past six years came to light in much media coverage, as described in the second section of *Sabaku no hana.* When Kobori died in 1959, leaving his former mistress and then wife (who had been Hirabayashi's trusted housemaid) and their child destitute, Hirabayashi went to their rescue and found a shelter for them, proving her identification with, and sympathy for, abused women and the poor to be genuine. Having survived many serious illnesses, including cancer operations on both breasts, Hirabayashi Taiko died of pneumonia in 1972. (This section is based specifically on *Gendai josei bungaku jiten,* or Reference on Contemporary Women's Literature, ed. Muramatsu Sadataka and Watanabe Sumiko, Tokyo-do, 1990.)

Career: At the start of her long, prolific career, Hirabayashi set the correction of social injustices as a primary goal of her life. Émile Zola's *Germinal* in Sakai Toshihiko's translation was instrumental in awakening her to the need for worldwide organization to fight social inequity. Her espousal of anarchism was due largely to the influence of her first common-law husband, Yamamoto, and her subsequent male companions, rather than intellectual understanding or commitment to ultimate ideological objectives. She saw Kobori as an embodiment of Zola's idealized character, Etienne. Her break with anarchist groups coincided roughly with her attainment of due recognition through powerful autobiographical fiction, "Seryōshitsu nite" (At Charity Ward, 1927), based on the hardship and family tragedy she suffered in Manchuria, followed by "Azakeru" (Self-Mockery, 1928; originally titled "Moshō o uru" [Selling a Mourning Badge], which won the New Writer's Award of the *Osaka Asahi* newspaper. Between 1928 and 1933, Hirabayashi was active in various women's groups, participated in organizing several labor groups, and wrote numerous articles that clarified her political stand.

In a short story, "Botsuraku no keizu" (Genealogy of Decline, 1933), she traces the history of her own family, whose income had been reduced to a subsistence level under the onslaught of Western-style capitalism in the late 19th century. As it became increasingly dangerous for writers to express their convictions freely under the repressive statutes, Hirabayashi seriously considered abandoning her writing career. During her illness incurred in police custody in 1937, she received financial help as well as moral support from women writers and activists, the principal fund-raisers on her behalf, including the future socialist politician Kamichika Ichiko (1888–1981) and novelist Enchi Fumiko (1905–86). By 1941, Hirabayashi was well enough to write an essay "Byōshō nite" (On a Sickbed, 1941) for a literary coterie magazine. In the meantime she was studying classical Japanese literature, including the 8th-century poetic anthology *Manyōshū* (which was most admired by the Araragi school), *The Tale of Genji,* and medieval historical works such as *Ōkagami* and *Masukagami.*

When World War II ended in Japan's defeat and the collapse of the military regime, a new era opened to writers of all types. Hirabayashi responded to the call for the formation of a leftist literary group, Shin Nihon Bungaku Kai (Association for New Japanese Literature) and was elected to their central committee. She insisted on exclusion from membership of those who had cooperated with the military government. Her voice fell on deaf ears, however, marking a critical juncture that eventually led to her separation from leftist causes. Opting to write on her own rather than in a group effort, she produced several pieces of great literary significance in 1946 alone, including a novel with a title that became her trademark, *Kōiu onna* (This Kind of Woman). In time her disillusionment with leftist causes grew into criticism, typified by "Nihon Kyōsantō hihan" (Criticism of Japan Communist Party, 1949). By 1960 she was absolutely opposed to radical movements such as the one against the renewal of the United States-Japan Defense Treaty.

In her busy schedule, she managed to serve as a juror for several literary prizes, as a social and literary critic, and as a columnist. Shortly before her death, she established the Hirabayashi Taiko Award, to be given to writers who contribute to the advancement of Japanese literature and literary criticism.

Major Works: "Seryōshitsu nite" (At Charity Ward, 1927), short story. Written during the process of Hirabayashi's transition from anarchist groups to socialist organizations, this story has a distinct flavor of proletarian literature in its treatment of theme and subject matter. The narrator is a pregnant woman. With delivery imminent, she is arrested together with her husband and two other associates on the charges of having staged a sabotage in a labor dispute. The stage for the sabotage is a planned rail track leading to an amusement center in southern Manchuria, Japan's undeclared colonial territory at the time. Because of her condition, the narrator is sent to a charity ward of the city hospital instead of a prison cell. She notes that the profit motives of a capitalist institution under

the guise of charity, in this case, the Salvation Army, are mirrored in the behavior of its director. She refuses to play the expected role of a grateful recipient
of charity, an insignificant gesture yet perhaps the strongest protest a woman
can make under the circumstances. Although the material is largely autobiographical, at the end the story departs from the author's real-life experience, for
the narrator chooses to leave the hospital and serve a prison sentence rather than
file an appeal for mercy. The resolution of this story proves Virginia Woolf's
contention that fiction can convey truer reality than mere fact.

Kōiu onna (This Kind of Woman, 1946), novel. The structural scheme of
''Seryōshitsu nite,'' centering around the narrator's firm commitment to her
beliefs, is elaborated again in this novel, with added analysis of the intricate
turns of the narrator's mind as powerful tools in developing the plot line. The
first-person narrator is in a hospital bed. She suffers from the complications of
multiple illnesses incurred in police custody. Her husband is now in jail awaiting
trial for his alleged involvement in a leftist conspiracy against the Japanese
government. The time frame is several months after the outbreak of the Sino-
Japanese incident in 1937, a critical point at which international socialist organizations were trying to gain a firm hold in Japan.

The second part delves more deeply into the specific events: the first police
summons for her husband, his escape, and his voluntary surrender after his
wife's arrest in his place. Interspersed with the unemotional, succinct narrative
describing the interrogation by Tokkō (the thought-control police) is the narrator's reflection over her relationship with her husband, or her mental journey in
search of fulfillment in a spiritual union with him. Now critical of Alexandra
Collontai's notion of free love between socialist comrades, Hirabayashi takes a
position that ideal love between man and woman should not be materialistic or
ideological but spiritual. In the narrator's eyes, her husband appears a strong
man of integrity, dedicated to working for labor's causes. This overwhelming
image of him changes when she sees him under arrest, alone and helpless. His
haggard image overlaps with that of her dead child, the hapless baby boy who
died of malnourishment due to dire poverty: she had been unable to buy milk
when her own dried up because of beriberi. The author demonstrates a remarkable skill in portraying the police system and its corruption. Characterizations
of a lieutenant and his subordinate are realistic and convincing, as are the descriptions of the animosity between the officers of the local and the central police
units, the merciless efficiency of their performance, and their treatment of suspects.

Chitei no uta (Song of the Underground, 1948), novel. A sincere believer in
labor's causes, Hirabayashi was disappointed with the Marxist leadership when
it exposed its weaknesses in setting its objectives after the war. She came to
realize that ideology forced writers to give only stereotypical treatment of the
subject matter at the expense of literature as an organic art. She expressed her
beliefs contrary to the proletarian credo through such pieces as ''Hitori yuku''
(I Go Alone, 1946), ''Kanashiki aijō'' (Sad Love, 1946), and ''Watashi wa

ikiru'' (I Will Live, 1947). By the time she wrote *Chitei no uta,* her effort focused on delineating the daily life of the people who led a sort of marginal existence, with no ulterior motives to promote socialism. Characterization is quite convincing, since the author had an intimate knowledge, through her husband, Kobori, of people who lived ganglandstyle. The heroine, Hanako, is a high school classmate of a daughter of the branch head of organized gangsters, or *yakuza.* Hirabayashi makes an ingenious use of Hanako's curiosity for the quaint manners and customs of gangsters in delving into the *yakuza* operations and its connections with the ultraright radicals. This novel provides a rare dissection of the dark forces in Japanese society, their influence over the outwardly rational and modern establishment, and the symbiosis of the two.

Sabaku no hana (Desert Flowers, 1955–57), novel. Serialized in a popular women's magazine, *Shufu no Tomo* (Housewives' Friend), this work proved to be a literary triumph for Hirabayashi. Here she combines all the autobiographical materials that had been published before 1954, covering the time span from childhood to her divorce, and presents it as the history of a woman's life. More mellow and more refined in her outlook and free of harsh criticism on men's behavior, she weaves in some newer elements, such as her effort to keep the marriage intact, while trying to live her life as a woman with a clear conscience. It is generally believed that Hirabayashi conceived this work in reaction to her divorce, but there is a strong possibility that she was more directly inspired by Guy de Maupassant's immortal work, *Une Vie,* a translation of which was entitled *Onna no Isshō* (a Woman's Life) and (One Life) widely read in Japan.

Biographies: Of the many biographical works that Hirabayashi produced, the most notable ones can provide valuable insights on Japanese modern literature and shed fresh light on the profiles of the people she knew as literary colleagues, political activists, or both. *Jidenteki kōyūroku, jikkanteki sakkaron* (Autobiographical Accounts of My Interaction with Friends, an intuitive critique on some writers, 1960) contains short essays on male writers, including Aono Suekichi, Nakajima Kenzō, and Ishikawa Tatsuzō, as well as a range of women novelists from Uno Chiyo, Kōda Aya, and Masugi Shizue, to the Hiroshima Holocaust writer Ōta Yōko. *Hayashi Fumiko* (1969) is a biographical novel in which Hirabayashi questions some generally accepted versions of events in her friend's life and gives her own interpretations based on documentary evidence, interviews, or her ''informed imagination.'' ''Hayama Yoshiki no omoide'' (Memories of Hayama Yoshiki, 1971) suggests that this advocate of workers' causes was already a ''convert'' *(tenkōsha)* who had abandoned his socialist beliefs by the May 15, 1932, incident, a coup d'état in which young military officers assassinated Prime Minister Inukai Tsuyoshi, who had been opposed to expansionist policies. Hirabayashi's last work before her death was *Miyamoto Yuriko,* on Miyamoto Kenji, the versatile proletarian novelist, wife of the longtime chairman of Japan Communist party, and Hirabayashi's greatest professional rival.

Translated Works: ''Azakeru'' (Self-Mockery, 1927), short story. The scene opens with the heroine's (Ryōko) concern over a pain in her breast, the pain so acute that she has to stop walking and check her chest. Ryōko has lived with three different men, one after another, since she left her first lover, who is now imprisoned in faraway Manchuria. The pain in the breast is a reminder of her past, in particular, of her baby, whose ashes she keeps in a small urn. The pain is also the symbol of her guilt and anger, guilt resulting from her abandonment of her first lover, who was the baby's father, and anger against a system that does not allow a woman to live freely. As she walks on, she witnesses a near accident in which a streetcar narrowly misses running down a track worker. The situation is analogous to Ryōko's current predicament: time and again she has indicated her wish to terminate her relationship with a current live-in comrade Koyama, but so far with no effect. If Ryōko is the streetcar operator who could not make the track worker remove himself from his path, Koyama is the worker who refuses to budge. She realizes that what causes the impasse is inertia.

In a highly charged style yet with emotional detachment, Hirabayashi demonstrates her masterful skill in depicting the psychological turns in Ryōko's mind as well as the despicable activities of anarchists who take pride in their parasitic life-style. Hirabayashi's view of woman's chastity is out of the ordinary in this story, which was originally entitled ''Selling Mourning Badges,'' after the black arm bands to be worn at the funeral service, arm bands that the heroine sells to raise funds necessary for feeding her comrades. In the author's words, the traditional price placed on female chastity is something that needs to be destroyed. A woman who appears to men's eyes to be selling sex is merely selling the used funeral band, a useless symbol of the old values regarding woman's sexuality. Ryōko never pretends that her predicament is unavoidable, for it is by choice that she lives as a sexually active woman. She does not apologize for her conduct, nor does she totally blame everything on men's parasitic dependence on women, both in financial and psychological terms. When she scornfully laughs at herself, that laughter envelops the men who exploit her as well. This naturalistic story won the cash prize in a short-story contest run by the *Osaka Asahi* newspaper.

BIBLIOGRAPHY

Translations

''The Black Age.'' Tr. Edward Seidensticker. *Japan Quarterly* 10.4 (October–December 1963): 479–93.

''Blind Chinese Soldiers.'' Tr. Noriko Lippit. In *Stories by Contemporary Japanese Women Writers,* ed. Noriko Lippit and Kyoko Selden. Armonk, NY: M. E. Sharpe, 1982, 44–48.

''The Goddess of Children.'' Tr. Ken Murayama. *Pacific Spectator* 6.4 (1955): 451–57.

''A Man's Life.'' Tr. George Saito. In *Modern Japanese Stories,* ed. Ivan Morris. Rutland, VT: Tuttle, 1962, 366–82.

''I Mean to Live.'' Tr. Edward Seidensticker. *Japan Quarterly* 10.4 (October–December): 469–79.

"Self-Mockery." Tr. Yukiko Tanaka. In *To Live and to Write*, ed. Yukiko Tanaka. Seattle: Seal Press, 1987.

"A Woman to Call Mother." Tr. Richard Dasher. In *The Mother of Dreams and Other Stories*, ed. Makoto Ueda. Tokyo: Kodansha International, 1986, 211–23.

Michiko AOKI

HIRATSUKA Raichō (1886–1971), essayist, social critic, magazine editor. Née Hiratsuka Haru; other names: Haruko; Okumura Haru (Mrs. Okumura Hiroshi).

Life: Hiratsuka Raichō was born in Kōjimachi, a residential section of Tokyo for the well-to-do. Named Haru at birth, she was the third daughter, though her eldest sister died prior to her birth. Her father, Teijirō, was the deputy director of the Board of Audit and played a prominent role in the Meiji Constitution Deliberation Committee, where he worked for the influential Itō Hirobumi. Haru's mother, the former Iijima Tsuya, was the daughter of a prominent physician. She had been raised in the old, plebeian sector of Tokyo and had been accomplished in the art of *tokiwazu* balladry before marriage. But this lower-class skill was not appreciated by her samurai-born husband, and upon entering his family she stowed her *shamisen* (three-stringed instrument) away forever.

Teijirō believed himself to be an enlightened man. Provincial by birth, he had reached his position largely through hard work and a quick intelligence. He put himself through school, where he studied European languages and so impressed his teachers that they helped launch his career in government. One year after Haru's birth he was sent to Europe on official business. Upon his return he brought back Western clothes and manners. He sent his wife to a private Christian academy where she might receive the polish of a true "lady" (that is, knitting, embroidery, and English conversation). With the installation of the new constitution in 1889 and the onset of nationalism, Haru's mother was taken out of school and put back in the home. She no longer wore Western dresses, and the family put away the fancy Western furniture Teijirō had brought back from Europe.

Haru began her education at age five. She was a good student, always the brightest in her class and known to be somewhat antisocial. But Haru preferred to be on her own. She was not considered beautiful by contemporary standards (though photographs show her to be quite striking). "Her skin was dark, her nose too high and her lips much too full. To top it off her hair was wavy." Her parents despaired that she had not been born a boy: all those brains gone to waste, and no beauty as a recourse. In 1898 she entered the girls' higher school affiliated with Ochanomizu Women's College. The following year the Meiji government passed the Ordinance for Women's Higher Education, which stipulated that the goal of a woman's education was the cultivation of *ryōsai-kembo* (good wives/wise mothers). The Ministry of Education declared, therefore, that appropriate subjects for women were needlework and the "domestic sciences." Haru, deeply interested in such "manly" subjects as philosophy and logic, was not at all pleased by the type of education she was receiving. She formed a reading group with several other dissatisfied young women. The friends she made in this group and in her subsequent institution remained close to her throughout the years and would later form the nucleus of *Seitō*, a journal she started.

With her mother's assistance and over her father's objections, Haru entered Japan Women's College in 1903, an institution founded by Naruse Jinzō (1858–1919) in 1901. Naruse, after studying in the United States, opened this school with the purpose of educating women "firstly as humans, secondly as ladies and finally as citizens of the nation." Haru was impressed by the breadth of Naruse's scholarship and by what she perceived as the progressiveness of his attitudes toward women. But she was bitterly disappointed when she later discovered the college was little more than a finishing school for upper-class women. Haru skipped her classes, particularly Naruse's course on ethics, and spent her time in the library reading works on Western and Eastern religion and philosophy. She began to attend lectures by the famous Christian evangelist Uchimura Kanzō and at the same time began to practice Zen meditation.

Haru graduated in 1906 with an essay on domestic science that incorporated religious history. Her classmates went on to marriages or to careers in education, and Haru, with little else to do, took classes at Seibi Women's Academy and Tsuda English Academy. She found a part-time position as a stenographer. At Seibi Women's Academy she became acquainted with Ikuta Chōkō (1882–1936), a novelist and influential translator. Chōkō chaired the weekly Keishū Bungakkai or Literary Circle for Accomplished Women. He was assisted by woman poet Yosano Akiko (1878–1942) and male novelists Baba Kochō (1869–1940) and Morita Sōhei (1881–1949).

Morita Sōhei was a recent university graduate and a rising young writer under the tutelege of the prestigious novelist Natsume Sōseki (1867–1916). When Sōhei went out of his way to compliment Haru on one of her compositions, she found herself attracted to him. The feeling apparently was mutual. Sōhei sent his wife and child back to his country home and began to spend more and more time with Haru, strolling about Ueno Park with her or discussing D'Annunzio's *The Triumph of Death*. It seems their relationship, though teasingly dangerous, remained platonic. Carried away by a morbid romanticism, Sōhei wrote to Haru suggesting that a woman was most beautiful at the moment before her death and that, as an artist, he should like to kill her and reveal her greatest beauty. Haru replied that the only way she could express her love for him would be to die by his hand. On March 21, 1908, she purloined her mother's heirloom dagger (luckily she overlooked her father's pistol) and ran off with Sōhei to the mountains of Shiobara. They trudged through the snow for several hours before Sōhei admitted he did not have the courage to kill her. He threw her mother's dagger into a ravine and sat down to finish off his bottle of whiskey. Fortunately the local constable discovered them before they froze to death. Haru's mother and Chōkō came to escort the couple back to Tokyo.

Love suicides, though common with the lower classes, were rare among the elite. The newspapers had a field day exploiting the failed attempt, blaming the couple's waywardness on the influences of naturalism and their Western education. Haru's name was stricken from the roster of graduates at Japan Women's College, and her father was encouraged to resign his government position, though he did not. Natsume Sōseki, in an effort to save his prize student, urged Sōhei to turn his experience into a novel. When Sōhei complied, Sōseki serialized the novel, *Baien* (Smoke), in the *Asahi Shimbun* from 1909 to 1910. The novel launched Sōhei's career and further scandalized the Hiratsuka family. Haru spent time between Kamakura and Matsumoto, quietly reading and furthering her studies in Zen meditation. She was so devout in her studies that her master priest graduated her to the first level of Zen achievement and gave her the Buddhist name Zenmyō. In the spring of 1910 she had her first sexual experience, with a young priest she had met four years earlier.

Upon her return to Tokyo, Ikuta Chōkō encouraged Haru to begin a journal for women. She did not know whether Chōkō was just being kind to her or if he really meant to encourage women. Haru did not have a great interest in literature and did not see an editorship as her calling in life. But her school friend, Yasumochi Yoshiko, encouraged her to accept Chōkō's challenge, and, when her mother offered her a portion of her dowry as start-up money, Haru decided to give the journal a try. She gathered several of her former classmates, and together they launched *Seitō* in September 1911. With this issue, Haru adopted the pen name Raichō, or snow grebe, after the bird that lives a solitary life high in the peaks of the Japan Alps.

Seitō (lit. Blue Steps, commonly translated as Bluestockings) was soon to capture the attention of other like-minded women. Many came from as far as Nagasaki and Nagano to join the journal. One was Itō Noe (1895–1923), who wrote letter after letter to Raichō from Fukuoka prefecture, begging her to help her extract herself from an unbearable marriage. Raichō responded by sending her a five-yen money order, and Itō was soon to become an important member of the *Seitō* staff. Another young *Seitō* fan was Otake Kōkichi (also known as Kazue), an art student from Osaka who joined as an illustrator. One evening when Kōkichi was soliciting subscriptions at a popular bistro, she was shown a fancy cocktail made of five different liqueurs. Kōkichi was so impressed she wrote a story describing Raichō drinking the "five-colored sake" with a handsome young paramour (who was actually the literary persona of Kōkichi herself). Newspaper reporters and other social critics took Kōkichi's story verbatim and, remembering Raichō's not-so-distant brush with notoriety, began to pillory her once again as an irresponsible, licentious "new woman" (a newly coined term with extremely negative overtones). Before this furor had even subsided, however, Raichō was soon embroiled in another fiasco—and one largely of Kōkichi's making. Kōkichi's uncle invited his niece to accompany him on a trip to the Yoshiwara, the old Tokyo pleasure quarter. Apparently he had taken Kōkichi with him on other occasions, and she always had a nice time conversing with the *oiran,* or high-ranking courtesans. Before going this time, however, she asked Raichō and another *Seitō* member to join her, which they did. Never one to keep a low profile, Kōkichi was soon boasting of their adventure, and the scandal rocked Japan. The *Yomiuri Newspaper,* for example, ran bold headlines: "Women Literati Dally in the Yoshiwara." The press made it appear that these "new women," in trying to assume an equal footing with men, went so far as to attempt the male pastime of disporting themselves with courtesans. The public was so outraged by the picture the press had painted of Raichō and her band of *Seitō* women that some stoned her house. Other *Seitō* members scolded Raichō and Kōkichi for exploiting the Yoshiwara women as shamelessly as men had. There were calls to expel Kōkichi.

The furor eventually took its toll on Kōkichi's health, and in the summer of 1912 she went to a sanatorium in Chigasaki to rest and recuperate from a touch of tuberculosis. Raichō visited her in August and there met the young art student Okamura Hiroshi (1891–1964), much to Kōkichi's distress. (Sources suggest that Kōkichi was in love with Raichō, an infatuation Raichō did very little to discourage.) Raichō has said of Hiroshi: "He was like a baby: one-fifth child, one-third woman and one-half man. Few men were as helpless as he in the face of reality. He couldn't nurse a sick child. He couldn't even sell one of his own paintings. And when we were penniless, he would go out and buy a piano." But Hiroshi, five years her junior, was the love of her life. (Sources suggest the relationship between Raichō and Hiroshi led to the coinage of the term *young swallow,* which came to describe a young man "kept" by an older woman.)

On New Year's Eve, 1913, Raichō and Hiroshi exchanged vows at the same bistro where Kōkichi had gone earlier to drink "five-colored sake." They did not marry legally because Raichō refused to do so under the present system, which rendered a wife her husband's property. The law, of course, did not recognize "free marriages," and neither did Raichō's parents. For a time they disowned her.

Raichō had to struggle to make ends meet. As Hiroshi did not work, they had to survive on manuscript fees that Raichō received from other journals. She could not afford a maid, and for the first time Raichō had to contend with day-to-day housework. Other *Seitō* women, such as Itō Noe, who had enjoyed less privilege growing up, came to Raichō's aid by showing her how to cook. In the spring of 1915 Raichō began to serialize a long autobiographical novel in the *Jiji Shimpō* newspaper, which promised to tell her side of the Shiobara suicide attempt. But shortly after serialization she began to suffer with her first pregnancy and discontinued the work. Her pregnancy became so difficult that she turned the editorship of *Seitō* over to Itō Noe. To compound Raichō's difficulties, Hiroshi fell ill with tuberculosis and had to return to the sanatorium in Chigasaki that fall. In December Raichō gave birth to a daughter, Akemi. Since this child was illegitimate, reporters tripped over one another in a rush to Raichō's bedside, where they sought her stance on illegitimacy.

In early 1916 Raichō moved to Chigasaki to be near Hiroshi. She had to struggle to pay his hospital fees. Since he refused to eat the hospital food, she had to prepare meals for him every day. The pressures were so great that her milk stopped, and she was afraid she would have to send her baby out to a wet nurse. But she managed to keep her family together. Then, just when Hiroshi was on the mend, Itō Noe, whom Raichō had left in charge of *Seitō*, ran off with Ōsugi Sakae (1885–1923), an anarchist and married man who was simultaneously having an affair with another *Seitō* woman. The scandal was too great, and Raichō was too weak to stave it off. The *Seitō* house, already shaky, came tumbling down. The last issue was February 1916.

Raichō returned to Tokyo in the summer of 1917 and gave birth to a son, Atsufumi, that fall. With the appearance of a grandson, her parents sought a reconciliation, and Raichō's mother bought her a house in Tabata. The house included an art studio for Hiroshi. By this time he had given up painting in favor of drama, and he used the space to stage plays with members of the Shingeki (New Drama) Association.

With the onset of World War I and the severe economic hardship it brought, Raichō found herself more and more involved in politics. Realizing the helplessness of an individual woman to render change, she joined other activist women (and former *Seitō* members), such as Yamada Waka (1879–1957) and Yamakawa Kikue (1890–1980), in their work to amend the Fifth Article of Japan's constitution, which precluded women from participating in politics. She also began to work to change marriage laws and to create laws that would protect mothers. The latter involved Raichō in a long and well-publicized debate with Yosano Akiko, who, herself a mother of thirteen children, felt special accommodations for mothers served only to hobble women further.

When efforts to amend the Fifth Article failed, Raichō grew even more active in work for women's rights, joining existing groups and creating new ones. In 1926 she moved to Seijō, then a residential suburb of Tokyo, where Hiroshi took a job as an art and drama teacher at Seijō Gakuen, a secondary school. Raichō's work began to slow somewhat, though she continued to publish articles and essays on women's issues. Following her son's graduation from Waseda University in 1941, Raichō feared his illegitimacy would hamper his chances for employment. She had her name placed in Hiroshi's family registry, thus becoming legally married.

During the latter years of World War II, Raichō and Hiroshi lived with her mother and sister in Ibaragi prefecture. She returned to Tokyo in 1947. From this time onward she began to work tirelessly for world peace. In 1964 Hiroshi died at the age of seventy-three; Raichō was seventy-eight. She devoted the last years of her life to securing peace in Vietnam. Cane in hand, she marched proudly at the head of the June 23, 1970, demonstration against the Japan-United States Security Treaty. This would be her last public protest. In August she was hospitalized for liver cancer. Although discharged shortly thereafter, she was again admitted in November. She died on May 24, 1971, at the age of eighty-five. Shortly before her death, her old friend and colleague Yamakawa Kikue visited her and asked, "If you were young and had it all to do again, what would be your focus?" Raichō answered, "Philosophy."

Career: The evolution of Raichō's career as a social critic parallels her development as a woman, lover, and mother. *Seitō,* the work that firmly etched her name in history, was initiated partly in an attempt to direct the terrific energies of a volatile young woman. Raichō had no particular interest in literature. But, denied access to political and economic spheres as a woman, literature and education were about the only venues left to her. More and more women had been emerging as writers since the turn of the century. Many had found their way into print through familial relationships, though a few, such as Tamura Toshiko (1884–1945), made their way largely unassisted. The popular coterie journals, such as *Subaru, Mita Bungaku,* and *Shirakaba,* regularly carried submissions by women. Though at least seven journals catered more or less exclusively to women, *Jogaku zasshi,* for example, there was as yet no journal run by women, for women, and about women. Ikuta Chōkō, well versed in the female romanticism of France, saw the need and the opportunity to launch just such a journal, and Hiratsuka Haru was ripe for the picking.

It would not be unfair to credit Chōkō with the creation of *Seitō.* He had suggested just such a journal to Raichō on several occasions, but she showed no interest until circumstances virtually forced her to consider his proposal. Chōkō offered the title, *Seitō,* as a direct translation of *Bluestocking,* the nickname of a predominantly female literary salon of 18th-century London. Even after Raichō gathered a staff of four women—Yasumochi Yasuko, Nakano Hatsuko, Kiuchi Teiko (all Japan Women's College graduates), and Mozume Kazuko (a graduate of Ochanomizu Women's College)—Chōkō remained a background force. For instance, when Raichō and her staff first drew up the goals and bylaws of the journal (which were printed in the back of each issue), they declared that their purpose was to "encourage women's self-awakening, to exhibit the multifaceted talents of these awakened women and thus to give birth to the female genius." Prior to publication, Chōkō had Raichō change "women's self-awakening" (*joshi kakusei*) to "women's literature" (*joryū bungaku*), thus imposing his interest in a literary journal on the young group. The bylaws continued by stating that members of the journal were to be women who are writers, who aspire to be writers, or who have a love of literature. Supporting members would include prominent women writers or any man who believed in the goals and principles of the journal.

The first issue was compiled and edited in Mozume Kazuko's house (as Raichō was afraid of irritating her father with production in her own house) and was ready September 1, 1911. In keeping with the literary outlook of the journal, the issue carried a poem by Yosano Akiko and stories by Mori Shigeko (1880–1936, novelist Mori Ōgai's wife), Tamura Toshiko, Kunikida Haruko (1879–1962, novelist Kunikida Doppo's widow), and others. In addition there was an essay on Hedda Gabler and Raichō's famous essay "Genshi josei wa taiyō de atta" (Original Woman Was the Sun).

The journal immediately attracted the attention of other women writers, and subsequent issues bore stories, poems, plays, and essays by Nogami Yaeko (1885–1985), Okamoto Kanoko (1889–1939), Koganei Kimiko (1870–1956, Mori Ōgai's younger sister), and Okada Yachiyo (1883–1962, playwright Osanai Kaoru's younger sister). Yet despite the stellar quality of contributions to the journal, the established literary world paid *Seitō* only lip service. The general press scrutinized the journal, and its interest was generated more by curiosity than art.

The press saw *Seitō* as a dangerous association of pampered and overeducated women who, with little better to do, spent their time in licentious and self-gratifying pursuits. *Seitō* women were compared with Ibsen's women. (*A Doll's House* began its first performance in Japan in September 1911, the same month *Seitō* was launched. The play, though given rave reviews as a theatrical piece, was castigated by the media for its sympathy with the home wrecker Nora. Hermann Sudermann's *Magda,* when performed in 1913, caused such an uproar it was banned from the stage.) Regardless of the fact that Raichō and her colleagues, in special *Seitō* issues devoted to *A Doll's House* (January 1912) and *Magda* (June 1912), wrote essays that condemned Nora and Magda for their selfishness and impetuousness, the popular press aligned them with the freedom-seeking heroines. *Seitō* women were defined as "new women," drunkenly disporting themselves with young men and corrupting the values of the Japanese family. Otake Kōkichi's indiscretions only increased public ire, and Raichō found her energies more and more devoted to defending her fledgling journal.

The April 1912 issue of *Seitō* was banned because of the story "Tegami" (Letter) by Araki Ikuko. The work, in the form of a letter from a married woman to her young lover, expressed the woman's unabashed joy over their secret meeting. The Home Ministry, contending that the work advocated adultery and challenged the family system, had the issue confiscated.

Reactions such as these, however, forced Raichō and the others to rethink their positions. They had not originally intended the journal as a forum of battle. It had simply been meant to encourage female expression, literary or otherwise. But when push came to shove, Raichō stood up to fight. In the 1913 January issue of the *Chūō Kōron,* Raichō published her proudly defiant essay "Watashi wa atarashii onna de aru" (I Am a New Woman). In this highly poetical essay Raichō accepts the mantle of the "new woman." She takes what the press had earlier corrupted as a term of shame and makes of it a title of valor. "A New Woman? Yes, I am a new woman. I hope and pray everyday that I will be a truly new woman." Shortly after this essay appeared, *Seitō,* with Ikuta Chōkō's direction, hosted its first public lecture on the issue of the new woman. Guest speakers included Chōkō, Baba Kochō, Itō Noe, and Iwano Hōmei (1873–1920). The hall was filled to capacity.

Raichō, herself considering marriage, was now more than ever inflamed by the injustices in the family system. She began publishing translations of *Love and Marriage* by Swedish feminist Ellen Key (1849–1926). In February 1913 another issue of *Seitō* was banned. This time the offense was the article "The Solution to the Woman Problem" by Fukuda Hideko (1865–1927), which seemed to call for a Marxist revolution. Women could not be free, she argued, if men were not free, and men could not be free under the present governmental system, which treats people unequally according to class. In April of the same year Raichō's essay "To the Women of the World" caught the eye of the censors, and Nakano Hatsuyo and Yasumochi Yoshiko were called before the Metropolitan Police, who warned them to curb their activities. But the women grew only more zealous. From October they rewrote the goals and bylaws of the journal, changing its direction from a literary one to one with more clearly feminist ends. The change was initiated without consensus of all the *Seitō* members, and, though many remained loyal, membership began to decline from this point onward. Not only were the ideas expressed in *Seitō* too radical for most women to accept, but known association with *Seitō* was certain to damage a woman's social and employment prospects. Kamichika Ichiko, for instance, was forced to resign from her position as a teacher when her earlier membership in *Seitō* was discovered.

By late 1913, Raichō had transferred most of the editorial responsibilities to Itō Noe, then barely twenty and also a new mother. But Itō had been one of the most ardent forces in the shift to a more political direction, and she worked tirelessly to meet the demands of her new responsibilities. *Seitō* began to include more and more translations from works of Western feminists, such as Olive Schreiner and Emma Goldman. Many *Seitō* members were concerned about this sudden interest in the women of other countries. They felt the issues could be better dealt with if the focus remained at home and that their needs could be better met if *Seitō* returned to the goals it had originally espoused. But Itō refused to compromise, and in 1915, when Raichō turned over the publishing as well as editing roles to her, Itō informed the other members that henceforth *Seitō* would have no overriding direction, policy, doctrine, or principle. Women who yet insisted on these were advised to join other magazines.

In keeping with her new direction of "no direction," Itō began to publish debates among *Seitō* members and other prominent women on highly controversial subjects. The first of these was the so-called chastity debate. Ikuta Hanayo published an essay in another magazine suggesting that, given economic hardship, a woman should be able to sell her chastity without censure. She was answered in the pages of *Seitō* by Yasuda Satsuki, who argued impassionately that a woman must guard her chastity at all costs. Itō and Raichō joined the debate by charging first, that chastity was a male-inspired concept and second, that female chastity could hardly be argued in an environment where men felt so little compunction in preserving their own.

The second debate centered on the issue of abortion and again involved Yatsuda Satsuki. In the June 1915 issue she wrote in "Gokuchū no onna yori otoko e" (To Men from Imprisoned Women) that women should be able to do with their bodies as they pleased. Pregnant herself, Yatsuda argued that since no one would be arrested for cutting off an arm or leg, why should a woman be arrested for removing a part of her own body? Itō, also pregnant at the time, countered with the argument that the fetus was an individual life. The issue, however, was banned due to the controversial nature of Yatsuda's article. Two months later, Yamada Waka, another *Seitō* member and a Christian, contributed an article in which she declared abortion, as well as birth control, a sin.

The abortion debate, introduced but hardly resolved, was followed by a debate on prostitution. Itō, no proponent of prostitution herself, argued that the Women's Temperance Union's attempts to abolish licensed prostitution were hypocritical and ill-founded, as they addressed the institution of prostitution without considering the society that allows and supports it. Itō realized that as long as women were destitute and men were in power, prostitution was inevitable. Besides, she found very little difference between the business brokering involved in contemporary marriages and that which took place between a prostitute and her patron. Yamakawa Kikue, however, challenged Itō from a Marxist stance, arguing against the sale of human beings. Although they held many ideas in common, Itō's emotional rhetoric was easily overcome by Yamakawa's cool and precise logic. Their argument continued up to the final issue of *Seitō* in February 1916.

Seitō was only a five-year enterprise, but it electrified an entire generation of women. As some have argued recently, the *Seitō* call was meant mostly for an educated elite, but even so, the voice of *Seitō* was a courageous one. So many young women dedicated their lives to the journal and to the movement it espoused that such dedication must not be forgotten. Raichō, when asked in 1927 what the role of *Seitō* had been, answered that the journal had been influential in awakening women to the fact that they had a self and that that self was important. It had alerted women to the fact that they were not inferior to men but were equal human beings entitled to equal rights. Finally, *Seitō* awoke women to the fact that they had been enslaved by the family system and that the system had to change. Despite Ikuta Chōkō's early direction, *Seitō* did indeed become the journal its early founders had envisioned. It became an instrument of female self-awakening.

Major Works: "Genshi josei wa taiyō de atta" (Original Woman Was the Sun, 1911)" This essay, in the inaugural issue of *Seitō,* marked Raichō's debut. It became the early manifesto for *Seitō* women and the battle cry for newly emerging feminists. The opening paragraph posits the assertion that "originally woman was in fact the sun. She was a genuine person. Now woman is the moon. She lives by the strength of others, she shines by the light of others and her pale moon face is as wan as an invalid's." In highly emotive rhetoric reminiscent of a dithyramb, Raichō lashes out at woman's present state and at the prejudices that have rendered her thus: "Is woman worthless? No! No, she is a genuine person. . . . Is she weak? No! No, she is a genuine person." She reminds her sisters that they have a genius implicit within them, and she urges them to unearth this genius. "We must now recover our sun which has been hidden for so long. 'Manifest your hidden sun! Your long-lost talents!' This is the cry that swells within us without ceasing. This is the thirst we find so hard to suppress, so impossible to slake. This, indeed, is the one instinct so central to our person that it overcomes all others.'' Giving birth to their genius will not be easy, she reminds her readers, because ''what women do today is always met with scorn and ridicule. But I am not at all afraid.''

''Genshi josei wa taiyō de atta'' is an inspired and feverishly impassioned piece. Horiba Kiyoko, a Raichō biographer, suggests that Raichō wrote the essay in late August 1911, after a session of intense meditation. The central motif of the essay, linking woman with the sun, refers to ancient Japanese mythology wherein the supreme Shintō deity was Sun Goddess Amaterasu, and militant, shamanistic female rulers took the throne. Somewhere along the line, however, patriarchal rule replaced the earlier matriarchy, and woman was relegated to a second-class position, her talents forgotten. Raichō enjoins women to recover their primeval strength.

From a literary point of view, Raichō's motif harks back to a time when female genius dominated the literary world, that is, to the Heian period, when Murasaki Shikibu and her literary sisters flourished. But, as the patriarchy divested women of their rights to self, by making it a virtue to be ''self-less,'' it also silenced their right to literary expression. Raichō offers *Seitō* as a forum for the recovery of that expression.

But ''Genshi josei wa taiyō de atta'' is not beholden solely to indigenous influences. Raichō was also stimulated by the rhetoric and philosophical polemics of Nietzsche. Half a year prior to the debut of *Seitō*, Ikuta Chōkō completed a translation of Nietzsche's ''Thus Spake Zarathustra,'' and Raichō's essay evidences this reading. She refutes Zarathustra's claim that women's sentiments are one-dimensional, ''like frivolous bubbles on shallow water; while men's are deep, like water cutting caves.'' Women have been so overcome with household chores, Raichō argues, that, of course, their mental powers have been blunted. But more than the content of Raichō's argument, the style of her essay bears traces of Nietzsche's influence. Like ''Thus Spake Zarathustra,'' ''Genshi josei wa taiyō de atta'' is a philosophical poem that seems to argue its points dialectically rather than analytically. Both are inspired by the impassioned genius of their creators. Whereas Nietzsche's ''God is dead'' engendered multifarious debate, so Raichō's ''original woman was the sun'' inflamed a nation.

''Dokuritsu suru ni tsuite ryōshin ni'' (On Becoming Independent, to My Parents, 1914). This essay, in the form of an open letter to her parents, is Raichō's attempt to mollify her parents' anger (and by extension the outrage of the patriarchy) over her decision to take up residence with Okamura Hiroshi (whom she refers to as ''H'' in the essay). Raichō explains her motives with typical cool-headed logic, addressing her parents courteously but candidly. She argues that it would be against her principles to participate in a marriage system that would have a couple united regardless of their feelings for one another; that rendered a woman nothing more than her husband's property; and that placed other unnatural demands on the woman, such as expecting her to accept her husband's parents as her own. H was also opposed to this system, she assured her parents; and theirs was, therefore, a union of love. Raichō dismissed her parents' concern for the fact that H was five years her junior. "H cannot stand the terms *danna-sama* (husband) and *okusama* (wife) and has said he is perfectly content for us to go through life as 'older sister' and 'younger brother.' " As for her mother's worries about the illegitimate status of the children of their union, Raichō asserts, "We have no intention of having children, at least not now (but I don't know yet how we'll feel in the future)." As reasonable and respectful as Raichō's arguments were, they apparently did little to mollify her parents and had even less influence on society at large. But the essay effectively encouraged other women in similar situations.

Translated Work: "Yo no fujintachi ni" (To the Women of the World, 1913), essay. In this treatise, Raichō defends herself and her *Seitō* colleagues against the kind of attacks that have so frequently been leveled at liberated females. "No, we are not celibates," Raichō asserts. "And no, we do not hate men." She writes how dismayed she is every time she is asked such questions. Raichō assures her readers, the women of the world, that the reason she is not yet married is not that she is too unattractive to be asked but that she refuses to enslave herself to a system that treats women like incompetents and invalids.

"To the Women of the World" reveals Raichō's frustration over being so little understood by the women around her. But her despair is not limited to women. She also takes a very direct dig at Naruse Jinzō, the educator who she felt betrayed her and the women he presumed to educate. He had recently criticized Raichō and other "new women" in the press by calling them "flappers" and by lauding Japan's "good wife/wise mother" education of women, as opposed to the vocational training popular in the West. Raichō responds by accusing Naruse of caving in to popular taste. She enjoins the women of the world to question what have been pronounced "womanly virtues." Maybe these are virtues only because they keep women weak.

BIBLIOGRAPHY

Translation

"To the Women of the World." Trans. Pauline C. Reich and Atsuko Fukuda. In "Japan's Literary Feminists: The *Seitō* Group." *Signs,* 2:1(Autumn 1976).

Critical Works

Andrew, Nancy. *The Seitōsha: An Early Japanese Women's Organization, 1911–1916.* In the Papers on Japan Series of East Asian Research Center at Harvard University, 6. Cambridge; 1972.

Miyamoto, Ken. "Itō Noé and the Bluestockings," *Japan Interpreter* 10: (August 1975).

Lippit, Noriko Mizuta. "*Seitō* and the Literary Roots of Japanese Feminism," *International Journal of Women's Studies* 2:2 (March–April 1979).

Reich, Pauline C. and Atsuko Fukuda. "Japan's Literary Feminists; The *Seitō* Group," *Signs* 2:2 (Autumn 1976).

Rodd, Laurel Rasplica. "Yasano Akiko and the Taishō Debate over the 'New Woman.'" In *Recreating Japanese Women, 1600–1945,* ed. Gail Lee Bernstein. Berkeley: University of California Press, 1991.

Sievers, Sharon L. "The Bluestockings." In *Flowers in the Salt, The Beginnings of Feminist Consciousness in Modern Japan,* Stanford: Stanford University Press, 1983.

Rebecca L. COPELAND

I / J

ISE (ca. 875–no earlier than 938), poet. Real name: undetermined.

Life: The woman known variously as Ise, Ise no go (Lady Ise), or Ise no miyasudokoro (Consort Ise) was born to Fujiwara no Tsugukage, who was a third-generation descendant of Manatsu (d. 829), the older brother of the powerful minister Fuyutsugu (775–826). Fuyutsugu's line produced many of the most influential political leaders of the Heian period (794–1185), while Manatsu's line, having been on the losing side in a power struggle of 810, had to settle for lower-ranking posts. Ise's father was nonetheless able to rise to junior fifth rank. One of the mid-level officials known as *zuryō,* Tsugukage spent part of his career moving from region to region as governor of the provinces of Ise, Yamato, Satsuma, and Oki successively. (His daughter's sobriquet was acquired when she entered court service during his tenure as governor of Ise.) As was the custom with such officials, Tsugukage received special training in history and Chinese classics at the Heian equivalent of university (*daigakuryō*) and went on to fill posts that required skill in writing. His father, Iemune, left his mark in history as the founder of Hōkaiji Temple at Hino, south of the capital Kyoto; and Ise's uncle and cousin both served as head of the university (*daigaku no kami*). Ise's upbringing amid a family of such prominent scholars and poets inevitably had an effect similar to what Murasaki Shikibu and the other famous literary court ladies were to experience several decades later.

The presence of such a talented woman as Ise would hardly have gone unnoticed at Heian court, especially by ambitious nobles in the highest positions of power and prestige. Ise's poetic reputation was, in fact, established while she served as a lady-in-waiting for Onshi (872–907), the consort of Emperor Uda (r. 887–97) and daughter of Regent Fujiwara Mototsune (836–91). There are various conjectures as to why Ise entered Onshi's service. The usual reasons would be that she was assigned the role as governess-tutor, attendant-companion to the empress or possible wet nurse to Onshi's hoped-for children to come.

More specific reasons have been suggested, such as that her grandfather took advantage of his close connections with the ruling Fujiwaras, or Onshi's aunt in particular, and planned early on to place her in court or that Fujiwara clan strategists viewed her as a kind of safety valve in the event that Onshi failed to perform her proper duties as empress, bearing children being the foremost of them. As Professor Akiyama Ken points out (*Ise,* Shūeisha, 1985), during Emperor Uda's reign, women from other families often attained the lofty positions of junior or senior imperial consort; the Fujiwara wish to see their own offspring produce future emperors and ministers would lead eventually to a virtual monopoly of the highest positions by their own women by the time of Emperor Ichijō (r. 986–1011); but the situation during Ise's time was still fluid and socially or politically ambiguous.

Ise, a master wordsmith, was able to use her literary ability to her own advantage in refusing the advances of those mainstream Fujiwaras who might have sought to profit from her court position. She is believed to have been a woman of great beauty, noted also as a first-rate musician. In any case, Ise seems to have been a focus of male attention throughout her long life. Apparently she was involved in a series of affairs with some of the most important figures of her time, such as the Minister of the Left Fujiwara no Tokihira (875–945) and the well-known poet Taira no Sadafumi (d. 923), who was to be memorialized as a Heian Don Juan by a poem-tale (*uta monogatari*) known as *Sadafumi nikki* (Sadafumi's Diary) or *Heichū monogatari* (Tales of Heichū), extant from the mid-Heian period. The loftiest of Ise's loves was Emperor Uta himself, who sired her an imperial prince, who died in childhood. Her last lover was Uda's fourth son and a notable poet, Prince Atsuyoshi (887–930), for whom she bore a daughter. Inheriting her parents' talents, the child went on to prove herself an accomplished poet known as Nakatsukasa and won fame in her own right.

Career: Shinsen zuinō, one of the earliest treatises on the art of *waka* (thirty-one-syllable poem) by Fujiwara no Kintō (966–1041), cites Ise's poem:

> I hear they are rebuilding   Naniwa naru
> Nagara Bridge in Naniwa.   Nagara no hashi mo tsukuru nari
> What is left for me now   ima ha waga mi wo
> To compare myself to?   nani ni tatohemu.

Accompanying it is the following note: "This is a poem that Lady Ise showed to [her daughter] Nakatsukasa, saying, 'Poems should be composed in this manner.' " Placed next to a poem by Ki no Tsurayuki (d. 945) opening Kintō's critical discussion, Ise's poem was to be prized by later poets as a fine example of how to employ poetic toponyms (*utamakura*)—Ise derived her double meaning on "Nagara Bridge" from an anonymous poem (*Kokinshū,* no. 890) in which it functions as a metonym for "aged":

> Those things that have aged   Yo no naka ni
> (or, been long) in this world—   furinuru mono ha

| Nagara Bridge in Tsu Province, | Tsu no kuni no Nagara no hashi to |
| And I. | ware to narikeri. |

Kintō attests also to Ise's reputation as one of the most highly regarded *waka* poets of her time, pointing out examples such as the following poem with an explanatory preface:

While she was staying at the palace, unknown to others a man sent a note saying, "I can't help but feel that you are hiding from me." This was her reply:

How can I vanish before meeting	Omohigaha
someone like a water bubble	tahezu nagaruru mizu no aha no
ceaselessly flowing	utakatabito ni
on a stream of thoughts!	ahade kiemeya.

The phrase *omohigaha* (thought-stream) is not found in literature predating Ise, but it was to be employed frequently by later poets, especially from the time of Fujiwara no Teika (1162–1241), a compiler of *Shin-Kokinshū* (New Kokin, 1205). The two examples indicate that Ise was considered something of a poet's poet with an innovative skill to create new possibilities for the native poetic language whenever necessary, duly recognized by poet-critics like Kintō and Teika, the acknowledged representatives of a larger tradition.

In the early Heian period, when official poetry (or literature in general) was still dominated by men, Ise won a place right alongside the venerable Tsurayuki, one of Japan's most illustrious poets and the most important of the compiler-editors of the first imperial *waka* anthology, *Kokinshū* (ca. 908). Various poetic texts of the time provide evidence of Ise's reputation. Counted among the so-called thirty-six Poetic Geniuses, she is the only female poet of note contemporary to the Kokin compilers. She is also the woman best represented in each of the first three imperially commissioned *waka* collections. In *Kokinshū,* which includes seventy-four poems by women, Ise with her twenty-two outstrips the legendary Ono no Komachi by four, placing seventh overall, while Tsurayuki tops the list at ninety-five, almost doubling the number of poems by Oshikochi no Mitsune (fl. 890–924), ranking second. Ise's showing in the *Gosenshū* (ca. 951) is particularly striking: her seventy-two poems place her second, a mere four poems fewer than Tsurayuki's seventy-six, whereas Mitsune comes in a distant third with twenty-three. *Shūishū* (ca. 1005), the third of the imperial anthologies, lists twenty-five, putting Ise again seventh overall, but only two behind Minamoto Shitago (911–83).

As important as quantity is the placement of Ise's poems in *Kokinshū.* Its editors seem to have taken special care in choosing the first and last entries of the different sections (of which there are sixteen major ones). The first poem begins a series in a particular manner that will affect the links with the succeeding poems, and the last one stands at a pivotal location that not only ends a cycle but often suggests a bridge to the next section. Ise's poems are found at the ends of four sections: first scroll of "Spring," third scroll of "Longing," second scroll of "Miscellaneous," and "Long Poems." Since poems by the editors themselves are often located at the divisions of the important sections, it is not difficult to imagine the esteem accorded Ise. Her reputation made her presence indispensable at *waka* contests (*utaawase*), sponsored quite often in the late 9th and early 10th centuries, when the renewed emphasis on poems composed in Japanese (*waka*), as opposed to ones in Chinese (*kanshi*), spurred literary competition. Ise was the only woman included in one of the earliest and most important contests, the one held in 893 to become known as the Empress's Poetry Contest in the Kampyō Era. In 913, Ise performed the prestigious role of recorder at another, the Poetry Contest at the Teiji Villa. Records show that Ise more than held her own at such contests, winning most rounds or tying even when her opponent was the formidable Tsurayuki, as in the following example:

Poem from the Left: Ise

Meetings with you	Afu koto no
have ended long ago;	kimi ni taenishi wagami yori
how many tears, I wonder,	ikura no namida
have flowed out of me by now.	nagare idenuramu.

Poem from the Right: Tsurayuki

When longing for you overflows,	Kimi kohi no amarinishikaba
try though I may to hide it,	shinoburedo
others will surely know—	hito no shiruramu
how depressing the thought.	koto no wabishisa.

Emperor Uda was partial toward Ise's poem but called the round a draw in the end, after Tsurayuki's side complained of biased judgment. Impressively, Ise is mentioned twice in *The Tale of Genji* (early 11th century) by Murasaki Shikibu, each time together with Tsurayuki, whose name appears four times.

Another striking aspect of Ise's career concerns the number of poems she was asked to compose for standing screens (*byōbu*). Seven types of screen-painting poems by Ise are extant, totaling seventy-one. Often commemorating a felicitous occasion (e.g., an emperor's fortieth birthday), composition of screen-poems was so formal and demanding that only the most eminent of poets were commissioned. Ise's screen-poems rival those of male poets like Tsurayuki and Mitsune, further attesting to her extraordinary talents. This category of poems was not always composed simply in praise of pictorial illustration but often represented the utterances of the figures in the picture. What stands out in Ise's poems is the particular "stance" adopted by the woman putting up a determined resistance to male advances, as in the following exchanges:

The same man arrives and, while loitering by the gate, hears a *hototogisu* bird in the orange tree. He composes a poem and sends it in:

Is it in pity for me	Toni tateru,
standing at the gate?	ware ya kanashiki
the nightingale is in song	hototogisu
perched upon the orange branch.	hanatachibana no eda ni ite naku.

The woman replies:

It takes no notice at all of you,	Nanika tomo kimi soba shiraji
the nightingale—	hototogisu
to perch on trees and sing,	kinagara naku ha
is that not its natural bent?	saga ni yaha aranu.

Having heard that she has come out into the autumn fields to view flowers, the man comes over and says:

You are indeed out in the autumn field,	Aki no no ni idenu to kiku wo
miscanthus in bloom.	hanasusuki
Aren't you beckoning me	shinobi ni ware wo
in secret invitation?	maneki yaha senu.

She replies:

If it knew where you were,	Izukata ni ari to shiraba ka
[i.e., if you stayed with one woman]	hanasusuki
would the miscanthus in bloom	hakanaki sora wo
be beckoning towards the empty sky?	manekitateramu.

These exchanges appear as part of a series of seasonal poems in *Ise shū,* Ise's personal poetry collection. Eighteen screen-painting poems in this section of *Ise shū* share an element of "poetic narrative" (*uta monogatari*) in that the participants are identified only by generic terms, "the man" or "the woman." This is no coincidence. The practice of composing poems for screens is believed to have been intimately connected with the rise of fictional narrative and, more important, with the manner in which narratives were received. A standing screen usually consisted of twelve panels forming six pairs. The poems composed by an assigned poet were transcribed onto a square blank area called *shikishi,* toward the top of the screen, by a noted calligrapher. When the panels suggest a romantic encounter, the poet would speak in both male and female voices and weave any number of fictional situations out of the pictures. The potential for fictionalization inherent in the *waka* form is activated as an indispensable part of the production stage, which is a component of the overall process of screen viewing. The figures in the screen paintings are usually given no distinguishing physical features so that the identities of the persons exchanging poems remain anonymous, except in scenes derived from literary or historical sources familiar to their contemporaries. Such a narrative register characteristic of screen-painting poems inevitably had an unfortunate effect on one particular expert of the genre: *Ise shū,* the major source of information about her life, is presented in a similar vein so as to leave more enigmas than contextual clues, to say nothing of concrete facts.

Major Works: Ise shū (The Private Collection of Ise's Works), poetry and narrative. The first substantial studies of Ise came out in 1985, in two books authored by the eminent contemporary Japanese scholars Katagiri Yoichi and Akiyama Ken, respectively. Katagiri bases his portrait of the poet primarily on a close reading of the first thirty-two poems in *Ise shū,* and Akiyama on thirty-three. This section of the collection has been generally called Ise's *nikki* (diary), since Ban Nobutomo (1773–1848) so dubbed it. True, the narrative section commemorates incidents and moments in Ise's relationships with various men, mostly through interpersonal poetic exchanges and lengthy headnotes that hint at a story line. Its topic is common to all *monogatari*—relations (often of an amorous nature) between men and women. The problem is that *Ise shū* is not a *monogatari,* or rather that it begins to put into question just what *waka, waka* collections, and *monogatari* are, raising a related issue of "genre" in Heian literature.

In most textual versions, *Ise shū* begins with the phrase *Izure no ontoki nika* (In the reign of I know not which emperor), from which the famous opening line of *The Tale of Genji* is believed to be derived verbatim. *Ise shū* continues on in a style as elusive and anonymous as the screen-painting poems: "There was in close attendance on an empress a woman whose parents were living in Yamato''; then a "brother of an imperial consort" courts her. Thus, the text resists referential closure. Flaunting the fictive potential that is constitutive of the brief *waka* form, the contexts of which are susceptible to tampering, *Ise shū* challenges its readers to put the pieces together. Parallel texts can assist in solving the puzzles. In *Gosenshū,* for instance, where the *"hototogisu* bird" exchange also appears (nos. 458 and 459), the man's poem is attributed to the Biwa minister of the left (Fujiwara no Nakahira) and the second poem to Ise by name. But discrepancies occur frequently: poem 4 of *Ise shū,* apparently by Nakahira, is attributed in *Kokinshū* (no. 1049) to his elder brother Tokihira; or poem 20 by Sadafumi receives no reply in *Ise shū* but is paired with a woman's poem in *The Tales of Heichū.* Rather than solving biographical puzzles, *Ise shū* invites attempts to reconstruct historical background out of the poetic sequences, even as it defeats any effort to establish the narrative as completely faithful to fact, leaving only an ambiguous line between history and fiction.

Such fictive processes involved in the reading of *Ise shū* necessitate a critical confrontation with the nature of biographical "fact" as it relates to *waka* discourse. Heian texts repeatedly demonstrate the limits to which the *waka* form can be manipulated and precisely in ways that always prefigure the possibility of misrepresentation. The "real-life" figure of the "author" is not the "origin" or "source" of the work bearing her name, but the texts or texuality "re-creates" the life and the figure of the author. It may never be possible to obtain clear portraits as such, but the adoption of certain reading strategies can nev-ertheless help in focusing not only on what lies at the heart of Heian literary studies but also on issues being debated in modern criticism, such as the matter of interpretive clarity itself, the rhetoric of sexual politics, and the relation be-tween biography and poetic discourse as well as between fact and fiction. Ise's screen-painting poems, for example, provide a hermeneutic model for analyzing the use of fiction and the issue of resistance.

The dynamics that set in motion the first section of *Ise shū* arise out of a crisis that must have been experienced by many a court lady in the mid-Heian period. A talented and beautiful woman enters the service of an imperial consort; courtiers get wind of the new arrival and begin making advances; an affair ensues, which often leads only to sorrow and anxious moments of waiting on the woman's part. Ise's situation can be reconstructed this way: she entered the service of Onshi toward the end of 888, soon after the latter was installed as a junior consort (*kōi*) and then almost immediately promoted to senior consort (*nyogo*); word spread of Ise's beauty and poetic talents, and she found herself involved with Onshi's younger brother, Nakahira; when he married into an in-fluential family, the abandoned Ise left her court post and sought refuge in Yamato, where her father was serving as governor (891–94). In highly elliptical language, *Ise shū* sets the time of its first poem at a point after Ise has left the capital. This is quite similar to the narrative *topoi* commonly found in the *mon-otagari* genre where an episode is begun somewhere beyond a crucial event, the event itself having been only briefly alluded to. After the mention of a trip to a temple in Nara, a lengthy passage tells of Ise's return to court at the urging of her parents and Onshi, with a firm resolve "not to give a second thought" to men. True to her "words," she begins to refuse the men, beginning with Nakahira, eager to rekindle their affair, and his brother Tokihira, trying to seduce her.

When *Ise shū* is read against parallel texts, however, a fictional guise can be discovered to be telling a different story: Professor Katagiri, for one, notes that, judging from the exchanges between Ise and Tokihira collected in *Gosenshū,* it may very well have been Ise who did the pursuing, even chiding Tokihira at times for his womanizing ways. Such referential enigmas also bear traces of greater sociopolitical concerns. It is easy, for instance, to read the initial section of *Ise shū* as a criticism of Heian marriage practices. It is that and much more. "The man" who follows in the heels of Onshi's brothers is referred to only as the son-in-law of a minister implicated in a disturbance at the capital, in which the son-in-law too was banished. Upon receiving a letter from "the man," the woman cannot help being moved to mark the moment:

| Your earnest words produce | Kakete iheba |
| an even swifter stream of tears— | namida no kaha no se wo hayami |

I find myself willingly   kokorozukaraya
swept away by its current.   mata ha nakaremu.

The minister in question is none other than the venerated scholar-statesman Sugawara no Michizane (845–903), and "the man" is believed to be Minamoto no Toshimi (dates unknown). It is possible to read in this poem Ise's sympathy with Michizane and his followers exiled to the distant Kyushu in 901. In the light of the historical fact that Tokihira was the minister who ousted Michizane and that Ise's paternal ancestors had been losers in a power struggle against Tokihira's branch of the Fujiwara clan, the stance of resistance taken by "the woman" toward Onshi's brothers in *Ise shū* assumes a social significance of great proportions.

Ise happened on the literary scene at a time when her skill in *waka* composition allowed her to compete on an equal footing with the best male poets of the day. The "whole" story of her life is never to be known, but the texts she has left behind (especially in her poetry collection) yield a fortuitous convergence of discourses—poetic, fictive, historical, political, sexual, and social—that can help to better situate not only the emergence of narrative fiction but also a mode of literary expression that must constantly depend on other contemporary discourses to supplement its representational deficiencies. The inevitable necessity in such a mode to (re-)contextualize the *waka* form was turned into a powerful means of criticism and protest by Ise. What she bequeathed posterity may have been more than a collection of technically sophisticated (though outwardly tame) poems, for her modern readers can detect a voice that kindred souls can enlist in other struggles at other times.

Translated Works: Twenty-two of Ise's poems are available in English translations of *Kokinshū*.

BIBLIOGRAPHY

Translations and Critical Works

Bownas, Geoffrey, and Anthony Thwaite. *The Penguin Book of Japanese Verse.* New York: Penguin Books, 1964.

Brower, Robert, and Earl Miner. *Japanese Court Poetry.* Stanford, CA: Stanford University Press, 1961.

Carter, Steven D. *Traditional Japanese Poetry: An Anthology.* Stanford, CA: Stanford University Press, 1991.

Encyclopedia of Japan, S. V. "Lady Ise."

Keene, Donald. *Anthology of Japanese Literature.* Grove Press, 1955.

McCullough, Helen C. *Brocade by Night.* Stanford, CA: Stanford University Press, 1985.

———. *Kokin Wakashu: The First Imperial Anthology of Japanese Poetry.* Stanford, CA: Stanford University Press, 1985.

Rexroth, Kenneth. *One Hundred Poems from the Japanese.* New Directions, 1964.

Rodd, Rasplica Laurel, with Mary Catherine Henkenius. *Kokinshu: Collection of Poems Ancient and Modern.* Princeton, NJ: Princeton University Press, 1984.

Sato, Hiroaki, and Burton Watson, eds. and trans. *From the Country of Eight Islands.* Anchor Press, 1981.

H. Richard OKADA

IZUMI SHIKIBU (fl. ca. 1000), poet. Real name: unknown.

Life: Izumi Shikibu was known by various sobriquets: as Omotomaro during childhood; as Kō Shikibu (the Sino-Japanese reading of her family name, Ōe, combined with the government department where her father probably held a post, meaning [Ministry of] ''Ceremonial''; as Masamune ga musume Shikibu, or Masamune's daughter, Shikibu; and finally as Izumi Shikibu, by which she is known today.

Her father, Ōe no Masamune, was the governor of Echizen, descended from a scholarly family from the middle ranks of the aristocracy. In addition to serving as governor, Masamune concurrently held the posts of director of the Bureau of Carpentry (*moku no kami*) and senior secretary (*daijin*) in the household of Shōshi (950–1000), the eldest daughter of Emperor Suzaku (923–52; r. 930–46), who later became empress to Emperor Reizei (950–1011; r. 967–69). Izumi's mother, Suke no Naishi, who served as wet nurse to Shōshi, was a daughter of Taira no Yasuhira, the governor of Etchū. Izumi's parents probably met while they were both in service to Shōshi and brought up their daughter at court.

Izumi Shikibu followed her mother's footsteps into Shōshi's service and maintained her residence outside court at the home of Tachibana Michisada (d. 1016), a close friend of her father's whom she eventually took as her first husband. According to two sources in Chinese—the diary of Fujiwara Sanesuke (957–1046), *Shōyūki* (also *Ono no Miya Udaijin no nikki* [Record of the Minister of the Right Who Lived in Ono Palace], ca. 982–1030), and the history *Nihon kiryaku* (The Abridged Japan Chronicle)—Shōshi died at Michisada's residence in 999. Scholars speculate that Izumi Shikibu married at around this time when she was about twenty.

Izumi Shikibu is believed to have been Masamune's oldest daughter and in her personal poetry collection alludes to her younger sisters, one of whom is also mentioned in *Akazome Emon shū* (The Collection of Akazome Emon) as the object of the affection of one of Akazome Emon's sons.

Izumi was twice married, both times to men from the provincial governor class, to which her father also belonged. The post of her first husband, Tachibana Michisada, as governor of Izumi, responsible for her final and best-known sobriquet, began in the second Moon of 999 and ended in 1003. Scholars propose that she may have married him in 996 or earlier, but the date remains unsubstantiated. But she accompanied him to his post in Izumi in 1000, writing thirteen poems en route, which are preserved in her poetry collection (*Izumi Shikibu kashū: zokushū* [The Continued Poetry Collection of Izumi Shikibu], nos. 673–85). In either 1000 or 1001, the second or third year of Michisada's five-year post as governor of the province, Izumi Shikibu returned alone to live in the capital of Heian-kyō (present-day Kyoto). It is conjectured that a liaison with

Prince Tametaka (977–1002) occurred during this period of separate residence. Apparently the relationship between Izumi and Michisada remained close and amicable, for she continued to correspond with him even after their separation. However, when Michisada set out for his new post as governor of Michinoku in 1004, he took with him a new wife. By then Izumi was already living with Tametaka's younger brother, having relinquished her position as Michisada's wife.

Her love affair with Tametaka, the third son of Emperor Reizei, had begun around 1001. It was considered scandalous due to the disparity in the social stations of the lovers and fueled gossip at court. Then the Prince died of an illness contracted in the course of nocturnal visits to her while a plague was raging throughout the capital, giving rise to her reputation as a femme fatale causing the early demise of her lover. Eight months later, Izumi Shikibu shocked the court circles by beginning an affair with his full-blood brother, Prince Atsumichi (981–1007), the professed love of her life and the primary subject of *Izumi Shikibu nikki* (The Poetic Memoirs of Izumi Shikibu). Taking up residence with Atsumichi and causing the departure of his principal wife, she lived with him until his untimely death in 1007. She mourned him for two years, writing 122 poems (*Izumi Shikibu kashū: zokushū,* nos. 940–1061) in sorrow over her loss. Izumi's son by Prince Atsumichi eventually took holy orders under the name Eikaku.

In 1009, Izumi married Fujiwara Yasumasa (958–1036), a retainer of Fujiwara Michinaga and successively governor of Higo, Yamato, Tango, and Settsu. A 1027 entry in Akazome Emon's *Eiga monogatari* (The Tale of Flowering Fortunes) contains the last reference to Izumi Shikibu, revealing that she was still married to Yasumasa at that time. They may have separated before his death in 1036, while he was governing the province of Settsu. Izumi Shikibu is believed to have died in her fifties.

Izumi's first marriage to Michisada had resulted in the birth of a daughter, Koshikibu (also Koshikibu no Naishi, ''Little [Handmaid] Ceremonial''), who was to become a poetess and follow her mother into service at the court of Empress Shōshi (988–1074), a daughter of the regent Fujiwara Michinaga (966–1027) and the consort of Emperor Ichijō (980–1011; r. 986–1011). Koshikibu bore a male child to Michinaga's son Fujiwara Norimichi (997–1075) in 1018. Her son was raised to become a monk under the Buddhist name Jōen and achieved distinction within the monastic hierarchy. Koshikibu died in 1025 while giving birth to a child by Fujiwara no Kinnari. Although short-lived, Koshikibu is remembered as a poet who displayed sparks of her mother's poetic genius.

Career: Izumi Shikibu and Ono no Komachi (fl. mid-9th c.) are regarded as two of the most gifted poetesses in Japanese history. Unlike Ono no Komachi, about whom almost nothing concrete is known, Izumi has several works attributed to her name, including *Izumi Shikibu nikki,* from which some information can be gleaned. Two personal poetry collections—*Izumi Shikibu kashū: seishū*

(The Main Poetry Collection of Izumi Shikibu) and *Izumi Shikibu kashū: zo-kushū*—contain a total of 1,549 compositions. Representation in poetic anthologies, beginning with the *Shūi wakashū* (Gleanings, ca. 985) amounts to 247 compositions, leading the list of women included in imperial anthologies.

Her literary talent was recognized even in her youth. In her teens she composed one of her most famous poems, *kuraki yori,* which was selected for the third imperial anthology, *Shūi wakashū,* testifying to her rising status as a respected poetess.

From utter darkness,	kuraki yori
I must embark upon an	kuraki michi ni zo
even darker road—	irinubeki
o distant moon cast your light	haruka ni terase
from the rim of the mountains.	yama no ha no tsuki

Addressed to a Buddhist cleric known as the Abbot Shōkū, the head of a temple on Mt. Shosha in Harima who was of the Tachibana clan related to her husband, Michisada, the poem alludes to the poet's desire to enter the path of enlightenment represented by the image of moonlight. Perhaps Izumi sought guidance from the abbot to ''light'' her way. Throughout Izumi's career, her poetry is threaded with the dichotomous theme of wishing to escape from the world of desires while being immersed in earthly love affairs.

Torn between worldly ties and physical desire, Izumi Shikibu left a wealth of passionate love poetry, fueling rumors that purported that she was a femme fatale with numerous lovers besides her two husbands and two princely lovers. There may have been some basis to the rumor, judging by the contents of the following poem, sent to the residence of a secret suitor on her departure for Tanba province with her husband, Yasumasa:

Am I all alone	ware nomi ya
in dispatching heartfelt thoughts	omoiokosemu
perhaps in vain	ajikinaku
to one whose destination	hito wa yukue mo
in life remains unknown?	shiranu mono yue

Scholars speculate that Fujiwara Takaie (979–1044), Minamoto Toshikata (960–1027), and Minamoto Masamichi (d. 1017) may be counted among Izumi's lovers (Cranston, 1969, 18). Because she does not always name her male addressees, she leaves the impression that there had been numerous casual lovers. For example, a poem she composed while waiting ''impatiently for a man she had trusted'' goes:

I am not of a mind	take no ha ni
to sleep alone	arare furu yo wa
on nights when hail	sara sara ni

noisily rains down upon   hitori wa nubeki
the leaves of bamboo.   kokochi koso sene

Perhaps one of her most famous love poems combines long black hair (*kuro-kami*), a powerful sign of the aristocratic lady, with intense physical passion:

I lay down   kurogami no
unaware of the tangles   midare mo shirazu
in my long, black hair,   uchifuseba
filled as I am with loving thoughts   mazu kakiyarishi
for my lover who stroked it clear.   hito zo koishiki

Her reputation as a writer of passionate verse, coupled with gossip about her various lovers, certainly generated abundant public interest in her worldly affairs.

Around 1009 Izumi was summoned to serve in the court of Michinaga's daughter, Empress Shōshi. Izumi Shikibu's reputation as a poet was certainly instrumental in the summons, but scholars speculate that the regent Michinaga's personal interest in the poetess may have played a pivotal role in the decision. Michinaga arranged for her to marry Fujiwara Yasumasa, his own retainer twenty years her senior, known for his martial prowess.

Shōshi's literary salon sparkled with the presence of brilliant women writers, including Murasaki Shikibu, author of the fiction *Genji monogatari* (The Tale of Genji); Akazome Emon, credited with the first history written in the vernacular, *The Tale of Flowering Fortunes;* and Ise no Tayū (ca. 987–1063?), known for her poetry collection, *Ise no Tayū shū*. Izumi apparently developed a close friendship with Akazome Emon in particular, who recorded anecdotes about Izumi and her daughter Koshikibu in her historical tale. *Midō kanpaku ki* (The Chronicle of the Regent Michinaga) also contains poetic exchanges with Izumi Shikibu regarding the birth of their mutual grandson, Jōen. Murasaki Shikibu mentions Izumi in *Murasaki Shikibu nikki* (The Diary of Murasaki Shikibu) with a decided note of approbation, in a candid moral critique of her peers at Shōshi's court. Moral judgment leveled against Izumi may have been repercussions for her numerous liaisons as revealed through the poetic exchanges with members of the opposite sex preserved in her personal collections.

A supreme tribute was paid to Izumi by the compilers of the fourth imperial anthology, *Goshūi wakashū* (Later Gleanings, ca. 1086), who selected sixty-seven of her compositions for inclusion. It indicates that in the course of half a century, her status as a poet had skyrocketed to a height of prominence, from which she had yet to fall in the centuries to follow.

The historical image of Izumi Shikibu underwent a series of drastic metamorphoses in the realm of legend, seen in the medieval short stories of *otogizōshi* (companion booklets) and *Nō* plays. Historical facts concerning Izumi's life are frequently subjected to blatant distortions, and the outlines of her life are reduced to oversimplifications, although some elements of her personality, such as her amorous nature and her longing for religious enlightenment, remain constant. A typical example of factual distortion can be seen in an *otogizōshi* tale entitled *Izumi Shikibu,* dating from the Muromachi period (1336–1477). In it she is romantically linked to Dōmyō Ajari, the son of Fujiwara Michitsuna (955–1020), the grandson of the author of *Kagerō nikki* and Fujiwara Kaneie, who is featured as her son in the story. Izumi, presented as a courtesan in the work, apparently conceives the child, later known as Dōmyō Ajari, through a liaison with Tachibana Yasumasa (a conflation of the names of her two husbands, Tachibana Michisada and Fujiwara Yasumasa). After giving birth to the child, she abandons it only to have an incestuous relationship with him after he has become an adult. After realizing it was her son, she gives up the world and goes to Mt. Shosha, where she presumably wrote the famous poem, *kuraki yori,* to Abbot Shōkū. In a similar vein, *Nō* plays, temple histories, and local traditions perpetuated the process of downgrading the image of Izumi Shikibu in subsequent centuries (Cranston, 20–24). However, the distortions in Izumi's life found in the medieval genres have perhaps contributed to the curiosity of the reading audience, a living testament to her enduring popularity.

Translated Work: Izumi Shikibu nikki (The Poetic Memoirs of Izumi Shikibu, ca. 1200), diary. About the authorship of this work there is much debate, due partially to the existence of a variant title, *Izumi Shikibu monogatari* (The Tale of Izumi Shikibu). Scholars are divided into two basic camps: those who support the traditional attribution of the work to Izumi Shikibu and those who propose that it is a fictional account by an anonymous hand. Assigning of probable dates of composition or compilation is influenced by each camp's stand in the controversy: the first group is limited by the life and death dates of Izumi Shikibu; and the second depends on conjectural interpretation.

Literary scholar Konishi Jin'ichi proposes an original approach for dealing with the issue of variant titles. According to Konishi, most compositions of the Heian period (794–1185) were originally untitled and assigned a title arbitrarily by later readers or copyists in accordance with the reader's perception of the work's contents. He believes that the existence of variant titles for the *Izumi Shikibu nikki/monogatari* dates the work prior to the mid-12th century, still within the range of Heian custom in receiving titles from others. (However, it became common practice for authors to name their own literary creations during the Kamakura period [1185–1333].)

Konishi's definition of the terms *monogatari, nikki,* and *shū* (poetry collection) suggests a useful way to approach such problematic issues as genre, tense, truth versus fiction, and narrative voice: *monogatari* is prose written in the past tense about either fictional or historical events; *nikki* is prose written in the present tense concerning a historical person; and *shū* is a composite of the *monogatari* or *nikki* style and a poetry sequence.

The classical *nikki* is not equivalent to a "diary" in the modern Japanese sense or to the Western notion of a "diary" proper as an autobiographical work.

Nikki bungaku as a whole contains so many aberrant traits that one cannot construct a paradigm for a typical or characteristic *nikki*. The *Izumi Shikibu nikki* uses the third-person narration in the present tense, referring to the female protagonist as the "woman" (*onna*), occasionally presenting an omniscient view not usually accessible to diarists. Thus, the genre definition does not necessarily tip the scale in favor of the theory for authorship by someone other than Izumi Shikibu, nor does it settle the case for traditional attribution.

The plot is simple: a woman meets a prince; they begin courtship via exchanges of poems; after some trials and tribulations, she decides to move in with him; the prince's principal wife leaves; and the woman stays in his home. The narrative spans nine months and contains 144.5 poems, including two *renga* (linked verses). While still in mourning after the death of this Prince Tametaka, the female protagonist receives a message from her deceased lover's younger brother, Prince Atsumichi. From the outset she shows her interest in him, immediately sending a coy reply. The rest of the work focuses on the development of their relationship from distrust (the prince of her other liaisons; the woman of his abandoning her), to happy trysts together, back to suspicion and separation, until finally the prince moves her into his own mansion in the subtle climax. The entire work is threaded with poetry exchanges between them that disclose nuances of their relationship. The prose involves little interior probing, thus limiting the reader's observations to the reactions of the lovers as they regard each other.

The author assumes an audience well versed in the poetic and *monogatari* traditions as well as the aesthetics of *mono no aware* (pathos of things) valued by aristocratic society. As Janet Walker suggests in her 1977 article, this work attempts to function within the paradigm of ideal Heian love as seen in imperial poetic anthologies but is caused to deviate from the paradigm by the dictates of factual realism concerning the historical personage, Izumi Shikibu. The first poem, opening the dialogue between the lovers, shows the eagerness of the woman to meet the younger prince.

Rather than compare	kaoru ka ni
the lingering memories	yosouru yori wa
this fragrance suggests—	hototogisu
o cuckoo, I wish I could hear	kikabaya onaji
your voice. Is it like his?	koe ya shitaru to

A dynamic tension is achieved by the ebb and flow of the lovers' feelings for one another as their relationship develops into one based on mutual love and trust.

It is interesting that nowhere does the work give any indication that the woman's beauty is what attracts the second prince to her. Rather the woman's wit and sensibility displayed in her poetry finally win him over. Time and time again the prince evaluates her as a woman worthy of consideration while reading a new verse they have exchanged. In the following sequence, the woman sends a poem to the prince during the rainy season:

> What kinds of things yomosugara
> went through my mind nanigoto o ka wa
> throughout the night omoitsuru
> as I listened to the ceaseless mado utsu ame no
> sound of rain striking my window? oto o kikitsutsu

"Although I am under shelter, somehow my sleeves are drenched," her note said. "This woman is not beneath my notice," thought the prince and replied:

> I, too, wondered how ware mo sazo
> you fared in your dwelling omoiyaritsuru
> with such inadequate ame no oto o
> eaves as I listened saseru tsuma naki
> to the sound of the rain. yado wa ikani to

Current Japanese scholarship favors the traditional attribution of this *nikki* to Izumi Shikibu. Edwin A. Cranston presents the most thorough analysis concerning the authorship of the *Izumi Shikibu nikki*. He states that unfortunately no concrete conclusion could be reached due to the evidence's falling equally between traditional attribution and later composition by an anonymous hand. However, it is clear that Cranston favors the theory of authorship by a later hand. He discusses Fujiwara Shunzei and his daughter as possible candidates for later authorship based on two colophons by Fujiwara Teika found on the manuscripts of both the *Izumi Shikibu nikki* and the *Kenshunmon-in no Chūnagon nikki* (The Diary of Kenshunmon-in no Chūnagon, ca. 1219) but admits this theory has few proponents. Essentially he concurs with the main argument proposed by Janet Walker.

A study by Janet Walker suggests that the author of the *nikki* was most likely a woman constructing a fictional romance controlled by alliances to two opposing conventions: one was to fit into the paradigm of love affairs portrayed in the poetic anthologies, and the other was to remain faithful to the events that occurred to two historical personages. Walker states that she detects a tone of self-defense in the work, suggesting that if the traditional attribution was correct, then Izumi may have adopted a defensive posture to demonstrate her sensitivity and vulnerability to leave a more sympathetic portrait of herself for posterity. Walker nevertheless also favors the theory of later authorship.

The dispute surrounding the attribution of authorship has been a major focal point in the study of the *Izumi Shikibu nikki,* but this controversy has in no way diminished the popularity of the *Izumi Shikibu nikki* or affected the attention accorded to it as one of the classics of the Heian literary canon.

BIBLIOGRAPHY

Translations and Critical Works

Aston, W. G. *A History of Japanese Literature.* Tokyo: Tuttle, 1972.

Brower, Robert H., and Earl Miner. *Fujiwara Teika's Superior Poems of Our Time: A Thirteenth-Century Poetic Treatise and Sequence.* Stanford, CA: Stanford University Press, 1967.

————. *Japanese Court Poetry.* Stanford, CA: Stanford University Press, 1961.

Cranston, Edwin A. *The Izumi Shikibu Diary: A Romance of the Heian Court.* Cambridge: Harvard University Press, 1969.

————. In *Kōdansha Encyclopedia of Japan,* S. V. "Izumi Shikibu."

Honda, H. H. *One Hundred Poems from One Hundred Poets.* Tokyo: Hokuseido, 1957.

Katō, Shūichi. *A History of Japanese Literature: The First Thousand Years.* Tokyo: Kōdansha, 1989.

Keene, Donald. *Travelers of a Hundred Ages.* New York: Henry Holt, 1989.

Konishi, Jin'ichi. *A History of Japanese Literature, Volume Two: The Early Middle Ages.* Trans. Aileen Gatten. Princeton, NJ: Princeton University Press, 1986.

McCullough, Helen Craig. *Tales of Ise.* Stanford, CA: Stanford University Press, 1968.

McCullough, William H., and Helen Craig McCullough. *A Tale of Flowering Fortunes.* 2 vols. Stanford, CA: Stanford University Press, 1980.

Miner, Earl. *An Introduction to Japanese Court Poetry.* Stanford, CA: Stanford University Press, 1968.

————. *Japanese Poetic Diaries.* Berkeley: University of California Press, 1969.

Miner, Earl, Hiroko Odagiri, and Robert E. Morrell. *The Princeton Companion to Classical Japanese Literature.* Princeton, NJ: Princeton University Press, 1985.

Morris, Ivan. *The World of the Shining Prince.* New York: Alfred A. Knopf, 1964.

Porter, William N. *A Hundred Verses from Old Japan.* Tokyo: Tuttle, 1979.

Putzar, Edward. *Japanese Literature: A Historical Outline.* Tuscon: University of Arizona Press, 1973.

Satō, Hiroaki, and Burton Watson. *From the Country of Eight Islands.* New York: Anchor Books, 1981.

Walker, Janet A. "Poetic Ideal and Fictional Reality in the *Izumi Shikibu nikki.*" *Harvard Journal of Asiatic Studies* 37.1 (June 1977): 135–82.

S. Yumiko HULVEY

JŪNII Tameko (ca. 1250–after 1315), poet. Real name: Kyōgoku (Fujiwara) Tameko.

Life: Tameko was born some time between 1250 and 1252, the daughter of Kyōgoku (Fujiwara) Tamenori (1227–79) and a woman known only as the daughter of Miyoshi Masahira (dates unknown), who served in the household of the powerful Saionji family. Together with her younger brother, Kyōgoku Tamekane (1254–1332), Tameko wrote verse and helped bring the Kyōgoku school of poetry, founded by her father, to a position of lasting importance in the history of Japanese court literature. Little is known of her life before the year 1270, when Tameko and Tamekane moved into the residence of their paternal grandfather, Fujiwara Tameie (1198–1275), where they lived off and on studying poetry until Tameie's death in 1275. In 1273, probably in her early twenties, Tameko served at the Kamo Festival as an assistant lady-in-waiting, with junior fifth rank, lower grade. No evidence suggests that Tameko ever married, so she may have remained single throughout her career.

Historians disagree on whether Tameko began her court service in the early 1260s or in the very late 1270s. One argument for the latter date holds that she would have been placed in the service of an influential patron during the last years of her father, who was to die in 1279, to ensure her continued rise through the ranks of court offices. She was appointed in the household of the retired empress Ōmiya (1225–92), the consort of Emperor Go-Saga (1220–72; r. 1242–46) and the mother of two emperors, Go-Fukakusa (1243–1304; r. 1246–59) and Kameyama (1249–1305; r. 1259–74).

The rivalry between these royal siblings divided the imperial household into two rival lines in the late 1260s, when the dispute over the installment of the next crown prince intensified. Kameyama, whose lineage would come to be called the junior or Daikakuji line, succeeded in having a son appointed crown prince in 1268, eventually to become Emperor Go-Uda (1267–1324; r. 1274–1287). But Go-Fukakusa, of the senior or Jimyōji line, had to fight hard to have his son appointed at all in 1275. Go-Fukakusa's son, the future emperor Fushimi (1265–1317; r. 1287–98), was already ten, relatively advanced in age in an era of infant emperors and ruling retired emperors.

In the household of Crown Prince Fishimi, Tameko and Tamekane received appointment as poetry tutors, Tamekane in 1280 and Tameko either at the same time or within a year or two of her brother. This appointment irretrievably tied the fate of their Kyōgoku school of poetry to the political fortunes of the Jimyōji line in the imperial clan, an event of lasting significance in Tameko's life and in the history of classical Japanese poetry. Over the next thirty years, Tameko held high positions in various quarters of Fushimi's extended household. Early in 1284, for example, Tameko joined another woman in Fushimi's service, the diarist Nakatsukasa no Naishi (fl. ca. 1250–92), as attendants to Fushimi on a poetry-writing excursion. This memorable event, as recorded in Nakatsukasa's poetic journal, was commemorated in poetry exchanges between the two women, to be repeated on the anniversary of the excursion over the next several years.

Beginning some time in the last years of the 13th century, Tameko seems to have served in the women's quarters of Fushimi's residence, for she was appointed *menoto* (nurse-guardian) to Fushimi's second son, who would later become Emperor Hanazono (1297–1348; r. 1308–18). The *menoto* was an important role in the upper-class household in premodern Japan, since she inevitably developed the closest and most enduring relationship with her noble charge while overseeing his education and training in socialization. Tameko's selection for this position shows the deep personal faith and trust that Fushimi had for her. On the occasion of Hanazono's enthronement in 1308, Tameko was given the ceremonial role, appropriate to the *menoto,* of raising the throne curtains and a promotion to junior third rank.

Tameko also served Fushimi's empress Eifuku (1271–1342)—the adopted mother of Fushimi's eldest son, Emperor Go-Fushimi (1288–1336; r. 1298–1301), and an important literary patron in her own right. Hanazono's diary records that during the Enkyō era (i308–11) following his enthronement, Tameko was Eifuku's most trusted lady-in-waiting. This series of Tameko's public appointments and her personal standing in the Fushimi and Eifuku households show how crucial a role the imperial family played in her life. Tameko's final promotion came in 1314, to *Jūnii* (junior second rank), an unusually high rank for a poet to hold. By the name of this rank she has come to be known to later centuries, as Jūnii Tameko.

The date of Tameko's death is unknown, but she must have died sometime after the year 1315, when she participated in a group composition of poems on the *Lotus Sutra.* Since it would seem natural for her passing to be mentioned in the diary of Emperor Hanazono, with whom she had had such a close relationship, some historians have surmised that Tameko's life must have ended during the years 1317–19, a three-year period that Hanazono's diary in its extant form does not cover.

Career: Tameko became active as a poet just as serious divisions developed between several rival poetic schools and two lines in the imperial clan. Her literary career cannot be understood outside this context. As the competing factions allied themselves with one or the other of the rival lines, Tameko's literary fortunes were inextricably entangled in both rivalries, demonstrating the inseparability of politics and cultural production in premodern Japan.

The division into three different schools of poetry grew out of the legacy of Tameko's grandfather, Fujiwara Tameie. During his lifetime Tameie had willed to three of his sons by two different wives three separate estates, together with a number of very valuable poetic documents attributed to his own father, the enormously influential poet and critic Fujiwara no Teika (1162–1241). In this distribution of family property, Tameie violated the Japanese tradition of primogeniture by favoring not his eldest son, Tameuji, but his third son, Tamesuke, by a second wife, known to history as Abutsu-ni (Nun Abutsu, ca. 1222–83; the author of *Izayoi Nikki*). Upon Tameie's death in 1275, the family split into three branches, whose descendants each founded a poetry school of their own, named after the estates given to the three sons: the Nijō school of Tameuji (1222–86), the Reizei school of Tamesuke (1263–1328), and the Kyōgoku school of Tamenori, the father of Tameko and Tamekane. The Kyōgoku and Reizei schools quickly aligned against Tameuji's Nijō school, which attained prominence both through the traditional authority of his position as the eldest son and through conservative poetic practice and aesthetic stand.

What may be Tameko's first known poem dates back to the years just preceding the deepening of divisions among Tameie's heirs, for it is found in the

Shokukokinshū, an imperial anthology compiled between 1259 and 1265 by Tameie and others. The poem is only tentatively attributed to Tameko, for the authorship is noted as Ōmiya Gonchūnagon, or lady-in-waiting of the Ōmiya household, a title that Tameko could have held if she had indeed entered Empress Ōmiya's service in the 1260s. Tameko must have written the poem in her early teens, and inclusion of such a youthful work was an honor not unknown for poets of great talent in Japanese court literary history.

Tameko and her brother received a very important gift from their grandfather Tameie: the copies of the canonically definitive first three imperial anthologies, with marginal notes that Tameie had used in teaching his students. Tameko and Tamekane soon had ample opportunities to make good use of these copies, which held enormous importance in a court tradition that so honored the Teika-Tameie literary heritage.

Shortly after Tameie's death, perhaps around the year 1276, Tameko's name began to appear in public and private poetry meetings, signaling her entrance into the court poetry circles. Her acceptance into the highly competitive and increasingly factionalized literary realm is evident in an imperial anthology of 1278, *Shokushūishū,* which includes the first poems definitely attributable to Tameko. The bitterness of the struggles between the Nijō and Kyōgoku branches can be seen in a letter of protest that Tameko's father, Tamenori, sent to the Bureau of Poetry in the following year: he complained that his brother Nijo Tameuji had slighted his children while compiling the anthology, for Tameko had only three poems selected for inclusion, and Tamekane only two. Later that year Tamenori died, leaving Tameko and her brother on their own to fight for the survival of the Kyōgoku school.

In 1280 the fortunes of the three poetry schools became inextricably entangled with the rival imperial lines when Tamekane was taken into the service of the crown prince Fushimi as poetry tutor, with Tameko to join him, probably soon afterward. By the standard of the day, the siblings were quite young for this important role, since she was around age twenty-eight and he only twenty-six. During the 1280s, Tameko and Tamekane, together with Fushimi, headed a small group of poets that included a senior adviser and important patron, Saionji Sanekane (1249–1322), the important woman poet Chikako (Minamoto no Shinshi) (fl. 1287–1317), and Fushimi's young empress Eifuku (1271–1342), who quickly matured into one of the most important poets of the school. Tameko worked with this group to lay the groundwork for what would become in two decades a clearly defined, distinctive, and influential school of poetry.

The 1280s and 1290s were years of Tameko's maturation as a poet. Sometime during the Kōan period (1278–88) she compiled the first of her several known poetry collections, a hundred-poem sequence known as the *Kōan Hyakushū,* which is no longer extant. Some of her correspondence from this period with other writers has been preserved, however, including poetic exchanges both with Tameie's second wife, Abutsu, in 1279 and with an important diarist at Fushimi's court, Nakatsukasa no Naishi, during the mid-1280s. Tameko is one of the more important participants in the first poetry contest of the group of poets around Fushimi in 1285, the *Kōan Hachinen Shigatsu Utaawase*. These contests and poetry meetings had become increasingly important by the 12th century as occasions for developing and establishing poetic innovations and conventions. The 1285 contest and the subsequent poetry contests and meetings of Tameko and other members of the group, which continued from the mid-1280s into the mid-1290s, were important forums for the Kyōgoku poets to experiment with and refine new techniques and diction, ideas and an aesthetic borrowed from Chinese poetry, and new styles.

Sometime during the years 1285 to 1287 Tameko's brother Tamekane completed a very important aesthetic treatise, the *Tamekanekyō Wakashū* (Lord Tamekane's Notes on Poetry), which laid out many of the fundamental poetic and aesthetic ideals of the school. In this work Tamekane argued that poetry should be fundamentally an art of the heart or mind (*kokoro*), a venerable foundation that contrasted with the Nijō school preoccupation with another of the central concepts in Japanese poetics, *kotoba,* or diction. This emphasis provided a convincing argument for innovation in the writing of poetry based on the feeling or intuition of the true nature of a subject or topic, rather than the more conservative Nijō tendency to have recourse to precedent in the treatment of particular subjects. Tameko's role in the writing of this treatise may never be known to historians, but her poems from this period reflect its tenets most faithfully.

Tameko compiled a collection of sixty-three poems, the *Tō Dainagon Tenshi Kashū,* in 1294 as part of the efforts of the Kyōgoku school to begin gathering poems for an imperial anthology that Emperor Fushimi commissioned in the previous year. Fushimi had charged a group of four poets to compile the anthology, which included the young Tamekane, his father's principal Nijō rival, Tameuji, and two other poets. Ultimately a series of disagreements between Tamekane and Tameuji ensued, and the anthology was never completed; Tameko's collection is no longer extant.

Tameko and the other Kyōgoku poets had developed a consistent and clearly distinctive style of poetry by the very end of the 13th century. Literary historians have selected a poetry contest in 1297, the Einin Gonen (1297) Hachigatsu Jūgoya Utaawase, to mark the beginning of a fully developed new movement in Japanese court poetry. The irony of this meeting is that Tameko's brother Tamekane could not join Tameko, Fushimi, and the young Eifuku, even though he has been described by historians as the central poet of the school based on the importance of the aesthetic principles outlined in his *Notes on Poetry.* The series of arrests and exiles that was to mark Tamekane's tumultuous court career had begun the previous year, and Tamekane was living in enforced seclusion when the poetry meeting took place, only to be sent into exile the following year.

While Tameko's central importance in the formative years of the Kyōgoku school seems to have been balanced by the younger Tamekane's role as a male who could be influential in court politics, with her brother's exile Tameko must have become, with Fushimi, the leading poet in the school. With Fushimi's line in the imperial household in relative decline, the next five years among the group members were a period of increased attention focused on a number of important poetry meetings and contests. While we have little documentation from this period, we can surmise that Tameko, while in her late forties, certainly played a leading role in these meetings. The respect for Tameko's experience with the most important Kyōgoku styles and techniques that she developed over the years can be seen, for example, in a diary entry written by Tamekane in 1303, the year he returned from exile. In this entry, her younger brother expressed great faith in Tameko's poetic judgment and recorded that he consulted with her regarding difficult points in some poems sent by the head of the Reizei branch, Tamesuke. While it might be expected that Tamekane would need to discuss with his older sister certain fine points of judgment after having been out of touch for five years with the elite circles of court poetry, his diary entry also provides a rare bit of evidence for the high esteem in which Tameko was held by her brother and other influential poets of her day.

The general topic of the importance of women poets in the Kyōgoku school has been little studied by modern scholars, except for the important work by Iwasa on Tameko's younger contemporary, Eifuku. We do know that Tameko and other women presided as judges at some poetry contests, but other women poets in the Kyōgoku school also had great importance in the literature written and the judgments passed. One measure of the predominance of women poets at the central forum of poetry gatherings is simple numbers, as seen in the statistics compiled by Iwasa, who has shown that females outnumbered the male participants in nine of eleven known poetry contests during the period 1285–1310. One other interesting gender-based phenomenon seen in the poetry contests from this period is the choice of teams for competition along gender lines: we know of at least one contest from 1303 with Tameko, Eifuku, and Chikako on one side, opposed by Fushimi, Fushimi and Eifuku's young son Go-Fushimi (1288–1336; r. 1298–1301), and Tamekane on the other side. The importance of this alignment is that teams for these poetry contests were chosen with careful regard to a close balance of skill on each side, which suggests that the senior female poets Tameko and Chikako were considered the approximate equal in talent of Fushimi and Tamekane, while the younger Eifuku was pitted against the youthful Go-Fushimi. While it is apparent from these various types of evidence that women clearly held their own in the Kyōgoku school, Tameko's leadership role also must not be overlooked.

In 1303 Tamekane returned from his exile, and one of the most important Kyōgoku poetry contests was held to celebrate his homecoming, the Sentō Go-jūban Utaawase, in which Tameko, of course, participated. The years of the Kagen era (1303–6) after her brother's return found Tameko busy compiling two more collections of her own poetry, neither of which is now extant. One of these collections, the *Kagen Hyakushū,* was probably put together in response to a call for hundred-poem sequences to be submitted to Nijō Tameyo (1250–1388), Tameuji's son, who was compiling the *Shingosenshū,* an imperial anthology completed at the very end of 1303. This anthology, which included nine poems by Tameko, also was important as the first imperial anthology in which a number of the Kyōgoku poets had their first poems, including Chikako, Eifuku, Fushimi, and Go-Fushimi.

The years 1311–13 marked the greatest single achievement of the Kyōgoku school: the compilation of an imperial anthology selected with the Kyōgoku school aesthetic as its guiding principles. As father of the reigning emperor, his second son, Hanazono (1297–1348; r. 1308–18), Fushimi had the authority to commission the anthology, and he chose Tamekane as its compiler. The importance of Tameko's poetry in the school can be seen numerically in the number of her poems that were included in the anthology, sixty, which was third among living poets only to Fushimi (ninety-three) and the still-influential Sanekane (sixty-two); Eifuku had forty-nine poems, while Tamekane's low number of thirty-six probably reflected his political troubles at court.

Contemporary records indicate that Tameko assisted her younger brother in compiling the anthology, although she is given no formal credit for her work. Tameko's work on the imperial anthology, while we do not know many details of her contribution, was perhaps the first time that any woman had taken an important role in assembling and editing one of these canonically all-important anthologies in the history of Japanese court poetry. In this respect her influence extended outside the private realm of poetry composition and poetry schools to exert itself even in the masculine world of public life at the imperial court.

Tameko's contribution to the *Gyokuyōshū* was to be her last major work, for her last recorded act occurred only two years later in 1315, when she participated in a meeting where poems were written on the *Lotus Sutra,* a subject that perhaps boded well for her future fortunes. Her reputation succeeded her, of course, in both happy and unhappy ways. The next imperial anthology was compiled by the leading Nijō school poet Tameyo, who slighted Tameko and Tamekane by completely excluding them and them alone among the Kyōgoku poets from the anthology. Then in 1346 the second Kyōgoku school anthology was completed by Hanazono, Fushimi's second son, and Tameko had the fifth largest number of poems included among the Kyōgoku poets.

Documents from the first few decades of the 14th century indicate that the last years of Tameko's life were spent as a poet commanding the highest respect and authority in the world of court literature. In these remarks her influence is often compared with that of her brother, yet modern scholars of court poetry have (with the exception of Iwasa's work on Eifuku) consistently focused on Tamekane's writings to the exclusion of Tameko. This is despite Tameko's importance in the male-defined canonical tradition, where the number of her poems in the imperial anthologies is third only to that of Fushimi and Eifuku. More significantly her central role as a leader in the formation of the Kyōgoku school style and aesthetic in poetry contests and meetings remains an important subject for further study in the larger field of women's studies in Japanese literary history.

Major Works: Tameko's main contribution to Japanese court literature was through her poetry. Of particular importance for the modern canon of classical poetry were those poems included in the two imperial anthologies compiled by members of the Kyōgoku school, the *Gyokuyōshū,* in whose compilation we have seen she participated, and the *Fūgashū.* In addition to these poems, however, Tameko's contributions to the development of the Kyōgoku school through her participation in, and also judgments on, poetry contests and meetings are central to her legacy in Japanese cultural history. Unfortunately, Tameko has been little studied by modern scholars in Japan and elsewhere, so much of her extracanonical contribution remains unknown, particularly in the area of her central role in the crucial formative years of the Kyōgoku school. As a result, the following section concentrates on her poems in the imperial anthologies.

The Kyōgoku poets introduced a number of innovations into the writing of court *waka* poetry, and Tameko's poetry provides representative examples of the school's new style and techniques. The two most important subjects of court poetry as seen in the organization of the imperial anthologies were seasonal or nature poems and love poems. Tameko wrote nature poems both in a style reflecting the authority of the court tradition and also in the distinctive Kyōgoku style. One of Tameko's better-known nature poems is in a more conventional style:

> Even the rain's legs   Ame no ashi mo
> grow aslant   yokosama ni naru
> in evening winds   yūkaze ni
> a straw cape blown along,   mino fukaseyuku
> the wasteland traveler.   nobe no tabibito
>
> (*Gyokuyōshū,* 1202)

The conceit of the wind blowing the cape across the fields is among several intriguing aspects to this poem, which also contains the striking image of "the rain's legs." The latter metaphor, as Brower and Miner have indicated, was a fresh image in the Japanese court tradition, even though it was a tired trope in Chinese poetry. Sung (960–1279) Chinese poetry was a common source for the Kyōgoku poets and provided many new ideas and vocabulary for them in their struggles over innovation with the Nijō school poets.

The conventionality of the previous example can be seen in comparison with Tameko's more distinctive Kyōgoku-style nature poems, which remove such explicit referents to the human subject as seen in the previous poem in the mention of the traveler. In the following poem on winter, Tameko eliminates all mention of the subjective human significance held by the natural imagery:

After the wind,	Kaze no nochi ni
hail in a brief burst	Arare hitoshikiri
falls and passes, and	Furisugite
again from clustering clouds	Mata mura kumo ni
the moon spills out.	Tsukizo morikuru

(*Gyokuyōshū,* 1005)

While Western readers might find this to be a simple, imagistic poem, the interpretive conventions learned by classical Japanese readers of court poetry demanded that a poem somehow indicate the subjective significance of objective referents. The Kyōgoku innovation was to eliminate even implicit suggestions of a subjective presence, whether of the narrator or individuals mentioned in the poem. This new development in nature poetry at the court effectively diffused the subjective presence of the narrator and poet throughout the natural scene described in the poem. The enigmatic meaning of these poems resulting from this innovation has challenged interpreters of Kyōgoku nature poetry since Tameko and other early Kyōgoku poets began composing them.

The extra syllables in the first two lines of the previous poem are examples of another important new poetic technique often used by the Kyōgoku school poets. The *waka* poetic form that dominated Japanese court poetry from the 9th through the 14th centuries traditionally employed a syllable count of 5-7-5-7-7, often depicted in English translation (as here) by line breaks at the end of each unit. Although *waka* can be found from earlier periods that varied by one or two syllables from the traditional count, one of the distinguishing characteristics of the Kyōgoku school poets was their frequent use of such variations. As Robert Huey has pointed out, Tameko used them in the lines describing the wind and hail to represent the intensity and unsettling rhythms of the passing storm.

The second major subject of the Japanese court tradition was love. One of Tameko's poems on this subject is considered representative of the love poetry in the first Kyōgoku anthology, the *Gyokuyōshū* (1527):

While longing,	Mono omoeba
among my wandering brush's	hakanaki fude no
diversions,	susabi ni mo
what echoed my heart	kokoro ni nitaru
was written.	koto zo kakaruru

In this poem, the narrator has discovered to her surprise that she has written the feelings of longing for her lover while playfully writing out whatever came to mind at her desk. This poem, as does much of Kyōgoku love poetry, contains penetrating observation on the ways particular everyday experiences subtly reveal the deepest feelings of affairs of the heart.

The course of love affairs in the court tradition was conventionally prescribed in great detail, and this path was followed in the arrangement of love poems in the five books on love in the imperial anthologies. The previous poem, which is taken from the third of five books on love in this anthology, would have been read as a signal that the affair was turning from its early stages of the woman's first rebuffing and then giving in to the man's ardent advances, to the longing of the latter phases of an affair, in which the woman languishes in sorrow as the man's attention wanes and then wanders to other objects of affection.

Tameko also wrote love poems about the fears of women trapped in this conventionalized course of an affair, which in the end inevitably took away much of the strength women held in the early phases of love affairs. Such a poem is found, like the last poem, in the third book of love poems in another Kyōgoku imperial anthology:

> Exhausted with longing,   Omoitsukusu
> soul, don't go   kokoro yo yukite
> to appear in his dreams: yume ni miyu na
> For with only that he   so o dani hito no
> may even come to hate me.   itoi mo zo suru
>
> (*Fūgashū*, 1178)

While knowing that the love affair is doomed conventionally to end in her own sorrow and despair, the female narrator of this poem still longs so fervently for her all-too-often absent lover that she knows her spirit may wander off and visit him. Such dream visitations were a common theme in Japanese court literature, often as a happier sign of missing a loved one during the earlier phases of the relationship. As the male's affection declines and the affair begins to degenerate into bitterness and resentment, however, she feels that even though she longs so deeply for her lover, she must not insist on receiving attention from him for fear of alienating him. In this poem, she wishes to tread so lightly that she feels she must avoid even the subtle influences on her lover of a dream visit. We can see how the conventionally defined course of a love affair forced poets at this point in a relationship to write as if their deepest longings and sorrows could lead only to alienation from, and even hatred by, males, without mentioning the internalized oppression and self-negation that this entailed for women. In this poem we can sense an awareness of the strains caused by the demands of the court tradition on women's esteem and self-image, as well as a self-consciousness of the direct opposition between a woman's innermost self, her spirit or heart, and the male's conventionally defined response to that self.

At least two types of stronger responses by Tameko to the male-defined course of love in court poetry can be found in her other love poems. The first questions the male's duplicity and insincerity in continually reassuring the female that he will visit, as convention dictated, when in fact he does not come to see her:

"Since something has come up,	Sawari areba
Next time definitely. . . . "	ato kanarazu no
is your consolation:	nagusame yo
How many times hearing this?	iku tabi kikite
How many nights waiting?	iku yo matsuran

(Fūgashū, 1059)

This poem is taken from the second book of love poetry and represents an earlier stage in the affair when the woman first realizes that her lover is no longer as interested in her as he has seemed. The intensity of her anger at his betrayal of their relationship and at her powerlessness to change the situation can be heard in the insistent questioning of the man with which Tameko ended the poem. The repetition of the words *how many* in these questions together with the parallel structure of the questions would have struck contemporary readers with substantially more force than modern readers, since both were new rhetorical devices introduced by the Kyōgoku poets that differ from classical techniques. The Kyōgoku school poets argued long and hard with the Nijō poets for the poetic qualities of repeated words and phrases and borrowed the parallel structure Tameko used here from Chinese poetry, where such constructions were common. In this poem the two devices are skillfully used to challenge male-defined conventions of love affairs and also to insistently assert in a new way the power of women at this stage in these relationships.

Tameko developed another response in her love poems to the man's fading affections at the end of a relationship, as in the following poem from near the end of the fourth of the five books of love poetry:

My heart,	Waga kokoro
if you turn to resentment,	urami ni mukite
then resent him completely,	uramihate yo
for if you grow sorrowful,	aware ni nareba
I cannot bear it.	shinobigataki o

(Fūgashū, 1297)

This love poem uses no images whatsoever in another Kyōgoku school innovation. The woman narrator argues that the resentment that inevitably arises in response to the male's unfaithfulness in these late stages of an affair is a more appropriate response than the conventional sorrow. Resentment or bitterness and sorrow were both quite conventional responses for women at this point in an affair. However, Tameko's explicit statement that resentment is better than unbearable sorrow shows her unwillingness to see women as deserted victims of the men's betrayal, which inevitably came in conventionally defined love affairs.

The same tendency to affirm sentiments resisting conventional, male-defined societal norms can be seen in Tameko's other poetry. One such poem reads:

> Even my heart   Kokoro da ni
> will not go along   waga omou ni mo
> as I wish: kanawanu ni
> there is no sense   hito o uramin
> in resenting him.   kotowari zo naki
>
> (*Fūgashū*, 1882)

Here the narrator struggles with the same feelings we have seen in Tameko's other love poetry, but defined in terms of two conflicting impulses: on one hand, conventional, masculine reason tells her that she should not resent her lover; on the other hand, in her own heart she feels this resentment. In openly expressing this contradiction, Tameko questions the masculine "sense" that defines her world, and she affirms a different way of thinking and feeling that accords more closely with her own impulses.

The placement of this last poem in the "Miscellaneous" category in the imperial anthology, not in the love sections where we might have expected to find it, indicates one of the most important areas of Kyōgoku school innovation, an area of particular importance for understanding Tameko's contribution to the school and to Japanese literary history. When Tameko's younger brother Tamekane compiled the first Kyōgoku school anthology, the *Gyokuyōshū*, he modified the traditional format of the anthology by increasing the number of "Miscellaneous" books. While this may seem to be an insignificant modification, one of the reasons for this increase would have been to increase the number of poems in the anthology by contemporary and ancient poets who had been innovative in their writing and whose poems would not have easily fitted under the traditionally defined topics of the canonically definitive imperial anthologies. The Kyōgoku school poets were interested in supporting their own innovations in the writing of poetry in their struggles with the Nijō school-defined orthodoxy, not only by including a large number of their own poems but also by compiling a large number of innovative poems by poets already fully accepted into the orthodox canon. Many of these poems could easily be included in the "Miscellaneous" section, and this was probably one reason for increasing the number of books of this section in the *Gyokuyōshū* and also in the *Fūgashū*.

This modification has particular significance for understanding Tameko's poetry, since a very high proportion of her poems in both of the Kyōgoku school imperial anthologies is found in the books of "Miscellaneous" poems when compared with other major poets of the school. At the most fundamental level the new developments found in the writings of the Kyōgoku school poets generally, and Tameko in particular, led in directions that did not fit easily into the categories of writing and of experience defined by the orthodox tradition and that formed the framework for the imperial anthologies. We would expect, then, that the poets who took the new directions of Kyōgoku school poetry the farthest wrote poems that fell outside those categories, and when they were included in the imperial anthologies, the compilers had no choice but to include them in such categories as "Miscellaneous." This clearly seems to have been the case with Tameko, as is apparent from another example of her new vision of the world, found again in a poem from the "Miscellaneous" section:

This human world is	Hito no yo wa
interminable, they say,	hisashi to iu mo
yet once,	hitotoki no
in a dream,	yume no uchi nite
it was not so long at all.	sa mo hodo mo naki

(*Fūgashū,* 1975)

The human world would indeed be interminable in duration if it was defined by the sorrow we can see was imposed on women in their affairs of the heart, yet Tameko has a dream about how the world might be if it were defined in her own terms. In this dream, the world of human existence would not be defined in Buddhist terms as a realm of suffering or *samsara,* but in terms that would make the time pass much more pleasantly and quickly.

It is not clear in this poem whether Tameko is rejecting only the conventional course of love, as she did in her love poetry, or also the Buddhist conception of human existence that defined the entire worldview of the medieval Japanese. However, Tameko does seem to be relying in her writing on her own life experience and her own vision of the world in a way possible for few women in court society. While we can only speculate on how this was possible for her, the central role she played in defining the values and leading the activities of the Kyōgoku school of poetry in its formative decades can only have affirmed her experiences and vision as having value and requiring expression and enactment. Modern scholarship could only benefit from further study of Tameko in order to explore in more depth her contribution to Japanese poetry and society.

BIBLIOGRAPHY

Translations and Critical Works

Brower, Robert H., and Earl Miner. *Japanese Court Poetry.* Stanford, CA: Stanford University Press, 1961.

Carter, Steven D. *Waiting for the Wind: Thirty-Six Poets of Japan's Late-Medieval Age.* New York: Columbia University Press, 1989, 110–19.

Huey, Robert N. *Kyōgoku Tamekane: Poetry and Politics in Late Kamakura Japan.* Stanford, CA: Stanford University Press, 1989.

Iwasa, Miyoko. *Kyōgokuha kajin no kenkyū.* Tokyo: Kasama Shoin, 1974.

Koya, Yōko. "Junii Tameko Nenshokō." *Rikkyō Daigaku Nihon Bungaku* (June 1967).

Kyōgoku, Tamekane. "Lord Tamekane's Notes on Poetry: *Tamekanekyō Wakashō.*" Trans. and intro. Robert N. Huey and Susan Matisoff. *Monumenta Nipponica* 40.2 (Summer 1985).

Joseph D. PARKER

K

KANAI Mieko (1947–), novelist, poet, essayist.

Life: Kanai Mieko was born in Takasaki, Gumma prefecture, November 3, 1947. After graduating from Gumma Prefectural Takasaki High School for Girls in 1966, the precocious Mieko wrote poems and stories instead of continuing on to higher education. About a year later her story "Ai no seikatsu" (Love Life) was designated as the runner-up for the Dazai Osamu Prize. Even though she missed the prize itself, her story was published in *Tembō,* a prestigious literary magazine. In the same year, she was also awarded a prize by *The Pocketbook of Modern Poetry.* In 1979, a collection of her stories, *Puratonteki Ren'ai* (Platonic Love), won the Izumi Kyōka Prize. She now lives in Tokyo.

Information about Kanai Mieko's personal background is hard to find as she explicitly intends to keep her work separate from her life.

Career: By 1988, Kanai Mieko had published more than fifty short stories, four novels, and numerous poems and essays. As soon as she began writing fiction, she quickly became obsessed by the psychic problem of the "other being who does not exist." More specifically, her self-consciousness, desperately attempting to verify her own existence, creates another person who reflects her own image. The relationship between the narrator-author and the other person may be that of the lovers in her story "Oenta" (a Greek phrase meaning "things that are," 1968). Most of the time, however, the "other being" is a mysterious, imaginary writer who sometimes claims that he or she actually wrote what the narrator-author supposed herself to have written, as in "Kyōsōsha" (The Rivals, 1976), and *Platonic Love.* This "other being" exists only in the author's psyche or consciousness, and it disappears at the end. Consequently, the narrator-author never verifies her existence. Also, since the other person writes what the author is writing, when this "other being" is gone, the author suffers a loss of language and is unable to continue writing.

In *Ren'ai <shōsetsu ni tsuite>* (On Love Stories, 1983), the male narrator says to his dead brother's girlfriend: "Funny thing is, I always wanted to talk to you about myself. Everybody has that kind of desire, I know, but nobody seems to know what exactly this desire is about." Jean-Paul Sartre clarifies this question. In *Sartre: His Philosophy and Existential Psychoanalysis* (New York: Delacorte Press, 1969), Alfred Stern argues that "our self-consciousness exists only because it exists for another person. Thus self-consciousness is basically 'acknowledgment' by another person; and our being-for-others is a necessary condition for the development of our self-consciousness" (116). In the case of Kanai Mieko, such acknowledgment is ultimately unattainable since the character she creates exists only in her mind. The character disappears the moment the author realizes that it was only the product of her imagination. There is a character named "P" in "Things That Are." It also appears in "Kimyōna hanayome" (The Strange Bride, 1970) and "Moeru yubi" (The Burning Finger, 1970). Although it is not quite clear why this "being who does not exist" is called "P," it is possible that "P" stands for "psychic existence."

To treat this major literary thesis in her fiction, Kanai Mieko resorts to the narrative technique of stream of consciousness. In *Stream of Consciousness in the Modern Novel* (Berkeley: University of California Press, 1954, 4), Robert Humphrey defines this technique:

Let us think of consciousness as being in the form of an iceberg—the whole iceberg and not just the relatively small surface portion. Stream-of-consciousness fiction is . . . greatly concerned with what lies below the surface.

With such a concept . . . we may define stream-of-consciousness fiction as a type of fiction in which the basic emphasis is placed on exploration of the prespeech levels of consciousness for the purpose, primarily, of revealing the psychic being of the characters.

"The prespeech levels of consciousness" indicate the stages of self-consciousness that defy intellectual analysis; the speech levels of consciousness are usually found in works that reveal psychological process in which a single point of view is maintained so that the entire novel is presented through the intellectual analysis by a single character (Humphrey, 4).

In Kanai's fiction, there is no established viewpoint: it can suddenly shift from the first person to the omniscient. Another conspicuous feature of her fiction is its lack of plot and disunity of action. This results in general elusiveness, which baffles the reader. But, again, this is precisely a characteristic of stream-of-consciousness fiction, the writer of which "is not usually concerned with plot of action in the ordinary sense; he is concerned with psychic process and not physical actions" (Humphrey, 86). Kanai Mieko's style clearly signifies her interest in the stream-of-consciousness technique. It has a kind of fluidity that is seemingly endless and uncontrolled. Paragraphs are often two or three pages long. She makes use of one particular linguistic characteristic in order to create her highly idiosyncratic style. In the Japanese language, the predicate verb always comes at the end of the sentence, and, therefore, the reader would not know whether the sentence is affirmative or negative until the very end of the sentence. This grammatical characteristic is especially conducive to developing the kind of rambling, undirected style that Kanai employs to relate the interior monologue of her psychic life.

Even though there are no patterns or forms in Kanai's fiction that are usually found in realistic novels, she resorts to some other elements to give a sense of unity to her stories. Probably the most important is the use of images. Images are almost always used as symbols. A symbol is an image that carries some hidden meaning, but not a huge expanse of meaning as a metaphor is able to express—a symbol is a truncated metaphor. The image of the sea is recurrent in Kanai's fiction, for example, especially in her earlier works such as "Shizen no ko" (The Child of Nature, 1968), "Yume no jikan" (Dream Time, 1970), and "The Strange Bride" (1970). This image is most significantly associated with death, more specifically with death by drowning. In "The Child of Nature," dead bodies washed ashore at the start of the story provide a sustaining image throughout the work. The metaphor here, as well as elsewhere, seems to be the lure and danger of the sea: nature represented by the sea and death in nature. The heroine of "The Strange Bride" strives constantly to reach the sea that she believes killed her husband.

Kanai Mieko makes use of various psychic landscapes to organize her stories: for example, her surrealistic daydreams totally ignore the myth of verisimilitude in the realistic novel. After all, insanity makes all kinds of improbable actions possible. Some of Kanai's leitmotifs are quintessential for her literature: she is obsessed by sex and other physiological phenomena like vomiting, sweating, bleeding, and especially menstrual discharge. Often these leimotifs are combined with sadomasochism and present quite grotesque scenes as in "Usagi" (Rabbits, 1972). These obsessions exemplify her sensuousness and play an important role in her stream of consciousness.

A narrative device known as cinematic montage allows Kanai to go beyond the usual limitations of time and space and over the boundary of the narrative viewpoint. Virginia Woolf, James Joyce, and other stream-of-consciousness novelists in the West extensively utilized this device in their writing. There are two types of montage devices. In time-montage, the flow of one's consciousness does not conform to the natural flow of rigid time progression so that the narrative can shift back and forth in time, mixing the past, present, and future; and images or ideas from one time are superimposed on those of another. In space-montage, one's consciousness, while staying at one time, may move around several spatial elements (Humphrey, 49–56).

In addition to these two montage types, Kanai Mieko uses transport vehicles to create fluid settings. In "Shizumu machi" (The Sinking Town, 1981) and in "The Rivals," for example, the narrator meets the mysterious person (the other being-for-herself) in a train. An automobile is a setting in "Dream Time" and "The Strange Bride." In the latter, a boat provides a scene of secondary importance. All these vehicles are spatial, rather than temporal, elements; but due to the nature of their linear locomotion from one point to another, they provide a fluid progression that resembles the flowing nature of time. This ingenious device adds a nonstatic and nonfocused quality to her narrative and, thus, enables her to present the extremely fluid state of her psyche.

Kanai Mieko's major technique in her poetry is also the cinematic montage of images. Her images, however, are not photographic but hazy and distorted, and in that sense, Kanai is not an imagist but a symbolist. Rene Taupin explains in *The Influence of French Symbolism on Modern American Poetry* (tr. William and Anne Pratt, New York: AMS Press, 1985) that the difference between the two is "only of precision. The symbolists tried to leave the image vague; they associated partial and multiple images in such a way as to render the emotion together with its overtones. The Imagists tried to make the image precise— sometimes to excess—and, through a total, unique image, to give the whole force of the emotion" (93). Kanai's poems are usually a succession of three- or five-line images. A poem usually runs two or three pages, sometimes more. She resorts to all sorts of parodies from popular culture such as pop songs and jingles in order to create images. These images therefore have metaphorical meanings. Seemingly nothing but meaningless hodgepodge, they are linked together to bring about rather shocking emotions.

Cinema director Sergei Eisenstein, who first formulated the theory of montage, emphasizes the importance of "collision" in montage in his *Film Form,* (tr. J. Leyda, New York: Harcourt, Brace and World, 1949): "Montage is conflict . . . the basis of every art is conflict (an 'imagist' transformation of the dialectical principle)"(38). To illustrate, Eisenstein makes an interesting observation of Japanese haiku (classical verse form of three lines containing seventeen syllables) and *tanka* (classical verse form of five lines containing thirty-one syllables) (31–32). A haiku poem is, to him, like a shot with a single impression; a *tanka* is more like montage phrases—shot lists. If this theory is applied to Kanai's poems, even though their forms and subject matters are far removed from those of haiku and *tanka,* the possibility is that her pieces are composed of many haikulike shots threaded together with the montage device.

One conspicuous feature about Kanai Mieko's poems is her use of language. She intentionally combines different levels of language in one sentence and, thereby, creates a sense of conflict, an important quality in montage. She starts out in an almost elegant, classical expression only to end up in a vulgar slang colloquialism. Kanai's poetic style is "free verse." It does not conform to any recognizable form from either the East or West. She sometimes writes "prose poems" in which there are several proselike paragraphs, except that each line is much shorter than in prose. She also experiments with Joyce-like punctuationless prose poems.

Major Works: Kanai Mieko shishū (The Collected Poems of Kanai Mieko, 1973). It contains sixteen poems, three short prose pieces, six essays, and five critical essays on Kanai Mieko by other poets. Due to the variety of its contents, it is impossible to treat this publication as a whole. The first two poems, chosen here for analysis, represent Kanai's literary tendencies: "Shinzō rambu" (The Dancing Heart) demonstrates her use of cinematic montage; "Hamputi ni katarikakeru kotoba ni tsuite no omoimegurashi" (Pondering How to Talk to Humpty Dumpty About Words) deals with her major theme of the "other being representing herself."

"The Dancing Heart" has seventy lines, with no clear demarcation of stanzas. A kind of refrain containing the phrase "shinzō rambu," appearing four times, might be considered a means of spacing the entire piece into five parts. This poem is exactly like a sequence of camera shots; each is an image presented in a three- to five-line unit. Some examples are a river and a railway over it; the heroine walking on the railway track, a scorching sun over her; a train coming; the heroine, tied with a rope, left on the track; the heroine taking a bath in a tin tub; cactus flowers; sandstorm. Most of these images are repeated with slight variation. The poet gives an endnote that the title "Shinzō rambu" is from that of a legendary action-packed silent film [*Perils of Pauline?*] that she has never seen. The extensive use of cinematic device in this poem is just one example of how erudite Kanai is about film. "‹Sakuhin› o koete" (Beyond ‹Works›) in *Kotoba to ‹zure›* (Language and ‹Its Discrepancy›, 1978) is an impressive, scholarly essay in which Kanai deftly analyzes movies from classical silent films to recent avant-garde pieces both of the East and the West.

The second poem is about Humpty Dumpty, who is, of course, the egg in the nursery rhyme found in Lewis Carroll's *Through the Looking Glass.* In the poet's consciousness, Humpty Dumpty becomes a poet and her lover. In this forty-six-line piece, the poet relates to him on a sensuous level. First, it is the sensation in her stomach, and then the dreamlike pink buttocks that she associates with him. Since Humpty Dumpty controls the "words," with which the author writes poetry, she desires some kind of relationship with him. The unstable state of Humpty Dumpty makes her mind unstable. In short, there is no Humpty Dumpty who provides the "words" for her to write poetry; it is only her own image reflected in the looking glass. At a glance, it is a highly enigmatic piece based on her psychic stream of consciousness; strangely concrete and sensuous expressions are combined in a unique and novel fashion. Kanai's main concern is, however, the theme of "the non-existing another being."

"Shizen no ko" (The Child of Nature, 1968), short story. This piece clearly establishes the image of the sea and of death by drowning. The setting is a summer resort where two young sisters and their governess are languidly passing the time. The girls skip around a dead body washed ashore, humming a rhythmic, impromptu ditty about death by drowning. Then, various ways of dying are superimposed over the original death image. For example, death by an accidental, delayed blast of a bomb dropped during wartime, children drowned in the sea at night who fly to the sky and turn into stars, a boy who falls in love with a girl dying of pneumonia only to commit suicide because he could not finish his summer homework, and, finally, a man in black appearing on the stage with the two sisters watching in expectation of his imminent suicide. This is probably the embryonic presentation of the concept of constantly watching the "other being," which Kanai develops fully in her later works. This also has something to do with one's own image reflected in the mirror, since the "other being" is inevitably none other than oneself. The sisters enjoy the distorted images of themselves on the surface of their spoons at breakfast. Eventually, the man in black throws himself into the sea, just as they had anticipated. They imagine that he crosses the sea to become part of the sea.

Strangely enough, in spite of all these death images, the work has a feeling of brightness. The author may be making an allusion to the Japanese creation myth in the *Kojiki* (The Record of Ancient Matters, 712) and *Nihon shoki* (Chronicles of Japan, 720). The name of the region where the sisters visited is *yomi* (lit. night see); but *yomi* is, of course, the land of the dead in the myth (with different characters), where death is only one of the states of being in the cycle of nature.

"Oenta" (Things That Are, 1968), short story. The story is set entirely in a psychic landscape; the stream-of-consciousness narration makes it extremely difficult to determine what actually happens in chronological order. It is divided into nineteen segments of various lengths; each can be considered as one cut in a film. The narrator A is a young woman, and the "other being," who probably does not exist, is called P. P is a writer, at least in A's consciousness, and A makes love to P in an attempt to relate her love to P's works. The sadomasochistic sex scene makes the reader physiologically uncomfortable with the description of the participants' bleeding and throwing up, immediately followed by a scene where A gets sick by eating spoiled fried fish. Kanai seems to emphasize the physiological aspects of life, especially the uncomfortable side, as a means of presenting the physical existence of her characters as she simultaneously tells of their inner lives.

Even though A sleeps with P, there is a strange sense of P's absence: A meets a group of people who insist that they killed P; finally she finds the figure of P sitting on a chair in the courtyard of an insane asylum. But ultimately P does not exist, and A realizes that the absence of P means the loss of language.

Yume no jikan (Dream Time, 1970), collection of three linked stories. The heroine is called Ai. Her name, presented in *katakana* (phonetic syllabary used for foreign words), could mean the English word *I* and/or the Japanese word for "love." All three stories deal with the same theme: the ultimate absence of the "other being" who is supposed to verify the heroine's existence.

In the title story, Ai tries to get to the beach in an automobile, and as it breaks down she falls asleep and dreams. It is not quite clear whether the rest of the story takes place in her dream or not. As she settles down at a place called "Mirror Hotel," she is unable to distinguish her own image from others in the mirror. She seems to be looking for a writer who stayed a long time ago in the same room, which turns out to be a part of the psychiatric ward of a hospital. There are images of death (a Japanese soldier killed in the war turns up as a white skeleton), of bleeding (a group of high school girls in menstrual cycle), of dismemberment (devoured by some huge animals), and of sex (a man and a hotel maid show how to make love to the heroine). Toward the end the heroine starts to live with the writer she has been looking for, but she knows that she has already had this experience. The implication is that she is going to lose him again as she did in the past.

Ai in "The Strange Bride" is completely enervated in a room filled with the smell of the decomposing corpse of a parrot who used to sing the line "everlasting love." She recalls sweet memories of a summer on the beach with her husband, P, who disappeared; a boat trip with him to an island; and a woman drowned in the sea. She refuses to eat so that she can die some day; but some mysterious organization sends nurses and a doctor to her. Ai wishes to determine her own fate and tries to escape from these people in order to get to the beach. She feels as if everybody watches her no matter where she goes. The image of the sea associated with death is the predominant factor in Ai's consciousness; without verification of her life by P, death is the only alternative.

The Burning Finger depicts an inexplicable situation in which Ai finds herself. Without her permission, she is placed in a huge house, a kind of dormitory for single girls in a town near the sea. Ai is disoriented, suffers from a loss of identity, dreams of a man-made city, of a railway track, and of her finger that starts to burn. The house, it turns out, is owned by a woman called Mrs. P, the wife of the P for whom Ai has been searching. She is told that P died recently. The dead P, however, shows up at the party, in a partially decomposed state and smelling terribly. Ever since Ai lost P, she has had no way of identifying herself. Feeling that her life is burned out, she dreams of committing suicide by throwing herself in front of an oncoming train. She discovers not only that P was married but that he is dead as well. Seeing his dead body disintegrating in front of her eyes, Ai finds the death of P an unmistakable fact.

Bunshō kyōshitsu (Writing Lessons, 1985), novel. Kanai Mieko continues to use the stream-of-consciousness style and the cinematic montage device to unify this full-length novel. The setting, however, is not a nightmarish psychic landscape any more. The heroine is a middle-aged woman named Ema living in the suburbs of Tokyo with her husband, Satō, and their daughter, Sakurako. The novel has a clearly traceable plot; it develops around Ema's awakening to her self-consciousness to tell of a somewhat complicated human relationship. Both the husband and wife are having extramarital affairs, and the daughter has a boyfriend who maintains an emotional relationship with an English girl in London. The main theme is the heroine's exploration of whether she should get a divorce in order to establish her own identity; in the end she decides against it. The young boy, Yoshino, sometimes called Y, with whom the heroine is supposed to have had an affair, is only superficially depicted. The writer who teaches the writing course Ema is taking at the municipal culture center is more clearly focused. He is probably an extension of the P whose existence Kanai pursued obsessively in her earlier works.

The novel also contains discussions on film, gossip about the Tokyo literati, and depictions of contemporary life-styles in Japan, including various fads. The author's frequent use of *katakana* words (borrowed words from Western languages) is a recent social trend.

Akarui heya no naka de (In the Bright Room, 1986), collection of short stories. Of the nine pieces in this publication, the longest is the title story. It resembles *Writing Lessons* in its theme and in its narrative technique. It concerns two families living next door to each other in a high-rise housing complex. The narrator-author's stream of consciousness freely moves from one topic of everyday life to another seemingly endlessly, with the narrative viewpoint shifting from one character to another. "Buta" (The Pig) and "Kazoku arubamu" (The Family Album) are enjoyable as traditional short stories, even though they unmistakably bear the Kanai's brand. "The Pig" is about a family who kills and eats the pig they have kept as a pet. In "The Family Album," the members of a family die one after another of some kind of food poisoning. "Shizukana hibi" (Quiet Life) depicts the everyday life of a family with a young boy. The other five pieces are fragmentary sketches of contemporary life in a stream-of-consciousness narration.

Translated Works: "The House of Madam Juju" (Madamu Juju no ie, 1971) and "In the Town with Cat-Shaped Maze" (original title unknown), poems. Both are composed of sensuous psychic images; in the former, the reader finds himself or herself in what can be metaphorically interpreted as the inside of Madam Juju's womb with a smell of semen. (The word *subways,* added by the translator, spoils the metaphor.) "Strawberry," a central image, stands for the menstrual bleeding of the girls who are loved by Madam Juju. (Another example of this symbol representing blood is found in the short story "Rabbits," to be discussed later.) The "whipping" probably symbolizes a sexual act, as a "shaft" of love does a phallus.

The sexual image in the second poem is the animal's male reproductive gland, which is a park located at the base of the cat's tail in this cat-shaped town. This image is overlapped with that of the moon. A girl waits for him. Some nights when he does not show up, she breaks a china cat out of frustration. The sensuousness created by the images pointing to the inside of the cat's body is blended with a sense of real life conjured up by such objects as amphitheater, park, restaurant, and harbor. Also bears wearing trousers and a hyena are the inhabitants of this nocturnal cityscape.

"Rabbits" (Usagi, 1972), short story. This is a well-told story, with a carefully calculated plot and a smashingly ironic ending. The narrator meets a crazed woman wearing a rabbit-fur costume who tells of how she ended up in it. This is a prime example of Kanai's obsession with blood. The custom of killing and eating their pet rabbits develops an affinity between the girl and her father, more specifically an affinity surrounding the bloody ritual of killing an unresisting animal. On the morning when this ritual will be performed, the daughter tries to communicate her excitement to her father. She recalls:

"The color . . . would be crucial to the analogy. We would have to eat something red. There were radishes and strawberries in the refrigerator and I used those to decorate the table. I was delighted since I knew my father would immediately understand what the radishes and strawberries stood for" (tr. Birnbaum).

Here clearly these two objects stand for "blood," as "strawberry" does in "The House of Madam Juju." As the father becomes bedridden because of obesity, the daughter kills and cooks the rabbit; she soon finds herself completely naked, killing several animals in order to obtain enough blood to bathe in. Gradually she herself becomes a rabbit and wishes to be killed and eaten by her father. On his birthday, she puts the rabbit blood all over her naked body and slips into a rabbit costume made from the fur of the butchered animals. Ironically, however, her father drops dead in terror, mistaking her for the ghost of the slaughtered rabbits.

The father's role here is that of the "other being," like the character P in Kanai's earlier works, whose function is to acknowledge the daughter's existence but who typically vanishes at the end. This same theme is repeated at the end of the story. The narrator, who has been listening to the rabbit woman's experience, now tries to relive that experience herself before the rabbit woman dies of a severe wound. The fact that the character P in many of Kanai's stories is always a writer who provides words to the author gives rise to an interesting question. The next piece deals with just that issue.

"Platonic Love" (Puratonteki ren'ai, 1979) short story. The narrator, a writer, receives a letter every time she writes a story, from someone who claims, "The piece published under your name is actually written by me." Once Kanai wrote a similar story, "The Rivals," in which the heroine, also a writer, meets a man on the train who has a notebook filled with exactly the same stories she wrote. Obviously, however, this man is conjured up by the writer heroine. By the same token, the author of the letters in "Platonic Love" is another Kanaiesque character.

In "Platonic Love," Kanai's fictive character writes a story, "Platonic Love," for the narrator. The narrator muses on this question: "I would remember to try and listen for the voice calling me to start the story I had been as yet unable to write . . . I would think that the absent 'he' or 'she' who had withdrawn from the protagonist was really the unwritten story itself" (tr. Heinrich).

When a character in a story starts to assert that he or she is its author, then who is the actual author? The actual author projects her consciousness entirely in the character, and, therefore, the character is an existence very close to the author. This exists only in fiction or in the author's psyche, not in the real world. In the stream-of-consciousness novel where the demarcation between the author's inner life and the outer world is blurred, this is an interesting but maddening question.

BIBLIOGRAPHY

Translations

"The House of Madam Juju." Tr. Christopher Drake. In *Contemporary Japanese Literature,* ed. Howard Hibbett. New York: Knopf, 1977.
"In the Town with Cat-Shaped Maze." In *The Burning Heart: Women Poets of Japan,* tr. and ed. Kenneth Rexroth and Ikuko Atsumi. New York: Seabury, 1977.
"Platonic Love," tr. Amy Vladeck Heinrich. In *The Showa Anthology: Modern Japanese Short Stories, Vol. 2,* ed. Van C. Gessel and Tomone Matsumoto. Tokyo: Kodansha International, 1985.
"Rabbits." In *Rabbits, Crabs, Etc.,* tr. Phillis Birnbaum. Honolulu: University of Hawaii Press, 1982.

Sanroku YOSHIDA

KŌDA Aya (1904–90), novelist, essayist, short story writer.

Life: Kōda Aya was born in Mukōjima, Tokyo, on September 1, 1904, the second daughter of the renowned man of letters Kōda Rohan (1867–1947). Her mother, Kimiko (1873–1910), died shortly after Kōda entered grammar school, and several years later, Rohan remarried.

The adults with whom Kōda subsequently had contact were an extraordinary group. Her two aunts were among the first Japanese to study Western music in Europe and, as well-respected performers and teachers, played a major role in introducing classical music to Japan. Among Rohan's other siblings, one became a famous military figure, and another became an authority on international commerce and economic history. Kodama Yayoko, Kōda's stepmother, devoted herself to the Christian faith, poetry, and intellectual pursuits.

Kōda's own life, in contrast, could easily be described in terms often used to discuss conventionally valued qualities of womanhood—the filial daughter, the patient, self-sacrificing wife, and the devoted mother. As a girl, she attended a middle school run by Christian missionaries called Kōjimachi Jogakuin. Because her stepmother was sickly and preoccupied with her own pursuits, Kōda did most of the cooking and housework. Significantly, Rohan took responsibility for training her in household chores. His approach was strict and meticulous and influenced by his own Confucian background. Specifically, he believed that one must "investigate and perfect one's knowledge" of all things (*kakubutsu chichi,* a Chinese concept found in the *Great Learning,* or *Daxue*). Rohan's insistence that Kōda not only perform her duties with the utmost precision but also become completely familiar with the properties and potential of the water she scrubbed with and the dust she wiped away gave her strength and, more important, a firm sense of pride and identity. Even so, she often resented the burden of housework, as well as her cold, remote stepmother. Her youth was darkened by several events: her older sister died in 1912, and her parents fought. Moreover, Kōda's younger brother, Ichirō, often got into trouble and was eventually expelled from school. Kōda, though, doted on him and always was his ally in family arguments. Ichirō died of tuberculosis in 1926.

In 1928, Kōda married the son of a wholesale liquor dealer, Sanbashi Iku-nosuke and, a year later, bore him their only child. When his attempts to participate in the family business failed, Kōda did more than half the work in starting and running a small liquor shop. Her husband's lack of resourcefulness, the family's resulting poverty, and a conflict of personalities all contributed to their divorce ten years later.

Meanwhile, Kōda's father continued to hold a unique position in the literary world. Though no longer one of the most celebrated novelists, as he had been in the 1890s, Rohan commanded respect as the author of many books and articles on a broad range of topics, from urban planning to classical Chinese literature. He became the first writer to receive the Order of Culture (*bunka kunshō*) from the Japanese government in 1937.

After her divorce, Kōda returned to Rohan's home with her daughter, Tama. There, she concentrated on raising Tama and caring for her now elderly and ailing father, who lived apart from his wife. The family lost its Tokyo home during the firebombing of 1945 and was still living outside Tokyo when Rohan died in July 1947.

Kōda herself began writing in April of that year, when she was asked to contribute a piece for a special issue about Rohan by the editor of a literary journal called *Geirin Kanpo*. It appeared after Rohan's death, so he never knew what talent his daughter possessed. Her readers, however, immediately recognized Kōda's abilities and pressed her for more. Initially, she wrote essays about Rohan and their family life but later found success with short stories as well. She edited several volumes of Rohan's correspondence and essays. Her own collected works were published in 1958. After more than two decades of active writing, Kōda devoted a great deal of effort to fund-raising and promoting the reconstruction of a three-story pagoda at Hōrin Temple in Nara. This act commemorated her father's best-known novella, *Gojū no tō* (The Five-Storied Pagoda, 1889; tr. Chieko Irie Mulhern, in *Pagoda, Skull and Samurai,* [Rutland, VT: Charles E. Tuttle, 1985]). In 1976, she was elected to the Teikoku Geijut-suin (Imperial Academy of Arts), of which her scholar-novelist father and pianist aunt Kōda Nobuko (1870–1964) had been members since its establishment in 1937. Kōda Aya died of heart failure on October 31, 1990, at the age of eighty-six.

Career: Kōda grew up in the shadow of a man whose life was devoted to writing, so she was well aware of its rewards and hardships. She did not feel drawn to this way of life; indeed, she disliked her father when he was writing, his back to the rest of the family. On Rohan's insistence, she read a wide variety of fiction in her youth, from the novels of Thomas Hardy to the Edo period romance *Shunshoku umegoyomi* (Spring Love—Plum Blossom Calendar, 1832–33, by Tamenaga Shunsui, 1790–1843), although she never professed a great love for reading either. Her relationship with Rohan, the great writer, had no literary basis, she says, only a very mundane one—she prepared meals, of which Rohan was the glad recipient.

The beginning of her literary career coincided not only with her father's death but also with the years immediately following World War II. Kōda insists that she became a writer out of mere financial necessity. Her new career doubtless had the double impetus of her own talent and the release of the literary world from censorship and the constraints of war.

Kōda's earliest works are autobiographical essays that concern her memories of Rohan's last days, such as "Zakki" (Random Notes, 1947) and "Sōso no ki" (Record of the Funeral, 1947). Subsequent writings deal with the author's own childhood and family: "Atomiyosowaka" (Household Work, 1948); "Misokkasu" (Good for Nothing, 1949); and "Kusa no hana" (Flowers in the Grass, 1951). In some shorter works, such as "Kunshō" (The Medal, 1949), the focus is on the contrasting fortunes of Rohan and his adult daughter. The story "Kansei" (An Evil Voice, 1949) examines her experience of being attacked and nearly raped by a man in her own home.

After a period of questioning her newfound career, Kōda stated her desire to discard the effortless "dealer in memories" role into which she had fallen. Critics cite the novel *Nagareru* (Flowing, 1955) as her first venture into fiction. The work concerns a declining geisha house in Tokyo and was both a critical and popular success. *Nagareru* does not, however, mark the beginning of a radical departure from Kōda's typically lyrical, autobiographically inspired early writings. In contrast to many of the up-and-coming writers of the day, Kōda did not have a postwar college education. Although highly psychological in nature, her works are not the conscious international style of many of her literary contemporaries, who possessed little memory of prewar Japan and who were influenced by contemporary trends in Western literature. *Nagareru* does indicate a willingness to experiment with longer narrative forms, to consider structural choices other than strictly chronological autobiography, and to write about more than her personal recollections. This functioned to broaden Kōda's audience a great deal: her works were on the best-seller list, and some were made into films and produced on stage.

Kōda's awareness of issues of narrative technique, characterization, and the imagination can be detected in short works from around this same period, such as the stunning "Kuroi suso" (Black Skirt, 1954). The author employs a third-person narrative stance and builds the narrative around a central image, a black funeral kimono, in her effort to depict the life of a woman who finds an identity outside the home. For this story, Kōda was awarded the Yomiuri Literary Prize. In the widely read novel *Otōto* (Little Brother, 1956), Kōda tells the story of a girl's love for her wayward, sickly brother. While clearly inspired by events in her own life, the novel captures the hearts of readers with its appealing characters.

Kōda excels at short stories and essays. She is at her best when, using her superb powers of observation, she spins a tale around a single, central image, as in "Hina" (Dolls for a Special Day, 1957) or "Fue" (The Flute, 1957). The influence of Rohan's philosophy becomes apparent in her many meditative essays.

After *Otōto*, Kōda wrote several more novels, including *Tō* (The Fight, 1965). It is an ambitious, though not entirely successful, attempt to depict a TB sanatorium from the various points of view of the patients and staff. In 1973, Kōda received the Joryū Bungakushō (Women's Literary Prize) for the novel.

Since the appearance of Kōda's collected works in 1958–59, many more of her short stories and essays have been published in journals. The most successful of these involve her views of old age, such as "Hitori gurashi" (Living Alone, 1962) and "Mono iwanu isshō no tomo" (A Friend for Life, 1966). In her later years, Kōda turned to cultural and natural subjects.

Major Works: Nagareru (Flowing, 1955), novel. The story centers on a geisha house in postwar Tokyo and the women who work there. It thus joins a long line of both premodern and modern prose narrative dealing with the demimonde. Kōda turns the genre on its head by neither looking at the gorgeous, beguiling performance aspect of this world (as did Edo writers) nor focusing on the hardships and exploitation of the profession. Instead, she has the house's maid, Rika, narrate this exploration of the aesthetics, personalities, and material realities of the quarters. Rika is no ordinary maid, but one with intelligence and wit enough to convey the rich atmosphere of life in the geisha house, replete with its smells, grime, and poverty. She may be an outsider (*shirōto*), but she describes the varied characters and behavior of the professional women (*kurōto*) with great insight.

For centuries, the geisha has had a powerful iconic grip on Japanese society. She is beauty incarnate, as the master of traditional dance and music and in her elaborate costume. She is romance and sexuality freed from the somber social bonds that marriage traditionally represents. In literature, the geisha has been viewed most often from the male point of view or, at least, in relation to men, rather than to other women and domestic society. Although geisha exist for the purpose of entertaining men, *Nagareru* does not offer even a glimpse of the actual performance, the male-female interaction. The narrative stance allows for an entirely different view—that of a closed society of working women, whose individual characters come forth only at the geisha house (their "office" and dressing room), not at the parties (*zashiki*) where they meet their customers. The owner (*shujin*) is a powerful but flawed woman. In this novel, it is a woman's world. Male customers are a mere appendage.

One of the chief thematic focuses in the novel lies in the dichotomy inherent in the geisha world, that is, the coexistence of a harsh, physical reality and art, or the traditional aesthetic sensibility. Kōda evokes this duality through patterns of imagery. Specifically, she depicts the sensual, material aspect by constant use of onomatopoeia and sound symbolism, which give the smells, sounds, and feeling of the quarters a stunning vividness. The aesthetic side reveals itself in fragments, as if to motion to its diminishing importance. Central are two scenes involving the older geisha in the house. Even in their most mundane actions, they cannot separate themselves from the stylized beauty that tradition dictates they embody. The barrage of physical sensations almost drowns out any shred of art, beauty, or tradition that is supposed to be an integral component of the geisha world. It is significant, furthermore, that Rika perceives this, for she has lost her family, and in her attempt to forget the sorrows of her own past, she turns to this detached world of beauty for release. At the end of the novel, in fact, she becomes the proprietress of the house.

Nagareru is a volume in Japan's cultural history and gives a fascinating view of the inside of the geisha world. Notable also is Kōda's beautiful, flowing style, little tainted by Western influence and an integral component of the work as a whole. Kōda actually worked as a live-in maid in a geisha house in Yanagibashi, so the work is based partly on her observations during that period.

Otōto (Little Brother, 1956), novel. Kōda focuses on a troubled family, especially the relationship between the oldest child, Gen, and her brother Hekirō. At age seventeen, Gen finds herself running the household single-handedly, with little help from her aloof stepmother and busy father, who will have little to do with family affairs. Keeping up with the chores as she attends school is not easy, but she is less concerned with this work than with her troubled brother. The novel is about a sister's unconditional love for her brother. Her friendship and loyalty survive despite all odds: Hekirō gets in trouble at school, is suspended, is questioned by the police, and falls in with a gang of rough boys. At home, his mother sides with his accusers, and his father simply neglects him. Only Gen perceives her brother's essential goodness and insecurity and realizes that many of his problems result from his adolescence. Kōda's portrayal of Gen's sincere desire to protect her brother and to show her feelings is convincing and touching.

Compared with *Nagareru*, *Otōto* strikes the readers as more accessible, in both theme and execution. The dynamic first part concerns Hekirō's descent into delinquency and Gen's fierce determination to save him. This section grows out of many incidents (mostly traumatic and negative), clashes between characters, descriptions of the crowded city, and a general atmosphere of darkness and oppressiveness.

In the second part, two years have passed and the family fortunes have changed considerably. Hekirō, a weak boy from birth, has been diagnosed as having tuberculosis. Only after this happens does the stepmother acknowledge his gentleness and youth and treat him with compassion. The psychology of the family and progress of the illness are described in detail. Ironically, this illness, which ends in Hekirō's death, functions as a release for him and salvation for the family. The relative lack of incident reflects this, as does the imagery. From the rainy, crowded city, the setting shifts to a hospital and Hekirō's airy, peaceful room.

Otōto is a remarkable portrayal of the problems of adolescence and families in conflict. The work is also interesting in its view of prewar Japanese society.

On the local level, Hekirō is ostracized at school. The rejection of his peers and school simply drives him deeper into delinquency. More alarming is the visit of the thought police to his neighborhood after reports of his antisocial behavior. The weak, insecure individual does not fare well in the hands of a society that demands uniformity. Also of interest is the portrait of Gen, who also functions as the narrator. She is the picture of a strong, self-reliant young woman.

Translated Works: "The Black Skirt" (Kuroi suso, 1954), short story. The author traces the life of an ordinary woman named Chiyo from adolescence to middle age. The reader sees her only at the many funerals she attends, but these, it turns out, are the focal point of her life and the source of her identity. The time spent at her parents' home or at a dull office job pales in comparison to funerals, where she can don her black kimono and be of service to others. Not only does she feel needed at funerals, but they are also her opportunity to meet and speak freely with other people. At a funeral she first encounters the out-spoken and handsome Kō. The story is about a woman's search for identity within a narrowly circumscribed society. It also explores the nature of hidden desire.

"A Fragment" (Kakera, 1948), essay. The narrator of this short work returns to the war-wrecked remains of her family's Tokyo home. Although she is ini-tially shocked by the desolation, she soon discovers that the "burnt ruins are a treasure chest" because they afford her the opportunity to remember her father and their life together. In particular, a broken piece of a sake cup spurs memories of her father's love of liquor.

"The Medal" (Kunshō, 1949), short story. This heavily autobiographical work centers on the unhappy marriage and desperate financial state of the nar-rator at the time when her father wins a great honor, the *bunka kunshō* (Order of Culture). The author employs the images of the father's Order of Culture medal and the apprentice's apron worn by the daughter in order to evoke the disparity between the fortunes of the two individuals. Metaphorically, this sug-gests the gap between the glorious ambitions of Japan in the late 1930s and the meager existence of many of the nation's citizens.

"Dolls for a Special Day" (Hina, 1955), short story. Kōda portrays the clash between youthful aspirations and the pragmatic demands of adulthood. As a young woman, the narrator purchased an expensive set of *hina* dolls for her daughter's first Girls' Day holiday. She soon comes to regret her extravagance, however. First, she has a glimpse of the misfortunes of another young family, and then her parents admonish her for failing to understand the aesthetics of incompletion in her planning of the celebration: "It's not so much that you overdid things, but that you didn't leave anything for us to do." The narrator explores the importance of incompletion, or asymmetry, in human relations and art and also provides a fascinating view of a woman's socialization.

"A Friend for Life" (Mono iwanu isshō no tomo, 1966), essay. In this dis-cursive essay about mirrors, Kōda presents her views on the changing sense of individuality in several generations of Japanese women. This is expressed in the placement of a woman's mirror in the home. Her mother "took the mirror and stand out of the closet only when she needed them. The moment she was done, she would put them away." In contrast, there "was great beauty in the boldness of those geisha who placed their mirrors in the most important room in the house. I felt a sense of pity and regret both for my mother and her mirror, so somber and inferior by comparison." Kōda also examines problems of aging.

BIBLIOGRAPHY

Translations

"The Black Skirt." Tr. Edward G. Seidensticker. *Japan Quarterly* 3. 2 (1956): 196–212.
"The Black Skirt." Tr. Edward G. Seidensticker. In *Modern Japanese Short Stories,* ed. Japan Quarterly Editorial Board. Tokyo: Japan Publications, 1961.
"Dolls for a Special Day"; "A Fragment"; "A Friend for Life"; "The Medal." Tr. Ann Sherif. In *A Dealer in Memories: The Works of Kōda Aya.* Diss., University of Michigan, 1990.

Critical Works

Mulhern, Chieko. *Koda Rohan.* Boston: G. K. Hall, 1977.
Sherif, Ann. *A Dealer in Memories: The Works of Kōda Aya.* Diss., University of Michigan, 1990.
Tansman, Alan. *With Her Apron Strings Tied: Trials of Remembrance and Creative Struggle in the Writings of Kōda Aya.* Diss., Yale University, 1989.

Ann SHERIF

KOMETANI Fumiko (1930–), novelist, essayist, critic. Real name: Fumiko (Foumiko) Kometani Greenfeld (Mrs. Josh Greenfeld); née Kometani Fumiko.

Life: A native of Osaka, Kometani graduated from the Faculty of National Literature, Osaka Women's University. Her main interest, however, was visual arts, which she successfully pursued while still in Japan: an oil painting won entry into the prestigious Nikakai Exhibition, and another work earned her the Kansai Women Artists' Award. In 1960 she was offered a scholarship to participate in an artists' workshop in Petersborough, New Hampshire. The summer in the New England artists' colony marked a decisive turning point in Kometani's life: first, she met the American writer Josh Greenfeld (b. 1927) and married him; second, the commitment to art demonstrated by other participants of the workshop inspired her and helped in sustaining her passion for creative expression for many years to come.

After three years in New York, Kometani and her husband moved to Japan, where they had their first child, Karl. Two years later, the family returned to New York and was soon joined by another son, Noah. The child rearing, particularly after her younger boy was diagnosed as mentally handicapped, left Kometani with no time for creative endeavor. She and her husband explored all possible medical and educational resources for the child. The couple's determination to find the best solution to his problem eventually led the family to

Los Angeles, where transporting him to a medical center for a series of tests and therapies became the parents' major activity. Motherhood nonetheless helped expand her interests by leading her to take a critical look at American society, particularly at the education it offered to minority and handicapped children. The care of the younger son also fomented in her a strong urge to find an outlet for self-expression.

Her husband, a literary critic, dramatist, and the author of works such as *A Child Called Noah* (1972); *Harry and Tonto* (1974); *A Place for Noah* (1978); *A Return of Mr. Hollywood* (1984); and *A Client Called Noah* (1986) stimulated Fumiko's literary interests and eventually led her to redirect her career from visual arts to writing. Josh Greenfeld himself has written books about their son Noah and his family, dealing with the problem of an interracial, intercultural marriage exacerbated by the tragedy of having an autistic child. Greenfeld's nonfiction books are very impressive for their direct and highly personal airing of these problems. Unlike a number of works of the family problem genre, his books do not seek solace in the spiritual sphere and are not written in an inspirational, self-help style. In her fiction, Fumiko would prove herself to be on the same wavelength as her husband.

While assimilating the American way of life, in the meantime, Kometani kept herself abreast of social changes in Japan by means of newspapers and magazines available to her. She became acutely concerned with mutual misunderstanding and friction between Japan and the United States. Having experienced prejudice directed at her as a Japanese wife of an American Jew, she was keenly aware of its devastating effects. Consequently, she decided to write about her American experiences in order to help the Japanese people overcome their biases against foreigners. She succeeded in having a lengthy article published in a prestigious Japanese magazine in 1970 and followed it with a series of articles on a variety of timely topics, providing Japanese readers with realistic and critical pictures of American life.

During this period Kometani also read novels, with particular interest in Henry Miller and Saul Bellow. Their works convinced her that writing fiction did not require strict adherence to a prescribed format. This discovery helped her overcome the fear of writing. She began to write short stories in Japanese around 1975. She made her literary debut in 1985 with two stories that turned her into an instant celebrity by winning prestigious literary awards.

Career: In her first essay, "Nihonjin-zuma no taikenshita jinshusabetsu" (A Japanese Wife's Experiences in Racial Prejudice, 1970), Kometani asserted: "I make an honest effort to point out what I find wrong about Japan and I do the same about the United States as well. There is a proverb, 'Do in Rome as the Romans do.' I have come to believe, however, that if I find the 'Romans' wrong, I must speak out against them. Such an act itself is my way of contributing to humanism" (*Asahi Journal* [December 27, 1970]: 118). With this determination, she began to write a series of essays on a variety of topics in major national publications. In her early writings, such as the one previously mentioned and

"Amerikajin no tsuma to natte" (As an American Writer's Wife, 1972), she introduced issues and trends in the United States. She also denounced the ignorance and conceit that manifest themselves in racial prejudices, being particularly critical of Japanese people's misconceptions about Jews.

Another subject of her essays was American celebrities with whom Kometani came to be personally acquainted. In "Nōman Meirā" (Norman Mailer, 1972), "Nōman Meirā no koto" (On Norman Mailer, 1976), and "Mirā-Meirā kaidan bōchōki" (A Dialogue Between Henry Miller and Norman Mailer, 1985), she reported her conversations with Mailer, which revealed his reserved yet sometimes explosive disposition. In the latter article, she compared the two writers, characterizing Mailer as a thoroughly mind-oriented prodigy and Miller as a visually oriented, sense-centered artist. Other prominent people whose artistic imagination enriched her mind include Art Carney, discussed in her essay "Karei na yoru no shuyaku-tachi" (Main Performers on a Splendid Evening, 1975), Zero Mostel in "Zero Mosteru no shi" (The Death of Zero Mostel, 1978), and Alan Schneider in "Ima wa naki Aran Shunaidā no koto" (In Memory of Alan Schneider, 1984).

Her political writings of recent years include "Shokku o uketa shushō hatsugen" (A Shocking Statement by the Prime Minister, 1986), in which she protests against Prime Minister Nakasone's discimination remarks about blacks and Hispanics; and "Soto kara mita abunai Nihon" (Japan Seen as Dangerous by Foreigners, 1986), a severe denouncement of two anti-Semitic books by Uno Masami (b. 1941). In addition, Kometani wrote open letters, "Chotto kiite kudasai" (Please Listen to Me for a Moment, 1986) and "Ojiue-sama ni" (To My Uncle, 1986), in which she defended her decision to cancel the publication of her novel *The Tumbleweed* in a Japanese journal that had previously printed an anti-Semitic essay. In 1988 Kometani wrote "Jidai e no okurimono" (A Gift to the Next Generation) in *Kokka Himitsu-hō: watashitachi wa kō kangaeru* (National Confidentiality Law: Our Reactions to It), edited by the Japan Pen Club. She has also been contributing weekly essays on a variety of topics to *Osaka Sankei* newspaper since June 1988.

Taking full advantage of a unique vantage point that has enabled her to experience a foreign culture as an insider and review her native country as an outsider, Kometani sought in these essays to contribute to an improved relationship among the peoples of the two countries. Her writings, invariably based on her personal experiences, are descriptive and episode-oriented. Her essays appeal to Japanese readers, who have long been accustomed to personal and experience-based anecdotal styles. In the fall of 1987, Kometani published the account of her much-belated "honeymoon" trip to the southwestern part of Japan in a travel journal, *Tabi*. Kometani translated the first two of her husband's Noah series into Japanese and published them in Japan in 1978 and 1979.

Around 1975, Kometani began to write fiction as well. It was not until a decade later, however, that she was able to publish her first story, "Enrai no kyaku'' (A Visitor from Afar, 1985), and its longer sequel, *Sugikoshi no matsuri* (Passover, 1985). Both were immediately successful: Kometani was lauded with the *Bungakkai* New Writer's Award for the former and with the double honor of the *Shinchō* New Writer's Award and the ultimate Akutagawa Award for the latter. They were followed by *Tamburu uiido* (The Tumbleweed, 1986); ''Giri no *mishabahha*'' (In-laws, 1986); and ''Umi no kanata no sora tooku'' (How Far Away Is the Sky Beyond the Sea, 1988).

Her publications in English include ''Pictures from Their Nightmare,'' a 1987 review of a book on the internment of Japanese Americans during World War II, and ''Silence Is Essential,'' a 1988 critique of *The Shooting Gallery* by Tsushima Yuko (b. 1947), both appearing in *The New York Times Book Review*.

Major Works: ''Enrai no kyaku'' (A Visitor from Afar, 1985), short story. Invariably based on her own life, Kometani's fiction belongs to the Japanese genre of the confessional ''I-novel,'' in which authors strive to explore their conflicts with dehumanizing forces of their world. Unlike the usual ''I-novel,'' the tenor of which tends to be serious and sometimes even oppressive, Kometani's stories are delightfully humorous, owing primarily to her skillful use of the Osaka dialect and highly imaginative metaphors. The humor creates tragicomedic pathos in her works despite the persistent theme of alienation and emancipation.

The protagonist of ''A Vistor from Afar,'' Michiko, is a Japanese woman in her late forties. Living in California with her American husband and two sons, she is seemingly well adjusted to the American way of life. Her freedom, however, is severely limited by her mentally handicapped younger son, who requires her constant care. Her frustration and exhaustion manifest themselves in the form of tension in her relationship with her husband, causing the couple to argue violently over trivial matters magnified by the culture gap. Their precarious relationship inevitably affects their older son, who withdraws into the security of his own room whenever his parents explode at each other.

The story opens with Michiko's busily preparing a dinner for her younger son, Ken, who is coming home for his first weekend visit from an institution for the mentally handicapped. Michiko's happy anticipation of the reunion, however, becomes clouded by an apprehension during the drive to pick up Ken, as her mixed emotions cause her to recall his violent behavior on the way to the institution three weeks before. Ironically, Ken behaves amazingly well throughout the weekend, but the parents remain tense and constantly argue with each other. To her husband's allegation that she has let sashimi, his favorite low-cholesterol food, spoil, Michiko bursts out:

Is this spoiled? You call this spoiled? Take a good look before you jump to a wrong conclusion. You haven't changed a bit since we got married. You remember what you did to me only a month after we were married. That time, it was roast beef. You got fuming mad at me because you thought it was well-done. How can I forget that? I was furious at you, too, but I couldn't even speak English very well then and I couldn't say anything to you even in Japanese because you didn't understand it. So the only thing I could do was to ask you, very calmly, to slice the roast and see for yourself. And how was it? Medium, just the way you liked it, right? I spent the whole night crying my eyes out. I couldn't believe I had married someone like you. And the next day, I wrote a note to you, saying over and over, "Please don't make any judgment on me until you *look* to be sure you're right." I had spent the whole night figuring out how to say just that much in English and I was crying the entire time I was writing that letter, too. That was all I could manage to say to you then. But you got mad at me for saying the same thing over and over, so we fought again, and you threw an ashtray at me. It scared me, and so I told you I was going back to Japan. . . . Then I pulled out my suitcases, packed, and asked you to get me a taxi.

The outrage, frustration, and sadness as well as the abject dependency stemming from cultural differences surface again later in the same evening. Giving Ken a haircut, Michiko tells him, "Good boy." Aggravated, her husband shouts at her, "Say, 'Be a good boy'! You skipped the 'Be' so you sound like you are praising him. You are confusing him!" Thus the first night of Ken's return passes with Michiko's again wishing to go back "home" to Japan. After the stormy weekend, the couple find themselves at peace with each other. Feeling both inadequate and empty as a mother, however, Michiko concludes that freedom is beyond her reach as long as she is the mother of a son who has become "a visitor from afar."

Modeled on Kometani and her family, the characters are vividly alive and convincing. The extensive psychological probing of the heroine, too, is highly realistic. The frustration and sadness of being "a visitor from afar" herself, as expressed in the section just quoted, effectively illuminate the struggle of a Japanese woman married to an American. The use of flashback contributes not only to capturing the protagonist's feeling toward her younger son but also to creating a structure that enables the author to present a full, dynamic account of her family life while treating the events of a mere three days.

Translated Works: Passover (Sugikoshi no matsuri, 1985), novella. This sequel to "A Visitor from Afar" portrays the same family. Its heroine is the same woman suffering from so-called culture shock, a stress reaction to the lack of familiarity with one's environment. Major symptoms of this phenomenon are anxiety and fear, which manifest themselves in hostility toward both one's native country and host culture and in withdrawal from social contacts. Culture shock thus has much in common with alienation and anomie, the symptom of which is social estrangement and isolation. Culture shock can also inspire the afflicted to aspire for higher goals than mere cultural adjustment, and availability of a network of supportive friends often plays a key role in realization of such goals.

The strain, not only of living in a foreign country but also of raising a mentally handicapped child, understandably creates neuroses in the heroine of *Passover,* but it also encourages her to strive for her personal freedom. Unfortunately, however, she finds that her Jewish husband and his relatives, the very people whom she expects to be her "network of supportive friends," only exacerbate her problem precisely because of her unfamiliarity with Jewish culture and customs. They, in other words, are the main source of her anxiety and, consequently, targets of her hostility. The irony explicit in this tragic situation is the key ingredient of this story: its main theme, as Kometani herself explains, is "liberation and emancipation that is the theme of the Passover seder" ("Trials of a Japanese Ruth Amid the Alien Corn," *New York Times,* April 13, 1987), but the heroine is forced to reject the Passover seder and Jewish culture as a whole in order to pursue her "liberation and emancipation."

The opening scene of this story captures the woman, her husband, and their older son on their way to New York City. After placing their mentally handicapped younger son in an institution at last, the family plans to vacation in the city. As foreshadowed by the air turbulence on their flight in, however, their week turns out tempestuous indeed. The problem begins when the family is invited to a Passover seder by the husband's relatives. Although a nonreligious Jew, the husband was raised in an orthodox Jewish family and is thoroughly familiar with this rite of liberation. Moreover, he is anxious to meet his relatives, some of whom he has not seen for about twenty years. The wife, however, is most reluctant to attend the ceremony for several reasons.

First, she is unfamiliar with Jewish culture. The invitation to a seder only reminds her of the humiliation she suffered on her previous meeting with her in-laws and the anger she felt toward them. Her nemesis is her sister-in-law Sylvia, who has, in the heroine's angry mind's eye, competed with her for the affection of her husband. Second, the religious gathering would force her to "confront the fact that I am totally different" from them. She recalls with bitterness that racial and religious differences had caused her in-laws to oppose her marriage and boycott their wedding. Third, she resists all social constraints that threaten her freedom, including all forms of organized religion as well as "the tradition of Japan, that sexist society." Religion and other human activities devoid of genuine mutual interest and affection are, in her view, nothing more than social constraints that would negate her individuality. An atheist in this sense, she asserts: "Were people who first spoke out against nuclear arsenals Christian ministers or Buddhist priests? No, the very first to oppose nuclear armament were people who had rejected religion, like Linus Pauling, Bertrand Russell, and Jean-Paul Sartre. Religion has always concerned itself with death and has glorified it. But virtue in the contemporary sense of the word has to do, not with death, but with an affirmation of life."

The protagonist nonetheless consents to attend the seder and even persuades her son to come along. Meeting the in-laws immediately makes her feel insecure about herself. She worries whether her "English with an Osaka accent" can be understood and if she is "being rude not to have worn any jewelry for an important celebration like this." The intimate and festive atmosphere of the occasion further contributes to her sense of alienation. She mutters: "I'm the only one here who's not a Jew. I don't belong to their race and, besides I am so much smaller than they are.'' Even her husband becomes a stranger, as she notes, ''The minute he put on a *yarmulka,* I was thrown thousands of kilometers away from him and into the loneliness of an outsider.''

Here the heroine is clearly in culture shock. The anxiety generated in her by the strangeness of the occasion manifests itself in anger, causing her to perceive herself as a victim and her in-laws as victimizers. The seriousness of her paranoia is explicit in her intensely hostile perception of Sylvia as the bejeweled, gluttonous oppressor pharaoh and of her own husband as one of her kind. The heroine cries out in her mind: ''Ah, he's picking his food up with his fingers— like sister, like brother! How disgusting! I must say that a person who can't take care of his own health without someone watching over him must be anxious to die. So let him go ahead and die. Don't expect me to straighten out his rotten body while he goes around abusing it. Let him do whatever he pleases. All this is too absurd!''

Her irrational thinking even leads her to conclude that the seder itself is nothing more than an antiquated ritual full of hypocrisy and that Judaism itself is responsible for Nazism. At the same time, she suffers profound fear, for instance, of misleading passages in *The Haggadah.* Plagued by anxiety and fear, she eventually decides to stage her own exodus from her ''oppressors''; she quietly slips away from the gathering to seek her own freedom elsewhere. It is interesting to read *Passover* and ''A Visitor from Afar'' along with Josh Greenfeld's *A Client Called Noah.* This record of Kometani's family life is extremely helpful in illuminating the scope of her literary imagination. In this work Greenfeld simply reports that the Passover with his relatives was ''enjoyable.'' Kometani agrees with him but has capitalized on the tension she had felt with his sister and let a full tide of creative imagination surge in *Passover.*

While criticizing Kometani's rough and crude style and unrestrained expression of excessive emotions, Japanese critics lavished their praise on *Passover* for its dynamic and realistic portrayal of a Japanese woman's life in America. They were also impressed by the freshness of the material, namely, Jewish tradition and kinship observed by someone who is neither an insider nor an outsider.

In the United States, however, this novella became the focus of a controversy. The dispute began with a report of what was conceived of as the recent upsurge of anti-Semitic literature in Japan (''Japanese Writers Critical of Jews,'' *New York Times,* March 12, 1987, p. A 13). In support of this contention, an American scholar of Japanese literature wrote claiming that *Passover* was an anti-Semitic story and that the fact that it had received the Akutagawa Award attested to the disturbing development of anti-Semitism in Japan (''Reason for Concern in Japanese Anti-Semitism,'' *New York Times,* March 25, 1987, and *Los Angeles Times Magazine,* June 12, 1988). He further characterized *Passover* as a neo-nationalistic and anti-West writing (''Portnoy-san's Complaint,'' *Newsweek,* May 25, 1987, p. 72). Kometani promptly protested, calling the criticism at once abhorrent and ironic (''Trials of a Japanese Ruth Amid the Alien Corn'').

Catholic novelist Endō Shūsaku (b. 1923) also responded to the American scholar, who had singled him out as the head of the Akutagawa Award Committee. Endō explained that there was no "head" in the committee and that he did not even support the committee's majority decision to grant Kometani the honor ("The Akutagawa Prize," *New York Times,* May 4, 1987). Although he had offered no comment on *Passover* in his printed appraisals of all five works nominated for the award, Endō's letter clearly indicated that he had detected anti-Semitism in the story. Simultaneously, another Japanese woman married to a Jew challenged Kometani. Using quotations from *Passover* itself, she charged that the story would have the effect of spreading in Japan the worst prejudices and stereotypes against the Jewish people ("A Painful Story of Japanese-Jewish Marriage," *New York Times,* May 4, 1987).

What does this controversy mean? The criticism does have some grounds. It is true that the heroine's resentment toward her in-laws is extremely intense, and the outburst of her emotion is entirely lacking in restraint. Even the Kometanish humor can easily be misunderstood as ridicule. It is therefore understandable that some readers find this novel offensive. Yet, crucial points should not be overlooked. First, this work is fiction, the focus of which is not Judaism or secular Jewish culture but an examination of the prolonged psychological effect of contact with an alien culture upon a Japanese woman. The effect is captured in this work in the form of her hostility not only toward her Jewish in-laws but also toward her native culture, including its religion. It is much too simplistic to brand *Passover* as an anti-Semitic, neonationalistic, anti-West novel. Furthermore, it is important to evaluate Kometani's treatment of Jewish motifs in terms of literary technique. Her psychological probing is at once extensive and realistic, and although the protagonist's raw emotions and subsequent decision to leave her family are disturbing, they are effective in showing both the devastating and sublimating effects of culture shock. With a skillful use of irony throughout this work, the motifs also contribute to substantiating the theme of liberation and emancipation.

In essence, what provokes criticism may be not so much Kometani's alleged prejudice against the Jewish people as her seeming lack of sensitivity in subjecting the reader to the unmitigated force of stark realism with little consideration for the sensitive racial nerve, particularly of the Jewish people. As *Adventures of Huckleberry Finn* has been accused of being an antiblack novel and, more recently, Alice Walker's *The Color Purple* of being a novel that encourages stereotype images of black men, so does *Passover* invite charges of being an anti-Semitic work in its own way. At the same time, this international controversy, quite rare in the history of Japanese literature, also seems to call into question the validity of the autobiographical "I-novel" tradition constituting the mainstream of modern fiction in Japan and illuminates its inherent risk in this age of international literary interchange.

The Tumbleweed (Tamburu uiido, 1986), novel. The theme of this work is, as the title suggests, the alienation of a Japanese woman uprooted from her native culture. The story covers the woman's mundane life, in which her reunion with her mother brings to the surface the differences in the cultures of her adopted home and her native country. The elaboration of the theme, however, falls short of being sufficient. Parts in this work appear more like an introduction to American customs aimed at the Japanese people than an integral part of the plot. Written a few years before the prizewinning works, this is an interesting piece against which to measure Kometani's growth as a fiction writer.

BIBLIOGRAPHY

Translations

Passover. Trans. Foumiko Kometani. New York: Carroll and Graf, 1989.

Original English Writings

"Help! His Best Friend Is Turning into a Sheep: Murakami Haruki's *A Wild Sheep Chase*." *Los Angeles Times,* October 1989.
"The Man/God." *Los Angeles Herald Examiner,* January 11, 1990.
"No 'Japanese-doll' Image for This 'Tom Boy' Writer: Respectful, Obedient Footsteps Are Not Her Trick." *The World Paper,* July 1989.
"Pictures from Their Nightmare." *The New York Times Book Review,* July 19, 1987, 9–10.
"The Press Has Found Its Villain and It's Japan." *Los Angeles Times,* August 16, 1991.
"Silence is Essential: Tsushima Yuko's *The Shooting Gallery*." *The New York Times Book Review,* July 31, 1988, 21.
"Trial of a Japanese Ruth Amid the Alien Corn." *New York Times,* April 13, 1987, A18.

Non-fiction by Kometani's husband translated into Japanese by Kometani

Greenfeld, Josh. *A Child Called Noah: A Family Journey.* New York: Rinehart and Winston, 1972.
———. *A Client Called Noah.* New York: Henry Holt, 1986.
———. *A Place for Noah: A Family Journey Continued.* New York: Rinehart and Winston, 1978.

Western Press Coverage

Abe, Patricia. "An Embittered Life in New Novellas." *San Francisco Chronicle,* December 19, 1989.
Chira, Susan. "No One Is Nice Here." *The New York Times Book Review,* October 22, 1989, 27.
Hinkemeyer, Joan. "Novella Focuses on Isolation." *Rocky Mountain News,* January 12, 1990.
Hopkins, Ellen. "Her Story." *Los Angeles Times Magazine,* June 12, 1988, 18–22.
See, Carolyn. "Japanese 'Passover': The Rudeness of In-Laws." *Los Angeles Times,* November 6, 1989.

Teicher, Morton I. " 'Passover' Conveys Passions with Understanding." *Miami Jewish Tribune*, April 6–12, 1990.

Wood, Helen. "Spring Cleaning the Psyche." *Asahi Evening News*, December 12, 1989.

Yoshiko Yokochi SAMUEL

KURAHASHI Yumiko (1935–), novelist. Real name: Kumagai Yumiko (Mrs. Kumagai Tomihiro); née Kurahashi Yumiko.

Life: Yumiko was born in Kōchi in Shikoku, the oldest of the five children of a dentist, Toshio Kurahashi, and his wife, Misae. Graduated from Tosa Senior High School in 1950, Kurahashi entered Kyoto Women's College and moved on to Nihon Joshi Eisei Tanki Daigaku (Japanese Women's Junior College of Hygiene) in Tokyo the following year. She graduated in 1952 and passed the national examination for dental clinicians. Then Kurahashi entered the French Department of Meiji University, graduating in 1960 with a B.A. thesis on Jean-Paul Sartre. She went on to graduate school but, upon her father's death in 1962, returned to Kochi. There she married Kumagai Tomihiro, an employee at Kochi N.H.K. broadcasting, in 1964. She enrolled in a creative writing program at the University of Iowa as a Fulbright Fellowship awardee from 1966 to 1967. On the way back to Japan, she stayed in New York for three months. Her first daughter was born in 1968 and the second in 1971. In 1972 she moved with her family to Portugal but returned to Japan because of a coup in 1973.

Career: While she was a student at Meiji University, Kurahashi's "Zatsujin bokumetsu shūkan" (Slaughter the Underclass Week) received the second-place nomination for the Meiji University Chancellor's Award in 1959. In the following year she won the award for her short story "Parutai" (*Partei* or Party). "Parutai" was also honored with the Joryū Bungaku-shō (Women's Literary Award) in 1961. She went on to produce more imaginative, antirealistic works of fiction, under the acknowledged influence of the European existentialist writers. All these works appeared in highly regarded literary magazines, and she was quickly recognized and accepted as one of the upcoming new writers. Her novel *Kurai tabi* (A Dark Journey), a journey into a writer's own creating psyche, appeared in 1961. In 1963 Kurahashi received the Tamura Toshiko Award for her accomplishment in literary works. Her experience at Iowa provided her with the ground for the novel *Bājinia* (Virginia), a portrayal of an American woman leading a life free from traditional sexual codes. *Sumiyakist Q no bōken* (The Adventures of Sumiyakist Q), a "surrealistic" novel on which she worked for three years, came out in 1969. Later, Kurahashi incorporated the framework of classical myths or legends into her fiction. Her short stories based on Greek tragedy were compiled as *Han higeki* (Antitragedy) in 1971. *Yume no ukihashi* (A Floating Bridge of Dreams), on the theme of swapping marriage partners, followed in the same year. After a hiatus of several years, Kurahashi published *Shiro no naka no shiro* (A Castle Within a Castle), a sequel to *Yume no ukihashi*, in 1979. Her recent works include *Shunposhion* (Symposium, 1985), a novel describing the graceful interactions of a selected small group of people in a secluded resort, with overtones of an impending catastrophe from a nuclear war; *Amanonkoku ōkanki* (A Record of a Round-Trip to Amanon Country, 1986), the Izumi Kyōoka Award-winning novel dealing with feminist issues; and *Saigo kara ni-banme no dokusō* (The Next to the Last Poisonous Ideas, 1986), a collection of essays.

Major Works: Yume no ukihashi (A Floating Bridge of Dreams, 1969), novel. This story of spouse swapping is framed in twelve chapters with elegant titles fraught with natural images, resembling those in the 11th-century narrative *The Tale of Genji* by Murasaki Shikibu. Both sets of parents of the heroine, Keiko, and her boyfriend, Kōichi, oppose their marriage, for they are afraid the young couple may be a half-brother and sister as the result of their own partner swapping, which started before the birth of their offspring and continues still. Keiko and Kōichi find out the older couples' secret and, without ascertaining their consanguinity, choose different spouses. The novel ends with Keiko and Kōichi spending a night together at an inn in Kyoto while their spouses are dating somewhere else. The second cycle of swapping has started.

Kurahashi, in one of her postscripts to the novel, describes Keiko as "a person who bets on the possibility of the non-existence of God." Kurahashi argues that while Japanese people do not feel fear as long as they are with others, Keiko is different in that "she has nothing to be afraid of, even if she is alone." Kurahashi sees Erich Fromm's belief that "only those who love themselves can love another" as a reference point for judging beauty, and this standard of beauty guides Keiko. Keiko, a daughter of an educated and well-to-do family, gives and takes only what appeals to her standard, including her partner for marriage and swapping. The idea is expressed in Keiko's term as fair "exchange."

While "grace" is Keiko's guiding principle, as it was appreciated in the old court described in *The Tale of Genji*, Keiko is not like the women in the ancient narrative. The women in the tale were carried away by the schemes of fate or by their own subconscious agitation, both beyond their control, but Keiko chooses her every step and is fully aware of her responsibility. Since her guiding principle is personal aesthetics rather than conventional moral codes, Keiko is free from either guilt or shame. She is a rare being among the heroines in modern Japanese novels. The title is the same as that of the last chapter in *The Tale of Genji*, where uncertainty of the emotional bond between man and woman is doubly emphasized by the image of "a floating bridge" and "dreams," but Kurahashi's title seems more to reflect her intention to create a fictional scheme that is essentially antirealistic.

Translated Works: "Parutai" (Party, 1960), short story. Kurahashi Yumiko admits that the work, this narration of a young girl's experience in a revolutionary party (*partei* in French), is influenced by Franz Kafka and Jean-Paul Sartre and especially by the style of Albert Camus's *Stranger*. The narrator speaks to "you," who is her lover and a senior party member, but the omission of quotation marks gives an impression of a mental discourse taking place within her stream of consciousness. The narrative is an antithesis of objective reportage. The heroine's recollections of encounters with various party members are translated into concretization of her sensory perception—an existentialistic technique. Even the buildings are described not only as mazes, echoing Kafka's *Castle,* but also as organic bodies that chew and spit out the scum of people who enter them. The composite effect of the work is immediate and personal.

The story is interspersed with the French word *honte* (shame) and the expression "I felt ashamed." The heroine feels *honte* whenever she senses that her life is defined by her past as recorded in the soiled sheets of curriculum vitae, and she is "ashamed" when sentimentality muddles her actions. Her sense of *honte* and "being ashamed" is intensified when she sees party members trying to conjure up camaraderie by confessing and sharing their personal life stories. Her *honte* has little do with the traditional Japanese notion of shame, which mainly relates to the group one belongs to and is triggered by betrayal of group trust or unfulfillment of its expectations. "Parutai" is a black comedy of people who try to force shapeless reality into patterns by applying prescribed formulas or concepts, which are in the original text placed within double hooks, as in ‹‹ ››. These words within hooks come to resemble phonemic symbols enclosed in slashes as indisputable elements in the analysis of actual sounds in a language.

Nausea, an important motif in Sartre's novel, also appears at a climax in "Parutai." The heroine vomits and at the same time laughs uncontrollably when her lover enthusiastically calls her "a comrade" after they are arrested for a party activity. The nausea is her revolt against the labeling, her realization of the absurdity of any enthusiast's incurable optimism, but the nausea is also caused by her pregnancy. In this story, there is no hint of a tragic hue, as is sometimes discernible in the European existentialist writers to whom Kurahashi is initially indebted.

"Kyosatsu" (The Monastery, 1961), short story. In one of her early essays, "Watashi no shōsetsu sahō" (My Manner of Writing Novels, 1965), Kurahashi states that "I create an illusory castle and give forms to meaning. I often use characters expressed by symbols of K or L. . . . They are like independent variables who move within a hypothetical condition I set. I observe and record their actions and, when the walls and the maze which enclose them take shape and the castle becomes visible, I disappear." Then, "words multiply words and they keep on spinning out a false world. I feel joy only when I trust words." Inspired by Goethe's *The Sorrows of Young Werther,* "Kyosatsu" centers on a love triangle involving the young daughter of an ancient monastery's (perhaps Tōdaiji in Nara) head abbot and two men. The heroine's emotional equilibrium is balanced on two men of contrasting qualities, her self-assured and realistic fiancé, who is to succeed her father, and a dreamy researcher of art history called K. The story consists of the heroine's narrative addressed to her fiancé, which perhaps was never meant to be read by him. The plot, which ends with K's suicide, is simple, and the dazzlement of the story comes from the richness and complexity of sensory imagery. Ideas take form as images and nuances of feelings change into colors. Even concrete human bodies are replaced by metaphors, and the narrative almost feels like the composite of a series of sensations. The monastery itself is overlaid with the image of the heroine's mind and body, which the two men covet. This replacement may be the reason that, in spite of a detailed description of the monastery, the scenery, and the people, the total world is translucent and escapes clear definition. In the "illusory castle" the logic of the characters' sensation is the reality.

Sumiyakist Q no bōken (The Adventures of Sumiyakist Q, 1969), novel. This work describes a revolutionary party member's attempt to plan a coup against the director and his regime at a juvenile reformatory on an island. Dispatched to the place by a political party most likely based on communism, the hero, named Sumiyakist Q, discovers that the main protein supplied in reformatory meals comes from inmates' corpses. In the end, the director himself becomes a food source, and the mob of juveniles leaves the reformatory to invade the town. The novel resembles science fiction, which is commonly understood as speculation on the human condition in an imaginative frontier of modern scientific and technological advancement. In Kurahashi's story, nightmarish encounters among grotesque people take place in a bleak geographical setting, ingredients common to many science fiction tales. The mazelike building and living quarters in the reformatory, as well as the housing for the juveniles, are strangely suggestive of ruins from a monstrous scientific catastrophe. As in the Hollywood movie *Soylent Green* (1973), starring Edward G. Robinson and Charlton Heston, the logic of cannibalism is not far removed from the present-day economical utilization of the underprivileged for the sustenance of the powerful, whether through mental or corporal means.

Q, who futilely tries to implant among the juveniles and menials an awareness of being exploited, can also be interpreted as a parodic representation of a Marxist. Yet, Kurahashi defies this notion in her postscript message to the readers, saying, "I do not feel any obligation to satirize or criticize the sterility of the Japanese left wing or the comical nature of Japanese Marxian people. . . . To bustle about looking for 'What does it mean?' is a bad habit of those 'antiquated intellectuals.' " She claims that this story happens at "a place which exists nowhere . . . with unusual people." Kurahashi also cites a comment on this work made by a critic called Mr. Y. K., who seems to stand for herself. The citation describes Q as a Don Quixote scion, whose actions are guided by his obsession, and the work itself as a series of dialogues taking place between Q and other characters who also personify various concepts. Kurahashi states that her hero is a "Christian/Marxist" prototype.

In this sense, the novel evolves from Kurahashi's earlier work, "Parutai," in which a heroine faces and argues with her boyfriend the communist ideology incarnate. Like the boyfriend in "Parutai," Q is conditioned by his urgent desire to save society. As in "Parutai," there is no open give-and-take, free exchange of ideas or any change or growth among the characters. As the title suggests,

Q's stay at the reformatory is an outsider's adventure in an exotic, esoteric terrain. The plot is not of so much importance as the brilliant exposé of the characters' ideology, not only through their words but through their physiques, which correspond to their ideas, such as the director's enormous, flabby, space-filling flesh. In the curious and powerful blending of metaphors and tangible sensory reality, portraying scenes and people in etched detail, Kurahashi constructs her "ideal" work, "a work which refuses to be resolved into a rationalistic interpretation," as extolled in her essay "Shōsetsu no meiro to hiteisei" (Maze and the Negating Nature of the Novel, 1966).

"Kakō ni shisu" (To Die at the Estuary, 1970), short story. In a postscript to *Antitragedy* (1971), a collection of five short stories, including this work, Kurahashi states that the stories are her attempt to transplant into novel form the mythos of tragedy, which is fundamentally antinovel in nature. Her adaptations concern "how characters would act if they were aware of the mythos in Greek tragedy and knew that they were about to be trapped in the same fate." The framework of "To Die at the Estuary" is Sophocles' *Oedipus at Colonus.* There are a Tiresias-prophet and an Oedipus character who blinds himself in living out the prophecy given to him. The human relationships are, however, doubled and tripled in "To Die at the Estuary," like a complex mesh of the modern psyche. Oedipus's fate of murdering his father and marrying his mother does not end with the counterpart in Kurahashi's novel, but it casts its net to the hero, old Takayanagi, who is not blood-related to the Oedipus figure. The characters' actions are more like chain reactions to the original prophecy, ensnaring several generations of people.

Yet the entrapment of fate has been changing its formula as the generations progress until it loses its mystic power and dimension. At least the Oedipus figure in "To Die at the Estuary" closely simulates the divine prophecy given to him. Takayanagi, a follower of the Oedipus man, on the other hand, only partially fulfills the pattern: he does not kill his father, and his sexual partner is but a stepmother, who also acts under the knowledge of the prophecy. Takayanagi's Antigone-daughter, Asako, senses the secret in her family and is almost willing to repeat the pattern, but she has no recourse to do so. In Sophocles' tragedy, the prophecy weighs on Oedipus's mind after he commits the transgression, and the plot follows Oedipus's discovery of self-identity, while in "To Die at the Estuary" the prophecy is given before the act and influences the characters' consciousness, like a fatal attraction that has to be consummated. Their interaction, therefore, becomes a matter of choice rather than inevitable fate. What binds the modern figures in the story is their concept of fate rather than a divine scheme. There is no frightening discovery, and, consequently, there is no need for Takayanagi to blind himself.

As in her novel, *Yume no ukihashi,* which reinforces Kurahashi's belief that when two characters find "exactly the same quality in each other . . . the voltage of love is heightened" (*Watashi no naka no Kare e* [To Him Who Is in Me], 1973), *To Die at the Estuary* hints at an attraction to incestuous love between

Takayanagi and his granddaughter, Asako. At the end of the story, however, when Asako suggests to Takayanagi that they leave on a journey, as Oedipus and Antigone roamed as inseparable companions, Takayanagi rejects the allure. He chooses to lead his life as an ordinary human rather than to follow the predestined course. Takayanagi comes to a town by the river where he grew up (perhaps Kochi, where Kurahashi also grew up) to find his eternal resting place. The river echoes Kamo no Chōmei's 13th-century collection of thoughts, *Hōjōki* (An Account of My Ten-Foot-Square Hut), which Takayanagi admires as one of the best final voices uttered by humans before their deaths. Chōmei's famous opening words, "The flow of the river never ceases and the water is never the same," carries his feeling of evanescence. It is the prescribed eternal destiny for all forms, living or nonliving. Takayanagi's decision to live by the estuary seems to show his acknowledgment that the flow of his life is near its natural end.

The irony is that the estuary where he hopes to rest is now reclaimed and changes into an artificial and mechanical sanctuary with shining oil refinery pipes. Takayanagi's acceptance of the estuary as the modern vice perhaps indicates his understanding and acceptance of the inevitable flow of time, like his recognition that he does not possess the stature of an old hero. He is not to be elevated to the rank of god after his death, as happened to Oedipus and to the Oedipus figure in the story, but will die as one of the ordinary men, to whom time is unequivocally equal. After all, to be a chosen one in this modern age is only a conceptual game.

BIBLIOGRAPHY

Translations

The Adventures of Sumiyakist Q. Tr. Dennis Keene. Queensland: University of Queensland Press, 1979.

"The Boy Who Became an Eagle." Tr. Samuel Grolmes and Yumiko Tsumura. *New Directions* 29 (1974):116–33.

"The End of Summer." Tr. Victoria V. Vernon. In *Daughters of the Moon,* ed. Victoria V. Vernon. Berkeley: University of California, Institute of East Asian Studies 1988, 229–40.

"The Monastery." Tr. Carolyn Haynes. In *The Showa Anthology, 2,* ed. Van C. Gessel and Tomone Matsumoto. Tokyo: Kodansha International, 1985, 218–31.

"Partei." Tr. Yukiko Tanaka and Elizabeth Hanson. In *This Kind of Woman.* New York: Perigee Books, 1984, 2–16.

"Partei." Tr. Samuel Grolmes and Yumiko Tsumura. *New Directions* 26 (1973):9–22.

"To Die at the Estuary." Tr. Dennis Keene. In *Contemporary Japanese Literature,* ed. Howard Hibbett. New York: Alfred A. Knopf, 1977, 247–81.

"The Ugly Devils." Tr. Samuel Grolmes and Yumiko Tsumura. *New Directions* 24 (1972):55–67.

Critical Works

Mori, Joji. "Drag the Doctors into the Area of Metaphysics: An Introduction to Kura-
    hashi Yumiko." *Literature East and West* 18 (1974):76–89.
Vernon, Victoria V. "The Sibyl of Negation: Kurahashi Yumiko and 'Natsu no Owari.' "
    In *Daughters of the Moon.* Berkeley: University of California, Institute of East
    Asian Studies, 1988, 107–34.
Yamamoto, Fumiko. "Kurahashi Yumiko: A Dream of the Present? A Bridge to the
    Past?" *Modern Asian Studies* 18 (1984):147–52.

Fumiko YAMAMOTO

M

MEIŌ Masako (1939–), novelist, essayist, translator, college instructor of American literature. Real name: Karatani Masako; (Mrs. Karatani Kōjin); née Hara Masako.

Life: A native of Tokyo, Meiō has spent her entire life in the city, with the following exceptions: six months in the mountainous Nagano prefecture during and immediately after World War II; two years and seven months in the United States; and a month in Europe. Despite the many years of residency in Tokyo, Meiō's fictional works are invariably set elsewhere. This fact perhaps has to do with the main theme common among her works: "split identity" consisting of past (the unconscious) and present (the conscious); her Japanese heritage and American influences; and her perception of who she is and who she wishes to be.

Meiō was a precocious, literary-minded child. She dreamed of writing stories at age six and actually began to work on one. Her topic for the work was her father, who would figure importantly later in her fiction. He was a schoolteacher and a fervent supporter of the Shirakaba-ha writers group, espousing Christian humanism. To the moralist teacher, Shirakaba-ha represented the "idealism" that he could understand intellectually but could not quite internalize as a viable value. He consequently imposed his rigid and stoic sense of the Shirakaba-ha morality on his family members, with little awareness of its stifling effects on their individuality. He turned even more domineering at home in the years immediately after the war, when he became a strong anticommunist and eventually joined an ultranationalistic religious group. Even after his death, Meiō remained highly critical of her father, who, in contrast to her empathic mother, was entirely lacking in affection toward her. The very fact that at age six Meiō gave her would-be fiction the title "In Search of My Long-Lost Father" reveals her profound need both for his love and for freedom from his molding power. The seriousness of her conflict with her father is also manifested in more recent years in her admiration for the psychoanalyst Alice Miller, who has been persistently warning against the devastating effects of parents' control on their children and society at large. Yet Meiō's frustration with her father has been responsible, at least in part, for her urge to seek self-expression in creative writing. Her literary endeavor can be interpreted as her way of confronting her own feelings toward her father and of freeing herself from the part of herself that has long been suppressed by his power.

Meiō did learn a taste of freedom in 1957, when she came to Norwood, Massachusetts, as an American Field Service exchange student and attended a local high school for one year. The event signified her "second birth," but it also made her somewhat of a stranger in her own country. The resultant problem of "split identity" subsequently became the focus of her personal and literary concerns.

Graduating from high school in Tokyo, she majored in British and American Studies at Tokyo University of Foreign Studies. Interested in acting as well, she joined the theater troupe Bungakuza. She also earned a master's degree in English literature from the University of Tokyo in 1967. Western writers such as Shakespeare, Laurence Sterne, Virginia Woolf, and Emily Brontë, as well as modern Japanese novelists Natsume Sōseki (1867–1916) and Arishima Takeo (1878–1923) attracted her literary interest. She was most impressed, however, by F. Scott Fitzgerald, particularly by his *The Great Gatsby,* and by Anaïs Nin.

Meiō was married in 1965 to Karatani Kōjin (1941–), who became one of the leading literary critics of his generation. She taught English literature at Ferris Women's University in Yokohama. After becoming embroiled in a campus dispute in 1975, she left teaching and accompanied her husband to Yale University in the same year. By then the mother of two young sons, she nonetheless took full advantage of the opportunity there and attended a seminar on Shakespeare at the university. Before returning to Japan a year later, the family took a trip to Europe. The couple returned to Yale for a brief visit in 1977. Her experiences at Yale and in Europe would later yield two works.

In 1983, Meiō was invited by Columbia University to spend seven months as a visiting research fellow. One of the courses she attended at Barnard College was in black women's literature, and she became profoundly interested in black women writers and intellectuals struggling to overcome the identity crisis of their "split selves," torn between their ethnic heritage and predominantly white, male-centered American culture. Perceiving herself as a minority in her own Japanese society, which has long discriminated against intellectual women, particularly those educated in the West, Meiō developed a strong empathy with female black writers. The role of identity crisis in the emancipation of minority women writers consequently became one of her major concerns, to be dealt with in her future novels. Since returning to Japan, she has been writing and teaching American literature, especially Afro-American fiction by female writers, part-time at Chūō and Musashi universities and at Aoyama Gakuin Women's Junior College.

Career: Although she had previously published critical essays on Western writers such as F. Scott Fitzgerald, John Updike, and Edward Albee, Meiō's first major works were the translations of Anaïs Nin's *The Novel of the Future* (Mirai no shōsetsu, 1969) and *The Diary of Anaïs Nin* (Anaisu Nin no nikki, Kawada Shobō Shinsha, 1973), for which she used her natal name, Hara Masako, and her married name, Karatani Masako, respectively.

After the trip to Europe, Meiō's husband encouraged her to write a novel on condition that the work would be of quality high enough to pass at least the first screening for the *Bungei* Award. Meiō consequently took advantage of her second visit to New Haven and gathered materials for her future novel, for which the city would be the setting. The entire folder, along with the couple's passports, however, was lost when the luggage containing them was stolen from their rented car. The loss of the passports forced them to leave the country immediately, and Meiō returned home empty-handed and discouraged. She nonetheless embarked on her project and completed her first novel, *Aru onna no gurimpusu* (A Glimpse of a Certain Woman, 1979), which, far exceeding her husband's expectation, won the *Bungei* Award in 1980. Upon completing the story, she thanked her "lucky stars" by choosing her pen name after her astrological sign Meiōsei (Pluto). All of her subsequent works have been published under this name.

A Glimpse of a Certain Woman was inspired by Anaïs Nin's account in *The Diary* of her relationship with Henry Miller and his second wife, June. Meiō's affinity with Nin goes deeper and further in the use of symbols in the complex synthesis of the past (the unconscious) and the present (conscious) for the purpose of self-actualization. For Meiō, writing a novel is reconstructing life "in remembrance of times lost." In her second novel, *Yukimukae* (Waiting for the Snow, 1982), the protagonist struggles to synthesize her past (in Japan) with her present (in the United States). Similarly, the first-person protagonist of "Shirouma" (Mt. Shirouma, 1983) delves into her childhood in the war years, tracing the painful process through which she has lost her sense of self. The heroine of "Gurando riyunion" (A Grand Reunion, 1984), too, gives an account of her participation in the reunion of a Massachusetts high school she had attended twenty-five years before: the occasion only forces her to reexperience the painful part of her past in which she was a mere novelty to her classmates. Meiō's latest work, *Temma kū o iku* (The Adventure of a Heavenly Mare, 1985), however, may suggest a turning point: it is a hilarious story of a Japanese family's travel through Europe, which metaphorizes the protagonist's urge to "move on" toward an ideal self. Meiō has also published several *zuihitsu* (personal essays) in recent years, but the focus of her literary interest remains fiction.

Major Works: Aru onna no gurimpusu (A Glimpse of a Certain Woman, 1979), novel. The story unfolds with a description of the area surrounding New Haven, Connecticut. Meiō cleverly capitalizes on the actual names of New Haven streets and nearby towns strongly colored by their British heritage in order to reinforce the archaic image of the city. She also points, however, to modern architecture and other contemporary elements in the town and defines the city as a crossroad between the past and the present. New Haven is characterized as a "miracle place" in which a mere stranger, enabling the residents to have the glimpses of "the other half of their selves that they have failed to pursue," might lead them to a new awakening regarding themselves and life in general. The city is, then, a symbol that represents the syntheses not only of the past and the present but also of the conscious and unconscious and of death and rebirth. This novel is about the protagonist's encounter with strangers and her subsequent discovery of the truth about herself.

The heroine, Yukiko, is a Japanese woman in her late thirties on her way to a high school reunion in Norwood, Massachusetts. An exchange student from Tokyo some twenty years before, she learned the spirit of rebellion against authority from the younger generation of Americans. Returning to Japan in the midst of anti-American sentiment building up toward the ratification deadline of the United States-Japanese Security Treaty set for 1960, however, she was forced to negate the America within herself in order to readjust herself to her native life. Tormented by her own split self between the two cultures, she entertained the idea of returning to the United States to pursue a law degree at Harvard University. She nonetheless married a literary critic, Tatsuo, who further discouraged her from retaining the American side of herself. Ten years and two sons later, Tatsuo was invited to Yale University. During the year in New Haven, Yukiko became embroiled in the lives of "strangers" who rekindled in her the flames of free spirit long suppressed since her Norwood days, as well as beginning to perceive her future as the author of a novel that she would entitle *The New Haven Story*.

Yukiko's second visit to New Haven signifies, then, not only a journey toward her past but also a descent into her unconscious in an effort to define her present self. The following passage captures effectively the image of the heroine struggling for self-actualization in the crucial moments of her life:

An automobile was one thing that she [Yukiko] could not live without. Sitting behind a steering wheel in the confinement of her own translucent and capsule-like universe, she enjoyed the secure feeling of being neither cut off entirely from the outside world nor forced to relate to it. There within a speeding car, she belonged to her own sphere far removed from Japan, America or any other place on earth. There she was free from mundane life full of constraints and coercions, and she was no longer the whimsical wife of Tatsuo nor the unattentive mother of Kazuto and Tsuguto. As long as she remained in this realm, she was not even an unemployed Shakespearean scholar or an aspiring writer struggling on a would-be-novel. . . . Driving, in short, transformed her into a mere entity who, creeping out of the depth of unconscious turned inside out to expose deceptions in her life, moved swiftly like the wind from one place to another in search of another incentive for life.

Yukiko recalled a certain Delores in New Haven as the antithesis of herself. Not only a successful attorney with a degree from Harvard Law School, Delores was also blessed with physical beauty and grace becoming the daughter of a deposed Puerto Rican aristocrat. Highly promiscuous despite her profound love toward her husband, Leonard, Delores manipulated Leonard, who vacillated between fury over her infidelity and a sheer adoration of her sensuous beauty. Yukiko watched the couple's struggle with mixed emotions, at once hoping for their reconciliation and criticizing them for their sexual indulgence and mutual abuse. Contemptuous of Delores but also deeply envious of her relationship with her husband, Yukiko was critical of Leonard but infatuated with him.

Yukiko came to see Delores as the "archetypal whore," Cressida, and Leonard as Troilus in Shakespeare's *Troilus and Cressida*. Yukiko suspected, however, that Leonard perceived himself at once a Leontes, the husband of the "wrong woman" Hermoine, in another Shakespeare play, *The Winter's Tale*, and Othello, the jealous husband of Desdemona. Infatuated with Leonard and wishing to identify herself with Delores, Yukiko even imitated her manners and attire in order to attract his attention. Yukiko's attempt failed, transforming her masochistic wishes into a maddening desire to destroy the couple's marriage. She consequently perceived herself as Iago, who fanned Othello's jealousy by maliciously informing him of Desdemona's alleged infidelity. Here, Meiō risks the possibility of alienating readers who are unfamiliar with Shakespeare's works. The analogy, however, effectively contributes to the characterization of Yukiko as a budding Shakespearean scholar. Having observed the entire development with the detached eye of an intellectual, Yukiko's husband helped her overcome the emotional turmoil by suggesting that she write a story about New Haven.

Back in town two years later, Yukiko simply wishes to know what has become of Delores. Yukiko's thoughts drift back to the memories of her stern, moralist father, whom she feared and resented until his death. She married Tatsuo because he was, in her mind's eye, the antithesis of her father. She has come to realize, however, that the two men, after all, differed little from each other. Small wonder she was strongly attracted by Leonard and Delores, who, with their uninhibited expressions of sexual love for each other, caused Yukiko to confront the effects on herself of her father's authority, manifested particularly in her negation of her own sexuality.

With this newly gained self-understanding, Yukiko meets Delores again, only to discover that the woman is not her alter ego after all but is a person who, like herself, has struggled between her native American culture and her Puerto Rican heritage. Moreover, Yukiko learns that Delores, now divorced from Leonard, has transcended her fragmented self and is ready to return to her mother's country to work with her people. After parting with her, Yukiko finds her luggage stolen. The suitcase contained her passport, her high school yearbook—the most precious keepsake from her past—and the materials she has gathered for her would-be novel, which was to be her major future project. Thus left with nothing but her own self-knowledge to rely on, she confronts the present anew.

Based heavily on the author's life, this novel is an exciting mixture of an "I-novel,'' biographical fiction, and psychological novel. Moreover, while it belongs to the category of ''serious literature,'' the story contains the elements of popular culture as well. What makes this synthesis possible is Meiō's creative imagination, a competent manipulation of literary techniques, and the seriousness and intensity of her self-search. The characterization of the protagonist gives not a glimpse, as the title indicates, but a rounded portrait (full image) of the heroine in the process of reconstructing and reaffirming herself as a woman and an artist. Particularly impressive are the extent of psychological probing; the deliberate style, built upon carefully chosen diction; and the tightly constructed structure that enables the author to retrace the protagonist's entire life from a clear perspective of her present state of maturity. Transcending the literary, geographical, and genre-specific bounds of conventional Japanese literature, this work was obviously considered by critics to signal the beginning of an exciting new era in contemporary Japanese fiction, richly deserving the coveted Bungei Award.

Yukimukae (Waiting for the Snow, 1982), novel. The subject matter is again Japanese women caught in a crevice between their native country and the United States and between who they are and what they could have been. Meiō is particularly skillful in characterization, creating two women with homonymic names (written in different Chinese characters) in order to illuminate the main theme of fragmented self. She also demonstrates her talent as a storyteller by adopting an unusual narrative technique: She has the third-person narrator describe the protagonist Yukiko, while having the other Yukiko (Yuki in this article to avoid confusion) give her first-person account of the heroine in alternate chapters. The story as a whole is woven into a complex and intricate tapestry of multivoiced accounts of the women's lives.

The two major characters in their thirties share the common background of having studied in the United States as high school exchange students. They represent a new crop of highly intelligent Japanese women who had to struggle to capitalize on the American experience in their personal and professional development. During their college and graduate school years in Japan, they were harassed by their peers for being *Amerika-gaerï* (returnees from America). Japanese society offered little chance as yet for them to make use of their unique insights and talents; the best they could do was to work as guides for American tourists. Eventually they find themselves in two separate and entirely incompatible worlds: Yukiko as associate professor of Japanese history at a state university in South Carolina and Yuki as an unemployed scholar of American literature in Japan.

During her one-year stay in New Haven, where her husband is a visiting scholar at Yale University, Yuki manages to visit Yukiko in the South. Despite her academic accomplishments, Yukiko is discontented with her life, her unhappiness manifesting itself in acute loneliness and an inability to commit herself to her career and her personal interests. She has declined a marriage proposal from her lover and is uninterested in her own tenure promotion, for the honor will not ensure her happiness. The pressure of having to demonstrate her professional competency by publishing only makes her even more resentful than ever of the intellectually unstimulating environment around her. She now yearns to return to her native country. Discontented with her own lot, the visiting Yuki experiences envy and resentment over her friend's professional achievement and disgruntlement. Little does she realize that Yukiko holds the same sentiments toward her.

Despite her colleagues' advice, Yukiko puts an end to eleven years of life in the United States and returns to Japan, only to find it extremely difficult to adjust back to Japanese life. This problem, coupled with an ongoing conflict with her tradition-bound mother, keeps her in inertia for days on end. Yuki returns from New Haven and persuades Yukiko to get together with their old friends who, like themselves, are former high school exchange students. Now engrossed in their role as middle-class mothers and wives, however, these women only exacerbate Yukiko's feeling of alienation. In the end, she decides to leave Japan, this time for Europe to be with a man whom she met during her brief vacation there.

Based largely on Meiō's own personal experience and observation, this novel realistically captures the difficulties that confront Japanese women who have studied abroad. The characterization is fully developed and convincing. The structure is highly effective, not only for depicting Yukiko and Yuki as the alter ego of each other but also for adding tension and depth to this story with a theme that is at once important and new in Japanese literature.

BIBLIOGRAPHY

Critical Works

Mitsutani, Margaret. ''Japanese Women and Studying Abroad: Fantasy, Identification, Rejection.'' In *The Proceedings of Symposium: The Walls Within; Images of Westerners in Japan and Images of the Japanese Abroad,* ed. Kinya Tsuruta. Vancouver, British Columbia: University of British Columbia, Asian Center, 1988.

                                                   Yoshiko Yokochi SAMUEL

MIURA Ayako (1922–), novelist. Real name: Miura Ayako (Mrs. Miura Mitsuyo); née Hotta Ayako.

Life: Miura Ayako was born in Asahikawa, on Japan's northernmost island of Hokkaido, on April 25, 1922, the fifth child of Hotta Tetsuji and Kisa. She has three older brothers, one older sister, four younger brothers, and one younger sister (who died at the age of six). Ayako's grandmother at the age of sixteen married a man she dearly loved. However, right after Kisa's birth, for an unknown reason, the young couple was forced to divorce by the bride's father. Thirty years later, the unfortunate ex-husband reappeared before his daughter, Kisa, who had given birth to Ayako a few months earlier. He picked up the baby girl and said to the mother: "Take good care of this child. She'll be a tremendous help to you. I can tell from her eyes." Kisa's father, who had remained single after the divorce, traveled to Sakhalin Island, where he died. Ayako later tried to re-create the misty world of her grandparents in a 1975 novel, *Tenpoku genya* (The North Plain). Kisa's mother eventually remarried a lumber mill owner by whom she had five children before he died at the age of thirty-nine.

Ayako's earliest fond memories are closely associated with this grandmother, who almost year-round helped her daughter raise the large Miura family. The ten grandchildren adored her. She told a fairy tale every night to the young Ayako, who had a hard time falling asleep. The bedtime storytelling whetted her literary appetite greatly. By the time she was old enough to understand things in the outside world, the grandmother was taking her to silent movies. A year after she entered Taisei Elementary School, a devout Christian family by the name of Maekawa moved in next door. They would play a crucial role in Ayako's perception of Christianity. She later wrote: "Their oldest son, Tadashi and I met again in 1948 when we were both TB patients. If I had not met him, I would not have become a Christian. If I had not become a Christian, I would not have even thought about writing novels. Because Christ is the point of origin (*genten*) for my life, for my writing."

When Ayako was a third grader, her classmates called her "book-maniac." She read everything and anything available to her: books and magazines handed down from her older siblings or from her aunt who lived in the already over-crowded Miura house for a time and the books discarded by her friends. Precocious and intensely curious, at the age of ten she took up the challenge of adult fiction, such as *Daini no seppun* (The Second Kiss) by Kikuchi Kan (1888–1948) and *Hasen* (A Wrecked Ship) by Kume Masao (1891–1952). Later in her life, as if to reverse this trend, the grown-up Ayako went back to the fairy tales of Hans Christian Andersen (1805–75) and Jacob Grimm (1785–1863).

Two years into high school, she came down with rheumatism, which forced her to stay in bed for three months. Upon graduation in 1939 she took a teaching post at an elementary school in Utashinai City for the next two years and another five years in Asahikawa City. During the seven years of teaching, it never occurred to Ayako to question the validity and propaganda of the government's educational policies that in the end brainwashed the entire Japanese population into believing in the divine emperor and the holy war in the Pacific. With Japan's unconditional surrender in 1945 came the American occupation forces and their strict order to delete all "patriotic" lines from the ethics textbook. When Ayako watched the innocent look on her pupils' faces as they obediently crossed out those lines with ink, she realized she could no longer continue teaching. It was March 1946.

Three months later she developed tuberculosis (TB) in the lungs, then a disease as fatal as any malignant cancer. This was the beginning of her battle against the disease, against her own cynicism, and against the terrible sense of guilt for having fed lies to the schoolchildren for seven years. As if falling deeper into her own self-deception, she gave her consent to marry two men—almost at the same time. One of them died later of TB. Her own confused psychological state of mind reflected that of her own countrymen brought to their knees in the midst of the postwar chaos and poverty. During these hard times, TB patients, with no antibiotics and less than inadequate diets, died in great numbers.

Although she briefly recovered enough to be able to take care of herself at home, she decided to recuperate at a sanatorium, where she also took a part-time job as a secretary for the three hundred-member TB Patients Club to pay part of her medical expenses. Her duties included the preparation and mailing of a newsletter and the acquisition of butter and other protein-rich foodstuffs. Her room was always alive with activity, filled with club members who would discuss various business matters or stop by just to talk with her. Her then fiancé, Nishinaka Ichiro, who had a job outside Asahikawa, took it upon himself to visit her on a regular basis, bringing meat and other nutritional food. (He once even sent her his entire one-month salary to help pay her hospital costs.) One of Ayako's sisters came to the sanatorium to prepare her daily meals. However, her life was still empty, purposeless. She lived for any kind of diversion that would distract her from depressing thoughts.

It was at such a time in her life that a childhood friend, Maekawa Tadashi, who had read about her in one of the club newsletters, began to visit her. At the age of twenty-seven Ayako had reached the bottom of her own private hell, desperate and frightened, her life in limbo. She broke her engagement to Nishinaka, who had patiently waited for three years for her to marry him. She turned a deaf ear to Tadashi's encouragement to hang on to life, continued to smoke, and refused to recognize how much he cared for her. She wrote in the first volume of her autobiography, *Michi ariki* (There Is a Way, 1966; tr., *The Wind Is Howling,* 1976), of how he tried to communicate with her:

"I think I know how you feel, Aya-chan. But I can't agree with you. The way you live your life is too miserable. You've got to find a way to really treasure yourself more. . . ." He broke off. He was crying. Tears streamed down his cheeks. My facial expression full of sarcasm, I just watched him and lit another cigarette. "Aya-chan! You mustn't do that. If you keep on like that, you'll die!" He cried out. He let out many deep sighs. Suddenly he began to strike his foot, bang, bang, bang, with a small stone he had picked up. He took me by surprise. I raised my hand to stop him. But he grabbed it, held it tight and said, "You don't know how desperately I've been praying for you that you'd live your live more fully. I thought I'd exchange my life for yours if you'd only live. But my faith is not strong enough, I've been forced to realize I don't have the power to save you. I want to punish myself because I'm good for nothing. That's why I am hitting myself." . . . I felt a ray of light shining on him. Sensing that it probably emanated from Christianity, I thought I wanted to seek out the Christ this man believes in, this man who loves me not simply as a woman, but as a human being, as an individual.

In October 1951 she was hospitalized once again, this time in Asahikawa, for a persistent low-grade fever. Even under medical treatment the fever did not

break, and Ayako instinctively knew she had spinal caries (Pott's disease) despite the fact that all of the x-rays she underwent revealed nothing. To her
chagrin, the doctors continued to dismiss her opinion as an "uninformed" di-
agnosis. In February 1952, she moved, at her own insistence, to the Hokkaido
University Hospital, where, after three months of extensive testing, her physi-
cians found she had "spinal caries." Ayako was thirty years old. But this time
she was not alone. She had Maekawa Tadashi. In July, lying in bed in a cast,
she was baptized by a Protestant minister, Onomura Rinzo, who had spent most
of the war years in jail for being an antiwar activist. By October Ayako began
immobilization therapy at home, a treatment that would last for the next four
years. In November Tadashi came to see Ayako for the last time. In 1973, their
correspondence was published under the title of *Seimei ni kizamareshi ai no
katami* (Mementos of Love Imprinted in My Life).

From her sickbed, Ayako began to correspond with TB patients across the
country. One of them was Sugawara Yutaka, a publisher of a small Christian
magazine, *Ichijiku* (Figs), which printed letters sent in by TB patients and con-
victs, some of them Christians, some of them wishing to learn about Christianity.
In May 1955 he wrote a postcard to one of his regular contributors, Miura
Mitsuyo: "Please pay a visit to Hotta Ayako," the card said. As far as Sugawara
was concerned, he was introducing a woman to a bedridden woman to keep her
company. He had no reason to suspect that this name, Mitsuyo, usually a girl's
name, had been given to a boy. Hotta Ayako and Miura Mitsuyo knew of each
other only by name through the magazine. In a society where gender separation
was still strictly observed, Miura was, understandably, a little concerned: he
might be visiting a young single woman, unannounced. However, with the postcard as his "letter of introduction," he visited Hotta Ayako.

Ayako would have jumped out of bed if she had been able: the visitor's
resemblance to Maekawa Tadashi was uncanny. His soft-spoken voice, his quiet
manner, his facial expressions, everything about him reminded her of her first
true love. Her astonishment was not unfounded: one day her father mistook
Mitsuyo for Tadashi's brother. This mistaken identification was later repeated
among many of her Christian friends. One of her former students, noticing
Tadashi's photograph next to the bed, looked surprised: "Do you mean to say
you know Mr. Miura?"

It had been two years since Tadashi died. With him, love was gone, she
thought. She should not, could not possibly fall in love with a man just because
he looked like her deceased fiancé. Mitsuyo's unexpected appearance was more
than she could handle. However, with his more frequent visits and correspondence, she began to improve markedly. In 1956 Mitsuyo proposed to her in a
letter and stated that he would wait as long as it took her to recover. Ayako
was then thirty-four, Mitsuyo thirty-two. Three years later, with a thirteen-year
battle against TB and caries behind her, Ayako married Mitsuyo, an accountant
at the Hokkaido Forestry Bureau. (He himself had contracted TB in the kidney
at seventeen but was cured by the miracle drug streptomycin.) He was to become
Ayako's best friend, adviser, and a most demanding editor for her novels.

Career: In 1961 Ayako submitted her first story, "Taiyō wa futatabi bossezu" (The Sun Will Never Go Down Again), to *Shufu no tomo* (Housewives' Friend) under the pen name of Hayashida Ritsuko. This autobiographical story of her battle against two ailments and her life as a Christian won first place in the magazine's short story contest and was reprinted in the 1962 January issue. It was a smash hit among housewives.

On New Year's Day, 1963, *Asahi Shimbun,* one of the three major newspapers in Japan, announced a ten-million-yen prize for the best novel to celebrate the eighty-fifth anniversary of the newspaper's Osaka office and the seventy-fifth for its Tokyo office. The deadline was exactly twelve months away. With encouraging words and moral support from Mitsuyo, she set to work. As the owner of a small grocery store, she had free time only between 10 P.M. and 2 A.M. The result of this labor of love was *Hyōten* (The Freezing Point), the winner of the prize of $27,777 and serialization in the *Asahi.* Considering the average schoolteacher's annual salary at that time was $2,500, the cash prize was a staggering sum. With the help of the television version, which was aired as a thirteen-part series, the novel had an unprecedented spiritual appeal to the ordinary Japanese.

This was the beginning of Ayako's fruitful career as a Christian writer. In addition to innumerable short stories and speeches that appeared in different magazines, by 1987, she had twenty-five novels to her credit, three collections of short stories, seven collections of essays (two of which are coauthored with Mitsuyo), and two candid autobiographies. She has also published *Kyūyaku-seisho nyūmon* (Introduction to the Old Testament, 1974), and *Shinyaku-seisho nyūmon* (Introduction to the New Testament, 1977), which are intended for the uninformed Japanese public, and a picture book on the life of Jesus Christ for children. By the time *Hyōten* appeared, the Japanese public had already been introduced to another Christian (Catholic) writer, Endō Shusaku (1923–). Both his *Wonderful Fool* (Obaka-san, 1959) and *The Silence* (Chinmoku, 1966) dealt with the theme of Christian faith and love. What Endō attempted to do in his work was to make this alien religion more familiar to Japanese. He likened this process to "retailoring the Western suit" to fit his own Japanese body. Contrasted to his intellectual approach, which frantically tries to assimilate and adapt Christianity, is Ayako's straightforward, undiluted message bubbling with evangelical fervor.

Major Works: Hyōten (The Freezing Point, 1964), novel. It tells the story of Yōko (the sun child), an adopted daughter of a physician, Tsujiguchi Keizo, and his lovely wife, Natsue. The popularity of this story is due to the fact that Miura painstakingly combines two literary genres familiar to all Japanese: *Bildüngs-roman* (which Japanese translate as *kyōyō shosetsu,* or something of an "apprenticeship" novel) and *mamako-ijime* ("ill-treated stepchild") tales. From the very beginning, Miura sets out the core argument of the novel: humans are imperfect, full of jealousy and mistrust.

The story progresses with the perfect loving mother fussing over the baby girl while the guilt-ridden, jealous husband, who knows the true identity of his adopted daughter, plays the role of mean stepfather. However, the situation completely reverses itself: the wife accidentally finds out the secret of the baby's birth. Now, an intense hatred of the infant is kindled with a vengeance, although the wife swears never to let the husband know what is burning inside her. To challenge the reader with the question, Can one love one's enemy? Miura sets up an elaborate psychological plot involving child kidnapping and murder, while contemplating unwed motherhood, incest, and extramarital affairs. Considering the conservative moral codes in the early 1960s in Japan, the novel explores many of the delicate issues the average Japanese reader found sensational.

In the manner of *Strange Interlude* by Eugene O'Neill (1888–1953), Miura lets the characters speak their mind to the reader through the dynamic interplay of what they really want to say but cannot (*honne*) and what they feel obligated to say (*tatemae*). The latter demands that one behave properly, according to the norm and ideal that society dictates, while the former forces one to be true to one's own feelings, regardless of their ethical content. Inevitably, *honne* tends to reveal the dark sides of human nature, the source of the "original sin," the message that Miura tries to drive home to her Japanese readers. Instead of using the stream-of-consciousness technique, Miura exposes the "unspoken true intentions" of each character in parentheses, which she distinguishes from spoken dialogues in direct quotations. The following passage, which describes the inner conflict of Natsue the stepmother, is typical of Miura's narrative style:

> She knew Yōko was without blame. But she could not help thinking that Yōko had killed Ruriko, and stepped into the Tsujiguchis' world as though nothing had happened.
> "Mother, by March the third, OK?"
> "March the third? What is it?"
> Natsue was distracted because Murai was coming back to Asahikawa soon.
> (My husband has betrayed me. I will betray him this time.)
> She knew that the best way to make him suffer was for her to approach Murai.
>   She turned around to Yōko.
>   Yōko smiled brightly.

Miura continues to build up this interplay of *honne* and *tatemae*. Yōko becomes the sacrificial lamb upon which all the sins of humankind are placed. By exposing the secret of Yōko's birth, the deceptions of Natsue, Keizo, and his accomplice are brought to light. A family drama is transformed into a parable on ethics. Miura uses a minimum of Bible quotations in an effort not to alienate the Japanese readers. However, the message is overwhelmingly clear, undiluted. Yōko writes in her suicide note:

> As long as I believed myself to be right, whether I was poor, badmouthed, or picked on, I regarded myself as a strong person, capable of living with a clear conscience.

Nothing of that sort would have injured me. . . . But when I learned of the possible existence of a sin inside me, I lost the hope to live. . . . I tried to live like a light of this world. You must have found me extremely irritating, Mother. But now I think there was always a freezing point (*hyōten*) inside my heart. It is frozen now. My freezing point is that "I am a criminal's child."

Miura keeps the reader in suspense till the very end of the novel. The denouncement comes with another revelation, the unknown story of Yōko's real parentage. The crime of selfish adults at play, jealous, deceptive, and egoistic, comes full circle. Miura lets no one escape from it. The reader must agree with the author that deep inside themselves, humans are indeed sinful. This persuasive power, which echoes throughout the novel, is her triumph.

Hosokawa Garasha-fujin (Lady Hoshokawa Gracia, 1974), historical novel. It focuses on the tragic life of an early Japanese Christian woman, the daughter of Akechi Mitsuhide (1526–82). In Miura's version of Mitsuhide's coup d'état against Oda Nobunaga (1534–82), Lady Gracia's father is portrayed not as a notorious traitor but as a vassal betrayed by his own lord. On June 21, 1582, Mitsuhide led his army against Nobunaga and drove him to suicide at Honnō-ji. However, Mitsuhide met an untimely death at the hands of a peasant. Lady Gracia was not allowed to follow her father in death and, like Hester in *The Scarlet Letter* by Nathaniel Hawthorne (1804–64), had to live in shame— branded a traitor's daughter.

Miura wrote in the "Postscript" of the novel: "Four hundred years ago when women were men's possessions, simply the tools for political intrigue, it must have been terribly difficult for women to live like human beings. Lady Gracia, who responded to a spiritual awakening and lived in faith in those uncertain times, moves me deeply." Lady Hosokawa Gracia (1563–1600), who inspired Mariko in James Clavell's 1975 novel, *Shōgun*, displays an inquiring and discriminating mind. A direct descendant of Murasaki in *The Tale of Genji* (11th c.), she is one of the most sympathetic and fully portrayed female protagonists in Japanese literature. Akechi Tamako, in Miura's imagination, possessed many of the attributes considered undesirable for a girl in Japan: intellectual, decisive, and articulate. She wed at the age of sixteen Hosokawa Tadaoki (1563–1645), a liberated man who greatly appreciated her talents. The novel follows her turbulent life, intricately bound with the civil strife that had raged in Japan for three hundred years. In the face of treachery, deception, corruption, and death, she desperately sought to maintain a measure of human dignity. Concerning how to best serve Christ and her politician husband faithfully, Lady Gracia allowed no compromise. She followed her husband's orders to the letter: she had one of her trusted bodyguards kill her rather than be taken hostage. In this final act, she proved her loyalty both to Christ and to her husband. She sacrificed her life to save Okitada's honor and yet remain a Christian. For Miura, Lady Gracia serves as the ideal symbol of faith and love.

Kairyō (Mountains Under the Sea, 1981), historical novel. This is a tale of three Japanese castaways who in 1833 drifted ashore at British Columbia in Canada, where English merchants rescued them out of slavery. When they tried to return to Japan in 1838, the Tokugawa government turned them away. Settling into a life of exile at Macao, with the help of English missionaries, the three Japanese were the first to translate the Bible into Japanese. The novel was made into a film by the Shōchiku Studio in 1983.

Translated Works: Shiokari Pass (Shikari toge, 1968), novel. This work was first serialized in a Christian magazine, *Shinto no tomo* (Believers' Friend). The public's enthusiastic response to the message of *Hyōten* enabled her this time to make a more direct appeal. She moved away from a fictional narrative and wrote a biographical account of a long-dead fellow Christian, Nagano Masao (1878–1909), from her hometown, Asahikawa. She also felt comfortable enough to incorporate fragments of her own autobiography into the story. She quotes the Bible at the very beginning of the novel: "Unless a grain of wheat falls into the earth and dies, it remains alone; but if it dies, it bears much fruit" (John 12.24 Revised Standard Version [RSV]). As this quotation makes clear, Miura tackles the now unfashionable concept of *gisei* (sacrifice) in contemporary Japanese society. The theme is a daring one—sacrifice of one's own life to save the lives of fellow countrymen. It challenges the traditional Japanese notion of ritual death, which occurs only to clear one's name or to avenge one's master. Renewal in death as in the case of Jesus Christ's sacrificial death for humankind or the idea that the old must die to make way for the new has never been dominant in Japanese culture.

Miura again adopts the role of an unpretentious storyteller, following Nagano's background chronologically: how the young boy finds out about his Christian mother, who was cast away by her mother-in-law; the reunion of his parents; his love for a crippled girl, Fujiko. The sequence of his proposal to Fujiko, who now lies in bed with TB and spinal caries, draws directly upon the event described in *The Wind Is Howling,* Miura's autobiography, which covers the period of her bedridden life till her marriage to Mitsuyo. The narrative voice of *Shiokari Pass* is unmistakably Miura's own. It would not be an exaggeration to say that Miura literature represents a *shi-shosetsu* ("I-novel") of hope and faith. She finds her kindred spirit in Nagano Masao; the humanism that motivates actions of this devout Christian, who stops a runaway train at Shiokari Pass with his own body, humbles her. She is considered the best evangelical Christian writer Japan has to offer. The success of her works, proven time and again, lies in the way she speaks to the reader, unabashed, straightforward, simple, and, above all, sincere.

The Wind Is Howling (Michi ariki, 1969), autobiography. It covers the period 1946–59, describing in clinical detail Miura's fight against TB and spinal caries and her encounters with Maekawa Tadashi and Mitsuyo, who led her to Christianity. This moving memoir, which Miura calls "a history of my spiritual journey," ends with her marriage to Mitsuyo.

BIBLIOGRAPHY

Translations

Shiokari Pass. Tr. Bill and Sheila Fearnehough. Old Tappan, NJ: Fleming H. Revell, 1976.
The Wind Is Howling. Tr. Valerie Griffiths. London: Hodder and Stoughton, 1976.
Michiko N. WILSON

MIYAMOTO Yuriko (1899–1951), novelist, essayist, critic. Other pen name: Chūjō Yuriko; née Chūjō Yuri (Mrs. Miyamoto Kenji).

Life: Yuriko was born in Tokyo, the eldest daughter of a well-to-do family. Her father was an architect, trained at Cambridge University, and had a warm personality and liberal beliefs. Her mother was the strong-willed daughter of a noted scholar-statesman who served as the principal of Kazoku Jogakkō (Women's School for Peers) and member of the House of Peers. Yuriko graduated from the exclusive Kazoku Jogakkō and entered Nihon Joshi Daigaku (Japan Women's University) in 1916 but left after one term, upon making her literary debut with *Mazushiki hitobito* (Flock of Poor People), which was published in a major monthly, *Chūō kōron* (Central Review), in September 1916.

In view of the family's reputation and social status, Yuriko's mother considered her daughter's unconventional behavior inappropriate, and she frequently quarreled with Yuriko. Her father took Yuriko to America with him, arriving in New York in October 1918. While auditing classes at Columbia University, she fell in love with Araki Shigeru, a man fifteen years her senior, majoring in ancient Iranian language. They were married in October 1919. Their life together was far from peaceful. Yuriko's mother, who was apparently opposed to the marriage, soon became ill and sent for Yuriko. Araki remained in America to finish his studies, returning to Japan the following year. For a while Yuriko and Araki lived at her parents' home. This arrangement did not work out well, creating emotional stress among the in-laws and magnifying the differences in age and cultural background between Yuriko and Araki. The young couple eventually moved out and attempted to make a financially independent, creative life together. Yuriko tried her hand at writing a play, a few prose pieces, and soul-searching essays. Araki tried to establish himself as a scholar but contracted tuberculosis. This stormy period of Yuriko's life ended in divorce in 1924.

Around that time, Yuriko met Yuasa Yoshiko (1896–1982), a well-known translator and specialist of Russian literature. Under her influence, Yuriko began to write an autobiographical fiction, her first novel, *Nobuko,* which would be serialized over twenty-four months in an intellectual magazine, *Kaizō* (Reformation), from 1924 to 1926. By 1925, Yuriko was living with Yuasa and taking frequent trips with her. In 1927, they went to the Soviet Union and lived in Moscow for about three years, during which they visited several countries in Europe and saw "signs of deterioration in capitalist civilizations." In July 1929, Yuriko joined her family in Marseilles and went on to Paris and London with them. Later she described this trip as a manifestation of the "corruption of the class in which she grew up." Yuriko and Yuasa returned to Japan in the fall of 1930. Communist writers and Marxist theoreticians were very active in Japan then, while nonpolitical novelists were producing introspective, personal, confessional stories. Yuriko joined Zen-Nihon Puroretaria Sakka Dōmei (All-Japan Proletarian Writers' Association) and began to write many essays on Russian life and culture. In 1931, she became a member of the Japan Communist party, which was still unlawful.

In February 1932, Yuriko married a communist leader and literary critic, Miyamoto Kenji (1908–19–), who would be a longtime chairman of the party in postwar years. At the time, however, Japan had already begun a military action in Manchuria, and proletarian literary movements and government censorship were both nearing their peak. Numerous protest meetings and arrests were occurring, and Kenji was forced to go underground within two months of their marriage. Yuriko was detained by the police and wrote up her experience of the eighty-two-day detention in *"1932-nen no haru"* (Spring of 1932). She went on to publish essays in such magazines as *Puroretaria Bungaku* (Proletarian Literature), *Hataraku Fujin* (Working Women), and *Yuibutsuron Kenkyū* (Studies of Dialectical Materialism). Censorship of publications and speeches became increasingly more severe, and the National Mobilization Law was enacted, as the entire nation geared toward the military government's war efforts.

By 1935, Yuriko had gone through four arrests, spending a total of nineteen months in detention, while her husband was ailing in prison since 1933. Before she received a suspended sentence, along with a ban on writing, effective throughout 1938, Yuriko had published a number of superior stories, including *Koiwai no ikka* (The Family of Koiwai, 1934). When World War II broke out in 1941, Yuriko was kept under police custody for the fifth time until the next summer, when she suffered heat stroke in her detention cell and nearly died. She was never to regain her health completely. Excused from serving out her sentence, she was released but saddled with a permanent ban on publishing. Accordingly, she wrote little except letters to her husband. Even a selection of the correspondence between Kenji and Yuriko that she published after the war as *12-nen no tegami* (Letters of Twelve Years) took up three volumes, and *"Gokuchū no tegami"* (Letters During Imprisonment), included in *Miyamoto Yuriko Zenshū* (Complete Works of Miyamoto Yuriko), published by Shin Nihon Shuppansha, amounts to one thousand. On the day the war ended, Yuriko was waiting for a ferry to take her from her grandmother's estate in northern Japan to visit her husband, imprisoned in Hokkaido.

To sum up the prewar stages of her life course, Miyamoto Yuriko not only was born into wealth and prestige but also was endowed with a superb power of observation and writing skills. Growing up a bright child, surrounded by influential family friends, faithful housemaids, and many books, young Yuriko knew little hardship, financial or otherwise. The leading scholar-novelist Tsubouchi Shōyō (1859–1935) arranged to have her first novel published in *Chūō kōron.* In New York, her father introduced her to important people to make her life easier and more fruitful. Her father also helped her first husband get his teaching position. When Yuriko was arrested, her father used his influence to have her released. Later on, family friends obtained visas for Yuriko and Yuasa to visit Russia.

Disagreement with her mother was one of the most important formative factors in her life. She refused to stay in college and instead took a trip to Hokkaido to do research for her novels. The adverse living conditions and tenacity of the peasants that she observed there made her aware of the differences that existed in society. She realized that the environment in which she grew up represented but one layer, or one privileged class, in a very large, complex world. To her then, America stood for freedom from her mother and a land where she could enjoy ''free'' love—the relationship of man and woman based not on family decisions but on mutual respect. In America she also learned that even some liberals were selfish and prejudiced. Back in Japan again, Yuriko's attempt at a meaningful marriage within her parents' household taught her that the Japanese family system could repress individual creativity and that financial independence was of great importance. Her quest for a creative life ended in divorce from Araki and led to a new life with Yuasa, both serving to broaden her perspective in the process.

Her Russian and European experiences were a revelation, for there she found that much of what she had heard and read was actually correct. People seemed freer, women livelier, and children happier in Russia. She thought she was witnessing the real workings of the communist doctrine. In contrast, she was particularly surprised by the large number of jobless people flooding parts of London and felt compelled to inform the Japanese public of her comparative observations. Having never experienced the plight of a proletarian personally, however, Yuriko was aware of the danger of falling into a vicious cycle of alternating between thought and action, and so she joined the Communist party upon her return to Japan. Her relationship with the party remained ambivalent, for she proved more a humanitarian than an ideological activist, as attested by her works, which are informative, balanced, and wholesome in viewpoint and execution.

One of her first works in the postwar period, ''*Utagoe yo okore*'' (Rise, Singing Voices!, 1946), is an essay with an elated tone published in the inaugural issue of *Shin Nihon Bungaku* (Literature of the New Japan), a new magazine of the Communist party, which was just legalized by the Occupation Authority. In it, Yuriko called for the people's active participation in rebuilding the devastated nation. She followed it up with more essays, one after another, on topics ranging from happiness and women, to democracy, in various commercial magazines, as well as the Communist party paper, *Akahata* (Red Flag). Soon she became popular as a public lecturer.

In the meantime, Yuriko began a novel, *Banshū heiya* (The Banshu Plain, 1946–47), depicting what she and the country were doing when Japan's defeat was imminent. *Fūchisō* (Weathervane Plant, 1946), its virtual sequel, recounts her husband's release from prison and their subsequent efforts to adjust their lives to the postwar situation. These two novels together won the *Mainichi* Publication Prize in 1947. Yuriko produced two more substantial novels, *Futatsu no niwa* (Two Gardens, 1947) and *Dōhyō* (The Signpost, 1947–50), extending her autobiographical coverage from the time of her divorce through her trip to Russia. In all, she published some eighty works of fiction and over seven hundred essays. Her latest "complete works" consists of twenty-nine volumes. With her health deteriorating all the while, Miyamoto Yuriko died of septicemia on January 21, 1951, at the age of fifty-two.

Career: The early stage of Yuriko's career in the 1920s and 1930s coincided with the flourishing of apolitical novels written by authors previously exposed to European naturalism. In an attempt to keep to an "artistic" stance during the time of extreme political turmoil, those novelists wrote mainly about their inner life. For many of them, fiction served as a means of catharsis in revealing the author's deepest thoughts and troubled, guilty conscience, in achieving some sort of reconciliation with life, or in reaching a height of spiritual exaltation. Yuriko apparently felt an affinity to such writers. She expressed her sympathy with Akutagawa Ryjnosuke (1892–1927), a novelist who felt pressure from both the proletarian literature and the naturalist novels and wrote some painfully confessional pieces before committing suicide. No doubt Yuriko aspired to write artistic novels like Akutagawa's, since she believed in literature as a means to accomplish her personal objectives and improve the world at large. Nevertheless, she was not as much concerned with technical experiments or innovations as many of her fellow novelists were.

Yuriko's literary career was quite different from that shared by many of her fellow writers, who not only produced far fewer works of significance but easily compromised their beliefs under government oppression only to write about their pangs of conscience in autobiographical fashion after the war. Yuriko did not emulate the abstruse interpreters of Marxism, nor did she subscribe to the criticism or defense of communism by popular theoreticians. Similarly, she was not particularly critical of any of the fashionable "bourgeois" schools of literature, such as Shirakaba-ha (White Birch School) and Shinkankaku-ha (New Sensitivity School). She managed to survive the period of intense thought control by immersing herself in the past, reading and writing about the classical works of women writers. She did not produce "literature of resistance," partly because it was impossible for anyone at the time to do so. She also survived the Allied occupation with its own brand of censorship. She refrained from getting involved in the internal strifes within the Communist party, which utilized literature as a tool in propagation and execution of its ideology, splitting the proletarian writers into factions. Nonetheless, Yuriko was subjected to criticism from the secretary general of the party, while her husband was confined to Kyushu for differing with the party on its policies.

Independent and intelligent, Yuriko did not allow her spirit to be crushed or her personal and ideological beliefs to be converted. As an intellectual, she was more concerned with perfecting her own self as well as contributing to the welfare of the masses. Concentration on these goals helped her to rise above the oppression that plagued her generation in one form after another.

Yuriko's novels defy her popular label as a communist writer, being autobiographical and containing no propaganda. They are barely distinguishable from *watakushi shōsetsu,* or the "I-novel," which constitutes a mainstream in modern Japanese literature. How is Yuriko different, for example, from Shimazaki Tōson (1872–1943) or Shiga Naoya (1883–1971), both of whom produced masterpieces by confessing their actions or narrating events in their personal lives? Yuriko did express admiration for Shiga's *Anya kōro* (Dark Night's Passing, 1919–37), a lengthy autobiographical novel delineating his past love for a woman and his reconciliation with the world. Some critics maintain that the perspective of the "I-novelists" is narrow and their techniques limited to a detached depiction of their immediate surroundings, whereas Miyamoto Yuriko's outlook is broader, more socially conscious, and intellectually challenging.

If, for Yuriko, the novel was an instrument of self-examination and humanistic growth, the essay was a tool with which to convey her knowledge and thoughts to the masses. Her essays are plainly descriptive, firsthand accounts of her observations, many focusing on Russia, her people and culture, and social conditions. Instead of discussing the Soviet political or economic principles, she depicted the life there in comparison with the Japanese one. Clearly she did not propose to advocate Marxist theories but hoped to induce the reader to admire Russia or to begin to think critically about Japanese ways. Even when faced with problems in interpreting certain policies of the Communist party that infringed upon her basic human rights, Yuriko chose not to make her dismay public through writing.

Particularly interested in education, she reported on Russia's Five-Year Plan and recommended equal educational opportunities, which would yield good production ratio and a relatively high literacy rate. She considered "education through literature" to be an effective weapon against poverty and ignorance, two issues of great concern since her childhood. Her essays address the function of literature in relation to the country's political, social, and economic affairs: literary works function to educate the masses whereas theories stimulate only their readers. In the postwar period, Yuriko's essays tended to sound academic. Many were presented in a manner similar to the methods used in reporting research results. Some were powerful arguments, substantiated by data, more concrete and straightforward than earlier works.

Major Works: 1. Fiction. Mazushiki hitobito no mure (Flock of Poor People; originally entitled *Nōmin,* lit., Peasants, 1916). This story is a sensitive study of peasants' life in northern Japan, where Yuriko's wealthy grandmother lived. A precocious city girl observes the ignorance and stubbornness of impoverished village people. The girl's goodwill is met with the villagers' apathy; there is a sense of frustration and pity, without a clear message. This work marked Yuriko's inititation into a world quite different from her own and the first step in her literary career.

Futatsu no niwa (Two Gardens, 1947). A sequel to *Nobuko,* her most famous novel, published some twenty years earlier, this story is populated by the same characters, including Nobuko, her ex-husband, and her mother. Directly following *Nobuko*'s time frame, the heroine recalls her divorce and reassesses the period during which she "created" Nobuko, in the tradition of the "I-novel" in terms of conception and treatment of the subject matter. A female character named Motoko, who lives with Nobuko, smokes a pipe, and speaks like a man, is described in detail. Motoko proposes a visit to Russia on their own, after discovering that she had not been chosen to attend the tenth anniversary of the Russian Revolution in Moscow. In examining their relationship, Nobuko realizes her life with Motoko is similar to her life with her husband before their divorce. As they travel through Russia, their relationship, rumored to be lesbian, slowly deteriorates.

The pace is slow, since the heroine spends a great deal of time reflecting on the past. She controls her ego better now than she did in *Nobuko.* She has grown more considerate, compassionate, and mature. She is able to recall and more fully appreciate her ex-husband's care and considerations, which she failed to notice before. Her action, nonetheless, is faithful to reality, for Nobuko leaves Japan for Russia with Motoko. The "two gardens" could refer to any one or all of the paired worlds contained in the novel, such as the adult world that Nobuko and Motoko share and the conventional world of man and woman. "Two gardens" are also contrasts between a "creative" life-style, which Nobuko thought she was leading, and her "bourgeois" environment, surrounded by influential family friends, housemaids, and chauffeur on one level and, on another, between communist Russia and Japan.

Dōhyō (The Signpost, 1947–59). In the afterword, Yuriko explains that an "aria" that had been *Nobuko* developed into a quartet of *Futatsu no niwa,* and the quartet has grown into a concerto that is *Dōhyō.* This novel, however, ends up not being an enlarged or developed version of the previous works but simply a sequel to *Dōhyō,* covering the author's life in Russia between 1927 and 1930 much in the same vein. This time, moreover, the novel does not contain much of a plot or structure, and the outcome resembles a detailed travel record full of tourist observations. At least the author does not fail to call attention to events and things that were not generally believed to exist in the Soviet Union at the time, such as the government cover-up of corruption, wealthy people's wasteful way of life in St. Petersburg, and misery of the deprived people. There is no constant viewpoint or well-defined stance. But the heroine does appear to grow, giving this novel a sense of history.

2. *Essays.* "Mosukuwa inshō ki" (Impressions of Moscow, 1928) describes the workings of communist society, while pointing to such negative elements as bureaucracy and the black market. Unconcerned with the broken elevator in

Moscow, she is greatly impressed by their welfare programs, labor unions, high status of women, and the physical facilities benefiting the masses.

"Kodomo, kodomo, kodomo no Mosukuwa" (Children, Children, and More Children in Moscow, 1930) pays special attention to working mothers and child-care facilities. Yuriko says that the future of a country is dependent on contented women and children.

"Shōgatsu to Sobieto kinrō fujin" (The New Year's Day and the Soviet Working Women, 1931) introduces Soviet women as contributing members of communist society, praising the gender equity in wages, as compared with the lamentable state of women in capitalist countries like Japan.

"Roshia kakumei wa fujin o kaihō shita" (The Russian Revolution Emancipated Women, 1932) even mixes envy with praise for the high status of Russian female workers resulting from the revolution.

"Sobieto Dōmei no fujin to senkyo" (The Women in the Soviet Union and Election, 1932) and other essays support women's suffrage against the backdrop of severe government suppression of leftist movements.

"Fujin no seikatsu to bungaku" (Women's Life and Literature, 1947) approaches women's issues from a historical perspective. Taking a small number of Japanese women writers as examples, Yuriko argues that for women, life and literature are inseparable as well as indispensable for happiness in the world, concluding that Japanese women must acquire a sense of history.

"Josei no rekishi" (A History of Women, 1947) surveys the state of women globally, introducing ancient Greeks, Italians in the Renaissance, Englishwomen in the 19th century, and Japanese women during various periods. Yuriko is critical of Japanese women, especially those in the feudal age, urging contemporary women to take a stand and develop class consciousness.

"Sensō to fujin sakka" (War and Women Writers, 1948) shows Yuriko's sympathy with women writers who, due to the absence of proper social systems and societal sanction, could not be financially independent and had to buckle under the military government's oppression.

Translated Work: Nobuko (1924–27), novel. Featuring a young woman apparently modeled after the author herself, this story opens with the heroine's meeting with her future husband in New York and ends with her divorce in Tokyo. The events and their dates in this novel parallel those in the author's real life. Some leftist critics interpret this story as an indictment of the feudal family system or as a thesis on women's liberation. However, the heroine's father is not really a domineering head of a premodern Japanese family, and her husband is not necessarily a man insensitive to her feelings or basic human rights. Nobuko senses in her husband a certain indecisiveness, which she takes as a sign of slyness, and thinks that their marriage fails to be dialectically elevating. This novel is a summation of the psychological struggles during which Nobuko's ego rejects her mother's ego and searches for a more compatible role model, that is, a woman with a creative life of her own. She takes objective lessons even from ideology. One of the characters compares a Marxist newspaper with a capitalist one and concludes that everything has two sides, so she must examine everything from at least two different angles. This same character then refuses to assist anarchists soliciting political contributions in a high-handed manner, as, just as in most of Miyamoto Yuriko's works, common sense rather than theories of dialectical materialism prevails. More than anything, *Nobuko* is a chronicle of the author's, or any thinking woman's, process of growth.

BIBLIOGRAPHY

Translations

"The Family of Koiwai." Tr. Noriko Lippit. In *Stories by Contemporary Japanese Women Writers,* ed. Noriko Lippit and Kyoko Selden. Armonk, NY: M. E. Sharpe, 1983.
"From *Nobuko.*" Tr. Brett de Bary. In *Longman Anthology of World Literature by Women: 1875–1975,* ed. Marian Arkin and Barbara Schollar. New York: Longman, 1989.
"Koiwai no ikka." Tr. Noriko Lippit. Bulletin of concerned Asian Scholars (1978).
"Nobuko." Tr. Brett de Bary. *Bulletin of Concerned Asian Scholars* (1975).

Critical Works

de Bary, Brett. "Wind and Leaves: Miyamoto Yurko's *The Weathervane Plant.*" *Journal of the Association of Teachers of Japanese,* 19 (1984-85): 7–33.
Keene, Donald. *Dawn to the West: Japanese Literature of the Modern Era.* New York: Holt, Rinehart and Winston, 1984, 1146–50.
Lippit, Noriko. "Literature and Ideology: The Feminist Biography of Miyamoto Yuriko." In *Reality and Fiction in Modern Japanese Literature.* Armonk, NY: M. E. Sharpe, 1980, 146–62. (Formerly, "Literature, Ideology, and Women's Happiness: The Autobiographical Novels of Miyamoto Yuriko." *Bulletin of Concerned Asian Scholars* (1978): 2–9.
Lyons, Phyllis. "Miyamoto Yuriko." In *Longman Anthology of World Literature by Women: 1875–1975,* ed. Marian Arkin and Barbara Schollar. New York: Longman, 1989.

James R. MORITA

MORI Michiyo (1901–77), poet, novelist. Real name: (Mrs. Kaneko Mitsuharu); née Mori Michiyo.

Life: Mori Michiyo was born on Shikoku Island but grew up in Mie prefecture on the main island after her father changed positions as women's middle school teacher. According to her husband, poet Kaneko Mitsuharu (1895–1975), Michiyo was a bright child who avidly read Japanese classical tales and other writings in her father's library. In 1920, she received a scholarship to attend the Tokyo Women's Normal College, the highest academic institution for women at the time. She majored in Japanese literature and soon began publishing poems in magazines. Through her literary friends, she met Mitsuharu and married him within a few months. The conservative college expelled her for marrying.

In 1924, Michiyo, Mitsuharu, and their friends launched a poetry magazine called *Fūkeiga* (Landscape Painting) but abandoned it shortly, for Michiyo gave birth to a son, Ken, and they had no money. Still, flamboyant Michiyo and Mitsuharu traveled to Shanghai in 1925 and visited some famous Chinese men of letters, including Lu Hsün. Their financial difficulties continued, but, due mainly to emotional problems, Michiyo separated from Mitsuharu and took Ken to her parents' house in Nagasaki. She left behind a lover, a young student and anarchist, in Tokyo. From Nagasaki, she was forced by Mitsuharu, who desperately wanted to sever her relationship with her lover, to accompany him to Southeast Asia in 1928. Mitsuharu earned a meager living by selling his paintings to Japanese residents in Malay and Java; then from Singapore, Michiyo traveled to France first, and Mitsuharu was to follow later.

In Paris, she had only part-time, low-paying jobs of dubious nature to sustain herself. After Mitsuharu caught up with her from Singapore, they visited Mitsuharu's old acquaintances, a Belgian antique dealer and his family, in Brussels, where Mitsuharu had sojourned in 1920 as a sort of the antique dealer's apprentice and a poet. Later, Michiyo moved from Paris to Antwerp for a better-paying job. She returned alone to Japan in 1932, stopping at Singapore to meet briefly with Mitsuharu. Mitsuharu had left Paris after the Japanese military invasion of Manchuria caused public outcry, and he warned Michiyo to leave Antwerp.

In 1937, Michiyo published her first fiction ''Shōshinshi'' (Little Gentleman) in a magazine. She wrote more works, mostly based on her travel experience. Around this time, both Michiyo and Mitsuharu benefited financially from the business success of Mitsuharu's sister. One winter, Michiyo and Mitsuharu traveled to China to survey the market for their business. Michiyo had a secret purpose: to learn about her Chinese lover, whom she had met and separated from before Mitshharu managed to return to Japan from Singapore.

In 1938, Michiyo and Mitsuharu bought a house in Tokyo and settled there. Michiyo produced short stories and essays. When World War II broke out, the Foreign Ministry wanted her to go to French Indochina to propagate Japanese culture. She complied, by touring there as a cultural envoy. After her return, American bombings on Tokyo became severe, Michiyo, along with Mitsuharu and Ken, vacated their house and moved to a remote village by Mt. Fuji. The isolated, inconvenient country life bonded them as a family. They feared that Ken might be drafted and did everyting possible to prevent it. Then the war ended.

The family returned to their Tokyo house, which had escaped bombing, and Michiyo started to publish again. However, she soon became ill and bedridden: an acute case of rheumatism deprived her of movement in her upper body. She managed to dictate several short stories, but as a writer she was overshadowed by Mitsuharu, who attained great fame with the publication of several poetry collections and numerous thought-provoking essays and with his eccentric conduct, which included affairs with young women. Michiyo suffered ill fate, having to protect both her status as his wife in the family register, which Mitsuharu had changed in favor of his mistress, and her name as a remaining member of the Mori family. Despite the adversities, she translated some Japanese classics into modern Japanese. Her grandchildren—Ken's daughters—who lived with her were her main solace and great joy, so she wrote about them. Back on her natal family's register, she died under the legal name of Mori Michiyo in 1977, two years after her husband Kaneko Mitsuharu's death.

Career: Michiyo published four books of verse: the first in 1927, the second in 1931, the third in 1934, and the fourth in 1942. Of these, the second and the fourth ones were in French. It is assumed that Michiyo wrote the poems in Japanese and, before publishing them, translated some of them into French. Mitsuharu has written of Michiyo's working on her Japanese poems with a French tutor in Paris. In fact, the majority of her poems in her second poetry collection, *Par Les Chemins Du Monde* (Sekai no michi kara, 1931), are translations of her own poems appearing in her third poetry book, *Tōhō no shi* (Poems from the East, 1934).

The title *Tōhō no shi* suggests that Michiyo intended to introduce the East to the West while attempting to establish herself as a poet on both sides of the world. The field of Japanese poetry lacked a powerful female poet then. Michiyo felt that she could become an international poet like, perhaps, Yone Noguchi (1875–1942), who attained fame both in English and Japanese. Not coincidentally, Yone Noguchi had written an introduction to Michiyo's first poetry collection, *Ryūjo no hitomi* (Dragon Woman's Eye, 1927). The poet Ōshika Taku (1898–1959), Mitsuharu's brother, also contributed, together with Mitsuharu and Yone Noguchi, a compliment to *Ryūjo no hitomi.*

Like the people to whom she was then close, she was an intellectual lyricist. She was skeptical of traditional Japanese lyricism, which she and her friends thought indistinguishable from sentimentalism. Critical also of both art-for-art's-sake poetry and plain, people's, or "democratic" poetry, she latently instilled art and social criticisms in her poetry, and her poetry was that of a modernist.

However, for Michiyo and Mitsuharu, who did not exactly belong to the main current of Japanese letters and who were plagued by poverty, any assistance was welcome. Michiyo's *Tōhō no shi* includes six illustrations by Francine Lepage, a daughter of the Belgian antique dealer and Mitsuharu's old acquaintance, Ivan Lepage, whom Michiyo had met when she visited Brussels from Paris. The book also carries F. Lepage's foreword in French. Likewise, Michiyo's second poetry collection, *Par Les Chemins Du Monde,* contains F. Lepage's frontispiece and is dedicated to Ivan Lepage. Moreover, the book is accompanied by a Japanese book jacket, on which its Japanese title, *Sekai no michi kara,* and the author's portrait are printed. Apparently, these books did not sell well either in Europe or Japan.

That was the period in which Japanese poetry on the center stage underwent a great diversification of style and content. Anarchism had waned before communism did as influential political and aesthetic thought. Particularly prominent among the countless number of poets were: Hagiwara Sakutarō (1886–1942), attacking sentimentality and reverting to the use of classical langauge; Nishiwaki Junzaburō (1894–198?), resorting to surrealism; Fukushi Kōjirō (1889–1946), insisting on people's poetry; and Nakahara Chūya (1907–37), singing about life's ennui—all against the backdrop of the government's relentless suppression of leftists and the phenomenal economic growth of publishers.

Michiyo's poems were relatively few in number, and she did not become a major force in Japanese literature. On one hand, she was out of Japan for prolonged periods and did not associate with influential Japanese writers or editors, which was, for aspiring writers, a crucial tactical disadvantage in channeling works to the literary world at that time. Michiyo's foreign journeys coincided, for example, with the duration of the important women's literary magazine, *Nyonin geijutsu* (Women's Art).

On the other hand, she was with Mitsuharu, a great loner in the Japanese world of letters and a total financial failure. Life with Mitsuharu was Michiyo's great literary stimulus. Their relationship was an enduring struggle of two egos, without a real winner. Respect existed between them, but so did doubt and deception. The two egos dragged each other from Nagasaki to Shanghai, Canton to Singapore, Java to France, Brussels to Antwerp, and deeper into life's abyss. In love and in hate, Michiyo and Mitsuharu nurtured each other, and their literary productions, let alone worldly success and financial fulfillment, looked insignificant in relative terms.

Michiyo's prose works include one long novel, *Kyonen no Yuki* (Last Year's Snow, 1959), delineating the love-hate marriage of her own, and a fictional biography of the 11th-century woman writer Izumi Shikibu, whose passionate love poems Michiyo had read fondly. When publishing was difficult and writers were expected to write in support of the government's war effort, Michiyo renewed her interest in Japanese classics. After she went to Indochina at the government's request and lectured on Japanese classics, she was able to publish a travel essay, a collection of short stories, and a book of poems called *Poesies indochinoises. Shōsetsu Izumi Shikibu* (Lady Izumi, A Fiction) appeared in 1943 and won the *Shinchō* Cultural Award.

It was bad luck that she was stricken by illness. Not only was her body incapacitated, but her thought appeared to have lost its once-defiant luster; nevertheless, Michiyo's eventful life, filled with passion and action, anguish and frustration, and glory and joy, was unique: it was literature itself. Her one-volume collection of works exists, but many of her works, especially poems, are uncollected.

Major Works: Fuka shizumu (Sharks Sink, 1927), poetry. This is an extremely rare work, a book of verse that Michiyo coauthored with Mitsuharu. The volume is small, containing eight poems, all set in China, with no indication as to which of the coauthors composed which poem. The cosigned preface states that Michiyo and Mitsuharu wanted to commemorate their trip to China and to express their gratitude to those who helped their trip. Neither Michiyo nor Mitsuharu ever again repeated coproduction of poetry with anyone in their long careers.

Ryūjo no hitomi (Dragon Lady's Eye, 1927), collection of poems. Michiyo composed these poems on specific occasions or on travel, juxtaposing her youthful, searching self with the nature scenes and crisp imagery. For example, the last half of a three-stanza poem called "*Kyoryūchi no sampo* (Stroll in the Foreigners' Residential District) reads:

> Under the heels of my shoes
> The red dry leaves crumble like ribs.
> Ah, how deep thought and fascination could run.
> In the foreigners' residential district from wall to sky
> This autumn a bird flies like a rock.

Par les Chemins Du Monde (Sekai no michi kara, or From the Roads of the World, 1931), poems in French. This book was printed by Leon Libbrecht in Brussels, Belgium in a limited edition of 320 copies. Judging by the circumstances, it seems to have been a private publication distributed among the author's acquaintances without going through a commercial channel. The fact that the book has a Japanese jacket supports this assumption. According to Michiyo's son, Professor Mori Ken, who teaches French literature at Waseda University, Michiyo herself wrote new poems in French or translated her previously published works, and Lepage polished them for her.

But these poems are not necessarily about Europe. One entitled *Shanghai* is a product of the author's travel to China.

> Dans la soie flamboyante de Fouchow
> Est enveloppé un pied de Chinoise,
> Comme un poing.
> La puanteur qui donne des nausées,
> La honte qui a perdu son lustre.

This poem depicts a visual effect of the foot-binding custom, a woman's foot that was deformed because it had been bound tight with a cloth in her childhood to restrict her movement beyond the boundaries of her household. The poet, herself troubled by love, society's criticism, her parents' disapproval, and her own sense of guilt at the time, approaches the subject without sentimentality. The attitude relfects the stance of anarchism and liberalism, which were sweeping across Japan those days. Michiyo concludes the poem with a scathing stanza:

> Mais coolies, wanpotzos et mendiants,
> Haletants et tremblants,
> Regardent fruieusement avec des yeux minces

Comme des aiguilles à coudre.
L'estomac, à ne jamais manger, se reverse.

Toho no shi (Poems from the East, 1934). Probably written much earlier than the book's publication date, these poems retain the liberal thought and modernist techniques prevalent in an earlier age.

Indian Ocean

How blue the water is!
But it's lumpy like thick glass bottles.
My body is twisted up
Like a saxophone.

In the shapelessness I seek
A path through which my thought can track
The keel of a ship cutting apart
My reason that has already turned to formless clouds.
The sea now resembles a green fruit.

Look,
The face swollen from hangover;
My eyes bloodshot. In the waves
Drifting eyeglasses, and a pistol;
A lizard, a top hat, a pair of scissors,
an umbrella, an anchor, and . . .

''Shō-shinshi'' (Little Gentleman, 1937), short story. Here Michiyo seems to be flirting with prose style. It depicts, from more than one viewpoint, a loving relationship between a boy and his mother, interweaving passages from the boy's diary and probing into the boy's psyche. The narrator, however, is too emotionally involved with another character, Mother. Besides, as a short story, it has structural weaknesses, and the boy, or the little gentleman, does not come across as the story's main character.

''Kunichigai'' (Foreigners, 1942), short story. In this better-structured narrative, foreigners are Japanese and Malaysians who work as rubber planters in the tropical jungle. One of them is Sonoko, who left Japan long ago and has been married to a Malaysian for decades. She looks Malaysian and is no longer fluent in Japanese. The story revolves around a Japanese journalist's plot to send Sonoko back to Japan. The author's intention is not to study Sonoko's dilemma caught between nostalgia and a feeling of shame, but to point out how foreign, that is, misunderstanding, human beings can be to one another. This work rises above a mere recitation of facts that can be observed in real life.

Shōsetsu Izumi Shikibu (Lady Izumi, A Novel, 1943). Michiyo's longest novel has a double structure: it is a tale about the first-person narrator, who writes a biography of the 11th-century Japanese diarist Lady Izumi Shikibu, incorporating a version of her own creation. In the text itself rather than in the afterword, Michiyo states:

As I look back upon finishing this novel, I cannot help feeling that I have after all written about myself, failing to produce a true Lady Izumi. However, if this were my autobiography, I would consider it an autobiography of a different kind, tracing the path that I myself did not take. Anyone is entitled to even three or four different autobiographies.

The decay of Izumi's grave and fallen leaves in the garden of her house had made Mori Michiyo decide to focus her novel on Lady Izumi's declining years. Moved by the passionate poems of Lady Izumi, now nine hundred years old, the narrator visits a temple in Kyoto and imagines many men and various events in Izumi's life. The narrator goes on to recount Lady Izumi's marrying her second husband, trying to find love, becoming ill, losing her daughter, and approaching a Buddhist understanding of life. The novel concludes with a remark on Buddha's acceptance of women on lotus leaves laid upside down. It is explained that the unusual upside-down lotus leaf, which Buddha uses in his mercy as a special device to extend salvation to sinful women, would have been appropriate for Lady Izumi and that the narrator herself would someday like to sit on it.

"Seishun no hōrō" (Youthful Wandering, 1951), short story. The characters bear the names of real people, including the poets Kusano Shimpei (1903–88?) and Kaneko Mitsuharu, and the events seem fact-based. The description of Michiyo's passionate love for an anarchist lover, for instance, is in accord with what both Shimpei and Mitsuharu have recorded elsewhere. The first-person narrator is obviously Michiyo herself. As the story opens, Mitsuharu just arrives from Shanghai and is taken by Shimpei to an apartment, where Michiyo and her lover are asleep. After an awkward reunion of husband, wife, and friend and the first meeting of husband and his wife's lover, Michiyo and Mitsuharu return to their own apartment.

Kaneko [Mitsuharu] pulled out an old *yukata* [summer kimono] from the closet and changed into it. The *yukata* is the one that I offered Teiichi to wear, when he was penniless and nowhere else to go and I brought him to this apartment, that is, when we slept together for the first time. Teiichi had abhorred touching Kaneko's clothes and worn my *yukata* instead. Moreover, after he lay on the bed, Teiichi had peeled the bedcover away and complained that it had the odor of Kaneko. But Kaneko is less sensitive; he put on the yukata which Teiichi might have used for all he knew, and stretched himself under the quilt. I moved my quilt to the adjacent room where my child was sleeping. Determinedly, I meant to show Kaneko that he and I were through.

I thought Kaneko had fallen asleep, but I heard his voice in the other room: "He seems to be a smart young man. He is . . . , Michiyo, are you asleep? Let's talk a while."

Two days later, the narrator puts on thick powder makeup, wears a Chinese dress and a single earring, and hurries out to see Teiichi. This story contains remarks on society's repression of the free love and anarchist movements. It also touches on the struggles and aspirations of some writers, including the woman dramatist-novelist Hasegawa Shigure (1879–1941) and Yoshida Issui (1898–1973). Certain narrative devices, such as flashbacks and diaries, and an analysis of the narrator's state of mind barely distinguish this work from a mere cluster of biographical sketches.

"Shinjuku ni ame furu" (Rain Falls in Shinjuku, 1953), short story. Dealing with a Japanese woman's love affair with a Chinese army officer, the story is presumed to be factual, and the narrator is apparently Michiyo. Other characters' names are easily identifiable with the real people around her. The time is a few years after the end of the war. As the narrator is trying to recover from a long illness, she receives a letter from her lover, whom she had not heard from for twenty years. She meets him in Tokyo's Shinjuku district in the rain. Her memory of love revives, blurs her present anxiety and passion, and numbs her senses.

In the mirror his eyes beamed with vitality, and though his complexion was that of a middle-aged man, his facial skin was taut, shining with a glow.
Ah, he is still so young.
She wondered how he will look the day he flies in from Taiwan next time.
"When can you come to Japan next?"
"Well, it may be sooner than you think, because this visit creates some business for me to pursue. In November, maybe. But I can't tell. It may be much later."
"Twenty more years later?"
"Sooner than that."
"Five years? Ten years? But if you come to Japan ten years from now and send for me, I will probably not see you."
"Why not?" He asked in surprise.
"Why not? But ten years from now, I will be . . . "

This work is melodramatic, a rather fantastic tale of a Chinese army officer who was reported to his Chinese wife as killed in action, then moved to Taiwan after the war, and rose to the rank of a general. The plot is too complex to be contained within a short story. The central theme is perhaps the continuity of lovers' passion through times of turmoil.

Translations (of Japanese classical literature into modern vernacular): *Tosa Nikki* (The Tosa Diary) and *Murasaki Shikibu Nikki* (Lady Murasaki's Diary). Extremely free and original in interpretation of the texts, these "translations" are quite readable but may be more accurately categorized as Mori Michiyo's own creative works.

BIBLIOGRAPHY

Original Publication in French

Par les Chemins Du Monde. Brussels: Leon Libbrecht, 1931.
Poesies indochinoises. Tokyo: Meiji Shobo, 1942.

Critical Works

Maki, Yoko. *Kaneko Mitsuharu to Mori Michiyo.* Tokyo: Magajin House, 1992.
————. "Shijoteki Mori Michiyo Ron." *Koganemushi* 1–6 (1987–1992).
Morita, James. R. *Kaneko Mitsuharu.* Boston: Twayne Publishers, 1980.

James R. MORITA

MORI Reiko (1928–), novelist, poet, dramatist, biographer, literary critic. Real name: Kawada Reiko.

Life: Born in Kyushu, Mori spent the first twenty years of her life in her hometown, Fukuoka (except for the years between 1931 and 1933, during which her family lived in Osaka). Kyushu has been the stronghold of Christianity since it was introduced to Japan in the mid-16th century. This fact may have contributed to Mori's decision to follow the faith later in her life. The significance of the hometown to this writer is also apparent in her fiction, often set in Kyushu.

Mori's early life was marred by a series of tragic events. She lost her architect father in 1933 and one of her elder sisters in 1945 immediately after the end of World War II. The war itself left on her many devastating effects, which she explores extensively in her writing. Mori was a frail child, susceptible to illness. She was consequently often kept home from school for prolonged periods of time. She spent those days reading world literature and grew into an avid reader. Encouraged by her teacher, she also wrote a play that was later performed by her junior high school classmates. She exhibited talent in visual arts as well, and her teachers encouraged her to pursue the field. Her family's financial hardship, coupled with the economic chaos in postwar Japan, however, allowed her no more than to audit courses in the Faculty of Theology at Seinan University in her hometown. The years at the university nonetheless had a significant impact on Mori's life. First, she became a Baptist in 1947. Second, while working in the university's library, she met a group of aspiring poets and decided to make writing her career.

By a happy coincidence, Kojima Naoki (b. 1919), the founder of the literary journal *Kyūshū Bungaku* (later changed to *Kyūshū Sakka*), moved into the house adjacent to Mori's in 1952. She subsequently published poems, short stories, and essays in the journal. She also wrote plays for local newspapers and radio programs. After moving to Tokyo in 1956, Mori was again fortunate to have the support of a famous Kyushu novelist, Hino Ashihei (1907–60), who encouraged her to publish in the journal *Taishū* (The Mass). Her 1960 encounter with a Protestant literary coterie, however, marked the turning point in her career. Recalling her meeting with Shiina Rinzō (1911–73), who led the group, Mori says, "For the first time in my life, my eyes became open to the essence of literature." Shiina, also a Christian, persistently probed in his writing the meaning of spiritual freedom. Reflecting her strong identification with Shiina, Mori's works share with his writing the theme of emancipation, particularly of people who live outside the mainstream of Japanese society, well on its way to economic prosperity. Her major topics in this vein include *kakure Kirishitan* (hidden or underground Christians), who had upheld their Christian faith for three centuries despite the severe official persecutions until the mid-19th century.

Mori traveled to Europe in 1972 and to the United States in 1975. The latter trip yielded *Mokkingubaado no iru machi* (A Town Where the Mockingbirds Live, 1979), which earned her the coveted Akutagawa Award. Mori took research trips to South Korea in 1980 and 1981, which resulted in a biographical fiction, *Sansai no onna* (The Woman of Three Colors, 1982). The women's liberation movement, which took a firm hold in Japan by the mid-1970s, had a significant influence on Mori's works as well. The protagonists of her stories since 1979 are predominantly women, and she published biographies of a noted actress and a poetess in 1981. Mori taught creative writing in 1982.

Career: Mori's literary career can be divided roughly into four periods. The first stage spans the 1950s, during which she emerged as an exceptionally versatile writer. While in Kyushu, she published poems and short stories in *Kyushu Bungaku/Kyushu Sakka* and wrote children's stories, drama, and essays for local newspapers and radio stations, winning an award for a 1954 film review. After moving to Tokyo in 1956, she regularly contributed her short stories and plays to the journals *Taishō* and *Bungei Shuto*. She earned important recognition in 1957, when she won the *Fujin Asahi* (Women's Asahi journal) New Writer Award for a short story, "Chinkonkyoku" (A Requiem, 1957; originally "Zaihyō" (A Signpost for the Guilty).

Mori's 1960 encounter with Shiina Rinzō marked the beginning of the second phase of her career. After coauthoring a play, *Warera wa shisha to tomoni* (We Live with the Dead, 1961), with Shiina and Watanabe Yasumaro, Mori concentrated her effort on drama and published in rapid succession plays such as *Shungiku* (Spring Chrysanthemum, 1964), *Warera no budōen* (Our Vineyard, 1966), and *Tōryanse* (Take This Path, 1970). Mori wrote short stories as well and won a nomination for the New Woman Writer's Award with her "Mikan no karute" (An Unfinished Chart, 1963). The English translation of her 1971 story depicting hidden Christians and exploited stone masons, "Usugurai basho" (A Twilight Place), was published in 1972. Evolved during this period were the Christian issue and the motif of death and emancipation, to become more clearly etched in Mori's later works.

The third period of Mori's professional life began in 1973, the year of Shiina's death, when she wrote essays and children's plays that were strongly colored by her religious conviction. Children's dramas such as *Kurisumasu no kodomo* (A Christmas Child, 1973), *Seiya* (The Holy Night, 1974), *Yona* (Jonah, 1975), and *Yoninme no hakase* (The Fourth Wiseman, 1977) are, as their titles suggest, invariably religious plays. Essays such as "Jiyū to akuma" (Freedom and the Satan, 1977) and "Rippō o koeru mono" (Beyond the Moral Law, 1978) also explicitly embody the author's religious views. Moreover, in her collection of literary criticism, *Ai to mayoi* (Love and Delusion, 1974), Mori discusses prominent writers such as Inoue Hisashi (b. 1935), Ōe Kenzaburō (b. 1935), Endō

Shūsaku (b. 1923), Ariyoshi Sawako (1931–84), and Pearl Buck, applying her religious perspective to her analyses of their fiction and drama.

During this period, Mori won another significant recognition, a nomination for the *Shinchō* New Writer's Award, with her "Yūenchi bokei" (An Evening Scene at an Amusement Park, 1975). This short story portrays a father desperately hoping for his daughter's release from a terminal illness. The daughter appears to have come to terms with her fate, but, anxious to distract her from the thought of death, the father takes her to an amusement park still desolate in early spring. There, while drifting on a power-controlled boat through the darkness of a horror house, the father sees the vision of emancipation, that is, of his daughter entirely free from the torment of her illness. A moment later, however, he dies of cardiac arrest. The theme of emancipation and death with an irony inherent in it is typical of Mori's third period, but this story is unusual for her in that it has little to do with Christian faith.

What marks Mori's fourth and the latest phase is her strong interest in women's issues. The award-winning 1979 fiction *A Town Where the Mockingbirds Live* explores the alienation and sublimation experienced by Japanese wives of U.S. veterans of World War II. "Ten no ryōken" (The Hound in Heaven, 1980) tells of a woman who becomes endowed with the vision of freedom. In "Yūwakusha" (A Seducer, 1985), a woman suffers because of an irreconcilable conflict between her husband and his hypocritical preacher father. Of the two 1981 biographies of women, *Matsui Sumako* captures the life and art of the famed actress (1886–1919), and *Bachelar Yaeko* puts spotlight on a little-known Ainu poet who was adopted by the British missionary, John Bachelar (1883–1908), and dedicated her life to propagating Christianity among her people.

Mori regularly contributes essays and book reviews to major newspapers and journals, while continuing to probe the theme of liberation in her fiction.

Major Works: A Town Where the Mockingbirds Live (Mokkingubaardo no iru machi, 1979), novella. In an obscure southern American town adjacent to "the largest missile base in the States," Keiko (Kay), a Japanese housewife in her late forties married to a retired veteran of World War II once stationed in Japan, leads a seemingly carefree life of the American middle class: their children are grown and gone, and they have few financial worries. Keiko nonetheless suffers an acute sense of alienation from her adopted home and from her true self. Left alone in a house darkened by the blinds pulled down to shield the intense summer heat that envelops this sleepy town, she recalls her childhood in a seaside town in Japan:

Here I am in the heart of America, Keiko thought as she looked at the face of an aging Japanese woman dimly reflected in a mirror in front of her. Why am I here, in a place like this? I was once so sure of my bonds to that sea. How could I have spent all these years—the years since I was only twenty years old or so—in a place like this? With a vacant look on her face, she swept her eyes over the things around her. Her bedroom, clean and tidy like a showroom display, suddenly looked totally strange to her.

Is this really my own home? Keiko felt as if she were tricked into the confinement of life that was not her own, only to busy herself with family chores. She wondered, too, if she had not been misled to believe that the children she has raised, and the man she has lived with, were actually the members of her own family.

How could this happen to me? I could have lived by the sea with a husband and children to whom I could talk in my own language, and in a house with tatami floors and sliding paper doors. Am I to spend the rest of my life here so very far from that sea, in this house where I am forced to live with the sound of an air conditioner? Would I ever be able to see that Ocean again? As if to break away from a bad dream, she asked the woman in the mirror.

While Keiko quietly suffers in her loneliness, her friend Sue—a Japanese woman no less isolated than Keiko—actively makes an attempt to break out of the rut by seeking the affection of a young artist, Edgar. The two women are the polar opposites of each other; their friendship is only a manifestation of their shared alienation. Sue's infatuation with Edgar is as superficial as her relationship with Keiko. Part Native American, he reminds her of Japanese men. He, too, is alienated; eager to be accepted by the white people, he has denounced his cultural heritage and now caters only to the aesthetic taste of the ethnic majority. He is, therefore, little different from the two Japanese women who have long been imitating the way of the white American middle class, like the mockingbirds mimicking the calls of other birds. Rejected by Edgar, Sue eventually leaves her husband and returns to Japan. Keiko remains a self-condemned ''do-nothing'' like Sue's husband, whose spirit seems to have been broken in his days in Japan as a prisoner of war.

Through the characterization of Keiko, Sue, and her husband, Mori delineates her perception of the impact of the war on the ordinary people of the two countries. Skillfully bringing up the issue of race, she provides a foil character in an Italian war bride who, unlike the Japanese women, Edgar, and Native Americans on the reservation, has assimilated well into the mainstream of American life.

Does Mori suggest, then, that there is no possibility of liberation for the minority people, particularly for the so-called Japanese war brides? Far from it. She has created another Japanese woman named June, who achieves sublimation in her own way, after suffering a series of tragedies throughout her life in the United States. June's American husband had abused her with racial slurs before deserting her, and her only child, Ronnie, had also humiliated her before his accidental death, for which she was blamed and imprisoned for seven years. Now quite ostracized by the Japanese community in town, she remains in her ''home'' for the simple reason that her son is buried in the vicinity. By following her native tradition to honor the land where the souls of one's family members rest, June succeeds in reaffirming her self-identity as Japanese as well as in establishing the sense of belonging to her adopted country. Mori also hints that Edgar as well will return to his people, helped by Keiko, who forces him to confront his own deception.

The characterization of the three Japanese women is quite well rounded and convincing. Sue's desperate attempt to attract Edgar's attention reveals her egoism and insensitivity toward her husband and Keiko, and June's use of a Japanese dialect in her conversation with Keiko helps effectively to capture each woman's state of mind. Keiko's feelings expressed in the quoted passages reinforce verisimilitudes by echoing the voice of Japanese wives of American servicemen living in the United States, as resounds in the personal narratives recorded in Enari Tsuneo, *Hanayome no Amerika* (Brides' America: Kōdansha, 1981).

Criticized by some for a seeming lack of vitality and individuality, Mori's style, nonetheless, is exceptionally suitable for portraying a town stifled by ennui and describing the scene of a Native American ritual dance on the reservation located on a stretch of barren land on the edge of the town. This work also demonstrates Mori's talent in translating her poignant observations into vivid images. Her diction, which incorporates a wide range of English words, is also effective, not only in achieving realism but also in elaborating on the twin themes of alienation and sublimation. Particularly impressive is the structure, which allows the story to unfold in a convincing yet smooth flow. The life of Japanese women residing in the United States is a subject seldom covered in modern Japanese literature with any depth before this novella.

The Woman of Three Colors (Sansai no onna, 1982), novel. Tracing the tragic life of a little-known woman named Otaa Julia from her birth in Korea to her final years on an obscure island in Japan, Mori again explores the theme of alienation and emancipation, this time until the heroine finds freedom in her worship of the Occidental God.

The story begins in Korea in the 1590s under the invasion of the Japanese forces dispatched by Toyotomi Hideyoshi (1536–98). Otaa's aristocratic mother committed suicide to safeguard her honor, and the girl is taken to the home of a potter, who found her. The Japanese forces, upon encountering strong resistance, retreat, taking captive Korean men, women, and children with them. Particularly vulnerable are potters. Since Hideyoshi, an enthusiast of the tea ceremony, craves refined Korean ceramic wares, the Japanese warriors are well aware that these artisans can be valuable assets to them back home. Otaa and her adoptive family are captured and shipped to the Island of Tsushima off the coast of Kyushu. She alone is rescued out of a slave merchant's hand by Sō Maria, the wife of the lord of Tsushima and, ironically, the daughter of Konishi Yukinaga, one of the leading commanders of the Japanese expedition. Lady Maria, as the name indicates, is a devout Catholic, as are her father and her husband. Although Hideyoshi had prohibited Christianity, he is still lenient and lax in enforcing the proscription, particularly in Tsushima and the Nagasaki area, where the foreign religion landed in 1949 for the first time in Japan's history.

The situation in *The Woman of Three Colors* parallels that of *A Town Where the Mockingbirds Live:* having survived the war that drastically altered her life, Otaa now lives in her conquerors' country but longs to return to her native land, suffering acute loneliness and anxiety in the midst of strangers who treat her kindly, as though she were their own kin. Hearing a rumor of a hamlet of Korean potters in the mountains near Nagasaki, she eventually seeks out her adoptive grandfather and brother. She desperately wishes to join them, but the old man reminds her of her indebtedness to the Sō family and persuades her to return to Tsushima.

Otaa decides to appeal to her lord on behalf of the community members so they be allowed to return to their homeland. But the death of Hideyoshi leads to a series of battles, from which Tokugawa Ieyasu (1542–1616) emerges victorious and Lady Maria's father is executed. Profoundly moved by Maria's beauty and strength born of her faith, Otaa consents to be baptized and receives the Christian name of Julia. After Maria's death in a convent, she finds herself obliged to accept an invitation from Ieyasu's wife, who is in desperate need of Otaa's expertise in herbal medicine for the cure of a son's illness. Serving her enemy once again but this time in Japan, Otaa faces Ieyasu's anti-Christian measures, which become progressively more severe. Adamant in her refusal to denounce the faith, she is exiled to a remote island, where she spends the rest of her life caring for her destitute neighbors.

This story reveals not only Mori's extensive historical research but also her talent as a storyteller. Written in contemporary vernacular interspersed with Korean words and neoclassical Japanese expressions, the style is at once poetic and realistic. Particularly pleasing is the scene of Otaa's first visit to the hamlet of the Korean potters, where Mori is exceptionally skillful in capturing the girl's complex emotions as well as the melancholy mood of the community. Equally effective is the use of irony, which accentuates the tragic events in the protagonists' life. The main characters' strength and weakness, self-assertion and resignation communicate well to the contemporary reader. The structure is not strictly linear, for the author's attention shifts from Otaa to Lady Maria midway through the story, making this work as much an account of Maria's life as of the title character.

Translated Work: "A Twilight Place" (Usugurai basho, 1972), short story. Since the proscription of Christianity in the late-16th century, the hidden Christians devised a unique cryptic mode in worshiping the forbidden God. The main character, Sagara, is a young resident of contemporary Tokyo who decides on a whim to accompany a journalist on his assignment to document the hidden Christians' life in a remote village in the lush mountains of Kyūshū. Witnessing exorcism performed on a woman by elderly hidden Christians, Sagara and his companion find the ritual incomprehensible and even comical: the supplication is offered in a mixture of "corrupted" words, with the names of Christian saints grafted onto the names of indigenous Shinto or Buddhist deities. The young men understand that the peculiarity of the incantation was intentionally garbled centuries ago in order to deceive the watchful authorities. They are nonetheless entirely mystified and bitterly disappointed when, at their request, the officials of the ritual show them "Amen-jozu Buddha," the most sacred object of their worship—a mere ordinary stone. Sagara and the journalist become flustered when they fail to see the cross that the old men insist is engraved on the stone.

On his return journey, however, Sagara suddenly realizes that "what he *couldn't see,* those old men *could see.*" This revelation leads him to understand the nature of difficulty he once had with his lover who is now deceased: she, too, was someone who could see what he could not see. Now he can perceive and accept the truth about himself. He mutters, "I'm a shipwreck of human life." Here, Mori clearly conveys her belief that modern people collectively are "a shipwreck" drifting aimlessly in the sea of a dehumanizing, advanced civilization, and that their sublimation is to be achieved through adherence to the tradition and faith.

BIBLIOGRAPHY

Translation

"A Twilight Place." Tr. Miriam L. Olson. *Japan Christian Quarterly* 38.4 (Fall 1972): 232–40.

Yoshiko Yokochi SAMUEL

MORI Yōko (1940–1993), novelist, essayist. Real name: Masayo Brackin (Mrs. Ivan Brackin); née Itō Masayo.

Life: Soon after her birth in Shizuoka prefecture, Mori moved with her parents to Inner Mongolia, where her father worked throughout the war years. She was repatriated to Tokyo at age four and in the following year began to study violin. Her upper-middle-class parents provided her, the oldest of their three children, with special care and comfort and encouraged her to become a professional violinist. Mori enjoyed films and literature, her preferences limited almost entirely to Western movies and novels. She was particularly impressed by the characterization of women in Françoise Sagan's works, who seemed to follow the dictate of their individual needs and accept the consequences of their actions with little sense of guilt. Fascinated by the ocean, Mori was also enamored of William Golding for his depictions of the sea.

Mori graduated in 1961 from Tokyo University of Arts, where she majored in violin. Frustrated with the limitations of her own potential, however, she relinquished the dream of becoming a virtuoso and obtained employment as copywriter in an advertisement firm that produced television commercials. In 1964 she married an Englishman, Ivan Brackin, and devoted the following eleven years to raising three daughters. After her youngest entered school, however, Mori began to think seriously about a career. An avid reader of fiction, she was keenly interested in writing but felt intimidated by her own misconception that one must have had academic training in order to become a writer. What eventually liberated her from the fear of writing was the emergence of a new writer, Ikeda Masuo (1934–), an artist of wood-block prints, who won the 1977 Akutagawa Award for his novella *Ēgekai ni sasagu* (Dedicated to the

Aegean Sea). Encouraged by his example, Mori determined to make writing her career. She spent the summer of 1978 writing her first story, "Jōji" (A Love Affair) and won the *Subaru* Literary Award. She soon joined the ranks of Japan's most prolific and sought-after writers, primarily of short stories and personal essays that belong to popular culture. She also traveled extensively to all parts of the world, capitalizing on her foreign experiences to create in fiction the unique ambience all her own. Mori Yōko died of cancer at the age of fifty-three.

Career: The successful "A Love Affair" in 1978 was followed by two collections of short stories, *Yūwaku* (Temptation) and *Shitto* (Jealously) in 1980; by a collection of essays and a book of short stories, *Kizu* (Scars), in 1981; and by three collections of short stories in 1982—*Manekarenakatta onnatachi* (Uninvited Women), *Ai ni meguriau yokan* (Anticipation of Chance Love), and *Atsui kaze* (A Hot Wind). Two 1983 novels are entitled *Kaze monogatari* (The Tale of the Wind) and *Yogotono yurikago, fune, aruiha senjō* (Nightly, Cradle, Ship, or Battleship). A 1984 novel, *Onnazakari* (The Prime of Womanhood), was adapted for a television drama. After many more collections, a large number of Mori's personal essays were compiled in 1987 into six volumes entitled *Jin wa kokoro o yowaseru no* (Gin Intoxicates My Heart), *Otoko jōzu onna jōzu* (Flirts), *Roppongi erejī* (Roppongi Elegy), *Wakare jōzu* (Breaking Up with Style), *Bijotachi no shinwa* (The Myth of Beautiful Women), and *Puraibēto taimu* (Private Time). Belying the suggestive titles, these essays are primarily Mori's accounts of her own life—of her childhood and student days; her relationship with her husband, children, English in-laws, and friends; her career; and her journeys abroad—all opulent and unique enough to stimulate Japanese readers' fantasy and curiosity. Her candid, intimate tone in these highly personal writings serves to minimize the distance between the author and the readers.

Mori's other major publications of 1986 include four collections of short stories, of which two from *Beddo no otogibanashi* (Bedtime Fairy Tales) have been translated into English.

Mori's fiction, falling almost invariably in the sphere of popular literature, can be divided roughly into three categories. The first group, which encompasses the majority of her stories, comes nearest to such Western genres as Harlequin romances, Gothic novels, and American soap operas. Tania Modleski (b. 1949) states in her acclaimed study of the romances, *Loving with a Vengeance* (Anchon Books, 1982), that the stories belonging to these genres are primarily written for and about women and that the plot is basically the same. Mori's stories are no exception.

Unlike Harlequin romances, which portray young women, their loves, and their eventual happy marriage as Modleski has observed, Mori often depicts middle-aged married women for whom there is no happy ending or moral victory in romance. Her main characters and narrators tend to be mature women who, like the heroines of Japanese and American daytime television drama, are acutely dissatisfied in their mundane life. Mori's stories nonetheless share with the female characters in Western popular fiction what Modleski calls "normal paranoia," abetted by the fear of aging, social isolation, sexual inadequacy, and their husbands' infidelity. Mori's women, too, blame their anxieties on their mates and become vulnerable to the possibility of sublimation in romantic relationships with other men. But after brief and generally arid interludes, they find themselves back in the same ennui, discontentment, and fear that had plagued them before. The male characters in these stories, like their Western counterparts that Modleski analyzed, are perceived to be almost categorically cynical, hostile, and mocking toward the women. They are of two types: chauvinistic, unsupportive, untrustworthy villain-husbands to whom the heroines nonetheless return after their romantic adventures; and sexually aggressive, yet passive and dependent lovers who become losers after their short-lived affairs with the heroines.

As in Western popular literature, the core element of Mori's works in this category is fantasy: illicit love affairs, often spiced with exotic settings and explicit descriptions of the heroines and their lovers in the sexual act, constitute the primary component of the fantastic. Indispensable ingredients that add flavor to this fantasy are impressionistic portrayals of the characters' physical beauty and magnetic personalities; their catchy pet names; pseudosophisticated conversations that read like direct translations of dialogues from Western fiction; the enticing foreign names of cocktails and music numbers; secret telephone calls; sentimental emotionalism; and such universal signs as lovers' eyes that "meet," "entwine," and "quietly consent." These stories keep readers frustrated and anxious, but not to the extent that they would actually hope to take action to change their mundane reality.

While sharing many characteristics with the first group, the works in the second category focus not on clandestine lovemakings but on conflicts between career-aspiring heroines and their unsupportive husbands. These protagonists eventually leave their husbands in order to pursue alternative lives. Most explicitly revealing Mori's criticism of men and her faith in women's ability to become independent, these stories can inspire readers to take an active role in defining their own lives. Still fewer works constitute the third category, which deals with a Japanese woman's relationship with her British husband and in-laws. Born of Mori's personal experiences, these stories resemble the traditional "I-novel" more than Western popular fiction.

What, after all, is the secret of Mori's enormous popularity? It appears that she owed her success largely to her own keen observation of contemporary Japanese reality and her insight into the psychological and social needs of Japanese women. The most salient characteristic of Japanese society in recent years is economic prosperity, and an astonishing 90 percent of the population perceive themselves as middle-class. Yet, polls indicate that they have been plagued, increasingly during the past decade and a half, by fear and anxiety over their present state and future security. Over 50 percent of Japanese women are now employed, though typically on a part-time basis, with both some money of their own and ample free time on their hands. Lacking specific goals and challenges in their mundane life, however, these women are at once bored, discontent, and mildly worried in their status quo. The recent trend toward the nuclear family system has eliminated close dealings with in-laws but has also isolated wives from kin and friends. The worldwide sexual liberation movement (which has generally been misconstrued by Japanese as sexual decadence) and the women's liberation movement appear to have contributed to the women's discontentment, most specifically with their tradition-bound husbands.

The same social climate has at the same time encouraged some Japanese wives to take a serious look at their domestic relationships and to take action to improve their own lot. It is understandable, then, that a large number of Japanese housewives and part-time working women find in Mori's works the source of diversion and escape from their daily life. The pleasure of withdrawing into a fantasy world, however, is inevitably short-lived, making the readers to crave more and more. Mori's writings fulfill the women's needs but can also perpetuate in them the very same problems, for the solution of which they reach out to her works. In a significant contrast to Western woman's fiction, nevertheless, Mori's works are avidly read by men, too. Responding to an unsatiable public demand, Mori kept producing collections of essays and stories, a large number of which were published in popular fiction monthlies catering to the male readership as well. Thus Mori effectively communicated women's feelings and desires to men.

Some of Mori's books have come out in both paperback and hardcover, some of the stories introduced to readers more than once, each time by publishers different from the original ones. There are consequently as many as sixty-six books by this writer on the market by 1987. Mori, regrettably, became much too prolific in her last years. Both the form and the content of her fiction suffered greatly as a consequence, rendering her dangerously close to being a writer of vulgar literature. One of her last best-sellers was a complete translation of *Scarlet* by Alexandra Ripley, the 1992 sequel to Mori's favorite novel—Margaret Mitchells's *Gone With the Wind.*

Major Works: Jōji (A Love Affair, 1978), novella. This award-winning story contains all the ingredients that make up a fantasy world typical of Mori. The first-person narrator, Yōko, is a beautiful, sophisticated woman irresistibly attractive to Western men who frequent the night spots on the fashionable streets of the Roppongi in Tokyo. As a translator of Western television drama, she has financial means and ample time of her own. Her British husband is wealthy enough to provide his family with the luxury of a cottage and a beach house, which become the main stage of the heroine's rendezvous with her Caucasian lovers. Yōko is bored and dicontented with her life: after eleven years of marriage, she is not only sexually frustrated but also fearful of losing her youthful beauty. Her anxiety has created in her a burning desire for "sex until I'm so sick of it that I can vomit."

She has had an affair with a certain David Hall, her husband's countryman and close friend, at her cottage in the romantic and prestigious summer resort of Karuizawa. Through David she meets an American named Lane Bradberry at Chalcott House, a cozy Roppongi bar patronized by Westerners. He and Yōko instantly fall in love with one another, and romance unfolds against the backdrop of his fashionable Azabu apartment and her beach house in an isolated village at a convenient distance from Tokyo. The affair ends in disaster when Yōko, who had told Lane that she was unmarried, is forced to introduce him to her husband. She suffers not the slightest guilt but profound remorse over the fact that she had never told Lane of her true love for him before the sad breakup.

The place and personal names, the deception that transforms Yōko into a secretive, mysterious woman in her lover's eye, and the explicit depiction of the lovers in their passionate lovemaking collectively contribute to heightening the quality of fantasy. Equally important are the urbane and sexually suggestive dialogues that the heroine exchanges with her admirers in the bar and the description of Lane's physical appearance. His "raven black hair," "silky-smooth hands," the "pained look on his face," and, above all, his "violet-blue eyes" that the heroine finds irresistible are powerful devices commonly used in Western romance fiction, but they work just as well in this story. Characterization of the major figures are typically two-dimensional, but style is appropriately ornate and poetic. Particularly effective are the smart dialogues that, as the critic Okuno Takeo notes, seem right out of Western fiction.

Yogoto no yurikago, fune, aruiwa senjō (Nightly, Cradle, Ship, or Battlefield, 1986), novel. One of Mori's few longer works, this fiction differs from her short stories in its structure and style, which add complexity and depth, and in its theme, which probes deep into the paranoia of contemporary Japanese women. Chapter 1 is an account of a childhood dream given by a thirty-eight-year-old narrator-protagonist, Yōko, to her woman therapist. Chapter 2 reveals that the entire first chapter is a recollection of the heroine while vacationing in a Malaysian seaside resort. She and her husband have traveled to this remote place in an attempt to salvage a "sinking ship," that is, their marriage, for the sake of their three daughters. The first two chapters thus cover three points in time and space—the present in a foreign land, Yōko's immediate past, in which the therapy took place in Tokyo, and her childhood in a obscure Japanese village. The same chapters also suggest that the dream, the significance of which is yet to be revealed, has something to do with the couple's marital problem and that Yōko aims to descend into her subconscious in search of self-revelation.

In the Malaysian resort, Yōko continues to recall one of her therapy sessions, during which she expressed her perception of her mother as a victimizer and of herself as a victim. Yōko fears her own perception that she has become an exact replica of her unloving mother. Unable to cope with this self-perception, Yōko abruptly returns to reality and complains to her husband of her sexual frustration with him. He in turn blames her for their marital problem and their daughter's autism, condemning Yōko for her excessive dedication to her career as a fiction writer as well as for being involved in the therapy. Here Mori voices her strong criticism of traditional Japanese husbands who stifle their wives' creative talents and hinder their effort to develop a better understanding of themselves. Helped by her therapist, however, Yōko comes to empathize with her mother and to develop a realistic image of her father, whom she has considered too meek and passive. Not surprisingly, the dream and the recurring memory of it turn out to be the manifestation of her long-suppressed fear of sexual intercourse, caused by her childhood experience in witnessing her parents in the act. Forcing her to plunge deeper into the realm of her unconscious, the therapy leads her back to the state of an infant, of death, or of prebirth—now she awaits to start her life afresh, as an independent new woman.

Nightly, Cradle, Ship, or Battlefield weaves a rich tapestry of events in Yōko's life taking place at three temporal and spatial points. As the heroine's thought shifts freely from her unconscious to conscious, from her past to the present, and from her mother to her husband, time and space become entirely obscured, as the following passage illustrates:

Anyway, it's hard for me to be talking about myself to my therapist. Does it do you any good? It certainly does. For one thing, I've become more accepting of myself, or rather, I've become more tolerant of myself. That's dangerous, muttered my husband as though deep in thought.

What would the ultimate changes be? An inversion of a victim to a victimizer, a powerless to a powerful, an adult to a child? And what else? From a woman to a man?

May I ask you a question? She asks, her eyes smiling teasingly. It may sound like a strange question to you, but do you think of yourself as a woman? What? I'm at a loss what to say. I know she is watching me closely while she waits for my answer. I believe I do. I feel myself blushing and, irritated at myself for it, I become incoherent. At least, I've never thought of myself as a man, not even masculine.

I see, says my therapist and is about to drop the subject altogether. You can't drop it now. It's as though you've just thrown a pebble into a pond, and you are leaving the whole thing at that. Flustered, I protest in silence. The rings of the waves spread rapidly in my mind, and I have no idea what to do about it.

Written entirely in the present tense, dialogues with no quotation marks such as these are intermittently followed by more conventional depictions of the scenery of the Malaysian resort. Such structure and style, along with a series of episodes from Yōko's past and present, create both tension and a dreamlike quality that are aesthetically pleasing, if rather confusing. Based on Mori's own involvement in therapy, the story in most parts is at once realistic and convincing. It is regrettable, however, that Mori was pressed by time to bring this work to a quick conclusion. The novel consequently suffers toward the end from a superficial elaboration of the main theme. An interesting experiment not only in structure and style but also in synthesizing popular literature and serious fiction, this novel is a significant work that merits critical study.

Translated Works: "Two Bedtime Stories: Be It Ever So Humble" (Beddo no otogibanashi-Sasayakana kōfuku, 1986), short story. The protagonist, Akiko, is a middle-class, married woman who commits adultery out of boredom. Her Japanese husband owns neither a cottage nor a beach house. Having no career of her own, she is obliged to spend most of her time alone either in her kitchen or in front of a television set. She has no friends to speak of, let alone a Caucasian admirer with "violet-blue eyes." She frequents not a high-class bar but a neighborhood supermarket, where one day she is approached by a "mousy kind of man," "precisely the type . . . who would accost a housewife with a yellow shopping basket in her arm." As characteristic of Mori's later works, this story lacks the element of the fantastic, which marks her earlier fiction. Precisely because of the realism, however, this short story is endowed with more power to satisfy, and at the same time further induce, the reader's fantasy and discontentment. This, in other words, is a disturbing work, not only because of its main focus on trapped life but also because of its trapping effect.

"Two Bedtime Stories: Spring Storm" (Beddo no otogibanashi-Haruno arashi, 1986), short story. Focusing on male chauvinism still prevalent in contemporary Japan, Mori illustrates in this work the difficulty that confronts career-oriented Japanese women. The heroine of this story, Natsuo, is an aspiring actress. She makes a painful effort to overcome her shyness in order to affirm faith in her potential and succeeds in earning a leading role. The story ends with an explicit suggestion that, like Ingrid Bergman, who was divorced by Roberto Rosselini for acting in a play directed by someone other than her husband, Natsuo would choose a career over her playwright husband, who cannot live with his wife's success. By incorporating the anecdotes about Western women's tribulations, Mori asserts, first, that male chauvinism is a universal problem. Second, she elaborates on men's sense of sex superiority, which, when threatened, manifests itself in jealousy and the denunciation of women's potentials and aspirations. Third, while depicting the cruel effects of chauvinism on women, Mori indicates that Japanese women are ready to fight against that form of oppression.

BIBLIOGRAPHY

Bedtime Tales. Tr. Sonya Johnson. Tokyo: Kodansha International, 1993
"Spring Storm." In *One World of Literature.* New York: Houghton-Miflin, 1993.
"Two Bedtime Stories: Be It Ever So Humble" and "Two Bedtime Stories: Spring Storm." Tr. Makoto Ueda. In *The Mother of Dreams and Other Stories,* ed. Makoto Ueda. Tokyo: Kodansha International, 1986, 117–24 and 125–32.
                                                                          Yoshiko Yokochi SAMUEL

MUKŌDA Kuniko (1929–81), playwright, novelist, essayist.

Life: Mukōda was born in Tokyo, the eldest of four children. The domineering father she was to portray in her works again and again was employed in an insurance company; he was repeatedly transferred to its various branches around the country, and his children learned the pain of parting from newly made friends and the agony of facing yet another classroom of strangers. In her collection of autobiographical essays, *Chichi no Wabijō* (A Letter of Apology from Father, 1978), Mukōda recounts how she and her siblings learned not to form attachments to places, things, or people, knowing what the price would be if they did. This stoic training may well be the background for the lack of sentimentality in Mukōda's works, remarkable even in her television drama, a genre traditionally "wet" with nebulous sentimentality in Japan.

As a first grader in Tokyo, Mukōda contracted an inflammation of the lungs, which required almost a year of treatment and recovery. The atmosphere of panic caused by this family trauma is reproduced in some of her short stories, such as "Daikon no tsuki" (A Moonshaped Wedge of Daikon, 1980), in which the disaster that befalls a child strains the relationship between his parents and opens the eyes of a young mother to the reality of the nature of that relationship. Mukōda's father was transferred to Kagoshima, at the southern tip of the island of Kyushu, soon after her convalescence. The sunny climate and fresh air helped the young girl to make a complete recovery. Before long the family moved to Takamatsu on the island of Shikoku, where Mukōda finished the last year of elementary school. Her father was transferred back to Tokyo, leaving her to finish out the first term at a girls' high school. After several months of boarding in a lodging house, she followed the family back to Tokyo, entering Meguro Girls' High School in September 1942.

These were the war years. Curiously, the war figures hardly at all in Mukōda's works except to provide a framework of dates or place-names used as markers for the more vital dramas occurring on the family front. Mukōda herself, in the wartime student mobilization program, was put to work in a munitions factory making screws for the "balloon bombs" that the military released into the jet stream flowing toward America. But, apart from the memory of getting covered with oil each day at the factory, the war seems to have meant little to Mukōda. What loomed much larger was the demand of her loving but tyrannical father that she excel in everything. A "self-made" man who rose in his insurance company from lowly clerk to manager of a department in its Tokyo head office, Mukōda's father believed in what could be accomplished through human effort and demanded the best from his daughter.

Mukōda lived with her parents in Tokyo until June 1946, when her father was transferred to Sendai in the northeast. Mukōda and her brother boarded with their maternal relatives in Tokyo, heading home to Sendai on weekends and during school vacations. When Mukōda graduated from the Japanese literature department of Jissen Women's College in 1950, the employment picture was bleak. She took night courses in an English secretarial training program and in 1952 found an editorial position with a magazine introducing new Western movies to Japanese audiences. Mukōda worked for the movie magazine for almost nine years, trying her hand at writing television and radio dramas and occasional essays. By December 1960 she had enough confidence in her ability as a freelance writer to quit the magazine. Working mainly for the radio, she wrote some dramas that, in their language and use of humor, were clearly superior to anything being done at the time. One of her scripts would eventually become the popular TBS television series *Shichinin no mago* (Seven Grandchildren, 1964). In 1960 she joined the women's free-lance writers' group Galina Club and began contributing pieces to weekly magazines like *Shūkan Heibon* and *Shūkan Kōron*. Meanwhile, her father had been transferred back to Tokyo, and she was once again living the life of a dutiful daughter, though the role was to become increasingly strained by the social demands of her life as a budding writer. Finally, in 1964, Mukōda left home after an argument with her father.

Her first novel, *Terauchi Kantarō Ikka* (Terauchi Kantarō's Family, 1975), was published six years after her father's death: it is an elegy to the man who had thundered through the lives of his children, the man whom Mukōda idealized "in lieu of offering up a stick of incense." What is particularly interesting is that the daughter in this story is crippled by a falling stone in her stonemason father's yard. Whatever the symbolic meaning of the crippling of her fictional alter ego. Mukōda herself was never to take on the role of wife or mother. She was forty-six when she made her novelistic debut. In the same year, her hospitalization for breast cancer brought home to her the importance of writing for herself. The operation successfully removed the cancer, which had been discovered in an early stage, but it was a different Mukōda who left the hospital, determined that she make the most of whatever time stretched before her. Six years later Mukōda was dead, not from a recurrence of the cancer she feared, but in the explosion of a China Airlines jet over the mountains of Taiwan.

Career: In 1980, barely a year prior to her untimely death, Mukōda won the Naoki Prize, one of Japan's most coveted literary awards. Her works in the six-year period following her hospitalization, which Mukōda called "the fishing derived from my bout with cancer," amounted to no fewer than eleven volumes of short stories, novellas, and essays. The Naoki Prize was awarded for three of her stories, which were being serialized in the fiction monthly *Shōsetsu Shinchō:* "Inugoya," (The Doghouse), "Hana no namae" (The Names of Flowers), and "The River Otter" (Kawauso).

Mukōda's fiction can be divided roughly into two categories. The first includes the semiautobiographical novels and essays in which she re-created a family dominated by the unreasonable, absolute rule of a well-meaning, loving, overly fussy father, around whom the rest of the household tiptoes. The second category consists of works that examine the precarious balance of the husband-wife, man-woman relationship, highlighting some of the elements involved in the play of power between the sexes. The tone that characterizes the works in the first category is elegiac: the daughter, in various guises, forgives and affirms her love for her father while re-creating the humor and pathos of their family life. Chief among the works in this category are *Terauchi Kantarō's Family* and *A, Un* (The Odd Pair, 1981), originally written as television serial drama. Their enormous popularity led Mukōda to condense them into novel form, inevitably sacrificing much of their original dramatic genius. *A Letter of Apology from*

Father marked Mukoda's growing power as a writer of fiction, presenting the most direct picture of her own family life.

Although these three works deal essentially with the same type of family situation, they differ in the focus and complexity of their vision. *Terauchi Kantarō's Family* is perhaps the simplest of the three, introducing the characters who would become familiar to Mukōda's viewers/readers.

Well aware of the typical Japanese viewer's all-too-easy belief that only a drama that seems ''serious'' can contain some truth, Mukōda asserted in her essay ''Hōmu dorama no uso'' (The Untruth of Home Drama, 1974) that what the reader does not realize is that ''there's a good chance that in the midst of all the banality, Reality is going to put in a fleeting appearance.'' First in her television dramas and later in her short fiction, Mukōda worked toward an understanding of a morality based on something deeper than conventional codes of behavior and consensus opinions. She also probed the theme of the balance between the sexes; the tone in her short fiction dealing with this theme is sharper than that adopted in the earlier television dramas and novellas, and the conclusions tend to be more ominous. The short stories share some elements that are recognizably parts of the familiar Mukōda world, such as the husband who comes from an impoverished background and has been educated, in various ways, by his wife.

In 1987, Mukōda's works were published in a three-volume collection, an unusual tribute paid to a ''popular writer.'' The set includes novels, short stories, and essays, but not her screenplays, many of which are still unavailable to the public in any form.

Mukōda's still-booming popularity is due in no small measure to her skill as a storyteller and to the comic touch she applied to stories that treat serious themes. It is also due to the compassion she displays for ordinary, somewhat cantankerous characters. The scope and seriousness of her work are not likely to be explored by Japanese literary critics, who categorically refuse to make popular literature the object of scholarly probing.

Major Works: Terauchi Kantarō Ikka (Terauchi Kantarō and His Family, 1975), television serial drama, then novel. Kantarō, the father, might be said to be typical of a certain type of prewar father; absolute in the governing of his family, he presents a stark contrast to the morally indecisive, family-neglecting father of the postwar years. Part of Mukōda's success, first on television and later in fiction, must be ascribed to her sense of continuity with the atmosphere of the prewar Japanese family. In this particular work the family members are secretly united against the tyranny of the father, and the mother plays the role of chief strategist in approaching him. Not as complex as the mother figure who will appear in the later *A, Un,* she is a self-abnegating figure of reconciliation. Much like the figure of Mrs. Ramsay in Virginia Woolf's *To the Lighthouse,* the mother in Mukōda's early works is the very soul of the household, suffering the unreasonable behavior of her husband while schooling their children in how to appreciate their difficult father.

But the grandmother is an irascible, ornery old lady who was to prove one of the most popular of Mukōda's characters, so popular that Mukōda would later write an essay on her origins. While explaining that 25 percent of this character is drawn on her own paternal grandmother, Mukōda reveals something of her father's unusual upbringing. He had never known his own father; he was born out of wedlock and raised by his strong-willed mother, whose unorthodox sexual behavior he was deeply ashamed of, so ashamed that he lived his adult years with her and let her go to her death without a single kind word. Mukōda's knowledge of this "skeleton in the closet" had a profound impact upon her. She sympathized with her grandmother and worked the complexities of her nature into a series of elderly characters whose grasp of reality and refusal to lead "pretty lives" for anyone else's sake lend them a stance that is almost prophetic. Mukōda's dislike of "prettiness" and pretense is obvious in her remarks near the end of the essay, "Terauchi Kantarō no haha" (Terauchi Kantarō's Mother, 1974):

Some people might call it the nastiness of the old; but I can't help feeling more humanity in the life that rants on about the things around it than in the life that prizes, "all action past," its lonely elegance.

Mukōda's awareness of her grandmother's past behavior and her father's inability to forgive her for it led Mukōda to a determination not to shrink from reality but to work to capture it in all its complexity and to present it with a humor that revealed an intrinsic acceptance of untidy lives and passions that could not fit into a socially approved pattern.

A, Un (The Odd Pair, 1981), television serial drama, then novel. This tragicomic story sketches the lives of a married couple, their eighteen-year-old daughter, and the grandfather who lives with them. What is new here is the introduction of a former wartime buddy of the father's. The two are a study in contrasts; the friend is handsome, talented, well-off, and socially gregarious, whereas the father is undistinguished-looking, fussy, and from an impoverished background.

The novel pitches and rolls through various comic situations brought about by a number of crises, but the seriousness of Mukōda's theme is clear: human beings have psychological and emotional needs larger than the institutions available to them. Each of the three characters—the mother, the father, and the friend—finds the most complete self possible only in the presence of the other two. While sexuality is an ambiguous force in the background, their relations are platonic. Though the work deals with a triangular relationship, it could not be more remote from the typical Japanese treatment of the motif. Though the work is too slight, as well as too different, to compare with Nathaniel Hawthorne's *Blithedale Romance,* Mukōda has more in common with Hawthorne's exploration into the possibilities of a human utopia than with other Japanese treatments of eternal triangles. What makes this work particularly poignant is that the daughter, who passes from girlhood to womanhood in the course of the novel, is observing the adults around her. When she comes home from a date and her first kiss to discover that her grandfather has passed away without ever speaking a word to his son about the flagrant three-way emotional interdependency, she comes to the conclusion that to be an adult means to be "a person who refuses to speak about the most vital personal issues of his/her life."

Satoko suddenly conceived a dislike for her mother. She was dividing herself between her own husband and this man. . . . And her father was no better. To go on for twenty years like this, knowing that his best friend was in love with his wife, saying nothing. . . . was it failure of the nerve, or craftiness?

"Father's just been using his friend as a kind of bait to maintain his relations with Mother!" How would they react if she threw that out at them? She wanted to confront the family friend as well: "If you really care anything for Mother, make her yours!"

All the resentment she could not express over not being allowed to meet her own boyfriend, desperate as she was to meet him, surfaced in this desire to confront the three of them. She wanted to shout something irrevocable and blast away their balance.

The book ends on an ambiguous note with the mother's reflections:

There was a movement on to save scraps of silver paper for the military effort. After things had gone sour between the two men the ball had hardly grown at all, with only the father's daily pack's worth to add to it. . . . but now the silver ball would start growing more rapidly again. Would this silver be used to make warplanes? Or would it be turned into bullets? It was hard to imagine what use the country would find for it.

Like the future of the three of them, it was quite beyond her. The tone of *A, Un* is elegiac, but what is being mourned is the human condition itself, which drives individuals to find a wholeness that may well, in realization, prove tragically impossible.

"Hamegoroshi mado" (The Window on the Landing, 1980), short story. The grandmother described in this story is clearly based on Mukōda's own renegade grandmother. She is a vital woman with a lusty thirst for tap water, while her husband is a frail, inconsequential man who can manage no more than a sip of boiled water for fear his innards will be affected. The story begins five years after her death and centers on her son, who has a vague memory of fleeing to a strange town with his mother because of a large, good-looking young man full of life. When he finds his daughter has a large thirst, he is alarmed. He remembers finding his mother staring at some high school boys naked to the waist, performing gymnastics in the schoolyard across the way. In a surprise ending, his anxiety about his daughter's potential sexual appetite proves to have been groundless. Instead, he becomes aware of something else; when a young doctor comes to the house to attend to his wife, he hears her speaking to him in a mellow tone he has never heard before. His daughter, on the other hand, happily married to a handsome young man of her own, confesses to her father that her husband seems to be having an affair. This story, as well as "Manhattan" (1980), concludes with father and child in the same situation, abandoned in some sense by their partners. The stories seem close, in tone and theme, to Mukōda's earlier works.

"Dara dara-zaka" (An Easy Slope, 1980), short story. This work presents a familiar situation: a middle-aged businessman has installed a young woman as his mistress in an apartment. She had applied for an opening in his company but was rejected by the all-male selection committee as being too big and ungainly. The man then secretly took down her name and address. What is remarkable about her is the degree of her expressionlessness, both physically and verbally. Nicknamed "Mouse" for his small size, the man finds the girl's large, white shapelessness exciting, like a pile of oval-shaped rice cakes. He fantasizes about prancing about on top of the pile.

One day he comes back a little early from a trip to Thailand and Singapore. When sunglasses appear behind the slit in the girl's apartment door, he gets alarmed, believing she's taken up with a member of the *yakuza* (crime syndicate). But the girl herself wears the sunglasses; she has undergone plastic surgery on her eyes while he was away. Her old, expressionless eyes are a thing of the past, and her new eyes resemble those of the middle-aged, attractive bar hostess who lives next door. The girl loses her pliability and begins to express herself. The story ends with the disheartened man's walking down the "easy slope" of the road past her apartment—the road that, only a short time before, he had believed to be his royal way, the flowering proof of his stature as a man.

"Otoko mamie" (Mannish Eyebrows, 1980), short story. This piece constitutes a montage of a woman's memories of having definitions of the self forced on her by other people. The woman's husband is the chief source of pronouncements that she "lacks finesse" or is the "stalwart" type of woman, as opposed to the "lovely" type. But the title derives from the pronouncement of the woman's grandmother that she—the main character as a young girl—has "mannish eyebrows." A patchwork quilt of past and present, the story finds its unity in these pronouncements, which always place the woman on the wrong side of what might be preferred.

An interesting scene involves a wartime memory. Thinking back on people she had met with well-shaped, separated "Buddha eyebrows"—as opposed to her own bushy, joined "mannish eyebrows"—the possession of which (according to her grandmother) could be the mark of fortunes as varied as restoring wealth to one's family or becoming a cold-blooded killer, the girl recalls a farmer she met during the war. The young girl and her mother, typical of the starving Tokyo populace of the time, went to the farmer in the suburbs with household goods to trade for sweet potatoes. Suddenly an American B-51 appeared in the sky, followed by a Japanese plane trying to intercept it; both planes fell out of the sky. The young girl's mother pressed her palms together in prayer, but the old farmer checked the quality of what they had brought to trade with one hand as he mumbled some prayers. The story finishes with a scene in which the grown woman scrambles to hide from her husband the equipment with which she has been plucking her eyebrows.

"Ringo no kawa" (The Apple Peel, 1980), short story. Mukōda's own figure as an adult is glimpsed here in the heroine, who is close to fifty and lives by herself. As she describes to her lover of a year's standing an image that orgasm conjures up in her mind, someone knocks at the front door. She opens the door, only to be slightly unsettled by the sight of her younger brother. Sensing that she is not alone, he bats his eyes a few times, then his eyes take on a glazed look as he makes an excuse and flees. Three days later she is still thinking of his glazed, unseeing eyes. She had seen that look on him before when she was going through the rough stages of divorce. She muses about the value of her solitary life. The things that surround her have all been chosen with care; suddenly it seems to her that the last thirty years of her life have amounted to no more than a fostering of taste, in things as well as in men. She can't help comparing the meaning of such a life with that of her brother, who has grown old with his family around him, paying little attention to the aesthetic quality of his life. She peels an apple, taking care, in her set way, to get the peel in one long piece. The peel has a beauty of its own; it is bright red on one side, and a greenish-white on the other, with a tinge of red. She puts one end of the peel in her mouth and throws the naked fruit out the window into the cold December air. She then turns to savor the peel.

Translated Works: "Doubt" (Dauto), 1984, short story. The protagonist is a middle-aged office worker whose father is dying. The focus of the story is on his attitude of self-complacency; he feels little compassion for those around him, even for his dying father, who was a stiff drudge of a man. The story progresses with the preparations for the funeral and the question of how to treat one of the relatives, a ne'er-do-well who is suspected of having stolen some money at a previous family funeral. The presence of this relative, who enjoys an enviable popularity with the women in the family, shakes the main character's complacency, for this fellow had been a silent witness to an act of cruelty the office worker would rather not recall. Unsure of the extent of the fellow's knowledge of his act, the protagonist decides to bait him as they are drinking after the funeral, but he cannot get a satisfactory response from the man. The baiting itself reminds him of a card game, Doubt, that he used to play with his father. Remembering his father's ineptitude at the game, which involves calling another's bluff, he recalls a day when his father was caught paying insufficient fare on a train. The feelings of guilt and memories of his father act, in the story, to bring the protagonist closer to genuine compassion for his father and for himself as a man like other miserable men. The story displays Mukōda's dislike of any righteousness that sets men apart from others.

"The River Otter" (Kawauso, 1986), short story. This enjoyable piece is typical of Mukōda in that it centers on the precarious balance between the sexes. The main character is an aging businessman who suffers a stroke, thus giving his energetic wife the upper hand in deciding to build an apartment house on the land that is their garden, a move her husband has repeatedly opposed. Mu-kōda's compassion for the harried breadwinner is evident here, as in other works, in scenes suggesting that a seat at the side of a silent garden is a restorative not to be done without. The treachery of the wife in going ahead with the deal is given a comic touch; she is only being herself, the same self who thrived through every disaster in her vicinity so far. Whether balance is possible in an institution that pits two people against each other is called into question, though the seri-ousness of the question is softened by the brilliance of Mukōda's comic story-telling. The end of the story is ominous, with the husband's suffering a second stroke as he tries to control his anger over what she has done.

"Manhattan" (1987), short story. The central character here finds himself deserted by his wife, apparently for his shiftlessness, but possibly because of her having taken up with the new dentist she hired at her clinic. The man collects unemployment and is lethargic in his daily schedule, leaving his couch at eleven to go and eat hard *yakisoba* (fried noodles), a penitential ritual. One day on the way home he finds a new bar being built, a place called Manhattan. The magic of the phrase sees him through several unpleasant encounters with his former spouse; it liberates him from the lethargy of his schedule. He starts wearing pajamas and sleeping in bed, and he splurges on Chinese noodles rather than on his usual self-punitive fare. Manhattan, Manhattan, he repeats, and it is in-cantation, a watchword against evil, a password to a new life. Putting his head round the door of the bar just before it is to be opened, he gets a whack on the head from the sign being carried in and is rewarded for his curiosity by a night in the hospital and a visit from the "Mama" of Manhattan.

He is chief among customers; he brings necessary supplies for the bar; he believes that Mama is a fellow creature, another "shiftless ne'er-do-well," as his wife put it. He believes that it is only a matter of time until Mama is his. But another customer comes and takes his favorite seat, and it turns out that this fellow is Mama's husband. Some three months later they abandon the place at night, and Manhattan becomes a memory. He hears a faint knocking at the door, a knocking he is sure will prove to be Mama, but it turns out to be a wizened old fellow looking for umbrellas to repair. When he has been turned away, the knocking comes again, and the memory clears; he realizes that the old fellow is his father come to him, turned out or abandoned by some woman. His mother had always said he took after his father. Injected at this point is a new note that seems to depart from the thrust of the story. Yet it is familiar in a sense, for it does suggest that, after all, the father and child are in the same boat, both having been turned out by a woman. Like much of Mukōda's work, this story is momorable for an elegiac tone for the misunderstood males.

BIBLIOGRAPHY

Translations

"Doubt." Tr. Dan Seymour. *Japan Quarterly* 31:3 (July–September 1984), 281–87.
"Manhattan." Tr. Adam Kabat. *The Magazine* 2:11 (December 1987).

"The River Otter." Tr. Marian E. Chambers. *Japan Quarterly* 33:3 (July–September 1986), 320–27.

Critical Works

Niyekawa, Agnes K. "Analysis of Conflict in a Television Home Drama." In *Conflict in Interpersonal Relations.* Honolulu: University of Hawaii Press, 1975, 61–84.

Paul McGRATH

MURASAKI Shikibu (fl. 1000s), court lady, poet, novelist. Real name: undetermined.

Life: As with most women writers of the Heian period (794–1185), there is scant biographical information available about Murasaki Shikibu, aside from what can be gleaned from the three prime sources: her collected poems, her diary, and her fiction, a prose masterpiece of classical Japanese literature, *The Tale of Genji.* While these works give some information about specific events in Murasaki's life, they do not contain facts such as the date of her birth or marriage. Murasaki's family background has been traced through the genealogy in the *Sompi bummyaku* (Genealogies of Main and Branch Families, compiled by Tōin Kinsada, 1340–99). Murasaki's father was Fujiwara Tametoki, a fifth-generation descendant of the founder of the northern branch of the family and a distant relative of the Regent Fujiwara Michingaga (966–1027), the most powerful political figure of the age, who would appear later in Murasaki's life and writings. Tametoki's branch of the Fujiwara line was not in the mainstream of political power, and Tametoki himself held only minor government posts and ranks: secretary in the Ministry of Ceremonial and, ten years later, in 966, governor of Echizen. In 1011 he went to Echigo province as governor and returned to the capital in 1014.

While of little political consequence, Tametoki's family was quite distinguished in the literary sphere. Murasaki Shikibu's most prominent ancestor was Tametoki's grandfather Fujiwara Kanesuke (877–933). He was a contemporary and friend of Ki no Tsurayuki (868–946), anthologist and author of the critically significant preface to the *Kokinshū* (Collection of Ancient and Modern Times, 905), the first of the imperially sponsored collections of Japanese poetry. Kanesuke's poems were selected for the *Sanjū-rokunin shū* (Collection of Thirty-six Poets, c. 1160), and many of his verses appear in the episodes of *Yamato monogatari* (Tales of Yamato, 11th c.).

The year of Murasaki's birth is not known. Scholars have placed the date somewhere between 970 and 978. Even the name by which the author of *The Tale of Genji* is now known was not the one she was given at birth but dates to her service at court. Except for members of the imperial family and royal consorts, it was not customary to record the personal names of women of the upper classes. In his diary *Midō kampaku ki* (Record of the Regent of the August Hall) Fujiwara Michinaga does mention some of the women in court service by name. In the year 1007, for example, there is a "Fujiwara Takako" (also read

"Kyōshi") listed. Some scholars have conjectured that this refers to Murasaki Shikibu, but the matter is still in dispute.

Most women at court were called by sobriquets derived from a combination of their family name or some related place-name and a post or title held by their father or husband. Thus, Shikibu refers to Murasaki's father's post in the Shikibu-shō (Ministry of Ceremonials). In some sources Murasaki is called "Tō Shikibu." Tō is the Chinese reading of the first element of "Fujiwara." Fuji means "wisteria," and its color is purple (*murasaki*), which may be the source for the use of Murasaki, rather than Tō, as her better-known sobriquet. The more likely origin of the name Murasaki, however, has to do with *The Tale of Genji* and probably dates to an incident recorded in her diary on the 1st day of the Eleventh Moon of 1008. The courtier poet Fujiwara Kintō (966–1041), in trying to search her out among the court ladies at a banquet, asks for "little Murasaki," using the name of the heroine of *The Tale of Genji*. Her reply protests that there is no one equal to Prince Genji at the banquet, so how can Murasaki be present. This is the first mention in her diary of the hero of her tale. Kintō was one of the most prominent literary figures of his day, so Murasaki Shikibu would no doubt have been pleased by his reference to her work and by the nickname he bestowed upon her. Her diary reveals that she was given another nickname by one of her court colleagues, "Our Lady of the Chronicles" (Nihongi no tsubone). This was supposed to be less complimentary than "Little Murasaki" because it was considered unbecoming for a woman to know Chinese, the "masculine" language in which the *Nihongi* (Chronicle of Japan, 712) was written. Since Murasaki did record this incident, however, she may have felt flattered by the nickname after all. In the same passage she relates how she used to listen in on her brother's Chinese lessons as a child. Chinese learning was the preparation for a career in government service, a career not open to women. When Murasaki proved to be a better student of Chinese than her brother, their father lamented that she was not born a boy. In addition to histories, her brother and his clandestine costudent studied other Chinese texts, such as *The Lotus sutra* and anthologies of Chinese literary classics, including the works of Po Chu-i (722–846), the most popular Chinese poet in Heian Japan. Murasaki no doubt also received training in the traditional feminine arts of music, calligraphy, and poetry.

She married a distant kinsman, Fujiwara Nobutaka, probably in 997 or 998. He was a fairly successful bureaucrat who served successively as secretary in the Ministry of Ceremonials and as governor of several provinces. Nobutaka was in his mid-forties at the time of his marriage to Murasaki, who was in her mid-twenties, rather a late marriage by Heian standards. In accord with contemporary customs of the polygamous aristocracy, Murasaki probably continued to live in her father's house, to which Nobutaka would commute. He already had several other wives and offspring. Murasaki and Nobutaka had one daughter, named Kataiko (or Kanshi). Fujiwara Nobutaka died in 1001, leaving Murasaki a widow after little more than two years of marriage. Murasaki's daily life, like that of most Heian women in her position, was probably quite uneventful. Left with ample leisure time on her hands while servants looked after her daughter and ran the household, she began writing *The Tale of Genji*. Murasaki probably shared her work in progress with her friends, who would copy it chapter by chapter to pass along and read again later.

Murasaki's reputation as the author of *The Tale of Genji* led to an invitation to enter court service with Empress Shōshi (988–1074; also referred to as Akiko). Shōshi was the eldest daughter of Fujiwara Michinaga and was married to Emperor Ichijō (980–1011; r. 986–1011). Murasaki most likely began her court service in late 1006. Her eyewitness account of events at court during the period from mid–1008 to the First Moon of 1010 is the core of her diary. She was in her mid-thirties when she joined the entourage of the nineteen-year-old Shōshi. Scholars have wondered why Murasaki would make such a momentous change in what was considered middle age for Heian women. Murasaki's diary records several poetic exchanges with Shōshi's father, Michinaga, and some scholars have inferred that Murasaki and Michinaga were intimates. But such exchanges of verses were routine in Heian society, and it seems more likely that Michinaga was interested in Murasaki as a literary talent than as an amorous conquest.

Michinaga had his daughter Shōshi installed at the palace initially as a secondary consort to Emperor Ichijō in 999, but he managed to have her designated empress the following year, an unprecedented event because it resulted in there being two empresses. The first was Fujiwara Teishi (Sadako, 976–1000), the daughter of Michinaga's brother and political rival Michitaka (953–95). The social and cultural life of Empress Teishi and her court has been immortalized in *The Pillow Book* of Sei Shōnagon (fl. ca. 1000). Besides Teishi, other women of high rank promoted cultural pursuits among members of their entourage. The emperor's aunt, Princess Senshi (963–1035), for example, presided over an elegant literary salon. Michinaga no doubt felt that his daughter must have an even more stellar cluster of women at her court. As the author of *The Tale of Genji*, Murasaki Shikibu would have been a desirable addition to Shōshi's coterie. For Murasaki too, the opportunity to partake of life at court must have been welcome, both for the prestige attached to serving the empress and for the wider scope of experience it afforded Murasaki to enrich her writings. Some of her observations were recorded in her diary, and others found their way into *The Tale of Genji*. In 1025 Murasaki's daughter, who had entered court service as well, was named wet nurse to the future emperor Go-Reizei (1025–68). She was later known as Daini no Sanmi and attained considerable fame as a poet.

It is not known exactly how long Murasaki remained in court service. With the death of Emperor Ichijō in 1011, the dowager empress Shōshi retired to one of the Fujiwara estates. Murasaki's name is not included in a roster of ladies-in-waiting for 1031, and for that reason it is considered the latest of possible dates for Murasaki's death, which range from as early as 1014, when Murasaki's father, Tametoki, suddenly returned to the capital from his post as governor of Echigo, possibly because his daughter had died. This final biographical question about her will probably remain an unsolved puzzle. Compared with the lives of some of her contemporaries, such as the flamoyant Izumi Shikibu (ca. 974–1030), Murasaki's life was fairly unremarkable, belying the magnitude of fame to be accorded her through the succeeding centuries.

Translated Works: Poetic Memoirs (Murasaki Shikibu shū), poetry. Poetic art was at the very core of *The Tale of Genji,* as well as of every Heian aristocrat. The earliest imperial anthology that attributes poems to Murasaki is the *Goshūishū* (Later Collections of Gleanings, 1068), but none of the four (compared with sixty-seven by Izumi Shikibu) included herein are found in the extant versions of her *Poetic Memoirs.*

Murasaki's *Poetic Memoirs* contains 128 verses, apparently arranged as a biographical sequence. As with all such private anthologies, copies were circulated in handwritten manuscript form and thus were subject to changes accidental and deliberate. Considered by some scholars to be the closest to the now lost original is the text edited by the poet and critic Fujiwara Teika (1162–1241). Teika also included eighteen of Murasaki's verses in the *Shinkokinshū* (New Collection of Ancient and Modern Times, 1206), an imperial anthology that he helped compile.

The first poem in her *Poetic Memoirs* is the best-known because it is represented in the popular *Hyakunin isshu* (One Hundred Poems by One Hundred Poets), compiled by Teika. The preface states that Murasaki met a friend whom she had not seen since childhood, and the meeting was so brief she hardly had time to be certain of her friend's identity. In the poem the moon is used as a metaphor for the friend. The preface does not specify whether the friend was male or female.

The verses, which are obviously directed to a lover, never specify him by name, although scholars have taken him to be Murasaki's husband, Nobutaka. The central poems in the collection (numbers 53–57) deal with the period after Nobutaka's death and reflect her grief in the melancholy tone that dominates the second half of the *Poetic Memoirs.*

The tone of some poems after her entry into Shōshi's court, however, is quite strong in comparison, especially when she counters the complaints of other ladies-in-waiting (poem 63). Some of Murasaki's verse seems skillful but lightweight, which may explain why most scholars have used the poetic memoirs as a biographical source rather than analyzing them as a work of art. Some of the information that has been gleaned includes the fact that she had an older sister who died (poem 15), that she traveled to Echizen province, where her father was governor (15, 20–24, 81–83), that she composed poems on behalf of Empress Shōshi (104), and the like. Some of the same events commemorated in the poetic memoirs are also included in her diary.

Diary (Murasaki Shikibu nikki). Murasaki's reportage and reflections on events at court cover the years 1008–10. One event depicted in great detail is the birth of Empress Shōshi's first son, Prince Atsuhira (future emperor Go-Ichijō, r. 1016–36) on the eleventh day of the Ninth Moon of 1008. Murasaki was also present in 1009 to record the birth of the second prince, Atsuyoshi, who would reign from 1036 to 1045 as Emperor Go-Suzaku. Both princes were born at the residence of their maternal grandfather, Michinaga, who would secure the undisputed control of Heian politics through them. Murasaki's diary does not focus on the political import of the births but describes the confinement of the empress, the attendant prayers and ceremonies, and the celebrations at court. She notes carefully the colors of the ladies' multilayered robes and the articles used in each sequence of ceremonies. These sections of Murasaki's diary were later used almost verbatim for the accounts of the events given in the *Eiga monogatari* (A Tale of Flowering Fortune, ca. 1045), a laudatory biography of Michinaga attributed to Lady Akazome Emon (ca. 960–1045). Besides the reports on the public occasions related to the births of the princes, Murasaki's diary contains private reminiscences and reflections. The episode of her earliest clandestine Chinese lessons leads into an account of reading the verses of the Chinese poet Po Chu-i in secret with Empress Shōshi. Although knowledge of Chinese was ostensibly considered unladylike, their efforts were supported by the emperor and Michinaga, who supplied them with copies of Chinese books.

Section 38 notes that the women were busy sending requests to calligraphers to copy sections of *The Tale of Genji*. Writing paper, a precious commodity in Heian times, was carefully selected and sent along with the requests. Meanwhile, Michinaga took advantage of Murasaki's preoccupation to sneak into her quarters and make off with draft sections of the tale in progress. This incident sheds interesting light on the nature of writing in the period and the precarious fate of handwritten manuscripts. Unfortunately, she does not say which chapters Michinaga took or whether she recovered the purloined draft. The diary records several poetic exchanges between Murasaki and Michinaga, as well as amorous overtures from other courtiers. On the whole Murasaki does not seem to enjoy this aspect of court life and depicts herself as trying to keep out of sight behind her screens. In her self-portrait (sections 68–69) Murasaki protests that she is misunderstood by the other women, who see her as a haughty, difficult person, though she admits to being ''perversely standoffish.'' Her haughty image might seem justified in the light of the sections devoted to critiques of her contemporaries. She is particularly harsh in her judgments of two women considered potentially her greatest literary rivals, Sei Shōnagon and Izumi Shikibu. Written in the form of letters, her critical remarks were perhaps intended for the edification of her daughter rather than for public circulation. The whole diary may in fact have been intended as a sort of handbook of court ceremonials and dress code for her daughter. Recording public events for future reference might also account for the rather dull style of the diary. Another possibility is that she made these events sound deliberately dull as a sort of private criticism of Michinaga's court. In any case, her acute powers of observation stood her in good stead as she translated the witnessed events into the work of fiction she was writing at the same time.

The Tale of Genji (Genji monogatari), fiction. Probably written during the first two decades of the 11th century, this is a work of remarkable complexity and psychological insight and amounts to 1,100 pages in English translation, encompassing fifty-four chapters. Murasaki's particular genius was to use elements from several different literary traditions to create her unique tale. One of her sources was the well-known narrative poem by Po Chu-i, "A Song of Unending Sorrow" (Ch'ang hen ko in Chinese, Chōgonka in Japanese), relating the love of the Hsuan Tsung emperor (685–762) for his consort Yan Kuei-fei and his grief at her death. Murasaki's narrative begins, "In a certain reign there was a lady not of the first rank whom the emperor loved more than any of the others." This is a direct allusion to the Chinese poem, from which there are nine quotes. The name Yang Kuei-fei also appears in the first chapter, "The Paulownia Court" (Kiritsubo). The influence of the Chinese history known as the "Records of the Grand Historian" (Shih chi) by Ssu-ma Ch'ien (145?–90? B.C.) has also been noted, and Prince Genji's exile has been compared with that of the Duke of Chou. Murasaki made use as well of the Japanese prose traditions, from the Buddhist tales of miraculous events to native mythology and folkloke, including The Tale of the Bamboo Cutter (Taketori mongatari), a fiction from the 9th century, and poem-tales such as the Tales of Ise (Ise mongatari), in which a number of episodes centering on the verse of Ariwara no Narihira (823–80) were linked together. These various prose genres were first merged by the anonymous 10th-century author of The Tale of the Hollow Tree (Utsubo monogatari), who relied heavily on fantastic elements for the first part but brought increasingly realistic episodes to the latter half of the narrative, which contains over nine-hundred poems. The author of this tale has generally been considered to be a male because the work lacks the feminine sensibility characteristic of Murasaki's novel as well as of the poetry and prose diaries of Heian women, typified by one known as the Mother of Michitsuna, who was the wife of the regent Fujiwara Kaneie (929–90). The confessional style and the sensibility and subjectivity in the depiction of the nuances of emotional experience in her work, the Kagerō nikki (The Gossamer Years), no doubt inspired Murasaki, for although the setting is physically much broader and is inhabited by hundreds of men and women, The Tale of Genji shares The Gossamer Years' subject matter, which is the inner life, the psychological and emotional effects of love, and the passage of time. Like the mother of Michitsuna, Murasaki would distinguish her own work from the "masses of rankest fabrication" and set it in the real world. In contrast to the narrative predecessors such as the Tales of Ise and The Tale of the Bamboo Cutter, which begin with the formula word mukashi (once upon a time), Murasaki begins her story with a phrase that narrows down the time element, "Izure no ontoki ni ka" (In a certain reign).

In its present configuration The Tale of Genji consists of fifty-four chapters. The overall structure of the work is generally divided into three broad segments: Chapters 1 through 33 (with the protagonist Prince Genji at the height of his glory); Chapters 34 through 41 (until Genji's death); and the remaining thirteen chapters centering on his "son" Kaoru and his grandson Niou. Murasaki peoples her vast stage with over four hundred characters, most of whom are related to each other, and her work spans nearly seventy-five years. The narrative does not follow a strictly chronological order, weaving back and forth between past and present, while some chapters represent simultaneous action. Murasaki Shikibu very rarely errs in her genealogies or chronologies, as later scholars have discovered after spending much effort in reconstructing her charts.

Murasaki employs some sophisticated structural and narrative techniques. One device is the "resemblance" motif, which threads through the plot, situations, and relationships. The attraction of Genji's father to Fujitsubo because of her resemblance to his favorite secondary consort, who is Genji's mother, is echoed in Genji's attraction to Little Murasaki (who reminds him of her aunt Fujitsubo) and in Kaoru's interest in Ukifune (half-sister of his departed first love). Likewise, Genji's seduction of his stepmother Fujitsubo is repeated in the adultery of Genji's second wife the Third Princess; the sons of both these unions share similar doubts about their parentage.

Another effective technique Murasaki Shikibu employs is creating memorable scenes for the introduction of the women in Genji's life: Little Murasaki is first seen by Genji as she is flushed with anger at her playmate, who has released her pet sparrow; Genji's interest in the Akashi Lady is aroused not by seeing her but by hearing her play the koto; the Third Princess is revealed on her verandah as her cat disturbs the curtains. Murasaki Shikibu can also make an event memorable by not describing it at all, as happens most dramatically with Genji's death, which is implied beforehand and reported as long past in Chapter 42, "His Perfumed Highness" (Niou), which begins the story of the next generation with the statement that the shining prince was dead, and there was no one to take his place.

The centrality and importance of poetry in Japanese literature are nowhere more beautifully illustrated than in *The Tale of Genji*. It contains nearly eight hundred verses, which form a vital part of its structure and tone. They convey heightened emotional awareness, whether the emotion is love, admiration, melancholy, or grief. The first poem is spoken by Genji's mother, the Lady of the Paulownia Court, on her deathbed. The titles by which the chapters are presently known were not assigned by Murasaki Shikibu, but by generations of her readers, who referred to each chapter by a poem in it. Murasaki creates sophisticated irony through the absence of poetry as well: Genji never exchanges verses with his first wife, Aoi. In the last ten chapters poetic imagery is used to emphasize the melancholy atmosphere of the isolated setting on the banks of the Uji River and mirrors the unsettled emotions of the characters.

The tone of the Uji chapters is much darker than the first two-thirds of the work. Quite different from the world Genji created and inhabited, the world of Kaoru and Niou is more often about the failure of love and perhaps a more accurate mirror of the late Heian society of Murasaki Shikibu's time. Here she fulfills the purpose of her tale, as stated by Genji in his famous comments on fiction. It is difficult to remember that Murasaki's work was written nearly one thousand years ago, so modern are the ideas, for example, that anything may be the subject of a novel, as long as it happens in the mundane world; that the novelist should relate both the good and the evil that are part of the world; and that the writer feels compelled to write lest the people and events she witnessed are lost forever. Even more remarkably, in these goals Murasaki Shikibu has succeeded perhaps even beyond her own expectations. The world of Genji is Heian Japan, just as Shakespeare's is Elizabethan England.

Murasaki is comparable to Shakespeare in many other ways. Her work too has inspired millions of pages of writing, both scholarly exegeses by Genji specialists and fiction, poetry, and plays. The scholar Motoori Norinaga (1730–1801) first captured the essence of *The Tale of Genji* in the term *mono no aware*—"the sadness of things" or, perhaps, the sensitivity to this sadness. *The Tale of Genji* is indeed a novel about sensitivity. Experiences are important to the characters insofar as they contribute to developing the sensibilities to the beauty and perishability of all things. Prince Genji is the ideal man because of his extraordinarily great range of sensibility. The last third of the novel depicts men and women of more limited sensibilities, living in a darker world that echoes the Buddhist emphasis on the transience and mutability of human existence. This brooding aspect of *The Tale of Genji* was inherited by the literature of succeeding periods, the Noh plays in particular. Murasaki Shikibu's novel has inspired many other works of literature but remains a unique achievement. The modern novelist Tanizaki Junichirō (1886–1965) translated *The Tale of Genji* from classical into contemporary Japanese more than once. Contemporary women writers such as Enchi Fumiko (1905–86) also translated Murasaki's novel and wrote extensively about it. The first complete English translation, done by Arthur Waley (1889–1966) and published between 1925 and 1933 in six volumes, has become a classic in its own right. The volumes written about *The Tale of Genji* seem to increase yearly, both in Japanese and in English. It is a fitting tribute to the creative genius of Murasaki Shikibu that her tale has come to be recognized as a classic of world literature, a source of literary inspiration, and a subject of scholarly researches and, most important, that it has continued to be the source of sheer reading pleasure that she most certainly intended her work to be.

BIBLIOGRAPHY

Translations

Bowring, Richard. *Murasaki Shikibu: Her Diary and Poetic Memoirs, A Translation and Study* Princeton, NJ: Princeton University Press, 1982.

McCullough, William H., and Helen Craig McCullough, tr. *A Tale of Flowering Fortunes: Annals of Japanese Aristocratic Life in the Heian Period.* 2 vols. Stanford, CA: Stanford University Press, 1980. Contains translations of sections of Murasaki's diary describing events at court.

Seidensticker, Edward G., tr. *The Tale of Genji.* New York: Alfred A. Knopf, 1979.

Waley, Arthur, tr. *The Tale of Genji*. New York: Modern Library, 1960. A one-volume
   edition of this translation.

Critical Works

Cranston, Edwin A. "Murasaki's Art of Fiction." *Japan Quarterly* 27 (1971): 207–13.
   An interesting analysis of three comparative translations of the section in which
   Genji discusses the art of fiction.
Fischer, Felice. "Murasaki Shikibu: The Court Lady." In *Heroic with Grace,* 77–28.
   Armonk, NY: M. E. Sharpe, 1991: *Legendary Women of Japan*. Ed. Chieko Irie
   Mulhern.
Morris, Ivan. *The Tale of Genji Scroll.* Tokyo: Kodansha, 1971. A beautifully illustrated
   volume of the handscroll in the Tokugawa family collection, Nagoya.
————. *The World of the Shining Prince.* Baltimore: Penguin Books, 1969. A study of
   court life based on *The Tale of Genji.*
Pekarik, Andrew, ed. *Ukifune: Love in the Tale of Genji.* New York: Columbia University
   Press, 1982. Essays on aspects of the last part of the novel.

Felice FISCHER

N

NAKATSUKASA no Naishi (Lady Nakatsukasa, fl. ca. 1250–92), diarist. Real name: Fujiwara Noriko.

Life: Nakatsukasa no Naishi or Lady Nakatsukasa is the author of one of the very last examples of the premodern court diary genre, which formed a central strand in the classical women's literature of Japan. This Lady Nakatsukasa is not to be confused with two earlier women writers known also as Nakatsukasa, a name associated with the posts that their significant male relations held in the Nakatsukasa or Ministry of Central Affairs. One is a poet (ca. 912–after 989) who, along with her celebrated mother, Lady Ise (ca. 877–ca. 938), is counted among the Thirty-Six Poetic Geniuses, and the second is a lady-in-waiting active in the late 10th and early 11th centuries in the household of Princess Senshi (964–1035). The poetic writings of these earlier women tell us about the aristocratic life of the Heian period (794–1192).

The subject under discussion here, Lady Nakatsukasa's work in the late 13th century sheds light on women's prose literature of Kamakura (1192–1333) Japanese court society. Virtually nothing is known about Lady Nakatsukasa's life other than the information found in her diary. She was born Fujiwara Noriko to an unknown mother and an influential father, Fujiwara Nagatsune (d. 1297), who was to become the minister of central affairs of the junior third rank. Like most court women after the 9th century, Nakatsukasa no Naishi was not known by her own personal name, Fujiwara Noriko: formal names as a rule were not widely used in premodern Japan because of a variety of taboos involving names so closely identified with the individual. Premodern Japanese women were commonly referred to by the titles, posts, or ranks of important male relatives, and Lady Nakatsukasa received her appellation from the highest position her father reached, minister in the Nakatsukasa-shō or Ministry of Central Affairs, which he held from 1286 to 1287. The second part of the name by which she was to be known to centuries of readers of her diary and poetry, Naishi, is her own title in the court of Emperor Fushimi (1265–1317; r. 1287–98). Lady Nakatsukasa's first formal appointment was in the women's quarters at the residence of ex-emperor Go-Fukakusa (1243–1304; r. 1246–59). When the diary opens in 1280, she is serving as an attendant to Go-Fukakusa's son, the sixteen-year-old crown prince who would become Emperor Fushimi in 1287 and whom Lady Nakatsukasa would serve until her retirement. During these early years, her life seems to have been a peaceful one, highlighted by her interaction with other women in Fushimi's service, visits of friends, her own writing and the study of poetry, and sojourns out of the palace. Lady Nakatsukasa showed her independence during this early period in the first of several journeys beyond the confines of the capital, duly recorded in the diary. She traveled to the port of Amagasaki in the early fall of 1286, accompanied only by a few attendants, and enjoyed seeing places she had only heard of in her reading of literature.

Nakatsukasa had fallen ill in the previous year and had been confined to her family home during her recuperation, which lasted until spring. The most detailed entries of her diary begin in 1285, and many authorities have speculated that this is when she actually began to keep the diary, filling in entries for earlier years from memory. Unfortunately, Lady Nakatsukasa seems never to have fully regained her health, and it may have been the same illness that eventually led to her retirement only a few years later.

In the twelfth moon of 1287 Lady Nakatsukasa was promoted from her previous, now unknown status to *naishi,* or lady-in-waiting, to the newly designated Emperor Fushimi. The elaborate enthronement ceremony, held in March of the following year, was itself a source of great pride to Lady Nakatsukasa, and she described the ceremony and the surrounding events in great detail. Lady Nakatsukasa's life thereafter changed to the busy schedule of the reigning emperor's court. But Nakatsukasa no Naishi still found time for another journey out of the capital that year, this time a pilgrimage to Hase near the ancient capital of Nara. Hase was famous both in the court poetic tradition and as the location of a famous Buddhist temple housing a statue of Kannon, the bodhisattva of compassion. In making this pilgrimage to Hase, Nakatsukasa no Naishi joined in the tradition of women diarists, such as Takasue's Daughter, who wrote *Sarashina Nikki* in 1059, and Lady Nakatsukasa's own close contemporary, Lady Nijō (1258–after 1306), who recorded her visits to many of the sacred places visited by the poet-monk Saigyō (1118–90) in *Towazugatari.* Lady Nakatsukasa's visit to Hase was only one of her several trips to places of religious importance, including one to the Iwashimizu Hachiman temple festival and another to Nara, the ancient capital and Buddhist center.

Lady Nakatsukasa records an important event in the male-dominated realm of public court politics in which she was involved: the assassination attempt on Emperor Fushimi by Asahara Tameyori in 1290. This is one of the few indications in her diary of the fierce rivalry between the two lines of the imperial family over accession to the throne, inheritance rights, and such cultural matters as the selection of poems for imperial anthologies. As a member of Fushimi's court, Nakatsukasa no Naishi was associated with the senior or Jimyōin line of Fushimi's father, Go-Fukakusa. The head of the junior or Daikakuji line, Emperor Kameyama (1249–1305; r. 1259–74), was implicated in the assassination attempt but officially protested his innocence to the warrior government in Kamakura. Although the event caused much disturbance in their lives, neither Lady Nakatsukasa nor her emperor was harmed in the attack.

Illness forced Lady Nakatsukasa to retire from court service in 1292, possibly a resurgence of the same illness that had stricken her in 1285. Her return to her family home upon retirement is the last in Nakatsukasa no Naishi's diary, concluding with a poetry exchange in which she compares herself with the falling blossoms. The year of her death remains unknown.

Career: Events at court significant enough to warrant extended treatment in Nakatsukasa's diary center around the composition of poetry and her relationships with various members of the circle of poets that had begun to gather at the crown prince's court in the 1280s. These poets were to build on the patronage of Emperor Fushimi to establish the innovative Kyōgoku school of poetry, whose members came, by the turn of the century, to rival the dominant Nijō school as arbiters of poetic taste, literary convention, and aesthetic theory. The early, core members of this group included the future emperor Fushimi, Kyōgoku (Jūnii) Tameko (ca. 1250–51–ca. 1315–16), Tameko's younger brother the accomplished poet and literary theorist Kyōgoku Tamekane (1254–1332), and Fushimi's empress, Eifuku Mon'in (1271–1342). One of the better-known events in Lady Nakatsukasa's relations with the Kyōgoku poets was a series of poetry exchanges inspired by a single call of the cuckoo in 1283 between Fushimi and Tamekane and also involving Lady Nakatsukasa. On another occasion, in 1284, Lady Nakatsukasa accompanied Fushimi on his visit to the Kitayama mansion of the influential Saionji Sanekane (1249–1322), an important poet and the father of Lady Nakatsukasa's future mistress, the soon-to-be empress, Eifuku.

Perhaps the most important single relationship that Lady Nakatsukasa seems to have developed with the members of this circle of poets, however, is her close friendship with Kyōgoku Tameko. Tameko had been appointed with her younger brother Tamekane as poetry tutor of the crown prince in 1280 or shortly thereafter, the same year that Lady Nakatsukasa's diary begins. The diary records a poetic correspondence that lasted for four years between Tameko and Nakatsukasa, triggered by their shared memories of a poetry excursion early in 1284 with the crown prince and his retinue. Even though Lady Nakatsukasa receives a poem from Minamoto Tomoaki (ca. 1259–87), a youthful but highly regarded man who had also joined them on the memorable journey, Lady Nakatsukasa's diary shows that her exchanges, repeated on the anniversary of the excursion, were not with him but with Tameko. The friendship that grew between Tameko and Lady Nakatsukasa is one aspect of the close ties between the women in Fushimi's service that developed independently of their relations with men. Women served in significant numbers at the courts of important members of the various branches of the imperial household and in the expansive households of high-ranking aristocrats. Although this institutional base of support depended to a significant extent on the patronage, marriage relations, or love liaisons with men, much of the women's social interaction centered on the other women at the court. In this women-centered social setting much classical Japanese prose literature, including Lady Nakatsukasa's diary, was composed, read, and appreciated.

Nakatsukasa's position as a member of Fushimi's court, which was the center of the Kyōgoku school of poetry, guaranteed her patronage of the highest order and opportunities to come in contact with the greatest literary talents of her day. One possible consequence was the inclusion of two of her poems in the first Kyōgoku-dominated imperial anthology of poetry, the *Gyokuyōshū* of 1312. Since these poems are not representative of the innovative Kyōgoku style, modern scholars now regard them as unimportant for Lady Nakatsukasa's literary career when compared with her diary.

Nothing is known about Lady Nakatsukasa's motive in beginning her diary or about its readership and contemporary critical response. Diary literature does contrast with several other important venues of literary activity, including the important institution of the imperial anthology of poetry, where the selection and editing process was often dominated almost exclusively by men. Diaries, in contrast, seem to have been, with a few very important exceptions, often written, reproduced, and read primarily or even solely in the context of the women's quarters in aristocratic and imperial households in medieval Japanese society. There does not seem to have been any institution for diaries comparable to what might be termed "publication," such as was served for poetry by the imperial anthologies. The circulation of diaries to their audience probably depended largely on informal channels, a practice that clearly reduced the number of their readers over the centuries, but this also meant that the writing, preservation, and reading of the diaries were largely independent of men's direct control and authority. Although the diaries provide access to the feminine voice in premodern Japanese literature, masculine-defined aesthetic elements still influenced women's diary literature through the pervasive role that poetics played in the formation of aesthetic taste generally and through the role of the masculine diary written in Chinese. In this context of cultural production and consumption the author of Lady Nakatsukasa's diary was given an important place in the eyes of later literary historians.

Translated Work: The Diary of Lady Nakatsukasa (Nakatsukasa no Naishi nikki). Nakatsukasa is known almost exclusively for a single literary work, her diary. Despite extensive association with the Kyōgoku school poets in Emperor Fushimi's court and the large number of her poems recorded in the diary, she has been granted standing as only a minor poet, and that for the only two poems included in the *Gyokuyōshū* imperial anthology. *The Diary of Lady Nakatsukasa* is positively attributed to Lady Nakatsukasa from internal evidence, though scholars find evidence for later editing by another hand. Nevertheless, specialists do agree that the title is a later addition.

The diary treats the period between the fifteenth day of the twelfth Moon of 1280, and the third Moon of 1292, with a substantial increase in the number of entries for the years 1285 to 1289. The earlier portions of the diary were possibly written from memory, beginning sometime after 1285. After the fourteenth day of the fourth Moon of 1289, the diary records only a brief notice in the second Moon of 1292 that Lady Nakatsukasa has retired from court service due to illness and subsequently returned to her homeland, followed by a poetry exchange late in the third Moon.

Defining the genre of this work involves several interrelated problems, although here for convenience the traditional Japanese term *nikki* (lit., "daily record") is translated as "diary" from Euro-American literary studies. In classical Japanese literature there was never any clear distinction between several genres: *nikki,* often translated as "memoir" or "diary"; *monogatari* or fictive tale; *shikashū* (often autobiographical) poetry collection, which generally included long prose headnotes for some or all of the poems; and *uta monogatari,* or "poem tale," which falls somewhere between *monogatari* and *shikashū.* These closely related types of literature often mix autobiography, lyrical poetry, and what might be termed fictive prose narration. As a result, students of works in the *nikki* genre often find that lyrical expression plays a dominant role in narration, placing the private or subjective experience at the center of what appears to be narrative fiction, although conventions of apparently "objective" factual and even public records of events are often interwoven. Western scholars trained in Western genre theory have generated several important critical studies of this problem, including Phillip Tudor Harries's introduction to his *The Poetic Memoirs of Lady Daibu* (1980), Edwin Cranston's introduction of *The Izumi Shikibu Diary* (1969), and review articles by Mark Morris, "Desire and the Prince: New Work on *Genji Monogatari*—A Review Article," *Journal of Asian Studies* 49.2 (May 1990), and Richard Okada, "Domesticating *The Tale of Genji,*" *Journal of the American Orientalist Society* 110.1 (January–March, 1990).

The disjunction of Euro-American genre distinctions and those of the classical Japanese literary tradition is further complicated by the important role that diaries written in Chinese prose played in the development of Japanese autobiographical narratives. Beginning possibly in the mid-7th century, diaries were written in Japan perhaps exclusively by men in Chinese language and as objective, factual records of public activities at the imperial court. Only in the 10th century did autobiographical narratives in the vernacular emerge. With only a few important exceptions they were written by women in a private vein and much more closely approximated the writing of poetry, especially in the format of the poetry collection. Diaries in later centuries mix the various conventions of these two types of diaries, and there are important examples in the vernacular showing the crossing of these constructed gender conventions.

The Diary of Lady Nakatsukasa is no exception in the evolution of *nikki* written since the 10th century, as it combined conventional narrative styles from both the masculine, public, Chinese-style diary and the feminine, private, Japanese-language diary. In line with the masculine tradition, Lady Nakatsukasa's diary is generally organized by daily entries, though rather irregularly, and somewhat less than half the diary is taken up with relatively prosaic reports of public events at court. Yet in several other aspects it reflects the feminine style. In surveying the subjects of the eighty-two total entries, Professor Fukuda Shūichi found that well over half of them focus on personal events outside public life at court, while a full fifth of the episodes are taken from life in the women's quarters or from the author's own purely private experiences. The use of poetry in the prose narratives also signals the presence of a private element in the diary, with the exception of public, occasional poems. Typical of the medieval diaries, even this brief work contains a great number of poems, amounting to some 150, scattered throughout the narrative. The poems often serve as the climax of a scene, placing their private, lyrical quality squarely at the center of the autobiographical narrative. Moreover, the generally reflective tone of many of the entries often gives the passages a distinctly personal flavor characteristic of earlier women's literature.

Both Japanese and Western scholarship has traditionally circumscribed this diary under the rubric of "women's literature," which is thought to have culminated in the early 11th century with the composition of such prose masterpieces as *The Tale of Genji* by Murasaki Shikibu. Based on this location of the peak of "women's literature," works composed after the middle of the 11th century have been dismissed as inferior works imitating the earlier "classics." *The Diary of Lady Nakatsukasa* is one of the very last of this line of later works, overlapping in time with *Towazugatari* (The Confessions of Lady GoFukakusa' in Nijō) and succeeded only by one extant woman's diary, the *Takemukigaki* of Hino Nako, which describes events between the years 1329 and 1349. As a result, Lady Nakatsukasa and many other later works have been little studied and are generally regarded as relatively unimportant. The neglect of women's diary literature from this period can be contrasted with the enormous corpus of scholarship on the autobiographical reflections and essays of male writers active at the imperial court from the 12th to the 14th centuries, such as Kamo no Chōmei (ca. 1155–1216) and Yoshida Kenkō (ca. 1283–ca. 1350).

The assumptions underlying this distinction between "women's literature" and (men's) "literature" in modern Japanese scholarship can be found in several areas. The modern Japanese historian's characterization of the imperial court as declining in power and wealth in the 12th and 13th centuries has led many modern scholars to read the literature of this period as the product of an effete, degenerate court society. The historian's premise has also misled scholars of medieval literature into concluding that the writers of diaries from this period saw their lives in terms of declining material wealth and enervated political power. Yet as Donald Keene has correctly noted, several of the women diarists of this period apparently perceived their own lives in the court as at the height of splendor. Nakatsukasa is a case in point: at the enthronement of Fushimi, for example, she describes the lavish preparations and robes not only in great detail but with considerable pride.

It is important to recognize that androcentrically or male-centered views of "reality" or of self, whether defined by Nakatsukasa's 13th-century contemporaries or by modern literary historians in Japan and the West, many of them male, are quite different from the worlds depicted by the women of the Japanese court. Their lives in the women's quarters of the imperial palace were in many significant respects free of the control that their fathers, uncles, husbands, or male children traditionally exercised in many other sectors of medieval society. In differing from other medieval women's diaries that concentrate on love affairs or marriages with male courtiers, Nakatsukasa's diary stands as an example of women's literature in which identity and subjectivity are constructed and delimited without the need for direct reference to male individuals. This raises an important question which has yet to be answered in the study of premodern Japanese literature: how was identity constructed for the women of the court, and in what ways did the differences between their reality and that of their male contemporaries contribute to different experiences and separately constructed identities and values?

Another common assumption found in the scholarship on Lady Nakatsukasa's *Diary* is that the zeitgeist of each age directly determines the personalities of its players. This has encouraged the scholars assuming a declining socioeconomic context to label the women writers of this period as ineffectual, melancholy souls adrift in a morass of lassitude and depression. An extreme example is Ikeda Kikan's condescending description of Lady Nakatsukasa as "a woman who, though she writhes and gasps, is unable to do anything about the terrible bitterness of her life, victim as she is to the pitiful anguish and desperation of a split personality" (*Kyūtei joryū nikki bungaku* [Women's Court Diary Literature, 1926]; tr. in Keene, *Travelers of a Hundred Ages,* 1989). Such a statement only suggests a question as to whether the identity of woman as victim is being defined within the context of women's experience or on the basis of androcentric assumptions about what a "whole" self is. As Sandra Buckley has pointed out in her review article, "Reading Women's Texts" (*Bulletin of Concerned Asian Scholars* 20.3 [1988]), the implicit masculine norm seems to have been violated in many women's texts, and yet it may be only through the disruption of this masculine-defined norm that women were able to establish their own voice. In further studies of Nakatsukasa's and other women's diaries, feminist critics may choose to seek out such differences from androcentric norms in order to define a distinctive feminine voice and identity in medieval Japanese women's literature.

The overall aesthetic of Lady Nakatsukasa's diary parallels many other works of the 13th and 14th centuries in its consistent reading of the world as *mujō,* or impermanent, and as *mono no aware,* or the pathos of things. Many passages express such a perception of the world as the one in Donald Keene's translation: "Living in the world, one naturally has many unforgettable experiences, and some of them are the cause of tears, but those are the ones I want most to preserve." Lady Nakatsukasa's interest in the sorrows of life is often evaluated in Ikeda's terms as "pitiful anguish," yet the same aesthetic is generally accepted in positive terms when found in men's literature from the same period, most notably in the "Tale of My Hut" or "Hōjōki" of Kamo no Chōmei and Yoshida Kenkō's *Essays in Idleness*. In men's literature, this same contemplation of the fleeting world is taken as a deeply philosophical appreciation of the impermanence of things. The unwillingness of critics to give Nakatsukasa's reflections the same value seems to be based on an assumption that women are incapable of deep intellectual reflection. Future study of this and other medieval women's diaries may lead to a revision of such assumptions through the consideration of possible gender differences in the construction of worldviews.

The genre and literary quality of Lady Nakatsukasa's diary, the questions of feminine voice and identity concept, the nature of the reality constructed, and the diary's overall aesthetic value all remain as potentially fruitful subjects for further exploration. Recently a Japanese woman scholar, Imazeki Toshiko, has suggested that such characterizations of the narrator as going through what Ikeda Kikan termed "agitation and disintegration of her identity" need to be reconsidered. Imazeki also argued against such facile, impressionistic criticism, contrasting the melancholy of *Lady Nakatsukasa's Diary* with the naive innocence of the diary by Lady Ben (Ben no Naishi) (active ca. 1246–52) of some two decades earlier. Imazeki's position suggests that Japanese scholars may also be joining Western students of Japanese women's diary literature in reevaluation based on feminist theory and other contemporary insights.

BIBLIOGRAPHY

Translation and Critical Works

Keene, Donald. "The Diary of Lady Nakatsukasa." In *Travelers of a Hundred Ages*. New York: Henry Holt, 1989, 149–54.

Muller, Klaus, tr. *Die Nakatsukasa no Naishi Nikki Zeit: Ein Spiegel Hofischen Lebens in der Kamakura-Zeit,* 1965.

Niwa, Tamako, tr. "Nakatsukasa Naishi Nikki." Ph.D. diss., Harvard University, 1955.

Joseph PARKER

NOGAMI Yaeko (1885–1985), novelist, playwright, essayist, translator, critic. Real name: Nogami Yae (Mrs. Nogami Toyoichirō); née Kotegawa Yae.

Life: Born in Ōita prefecture on the southern island of Kyushu, Yaeko was the first daughter of a sake brewer who was an active supporter of political figures such as Itagaki Taisuke (1837–1919, head of the Liberal party) so that she was accorded an unusual look into the inner workings of political and financial machines. Her father's large establishment, with a great number of live-in employees, was a rich reservoir of old stories that stimulated the girl's imagination. One story that impressed young Yaeko the most was an anecdote about her mother told by her grandmother, and it yielded Yaeko's first published story, *Enishi* (Preordained, 1907). A significant juncture in her life came at the turn of the century, when she was allowed to leave home to study in Tokyo. This decision, unusual in the light of social custom at the time, was made largely by her mother. Yaeko entered Meiji Jogakkō (Meiji Women's School), which was founded by Japanese Protestants. Its vice president and de facto leader, Iwamoto Yoshiharu (1863–1943), was an effective advocate of women's education and the principal editor of *Jogaku Zasshi* (Women's Learning), which played a significant role in fostering a new type of woman as well as launching a new generation of male writers espousing romantic ideals, such as Shimazaki Tōson (1872–1943) and Kitamura Tōkoku (1868–94), who taught at Meiji Women's School. Yaeko's experience at this school made a profound imprint on her, culminating more than eight decades later in her last novel, *Mori* (The Forest, 1972–85).

In 1902, Yaeko met Nogami Toyoichirō (1883–1950) from her hometown and married him four years later upon her graduation from the college division of Meiji Women's School. An English major studying under novelist-professor Natsume Sōseki (1867–1916) at Tokyo Imperial University, Toyoichirō was an ardent student of the Nōh theater who would become a highly respected scholar of Greek and Japanese drama. Soon Yaeko started taking lessons in *utai* (chanting of Nōh play lyrics) and *tsuzumi* drum accompaniment, which would later play an indispensable role in her fiction. Her decision to marry was motivated primarily by a wish to continue her study in Tokyo, but it proved most crucial in Yaeko's growth as a writer. Before long Toyoichirō's mentor, Sōseki, took her under his wings indirectly via her husband and began to steer her into a literary career with genuine enthusiasm and high expectations.

While Sōseki's acceptance gave her invaluable advantages, it also subjected her to her husband's intense jealousy. Kind and gentle though he was, Toyoichirō also had a possessive and patronizing attitude. He was especially disturbed by Yaeko's friendship toward Sōseki's other students, such as the future novelist Naka Kansuke (1885–1965) and Iwanami Shigeo (1881–1946; founder of Iwanami Shoten, later the principal publisher of Yaeko's works). The diaries that she kept from 1923 until her death abound in anecdotes relating to Toyoichirō's jealousy, particularly in their late thirties and early forties, as well as her laments and critical comments not only on her husband's but also men's egotism in general. Yaeko was by no means guiltless in aggravating her husband's jealous fits. The diaries have posthumously revealed her feelings toward Naka Kansuke, comparable to those of Charlotte's toward Werther in Goethe's romantic novella *The Sorrows of Young Werther* (1774), explosively popular in Japan. By the time she wrote a short story, "Kokoro" (Heart and Mind, 1935), alluding to her platonic relationship, she had apparently reconciled her conflicting emotions toward Naka and her husband. Such personal experiences and observations undoubtedly motivated her in mid-career to write plays dealing with conflicts between men and women such as *Himitsu* (The Secret, 1916), *Reikon no akambō* (Spiritually a Babe, 1918), and *Aru otoko no tabi* (One Man's Journey, 1921).

Nogami Yaeko never took a job or position other than honorary ones, and her career as a mother of three children played a significant role in her personal development while working at home as a writer and translator. In the 1920s, when Japanese intellectuals were attracted to the gospel of Marxist literature, Nogami's sons were growing into adulthood. Yaeko's major concern turned to the young people's espousal of leftist ideologies. Adamantly independent in thought, though conservative in leaning, Nogami lived up to her conscience and counseled her children against radicalism. The experience materialized into her novel *Machiko* (Machiko, 1920–30), through which she established her name as one of the most intellectual, yet humanitarian, thinkers of the time. A rare eyewitness to Japan's turbulent transitional period, Nogami Yaeko lived through drastic social changes following the nation's confrontations with foreign powers, especially the two world wars. Through her astute contemplation of the real causes underlining those changes and her empathy with the fictional characters she created, Nogami succeeded in defining her moral values for the world in which she lived. Nogami died in 1985, five weeks short of her one hundredth birthday, leaving unfinished only a few pages of her last work, *The Forest,* which was to crown her award-rich, eighty-year career by posthumously winning the Japanese Literature Grand Prize (Nihon bungaku taishō).

Career: Formative to Nogami's career was her exposure to a wide range of Western literary works available in the English language. Natsume Sōseki, upon reading one of her earliest short stories, advised her to rid herself of the influence of the Japanese popular literature that flourished in the Meiji period (1868–1912). Nogami took his counsel to heart and wrote ''Preordained,'' which was published in *Hototogisu,* a literary magazine that would become an influential vehicle in promoting post-Meiji literature. It was followed by a series of short stories dealing with subject matter and themes taken from the daily lives of middle-class Japanese. Nogami's effort at this time was focused on finding a way to reconcile the traditional techniques of storytelling with modern rationalistic thinking, an objective that Sōseki himself had tirelessly pursued. Nogami achieved this goal in two subsequent sister volumes, *Chichioya to sannin no musume* (Father and Three Daughters, 1911) and *Terejia no Kanashimi* (Theresia's Sorrow, 1912), which vividly illustrate that women's values as well as personalities are conditioned by the circumstances of their formative years.

When Hiratsuka Raichō (1886–1971) started her liberal women's literary magazine *Seitō* (Bluestockings, 1911–16), Nogami contributed partial translations of such works as Alfred de Musset's *La Confession d'un enfant du siecle* (1836, from an English translation of 1905) and the Russian-born mathematician's memoirs from an English translation, *Sonya Kovalevsky: Her Recollections of Childhood* (1895). Nogami's dedication to children bore fruit in 1913 in the form of her first book, a translation of Thomas Bulfinch's *The Age of Fables.* The book was dedicated to her eldest son, who was then three years old. *Atarashiki inochi* (The New Life, 1914), *Futari no chiisana vagabondo* (The Two Little Vagabonds, 1916), and *Hahaoya no tsūshin* (Letters from Mother to Mother, 1919) followed, and by 1920, when she wrote *Arupusu no yama no musume* (The Girl in the Alps), an adaptation from Johanna Spyri's (1820–1901) *Heidi* (1880–81; English tr., 1884), Nogami Yaeko had become a household name. A 1921 adaptation of Swedish author Selma Lagerlof's (1858–1940) *The Story of Gösta Berling* (1891; English tr., 1898) fascinated young readers with the warm, emotional tone of country life, the depiction of such being one of Nogami's real strengths. The moral theme of Gösta's redemption sent a powerful message to the young audience. While she found some elements of traditional Japanese fables to be injurious to young minds, her adaptations from Western authors laid the foundation for her own growth as a writer and nurtured the forthcoming generations of readers as well.

In response to a new surge in the theatrical arts during the late 1910s, Nogami presented her plays, *Hōka satsujinhan* (Arsonist-Murderer, 1916; later changed to The Secret) and *Spiritually a Babe*. Adapting both theme and technique from Greek drama as well as Japanese Noh theater, Nogami demonstrated her insightful speculation on social issues and her in-depth observation of human psychology in writing *Fujito* (The Fujito Shallow, 1920), *Kantan* (Han-tan, Young Lu's Dream, 1920), and *Aya no tsuzumi* (Tangled Drum, 1922).

Of her plays of this period, perhaps the most significant for the history of Japanese women's literature was *Spiritually a Babe* (1918), for this piece prompted Miyamoto Yuriko (1899–1951) to write to Nogami, critically commenting on her literary concepts and social attitude. Nogami graciously accepted the criticism and began corresponding with Miyamoto, who was on her way to blossom into a major leftist writer. Nogami's awareness of social ills as well as the nation's slide toward militarism intensified, as her own sons grew older and became critical of the authorities dictating to them how to behave. *Machiko* was followed by ''Wakai musuko'' (A Young Son, 1932) and ''Kanashiki shōnen'' (Sorrowful Boy, 1935). Nogami's interest in this area led to further investigation into the lives of young liberals who recanted under severe persecution and brainwashing. *Kuroi gyōretsu* (Mournful Procession, 1936) and *Meiro* (Labyrinth, 1937) are the first parts of a sextet on this subject that was suspended during the war years, to be completed in 1956 under the comprehensive title, *The Labyrinth*.

In 1934, her husband was suddenly dismissed from the university deanship, and this incident yielded *Ko-oni no uta* (Song of a Demi-Devil, 1935), a novella notable for a mild ridicule of the rather licentious life led by novelist Morita Sōhei (1881–1949), a fellow disciple of Natsume Sōseki. In the same year, she started serializing *Niji no hana* (Rainbow Flower, 1935–36), an adaptation from Jane Austen's *Pride and Prejudice*. Her trip to Taiwan in 1935 became an inspiration for ''Satō'' (Sugar, 1946). In 1938, she accompanied her husband, who was appointed exchange professor to teach in England, and traveled through Western Europe and the United States as well.

Since literary works with alleged touches of liberalism or individualism were banned in Japan from 1937 on, Nogami's major activities until Japan's defeat in August 1945 were limited primarily to writing travelogues and children's literature. Her translations during this time include George Bernard Shaw's *Caesar and Cleopatra* (1898). In an "I-novel," *Yamauba* (Mountain Witch, 1941), nevertheless, she found a way to reconcile her suppressed intellectual self with the rustic yet quiet lives of the simple folks in the foothills of Mount Asama, where she would continue to live until 1948. In the postwar period, Nogami's views as a social, cultural, and political critic were eagerly sought after by the media, and she produced essays, short stories, and translations, while reworking the ongoing sextet novel, *The Labyrinth.* This longest of Nogami's works earned her the Yomiuri Award for Literature in 1957 and in the following year an invitation from the Chinese Writers Association and Overseas Cultural Council for her to travel in China, which had provided the fictive setting for the last stage of her labyrinthine drama.

Her search for the truth hidden beneath the surface of utter simplicity was carried over into the next novel, *Hideyoshi to Rikyū* (Hideyoshi and Rikyū, 1962–63), which traces the inner journey of a master of the tea ceremony and originator of the rustic-style tea. Nogami received numerous awards, including the Order of Culture in 1971, the highest honor available to the citizen of Japan today. In addition to working toward the betterment of Japanese society in social, cultural, and education spheres, for example, as honorary headmaster of Hōsei High School, she had the distinction of sitting on the Women's Literature Prize Committee and the traditionally male-dominant Akutagawa Prize Committee.

Major Works: Machiko (Machiko, 1928–30), novel. Set in the late 1920s, the events evolve around a young woman of a middle-class family. By depicting Machiko's thirst for knowledge and sincere search for self-identity, Nogami successfully presents the problems facing educated single women in prewar Japan. The heroine's mother is modeled on Mrs. Bennet in Jane Austen's *Pride and Prejudice,* whose chief concern is to find a suitable husband for her daughter. Machiko's position is contrasted with that of her college classmate, Yoneko, sister of the heir to a landed gentry with declining fortunes, whose predicament is continued from Nogami's earlier play, *Kusarekaketa Ie* (Decaying Family, 1927). By detailing the life of Yoneko's ailing brother, Nogami delineates the inherent problems plaguing Japanese society after modernization. Adopting the position of *narodnik,* Yoneko wants to dedicate herself to working for the poor. Interwoven between her criticism of the privileged and her sympathy with the liberals are Machiko's romantic association with an activist, Seki, and her disillusionment upon discovering his real intentions. Many a minor character in the story, such as Machiko's brother-in-law, who is the dean of students at a college preparatory school, reflects real people involved in the "thought control" of students enforced by the authorities.

"Wakai musuko" (Young Son, 1932), short story. Attracted to Marxist gospels without understanding exactly what they would entail, many young men and women were actively participating in ideological movements in 1932 and

1933. Nogami views the so-called leftist activities in these years as a sort of spiritual movement joined by those who hoped to cleanse the sins of the world. Young Son traces this process of youthful thinking and casts doubt on the ulterior motives of the hidden but real leaders of the movement. Her skepticism is projected onto the mother of Young Son, who is sympathetic to her son's feelings toward his fellow activists yet critical of the political goals of the leftist leaders. The only thing the mother of such a son in such an age can do, Nogami seems to say, is to watch his spiritual growth with affection and moral support. Two years later, Nogami elaborated on this theme in an essay, "Wakai oi ni tsuite itoko e" (To My Cousin Concerning Her Son, 1934).

Hideyoshi to Rikyū (Hideyoshi and Rikyū, 1962–63), novel. This historical story focuses on the events leading to the tragic death by forced suicide in 1591 of Sen no Rikyū at Hideyoshi's command. The two men, with equally driving ambition, represent the two burgeoning classes of their fast-moving time: Hideyoshi, a former foot soldier of low rank who won the de facto rulership of Japan by wit and might; and Rikyū, an independent spirit nurtured in the mercantile community who perfected the art of tea ceremony. Utilizing a vast number of primary sources, Nogami re-creates a dynamic history of the 1590–91 period between the fall of Hideyoshi's last foe and his fateful attempt to invade Korea in the hope of subjugating Ming China. While the real reason for the rift between the two men and the ultimate tragedy of Rikyū is hidden by the shrouds of legend, Nogami interprets it as a psychological conflict between two geniuses caught in changing times as well as their own ambitions and successes.

Written six years after the completion of *The Labyrinth,* some parts of *Hideyoshi and Rikyū* constitute an allegory for Japanese society in the 1930s, in which Hideyoshi stands for the zealot militarists and Rikyū stands for any number of liberals opposed to war. The famed tea master Rikyū's honorable death without compromising his moral integrity signifies his victory over power for Nogami, who never wrote a single line in support of the war effort. The most successful fictional creation is Rikyū's third son, etched against a vivid background of the life and ethos in the bustling port city of Sakai, prospering in foreign trade in the late 16th century. No less impressive is Rikyū's brother-in-law, a Noh actor, forging a bridge between the two worlds, aristocratic and plebeian, through his teaching of the art of Noh theater.

Mori (The Forest, 1972–85), novel. Partly autobiographical yet largely fictional, *The Forest* is a historical romance featuring interwoven plots and characters that demonstrate such qualities as wit, ambition, humor, generosity, compassion, and, most important, the sense of justice in the three years preceding the Russo-Japanese War of 1894–95. At a time when various social ills were surfacing as inevitable costs for the hastily built modern economy precariously balanced on the quasi-modern political system, the editor in chief of a progressive women's magazine, *The New Woman,* presides over the Forest, the former estate of a shogunate vassal, now a boarding school for women established by an ex-samurai who became a Christian after thirteen years in the United States. The narrator, a commuting student introduced to this unique community, reflects the author herself in her mid-teens.

The novel consists of three parts and an epilogue. The first five chapters introduce the narrator to the mystery surrounding the present headmaster, who is attired like a Shinto priest but preaches Christianity with fervor. A major role in gradually lifting the fog of mystery is played by one young art student, the only male student permitted to live on campus, and two girls who are interested in him until his departure to study abroad. The next five chapters bring a shock to the entire Forest community with the news of a political assassination committed by a former instructor of the school. The narrative extends to the history of the institution, including the rift between the present headmaster and his predecessor, echoing the actual schism in the Japanese Protestant world. The last five chapters offer the most fictional of the subplots, a secret relationship between the headmaster and a student. When an admirer of the headmaster, a male medical student from outside the Forest and now a lover of the girl, belatedly learns of their affair, the drama reaches its climactic height.

Through the delineation of the mid-Meiji society and natural landscape, the author contemplates the essential question of how to reconcile the old values with the new. A number of supporting characters, including the narrator's classmates, their seniors, and two teachers of English, both of whom have studied in the United States, perform functions highly reminiscent of the chanters and secondary characters (*waki*) of the Noh drama, their ever-curious mind and animated chatter revealing and assessing incidents. Providing valuable historical material that had been largely unavailable, such as the sources on the Christian movement in Japan prior to the Russo-Japanese War, the book can serve as a supplementary cultural history of Japan at the turn of the century. Detectable in Nogami's narrative technique is a subtle yet profound influence from the storytelling tradition of English literature, especially of Jane Austen but with a Dickensian magnitude. Unfortunately, the author's death cut the epilogue short in the middle of a new sentence leading to the concluding section.

Translated Works: The Neptune (Kaijin-maru, 1922), novella. Set in a small boat driven off course by bad weather and adrift for fifty-nine days, the story explores the psychology of four men in a no-exit situation. Based largely on a true incident of near cannibalism at sea, Nogami personifies human weaknesses in two sailors who kill the captain's young nephew with the intention of eating the corpse. The gruesome imagery has been traced variously to the author's knowledge of a story in the *Epic of Gilgamesh,* Greek mythology, and an episode in Dante's *Divine Comedy,* but in fact Nogami has a denouement that is typically Japanese. Neither of the killers dares commit cannibalism after all, and one of them dies in rapture from acute relief upon being rescued by a freighter. Redemption comes to the surviving killer, for the captain tells the authorities that his nephew had died of an illness, thereby saving the killer from indictment.

The author credits the religious nature of the captain, who is an ardent believer in Kompira (Kumbhira), the guardian deity of seafarers.

"The Full Moon" (Meigetsu, 1942), short story. Centering around the terminal illness and subsequent death of an aged mother, the story is set in the early spring of 1941, ten months before Pearl Harbor. This seemingly autobiographical narrative conveys Nogami's anxiety over the impending disaster, foreboded by Japan's rejection of international accord. Nogami's own observation of current events in Europe and East Asia on her travel in 1938–39, astutely yet sparingly stated in this story, would be further elaborated in her subsequent travelogue, Ōbei no tabi (Journey Through Europe and America, 1942).

In "The Full Moon," the hairdresser, having taken care of the narrator's hair for the past ten years, has become a part of the family to the point that she does not mind even running errands for her client. Such an attitude was not unusual in former times but has been rapidly disappearing in changing Japan, especially after the passage in 1938 of the National General Mobilization Law, which gave the prime minister broad discretionary powers over the conduct of domestic affairs. The principal theme is the narrator's contemplation of the values of the older generations, of women in particular, especially those who were trained not to want anything for themselves but to devote their life to the welfare of the ie, the institution of the extended family. Succinctly depicting the idiosyncratic habits of her own mother, the narrator assesses the mores of the society in which her mother and her contemporaries were reared. Her mother's death and funeral bring out the villagers' sense of community, continuity, and loyalty. The equilibrium of such traditional existence, however, is bound to be broken, washed away by the overwhelming tide of time. The cries of the crows in the opening scene, then, may be interpreted as a warning of approaching death, not only of the narrator's mother in her sickbed, as the characters assume in the story, but also of the old community as such. When the narrator buries her mother's ashes at the foot of Mount Asama, the night is bright with a full moon, symbolizing the full life of the mother and forecasting the life that the narrator would lead in the mountain villa in central Japan, writing her aphoristic and even apocalyptic literature.

"The Foxes" (Kitsune, 1946), short story. Nogami forthrightly identifies greed, whether individual or nationalistic, as the cause of the conflict and suffering in the civilized world. Three characters, the protagonist, his university friend, and his uncle the vice admiral, embody the critics of the reckless policies of Japanese militarists, especially of the faction that gained political power through its aggressive venture into northeast China. Counterbalancing them is the protagonist, an ailing man who has quit his job in Tokyo and come to live in the rustic village in northern Karuizawa. Detailing his reasoning for renouncing a prominent bank position is the author's device to emphasize the financier's role as the real culprit behind Japan's imperialist aggression. Marriage to an innocent young woman of his own choice underscores his integrity. His rejection of the time-honored convention known as marriage politics so as not to become part of power mongers and his decision to leave Tokyo earn him bliss in the bucolic life on the farm, raising foxes—a humanistic resolution that betrays the Tolstoyan influence on the author Nogami's idealism.

The time frame of the story is highly metaphorical, spanning the eve of World War II in 1941 and the aftermath of Japan's defeat in 1945. The ailing protagonist may be an aphoristic metaphor of the flagging Japanese economy or even the broken spirit of the populace. As he has taken the passive option of living away from his greed-filled clan rather than actively trying to solve his personal problems, so did the Japanese majority take the passive alternative of going along with the militarist government without much protest. This stance of the populace has been credited for their orderly acceptance of unconditional surrender, but Nogami provides another insight. Shortly before the end of the war, the protagonist dies, leaving his widow a hollow person, a spiritual invalid. The period of her bereavement overlaps that of the nation, dispirited and devastated as never before—the majority of the Japanese survived the wrenching agony of the defeat by becoming spiritually "invalid," Nogami seems to say. The concluding section of the story covers the process of reconciliation and reconstruction. When her husband's uncle returns, the widow finds her strongest moral support in continuing her life on the farm: this former admiral, wounded in the Battle of Midway and repatriated, climbs the watchtower of the fox farm and affirms a new life in the legacy of his nephew. The foxes, then, become the symbol of innocence and sanity, of which the nation has long been deprived.

Minor characters are also significant: the fox farmer who refuses to give up his animal (symbol of innocence) at any cost stands for an indomitable determination not to compromise art; his wife and a farmhand portray the realistic no-nonsense ethos of the ordinary Japanese. The protagonist is a forerunner of Ejima Munemichi, the principal character that was to be added two years later to the ongoing novel *The Labyrinth,* who also finds the purpose of life in his new vocation, as Nogami herself did during the war years and duly recorded in *Mountain Witch.*

The Labyrinth (Meiro: 1 and 2, 1936–37; 3, 4, 5, 1949; 6, 1956), novel. Set between the years 1935 and 1945, this story has thematic continuity with Nogami's earlier works, especially with Machiko and Young Son. The principal character in the first parts is a former activist student who suffers from a deep sense of guilt for having recanted his political beliefs, groping for a way to reconcile his conscience. His association with an aristocratic employer is a novelistic device to connect his hometown in Kyushu with Tokyo and values of the middle class with those of the upper class. His desire to know more about the heritage of his hometown sets the history of early modern Japan to unfold, leading into the international conflicts and their consequences in the mid-20th century. In her postwar chapters, Nogami created a second major charater, Ejima Munemichi, a former count who devotes himself to preserving the art of Noh theater through his patronage of a Noh master. He reads extensively in world history, thereby fulfilling the role as critic of the time.

Her hope for the future of Japan is expressed in two specific terms: the liberation of thought and the supremacy of art. The former is illustrated by the young protagonist, who deserts from his regiment in China. The latter is represented by the Noh master, who evacuates himself from air-raid-prone Tokyo in 1945, transcending the chaos of time. In *The Labyrinth,* Nogami aims at uniting the reader's stream of consciousness with the author's to produce what her mentor Natsume Sōseki believed to be the ideal way of appreciating literature. Minor, but no less significant, figures such as the protagonist's cousin and his former activist friend memorialize young people who were caught in the crucible of time in which Japan dashed through a labyrinth of ambitions that seemed to know no end.

BIBLIOGRAPHY

Translations

"Foujito." Tr. M. Yoshitomi. In *Femme japonaises et leur literature.* Paris: Chariot, 1924.
"The Foxes." Tr. Ryozo Matsumoto. *In The Neptune-The Foxes.* Tokyo: Kenkyusha, 1957.
"The Full Moon." Tr. Kyoko Selden. In *Stories by Contemporary Japanese Women Writers,* ed. Noriko Lippit and Kyoko Selden. New York: M. E. Sharpe, 1982.
Labyrinth. Tr. C. Guterman. Moscow: Foreign Literature Publishing House, 1963.
"The Neptune." Tr. Ryozo Matsumoto. In *The Neptune-The Foxes.* Tokyo: Kenkyusha, 1957.
"A Story of a Missing Leg." Tr. Yukiko Tanaka. In *To Live and to Write,* ed. Tanaka. Seattle: Seal Press, 1987.

Synopses

"A Certain Socialist." In *Introduction to Contemporary Japanese Literature 1902–1935.* Tokyo: Kokusai Bunka Shinkokai, 1939, 274–79.
"Hideyoshi and Rikyū" and "Labyrinth." *Japan PEN News,* 15 (July 1965): 12–14.

Michiko AOKI

O ————————————————————————————

ŌBA Minako (1930–), novelist, short story writer, essayist, poet, playwright. Real name: Ōba Minako (Mrs. Ōba Toshio); née Shiina Minako.

Life: Ōba was born in Tokyo on November 11, 1930, the eldest daughter of a navy doctor, Shiina Saburō, and his wife, Mutsuko. Her childhood was an unsettling one because of her father's frequent transfers: she changed elementary schools six times, once every year. She was six when the China incident broke out, the beginning of Japan's aggressive involvement with China, leading to World War II. By seven or eight, she had read the fairy tales of every nation imaginable; the stories by Hans Christian Andersen (1805–75), in particular, deeply influenced the young Ōba. Later on, her love of fairy tales and folklore would be rekindled when she had an unexpected encounter with the Inuit (Eskimo) culture of Alaska. At the age of eleven, she began to read Victor Marie Hugo (1802–1985), and his humanism moved her so much that she knew then what she wanted to be when she grew up. In a questionnaire passed around in class she happily put down "writer" as her desired profession. The homeroom teacher corrected her by saying, "What you mean by 'writer' is that you want to go on to high school." This was the first of a series of childhood experiences that would be etched in her curious mind, establishing the notion that grown-ups are indeed strange creatures.

World War II broke out during her fifth year in elementary school. By the time she entered Toyohashi Girls' High School, reading narrative fiction was her sole occupation, a tendency that provoked great displeasure from the teachers. In 1944 her family moved to Seijō City near Hiroshima. In its desperate struggle to fight a losing war, Japan mobilized all the students to work eleven hours a day (with only a one-day holiday each month) at the school-turned-uniform-factory. Ōba looked forward to the air-raid alarms, which came two to three times a day; due to the shortage of shelters, the students were evacuated to the nearby wheat fields, where they could rest a bit, temporarily freed from relentless, backbreaking labor. The alarm was particularly a welcome break for Ōba because she could read a book, which she never forgot to grab before she ran into the fields. She wrote: "I saw nobody else doing what I was doing. Over my head flew B-29s dropping bombs everywhere. They were so close that I could often count the number of bombs jettisoned from each bomber."

During the tender adolescent days of high school, Ōba had already earned the label *chūi jinbutsu* (a "dangerous" character) for the kind of *nan bunqaku* (soft literature) she avidly read. According to the military regime, it meant any fiction that was entertaining and therefore unconnected with maintaining a patriotic spirit. Once when a factory supervisor made an inspection tour of the school, one of Ōba's teachers, who had already taken an intense dislike to the youngster's indomitable spirit, accused her of being *defiant* in front of the visitor and slapped her face repeatedly.

On August 6, 1945, in Seijō City, she saw a huge mushroom cloud hanging over the Hiroshima sky. A few hours later, a long procession of terrifying, disfigured A-bomb victims made their way to Seijō. A student rescue squad was hastily formed and sent into Hiroshima. What Ōba witnessed in the aftermath of the A-bomb "was not of this world," and she would forever be hounded by the image of unspeakable devastation, "constantly inhabiting her subconscious."

At sixteen, she graduated from Iwakuni Girls' High School in Yamaguchi prefecture. That same year, her family moved to Niigata, her mother's birthplace, where Dr. Shiina opened a clinic. Around this time her literary attention was focused on Japanese classical literature, of the Heian period (797–1190) in particular. She was bored to death at the school where she was enrolled in 1947, the three-year Home Economics School for Girls. None of the courses offered there challenged her intelligence. Although she had made the highest score on the entrance exam, after only one semester she found herself at the bottom of her class, never failing to invite the teachers' fury. She was permanently branded a "rebellious student" and was often dismissed from class. At the end of the term the administration advised her to withdraw from school. Her parents then moved her to Shinhotta Girls' High School. Under the 1948 Educational Reform, the Niigata Home Economics School for Girls she had just left became a new senior high school. She was readmitted into a new third-year class. She still maintained her voracious appetite for literature, and one of the literary giants in particular who won her soul during these turbulent times was Dostoyevski (1821–81).

Between 1949 and 1953 Ōba found the quiet, uneventful academic life at Tsudajuku Women's College in Tokyo quite to her liking. During her freshman year she met her future husband, Ōba Toshio. Drama became her love at this time, and she seriously debated the possibility of pursuing an acting career. She had the opportunity to play roles in several Chekhov (1860–1904) pieces, and his dramatic works became sources of literary inspiration later on in her writing career. Her college studies also awakened an interest in poetry, chiefly through the works of T. S. Eliot (1888–1965), and she began to try her hand at writing verse. In the end, however, she chose American literature as her major. She particularly enjoyed William Faulkner (1897–1962), Ernest Hemingway (1899–1961), and John Steinbeck (1902–68).

Upon graduation with a B.A. in 1953, she decided to remain in Tokyo rather than return to Niigata, and she took a part-time job teaching at several different local junior and senior high schools. In the summer of the same year she fell ill, quit her job, and went back to her parents' home in Niigata, where she devoted her time to reading fiction and writing poetry. In December 1955, she married Ōba Toshio on the condition that she be allowed to continue fiction writing. In 1959 Ōba's life took a radical turn: appointed as the Japan-Alaska Pulp Company representative, Mr. Ōba, an engineer, was stationed in Sitka, Alaska, where the Ōbas made their second home for the next eleven years. They have one daughter, Yū.

Career: The new life in Alaska meant the beginning of Ōba's literary career at the age of thirty-one, as well as the moment of her intellectual, psychological, and physical liberation. There were two things that she always wanted to do but was not able to do in Japan: to travel and to pursue graduate education. She took full advantage of the opportunities given her in the States to take up both avocations. In the summer of 1961 the Ōbas took a three thousand-mile tour of the West Coast by car; the following year she enrolled as a graduate student in the Art Department at the University of Wisconsin at Madison in her attempt to express herself in painting. This was where she was able to complete her first short story, "Kōzu no nai e" (A Picture with No Composition, 1963).

Four years later, she still believed painting was the medium of her self-expression and enrolled again as an art graduate student in the summer school, this time at the University of Washington at Seattle. Her English was proficient enough by then for her to audit many literature classes. She produced a second short story, "Niji to ukibashi" (A Rainbow and a Bridge of Dreams, 1967), during what she calls "her college dorm life" in Seattle.

Back in Sitka, where she once again settled into a domestic life, she began to write what turned out to be a gem of a short story, "Sanbiki no kani" (Three Crabs, 1967). A prestigious intellectual magazine, *Gunzō,* printed the manuscript in the June issue of 1968. The story was an immediate success: it won the Gunzō New Writer's Prize and the most coveted Akutagawa Prize in the same year. In 1969 she published five short stories, visited an Inuit (Eskimo) village at the Bering Sea, and made a brief stay in Paris during November and December.

Between 1971 and 1980 a trip abroad became an annual rite for Ōba as she traveled extensively in Europe, Southeast Asia, Africa, Canada, and the United States. With her maturity in technique and popularity steadily on the rise, she was invited as a visiting scholar by the University of Oregon, where she stayed for a semester in 1979; she also participated in the International Writers' Seminar for four months in 1980 at the invitation of the University of Iowa. In May 1987 she was selected as one of the judges for the Akutagawa Prize, only the second woman novelist after Kōno Taeko (1926–) to serve on the committee. She has to her credit eleven novels, eight collections of short stories, five collections of essays, four plays, and a book of poetry. A novel, *Ōjo no namida* (The Princess's Tears), was published in 1988.

Major Works: Urashima-sō (The Urashima Plant, 1977), novel. In this ambitious futuristic novel, Ōba's narrative voice turns philosophical as she contemplates the future of civilization, technology, Japanese, Americans, sexual equality, and ultimately human life itself. The novel draws upon a familiar Japanese folktale: Urashima Taro, who once saves a turtle harassed by children on the beach, is carried by the grateful creature to the Dragon Palace in the depths of the ocean. When he begins to miss his family and asks for permission to return to the land, the Dragon King gives him a *tamatebako* (a Pandora's box) as a farewell gift, with strict instructions never to open it. Once back on the shore, unable to find his home, he feels lonely and opens the small box. Out comes a puff of curling white smoke, and Urashima turns into an old man with white hair.

In Ōba's version of the Japanese Rip Van Winkle story, Urashima is the twenty-three-year-old Yukie, who decides to visit Japan after eleven years of living in the United States. First, curious to rediscover her own childhood and Japan's recent historical past, she seeks out her stepbrothers, Morito and Yoichi, who in turn bring her into contact with a mixed-blood beauty with a boy's name, a retarded son, a calculating wife, and an American hippie married to a Japanese. All of these characters have a story to tell, and Yukie, an uninvited guest in her own native land, proves to be indispensable: she is the listener of this stories-within-a-story narrative. The more curious she gets, the further she is dragged into the deeper recesses of the storytellers' psychic world.

The dual narrative structure of *The Urashima Plant* blends the contemporary stories with the old stories of those who are long dead, including Yukie's mother and her two husbands. Furthermore, Ōba layers another set of stories, a *ménage à trois,* an eyewitness account of the Hiroshima holocaust, Yukie's eleven-year American odyssey, her two-year relationship with Merrick, and his own biographical background. Interspersed with all these data are dramatic monologues of Yukie and Merrick and their dialogues, commenting on everything under the sun.

In the hands of a less mature and accomplished writer, the sheer bulk of the information involved would have been overwhelming. However, Ōba is quite successful in delivering a novel that combines the qualities of legend, fairy tale, myth, satire, and critique. One of the most effective devices employed in this novel is her deliberate omission of direct quotation marks, which re-creates the dreamy, fluid style of the Heian narrative, as in *The Tale of Genji* (11th c.). Yukie is like a ghost figure who is able to go in and out of physical barriers or, in a futuristic high-tech society, someone who overcomes the barriers of matter-antimatter. Japan becomes a different type of imaginary Dragon Palace for Yukie, who longs to go back to her second home, the United States, where a happy life with Merrick is not assured, but possible. The "*tamatebako* that begins to weigh in her hands" in the end shows the symbolic state of her own psyche: her vacillation on whether to stay behind in Japan a little longer or to leave with Merrick for good. Ōba's Pandora's box also symbolizes the unknown, potentially destructive nature of the future of civilization and humankind.

Katachi mo naku (Without a Shape, 1982), novella. This short novel won Ōba another prestigious prize, the Tanizaki Junichirō Award. The title is taken from a four-character line in Chapter 25 of *Tao-te Ching* (The Book of Tao): "something nebulous yet complete" (*Sources of Chinese Tradition,* vol. 1, p. 56). Ōba liked the four-character phrase, which, in the modern Japanese rendition, means "lonely and desolate," but she assigned her own *hurigana* (phonetic scripts) to read it, "without a shape." As the allusive title suggests, this novella (only 197 pages long, printed in unusually large type) explores the quintessential Japanese sensibilities of *mono no aware* (a nostalgic longing for the past and sadness for the impermanence and ephemerality of things) and *iroke* (eroticism). The narrative voice is impregnated with the drowsiness of the dream state, something indirect, suggestive, and sensual. The characters' names, directly taken from the twentieth chapter of *The Book of Tao,* imply Ōba's Taoistic outlook on life: Ton, the state of being dim and weak like a fool; Haku, not knowing where one is, like a newborn babe before it learns to smile; Ryū, the restless wind that never ceases; Mayuko, the ten thousand things of the universe, and so on. The basic story line centers around three characters who have grown up together: two brothers, Ton and Haku, and the girl next door, Mayuko. Mayuko and Haku remain neighbors but lose their spouses, who are killed together in an accident on their way to a hot spring. Ōba does not present this simple story in a linear movement but goes back and forth between the main characters' childhood memories and the postaccident relationship of Mayuko and Haku. Dream sequences and an excerpt of Haku's unfinished soft-core pornographic story point to Ōba's attempt to free herself from the constraints of intellect, reason, and consciousness. Some critics called the novella "a masterpiece of pornography," and Ōba calls it "a work born out of the conscious subconscious."

Translated Works: Naku tori no (Birds Singing, 1985), novel. A winner of the Noma Literary Prize, this work deals with another subject with which Ōba feels very much at home: the marital relationship of man and woman in a changing society. Ōba spent considerable time on what title to give to this narrative. "Naku tori no," which can be a five-syllable opening line in a haiku poem, is open-ended and literally invites another line to follow: "I've had a hard time coming up with a title I liked. I wanted something expansive . . . a fictional world is basically a human world, and in a larger sense it is a universe, within which exists every conceivable kind of space and time, etc. That is to say, there is no such thing as a state of completion as the fictional world expands to infinity. And yet it exists at this very moment." Another symbolic meaning of the title is related to Ōba's Wordsworthian approach or the Japanese traditional aesthetics expounded by Ki no Tsurayuki (?–945, a *waka* poet): a spontaneous overflowing of emotions, which she likens to singing.

One of the central characters in the story, Yurie, is a free-spirited, "spacey" novelist happily married to Mama (lit., "Mr. True-Space," one of Ōba's delightful puns) who has retired early from his profession in order to enjoy his life as a house husband, bookkeeper, and dependent. He represents the prototype of the liberated Japanese male experiencing a role reversal in a rite of passage. Side by side with this radically unconventional couple is the *kokusai kekkon* (lit., international or mixed marriage) couple of the younger generation, Mizuki and her husband, Carl, and their two adopted children, a half-Chicano, half-Japanese Leonard and a blue-eyed Scot, Mary. All kinds of "birds" come to "sing their tunes," that is, stories, before Mama Yurie and Shōzō: their old-time friends Lynn-Anne and Henry; Mizuki's uncle, who has just come back from a monastery in Bulgaria; Yurie's daughter and her husband. Their quick-paced, tongue-in-cheek dialogues are the "songs" put together for a "singing contest" among the characters, the triumph of this novel. The following dialogue exchanged between Mama Shōzō and Yurie's cousin, Mizuki, is a typical example:

"Shōzō, Yurie certainly writes what she damn pleases in her novels."

"Yes, I know. She's apparently making lots of men angry out there. But I'm her husband, and what she's saying doesn't make me angry, so why should they be?"

"Probably they're angry at you as well. You're such a bad example of a husband. Because there's a husband like you, there's a wife like her, they're saying."

Mizuki wanted to see him angry, but her provocation had no effect on him. He simply went along.

"I guess so. You may be right. Seiichiro was just like that."

He cleverly shifted the topic to her dead father.

"Yurie's female protagonists are so uninhibited, doing what they damn please with men."

"A bit like me, those male characters, it seems. Always daydreaming, cuckolded, typecast as a quack doctor, a dumb scholar, or a trashed white-collar still kept on the payroll, so I understand."

"Do you mean to say you enjoy reading that kind of stuff?"

"I guess so. You certainly don't get bored living with a female like Yurie."

There are several messages in this novel that Ōba playfully tries to send to the opposite sex in Japan: men should start rebelling against women who take it for granted that men exist only to feed women and children; it is time that men start enjoying more freedom, a more humane life; they must start thinking about the quality of their life, what to do with themselves, especially after their retirement. However, once men have been properly informed, there is the other side of the coin—the women. The inseparability of both sexes is, in Yurie's words, like *kingyo no fun* (the goldfish dung that always clings to the creature as it swims around). Ōba discusses this gender question in many of her essays, collected under the titles of *Josei no danseiron* (Discussions on Men by Women, 1979) and *Onna, otoko, inochi* (Women, Men, and Life, 1985).

Garakuta hakubutsukan (The Junk Museum, 1975), novel. A recipient of the Women's Literature Prize, this work is the sum total of the sojourn in Sitka, which Ōba declared her "salvation." She hardly ever got homesick and found in her life abroad the absolutely blissful experience of discovering what it is to be articulate, to be able to say what she was not supposed to say at home without risking society's disapproval. Despite the linguistic obstacles she had to overcome, Ōba was able to take advantage of a situation in which she could create her own language to communicate with people around her. She often speaks of the total verbal isolation she had experienced in Japan before she left for Alaska: "There were too many things I could not say. I believe this had a lot to do with being a woman in Japan. I could not say anything that was really on my mind."

This frustration and, in her own words, a *urami* (grudge) she holds against her own society generate the dynamics of *The Junk Museum*. In turn, this makes her one of the most truly articulate Japanese writers of all time. Her style is invariably tongue-in-cheek; her tone witty, wise, sarcastic, merciless yet forgiving. Her characters, often full of venom, spewing spiteful yet realistic comments about Japanese, humankind, society, the world, and civilization, operate as Ōba's mouthpiece time and again but always with wit and humor.

The Junk Museum takes the format of "stories within a story." Like novelists Ōe Kenzaburo (1935–) and García Márquez (1928–), Ōba repeats characters and events not within a single text but between texts. Each story is independent, yet each is part of a larger narrative. The first story, "The Mistress of the Dog Palace," is the tragicomic odyssey of Maria Andrevena, as related in her diary. A red-haired and dark-skinned Russian refugee who was elbowed out of her society in the throes of a revolution, she lives with four wolflike Siberian dogs in her large "dog palace." She talks gibberish with a heavy accent and struts around the town, sometimes in rags like a beggar, sometimes in a fancy dress like an aristocratic lady. Another personality of the "junk museum" introduced in this first tale is Aya, Maria's "bosom friend": despite her light brown eyes and almost white skin, she is a "dyed-in-the-wool Japanese," the storyteller assures us. Aya is married to an American called Russ, who owns an old abandoned ship turned into a junkyard, which the townspeople began to call "the junk museum." Maria works as a clerk-bookkeeper at the gift shop, also the only print shop in town, owned by Carlos Semprin, a Spanish Don Juan. These characters share certain common characteristics: they are "a bit arrogant, standoffish, but extremely curious and love people and love to talk."

The tale shifts to the personal history of Aya in "The Handyman's Wife," how she abandoned Japan and came to the States with Russ and her visit to Japan, where she meets her ex-husband, accompanied by their daughter Chizu. "The Gooseberry Island" deals with Sue, a mysterious Korean woman casually mentioned toward the end of the first tale. All three tales can be enjoyed either as separate stories or as part of a long narrative, to which Ōba, if she wishes, can add later. This open-ended structure, a favorite of Kawabata Yasunari (1899–1972) and other traditional Japanese writers, is a symbolic one for Ōba, whose curiosity is inexhaustible, in constant search of uncompromising individuals to add to her memory bank.

(*The Junk Museum,* is being translated by Stephen W. Kohl, Toyama Ryoko, and Marian Chambers.)

Translated Works: ''The Three Crabs'' (Mittsu no kani, 1968), short story. Yurie is a housewife living in the United States, bored to death by the pretensions of the people around her and refusing to play the diplomatic role imposed upon her. Through the casual, bantering kind of party conversations of the mixed company of Japanese and Americans, the story explores many of the troubling issues of the 1960s in the United States.

''Fireweed'' (Higusa, 1969), short story. The mysterious beauty and power of the Alaskan wilderness and its native people are told in a surrealistic atmosphere. As she so often does, Ōba deliberately begins the story with its conclusion, in this case, the death of a sensuous, goddesslike creature, Fireweed, loved by two men. The story unfolds in flashbacks, keeping the reader in suspense till the end: how does she die? An accident, a suicide, or is there a murder involved? The death-birth cycle of human life blends with the primordial rhythms of nature.

''The Pale Fox'' (Aoi Kitsune, 1973), short story. A woman dreams of catching a beautiful fox in a forest while in real life she plays to perfection the roles of ''slave'' and ''mother.'' This piece captures humankind's primordial urge to be free in the wilderness where one plays the double role of prey and predator. The interesting twist of the story is that while a man thinks a woman is forever catering to the needs of the opposite sex, a woman is the one who actually holds power over him. However, Ōba never falls into the folly of assigning both sexes roles from which they cannot escape.

''The Smile of a Mountain Witch'' (Yamauba no warai, 1979), short story. This satire on the stereotyped relationship of a man and woman begins in the style of folklore, disarming the reader on the spot. A Japanese mountain witch endowed with the power to read people's minds and to transform herself into any form that may please the opposite sex is a cursed creature, the embodiment of woman in Japan. She is not taken seriously and has to pretend she is not what she really is. Ōba gives no names to her characters: it is simply a story of a real mountain witch who ''spent her entire life in the dwellings of a human settlement,'' going through the usual rites of passage, childhood, adolescence, marriage, and death. At each stage, the witch deepens her knowledge of how not to offend others in interpersonal relationships: careful not to verbalize what is on her mother's mind, she adjusts her perception to meet her mother's needs; at school she spends ''an incredible amount of mental energy'' matching everyone else's mood and behavior; in marriage her role-playing techniques become more refined. Like Chekhov's ''The Darling,'' the sole purpose in life for this mountain witch is to decipher, to assimilate the likes, dislikes, and needs of the opposite sex. Ōba seems to be giving the reader a dual message: the mentality and approach of this mountain witch resemble those of Japan (as a collective body), which spends a tremendous amount of energy incorporating and assimilating Western technology, while the culture willingly pays a high price for the absence of, in Masao Miyoshi's words, "universalist knowledge, skeptical observation, and individual reflection in order to sustain a close and coherent community inherited from the long past" (*As We Saw Them: The First Japanese Embassy to the United States [1860]*, 124).

"The Sea Change" (Tanko, 1978), short story. It describes "a casual friendship" (the original title of the story) of a woman who, despite her revulsion toward masculine vanity, plays along with different men. In a neutral narrative voice, Ōba playfully satirizes a misguided conviction and inflated ego of a world-famous cellist. Neither does a female fare well in this story. Many of the stereotyped characteristics of both sexes are discussed in the open. None of the characters has a name; the tone is erotic, dreamy, and surrealistic.

BIBLIOGRAPHY

Translations

"Candle Fish." In *Unmapped Territories: New Women's Fiction from Japan.* ed. Yukiko Tanaka. Seattle: Women in Translation, 1991.
Birds Crying (Naku Tori no). Tr. Michiko Wilson. In preparation.
"Birds Crying (Chapter 1)." Tr. Michiko Wilson. *Chicago Review* 39, 3 (Fall 1993): 186–195.
"Birdsong (Tori no Uta)." Tr. Seiji Lippit. *Review of Japanese Culture and Society—Josai University*, 4 (December 1991): 84–93.
"Firewood." Tr. Marian Chambers. *Japan Quarterly* 38, 3 (July–September 1981): 402–27.
"Ōba on Ōba." In *World Authors, 1985–1990.* New York: H. W. Wilson, (forthcoming).
"The Pale Fox." In *The Shōwa Anthology: Modern Japanese Short Stories,* 2, ed. Van C. Gessel and Tomone Matsumoto. New York: Kodansha International, 1983, 337–47.
"Repairman's Wife." Tr. Tomoyoshi Genkawa. In *Kyoto Collection: Stories from the Japanese.* Ed. Bernard Susser. Osaka: Niheisha, 1989, 87–132.
"Sea-change." Tr. John Bester. *Japanese Literature Today,* 5 (March 1980): 12–19.
"The Smile of a Mountain Witch." In *Stories by Contemporary Japanese Women Writers.* Tr. and ed. Noriko Mizuta Lippit and Kyoko Irye Selden. Armonk, NY: M. E. Sharpe, 1982, 182–96.
"White Wind." Tr. Joel Cohn. *Mānoa: Pacific Journal of International Writing,* 3 (Fall 1991): 12–16.

Critical Works

Wilson, Michiko. "Becoming, or *Un*becoming: Female Destiny Reconsidered in Ōba Minako's Narratives." A paper presented at the Conference on Japanese Women

Writers at Rutgers University in April 1993, forthcoming in a book edited by
Janet Walker and Paul Schalow.

————. ''Ōba Minako.'' In *World Authors, 1985–1990.* New York: H. W. Wilson,
(forthcoming).

Michiko N. WILSON

OKAMOTO Kanoko (1889–1939), poet essayist, novelist. Née Ōnuki Kano
(Mrs. Okamoto Ippei).

Life: Kanoko was born in Tokyo to the wealthy Ōnuki family of Takatsu
(Kawasaki City), formerly purveyors under the patronage of the Tokugawa shogunate. Named Kano after an esteemed female ancestor, she was raised by her
nurse, who treated Kanoko like a princess. This nurse, well educated herself and
the widowed daughter of a former samurai, tutored Kanoko in the feminine arts
of *waka* (Japanese verse of thirty-one syllables), calligraphy, dance, and *koto*
(Japanese harp). Kanoko read Japanese classics at home and studied Chinese.
Despite her poor health and an eye affliction (which required lengthy treatment
at a hospital in Tokyo), she was a lively girl. Her parents and an older brother
doted on her. In 1902 she was sent to Tokyo with her nurse for more eye
treatment and while there enrolled in the Atomi Girls' School. The headmistress
of this prestigious school was an outspoken advocate of women's education and
nurtured individuality and creativity in her students. Kanoko, largely at her
brother's urging, began publishing her *waka* in the school journal and several
other small poetry magazines.

In 1909 Kanoko met Okamoto Ippei (1886–1948), a graduate of the Ueno
Art Academy. He proposed to her, but because he was from a lower-class family,
Kanoko's father objected to the marriage. In the summer of 1910 Ippei waded
across the flooded Tama River and walked to Kanoko's home, whereupon he
wrote out an oath sealed in blood, promising never to give Kanoko cause to
suffer. Her father relented, and they married in August. Their first child, Tarō,
was born the following year in February. (Some biographers suggest that Tarō
was fathered by Kanoko's earlier lover, Fuseya Taketasu, a wealthy literature
student whom she met in 1908.)

Life was not easy for the young couple. Ippei hardly earned enough to feed
his family, and Kanoko, pampered all her life, knew nothing of housekeeping.
When Ippei secured a job with the *Asahi Newspaper* as an illustrator, he began
to draw a sizable income, but he spent his money in the pleasure quarters, rarely
coming home. Kanoko and the infant Tarō were left to starve. To make matters
worse, her older brother died suddenly in 1912, soon followed by her mother,
and her father was facing bankruptcy.

Amid this tragic family situation Kanoko met Horikiri Shigeo, a young Waseda University student and ardent admirer of her poetry, and they began to
have an affair. In 1913 Kanoko gave birth to a baby girl, acknowledged as
Ippei's child but believed to have been Horikiri's. In the fall of 1913 Kanoko
was hospitalized for a nervous breakdown. Soon after she was released in 1914,

her daughter died. It is no wonder that Kanoko termed this period in her life "my days of hell." Ippei returned home in the fall that year, determined to dedicate his life to Kanoko and her career. In 1915 she gave birth to her third child, a boy, who died in infancy. (This child, too, is believed to have been fathered by Horikiri, who remained in the Okamoto house for several months after Ippei's return.)

Ippei and Kanoko began to search for spiritual solace in an effort to heal their marriage. They looked first to Christianity but, unsatisfied, turned to Buddhism. Kanoko began to attend study meetings and lectures. Meanwhile, she and Ippei accepted Tsunematsu Yasuo, a Keio University student, into their home as a boarder. He eventually became Kanoko's lover, a fact Ippei accepted. Kanoko entered a hospital for minor surgery in 1923 and fell in love with her doctor, Niida Kamezo. Dismissed from his position on account of their affair, he was forced to take his practice to Hokkaido. From 1925 to 1928 Kanoko spent her time traveling between Hokkaido and Tokyo, leaving Ippei and Tsunematsu at home.

In 1929 her son, Tarō, entered the Ueno Art Academy. He would later become an internationally recognized artist, specializing in boldly abstract mosaics, reliefs, and sculptures, often monumental in scale. In December of that year the family set sail for Europe, taking with them Niida as Kanoko's personal physician and Tsunematsu, on his way to study at a university in London. Ostensibly they went so that Ippei could attend the Disarmament Council in London as a representative for the *Asahi Newspaper,* but they also took the opportunity to put Tarō in an art academy in Paris, where he found himself under the influence of such artists as Pablo Picasso. Kanoko and Ippei stayed in England for a year with Niida and Tsunematsu and then, after touring Europe and America, returned to Japan in 1932.

In 1933 Kanoko suffered her second stroke and was hospitalized. In December 1938 she had a third stroke. Ippei and Niida nursed her at home (Tsunematsu, by this time, had left) until her condition deteriorated, and she had to be hospitalized. She died the following day, February 18, 1939. Ippei and Niida personally saw to her funeral, dressing her and fixing her hair and makeup. They festooned her coffin with flowers and had her buried privately February 21.

Career: Okamoto Kanoko began her career as a *waka* poet and in the early stages was greatly influenced by her brother Yukinosuke, who was interested in the new poetics of Yosano Tekkan (1873–1935), and his wife, Akiko (1878–1942). In 1906 he entered their salon, the Shinshi-sha (Circle of New Poetry), writing under the name Ōnuki Shōsen, and encouraged Kanoko to join. Recognizing in the young woman a talent that far surpassed her brother's, Yosano Akiko asked Kanoko to contribute to *Myōjō,* the poetry magazine that Tekkan had launched in 1899. Kanoko began to publish her poems in *Myōjō, Subaru,* and several other poetry journals, first under the name Ōnuki Nobara (Wild Rose) and later Ōnuki Kanoko, the name she would use until her marriage in 1910. In 1908 she met Hiratsuka Raichō (1886–1971), one of the early leaders of the women's movement in Japan, who asked her to participate in the feminist journal *Seitō* (Bluestocking).

In 1912 Kanoko published her first collection of poetry, *Karokinetami* (Delicate Envy) at Ippei's urging and under the auspices of the Seito Company. In 1918 she published her second collection, *Ai no Nayami* (Love's Anguish), rich with songs of passion and lament. Shortly after this volume appeared, Kanoko began her study of Buddhism in an earnest effort to quell her "love's anguish." Inspired by her studies, she began writing essays such as "Sangeshō no Bungakuteki Kaishaku" (A Literary Approach to the Buddhist Flower-Scattering Ceremony), which was serialized in the *Yomiuri* newspaper from March to December 1928. Her Buddhist writings were highly regarded, and she was heralded as a distinguished "woman scholar." Around this time, however, Kanoko began to feel the need to write fiction. Long confined to the brevity of *waka,* she now sought a more substantial literary medium for expressing her complex and varied emotions. Many of her popular Buddhist essays incorporated anecdotes and parable-type stories, yet, grounded in religion, these essays hindered her personal expression. As early as 1919, she had published her maiden work of fiction, "Kaya no Oitachi" (Kaya's Childhood), in the journal *Kaihō,* but it received no critical attention. For a period of ten years Kanoko assiduously studied fiction, covering both Western and Japanese modern literature. She joined study groups and developed friendships, largely through Ippei's maneuverings, with such prominent novelists as Akutagawa Ryūnosuke (1892–1927) and Kawabata Yasunari (1899–1972), who was to be Japan's only Nobel laureate. She sent samples of her work to Tanizaki Junichirō (1886–1965), who had been her brother's close friend. But Tanizaki clearly disliked Kanoko, calling her pushy and her works childish, and he would have nothing to do with her.

Before Kanoko left for Europe, she published *Waga Saishū no Kashū* (My Last Collection of Poems), as if to signal to the world that her career as a *waka* poet had run its course. Kanoko did not abandon poetry, however, and was to continue writing *waka* until her death. Nor did her overseas journey guarantee literary success. Although she was able to publish several travelogues and essays upon her return to Japan, she did not publish any notable work of fiction until four years later, in 1936, when her story "Tsuru wa Yamiki" (The Crane Is Sick) was published in *Bungakkai,* a literary journal associated with Kawabata. The story describes Kanoko's relationship with the celebrated writer Akutagawa, who had committed suicide some years earlier, and though she gave her two main characters fictitious names, the identities of both were obvious.

This work was followed by the short story "Konton Mibun" (Chaotic Circumstances, 1936). Although the protagonist in this story is a young swimming instructor and therefore not identified as Kanoko, her descriptions of the young woman are obviously self-enamored. She breathlessly describes Kohatsu's plump, suntanned body, the firm white underside of her arms, her big, round eyes and full, pouting lips. She is the very image of Kanoko, and the passion she portrays in describing Kohatsu becomes so obviously self-directed that it is uncomfortable. This penchant for narcissism continued in her next work, *Boshi Jojō* (Mother and Son, A Lyric, 1937), in which she describes her overwhelming love for her son. This work met with excellent reviews, and journals began to clamor for Kanoko's manuscripts. She wrote prodigiously, turning out within the three-year period before her death over fifteen short stories and novellas, among them such highly acclaimed works as "Hana wa Tsuyoshi" (Flowers Conquer All, 1937), "Kingyo Kyōran" (Goldfish in Profusion, 1937), "Michinoku" (North Country, 1938), *Pari Sai* (Bastille Day, 1938), "Tokaidō Gojūsan tsugi" (The Fifty-Three Tokaidō Stations, 1938), "Sushi" (Sushi, 1938), "Karei" (Family Ghost, 1938). The work most often cited as her masterpiece is "Rōgishō" (The Story of an Old Geisha, 1938), which was nominated for the prestigious Akutagawa Literary Prize. Even after she was bedridden in 1938, she continued to write, completing the two novella-length works *Oshaku* (The Geisha Apprentice) and *Kawa Akari* (River Reflections) just before she died and leaving for posthumous publication several unfinished manuscripts, including *Seisei Ruten* (Life's Changes), her only novel-length work.

Kanoko was, as critic Kamei Katsuichirō (1907–66) has suggested, "a star that glitters brilliantly but once and then slips forever from sight." During her brief career as a novelist she was able to imbue the Japanese literary scene with unequaled verve and beauty. She was a writer of extraordinary breadth and vitality. Her works drew on sources as disparate as Buddhism and French literature, on the classical *waka,* and on the spirit of the feudal age. Moreover her works evidenced a versatility rare in serious Japanese fiction. She was able to sing of the sweet pain of her own life as easily as she wrote of characters quite unlike herself, characters who belong to downtown Tokyo and to the plebeian milieu—shop owners, traders, and geisha. Of importance in all of Kanoko's stories is an insistence on beauty. Of even the most mundane objects—sushi, steamed eels, goldfish—she creates a sensuality of explosive potential. Furthermore, though frequently simple in construction, Kanoko's language is anything but simple, with most of her stories cloaked in a gorgeous brocade of words. She makes use of a lush and varied vocabulary, often creating her own words in the process. Kamei has noted that the special character, indeed, the power of Kanoko's works, lies in the "combustibility" of her language.

Major Works: "Tsuru wa Yamiki" (The Crane Is Sick, 1936), short story. Although the focus of the story ostensibly is on Asakawa Shōnosuke (modeled on novelist Akutagawa Ryūnosuke), the work serves as a showcase for the sensitivity and beauty of Sakamoto Yōko (modeled on Kanoko herself). Yōko continually compares herself with the other women in Asakawa's life, primarily to Akiko (the fictional surrogate for Tanizaki's beloved sister-in-law), who, she observes, has a vulgar profile and lackluster skin "the whiteness of a peeled potato." Yōko, by comparison, is superior. Although she does not speak forthright of her own virtues, by denigrating Akiko's charms, she suggests her own. Moreover, she very clearly describes Asakawa's admiration for her, writing that in his diary he praised her as the most intelligent and comforting woman he knew. She even suggests that had she known of his despair, she could have effected some kind of change in his life, perhaps even have saved him from suicide. The work is flawed by this type of narcissism but was successful nevertheless when first published because of the very intimate view it offered into the world of celebrated novelists.

"Karei" (Legacy, 1939), short story. Kumeko, the heroine of this work, is a college student who is compelled, when her mother falls ill, to take over the family restaurant, Inochi (Life). The restaurant is so named because the dishes it serves of turtle, catfish, and young eel were all thought to be sources of energy. Soon Kumeko meets Tokunaga, an old metal engraver, whose account is in arrears. He explains that years ago, when he was destitute, her mother agreed to feed him if he would pour his heart and soul into his work and present her with the fruit of his labor. He showered her with gifts of hair ornaments, all exquisitely engraved, and she fed him. Her mother was young then and, because her husband was blatantly unfaithful, often sad. But when she wore one of the hair baubles the man had made, she brightened.

The title of this story, "Legacy" operates on multiple levels. Kumeko's legacy is the restaurant and a family history of strong yet unfulfilled women. As her mother tells her, both her grandmother and her great-grandmother suffered from unfaithful husbands just as she has, and she speculates that that is why the restaurant flourished—it was their escape. The legacy is grim, but there are also those fragile combs, symbols of a love so passionate it surpasses time. *Karei* literally means "family ghost," and, as the story opens, Kumeko's mother is already something of a ghost. Kumeko is dark and robust, but indications are that she too will become a ghost as pale as her mother. The prospects are sad, but the family ghost will comfort her and give her strength, just as the box of combs comforted her mother.

Translated Works: Boshi Jōjō (Mother and Son, A Lyric, 1937), novella. This work (half of which is translated) is an "I-novel," and the family described therein, Issaku and Ichirō Okazaki and "she," are easily identified as the author's own. The work focuses on the heroine's love for her son—a love so obsessive it compels her to find a surrogate son when Ichirō is away in Paris. From the very outset the tone of the narration is gauged to alert the reader that she is not the "run-of-the-mill 'good mother'" but a woman of extreme passion. Her sensuality is clearly evoked in the opening pages when she is strangely excited by the sight of young red buds on the ivy trellis. Later, she is equally stirred by the "red passion" she senses in the young man Kikuo, who will become her surrogate son.

The relationship that ensues between the woman and Kikuo is frought with a teasing sensuality. She is at once motherly and coquettish. The intensely sexual undercurrent in their relationship suggests a parallel to that between the mother and her real son. The untranslated sections of the novella generally depict the heroine as she dallies with Ichirō in the cafés of Paris. Here she is shown to be vibrant and youthful, almost flirtatious. At one point she scribbles down,

"Mother is woman; son is man." Her son responds in kind, boldly confirming that he is a man and she a woman. The incestuous tension that is thus created between the heroine and these young men grows more and more intense until finally it reaches its apex when Kikuo approaches her as a potential lover. She rebuffs him—terrified that to submit would be to betray her son. Nothing, however, is resolved. As the story ends, the woman still seems to be toying with the idea of encouraging Kikuo, obviously enjoying the sweet torture engendered by her ambiguous feelings for her man/son.

Mother and Son embodies many of Kanoko's representative themes. Not only does it concern a mother's manifestly erotic love for her son, but it also treats the image of a beautifully passionate woman who madly pursues an object she knows she cannot obtain. Furthermore, the novella reveals Kanoko's stylistic prowess. The language she employs is precise yet surging with emotion. But just as *Mother and Son, A Lyric* displays Kanoko's skills, it also caters to her excesses. The narcissism expressed in her portrayal of the heroine, the most perfect, most beautiful mother, is disturbing, and her excessive references to things Western are obtrusive. Nevertheless the work is her early masterpiece.

"Hana wa Tsuyoshi" (Flowers Conquer All, 1937), short story. This work similarly depicts a woman of beauty and passion who, in her fierce desire to love, cripples the object of her affection. Unlike *Mother and Son,* the subject is treated on a more objective level. The protagonist, Mionoya Keiko, a flower arrangement teacher, loves Kobuse, a tuberculosis-stricken painter. But her love is overwhelming and threatens to drain away what little strength the man has left. It is little wonder that Kobuse finally chooses to marry the placid, sensible Senko, Keiko's niece and apprentice.

As in the earlier work, the heroine's sensuality and strength are symbolized through floral imagery. She is ever surrounded by vibrant, blooming, fragrant flowers. Her flowers may be delicate, but they are also mighty, as is suggested by the image in the opening paragraph of a potted flower with stamens so powerful that they stand out firmly. The beautiful Keiko is just as strong. Even though she realizes she is destined to live alone, as no man is truly equal to her love, she is not overcome by her sorrow. Supported by a bower of brilliant, burgeoning flowers, she conquers all.

"Michinoku" (North Country, 1938), short story. This work is a story within a story, a formula Kanoko often employed. The first-person narrator travels to an ancient town in the remote countryside to give a lecture on Buddhism and there discovers the portrait of a beautiful young man. She learns that he was known as "Shiro-Fool" because he was retarded. Yet Shiro, uncorrupted by knowledge, is gentle and virtuous. A shopkeeper takes him in and cares for him, and in exchange Shiro cleans the store. But before long he takes an interest in Ran, the shopkeeper's daughter. The love that gradually transpires between them is pure and innocent, yet hopeless. Shiro is tricked into leaving, and Ran, against her better judgment, waits loyally for his return.

The events depicted in "North Country" seem extraordinary in summary.

Yet the strangeness adds to the charm of the work, evoking a sense of mystery. Moreover, Kanoko treats the events with the simple suggestiveness of a Buddhist parable. The love that she describes, so gentle and sweet, is sullied by knowledgeable adults and can remain pure and profound only in the heart of a child or of one childlike.

"Rōgishō" (The Old Geisha, 1938), short story. Kanoko's masterpiece, this work concerns an old geisha who offers to support a young electrician aspiring to be an inventor. He is suspicious of her offer, imagining that by supporting him, she means to assuage her guilt for a lifetime of deceiving men. Later he begins to suspect that she has befriended him in the hopes of marrying him to her willful and modern adopted daughter. But finally he realizes that the old geisha is trying to give him a chance to accomplish what she could not, to live out a dream. As a geisha and a mistress to a variety of men, she has been able to grasp at only fragments of life—bits and pieces that do not add up to a whole. She wants to live a whole life through the young man. But the prospects are too intimidating for him. After several unsuccessful attempts, he leaves the old geisha and returns to his life of poverty.

In her preface to her translation, Kazuko Sugisaki indicates that Henry Miller was disappointed that nothing ever happened in the story. As the outline just given indicates, the story is practically devoid of action, yet it is propelled by a subtle yet sophisticated psychological drama. So much depends upon the emotional tension generated between the young man and the old geisha. Their relationship is forged on an implied sexuality. He first converses with the older woman because he imagines her profession to be one of passion and eroticism whereas his own is strictly business. (He does not know that for the geisha, passion is business.) The old geisha is able to bind him to her with money, but also with the mysterious, threatening sexuality she exudes, a sexuality that is most suggestively revealed when she thrusts her arm before him, slides back her silken sleeve, and demands that he pinch the white flesh of her upper arm.

Of equal interest in this relationship is the ambiguity implicit in her arrangement with him. She provides him the financial freedom he craves, yet her support creates a prison for him. He loses his desire to invent and becomes little more than the woman's property. The more dependent he becomes on her, the more she longs for him to break away. Yet, the more he struggles to free himself, the tighter she binds him to her. Thus, in the end, when the man finally escapes, the reader is overcome with a sense of catharsis, as though the curtain has finally fallen on a dramatic battle. Yet at the same time the image of the old geisha left alone to once again pick up the fragments of her broken life is heartrending.

What makes "The Old Geisha" such an impressive work is the fact that the emotional tension in it is drawn with deft understatement. The reader is not assaulted by the heavy narcissism of *Mother and Son* nor stunned by the gorgeous sensuality of "Flowers Conquer All." But in her subdued yet lovely prose, Kanoko is able to evoke the pathos in the life of this woman, who, having struggled unsuccessfully to find love, must accept the fact that she will be forever unfulfilled.

"Sushi" (Sushi, 1938), short story. This brief work, written shortly before Kanoko's death, reveals her brilliance as a storyteller. The story is set in Fukuzushi (good-luck sushi), a small restaurant in downtown Tokyo, where the customers are immersed in an atmosphere of warm camaraderie. Tomoyo, the proprietor's beautiful daughter, becomes acquainted with an older customer whose quiet manner intrigues her. He tells her that as a child he refused to eat, fearing that food would sully his otherwise pure body. His mother, at her wit's end, made him sushi, going through an elaborate ritual of washing her hands, the knife, and the cutting board. The boy was able to eat and, thanks to his mother's loving ministrations, grew into a beautiful youth. Now old and alone, he begins coming to the sushi shop, hoping to revive his memories of his mother. Having learned his story, Tomoyo is even more enchanted with the old man. But before she can query him further, he leaves, never to return. As time goes by, she forgets him.

Kanoko's representative themes are evidenced in this story: a loving, profoundly sensual relationship between mother and son and an interest in the mysterious, potent world of passion. Moreover, as in "North Country" and "Legacy," she writes with an artlessness that is both endearing and deceptive. "Sushi" can be read as a charming little tale and nothing more or plumbed for a wealth of meaning.

BIBLIOGRAPHY

Translations

"A Floral Pageant." Tr. Hiroko Morita Malatesta. In *To Live and to Write: Selections by Japanese Women Writers 1913–1938,* ed. Yukiko Tanaka. Seattle: Seal Press, 1987, 195–225.

"Kōmori, the Bat," *Nippon* 28 (1940): 39–44

"A Mother's Love." Tr. Phyllis Birnbaum. In *Rabbits, Crabs, Etc.* Honolulu: University of Hawaii Press, 1982, 49–97.

"Scarlet Flower." Tr. Edward Seidensticker. *Japan Quarterly* (July-September 1963): 331–48.

"Selected *tanka.*" Tr. Asataro Miyamori. In *Masterpieces of Japanese Poetry, Ancient and Modern.* Tokyo: Maruzen, 1936, 782–84. (Reprints. Tokyo: Taiseido, 1956, and Westport, CT: Greenwood Press, 1971.)

"Sushi," "The Tale of an Old Geisha," and "North Country." Tr. Kazuko Sugisaki. In *The Tale of an Old Geisha and Other Stories.* Santa Barbara, CA: Capra Press, 1985.

"Tanka." In *The Moment of Wonder,* ed. Richard Lewis. New York: Dial Press, 1964, 16.

"Tanka." In *The Burning Heart,* ed. Kenneth Rexroth and Ikuko Atsumi. New York: Seabury Press, 1977, 70.

Synopses

Kawa akari (Shining River). In *Introduction to Contemporary Japanese Literature 1936–1955*. Tokyo: Kokusai Bunka Shinkokai, 1959, 60–61.

Kawa akari (Shining River). In *Synopses of Contemporary Japanese Literature II*. Tokyo: Kokusai Bunka Shinkokai, 1970, 75–76.

"Rōgishō" (The Old Geisha's Tale), with a brief biographical introduction. *Japan PEN News*, 13 (October 1964): 13–14.

Critical Writings

Keene, Donald. "The Revival of Writing by Women." In *Dawn to the West: Japanese Literature of the Modern Era*. New York: Holt, Rinehart and Winston, 1984, 1113–67.

Tanaka, Yukiko. "Okamoto Kanoko." In *To Live and to Write: Selections by Japanese Women Writers 1913–1938*. Seattle: Seal Press, 1987, 197–203.

Rebecca L. COPELAND

ONO no Komachi (fl. 800s), poetess. Real name: unknown.

Life and Career: Most Japanese are familiar with Ono no Komachi's most famous poem, included in the *Hyakunin Isshu* (One Hundred Poems by One Hundred Poets), a New Year's card game based on the famous collection of one hundred verses:

The color of the flowers	Hana no iro wa
Has faded away,	Utsurinikeri na
In vain	Itazura ni
I spent my days in this world	Wa ga mi yo ni furu
Gazing at the long rains falling	Nagame seshi ma ni

(All translations are by Felice Fischer unless otherwise indicated.) But for all her fame as a poet, reliable historical information about Komachi is hard to find.

The earliest genealogy that includes Komachi's name is that of the Ono family found in the *Gunsho ruijū* (Classified Collection of Japanese Classics, 1779–1819). Komachi appears as one of two daughters of Ono no Yoshizane, son of Ono no Takamura. This Ono family line boasts many famous politicians, military men, and poets. Takamura (802–52) was a noted poet of Chinese and Japanese verse. Although Yoshizane is listed as the governor of Dewa province, his name does not appear in any official records. It may be that the *Gunsho ruijū* version of this Ono family genealogy was amended to include both Yoshizane and Komachi, for in variant editions of the genealogy neither name appears at all. About all that most scholars agree on concerning Komachi is that she belonged to a branch of the Ono family, was probably born in Dewa, and had at least one older sister. It is not even clear to which social class Komachi belonged. There are two main theories on the subject.

One theory proposes that Komachi served at court in the capacity of an *uneme* (palace woman). The *uneme* were lower-ranking women whose duties included serving at imperial meals. Originally, sisters or daughters of provincial officials seem to have been sent as *uneme* as a kind of tribute or display of loyalty to the court. If her father, Yoshizane, was in fact governor of Dewa, Komachi could have entered court service as an *uneme*. This theory has been disputed on several grounds, however. Some scholars, for example, doubt that any girl raised in the remote provinces far from the literary circles of the capital could have developed the talent and versatility in poetry that Komachi did.

Another line of conjecture, based on her sobriquet, suggests that she lived at court in the capacity of a secondary imperial consort (*kōi*). The section of the palace grounds where the empresses, secondary consorts, and their ladies-in-waiting lived was called the Joneiden, also known as *kisaki-machi* (empress's quarters). There are two sisters whose verses appear in the first imperial anthology, the *Kokinshū* (Collection of Ancient and Modern Times, 905), and whose court names include the element *machi*. They were Mikuni no Machi (real name, Ki no Taneko) and her younger sister Sanjō no Machi (real name, Ki no Shizuko), consorts of Emperors Ninmyō (54th r. 833–50) and Montoku (55th r. 851–53), respectively. The history of the reign of Emperor Ninmyō, the *Shoku Nihon kōki*, contains an entry for the year 842 that mentions the promotion of one Ono Ason Yoshiko, possibly a secondary consort of the emperor. Some scholars believe this Yoshiko to be the poetess Ono no Komachi. But the evidence is inconclusive, as there is no other mention of Yoshiko.

The "ko" (small, little) in Komachi's name may have been used in the sense of "junior." It is known from poems in the imperial anthologies that Komachi had an older sister who may have served at court at the same time as Komachi. The "ko" would have been added to distinguish the sisters, the elder's appellation having been Ono no Machi, perhaps.

The most tangible source of information about Ono no Komachi is actually her own poetry. Some of her verses provide clues about her biography, including the probable dates of her life span. For example, Komachi exchanged poems with several men about whom some historical facts are known. From the circumstantial evidence provided by such poetic exchanges, Komachi's date of birth has been estimated around 834 and her death around 899. It is also evident that she served at court in some capacity, though most likely not in as exalted a position as imperial consort. If the latter had been the case, there might have been more reliable genealogical data available, as is the case with the Ki sisters previously mentioned. That Komachi was intimate with a number of men is evident not only from the poetic exchanges with several named men but also from the many love poems in her collection of poetry. Numerous legends subsequently arose to supplement the paucity of provable facts about one of the most famous women poets of the Heian period.

Works and Legends: The *Kokinshū* anthology contains eighteen verses attributed to Ono no Komachi, the primary theme of which is love. From the 9th century on, the dominant poetic form in the Japanese language was the *waka* (also called *uta,* or "song"), a thirty-one-syllable form. During the Heian period

(784–1185) *waka* served largely as a vehicle of communication between men and women, especially of an amorous nature. Owing to the brevity of the poem itself, a knowledge of the circumstances under which it was written often adds greatly to the understanding and appreciation of the verse. Hence, poems included in the imperial anthologies and private collections often bore headnotes giving the background of the composition. Sometimes a group of poems would be used to create a story, as happened in the genre known as *uta-monogatari* (poem-tale). The various legends that have developed about Komachi are inspired by her poetry, some directly, some more indirectly from the mood or tone of her verses.

One line of legends deals with "Komachi the amorous woman," of which the earliest example is found in the *Tales of Ise* (Ise Monogatari, completed in the mid-Heian period). This is a typical "poem-tale," consisting of a number of episodes, each of which revolves around one or more poems set in a prose narration. The *Tales of Ise* is based on the poems of Ariwara no Narihira (825–80) in the *Kokinshū*. Although Komachi is never identified in any of the episodes, her poems appear in three of them.

Episode 25 gives a verse by Narihira, meant to be an inivitation to a woman who seemed undecided about meeting him. The reply to the man's verse is a coquettish but firm refusal. In episode 115 of the *Tales of Ise,* a man who had been living with a woman in the provinces was about to leave her to go to the capital. The woman, in great distress over his departure, composed a passionate poem. The third episode containing a verse by Komachi is number 113. This also contains a poetic exchange. In reply to a man who seemed to be tiring of her, she sent the poem:

Now is the time	Ima wa tote
You think to leave me,	Ware ni shigure no
I am growing older	Furiyukeba
Your promises too	Koto no ha sae zo
Are leaves of turning colors.	Utsuroinikeru

In each of these episodes, the woman's verse by Ono no Komachi is from the *Kokinshū*. The verses in the first episode are numbers 622 and 623 in the *Kokinshū*, but neither poem has a preface, so the idea of linking the two in a poetic exchange was that of the author of the *Tales of Ise*. The poem in episode 115 has only the place-name that was to be the topic of the poem "Okinoi Miyakoshima." There is no indication of any actual parting, which was also the invention of the later author of the poem-tale.

The exchange of verses in episode 131 is listed as such in the *Kokinshū*, although the link is a terse "Reply" as the headnote for the man's verse. In the *Kokinshū*, however, the man is Ono no Sadaki (fl. ca. 850), not Narihira. Komachi is never mentioned by name in the *Tales of Ise*, although, or perhaps because, the readers of the time were familiar with the verses of these famous poets and did not need to have them identified.

Part of Komachi's fame as a poet rests on the fact that she is named in the Japanese preface to the *Kokinshū*. Five other poets are cited there as well, Ariwara no Narihira, the Bishop Henjō (816–90), Bunya no Yasuhide (fl. ca. 870), Ōtomo Kuronushi (fl. ca. 860), and the priest Kisen (fl. ca. 810–823). Collectively they became known as the Rokkasen (Six Poetic Geniuses). Lacking any proof to the contrary, it would be natural for Komachi's name to become linked with the other Rokkasen, as happened in the *Tales of Ise*. The tone of Komachi's poems and the prefaces supplied by the *Tales of Ise* describing her as an amorous woman (*irogonomi onna*) formed the basis for later works depicting Komachi in this way.

Tales of Yamato, an 11th-century collection of stories, links Komachi romantically to another of her famous contemporaries, Bishop Henjō. Episode 168 depicts Komachi on a pilgrimage to a temple, where she sends Henjō a flirtatious inquiry as to whether he would lend her his priestly robe to keep her warm.

The literary culmination of the Komachi legends, however, is found in a series of plays written for the Noh theater in the 14th and 15th centuries, collectively called the *nana Komachi* (seven Komachi), five of which are still in the Noh theater repertory. The themes of the plays vary with the aspect of the legend being emphasized but deal with Komachi as a poetess, an amorous, haughty beauty, and an old woman.

Sōshi arai Komachi (Komachi Clears Her Name) depicts the poetess at the height of her glory at court. Its authorship has been attributed to either Kan'ami Kiyotsugu (1333–84) or his son Zeami Motokiyo (1362–1443). As in the poem-tales, the author of this play has relied heavily on the *Kokinshū*. Komachi is here matched with the Rokkasen Ōtomo Kuronushi, not romantically, but as competitors in a poetry contest at court. The three compilers of the *Kokinshū* also appear in the play. The prose prefaces of the *Kokinshū* and verses from the anthology are quoted. Curiously, none of the poems quoted in the play are by Komachi. Even Komachi's winning poem in the contest is not hers but is apparently original to the play.

Ōmu Komachi (Komachi's Parrot Answer Poem) is another of the works that emphasize Komachi's fame as a poet, although she is not seen in the splendor of the court, but as an old woman living near Sekidera Temple. Emperor Yōzei (r. 877–84) has sent a messenger to seek out Komachi, present her with an imperial verse, and ask for a reply poem from her. Her return poem is composed by altering one syllable of the emperor's original verse. This incident is taken from a collection of tales, the *Jikkinshō* (Ten Moral Tales, 1252), and the verse is attributed to Komachi. The plot of the play is again supplemented by references to the *Kokinshū* prefaces.

The second half of the play consists of a discussion of various modes of poetry. Then Komachi performs a dance depicting the pilgrimage of Ariwara Narihira to the Tamatsushima Shrine. The imperial messenger returns to the capital, and Komachi totters back to the temple.

Sekidera Komachi (Komachi at Sekidera) by Zeami exemplifies the most successful use of the *Kokinshū* as the poetic inspiration for a play. On the seventh day of the lunar seventh month, the *Tanabata* star festival celebrates the once-a-year meeting of the Cowherd star (Altair) and the Weaver girl star (Vega) across the Milky Way. During the preparations, the priests of the Sekidera Temple call on an old woman living nearby who is said to know the secrets of poetry. As they discuss poetry with her and ask her about Ono no Komachi, the old woman is overcome with grief as she reveals that she is in fact Komachi. During the festival Komachi joins the celebrants, for a few moments forgetting her age and performing a beautiful dance. When it is over, she slowly walks back to her hut, leaning on her staff for support.

This beautiful piece derives its lyrical quality not only through references to the *Kokinshū* prefaces but also through its quotations of many of Komachi's own poems. When Komachi reveals herself in the play, she recalls her former beauty and life at court when she composed verses such as

A thing which fades	Iro miede
Without seeming to outwardly—	Utsurou mono wa
Such indeed is the flower	Yo no naka no
Of the heart of man	Hito no kokoro no
In this world.	Hana ni zo arikeru

Another of her *Kokinshū* poems is quoted to describe her present wretched state:

In my loneliness	Wabinureba
I am as floating grass	Mi o ukigusa no
Cut from its roots—	Ne o taete
Were there water to entice,	Sasou mizu araba
I would follow it, I think.	Inan to zo omou.

Zeami has taken Komachi's own poetry for the core of his work, weaving the verses masterfully into the context of the play. The ambiguity afforded by the compact *waka* form is brilliantly used to full advantage. As in *Ōmu Komachi,* the poetess is portrayed as an old woman begging for alms to survive.

Kayoi Komachi (Komachi and the Hundred Nights), another Zeami play, also depicts her as a poor old woman, bringing daily offerings of fruit and firewood to a temple at Yase. The priest of the temple questions her about her offerings and identity, but she vanishes after reciting part of a verse,

My name—Oh, no—I cannot speak it;	Ono to wa iwaji
The pampas grasses grow	Susuki oitaru

The priest recalls the first part of the poem:

Autumn winds—	Akikaze no
Each time they blow	Fuku ni tsukete mo
What emptiness and pain!	Aname aname

In the second half of the play the priest begins to recite prayers for Komachi's salvation, as she requested. He is interrupted by the ghost of the Commander, Shii no Shōshō, who wants to prevent Komachi from attaining salvation. He then relates how the haughty beauty Komachi assigned him his cruel task. She would consent to meet him only after he visited her house one hundred nights in succession. As proof of his visits, each night he carved a notch on the bench used to support the shaft of her carriage. He did this for ninety-nine nights but died on the last night before the tryst was to take place. Such was the bitterness he carried into the next world that he could not free himself of it to attain salvation and wished the same fate for Komachi. In the end both souls are freed through the priest's prayers.

The verse of the first section just quoted and the legend of the skull have long been associated with Komachi. The poem is found in the variant text of Komachi's poetry collection and in the *Waka dōmōshō* (A Child's Jottings of Verse), a work dated 1139. An even earlier version is found in the *Gōke shidai* (Ceremonial Usages of the Ōe House) of 1111, by Ōe Masafusa. Here the story tells of Ariwara Narihira journeying through the province of Mutsu. One night he hears a voice reciting the first half of the poem. The next day he finds a skull in a field with pampas grass growing through it. He recites the second half of the verse and buries the skull. The legend is also noted in the *Mumyōshō* (Untitled Notes) of Kamo no Chōmei of 1209–10.

The association of the legend of the one hundred-night visit with Komachi seems to have been Zeami's invention. The story itself is found in early 12th-century works such as the *Ōgishō* (Mysterious Tales, 1124–44), and it is referred to in the poetry of the age. It may well have been the haughty tone of some of Komachi's poems that inspired Zeami. There is, for example, a reply Komachi sent Abe no Kiyoyuki (825–900) recorded in the *Kokinshū,* which exudes her skepticism concerning the depth of male feelings expressed in their amorous verses. From the tone of Komachi's poem, one might readily imagine that she would demand further ''proof'' of the devotion of a would-be admirer.

In the Noh play *Sotoba Komachi* (Komachi at the Stupa), Kan'ami also used the legend of the one hundred-night visit. Two priests meet an old woman sitting on a stupa by the roadside. She laments that despite her former beauty and comfortable circumstances, she is now nearly one hundred years old, begging for alms, ashamed to be seen by anyone. They engage her in a religious debate in which she proves the superior. The priests ask her name, which she promises to tell in return for their prayers. As she relates the details of her former beauty and pride, the spirit of Commander Shii no Shōshō speaks through her, telling of his suffering on the hundred-night visit. At the close of the play Komachi's troubled soul is able to find respite through the priests' prayers.

Tamatsukuri Komachi sōsuishō (Tamatsukuri Komachi Chronicle) is an anonymous mid-11th-century work that is a source for the legends about Komachi's arrogance and the subsequent retribution her soul must suffer before attaining repose. The *Tamatsukuri Komachi Chronicle* is written in *kanbun* (in Chinese, with diacritical marks for reading in Japanese word order). It depicts an aged woman who recollects her former life at the palace in florid passages, such as: "In the times of my glory, my haughtiness was most extreme . . . my graceful form might have been confused with a willow swaying under the spring breeze." Such descriptions are used almost verbatim in both *Ōmu Komachi* and *Sotoba Komachi,* as are those portraying her in her old age. The *Chronicle* ends with the woman's desire to become a nun and with depictions of the Buddhist paradise. How the character in this Buddhist tract, Tamatsukuri Komachi, became identified with Ono no Komachi is not clear, but it began quite early. Thirteenth-century works such as the *Kokon chōmonshū* (Collection of Ancient and Modern Works, 1254) quote the *Tamatsukuri Komachi Chronicle* as genuine biographical data about Ono no Komachi. The previously mentioned *Mumyōshō* also cites it, though Chōmei questions the identification of Tamatsukuri Komachi with Ono no Komachi.

Thus authors of the Noh plays had not only Komachi's verse in the *Kokinshū* as inspiration but also a fund of legends associated to various degrees with the elusive poetess. Komachi legends extend into the 20th century, including a play by Akutagawa Ryūnosuke (1892–1927) entitled *Futari Komachi* (The Two Komachis), which is a tribute to the beauty, variety, and vitality of Komachi's poetry, which has left such a lasting imprint on the imagination of so many Japanese writers.

Translated Works: Although there is an extant collection of verse called the *Komachi shū* traditionally ascribed to her, only the eighteen poems in the *Kokinshū* are indisputably Komachi's own. All eighteen are available in the English editions of the *Kokinshū,* but the translations quoted here are by Felice Fischer. Despite the relatively limited vocabulary of about two thousand words used in the composition of *waka* during the Heian period, Komachi expands the possibilities of poetic diction to the utmost.

Her best-known poem starting with the phrase, "The color of the flowers," is classified as a spring poem in the *Kokinshū,* but the complexity of its rhetoric reveals deeper layers of meaning beneath the surface imagery. One of the characteristic poetic devices of the age is the *kakekotoba* (pivot word), consisting of a series of sounds used in two or more meanings. Thus, in Komachi's poem, *furu* is used to mean both "to fall" (for rain) and "spend my days, grow old," and *nagame* is used to mean both "gaze" and "long rains." The word *iro* in the first line contains a rich variety of meanings—"color," "appearance," and also "passion." Thus the *iro* already signals in the first line that the poem is not only about blossoms but also about the poet's own appearance and love. The scene from nature provides the stimulus for her realization of the passage of time and the perishability of beauty. The *itazura ni* (in vain) of the third line also serves a double function, referring both to the vanity of her own life and of the beauty of the blossoms. Yet the correspondence between nature and human life is not complete. Komachi may see in the fading blossoms a reflection of her own advancing age, but she knows the flowers will bloom again next spring, while there is no such reprieve from the forward press of time for herself. Time is the controlling force over love and life. The image of gazing into the spring rains is a hauntingly beautiful evocation of the resigned despair over a lifetime of deep yet transient experiences conditioned by a poetic sensibility and transformed into a body of poetry with universality that transcends any one place, time, or individual. The preeminent critic and poet of his time Fujiwara Teika (1162–1241) singled out this poem for inclusion in several anthologies he compiled, such as the *Kindai shūka* (Superior Poems of Our Time, 1215–22) and the *Hyakunin isshu* (One Hundred Poems by One Hundred Poets, 1237).

Thirteen of Komachi's eighteen *Kokinshū* poems are classified as love poems, three of them heading the second section:

Was it that I fell asleep	Omoitsutsu
Longing for him	Nureba ya hito no
That he appeared?	Mietsuran
Had I known it was a dream	Yume to shiriseba
I should not have awakened.	Samezaramashi o

In a doze I saw	Utatane ni
The one I am longing for;	Koishiki hito o
Since then	Miteshi yori
I have come to rely	Yume cho mono wa
On my dreams.	Tanomisometeki

When I long for him	Ito semete
Oppressed by the thoughts I have,	Koishiki toki wa
I wear my robe,	Mubatama no
Jet black as the night,	Yoru no koromo o
Turned inside out.	Kaeshite zo kiru

Komachi's verses derive much of their emotional intensity from the lack of contact with the ''real'' world they reveal. Komachi's feelings of helplessness and hopelessness are such that dreams become not an extension or portent of the waking world but a substitute. Only in her dreams can she meet her lover, so she wears her robe inside out to guarantee his appearance in her dream, in accordance with popular belief. The intensity of her longing is such that dreams take dominance over reality. The contrast of the two worlds is poignantly expressed in another verse about her fear over the exposure of a love affair:

In waking daylight	Utsutsu ni wa
One might well act that way,	Sa mo koso arame

But that even in my dreams	Yume ni sae
I see myself hiding from people's eyes—	Hitome o moru
This unhappiness indeed.	Miru ga wabishisa

The discrepancy in the relationship between "waking daylight" and "dreams" is focused here in the almost startlingly concrete image of *hitome* (people's eyes). The image of eyes is usually associated with the beauty of the beloved's eyes. But here they are intruders, penetrating the night and even dreams as a visual manifestation of Komachi's fears. In the preceding poem, *hito* refers to her lover, the person she longs for but who comes to her only in her dreams. But in this last verse it is not her lover who appears, but the hostile eyes of a censuring world.

The legends about Komachi's passionate nature were no doubt stimulated by poems such as this:

On a moonless night	Hito ni awan
When I will not meet him,	Tsuki no naki ni wa
I lie awake longing for him, my mind aflame,	Omoiokite
My heart burns amidst	Mune hashiribi ni
The leaping fire in my breast.	Kokoro yakeori

This verse is also a rhetorical tour de force, containing several "pivot words," the primary one being *omoiokite* ("to lie awake longing" and "to set aflame"). It also serves as the pivot for the contrasts of imagery and movement of the whole poem. The two lines preceding it are negative: there is no moon, and she herself is passive, lying awake in the darkness. With *omoiokite* there is a sudden shift. The final two lines are alive with activity, and Komachi's brooding has given way to intense passion. The images become ones of fire and light. The increasing emotional intensity is expressed by the highly active verbs and adjectives "aflame," "burning," and "leaping." The fluidity of the six syllables of the third line, *omoiokite,* sets in motion the urgent forward movement, with its climax in the final *yakeori* (burns). Although this is obviously a love poem, it was not classified as such in the *Kokinshū,* where it was placed in the section called "Miscellaneous Poems." Perhaps the strong emotion of the verse offended the compilers of the anthology, who would have preferred an elegant sigh. Yet the beauty of the poem lies precisely in its intensity and its perfect merging of imagery and emotion, which imparts to it a significance beyond one particular poet's experience.

In the centuries after Komachi there came a succession of women writing in the "passionate style," reflecting concerns, sometimes to the point of obsession, with the anxieties of unrequited love and the perishability of beauty in human life. Among them were many outstanding poetesses, from Lady Ise (fl. ca. 935),

Izumi Shikibu (ca. 970–1030), Lady Sagami (fl. ca. 1050), and the Ex-empress Eifuku Mon'in (1271–1342), to Yosano Akiko (1878–1942), who championed romanticism in Japan. Many men, such as Fujiwara Teika, also tried that style, often writing in the guise of women. As Japanese poetry evolved from one period to the next, the flame of the passionate style that Ono no Komachi kindled remained alive, at times reduced to a flicker, at others blazing radiantly as a tribute to her genius.

BIBLIOGRAPHY

Translations and Critical Works

Brower, Robert H., and Earl Miner. *Japanese Court Poetry.* Stanford, CA: Stanford University Press, 1961. Gives translations and analyses of several of Komachi's poems, as well as an excellent narration of the poetics of the period.

Fischer, Felice. *The Collected Poems of Ono no Komachi.* Master's thesis, Columbia University, 1967. A complete translation of the *Komachi shū.*

———. *Ono no Komachi: A Ninth Century Poetess of Heian Japan.* Ann Arbor, MI: University Microfilms, 1972. Doctoral diss., Columbia University.

Keene, Donald, ed. *Anthology of Japanese Literature.* Rutland, VT: Charles E. Tuttle, 1968. Translations of some poems and of *Sotoba Komachi.*

———. *20 Plays of the Nō Theater.* New York: Columbia University Press, 1970. Translations of *Kayoi Komachi* and *Sekidera Komachi.*

McCullough, Helen Craig, tr. *Kokin wakashū: The First Imperial Anthology of Japanese Poetry.* Stanford, CA: Stanford University Press, 1985. Complete translation, including Komachi's verses.

———. *Tales of Ise.* Stanford, CA: Stanford University Press, 1968.

Rodd, Laurel Rasplica, with Mary Catherine Henkenius. *Kokinshū: A Collection of Poems Ancient and Modern.* Princeton, NJ: Princeton University Press, 1984.

Teele, Roy E., tr. "*Ōmu Komachi:* Komachi's Parrot-Answer Poem." *Jinbun ronkyū* 7.5 (December 1956): 15–28.

———. "*Sōshi arai Komachi:* Komachi Clears Her Name." *Jinbun ronkyū* 5.5 (February 1955): 16–34.

Felice FISCHER

ŌTA Yōko (1903–63), novelist, essayist. Real name: Ōta Hatsuko.

Life: This author was born in Hiroshima. At age seven, her parents were divorced. Two years later, her mother remarried for the third time, and the young Yōko was adopted by her stepfather, a wealthy landowner who loved literature and provided the future novelist with a fertile literary environment, initiating her to Heinrich Heine, Walt Whitman, and Tamura Toshiko, along with other authors. Under his influence, while still in school, Ōta set her goal to be a writer and began writing *tanka* (thirty-one-syllable classical poem) and other types of verse, some of which were published in local newspapers and periodicals. After graduation from high school, she taught for a year and worked as a typist for a while. In 1925 she met and soon moved in with a journalist, Fujita Kazushi. She was deeply hurt to discover that he was married, with two children. She left him and went to Tokyo alone, only to return to Hiroshima and to Fujita in less than a year. In the next three years Fujita divorced his wife, married Ōta, and began dental practice. But shortly after their son was born in 1928, Ōta abandoned her family and went to Tokyo, driven apparently by her desire to pursue a literary career. Her second marriage failed in 1937 after only seventeen months. In January 1945, as Tokyo became subjected to fierce bombing raids, Ōta returned to Hiroshima. She was at her sister's home when the atom bomb was dropped on August 6. She escaped with minor wounds, as did her mother, sister, and infant niece. But this experience became a crucial turning point in her literary career and determined the course of action for the rest of her life. In 1947 she married for the third time. A member of the Communist party, the husband was eight years her junior, but this marriage too lasted no more than a year. She died of a heart attack in 1963 in Fukushima prefecture, while gathering materials for her ongoing novel, *Naze Sono Onna wa Ruten Suru ka* (Why Does the Woman Wander?).

Career: Her debut as a writer came in June 1929, when her short fiction "Seibo no Iru Tasogare" (The Holy Mother in the Dusk) appeared in *Nyonin Geijutsu* (Women's Art), a leading journal founded by women for women writers. In the following years, now living in Tokyo, Ōta published a number of short stories and essays. Unfortunately for her, *Nyonin Geijutsu,* which had served as a support basis for her creative efforts, ceased its publication in 1932 primarily for lack of funds, following the government ban on the journal for two months in 1930. The next several years marked professional stagnation for her. Instead of critical acclaim or recognition for her numerous works, she gained notoriety for her decadent life-style. In 1938 she completed an autobiographical novel, *Ryūri no Kishi* (The Shore of Solitary Wandering) but found no publisher for it. In the fall, she traveled to China to collect materials for a new novel. In 1939, she won first prize from the *Chūō Kōron* magazine for a short story *Ama* (Woman Diver). In the following year her *Sakura no Kuni* (The Land of Cherry Blossoms), a novel based on her travel to China, won first prize from the *Asahi* newspaper. These two first prizes in literary contests established her as a novelist, and until the end of 1943, Ōta enjoyed fame and recognition for a number of works of fiction and essays. As the war progressed, journals and newspapers cut down publication for scarcity of paper supply, and Ōta was forced to curtail her literary activities.

Ōta was among the first writers stirred by a sense of mission to write about her experience as a Hiroshima *hibakusha* (surviving victims of the atomic bombing), the utterly incomprehensible catastrophe that fell upon her and fellow citizens without any warning. She began her writing almost immediately after the incident. Her first recording of the experience, entitled "Kaitei no yōna Hikari—Genshi Bakudan no Kūshū ni atte" (Like a Flash from the Depths of the Sea—The Atomic Bomb Air Raid), appeared in the *Asahi* newspaper on August 30. *Shikabane no Machi* (City of Corpses), her first full-length work dealing with the immediate aftermath of the destruction of Hiroshima and its people, was completed in November 1945, but its publication was postponed because, from September 1945 to September 1951, the occupation authorities enforced the press code, which imposed prior censorship on everything written for publication or broadcasting. Even the delayed first edition of *City of Corpses* (November 1948) had a section containing statistical, medical, and other reports of the effects of the bombing deleted as a result of self-censorship by the publisher. The restored, unexpurgated version was finally published in May 1950.

Encouraged by the positive responses to *City of Corpses* and by the gradual loosening of the press code enforcement, Ōta delved into the subject of atomic bombing more intensely. At the same time, her neuroses caused by the trauma of the atomic bombing and aggravated by the agony of writing about the experience worsened to such an extent that she had to be hospitalized. With the publication of *Ningen Ranru* (Human Rags) in 1951, for which she received the Woman Writer's Award, Ōta firmly established her reputation as a writer of atomic bomb literature. Her next work, *Han Ningen* (Half-Human, 1954), was awarded the Japan Cultural League's Peace and Culture Prize, followed by *Yūnagi no Machi to Hito to* (The Town and People in the Evening Calm, 1954).

Despite her deteriorating physical condition, Ōta continued to write both fiction and essays, pursuing the uncertainty of atomic bomb survivors, who were living one day at a time, in fear of radiation diseases that might strike them at any moment and of another world war that could be triggered by the ongoing Korean War. In her last years, Ōta grew tired of atomic bombing as the subject for her writing and turned to a new field of psychological novels, such as *Hachijussai* (Eighty Years Old, 1960) and *Hachijuyonsai* (Eighty-Four Years Old, 1961). However, Ōta could never dissociate herself completely from the Hiroshima experience.

Although Ōta Yōko began her literary career before August 1945, her importance as a writer in Japanese literature lies in her contribution to *genbaku bungaku,* or the atomic bomb literature. Like Ōta, the earliest writers of this literature were *hibakusha* such as Hara Tamiki (1905–51; poet, novelist); Tōge Sankichi (1917–53; poet); Shōda Shinoe (1910–65; poet); and Kurihara Sadako (b. 1913; poet, essayist). Subsequent atomic bomb literature has been written by both *hibakusha*—such as Hayashi Kyōko (b. 1930)—and non-*hibakusha* writers, the best known among the latter being Ibuse Masuji (b. 1898), novelist and author of *Black Rain* (1965–66; tr. 1969).

Ōta Yōko was deeply involved with the atomic experience, her writings characterized by heavily autobiographical elements, an unflinching objectivity in recording the facts, which she calls the "reality of Hiroshima," a critical awareness of social and political environments, and her compassion for fellow human beings in pain and suffering. Despite the mental and physical tortures of writing about Hiroshima, Ōta Yōko was driven by a strong sense of mission, made a conscious search for a new language and a new novel demanded by the unprecedented experience, and dedicated the rest of her life to the causes of humanity and peace.

Major Works: Ningen Ranru (Human Rags, 1951), novel. In her 1950 preface to *City of Corpses,* Ōta writes, "Some day I wish at all costs to write a 'novelistic novel' which should make up for my incomplete memoir [*City of Corpses*]." *Human Rags* may be considered such a "novelistic" novel, for it achieves a greater degree of inclusiveness, encompassing much wider geographical areas of Hiroshima, and a markedly more novelistic structure, especially in relations and interactions among a large number of characters. Instead of a single principal character, this novel focuses on multiple characters who share what constitutes "the reality of Hiroshima," which is the central subject of the book. An omniscient narrator follows the movements of characters scattered at various parts in and around the city at the time of the bombing. Shortly after the blast, Yamakawa Sugita, a twenty-one-year-old student soldier, leaves the Kanawa Island by boat, in search of his foster parents living within the city. He is accompanied by Tamura Kikue, who is five-months pregnant. Despite the spreading fire in the city, they eventually make their way to the empty house of Sugita's foster parents, who had evacuated to safety across the river. In another part of the city, Sugita's natural mother, Toshiko, witnesses her husband's death and then evacuates to Mount Hiji. In yet another part of the city, Dr. Umehara was making a house call at the time of the explosion. He tries to return to his clinic-residence in the northern suburbs. On the way there, he comes upon Sugita and Kikue and treats her miscarriage in the grass. What these surviving characters go through in the immediate aftermath of the bombing—including pain of their own injuries, agony of their bereavement, and uncertainty about their future—is portrayed with the disciplined objectivity of a writer, yet unmistakably tinged with the author's deep compassion for fellow human beings in pain and suffering.

Human Rags presents, on one hand, the universal theme of survival, or self-preservation, everyone fending for himself, in the face of certain death by the spreading fires or under collapsing buildings. It also deals with compassion, human solidarity, and self-effacing devotion to the helpless victims lying in the atomic wasteland. Another important theme is disconnectedness, the phenomenon that the entire city of Hiroshima, its people, and its history experienced. This condition of disconnectedness, which affects nearly everyone, is most apparent in the complicated love triangle of Sugita's foster-father Eizō, his mistress, Yae, and his wife, Sumiyo. The atomic blast pulls Eizō away from Yae as he trudges toward safety with his wife, carrying household goods on his back. Ironically, however, his wife, who has endured his infidelity until then, begins to sense a deep chasm between them that later proves to be unbridgeable. Nor does Yae return to Eizō again. The novel thus provides not only accurate information on the physical facts of destruction, but, more important, it tells about the effects of atomic bombing on citizens' entire existence, on their souls as well as their bodies, on their spiritual lives, and ultimately on the destiny of humankind.

Yūnagi no Machi to Hito to: 1953–nen no Jittai (The Town and People in the Evening Calm: The Real Condition of 1953; 1954), novel. Ōta's last major fiction dealing with the atomic bombing, this work again features Oda Atsuko, a *hibakusha* writer and the protagonist of *Half-Human,* who returns to Hiroshima, eight years after the blast, to see, hear, and record "the real conditions of 1953." Atsuko spends days and evenings meeting with people, mainly *hibakusha* and a few returnees from overseas. She finds the majority of them "broken" or "damaged" in body and mind. They are "lost humanity" reduced to "prehuman" existence physically as well as spiritually. As shown in Ōta's earlier works, Atsuko represents a writer who cannot dissociate herself from the subject of the atomic bombing, even though her doctor tells her that she will not be cured of her neuroses as long as she is involved with that subject. Her reply is: "I will never be able to withdraw myself from this issue. To me it is the question of the soul"; "She knew she would again, some day, write about this town. . . . Below the surface of this town existed the reality which was beyond the limit of what the conventional literature was capable of." Atsuko's work will be an unconventional or unnovelistic novel, in which "the entire surviving humanity" will be "heroes and heroines."

To a large extent *The Town and the People* is exactly such a novel, marking a culmination of Ōta's literary techniques. It also takes the strongest stance of protest on the subject, emphasized with the subtitle, "The Real Condition of 1953." It exposes the extreme poverty and misery of the A-bomb survivors living in subhuman conditions, without running water, indoor bathrooms, or sewage, eight years after the bombing, while the city planners dream of creating a Venice of the Orient. Anger and frustration at the seemingly helpless situation are pervasive, but there are also elements of hope—the novel affirms underlying values such as compassion for the suffering and striving for love and happiness of all humanity; most significantly, at its close, the novel calls for international efforts for a better world and future for the human race.

Translated Works: City of Corpses (Shikabane no Machi, 1948 and 1950), novel. For its form and structure, this work can hardly be called a novel in the ordinary sense of the word. It is essentially a recording of the unprecedented event of the bombing, characterized by a reportorial objectivity with occasional lyricism that adds poignancy to the entire work. Using the first-person narrative, the author makes conscious efforts to record accurately the nature of the devastation and destruction of the city of Hiroshima and its people. With graphic details and photographic precision, she incorporates facts gathered from newspaper articles and scientific reports, recordings of interviews, and narrations by survivors of the bombing. Yet, this work is not a mere reporting of some tragic event in history. It is also an expression of the author's strong personal beliefs and convictions, crying out against all wars—nuclear and conventional—and pleading for world peace.

"In the tragedy of humankind which cannot progress without acts of destruction, the time for revolution has now come. There is no other way for peace but to make progress without acts of destruction. I sincerely hope that the defeat of Japan will bring true peace to this nation. In all the pain I am suffering, I write this book for that one hope,'' says the narrator. Both the story and its 1950 preface clearly show the author's sense of mission to write about her experience and the urgency of the task, which is an important and notable motive for most of the earliest writers of atomic bomb literature. Ōta's narrator says, "I am watching with two eyes, one a human being's and one a writer's . . . I must write about [this experience] some day as a duty of a writer who witnessed it.''

Furthermore, so overwhelming are their memories and visions that most *hibakusha* writers try to find a new language or new form to describe the unprecedented experience. Ōta speaks of the need for, and the difficulty of, creating new vocabulary to depict what she calls "the reality of Hiroshima.'' In Ōta's case, her "unnovelistic novel,'' *City of Corpses* being its clearest example, may be considered as a new form, and her chosen approach in dealing with the subject is her striving for inclusiveness, so as to lend her pen to the entire city and beyond, to warn against the impending tragedy of humankind. This earliest work of atomic bomb literature by a *hibakusha* writer indicates a certain direction in which this body of literature is moving: from a recording of direct, personal experience of atomic bomb victims to an artistic expression of greater concerns for the present condition and for the future, if any, of humankind in the nuclear age.

Half-Human (Han Ningen, 1954), novella. This prizewinning autobiographical short novel focuses on a woman *hibakusha* writer, hospitalized for treatment of drug dependency and neuroses. This character, named Oda Atsuko, cringes at the "insincere label'' of "atomic bomb writer'' but feels compelled by a strong sense of duty to write about the subject. With skill and effectiveness the author presents the protagonist Atsuko's grief, agony, and torment of having to relive the experience of Hiroshima in her writing as well as her anxiety and fear for the uncertain future not only as a professional writer but as a concerned citizen of the volatile world where the Korean War has just ended. Gnawed by the haunting memories of the blast and its aftermath, Atsuko wonders if she could have been spared her current illness had she not been exposed to the bombing. Her chief doctor evades the question, maintaining that Atsuko shows no apparent symptoms of radiation sickness. Like most *hibakusha*, Atsuko would rather forget her experiences if she could. She yearns for a normal, quiet life denied to her. She tells her doctor, "Since the end of the war, . . . my thought has been that I have only three choices: to commit suicide, to run away, or to live by writing good work.'' The implication is that she could neither commit suicide nor run away but that writing "good work,'' which was her mission, was extremely difficult, nearly impossible. Born of much pain and anguish, *Half-Human* intimates that the heroine's, hence the author's, personal misery and fear are ultimately shared by all humanity. This implied affirmation of solidarity seems to justify the hopeful tone of the ending, despite the pervasive sense of hopelessness.

''Fireflies'' (Hotaru, 1953), short story. Representing characteristics of many of Ōta's works on the subject of Hiroshima, this autobiographical narrative is a first-person description of Hiroshima through selected scenes and characters seven years after the blast. The female *hibakusha* narrator, a professional writer, returns to the city for a visit in 1952. As she visits the proposed site for the monument of the *hibakusha* poet Hara Tamiki (1905–51), who committed suicide the previous year, the colors of the stone wall at the site where the famous castle once stood evoke the memories of August 1945. The story emphasizes the poor living conditions of *hibakusha,* with the infestation of slugs inside the houses symbolic of the pervasive situation. Further, the indelible scars of the blast are graphically shown in the severe burns and deformities of some characters whom the narrator meets. At the end of the story, the low-flying fireflies, associated with ephemeral beauty and elegance in traditional Japanese literature, are seen as the spirits of dead soldiers unable to rest in peace.

BIBLIOGRAPHY

Translations

City of Corpses. Tr. Richard H. Minear. In *Hiroshima: Three Witnesses.* Princeton, NJ: Princeton University Press, 1990, 147–273.
''Fireflies.'' Tr. Koichi Nakagawa. In *Atomic Aftermath: Short Stories About Hiroshima and Nagasaki,* ed. Kenzaburo Oe. Tokyo: Shueisha, 1984, 93–119.
''Half-Human.'' Tr. Naomi Matsuoka. In preparation.

Critical Works

The Atomic Bomb: Voices from Hiroshima and Nagasaki, ed. Kyoko Selden and Mark Selden. Armonk, NY: M. E. Sharpe, 1989.
Tsukui, Nobuko. *The Atomic Bomb Literature of Japan: An Introduction.* In preparation.
                                                                 Nobuko TSUKUI

S

SAEGUSA Kazuko (1929–), novelist, dramatist, essayist, literary critic. Née Yotsumoto Kazuko (Mrs. Saegusa Kōichi).

Life: A native of Kobe, Kazuko was born the eldest of the four children of Yotsumoto Masatoshi and his wife, Sada. Kazuko's only brother, a frail and sickly child, died in 1954 at the age of thirteen. Descended from a retainer of the feudal lord of Satsuma (today's Kagoshima prefecture), Kazuko's father worked on postal ships until 1935, when he was hired by the Kobe City Water Police Bureau. In the period from 1935 to 1943, Kazuko frequently changed schools because of her father's repeated transfers to different locations within Hyogo prefecture. Her mother had been a schoolteacher until she resigned from her position upon the birth of her first daughter. She was a devout Protestant who would often take her children to church without attempting to impose her faith on them. She was more emancipated in her thinking than her husband, who professed contempt for ''women's inferior intelligence'' and maintained that they should be content with their traditional domestic and nurturing roles. Sada tried to instill in her children an egalitarian, Christian, humanist view of history and a love of learning. Saegusa later acknowledged that her keen interest in Western philosophy, literature, and religion was stimulated by the liberal education she received from her mother. Sada died in 1943. Unable to look after his children on his own, Kazuko's father remarried within a few months.

In 1944 Kazuko, now a student at a girls' high school, was sent to a military airplane supply factory in Kawasaki under the Student Mobilization Act. In April 1945, she enrolled in the tuition-free Hyogo Prefectural Normal School, partly motivated by her desire to escape from compulsory work in the military factory, but primarily as a compromise with her father: Masatoshi wanted his eldest daughter to achieve financial independence as soon as possible in order to avoid clashes with her stepmother, who objected to the costs of Kazuko's education. At the normal school, Kazuko joined the Dostoyevsky Study Group and the theater club, in which she directed, and even acted in, several plays.

In 1948 she enrolled in the philosophy department of the Kansei Gakuin University. Due to the reform of the educational system that year, Kazuko was able to skip two years and earn her bachelor's degree within two years. She specialized in Hegelian philosophy but chose to write her graduation thesis on Nietzsche. In graduate school, she continued to study Hegel as well as other 19th- and 20th-century Western philosophers. She also became interested in the Bible, which was required reading for all their philosophy courses. While doing research for her master's thesis, Kazuko became involved in the activities of the Nishinomiya Culture Circle, a local literary coterie.

Also she regularly attended the meetings of the Vernunft (Reason) Association, a reading group organized by Kyoto University philosophy students. At one of these occasions she met Saegusa Kōichi (b. 1922), who was to become a respected literary critic, better known by his pen name, Morikawa Tatsuya. Kazuko and Morikawa were married in 1951 and moved to Kyoto, where they lived until 1963. From 1956 to 1957 they both worked as middle school teachers and published the literary magazine *Bungeijin* (The Literati), together with a group of fellow teachers. In 1958 Morikawa and Kazuko started their own journal, *Mushinpa bungaku* (Freethinkers' Literature), which appeared at first bi-annually, then annually till 1964, eight issues in all. In 1963 Kazuko's husband succeeded his father to the hereditary office of head priest of Kōmyōji, a small Shingon temple in Takino, Hyogo prefecture. The couple gave up their Kyoto apartment and moved into the temple at Takino.

In 1964 Morikawa started the journal *Shinbi* (Aesthetics) with the aim of creating a publishing forum for the writers of the Showa period (1926–89). The sixteen issues of his journal that appeared from 1964 to 1973 carried fiction, poetry, and critical articles by such writers, poets, and critics as Haniya Yutaka, Noma Hiroshi, Nakamura Shin'ichirō, Inoue Mitsuharu, Shimao Toshio, Yoshiyuki Jun'nosuke, Isoda Koichi, and Akiyama Shun, all of whom are generally regarded as leaders in postwar Japanese literature and literary criticism. Kazuko, who became associate editor of the journal, published in it most of her writings from the late 1960s and the early 1970s. It also carried some of Morikawa's seminal critiques: his most notable critical studies include "Shimao Toshio-*ron*" (on Shimao Toshio, 1965), "Haniya Yutaka-*ron*" (On Haniya Yutaka, 1970), and "Bungaku no hiteisei" (The Negativity of Literature, 1972).

Since the beginning of the 1980s, Kazuko has divided her time between To-kyo, where she engages in creative writing, and Takino, where she helps her husband run the Kōmyōji temple. Morikawa has been equally busy trying to meet the demands of his three professions as Shingon priest, literary critic, and professor of Japanese literature at Kobe Women's University. Kazuko is an assiduous visitor to Greece, where she has been spending two or three months every year since 1983, studying ancient Greek literature, art, and religion, visiting archaeological sites, and searching for vestiges of a long-lost matriarchal culture.

Career: Saegusa Kazuko's oeuvre consists of novels, poetry, dramas, essays, and literary criticism. The first among her works to receive public attention was the collection of short stories *Shokei ga okonawarete iru* (Execution Is in Progress, 1969), which was awarded the Tamura Toshiko Prize. The neat periodization of her literary career that Saegusa herself suggested in a 1985 interview (*Genten,* no. 5, 1985) is somewhat problematic, but there is a progressive development traceable through her works. The avant-garde short stories and novellas she wrote in the 1960s show her still groping for a personal style. Later novels such as *Hikaru numa ni ita onna* (The Woman in the Shining Marsh, 1986) and *Murakumo no mura no monogatari* (Tales of a Cloud-Swept Village, 1987) demonstrate artistic maturity.

From the outset of her career, Saegusa has consistently pursued a clearly defined, sharply focused set of themes and motifs: the significance of Japan's defeat in World War II; the correction/displacement of male views of womanhood and motherhood; death, love, and sexuality; the disintegration of historically sanctioned social institutions such as traditional village communities, marriage, and the family; and the collapse of a modernist utopia of a unified self; language as an art form and as a means for apprehending and/or (re)creating reality and history. Within the context of Saegusa's oeuvre, these concerns interact in such a way as to produce two distinct patterns. One is circularity or cyclical occurrence. The other is horizontal kinship, that is, similarities in subject matter, plot structure, and formal and stylistic devices between works that are otherwise dissimilar.

The latest three novels are related in terms of subject matter. *Sono hi no natsu* (Summer on That Day, 1987) records the changes in the thinking and behavior of six girl students at a provincial normal school during the first ten days after Japan's unconditional surrender to the Allies on August 15, 1945. *Sono fuyu no shi* (Death in That Winter, 1988) recounts the stories of several characters who were displaced or suffered losses because of the war. *Sono yoru no owari ni* (At the End of That Night, 1990) traces the destiny of Someyo, a streetwalker who, still haunted twenty-five years after the war by the memories of her experiences as an army prostitute in Southeast Asia in the early 1940s, commits suicide. In all three novels, the dialogue takes up a good part of the text, and rape and prostitution as archetypal women's situations are recurring motifs. Though not a trilogy in the commonly accepted sense of the word, these three novels certainly form a loosely structured unit: in the ''Afterword'' to *Sono yoru no owari ni,* Saegusa insists that these novels should be read as a trilogy.

The patterns of circularity and horizontal kinship extend to other groups of works as well. In the novella *Eguchi suieki* (The Port of Eguchi, 1982), the protagonist, Yuko, tries to reconstruct the life story of her dead mother, Yukie, who worked as an army prostitute in Southeast Asia during the war. Based on the 14th-century No play *Eguchi,* Saegusa's story in its turn exhibits structural, thematic, and formal similarities with two other novels of her own: *Hachigatsu no shura* (Asura in August, 1972), which is structured like a No program, and *Hōkai kokuchi* (Annunciation of the Fall, 1985). Another three, *Kōhikan mokuyōsha* (Coffee Shop Thursday Society, 1973), *Ren'ai shōsetsu* (Love Story, 1976), and *Omoigakezu kaze no chō* (A Butterfly on a Gust of Wind, 1980), are novels about the process of creating fiction through language. Three complex novels are related inasmuch as they all depict mythic village communities that exercise a fatal power over their inhabitants: *Tsuki no tobu mura* (Village of the Flying Moon, 1979), *Onidomo no yoru wa fukai* (Deep Is the Night of the Demons, 1983; winner of the Izumi Kyōka Prize), and *Murakumo no mura no monogatari* (Tales of a Cloud-Swept Village, 1987).

Circularity and cyclical occurrence are salient features of Saegusa's treatises as well, apparently attributable partly to the influences of such divergent traditions as Mahayana Buddhism (e.g., the important treatise *Daijō Kishinron,* or The Awakening of Mahayana Faith, which she began to study in 1976 under her husband's guidance); the texts of the No theater; women writers of the Heian period (794–1196); and European modernist and postmodernist writers from Kafka to Alain Robbe-Grillet and Michel Butor. At the same time, such features seem to derive also from Saegusa's conscious effort to create, as she puts it, a literature like "a living being," like a great continuous flow in which the writer's subjectivity or ego is totally irrelevant.

The postmodernist tenets of the denial of authorial power, of the affirmation of intertextuality and heterogeneity of the text(s) of history, are already detectable in the experimental fiction Saegusa published in the early 1970s, but it was not until a decade later that a preoccupation with feminist themes surfaced in her writings. In the essay collection *Sayonara, otoko no jidai* (Goodbye, the Age of Men, 1984), she advances a feminist revisionist critique of past as well as contemporary sociocultural traditions. Her recent study, *Ren'ai shōsetsu no kansei* (The Fallacy of Romance, 1991), directs attention to the unmistakable imprint of patriarchal ideologies in the representation of the love theme in a range of texts by ten modern Japanese male authors, from Natsume Sōseki (1867–1916) to Murakami Haruki (b. 1948). The motif of gender inequality and the oppression and suffering that women have had to endure as a result of the psychosexual, cultural, and political ramifications of the construct "woman" are elaborated upon in most of the fiction Saegusa has published since the beginning of the 1980s.

One of her recent projects is the retrieval of the ideal of matriarchy from ancient Greek literature and art. This search is apparent in the novels *Hōkai kokuchi,* which attempts to trace matriarchal thought patterns in Aeschylus's *Oresteia* trilogy, and *Onna tachi ha kodai e tobu* (Women Fly Off Toward Ancient Times, 1986), in which three "liberated" Japanese women speculate on the transition from a matriarchal society to a patriarchal one that took place in ancient Greece. Another of her projects concerns the reinscribing of the life and works of famous women writers and poets from the Heian period in an exclusively female literary/critical tradition. To date, Saegusa has produced two historical novels dealing with two outstanding women of that period: *Sei Shōn-agon—Nagako no koi* (Sei Shōnagon—Nagako's Love, 1988), a fictionalized biography of the 10th-century author of the celebrated essay collection *Makura no sōshi* (The Pillow Book); and *Michitsuna no haha—Yasuko no koi* (Mich-itsuna's Mother—Yasuko's Love, 1989) featuring Fujiwara Michitsuna's mother and author of *Kagerō nikki* (The Gossamer Years), which is one of the four major Heian diaries.

Major Works: Tsuki no tobu mura (Village of the Flying Moon, 1979), novel. The setting is Sumiyoshi village, a rather isolated rural community consisting of six hamlets with some eighteen hundred souls. The time is the 1970s. This novel in six chapters tells stories of several villagers. Teruji, the poultryman, is scrupulously avoided by the villagers, because his chicken farm is believed to be cursed by evil spirits: as if to confirm their superstitious fear, the poultry house catches fire and Teruji dies in the blaze. Another virtual outcast is Rui, the aunt of the present owner of the lumber mill: she had left the village at age eighteen but, having failed to establish a reputation as a musician, returned when she was thirty-seven, only to commit suicide at the age of seventy. Like Teruji the poultryman, with whom she had an affair not long after her return to the village, Rui becomes a local legend herself. Her favorite great-nephew does not seem to have been born under a lucky star either: the eldest son destined to take over the Nagano lumber mill after his father, he flees from the village at the age of twenty with his lover, Toyoko, a strange young woman with shamanistic and visionary powers. Three years after his escape with Toyoko, however, he comes back and rebuilds the poultry house to eke out a meager living by selling eggs. In time, he becomes obsessed by a desire to kill all the old men and women in Sumiyoshi village and to blast the village to pieces.

Not only the so-called deserters and outcasts but even the people who have spent their whole life in the village and who have never rebelled against its norms and codes are undone by the evil spell hovering above it. There is the "cousin wife" Yoshiko, who, at age forty-five, throws herself into a well to put an end to the suffering caused by her loveless, childless marriage and by the cruel treatment to which her in-laws subject her. There is Yufu, the old idiot woman who hangs herself a week after Yoshiko's death, leaving behind her mentally retarded brother, Sata, with whom she has had two children. In the final scene, a group of angry young men donning goblin masks set fire to eight big drums that have been brought out for the annual festival. The surrealistic vision of destruction following upon the description of this act of vengeance has an ominous apocalyptic ring: if it is a natural denouement and a logical conclusion that Sumiyoshi village perish in a conflagration, as prophesied by the main characters and portended by the deaths that keep piling up as the narrative progresses, then, a worse fate could befall the whole world.

Gathering around the scorched remains of the big drums, the old villagers wept pro-
fusely. "Why did they have to burn the drums?" The reason why the masked young
men had set fire to the drums was beyond their comprehension. "The drums are village
property. Why did they have to do such a reckless thing?" Still moaning ruefully, the
old men and women carefully gathered the charred remains of the drum, still soaking
wet from the water with which the fire brigade had extinguished the blaze. . . . While
they busied themselves with the dirty carcasses of the burnt drums, the old men and
women slowly turned into maggots. Big, fat maggots. Like a heap of garbage thrown in
the incinerator for quick disposal, the whole area suddenly began to wriggle with maggots, crawling on top of one another, lying interlocked in motionless lumps or struggling
to disentangle themselves from the mass. White sunlight poured down on them from
above as mercilessly as ever.

"I'll throw the whole damn lot in an old folks' home, set the house on fire and let
them roast in the blaze," muttered Nagano's son, his head throbbing from a bad hangover
as he tried to visualize old villagers burning to death in the village incinerator.

The maggots died one after another in quick succession. . . . The door of the incinerator
was suddenly slammed shut. Once the door was shut, the incinerator began to pour forth
billows of white smoke. The stench of burning maggots filled the air. Now wholly
transformed into a bad-smelling smoke, the maggots rose slowly to the sky.

The village was about to go up in flames.

Tsuki no tobu mura is an extremely complex novel that works on several
levels. On the literal level, there is little doubt that it takes to task traditional
Japanese rural communities for their political and ideological conservatism, cultural backwardness, moral orthodoxy and opportunism, and male chauvinism.
This criticism is reflected in the rebellious attitude of the young generation
toward the middle-aged and old generations in Sumiyoshi village; in the contention of the latter generations that those who attempt to escape to the outer
world will inevitably die in their flight; and in the discriminatory treatment
meted out to former runaways who have returned to the village. The stories
about the "cousin wife" in Chapter 2 and Nagano's seventy-one-year-old
brother in Chapter 3, who returns to the village ostensibly because he wants to
die in his hometown, may both be interpreted as a strong indictment of women's
oppression in the traditional rural context. The Nagano narrative conveys a
scathing condemnation:

"It's because you allow yourself to be ruled by such stupid things as rumors and
gossip, Mother, and keep worrying about appearances that you've come to lead such a
miserable life, looking after three old fools and with a daughter who walked out on you
never to come back again."

"Are you saying that Yasuko left home because of me?" asked Nagano's wife, turning
pale.

"Shall I tell you what Yasuko said before she left?" said her son coolly. " 'Looking
at Mother's way of life, I've come to understand that Sumiyoshi Village is no place for

a woman to live as a human being. It's pointless trying to change anything here. I'm leaving before it's too late.' ''

"What's this supposed to mean? Why do I have to hear this, after I've spent all my life working like a slave for all of you, never thinking of myself?"

"Why can't you see it, Mother? It's because you work so hard for others and never think of your own needs that Yasuko ran away from home. She didn't want to become like you."

This novel also levels criticism at the superficial, fetishist popular culture and the mindless throwaway consumerism fostered by contemporary Japanese society. What Saegusa is primarily concerned with, however, is not so much decrying the irreparable damage that postwar Japanese society has done to the sense of identity in traditional rural communities but rather constructing a mythic space in which familiar philosophical themes may be restated, and structural and stylistic innovations may be attempted without the prerequisite of rituals of legitimation such as parody form. Seen from this standpoint, Sumiyoshi village appears as an allegory or an extended metaphor in which converge several mythic narratives peopled by characters more or less intended as illustrations of ideas. Thus the village may be seen as a kind of no-man's-land that blurs the distinctions between life and death, time and no-time, history and amorphous chaos. It could be a secularized version of the Land of the Dead (*yomi no kuni*) that recurrs in Japanese literature and folklore: the poultryman is a living apparition emanating the smell of death; Yufu and Sata may be Izanami and Izanagi, the mythical, incestuous parents of the Japanese archipelago described in Japan's first official chronicle, *Kojiki* (Record of Ancient Matters, 712); and the ghosts of the "cousin wife" Yoshiko, Teruji, and Rui attain the dreams and aspirations they could not fulfill during their lifetime in an ideal landscape. Sumiyoshi village may also be interpreted as a metaphoric amalgam of the features of the *hachinetsu jigoku* (Eight Burning Hells), the most horrifying realm in the Buddhist cosmology, or as a stage on which an absurd drama of death and rebirth, award and retribution endlessly repeats itself. Such interpretations can account for the circularity of the plot (even if Sumiyoshi village burns down, another village will rise from its ashes, and young people will repeat the mistakes of the preceding generations); for the motif of reincarnation (the eldest son of the lumberer as reincarnation of Teruji the poultryman, Tokoyo as that of the village shamaness); and for the horrible death of the poultryman as well as the suicides of Yufu and Rui.

In an archetypal-psychoanalytic reading of this novel, the young villagers' sadistic impulse to abuse or even kill their parents and grandparents reveals a perspective as the primitive fear of death, as refusal to grow up, and as unconscious longing for a state of eternal youth. This perspective also renders Sumiyoshi village into a powerful symbol of female sexuality; or rather, it can stand for men's unconscious dread of women's sexual drive as a monstrous vampiric force that threatens to annihilate them, or even as an emblem of the male longing for, and terror of, the reunion with the preoedipal mother. This archetypal scenario is vividly enacted in the following passage from Chapter 1 in the mind of the eldest son of the lumber mill owner:

> The extraordinary tenacity and durability of his mother's and grandmother's sexual organs were qualities that in their turn seemed directly related to the two women's unabashed affirmation of their reproductive functions. . . . The burning hatred he had felt at that time toward his mother and grandmother was coupled with an equally intense desire, both to kill the two women and to destroy himself in the process. . . . Reliving the murderous impulse of that time, he gradually became aware that it was spilling out of his mind, threatening to submerge the whole village.

Tsuki no tobu mura not only points to the causes of women's oppression in traditional rural communities with their feudal-patriarchal habits of thought and attitudes and the age-old division of labor and sexual roles but also celebrates female biological, intellectual, and spiritual superiority: Rui and young Toyoko are both outstanding women endowed with a keen intelligence and supernatural abilities.

In view of Saegusa's indebtedness to classical Japanese literature and her adherence to postmodern intertextuality as a means to revitalize the language of literature, it is certainly not accidental that *Tsuki no tobu mura* displays stylistic similarities with the *setsuwa* (shorter tales commonly Buddhist and didactic in intent, often interspersed with legendary and folklore elements) collections of the Heian and Kamakura periods, or even with Ueda Akinari's masterpiece, *Ugetsu monogatari* (Tales of Moonlight and Rain, 1768). Such similarities may be seen in the Gothic romanticism of some passages describing stormy or moon-lit nights or in the moralistic intent and episodic character of the narratives. At the same time, Saegusa's novel shows intersections with such contemporary novels as Gabriel Garcia Marquez's *Cien años de soledad* (One Hundred Years of Solitude, 1967) and Nakagami Kenji's *Sennen no yuraku* (Thousand Years of Pleasure, 1982) and *Kiseki* (Miracle, 1989) in that the actions and responses of their characters are determined by a mythic place or community that occupies a central position in the plot (Marquez's Macondo; Nakagami's Alley). According to Saegusa, any geographic locality in literature possesses a power to manipulate fictional characters at will, a power she calls "principle of location," which in essence is a kind of topographic determinism. Saegusa discusses this principle at length in her novel *Omoigakezu kaze no cho*.

Translated Works: Sono hi no natsu (The Summer on That Day, 1987), novel. The "day" refers to the immediate aftermath of Japan's surrender on August 15, 1945, encompassing exactly ten days following the historic broadcast of the Imperial Rescript of Surrender. Ten short chapters arranged in chronological order present the happenings, one chapter for each day. The events unfold through a first-person narrative related by the protagonist, sixteen-year-old

Yoshii. In spite of the fact that the narrator and the protagonist are identical and that the novel is autobiographical, Saegusa's text is nothing like the narrowly focused, narcissistic type of confessional novel known as *shishōsetsu,* or the "I-novel." In an essay included in the collection "Sayonara, Otoko no jidai," she confesses that the setting, characters, and events described in *Sono hi no natsu* are faithful reproductions of her own experiences at the end of the war. Yet, this novel presents a multitude of perspectives that may supplement, but also clash at times with, the protagonist's views. The result of this conscious break from the *shishōsetsu* pattern is a kaleidoscopic structure that is ideally suited for expressing various kinds of criticism, precisely because it allows for various interpretations of the same story.

Yoshii and her five roommates in the dormitory of H Normal School listen to the emperor's unprecedented radio broadcast and, like everyone else, weep heartbrokenly. But as time goes by and the historic date of Japan's defeat becomes more and more removed from their immediate range of perception, the girls begin to question their spontaneous expression of grief on that day and to have doubts about the cult of the emperor propagated by the militaristic government, about the chauvinistic ultranationalism that had pervaded formal education during the war, and about the justice of this war, officially dubbed "holy." The girls also witness the gradual slackening of the strict regulations and the rigid military discipline that had dominated school life up to August 15 and puzzle over their teachers' ambiguous attitude, which provides no clues for them as to how to fill the ideological, religious, and philosophical vacuum created by the end of the war. As they read in the newspaper about the suicide of military men who had played key roles during the war, about the incalculable human casualties and property losses caused by the atomic bombs in Hiroshima and Nagasaki, and about the devastation and misery of all Japanese cities, the girls become increasingly aware of the horror and inhumanity of war.

On August 24, most of the girl students, availing themselves of a three-day holiday granted by the school, leave for home. Yoshii, who finally arrives home after an exhausting ride on overcrowded trains, is no longer the naive "patriotic girl" who had firmly believed in the myth of the emperor as a living god, even comparing him with Jesus Christ. In recording her groping reflections and painful efforts to shake off the hypnotic effect of the wartime propaganda with devastating honesty, the text implies that the protagonist has matured and is now able to pass a more objective judgment on the events she witnessed during the war. The kaleidoscopic perspective abounds in scenes such as discussions between Yoshii and her roommates on current events, the war, and the extent of the involvement of the Showa emperor (Hirohito) in the war; Yoshii's reflections and reminiscences in which her own attempts at evaluation and interpretation are weighed against the opinions of her family members still colored by the jargon of wartime propaganda; and passages in which extensive quotations from the press in the first days after Japan's surrender are used as a foil to the views of Yoshii and her roommates. A characteristic instance is the scene in which the six girls engage in a heated debate on the meaning and literary value of a poem by the leading poet and artist Takamura Kotaro (1883–1956), a work that laments Japan's defeat and, notwithstanding the new historical circumstances, still addresses the emperor as an awesome supernatural being transcending human errors. The issues at stake in this episode are wartime education and its devastating effects on the psychology of the young generation and the active support lent by many Japanese intellectuals to the totalitarian rule at home and to the imperialist war waged by Japan in East and Southeast Asia. Though formulated in indirect terms, the condemnation of the war and those responsible for it in this section is unequivocal.

This novel has recourse to several strategies to put forward a critique of World War II: the unmistakably feminine, even feminist, flavor of the protagonist's narrative; what may be called the "literariness" or "fictional unreality" of the situation in which Yoshii and her friends find themselves; and the anxiety and insecurity expressed by all characters with respect to Japan's future, which, insofar as it must stand without the support of the emperor symbolism, appears strangely empty and meaningless. The manner of speech of Yoshii and her classmates is distinctly that of young girls, and their preoccupation with romance, idealistic notions of love and friendship, and their coquettish behavior in front of their male classmates and teachers is as feminine as can be, but there is a dim awareness of gender discrimination in their envy of certain privileges only boys enjoyed during the general mobilization of students in the labor force or in their unrestrained joy when they were treated on the same footing with the boys during a visit of the prime minister, General Tojo Hideki, to their school. This vague awareness turns into uneasiness and even angry attacks on the wartime ultranationalist ideology for its feudal-patriarchal bias and into the realization that the war has not only failed to resolve the age-old problem of the oppression and discrimination of women but, on the contrary, aggravated it. In a passage in which the girls discuss the possibility of Japanese women being sexually assaulted by soldiers of the occupation forces, it is suggested that a tacit alliance between the foreign soldiers and Japanese men might come into being should such assaults occur.

Irmela Hijiya-Kirschnereit in the preface to her German translation of *Sono hi no natsu* notes that there is an undeniable "literary" quality to the girls' confinement in the school dormitory in the first few days after Japan's surrender: Yoshii and her roommates spend most of their time reading novels; and Yoshii expresses a close affinity with the world of the *Tale of Genji,* finding similarities between her present predicament and the life in the golden age of the court ladies described in the 11th-century masterpiece by Lady Murasaki; and besides, the girls' only link with the outside world is the newspaper, "literature" in the broad sense of written information. This situation is emblematic in several ways. On one hand, it delineates the sense of liberation and the great thirst for knowledge that the Japanese people, especially the young generation, felt after the ruthless suppression of all criticism of governmental activities and even of what was deemed unpatriotic and morally objectionable literary and artistic heritage during the war. On the other hand, the girls' confinement alludes to the conventional roles of women as mothers, housewives, and guarantors of the survival of any society. Saegusa's novel shows with great clarity that these traditionally female roles are given new luster and even an aura of sanctity in times of war or politicoeconomic crisis. The "literary" seclusion of the girl students in the novel also ironically echoes the classical pattern of withdrawal from the secular world in times of social unrest, a life-style chosen by male literati who contributed to fostering the Japanese and Chinese literary, religious, and philosophical traditions.

Finally, as seen in the following highly significant passage, *Sono hi no natsu* advances a view that the emperor played a much more active role in the war than conservative historians in the postwar era ascribed to him and that the web of myth created around him by right-wing politicians and the military in the 1930s was a major factor in the successful mobilization of the nation for war.

I stared at the small fissure in my heart. Today at noon the hour count since the broadcast of the Imperial Rescript of Surrender had reached exactly 144. The changes in my thoughts and feelings went on at an incredibly rapid pace. These changes were due neither to the instructions of our teachers, nor to the opinions of specialists as expressed in the press or in radio broadcasts, and even less to the text of the Rescript itself: they occurred naturally and spontaneously, as if from an inner impulse. The Imperial Broadcast had destroyed all the values and ideals on which my inner world rested, without replacing them with any guidelines for the future, or indicating how to build a new system from the simple but fundamental realization that there weren't any guidelines any longer, neither for the present nor for the future, and that as long as we lived we would never receive instructions from a supreme authority again.

I found the tone and style of the press reports we read every day not only extremely remote from my feelings about the situation since the surrender, but also irritating and disconcerting. Especially phrases like "Absolute obedience to the Imperial Rescript (of Surrender)" sounded unacceptably hypocritical. I wanted to cry out in protest: "Then, what about the Imperial Edict of December 8, 1941? [As Japan's official declaration of war to the United States, the edict marked the beginning of the war.] Have you forgotten it?" (My roommate) Uda Noriko's comment on the newspaper articles, which I had found so revolting, came closest to how I felt: "A very clever strategem that, blaming everything on the Emperor!"

"His Majesty the Emperor: a very convenient excuse, indeed," Noriko had added sarcastically, and now again I found myself agreeing with her. The edicts on the beginning and the end of the War had of course been proclaimed by the same Emperor. . . . There was also the belief that the Emperor's words, once pronounced, cannot be rescinded, but it was of no help in resolving my contradictory feelings about the emperor and the war, and about what was now being said and written on both.

Though written in a plain, unadorned style and containing much less of the horrifying descriptions of mutilations and carnage or of the moral torment caused by the war than the fiction and documentary narratives by male novelists

Ōoka Shōhei (1909–90) and Takeda Taijun (1912–76), *Sono hi no natsu* deserves a conspicuous place in the large and heterogeneous body of contemporary Japanese writings dealing with World War II.

BIBLIOGRAPHY

Translations

Der Sommer and jenem Tag (Summer on That Day). Tr. Irmela Hijiya-Kirschenereit. Frankfurt am Main: Isel Verlag, 1990.
''The Narcissism of Female Representation and the Professional Writer.'' Tr. Nina Blake. *Review of Japanese Culture and Society—Josai University* 4 (December 1991): 18–22.
''The Rain at Rokudo Crossroad.'' Tr. Yukiko Tanaka. In *Unmapped Territories: New Women's Fiction from Japan,* ed. Yukiko Tanaka. Seattle: Women in Translation, 1991, 3–17.

Critical Works

Mulhern, Chieko. ''Japan.'' In *Longman Anthology of World Literature by Women 1875–1975.* New York: Longman, 1989, 1152–62.
Tanaka, Yukiko. ''Introduction.'' In *Unmapped Territories: New Women's Fiction from Japan,* ed. Yukiko Tanaka. Seattle: Women in Translation, 1991, vii–xvi.

Livia MONNET

SANUKI NO SUKE (1079?–after 1119), memoirist. Real name: Fujiwara Nagako.

Life: Fujiwara Nagako, more commonly known by her court title, Sanuki no suke (the Sanuki Assistant Handmaid), is thought to have been the youngest daughter of Fujiwara Akitsuna (d. 1107?), an official of the mid-level *zuryō* class. Akitsuna held various provincial governorships (the governorship of Sanuki among them, hence his daughter's sobriquet) and enjoyed close ties to the imperial household, particularly during the life of Emperor GoSanjō (1034–73; r. 1068–72). He was foster father to one of GoSanjō's sons and served for a time as director (*bettō*) of GoSanjō's Office of the Retired Emperor (*in no chō*). Related by marriage to two of the most politically well connected poets of his day, Fujiwara Akisue (1055–1123) and Fujiwara Michitoshi (1047–99, compiler of the fourth imperial *waka* anthology *Goshūishū*), Akitsuna was himself a well-known poet and literary scholar. Twenty-five of Akitsuna's poems are included in imperially commissioned *waka* anthologies (*chokusenshū*), beginning with *Goshūishū* (1086), and a personal poetry collection (*Akitsuna ason no shū* or *Sanuki Nyūdō shū*) also survives. A poem from his collection, written upon returning a borrowed copy of *Genji monogatari* (The Tale of Genji, early 11th c.), attests to his interest in that work. Akitsuna is also thought to have made copies of the *Man'yōshū* (Collection of Ten Thousand Leaves, late 8th c.) and the *Kokinshū* (Collection of Poems Ancient and Modern, ca. 908). It thus seems his household would have provided an ideal environment for the cultivation of his daughter's literary talents.

Yet, Sanuki is one of the more shadowy figures among the great female memoirists of the Heian period. Scholars confused her for generations with her elder sister Fujiwara Kaneko (1049–1133) (also known as Tōzami or Iyo no sammi), a wet nurse to Emperor Horikawa (1079–1107; r. 1086–1107). It is now thought that Sanuki was roughly thirty years Kaneko's junior and more or less an exact contemporary of Horikawa himself. Biographical information on her is based in part on the evidence of her memoir, *Sanuki no suke nikki* (The Memoir of the Sanuki Assistant Handmaid, ca. 1109), in part on other memoirs of the day, and may be briefly summarized. She entered Horikawa's service in 1100. In late 1101, she was made *naishi no suke* (assistant handmaid) and spent the next six and a half years, until the emperor's early death in 1107, attending to his daily needs in this capacity. The duties of a *naishi no suke* varied depending on her status and the degree of imperial favor that she enjoyed. While the extent of Sanuki's duties is not clear, her memoir implies she attended Horikawa in morning prayers and religious observances. Their relationship, though not necessarily sexual, would thus have been of an intimate, daily nature. The confusion of Sanuki's identity with that of her elder sister seems to have stemmed in part from the lack of eroticism in her memoir, an absence judged curious in the case of an assistant handmaid's memoir about an emperor. Many *naishi* bore children to the emperors they served and were in general considered a sort of concubine. The question of whether Sanuki was also sexually intimate with Horikawa has not been solved. Whatever the case may have been, she bore the emperor no children. When Horikawa became terminally ill in the summer of 1107, she waited upon him constantly, remaining with him until his death. She was called out of mourning before the end of the mourning period in the twelfth Moon of 1107 by order of Horikawa's father, the Retired Emperor Shirakawa (1053–1129; r. 1072–86), to assist at the accession ceremony of Horikawa's son and successor Toba (1103–1156; r. 1107–23). In the first Moon of 1108, she was asked to take up service at court again as assistant handmaid to Emperor Toba. For the next eleven years, she served at Toba's court until she was suddenly dismissed in 1119, ostensibly for reasons of mental illness. No record remains of her activities after this date.

References to Sanuki's dismissal are fragmentary and tantalizingly vague, and their interpretation has long provided a problem in traditional biographical scholarship, coloring the way some scholars interpret her *nikki* (memoir, lit., "record of days"). According to the brief, thirdhand account recorded in *Chōshūki* (Diary of Minamoto Morotoki, 1077–1136), in the eighth Moon of 1119, she was relieved of court duty, and her brother Fujiwara Michitsune (fl. 1072–1129) was called in to take custody of her as a result of claims she had been making since the previous year to being possessed by the spirit of the late Horikawa. In the autumn of 1118, she had prophesied the birth of an imperial prince to Empress Taikenmon'in (1101–45), who had entered Toba's court in the twelfth Moon of

1117. The child (the future emperor Sutoku, 1119–1164; r. 1123–41) was born in 1119, and Sanuki, again claiming the authority of Horikawa's ghost, demanded that she be rewarded for her prophecy. Toba was to do as Horikawa's medium wished, and Sanuki as medium wished that her brother be granted the governorship of ōmi province and that she herself be provided with a new residence (her own having been recently destroyed by fire). Since these wishes had not been granted, the spirit vowed that it would haunt to death the descendants of Lady Nii (fl. ca. 1095; Taikenmon'in's mother, who had been one of Sanuki's older contemporaries at Horikawa's court). The incident came to the attention of Shirakawa, and he ordered Sanuki's dismissal.

Shirakawa's motives appear to have been deeply entangled in the bedroom politics of the day. Taikenmon'in had been raised in his household as his foster daughter, and it was rumored that their relations had been sexual as well as familial. It became common gossip, recorded in later years in the *Kojidan* (Conversations About Ancient Matters, compiled ca. 1212–15 by Minamoto Akikane), that Taikenmon'in's son Sutoku was not Toba's child at all, but his half-uncle, the offspring of Taikenmon'in's early intimacy with Shirakawa. It would seem, then, that Shirakawa had Sanuki dismissed in an effort to prevent her further manipulation of rumors about Taikenmon'in and the paternity of the infant prince. But the incident was to create friction anyway, at least for a time, between Shirakawa and his reigning grandson. Toba initially opposed the dismissal and threatened to cease visiting Taikenmon'in if Sanuki were removed from court. Some scholars have suggested that years later, the affair contributed to the political rivalries between Toba and Sutoku that culminated finally in the Hōgen rebellion of 1156.

Whatever the actual circumstances surrounding Sanuki's dismissal, it seems clear that her position in later years was a politically vulnerable one. She was apparently childless, and though her father had represented the interests of an important client family of the imperial house, he died the same year that Horikawa did. Horikawa's death deprived her of her elder sister's support as well since Kaneko took the tonsure a month after Horikawa's funeral.

Career and Major Works: During her seven years as assistant handmaid to Horikawa, Sanuki lived in daily contact with one of the most active patrons of *waka* the imperial court was to know for many generations thereafter. Though short-lived and somewhat sickly, Horikawa was the center of a dynamic, if technically conservative poetic circle that produced several important *hyakushu-uta* (hundred-poem sequences) and numerous *utaawase* (poetry competitions). Horikawa's empress Atsuko (1060–1114) and her kinsmen also seem to have provided a focus of poetic activity. During the decade and a half between Atsuko's entrance to court in 1091 and Horikawa's death, poetry was composed on twenty-four different court occasions. Music also flourished during Horikawa's reign, and Horikawa was himself a skilled flutist. Perhaps in part because of the greater brilliance of those surrounding her, Sanuki's own talents have been judged rather dim. Youngest daughter in a family of sought-after contemporary poets, she was apparently unsuccessful in displaying skill in the art of *waka;* there is room to believe she had little to display. Certainly, there remain very few *waka* by which we might judge her. No record remains of her participation in the many *utaawase* or *hyakushuuta* of her day, and only one *waka* by her appears in the *chokusenshū* (in the ninth, *Shinchokusenshū,* 1235). The *waka* included in her *nikki* confirm the impression of her lack of poetic talent. In fact it has become commonplace to remark that her *nikki* is unique among Heian female-authored *nikki* for the meagerness of its included *waka,* particularly those composed by the author herself. The first volume is completely devoid of *waka,* perhaps due to its format and subject matter: an almost day-by-day account of Horikawa's final illness and death. Volume 2, on the other hand, contains a total of twenty-three *waka,* a sum that, as Miyazaki Sōhei has pointed out (*Heian joryū nikki bungaku no kenkyū* [Kasama shoin, 1972] 352), creates a prose-to-poetry ratio comparable to that in other well-known Heian women's *nikki.* What distinguishes Sanuki's memoir from other ''poetic diaries,'' however, is the extent to which it relies on quoted *waka.* Only eleven of the twenty-three *waka* included in the *nikki* are attributed to Sanuki herself: five *dokueika* (*waka* composed without a specific addressee in mind) and six *waka* composed as part of poetic exchanges between Sanuki and someone else. The six exchanged poems are without exception rhetorically spare, eschewing in every case but one *honka dori* (allusive variation) and *engo* (associative language), two of the tropes frequently used to showcase a poet's skill at manipulating conventional poetic language in the give-and-take of a poetic exchange. On the other hand, her *dokueika* rely so heavily upon the *honka dori* technique that some argue they are not allusive variations at all but rather represent little more than quotations of older poems. Indeed, of these five *waka,* four present only minor variations on more illustrious predecessors. Typical of the extreme rhetorical minimalism of Sanuki's *waka* is the following *dokueika,* from one of the final passages in the *nikki:*

If this year I've spent	Nagekitsutsu
lamenting him draws to a close,	toshi no kurenaba
how much further will	naki hito no
that last parting	wakare ya itodo
sink into the past?	tōku narinamu
	(Nihon Koten Bungaku Zenshū 18,
	454; all translations in this entry by
	Edith Sarra)

The only difference between this poem and the famous one by Ki no Tsurayuki (ca. 872–945) to which it alludes is a matter of five syllables. The first line in Sanuki's poem, ''[I] go on lamenting'' (*nagekitsutsu*), appears as ''while [you] yearn'' (*kōru ma ni*) in Tsurayuki's version (''If this year you've spent/yearning for her draws to a close/how much further will/that last parting/sink into the past?''). Given the sheer consistency of her citation and repetition of prior *waka*, one wonders whether repetition itself was intended as a deliberate rhetorical technique. Certainly techniques of repetition play a considerably more interesting role in the narrative structure of the *nikki,* as is argued later.

If the *waka* in her memoir suggest a woman of minor poetic talents, its intricate narrative structure hints at greater accomplishments in narrative technique. For centuries, the memoir seems to have been read primarily for the vivid, intimate images it bequeaths of Horikawa. The title appended to some copies of the text—*Horikawa'in no nikki* (The Emperor Horikawa Memoir)—reflects this source of its appeal, as do the mentions it receives in late Heian and early Kamakura collections, where it is identified as a source of anecdotes about Horikawa. This tradition is carried on by the work of Jennifer Brewster, who made the first translation of the work into English, entitling it *The Emperor Horikawa Diary.* Indeed, the anecdotes the memoir relates about Horikawa and Toba may have helped save the work from oblivion. But the charm of these anecdotes owes much to the manner in which they are told, their striking immediacy to a number of innovative experiments in the art of narrative.

Translated Works: The extant manuscript copies of *Sanuki no suke nikki* (The Memoir of the Sanuki Assistant Handmaid, ca. 1109) show it to be a work in two *maki* (volumes). Volume 1 gives a detailed account of the stages of Horikawa's final illness, structuring time in a pattern familiar from earlier *nikki.* As in *Kagerō nikki* (The Gossamer Memoir, after 974 by Michitsuna's Mother) and *Sarashina nikki* (The Sarashina Memoir, after 1058 by Takasue's Daughter), events recounted in the narrative conform to the order of their occurrence in a remembered past. For the most part, the narrator describes past events and feelings in the sequence in which they presumably arose in the past and typically makes only a few scattered references that mark her perspective as retrospective. This effacement of the distance between past event and narrating present is further heightened by the predominant use of imperfective verbals and auxiliaries. In this latter respect in particular, both volumes of Sanuki's memoir follow the conventions of other Heian female-authored *nikki.*

But the temporal structure of volume 2 is only partly determined by the essentially linear (auto)biographical chronology employed in the first volume. Volume 2 opens as Sanuki is recalled to court service in the twelfth moon of 1107, and it loosely chronicles her life at court during the twelve months of the following year (1108), closing with several undatable passages that seem to refer to episodes that postdate 1108. Yet the account of Sanuki's first year of service under Toba is interwoven with a series of analepses, paradigmatic scenes recalling her earlier years of service under Horikawa that she relates, not in the order of their occurrence in the past, but in the order of their recurrence to her as memories in the recent past of her ongoing service at Toba's court. Their link to the temporal macrostructure of the *nikki* is thus highly associative, with each remembered anecdote triggered by the narrator's description of her duties and events at Toba's court. The cycle of yearly festivals and court rituals (*nenjū gyōji*) provides the overall chronology for the volume as a whole. Yet within this linear order, the forward momentum of the narrative is periodically checked, halted, and reversed by the interpolation of anecdotes referring to much earlier moments. The account of each month of 1108 becomes a commemorative locus, an occasion for recalling events from the same month in other years. The second volume thus concerns itself with Sanuki's obsessive memories of Horikawa and the way these memories continue to intrude and at times overwhelm the narrative of her present life at court. It is as much "about" the narrator-heroine's entrapment in the repetitive paradigms of memory as it is "about" the dead emperor.

In this respect, the second volume of the *Sanuki* memoir recalls the radically paratactic strategies and seasonal themes of "The Wizard" chapter of *The Tale of Genji,* in which Genji passes a year mourning the death of his wife, Murasaki. In this chapter, each festival and change of season is contrasted with those of the past and provides the occasion for the extensive use of *waka* and poetic allusions that heighten the lyricality of the narrative and deepen the pathos of the figure of the mourner. Genji's young grandson Niou (like Toba with Sanuki) is "his sole companion" during this year of intense reverie, his pranks and innocent remarks providing a poignant counterpoint to the aging Genji's melancholy. Though its slight, intricate sketches cannot compare with the *Genji's* majestic weave of *waka,* prose, and poetic allusion, the memoir develops a number of interesting possibilities left unexplored by the densely lyrical prose of *Genji.* Commentators have frequently remarked on the interesting use of "flashbacks" in the second volume of the *nikki.* In fact, the temporal structure of the volume is more complicated than the term *flashback* would suggest. Examples of a few of the tropes involved are sketched later.

Like other Heian female-authored *nikki,* the *Sanuki* memoir proceeds upon a general assumption of temporal duality. In certain passages of the second volume, however, this temporal duality is complicated by the introduction of a third level of past time that Ishino Keiko terms "the remote past" ("*Sanuki no suke nikki* ni okeru jikan no kōzō," *Nikki bungaku sakuhinron no kokoromi,* eds., Chūko bungaku kenkyūkai [Kasama shoin, 1979] 252). To use the language of narratology, these passages constitute something like double analepses: they refer to or describe occasions that themselves depict the narrator-heroine in the act of remembering yet earlier events. In other words, the narrator in volume 2 has a propensity for recalling moments that show her (and sometimes other characters as well) recalling even earlier times. These passages commemorate the act of remembrance itself and thus place the reader (and Sanuki as narrator) at a third remove from the instance ultimately recalled.

Repetition also becomes an obtrusive device for linking various parts of the *nikki.* Certain images recur in the narrative again and again as the narrating voice doubles back to them to find new discoveries concealed beneath old ones. Of these, perhaps the most richly evocative are memories of snowfalls, snowy mornings in particular. The imagery of snow in Heian *waka* and in Heian women's writings in general appears closely associated with the idea of memory and

forgetting. We might look again at ''The Wizard'' chapter in *Genji,* which opens
and closes with striking snow scenes. Of particular note is the one that describes
a moment in early spring when Genji falls into a fitful sleep, sadly recalling a
snowy morning when he had returned from the Third Princess's bed to Murasaki's quarters before dawn. He had hurried back, alarmed after seeing Murasaki's face in a dream, and he remembers especially the chill of the dawn air
as he waited outside her doors. Suddenly the voice of a lady-in-waiting, surprised by the heavy snow as she returns to her own rooms, awakens him—from
his sleep and from his remembrance of the past—to the sight of another snowy
dawn:

He heard a voice call out ''just look at how deeply the snow has piled up!'' and he feels
in that moment just as he had that other dawn, but she was gone from his side now and
his loneliness brought a sorrow beyond words (NKBZ 15, 510).

The reader who follows the trajectory of Genji's musings back into the memory
of his past life with Murasaki (the past of the *Tale*) will also falter, like Genji,
at the voice of the lady-in-waiting astonished at the depth of the snow. The
syntax of the passage itself enacts the involuntary slippages between past and
present to which Genji in his mourning is prey. Its peculiar effectiveness arises
from its power to involve the reader in the same disorientations that plague the
mourner.

There are signs of experimentation with a related trope in the later pages of
Sanuki's memoir, where we find a number of passages ordered by something
that might be called a syntax of involuntary remembrance:

The year before—perhaps because it was the last time?—he was unusually taken by
it all, and from the evening the dancers arrived at court he was up, bustling here and
there. Then there was the rehearsal until late that same night, so he slept longer than
usual the next morning. But when he heard that it had snowed, up he got. The Empress
was also with him that time—they were going to send letters to the Gosechi dancers—
and since I was in attendance, we made the decorative hair-garlands together, and they
tied and fastened them; we were in the Empress's chamber, with thoughts of the past
welling up in me till I was blind and deaf to all else (NKBZ 18, 441–42).

Because of the structure of this passage (which reads as one long sentence in
the original), we cannot place the narrator-heroine or identify what triggers this
particular reminiscence until we read through to the end of it. She has been
sitting in the empress's chamber, it seems, just as she had at the same time two
years before. The reconvergence of a particular site and time of year dissolves
for a moment the distance between past and present.

In the passage immediately following the one just quoted, we are led through
an even more radical elision between reminiscence and reportage. Drawn back
to the present momentarily by Toba's fascination with the carpenters who have

come to build the Gosechi dancers' bridge, the narrator plunges again, this time in mid-sentence, deep into a sustained evocation of yet another snowy morning. Unlike the quoted passage, the transition between this scene and the older scene is completely unmarked, as the narrating voice shifts abruptly, without signaling the change of topic, from talk of Emperor Toba's delight in this year's Gosechi preparations, to the way Emperor Horikawa had overslept one snowy morning during the same festival in some other year. Note that the empress and all other attendants are excluded from this deeper layer of the past: this second return to the *topos* of snow and memory nets an idyll of nearly perfect intimacy between Sanuki and Horikawa. (In the following translation, I have identified the two emperors by name in brackets; no such distinction is made in the original):

The carpenters came to construct the long veranda the dancers use to mount into the Palace; it was the usual sort, linking the steps at the southwest corner of the Sogyōden to the edge of the northeast corner of the Seiryōden, just as in times past. The Emperor [Toba] found it all very novel, and since he was watching them I stayed with him until it got dark—there was that snowy morning he [Horikawa] had still been asleep when we heard the news of a very deep snowfall—that was the morning we got up to see the snow together, because I had spent the night before at his side. And though I always find snowfalls beautiful, this one was especially so; why, even the commoners' poor hovels were a sight to behold in all that whiteness, but how much more so was the Imperial Palace, gleaming like a polished jewel or mirror, and we two gazing together at the scene—if I had been a painter, I would have painted it just as it was without changing a jot, and shown it to the others—when he had the shutters opened, we found where we supposed treetops to be that the snow had piled up so much it was hard to say which one of them was a plum. The stand of bamboo in front of the Jijūden was bent over till it looked like it had snapped. Even the fire-huts by the Palace were buried, and I marveled at how even now the snow was still falling down out of the gloom. How lovely it was, lodged in the interstices of the wattle fence in front of the guards' quarters. He was radiant—was it because of the moment? or because my own heart made me see him that way? I became embarrassed at the thought of how disarrayed I must appear. "This is a morning to make a person wish she might look more beautiful than usual" I exclaimed.

He seemed amused by this, and replied, "But you always do look so." I feel I could be there before him even now, facing that bright, smiling countenance he had as he spoke to me.

I was wearing the kind of things one wore for the Gosechi season, a pale mauve Chinese jacket I believe it was, over a brilliant layering of maple-leaf robes that ranged from yellow to scarlet, colors made all the more splendid by their contrast to the glowing white of the snow. The Emperor gazed on at me, unable to go back inside.

Then we heard women's voices, servants from the guardhouse it seemed, who had come close to the wattle fence by the guards' quarters. They seemed to be looking at the snow, and we heard one call out "Just look at how high this awful stuff has piled up! What are we going to do? We can't get through it in these skirts." The Emperor heard them and laughed. "Listen to that," he said, "it's just that it created such a bother for them that they are raising a fuss. I feel I've been jolted awake from a splendid dream of snow." And I was remembering these things, completely caught up in their contemplation when the boy tugged at me with an uncomprehending stare: "Ask that workman for that thing he's got. Hurry up and go on out there! Go on before he goes away and ask him for it. Ask him, hurry!" I felt I had been roused from all my dreams of beauty. Answering his questions distracted me for awhile, but when I said "I'd like to retire," the others muttered among themselves "Isn't she awful! Why leave now, without even seeing anything of the performance?" (NKBZ 18, 442–44).

As if she would replay the old paradigms of her intermittent intimacy with Horikawa, the narrating voice embeds this reminiscence in a narrative frame that is a latticework of interruptions and broken illusions. The reverie itself intrudes abruptly into her account of Toba's delight in the carpenters; it moves on to dilate upon an episode of unequivocal intimacy that had been brought to a precipitous close long ago by the threatened intrusion of others (serving women approaching from the guards' quarters, commenting loudly upon the snow, which they found, for their part, to be *ana, yuyushi*, "just awful"). Finally, even the memory of her interrupted intimacy is broken, just as Horikawa's delight in the snow had been, by the intrusive cries of people around her as she sits musing on the past (Toba asking her to fetch one of the workman's tools, the remarks of the other court women who find her retiring behavior to be, as the snow was to the other women long ago, "just awful," again, *ana, yuyushi*).

It appears, then, that both the prose and the poetry of *Sanuki no suke nikki* attempt to transcribe the experience of memory itself—its obsessive repetitions and returns, the vertigo of involuntary recollection—implicitly as well as explicitly, at the level of style and narrative sequence. It marshals and elaborates for this purpose a number of sophisticated techniques borrowed from other Heian works. The fascination with memory inscribed in this *nikki* is also, I would argue, deeply involved with a desire that the reader be called upon to remember. Volume 2 is full of vivid descriptions of particular scenes. But its art lies not simply in the inventory of detailed images that memory brings to light. It also lies in the way the narrative reenacts the movements and repetitions of its narrator-heroine's memory as she wanders the same rooms of her former life at court. In such a text, remembrance is more than a means of turning up a clutch of striking anecdotes. It also becomes both the subject and the goal of the text. If we understand texts as constituting all that remains of their "authors," then this feature of the memoir, coupled with the obscure scandal of its author's shamanistic claims in later years, inscribes Sanuki as a far more complex figure than many of her modern readers may have imagined.

BIBLIOGRAPHY

Translation

The Emperor Horikawa Diary by Fujiwara no Nagako. Jennifer Brewster, trans. Honolulu: University Press of Hawaii, 1977.

Critical Works

Keene, Donald. ''The Sanuki no Suke Diary.'' In *Travelers of a Hundred Ages*. New
    York: Henry Holt, 1989.
Sarra, Edith. ''Fujiwara Nagako and *Sanuki no suke nikki:* The Writer as Medium.'' In
    ''The Art of Remembrance, the Poetics of Destiny: Self-Writings by Three
    Women of Heian Japan.'' Ph.D. diss., Harvard University, 1988.

Edith Lorraine SARRA

SEI Shōnagon (fl. 10th c.), essayist, poet. Real name: undetermined.

Life: The Pillow Book (Makura no sōshi) by Sei Shōnagon is a veritable
sourcebook of court life in the Heian period (784–1185), especially during the
last decades of the 10th century. Its author recorded the world around her in
vivid detail and did not hesitate to state clearly her own opinions and tastes.
Unfortunately she remains silent about the particulars of her life that interest
modern biographers, such as when and where she was born, if and to whom
she was married or if she had any children, or even what her real name was.
The ''Sei'' of her sobriquet is the Chinese-derived pronunciation of the first
element, ''Kiyo,'' of her family name, Kiyowara. The sobriquets of Heian
women were often derived from the titles or positions held by their fathers or
husbands, but this does not seem to be the case with Sei, and the origin of the
use of ''Shōnagon'' remains a mystery.

The Kiyowara family traces its line back to Emperor Temmu (630–86). Sei's
great-grandfather Fukayabu (fl. ca. 905–30) was a poet of note whose verses
appear in the imperial anthologies such as the *Kokinshū* (Collection of Ancient
and Modern Times, 905) and the *Gosenshū* (Later Collection, 951). Sei Shōnagon's father, Motosuke (908–90), was a scholar and poet, one of the five compilers of the *Gosenshū* who were collectively known as the ''Five Poets of the
Pear-Jar Room.'' Motosuke was also a lower-ranking bureaucrat who served as
governor of Higo province. The exact birth date of his daughter, later known as
Sei Shōnagon, was not recorded, but scholarly opinions center on 965.

This date has been inferred from what is known about the men in Sei's life.
In *The Pillow Book* she refers to Tachibana no Norimitsu (b. 965) as her ''elder
brother,'' a term often used in this period to mean ''husband,'' and some scholars conjecture that Sei was the mother of his son Norinaga (982–1034). But Sei
describes Norimitsu as somewhat of a boor, incapable of appreciating poetic
allusions, and he seems an unlikely husband for a woman who would have
considered such a failing a major handicap. If they had been intimate at all, it
was most likely before Sei entered court service. They parted on bad terms in
993, according to Sei.

Another man often mentioned in her work is Fujiwara no Tadanobu (967–
1035), and it seems likely that they were lovers. He was a man with a reputation
as a poet as well as being a high government official. Fujiwara no Sanetaka (d.
998) is also believed by some scholars to have been an intimate of Sei Shōnagon.

Sei began *The Pillow Book* during her years at court in the service of Empress

Teishi (also pronounced "Sadako"; 976–1000), consort of Emperor Ichijō (980–1011; r. 986–1011). The date of Sei's entry into court service is not known but is conjectured to be sometime between 990 and 993. Sei does not write why or how she came to Teishi's court. She does give a memorable description of her first impressions as a flustered and easily embarrassed fledgling among the sophisticated aristocrats she had until then admired only from afar. Totally tongue-tied at the thought of even being glimpsed through her blinds by the empress's brother Korechika (975–1010), Sei expresses an uncharacteristic lack of confidence in her choice of career.

But in fact Sei seems temperamentally best-suited for life at court and soon conquered her initial fears. The visit of Korechika mentioned previously occasioned an incident that seems to bode ill for Sei's relationship with Empress Teishi. The empress asked Sei if she was fond of her, and as Sei was asserting that she was, someone sneezed in the next room. Sneezing apparently implied in Heian times that the last person to speak had not told the truth. The empress did, however, believe Sei and showed her such favor that the envy of some of the other ladies was aroused.

This same section describes the events of 994 related to a ceremony dedicating a set of Buddhist sutras at the Shakuzen Temple, which had been founded by Teishi's father, Fujiwara no Michitaka (953–95) at the height of his power and political influence. As chancellor and de facto ruler, Michitaka had married his daughter Teishi to Emperor Ichijō in his early teens, as part of the "marriage politics" that would become the hallmark of Fujiwara power manipulation. After Michitaka died in 993, his younger brother Michinaga (966–1027), whose daughter Shōshi (988–1074) was a secondary consort to Ichijō, managed to have her name empress as well, and to have her son succeed to the throne. Teishi's brother Korechika was also maneuvered out of power through the machinations of his uncle Michinaga. Korechika was exiled from the capital in 996, but *The Pillow Book* is silent on the subject. Sei does mention that some of Teishi's ladies-in-waiting were whispering that Sei was partial to Michinaga after Michitaka's death. But Teishi does not seem to have questioned Sei's loyalties, and Sei remained in the empress's coterie until the latter's death. *The Pillow Book* ends before Teishi's death in childbirth in 1000, and there is no record of Sei extant after that date.

One tradition has it that after retiring from court service, Sei married Fujiwara no Muneyo (fl. ca. 995–99) and had a daughter by him called Koma no Myōbu. There are also legends that Sei became a nun and lived to a wretched old age, begging for alms. There is a verse by Sei included in the imperial anthology *Shokusenzaishū* (Collection of One Thousand Years Continued, 1320), with a preface stating that it was sent to her when she was old and living in retirement by someone who came to visit. It is possible that the preface was added later when the legends about Sei's old age were already in circulation. There is also a famous reference to Sei Shōnagon in the diary of the other great prose writer of the era, Murasaki Shikibu, written between 1008 and 1010. Murasaki says of Sei that she was very conceited, especially when it came to her own literary abilities. Murasaki faults Sei as being too clever for her own good and predicts that her future will not turn out well. This entry in Murasaki's diary does not state whether Sei was still alive or at court or, in fact, whether the two actually ever met. They probably did not, since Murasaki was in the service of Empress Shōshi, who displaced Empress Teishi. Murasaki's comments seem to have been on her reading of *The Pillow Book,* and her remarks about Sei and her ilk being bound to come to a bad end owe more to literary rivalry than to historic fact. Similar legends grew up around other famous women of the day such as Ono no Komachi or Izumi Shikibu. Perhaps the legends about Sei were even prompted in part by her own satirical depiction in *The Pillow Book* of the old nun Hitachi no Suke, who came to beg for alms at the palace.

Major Work: Sei Shōnagon shū (Collection of Sei's poetry). This small collection has two textual lines, both of which include the sixteen poems in *The Pillow Book.* Fourteen poems are also found in the imperial anthologies. Sei's best-known verse is the one selected for the 13th-century compilation of "One Hundred Poems by One Hundred Poets" (Hyakunin isshu), which is the basis of a New Year's game still played today. In *The Pillow Book* the verse is presented as part of a poetic exchange between Sei and Fujiwara no Yukinari (971–1037), noted poet and calligrapher. The section describing his visit alludes to a Chinese legend of a barrier keeper who was deceived into opening the gate before dawn by a man imitating the cock's crow. The exchange is just the kind Sei delighted in, allowing for allusions to Chinese literature and an apt and elegant use of Japanese verse. The social context of poetry at the Heian court emphasized the speed and aptness of the poetic repartee rather than its originality or depth. The verses found in Sei's collection tend to be of this type, clever rather than passionate or philosophical.

The Pillow Book records many such incidents, which illustrate the role of poetry in Heian social life. One day a message arrived from the famous critic and poet Fujiwara Kintō (966–1041), giving two lines of verse for which Sei was expected to produce opening lines. Kintō's judgment would count for a great deal in court circles, and Sei was very pleased with his complimentary remarks on her lines. No greater embarrassment could arise than failing to recognize an allusion or being unable to produce a verse. In another section Sei depicts her annoyance at not being able to recall the lines of an old familiar poem to which the empress had alluded in her message. Sei is rescued by a page boy who recites the lines. On another occasion Sei and a group of women from the palace go on an outing to hear the *hototogisu* (cuckoo) singing near the Kamo Shrine but return without any poems about the trip. Any aristocrat with proper breeding and sensitivity would have been moved to write a poem on such an occasion. When the empress requests Sei's composition, the latter protests that she is always being singled out to compose poems, though she cannot even keep proper count of the syllables and feels she is disgracing her poetic ancestors with her feeble efforts. Sei is perhaps displaying some false modesty here, but she is probably being honest about her poetic talents. She was not a great poet in her verse. Her poetic impulse is manifested best in her prose work.

Translated Works: The Pillow Book of Sei Shōnagon (Makura no sōshi). The concluding section in several extant versions of *The Pillow Book* describes how one day the empress's brother Korechika brought a packet of old notebooks to her quarters. Sei immediately requested them to make a "pillow" to use for recording stories, poems, and all sorts of trivia and events. This section is traceable to the year 994, although its authenticity has been questioned by some scholars. The passage is of interest because of the use of the term *pillow* to refer to this type of journal, and it seems likely that many more such "pillow books" existed but failed to survive. Murasaki Shikibu in her diary also mentions the gift of some paper for copying her tale. The supply of good writing paper was limited and would be a valuable and highly prized gift. Sei claims that she wrote her jottings solely for her own amusement, never intending them to be read by others. A preceding passage describes how her notebook was accidentally discovered and made off with by a gentleman caller, resulting in its circulation at court. The extant versions of *The Pillow Book* fall into two main lines: those in which the sections are in "random" (*zassanteki*) sequence, and those in which sections are arranged by groupings of topics (*bunruiteki*). None of the manuscripts predate the 13th century. Datable but not set in chronological sequence in the modern editions are accounts of court events or anecdotes about life at the palace. Mixed in among these sections is a second type, listing names of places and natural phenomena as well as categories such as "Charming Things" or "Bad Things." Scholars speculate that these lists may have been the first sections Sei wrote. She may have been inspired by Chinese models. There is a Tang dynasty collection of lists by the poet Li Shang-yin (813–58), but it may not have reached Japan until after *The Pillow Book* was already finished. Some of Sei's lists are similar one- or two-line listings of categories such as "Unreliable Things" or "Things That Belong in a House." Many of her lists are, however, embellished with anecdotal materials that make them lively and memorable. Even terser listings amply display Sei's keen wit and ability to focus on the essential. Among "Things That Seem Better at Night Than in the Daytime" are items such as the luster of dark red, glossed silk or an ugly person with an agreeable disposition.

Perhaps after her manuscript was discovered, Sei expanded her journal to include the lengthier sections of events, personal reflections, traditional stories, and some of the fictional imaginary scenes. In these entries Sei gives a vivid glimpse not only of the lives of the 10th-century aristocracy but also of herself as a high-spirited and tireless observer and recorder of everything and everyone around her. *The Pillow Book* is like the beam of a lighthouse, briefly illuminating whatever crossed its path. To modern readers the world of the Heian court may seem quite limited, but to Sei it held unlimited possibilities for her writings. She obviously enjoyed life in Teishi's service and admired the empress and the imperial family unconditionally. The descriptions of the emperor and empress during poetry exchanges or musical recitals or the great festivals at the palace reveal Sei's pleasure at being part of their elegant court. Vignettes of court life stand out, such as the outing to hear the cuckoo or another about the snow mountain that was built in the empress's garden and the lively wagering that ensued over the length of time the mountain would last. Sei lost the wager with the empress but only because the empress had the remains of the snow mountain removed the night before the day on which Sei would have won. In retaliation, Sei refused to compose a poem as requested by the empress.

In her dealings with competitors other than the empress, especially male ones, Sei is not so lenient. One courtier, Fujiwara no Nobutsune, took credit for a witty remark that Sei made and then went on to boast of his prowess as a poet. But when an attempt is made to test his boast, Nobutsune made an excuse and escaped. One day after this incident, Sei happened to see a document with Nobutsune's calligraphy. She found to her satisfaction that it was quite atrocious. Sei wrote a comment to that effect on the margin and sent it along to the imperial apartments, to the amusement of all but Nobutsune. Sei recognized the absurd in human behavior and pointed it out, often with quite devastating effectiveness. She was also able to laugh at herself, as when the empress, in reference to a visitor who came to see Sei one rainy night, sent her a line of poetry with a drawing of a large umbrella. Or in another famous passage, Sei berated herself for writing that a preacher should be good-looking so as to hold our full attention during his sermon. One of the words most often found in the original Japanese text of *The Pillow Book* is *okashi,* meaning "amusing." To call someone or something amusing was the highest praise, while being boring or dull was the worst offense.

Another term that summarizes Heian court standards was *miyabi* (courtliness, elegance). This elegance and refinement pervaded all aspects of aristocratic life, including the conduct of a love affair. Under "Hateful Things" Sei relates an incident about a lover leaving at dawn after a tryst. Before departing he bustled about in the darkness, searching for his fan and papers. Having found them after many complaints and bumping into furniture, he finally made his exit, noisily adjusting his robes and fanning himself. "Hateful" is an understatement for this kind of boorish behavior, according to Sei—hateful because the lover failed to observe the rules of taste and refinement. Sei describes the proper way of taking leave and notes that her attachment to a man depended largely on the elegance of his leavetaking. Equally important is the letter he was expected to send the morning after their night together. The woman will judge not only its contents but the quality of the paper and calligraphy, the incense on the paper, the blossom spray attached to the letter, and the like. One elegant bachelor dispatched his letter and then began his morning recitation of the Buddhist sutras, but as soon as the messenger arrived with the lady's reply, the man transferred his attention from his sutras with seemingly sinful haste. Most of the people Sei ridiculed became her targets because they lacked the proper sense of refinement.

Minamoto no Masahiro was one such person. His way of speaking and some of the quaint terms he used were a constant source of her amusement. On one occasion he was discovered stealthily eating a dish of beans when he thought no one would see him. On another he was seen dragging a lamp behind him after his foot got stuck on the oily lamp cloth. In his clumsiness and incongruous behavior, Masahiro was the opposite of the ideal courtier. Some of the situations that seemed humorous to Sei may not seem so now, such as the story of the man who received a mocking poem instead of the donation he was expecting for his house lost in a fire. But Sei could take for granted the understanding reception of her work by her peers since they belonged to the same social milieu and held the same attitudes. For them her comic observations of manners and behavior were a source of shared delight.

Most of her personal observations convey her sense of wonder and her vivacious character. Many of her most endearing remarks are found in her comments on children. Sei delights in watching the way a baby crawls along and, spotting some object, picks it up with his small fingers to show to an adult. Sei says that babies and provincial governors should be plump. If either is too thin, we suspect them of being mean-spirited and cross. Sei can capture in a quick sketch a scene or a character, such as the passage in which she describes the wonderful scent of sagebrush as it wafts up to the riders in a carriage after a branch has been crushed under the carriage wheels. Her ability to describe with precision and aptness is particularly notable in her observations of nature. The opening section of *The Pillow Book* is justly famous as a model of lyrical conciseness in describing the beauties of a spring dawn, summer nights, autumn evenings, and early mornings in winter. Her brief apotheosis of the four seasons is exactly right. The sights and sounds, even the tactile beauty of a cold morning, are captured with typical aptness and terseness that set the poetic standards for later writers. Sei can reproduce the texture and atmosphere of a scene and fix it by the precision of a similie, as in the image of the water scattering in showers of crystal under the oxen's feet in bright moonlight. The lapidary quality of her prose is conveyed in a series of deft details such as the image of dew dripping from a chrysanthemum onto tatters of spider webs on which raindrops hung like a string of white pearls. Passages such as these prompted Arthur Waley in his translation of *The Pillow Book* to cite Sei as the greatest poet of her age.

Sei Shōnagon was one of a group of extraordinary women writers who lived during the Heian period, many of whom kept journals in one form or another. The Japanese literary term for these journals is *nikki,* or ''diary.'' While some of the works, such as *Kagerō nikki* (The Gossamer Diary) of Michitsuna's Mother, resemble a diary format in the use of factual narrative (for the years 954–74, in this case), the term *nikki* also included fictional narratives such as the *Tosa nikki* (Tosa Diary, 935), written by the poet Ki no Tsurayuki (868–945) in the guise of a woman. *The Pillow Book* has both these elements. It contains narrative passages relating incidents from her personal life as well as some fictional scenes, which serve as important historic documentation on court costume and etiquette. For some sections such as the sutra dedication at Sha-kuzen Temple, Sei must have taken notes with the intention of writing them up later.

In the over 160 listings, transformed into lyrical passages of exceptional beauty, *The Pillow Book* differs from all other extant *nikki*. The original se-quential arrangement of sections will probably never be known, but most schol-ars believe it was the "mixed, random" format rather than an arrangement by subject groupings. A more unstructured format would seem eminently suited to Sei's quick mind and wide-ranging curiosity. She would have delighted in the juxtaposition of dissimilar and unexpected things. Her personality and style were not likely to produce an extended narrative fiction such as *The Tale of Genji*. The journal format allowed for the crisp and spontaneous style that became the hallmark of Sei's writing. This characteristic was singled out by scholars begin-ning in the 18th century, who coined the term *zuihitsu* (essay; lit., "following the writing brush") for *The Pillow Book,* distinguishing it as the first such work. The miscellaneous essay format of *zuihitsu* writing has proved to be a lasting genre, characteristic of Japanese literature. It has been flourishing ever since Sei's day, boasting outstanding examples from the *Tsurezuregusa* (Essays in Idleness) of Yoshida Kenkō (1282–1350), down to contemporary authors such as Mukoda Kuniko (1929–81) and Enchi Fumiko (1905–86). The personal tone, the informality of structure, the brevity of the individual units, the poetic sub-jects, and the lyrical quality of language make *The Pillow Book* a work of lasting appeal, influencing centuries of Japanese writers and readers. Above all, the intelligence, enthusiasm, observant eye, and sharp wit of Sei Shōnagon shine through the veils of time and translation.

BIBLIOGRAPHY

Translations

Morris, Ivan, tr. *The Pillow Book of Sei Shōnagon.* New York: Columbia University Press, 1967, 2 vols. There is also an abridged edition, Penguin Books, 1970.
Waley, Arthur, tr. *The Pillow Book of Sei Shōnagon.* New York: Grove Press, 1960. Selections from the work, with commentary by the translator. A good, brief in-troduction to the work.

Critical Works

Morris, Ivan. *The World of the Shining Prince.* Baltimore: Penguin Books, 1969. Back-ground material on the Heian court.
Morris, Mark. "Sei Shōnagon's Poetic Catalogues." *Harvard Journal of Asiatic Studies* 40.1 (June 1980).

Felice FISCHER

SETOUCHI Harumi (1922–), novelist, biographer, esssayist. Buddhist name: Setouchi Jakuchō.

Life: Setouchi Harumi was born on May 15, 1922, second daughter in a well-to-do merchant family dealing in Shinto-Buddhist altar furnishings in the city of Tokushima on the island of Shikoku. While she was still a student majoring in Japanese literature at Tokyo Women's College, her parents arranged for her to marry. A few days after the wedding, her husband, Sakai Tei, went to China, eventually to become assistant professor at Beijing University. Harumi, upon early graduation from college, joined him about eight months later in October 1943.

She returned to Japan in August 1946, one year after Japan's defeat in World War II, with her husband and a two-year-old daughter. Within a year and a half, however, she left her family in Tokyo to live alone in Kyoto. This escapade was triggered by her infatuation with a former student of her husband's, but it was in essence the declaration of her spiritual independence. She was divorced in 1951. The fact that Setouchi was born toward the end of the Taisho era (1912–25), when Japan's military jingoism was yet in its cradle and social trends were predominantly liberal and egalitarian, seems conducive to her later development into a writer. Also it is symbolic of the age that she married in such a manner as the society mandated and that she broke out of the marriage in the iconoclastic postwar period to seek a life of her own choosing.

Harumi had been an extremely precocious girl: she started reading the poems and stories by such romantic writers as Kitahara Hakushū (1885–1942) and Shimazaki Tōson (1872–1943) when she was a third grader; her favorite books in her high school days were *The Tale of Genji* by Murasaki Shikibu (fl. ca. 1000), the realistic fiction by Ihara Saikaku (1642–93), and the plays by Chikamatsu Monzaemon (1653–1724). Such immersion in native classics at an early age and her college education in Japanese literature form the basis for the world of Setouchi's fiction. After her divorce, she struggled on her own for about ten years, taking up various jobs and writing for children's and teenage girls' magazines. She finally established herself as a professional writer by winning the Tamura Toshiko Prize in 1961 and the Women Writers' Prize in 1963.

As a writer, Setouchi is astonishingly prolific; by 1987, she had written more than thirty full-length novels, some fifty short stories, and numerous essays. Her representative works have been included in several major collections of contemporary Japanese literature, and at least two sets of her collected works have been published. She took a month-long trip to Russia in 1961 to attend the Russo-Japanese Women's Conference and to China in 1973 as a member of the Sino-Japanese Cultural Exchange Association. Privately, she traveled in Europe for about a month each in 1964 and in 1965.

To the consternation of the Japanese reading public, Setouchi suddenly took Buddhist vows in November 1973. Now living in Kyoto as a Tendai-sect nun, she continues to be just as productive in fiction and critical essay writing as ever.

Career: In 1955, four years after her move to Tokyo, she published two stories in a *dōjin zasshi* (literary coterie magazine) called *Bungakusha* (Writers) presided over by the leading novelist, Niwa Fumio (1904–). After it folded,

Setouchi joined a group of would-be writers to launch another magazine called Z. In 1957, she was awarded the Shinchō Dōjin Zasshi Prize for her story in Z, "Joshidaisei, Kyoku-airei" (Quai Ling, A Coed). By virtue of this award, her next story in the same year, "Kashin" (The Pistil, 1957), was carried in *Shinchō*, a prestigious literary magazine. "The Pistil" is a story of a woman who reduces herself from respectable housewife to high-class prostitute because of her obsession with sex. Setouchi's repeated use of an anatomical term for the female reproductive organ instead of the traditional euphemism led some critics to accuse her of resorting to sensationalism for quick recognition. Consequently for about five years, she found it difficult to get her works published in major literary magazines.

Tamura Toshiko (1961), for which she won the Tamura Toshiko Prize, newly established in honor of the writer who happened to be her subject, was the first of at least eight biographies of women from the Meiji period (1868–1912) that she was to write in the next quarter of a century. In 1963, she received the Women Writers' Prize for her short story "Natsu no owari" (The End of the Summer), the best-known of a series of works closely modeled on her own life. This award at last established Setouchi's reputation as a writer of serious literature. She finished her autobiography entitled *Izuko yori* (Whence) in 1968 and translated a classical autobiography, *Towazugatari* (The Confessions of Lady Nijō, ca. 1313–24), into modern Japanese in 1973.

Parallel to these serious works, Setouchi started in 1962 to churn out lighter and more entertaining novels, mostly serialized in weekly magazines. Even though it is not easy to draw a clear line between serious and lighter works, Setouchi wrote at least seventeen potboilers by 1987.

The most ubiquitous and pervasive theme in Setouchi's serious fiction is her utmost emphasis on emotional sincerity. This can, of course, be very easily traced back to the characteristics of the literature of the Heian period (794–1185), when it was socially acceptable to behave according to one's emotions, provided they were sincere. Now, in modern Japan, such total surrender to one's emotions tends to be considered a weakness, just as in any other modernized society in the world. Yet with a poignant insight, Setouchi explores the depths of female emotions, including, typically, the heroine's longing for men in her sexual loneliness, inevitably resulting in promiscuity. The characters in Setouchi's stories are almost always promiscuous married men, their mistresses, and the mistresses' young lovers. The characters in the Heian literature are also promiscuous, but their behaviors cannot be considered antisocial by the moral standard of the polygamous society of their day. Similarly, Setouchi's heroines, even when they act against the modern middle-class social norms, are not ignoring morality. In fact, not only are they keenly aware of the fact that they are breaking social norms, but they measure the degree of their own emotional sincerity by that fact. The lovers in Setouchi's stories, however, are never triumphant. They sheepishly attempt to sever their relationship so that they need not feel so guilty, but always in vain.

Setouchi defines the novel as "an expression of an inner voice of the inexplicable creature called 'human being,' or of the pains he feels as he vomits, being unable to contain any longer the dark, frustrating part of his life" (*Setouchi Harumi no sekai* [The World of Setouchi Harumi], ed. Kokubo Minoru et al., Sōrinsha, 1980, 88). If this theory of literature as catharsis is applied to Setouchi's own stories, the dark, frustrating part of life is the heroine's strong attachment to a married man and pity toward her young lover. The heroine suffers from an interminable dilemma within herself: should she conform to the social norms and give up her illicit love or continue to be sincere to herself?

What distinguishes Setouchi's novels is her skillful use of the image of death, often juxtaposed to painful love, right in the mainstream of traditional Japanese literature. In the world of Setouchi's love stories, however, the role of the death image, presented in various forms, is not quite so clear. It can be interpreted as something to make the vitality of love stand out or to foreshadow the fate of illicit love. This ambiguity, interestingly enough, gives a modernistic outlook to Setouchi's stories, which otherwise might be seen as nothing but tear-jerking sentimentalism. Another feature prominent in her narrative is a genre developed in Japan after the Meiji Restoration of 1868, *shishōsetsu* (the "I-novel"). The "I-novel" is usually a confessional narrative in the first-person viewpoint directly based on the author's actual experience. The literary merit of a work is often evaluated by the extent to which the actions described in the work violate the social norm, by the degree of sincerity with which the author-narrator takes such actions, and, most important, by the degree of honesty with which he or she confesses. It often seems as if the authors presuppose that the reader knows them as persons in real life. In short, actuality counts more than fictionality. One characteristic of the "I-novel" genre that does not apply to Setouchi Harumi in her serious works is the technique to render narrative consciousness. She uses the third-person viewpoint, though it is far from being omniscient, strictly concentrating on the heroine, never to stray—her viewpoint is so deliberately limited that the effect is nearly the same as first-person narration.

Setouchi's autobiographical works fall roughly into two groups of linked stories: what can be called the Tomoko series and the Makiko series, by the heroines' names. In general, the plot centers around a financially independent but emotionally insecure woman. Dealing with mundane incidents involving the heroine and her two lovers, one story takes up where another has ended, in the setting taken from the author's life as described in her autobiography, *Whence*.

Major Works: Hōyō (Embrace, 1973). Death plays a much more central role in this novel, set in a high-rise apartment in Tokyo, where three different relationships are acted out. The narrative viewpoint is omniscient this time, and the image that connects these three pairs of man and woman is the mirror in the bedroom of a woman named Masako on the eighth floor. At the outset of the novel, Masako sees in her mirror a female figure climbing out of a window in another wing. It is never clear, though, whether it is an actual suicide or simply Masako's hallucination. Another example of suspected suicide is a pair of shoes found in a descending elevator in the middle of the night. All these eerie suggestions of suicide, together with the sound of sirens from ambulances and police cars, lead to the final suicide of Masako, who jumps off the top of the building.

Masako kills herself at the age of fifty-four, probably in order to break her relationship with a married man called Hatano. Masako and Hatano are the only characters that are named. The other two pairs, including a woman who has not been intimate with her husband for years because he has a girlfriend somewhere and a woman who is annoyed by constant telephone calls from her husband's neurotic sister, are all referred to by the generic term *onna* (woman) or *otoko* (man). It is very difficult, therefore, to determine what is happening to whom. This difficulty is exacerbated by the hallucinatory and surrealistic presentation of the characters and incidents. Three pairs of lovers represent a relationship between man and woman with all its emotional, psychological ramifications. The novel treats female psyche extensively and seems to suggest that the only way out is death.

Setouchi started writing this novel for a monthly literary magazine *Bungakukai* (Literary World) in January and finished it in December 1973. In November of the same year, she had taken the tonsure at Chūson-ji, an ancient temple in the Tendai sect, which has its headquarters on Mt. Hiei in Kyoto.

Hiei (Mt. Hiei, 1979) features a woman called Toshiko, who can be identified easily with the author herself, depicting Toshiko's colorful life as a popular writer with many lovers. Since these lovers are again referred to by the word *otoko,* it is hard to tell one from another, but clearly there are more than one during the course of her life. The heroine, tired of the emotional and sexual turmoil resulting from involvement with these men, gradually starts to seek and finally attains a Buddhistic salvation. The narrative viewpoint is third person, focused on the heroine Shun'ei (Toshiko's Buddhist name). The plot consists of incidents in the heroine's current life juxtaposed to her reminiscences of past events, including the shadow of death surfacing out of her days in a Tokyo high-rise apartment. One recurrent image is that of a suicide who jumps off a building.

Both novels, *Mt. Hiei* and *Embrace,* treat female emotionality, but *Embrace* ends in the heroine's death, and *Mt. Hiei* in the heroine's salvation. One prime example in classical literature of a woman who is plagued by emotional entanglement with two men and seeks Buddhist salvation is, of course, Ukifune in *The Tale of Genji.* As Ukifune throws herself into the Uji River, she conjures up the image of Prince Niou, who seduced her on the Islet of Oranges: ''It had been wrong to permit even the smallest flutter of affection for Niou. The memory of her ultimate disgrace brought on by his attentions, revolted her. What idiocy, to have been moved by his pledge and that Islet of Oranges and the pretty poem it had inspired!'' (Murasaki Shikibu, *The Tale of Genji,* tr. Edward Seidensticker, New York: Alfred Knopf, 1979, 1065). This outright denial of emotionality by Ukifune in the final chapters is considered to signal that the romantic age, the age of *The Tale of Genji,* was over. There is no outright denial of emotionality in Setouchi's novels, but her heroines seem to try to gradually overcome their emotional intensity.

For example, Shun'ei in *Mt. Hiei* takes every precaution, for she is a celebrated writer, against the possible leak to the media of the news that she is going to take the tonsure at Hiraizumi. Nevertheless, she discusses the matter with her lover. On the day of her tonsure ceremony, he waits at the gate of the temple and stays with her at the inn that same night. Although this man's image remains in the heroine's mind even during the sixty-day-long training for new clergy at Mt. Hiei, the author's concern about the heroine's emotions is much less intense and her preoccupation with the male less concentrated than in her earlier works. Instead, Setouchi's perspective is now much broader, including all kinds of emotional relationships in addition to those between man and woman.

The type of salvation achieved by Shun'ei is different from the one sought by Ukifune, who is much younger and less experienced. Setouchi has her heroine comment about Ukifune's way of seeking Nirvana: "Ukifune's flat refusal even to open the letters sent by Kaoru after she has taken the tonsure is a manifestation of how far she is from attaining Nirvana" (Setouchi Harumi, *Shinchō Gendai Bungaku* 59 [1980]: 281). Forced into a difficult situation by the handsome prince Niou, Ukifune seeks desperately for a shelter, denying all the emotions associated with her love adventure on the Islet of Oranges. This fits the thematic scheme of *The Tale of Genji.* In Setouchi's novel, on the other hand, the heroine is responsible for all her encounters with, attachment to, and longing for, men as well as the guilt that all the relationships cause her. This is the price that a liberated, independent woman has to pay. Both Shun'ei and Ukifune, nonetheless, reach beyound the shadow of death, saved by faith. *Mt. Hiei* is Setouchi's most significant work in that it shows the process through which total submission to emotions takes on the power of spirituality.

Kanoko ryōran (Kanoko in Bloom, 1963). Setouchi became seriously interested in Buddhism while she was writing this fictionalized biography of novelist Okamoto Kanoko (1889–1939). It covers not only the life of Kanoko extensively but also the life of her husband, Okamoto Ippei (1886–1948), a famous political cartoonist, as well as the age and society in which they lived. Kanoko had already been a celebrated essayist-lecturer on Buddhism and an accomplished *waka* (thirty-one-syllable classical verse) poet, before she became known as a novelist. Setouchi's later devotion to Buddhism was nurtured by studying Kanoko's works advocating Buddhist ideas. It seems ironic that Kanoko led a colorful life far removed from Buddhist enlightenment and that Setouchi, influenced by Kanoko, actually became a nun.

Compared with the first biography, *Tamura Toshiko* (1959), *Kanoko in Bloom* is much more novelistic. The author's voice is not heard very much until two-thirds into the telling. Setouchi's technique of synthesizing factual materials into a narrative is superb, and detailed description of social and historical background makes the characters come alive. The most unusual element in Kanoko's life is her relationship to her husband, Ippei. After several years of playing the tyrant in their marriage, Ippei suddenly became a most dedicated servant to his wife and ardent supporter of her literary activities. He not only tolerated the presence of Kanoko's lover in his household but also encouraged her to write novels. Setouchi explores the conflicting forces of art and love driving a woman writer that can bloom magnificently despite untold emotional costs to her.

Other Meiji women whose biographies Setouchi wrote include socialist Itō Noe (1895–1923) in *Bi wa ranchō ni ari* (Beauty Is in Atonality, 1965), soprano Miura Tamaki (1884–1946) in *Ochō fujin* (Madame Butterfly, 1968), anarchist Kanno Suga (1881–1911) in *Tōi koe* (A Faraway Voice, 1968), women's historian Takamure Itsue (1894–1964) in *Jitsu getsu futari* (The Sun and the Moon in a Pair, 1975), and feminist Hiratsuka Raichō (1886–1971) in *Seitō* (Bluestocking, 1984). The most conspicuous element threading through the lives of these women is, of course, their revolutionary stand on women's social status and the freedom of their minds. It was not just these abstract notions and ideals for which they lived, but it was their implementation in real life that had the greatest impact on society and the course of history. More specifically, most of these women were first awakened to their individualistic philosophies upon rejecting a marriage that their parents imposed on them. Often the scandalous way of life that most of them chose to lead after they liberated themselves from the familial control and their antisocial behaviors, such as falling in love with married men, were, in fact, their political statements. For example, Hiratsuka Raichō, who was educated at Japan Women's College and started the epoch-making feminist journal called *Seitō* (Bluestocking) in 1911, experimented with ''free'' love and attempted double suicide with novelist Morita Sohei (1881–1949). Later she had a lesbian love affair and wrote in her journal about her experience. Kanno Suga once lived with leftist Arahata Kanson (1887–1981) and later with anarchist Kōtoku Shūsui (1871–1911), eventually to involve him in the high treason incident of 1910, an alleged plot to assassinate the Meiji emperor. Suga was executed along with Kōtoku and ten other men.

In the Meiji period, activists in the feminist movement were often influenced by Marxist and anarchist philosophies, which implied sexual equality in principle along with class equality. Even though feminists were usually either punished by repressive laws or severely castigated by moralistic society, they refused to conform and used writing as their weapon for fighting tradition. Obviously there are many factors in life that Setouchi Harumi shared with these early feminists: breaking up family ties, having affairs with married men, and flaunting one's own experience through writing. Setouchi seems to have a great affinity and sympathy for these women and what they believed in, probably identifying herself with the heroines of the biographies she writes. Though still much concerned with feminine emotions, Setouchi is interested in reforming society, and her works in this genre direct the reader's attention toward the future of mankind. This is a refreshing change from her short stories, which almost always deal with the inescapable shadows of the past. Setouchi's social contributions are greater in her biographies than in her serious "I-novels." These biographies are all greatly detailed, well researched, and well written, even though sometimes digressive and lengthy. Setouchi gives life to these legendary women and resurrects an important segment of Japanese history.

Translated Works: "The End of Summer" (1963), the prizewinning short story. In the opening scene, the heroine, Tomoko, returns to Japan by boat from her month-long trip to Russia. Her concern centers around her married lover, Shingo, who divides his time equally between his wife and Tomoko. Assailed by a fleeting fantasy that Shingo had died while she was in Russia, Tomoko realizes how many tears she has to shed even for the imaginary death of Shingo. Overwhelmed by her guilt toward the man's wife, she makes a hasty decision that she must break up with Shingo, if he is still alive. He is still alive, and she, of course, cannot carry out her decision. Pressed by another lover of hers, she finally goes to Shingo's home, hoping that a meeting with his wife will make it easier for her to sever the relationship. But his wife is out shopping, and Tomoko is prevented from acting on her decision. In this story, the image of death gives the heroine a chance, first, to reconfirm her strong feelings for the man and, second, to reevaluate what she is doing from a moral point of view.

"Lingering Affection" (Miren, 1963) is also a story from the Tomoko series, chronologically following right behind "The End of the Summer." "Lingering Affection" seems to suggest that it is totally impossible to break up a relationship between a man and a woman, even when it is no longer passionate and merely coasting on nothing but force of habit. Tomoko tries to straighten out her life and start all over again, for she would keep feeling quilty toward the man's wife otherwise. It is not clear, however, whether her lingering affection for the man or her fear of the sadness inevitably to accompany a separation makes it so hard for her to break up with Shingo.

Toward the end of the story, Setouchi utilizes the image of death as she almost always does in her works of serious literature. Here she refers to the archetype of a historical suicide. In 1903, an eighteen-year-old student named Fujimura Misao killed himself by throwing himself into the scenic Kegon Falls at Nikko, after he had carved his philosophical suicide note on the trunk of a tree. The incident not only induced many adolescents to copy the act but also left a long-lasting impact on the mind of Japanese intellectuals, for the incident was considered the first example of suicide for philosophical reasons. When Tomoko takes a trip to the inner mountains of Nikko, therefore, the notion of death immediately comes to the mind of the Japanese reader, as it does to the mind of Tomoko. The death depicted in "Lingering Affection" involves the suicide of two lovers, a young girl and an older man who had appeared to Tomoko in the hotel dining room to be having an illicit love affair.

"Pheasant" (Kiji, 1963) belongs to the Makiko series. This story abounds in allusions to classical Japanese literature. First of all, the title represents a metaphor for love between parent and child used by the haiku master Matsuo Basho (1644–94). The heroine, Makiko, has left behind a daughter, who has the phonetically same name as the daughter of the man she is meeting. This device of substitution of someone lost recurs in *The Tale of Genji*. The last page of the story is reminiscent of the scene from *Koshoku ichidai onna* (The Life of an Amorous Woman, 1682) by Ihara Saikaku, where a woman of the street sees a vision of the babies to whom she should have given birth. The same page also evokes an equally eerie atmosphere related to death in the famous double-suicide journey in *Sonezaki shinjū* (The Love Suicide at Sonezaki) by Chikamatsu Monzaemon. ''The gray tombstones at Asashino'' refer to the Nembutsu-ji Temple, where aborted, or stillborn, babies are buried.

In her serious fiction, Setouchi employs the ''I-novel'' format, in which the basic setting is directly taken from the author's life, and plot scheme is virtually nonexistent. The recurrent theme is female sexuality, longing, and guilt. Of all the images, only those pertaining to death are not directly traceable to the author's own life. Setouchi's biographies of the Meiji women enjoy a wider range of readers than her fiction, since they pack much more impact on social, historical, and cultural levels. Undoubtedly, Setouchi Harumi is a first-rate biographer. In all her writing, her style is straightforward and lucid and, therefore, is suitable as reading material for advanced foreign students of the Japanese language.

BIBLIOGRAPHY

Translations

The End of Summer. Tr. Janine Beichman. Tokyo: Kodansha International, 1989.
''Lingering Affection.'' Tr. Mona Nagai and Akiko Willing. In *This Kind of Woman: Ten Stories by Japanese Women Writers, 1960–1976*, ed. Yukiko Tanaka and Elizabeth Hanson. Stanford, CA: Stanford University Press, 1982.
''Pheasant.'' Tr. Robert Huey. In *The Mother of Dreams and Other Short Stories: Portrayals of Women in Modern Japanese Fiction*, ed. Makoto Ueda. Tokyo: Kodansha International, 1986.

                                                          Sanroku YOSHIDA

SHIBAKI Yoshiko (1914–91), novelist, essayist, art critic. Real name: Ōshima Yoshiko (Mrs. Ōshima Kiyoshi), née Shibaki Yoshiko.

Life: Shibaki Yoshiko was born in Tokyo's mercantile milieu, her father a well-to-do kimono merchant with a samurai lineage and her mother from the family of a wealthy cosmetics wholesaler. Around six years of age, Shibaki was initiated into the tea ceremony, composition of *tanka* (thirty-one-syllable Japanese poetry), Japanese painting, and chanting of *gidayu* (lines from Kabuki plays) accompanied by the three-stringed *samisen.* Even in her elementary school days, she was often taken to the Kabuki theater, an extracurricular education that would contribute to developing her sense of estheticism. Except for a brief period after the great earthquake of 1923, which devastated the entire "lower-town" of Tokyo, Shibaki lived in the Asakusa district from 1920 until her father's death in 1932.

She attended the Tokyo First Women's Higher School and Surugadai Jogakuin (Women's Academy, housed in the Tokyo Young Women's Christian Association [YWCA] complex) for 1932–33, where she studied English and acquired the skill of typing. Soon after the severe trauma from the loss of her beloved father, she began contributing her writings to magazines for young women. For a few years, she attended the YWCA lectures given by well-known literary figures such as critic Kobayashi Hideo (1902–88), novelist Funahashi Seiichi (1902–76), and novelist-critic Abe Tomoji (1903–1973). For several years Shibaki worked at Mitsubishi Economic Research Institute in the Marunouchi business district. In 1941, she married a young economist, Ōshima Kiyoshi, later a vice president of Tsukuba University. Among the many awards Shibaki Yoshiko went on to earn in her career, the most recent included the Women Writers' Award (1986) and the Governor of Tokyo Award for Outstanding Citizens (1987).

Career: By 1933, Shibaki was contributing to the readers' column of such magazines as *Reijokai* (Ladies World) and *Wakakusa* (Young Grass), more or less in a reaction to her father's untimely demise the previous year. By 1936 her work caught the attention of Hayashi Fumiko (1803–1951), then one of the most sought-after women novelists, who served as a judge for the readers' column in *Reijokai*. Shibaki often won the Hayashi Fumiko Prize for her contributions to the magazine. Hayashi was criticized by some for not promoting the younger generation of female writers, but she did encourage Shibaki, who in turn became her ardent admirer and avidly read Hayashi's works.

Shibaki Yoshiko came of age in the literary world when advocates of the military expansionism succeeded in entering the mainstream of Japanese politics and suppressed any artistic activities that did not conform to their national policies. This made it necessary for any potential writers to confine their area of interest to cooperation with the war effort, to children's literature, or to such traditional subjects as reminiscences of things past. Shibaki chose the latter two as her primary concern. After she was selected for membership in the Bungei Shuto (Literary Capital) group in 1938, she eventually culminated her interest in children and nostalgia into *Futabaki* (Records of Young Shoots, 1940). Shabaki's interest at this stage was principally focused on her childhood and the ambience of her hometown, Asakusa, with much affinity to the world described by Higuchi Ichiyo (1872–96) in her most acclaimed novella, *Takekurabe* (Growing Up, 1895–96). Shibaki identifies her heroine, Kimiko, with *Takekurabe*'s Midori, through delineation of a young girl in puberty and her disheartening discovery of the pains of growing up.

Shibaki's work experience at an economic research institute and her subsequent marriage to an economist certainly helped in widening her perspective as a writer. In 1941, she published in *Bungei Shuto* the first of her major stories, "Seika no Ichi" (Greengrocers Market), based on extensive research on the peculiar tradition of *seri* (bidding) at the distribution center. It won her the Akutagawa Prize. In the fall of 1942, she was introduced to novelist Tsuboi Sakae (1900–67), a significant event in her career, for from this time on, Shibaki received subtle influence and continuous support from Tsuboi, who was able to move the reader with her own poignant stories charged with empathic under-standing of human nature.

In 1943, the government, now deeply committed to expansionism, sponsored a trip for Shibaki and two other women writers to survey the Japanese settle-ments in Manchuria. After yielding a work in the vein of government propa-ganda, *Manshū Kaitakuchi no Josei* (Women in the Newly Opened Settlements in Manchuria, 1943), this travel experience apparently incubated in Shibaki until it bore fruit in *Asu o Shirazu* (Not Knowing Tomorrow, 1968) a quarter-century later. Through the war years, in the meantime, Shibaki kept writing, even though hopes of getting her kind of works published were slim. After Japan's surrender in 1945, the literary world became that much richer for the steady flow of finished works from Shibaki's portfolio. *Nagareru hi* (Drifting Days, 1946), "Onna Sannin" (Three Women, 1946), "Kibō" (Hope, 1946), "Onna hitori" (Woman Alone, 1946) and "Kano hi" (Those Days 1946) all appeared in 1946.

Shibaki Yoshiko in her mid-career benefited from the postwar publishing boom, which provided a ready stage for her short stories, such as "Tamashii no moeru made" (Till This Heart Burns Out, 1947), "Otto to tsuma" (Husband and Wife, 1947), "Kōfuku" (Happiness, 1948), "Sugishi hi no kage" (Reflec-tion of the Bygone Days, 1950), "Umi no nai machi" (The Town with No Seascape, 1951), "Yūkaisha" (Seducer, 1951), "Ikyō" (Strange Land, 1953), and "Akuen no Kizuna" (Unblessed Bond of Destiny, 1953).

The two-year period 1954–1955 marked a discernible change in Shibaki's thematic interest, as she turned out a series of stories on the women of "pleasure quarters," partly prompted by the intense media coverage of the new breed of women, street girls or *yoru no onna* (night women), a euphemism for prostitutes. This shift in Shibaki's focus was mostly inspired by the women's movement, organized in 1953 by such activists as Kamichika Ichiko (1888–1981) and Hir-abayashi Taiko (1905–72), which ultimately led to passage of the Anti-Prostitution Act of 1958. A studious and observant reporter, Shibaki is said to have carried out her frequent field trips to the pleasure districts with her husband as escort. The effort proved a worthy venture, yielding the acclaimed "Susaki series" including "Susaki Paradaisu" (Susaki the Paradise, 1954), "Kanraku no machi" (City of Pleasure, 1955), "Susaki no onna" (Women of Susaki, 1955), and "Chō ni narumade" (To Become a Butterfly, 1955).

In 1956, Shibaki found an opportunity to tour Southeast Asia with three other women novelists, Sono Ayako (b. 1931), Miyake Tsuyako, and Yuki Shigeko (1902–69). The month-long trip yielded nothing but a few travel impressions, yet the experience of being away from home in a foreign land for the first time after the war with fellow writers provided Shibaki with much-needed incentive and chance to reflect upon her art. Beginning in 1958, Shibaki started writing longer, more lyrical pieces in which her heroines played her own alter ego. It was a giant step for Shibaki, who until then had mostly kept her distance from her protagonists with what critics called the Saikaku-esque (meaning, cold) detachment. Unlike some women writers of a new generation, such as Sono Ayako and Ariyoshi Sawako (1931–84), who burst upon the literary scene with a dazzling light of instant acclaim, Shibaki was to take slow but steady footsteps in growing into a mature writer. Many of her short stories demonstrate her skills in developing well-thought-out, solid, yet intricate plots, often compared with those of Akutagawa Ryunosuke (1892–1927), one of the rare accomplishments among Japanese writers, most of whom are given to a loosely strung, episodic plot.

Shibaki Yoshiko established herself as a leading novelist with *Yuba* (Soya Extract, 1960), the first of her biographical trilogy, which earned the prestigious Women Writers' Award in 1961. She followed it up with *Sumidagawa* (The River Sumida, 1961) and *Marunouchi Hachigokan* (Marunouchi Building Number Eight, 1962). Her trip to the West had broadened her horizon and made her aware more than ever of her identity as a woman who grew up in traditional Japan. With renewed enthusiasm she pursued performing arts such as Japanese music and dance, flower arrangement, and the tea ceremony. A direct outcome of her new awareness is *Yoru no Tsuru* (Cranes in the Night, 1964), a three-part novel.

The next stage, her inquiry into the lives of real-life artists, began when she encountered a fine piece of celadon (porcelain) produced by a contemporary potter, whose extraordinary dedication to his art is delineated in ''Seiji Kinuta'' (Celadon Vase, 1971). Similar inspirations gave birth to *Sensai* (The Art of Dye and Print, 1957), *Hinoyama nite tobu tori* (Phoenix in Flight over a Volcano, 1973–74) and its sister volume, *Habataku tori* (Soaring Bird, 1978–79), as well as *Kai murasaki gensō* (Illusory Phoenician Purple, 1980–81). Shibaki also serialized essays on traditional handicrafts, eventually to be collected into *Nihon no dentōbi o tazunete* (In Search of Traditional Beauty of Japan, 1972) and *Bi o motomete* (Seeking Art, The Infinite, 1974). Shibaki created what may be called her ultimate image of a woman who makes art as the sole purpose of life in *Yukimai* (Snow Dance, 1984–87).

Major Works: ''Seika no ichi'' (Greengrocers Market, 1941), short story. The theme of Shibaki's first major work is a woman's will to live a purposeful life despite adverse circumstances. The setting is the wholesale produce market at Tsukiji in Tokyo between the great earthquake of 1923 and the outbreak of World War II in 1941. The focus is on a small wholesaler's life portrayed through Yae, who has given up her high school education and prospect of marriage to devote herself to keeping her family together over ten years. By a single-minded loyalty to her family, Yae survives in what is considered a man's world and manages to bring them a period of respite.

As proved in her later works as well, Shibaki's interest in ''Greengrocers Market'' centers around the traditional systems and institutions that require staunch supporters to survive. Yae's struggle proves successful in safeguarding the institution of family, yet it is less effective in business, promising only temporary financial rewards. The time-honored middleman system is about to be absorbed into the government-controlled semipublic Central Wholesale Market. With admirable dexterity, Shibaki weaves her knowledge of economic history into this fiction. She casts a typical second-generation merchant as Yae's father, who is a spendthrift, the archetypal Edokko harking back to the feudal Edo (Tokyo's former name), or knight errant of a sort on a personal mission to enjoy life. In contrast, Yae's brothers are more serious businessmen, the embodiment of the burgeoning new Tokyoites, the cream of the middle class to be.

"Yuba" (Soya Extract, 1960), short story. One of Shibaki's recurring characters, a woman with an urge to live life to the fullest, make the most of any situation, and find fulfillment, is further developed in this story. Here the heroine is a samurai's daguter, Fuki, who was adopted at the age of fourteen by a merchant family and later was given to their son in marriage. Her adoptive family is a manufacturer of *yuba* (soya extract dried and pressed for cooking), a by-product of *tofu* (bean curd), which had once enjoyed considerable popularity thanks partly to the patronage of the Tokugawa shoguns. But Fuki finds that it is quickly losing its appeal to the tastes of an "enlightened" age, being replaced by imported protein food such as beef. Through Fuki, Shibaki depicts a disappearing breed among the Japanese of the day, dedicated to the hereditary cause and a situation in which they have been conditioned to live. Fuki is happy if she can "work hard in the day, and if the day is filled with cheerful liveliness," for work provides a sense of fulfillment despite the unfaithfulness of her wastrel of a husband. Born largely of the author's loving memories and respect for her own maternal grandmother, "Yuba" and its critical acclaim gave Shibaki confidence to continue writing about what she felt most familiar at the time.

Sumidagawa (The River Sumida, 1961), novella. Here the story moves ahead to the next two generations, featuring Fuki's daughter and her family. Her father-in-law, the owner-artist of a venerable dye and print shop, is a close likeness of the author's own father: he loves to make himself appear larger than life by living beyond his means, not a rare disposition among the men of the times. His eldest daughter, Kyōko, is modeled on the author herself in high school years. The setting is in Asakusa in the aftermath of the Manchurian incident of 1931. The main focus is on Kyōko's agony and ambivalent reactions to her father's flamboyant life-style, which includes an extramarital relationship with a proprietress of an inn. Critical of her father's conduct, Kyōko is still unable to tell her mother what she has witnessed, out of concern for her feelings. Before she can decide which side she should take, the father falls ill and then dies of a stroke. Against the backdrop of the world of small merchant families lining the banks of the River Sumida, Shibaki unfolds an excellent tableau of Asakusa, the heart of Tokyo's *shitamachi,* or the "lower-town." The minor characters, such as Kyōko's cousin, who falls victim to police surveillance of liberals, and

BIBLIOGRAPHY

Translations

"Behind Every Great Man." *Journal of Japanese Trade & Industry,* No. 3 (1985): 53.
"Blowing a Muted Horn." *Journal of Japanese Trade & Industry,* No. 6 (1985): 53.
"Food for Thought." *Journal of Japanese Trade & Industry,* No. 5 (1985): 85.
"Four Keys to Success." *Journal of Japanese Trade & Industry,* No. 2 (1985): 49.
"Fuji." Tr. Phyllis Birnbaum. In *Rabbit, Crabs, Etc.,* ed. Phyllis Birnbaum, Honolulu: University of Hawaii Press, 1983, 17–23.
"Letter to the Editor." *Journal of Japanese Trade & Industry,* No. 4 (1985): 53.
"Love." Tr. Edward Putzar. *Japan Quarterly.* In press.
Watcher from the Shore (Kami no yogoreta te). Tr. Edward Putzar. Tokyo: New York: Kodansha International, 1990.

Fumiko Y. YAMAMOTO

SUGAWARA Takasue's Daughter (ca. 1008–after 1059), memoirist. Real name: undetermined.

Life and Career: The writer known as Takasue's Daughter was born into the Sugawara clan, one of the three families of the mid- to late-Heian period (900–1185), from which professors of literature (*monjō hakase*) were regularly chosen to fill posts at the university. Her father, Sugawara Takasue (ca. 973–?), was a fifth-generation descendant of Sugawara Michizane (845–903), the great poet, court minister, Confucian scholar, and political exile, who by mid-10th century had been enshrined at Kitano as a heavenly deity (Tenjin) and was beginning to be worshiped as a patron of various bookish arts such as Chinese and Japanese poetry, Confucian learning, and calligraphy. Michizane had been on the losing side in a power struggle that culminated eventually in the monopoly of political power by the northern branch of the Fujiwara family. After his exile, the Sugawara clan declined in political power, though they retained their connection with the university and its bureaucracy. Takasue's father, grandfather, and great-grandfather had each occupied the posts of head of the university (*daigaku no kami*) and professor of literature (*monjō hakase*). Takasue's own eldest son and heir, Sadayoshi (d. 1064?), regained these positions during his sister's lifetime. But Takasue himself began and ended his career in less-distinguished positions as assistant governor of Kazusa and, finally, assistant governor of Hitachi. Though still reasonably well connected, the family witnessed a further eclipse of fortunes in Takasue's day. Certainly the frustrated ambitions and the social stigma, as well as the romance of provinciality associated with literary daughters of the provincial governor class, figure largely in his daughter's memoir. Her mother was also a member of this class, thought to be a daughter of Fujiwara Tomoyasu (d. 977) and thus a younger sister of one of the great female memoirists of the 10th century: Fujiwara Michitsuna's Mother (ca. 936–95), the author of *Kagerō nikki* (The Gossamer Memoir, after 974). Early commentators traditionally underscored the family link between the two memoirists, but the her uncles and aunts, complete the picture of Japanese society in the early 1930s, with irreconcilable conflicts of values between the young and the old.

Yoru no tsuru (Cranes in the Night, 1964), novel. This three-part work, which won the Shōsetsu Shinchō Prize, features three generations of women at a geisha house, Tsurunoya (Cranes' Nest), located in the lower-town and run by a former geisha named Seki. The first two parts, entitled *Shinobazu no Ike* (The Shinobazu Pond) and *Yoru no tsuru*, present the lives of Seki and her adopted daughter, Kotsuru (Little Crane), as viewed through the eyes of Kotsuru's daughter, Chikako. Covering the time span from a few years prior to the outbreak of World War II through the early part of the war years, the narrative effectively conveys the values, ethos, joys, and sorrows of the women in the entertainment profession. The novel's third part, *Otokozaka* (Male Hill), follows Chikako's development into a grown woman against the unsettled background of the postwar period.

Kotsuru is highly regarded in the pleasure district in Shitaya as a master of traditional dance and music. Though extremely popular among her clients, she is deeply attached to Asakage, a painter with whom she lives in his studio. Her daughter by a former patron, Chikako, lives at the geisha house with Seki, who showers her with love and attention. Although Chikako attends private school, she knows little of the life outside the entertainment world. Yet, she is determined not to become a geisha (lit., a "person of talent"), even as she demonstrates considerable talent in the performing arts. Partly, her determination derives from criticism of her mother, who suffers from hysterical fits of jealousy every time Asakage goes out with another woman. Chikako takes a job as editor of a theatrical magazine. After the war, Kotsuru's half-brother Koji, whom she had supported through his days as art student, returns from the service overseas, and Chikako falls in love with him, knowing that no relationship is possible. The author's view of "woman in love" is illustrated by the treatment of Chikako as well as by the case of Asako in another story, "Not Knowing Tomorrow" (1968).

Katsushika no onna (Woman of Katsushika, 1965), novel. With a strong inclination to be a painter herself, Shibaki turned her attention next to the making and unmaking of women artists. This story is about an aspiring painter, Maki, and her teacher, Takikawa. The setting is in the late Meiji period, around 1910. It was the time when the women's movement started to reach into the upper stratum of urban society, advocating improvement of women's status. Yet, for Maki, who grew up in a highly conservative merchant family in the lower-town of Tokyo, such a notion of liberation seems remote. Taking inspiration from a painting by a famous real-life artist entitled *Woman of Katsushika*, Shibaki creates a young heroine who is devoted to the art of traditional Japanese painting. The scenes are mostly related to the river system connecting the lower-town of Tokyo and its eastern suburb, in the rustic beauty of which lies Katsushika, a town noted for iris blossoms. Maki's tragedy is presented via recollections of her daughter Hisako, now a grown woman and aspiring artist.

Using a masterpiece by Takikawa in Hisako's memory as a visual trigger is a fine technique with an effect of softening the unsparing intensity of the narrative. Maki's fate bears a subtle reference to the popular folk legend associated with Katsushika, about a woman who killed herself to resolve a love triangle. Although in Shibaki's story the painter's relationship with the heroine is platonic, her devotion and admiration for him go beyond that between teacher and disciple. When her husband, a scholar from Katsushika, threatens to file a suit against Takikawa for adultery, Maki finds that the only way left for her to protect his professional reputation is to commit suicide. The teacher's grief, coupled with his affection and sympathy toward this talented but hapless student, crystallizes into a great painting depicting a young woman with pensive eyes standing by a river in twilight. Shibaki's exploration of the heroine's heart and mind constitutes a study of Japanese female psychology, which still retains the notion of dying as the ultimate solution to a no-exit situation. At the close of the story, Maki's daughter declares her intention to become an artist and explains that her decision has nothing to do with her mother's life or her death. The author identifies this stance with a small number of independent women of her own generation who actually learned to live to the full by pursuing what they loved most.

Asu o shirazu (Not Knowing Tomorrow, 1968), novel. When the Japanese empire collapsed in the summer of 1945, so did the dreams of approximately three hundred thousand Japanese farmers who thought they had found a home in Manchuria. Based on the author's travel observations, this saga of Japanese refugees fleeing from the Soviet forces that invaded Manchuria three days after the bombing of Hiroshima describes the horror of evacuation. The central figure is Ogata, a college-educated idealist who had believed in the Japanese settlement program and proved himself a tireless associate director of one settlement. The heroine, Asako, is a young widow whose husband was killed in the early stage of the war. Now in 1943, she is visiting her aunt, working as a journalist in Manchuria. Being a family man, Ogata shows little interest in anything but helping settlers by organizing community affairs and even midwifing at animal births. Asako is attracted to him for his devotion to work, one of the ideal traits in Shibaki's male characters. Before long the two somehow begin seeing each other clandestinely, and even after Asako gets a job in Harbin, Ogata visits her there periodically.

The first part of the novel focuses on historical events in Manchuria, and the second on the protagonists' experience in postwar Japan. The first part shows an evocative use of the setting, reminiscent of Hayashi Fumiko's novel *Drifting Clouds* (1949–51), in which the exotic landscape of Indochina plays a memorable role. Of note among the supporting cast is Asako's aunt, Wakako, who, in fact, sees a mirror image of herself in young Asako with the same indomitable spirit of independence. Wakako maintains an ambivalent attitude toward her niece's love affair, which may well reflect the moral confusion of adult society at the time. Written after the waves of nationwide protest against the 1960 renewal of the United States-Japan Defense Treaty, this saga concludes with a scene of the huge demonstration on the Ginza, in which Asako, now the wife of a businessman and the mother of a child, catches sight of Ogata, aged yet still working for causes in which he believes. In the author's view, the participants in the demonstration have the potential to change the course of history, while the watchers remain mere bystanders. Asako feels her life is vacuous, suggesting Shibaki's prediction about Japanese women's situation in the years to come.

Tsukijigawa (Tsukiji Canal, 1967), novella. Shibaki's interest in the theme of conflict between the old and new generations in the mid-1960s is illustrated in her portrayal of a young woman transforming from a junior college art student into a successful handicraft designer. In her early twenties and only recently recovered from a respiratory illness, the heroine is working in the Ginza at her relative's shop, selling women's accessories. The physical setting is Shibaki's ever-cherished location, by the Tsukiji Canal, which once drew water from the River Sumida to serve not only for transportation through the city of Edo but also to supply water for landscaping at feudal lords' mansions. The canal has been turned into one of the superhighways running beneath the bridge that remain intact. The author uses this bridge as a symbol that connects the past with the future: it carries the childhood memories of the two principal characters, Mariko and her older brother Yasushi, who grew up together sharing the joys and sorrows of life after the loss of their parents.

Both characterization and physical setting reflect the rapidly changing society of postwar Japan. Now old and decaying, their house is the legacy of their grandmother Sei, who had been the virtual head of the household ever since she branched out of the proud Morimura family, the owner of the Ginza shop. Her husband was a docile former employee of the shop selected to marry her and take on her family name. Supporting characters such as Mariko's cousin, the would-be successor to the Morimura shop, named Nobuo, and a leather goods craftsman, Toroku, and his wife represent the new and old breeds of Japanese people who are basically minding their own business, yet not entirely without kind concern over the young Mariko's growth as a woman. Interspersed with the scenes in the Morimura store, at Toroku's workshop, and at the aggressively managed business of Nobuo's is a sensitive home drama in which a young woman and her brother wean themselves from each other to outgrow their childhood unhappiness. The ultimate fate of the venerable house, which had been adamantly sustained by the grandmother, is suggested by the decision of the elder sister to move into a newly fashionable condominium. Shibaki's love for the old Tsukiji district is well demonstrated in this story as well as in her shorter stories such as ''Onna no hashi'' (Woman's Bridge, 1973) and ''Kōrin no kushi'' (Korin's Comb, 1979), depicting the lives of a new type of geisha and their values.

Pari no mon (The Gate of Paris, 1966), novel. A direct fruit of Shibaki's three-month European tour in 1963 was this work, the main theme of which is a young woman's struggle to become independent as a graphic designer working and studying in Paris. Reflecting the taste as well as the problems of postwar Japanese society, the story reveals the conflicts of values. The heroine Natsuko is a postwar version of Maki in *Woman of Katsushika,* in trying to make her husband understand that their marriage has been a mistake from the beginning and that it is best for both of them to dissolve it. Her husband, who stands for the old values, is incapable of perceiving his wife's need for time to be alone and for self-respect arising from a sense of achievement.

Translated Works: Yukimai (Snow Dance, 1984–87), novel. This story summarizes Shibaki's long-held conviction that a woman should be able to live her own life pursuing her art. It is the message presented in her earlier works, such as *Omokage* (Image, 1969), ''Art of Dyeing and Print'' (1975), and ''Soaring Bird'' (1978–79). Yet, until the completion of *Yukimai,* no heroine of Shibaki's has been able to develop her talents fully while at the same time living a full life as a woman. Here at last, Shibaki places Yuki (Snow) in a different situation. The man whom she encounters is an accomplished painter, while she is a dancer so talented that her teacher hopes to make her the heir to the ultimate teachings of her art, the Yamakage school of *jiuta* dancing, a genre of Japanese traditional dance that can compare with the Petipa school for Russian ballet. Yuki has been adopted by a successful geisha restaurateur, Hanamaki En, to be her successor. Although Yuki's position requires her to behave like one, she is not a full-fledged geisha as yet, and her dancing alongside other geisha is voluntary. By placing her heroine on the sidelines, Shibaki depicts the world of geisha from inside and outside as it went on changing a great deal after World War II.

An impressionistic social chronicle and a poignant romance, the narrative covers the thirty-year period beginning in 1955. The author describes with scholarly accuracy what exactly has changed and what has remained unchanged in the old, peculiarly Japanese institution of geisha and its function in modern society. The pleasure quarters that appears in this story is first-rate. The customers who make use of their services to fill social needs epitomize the Japanese business ethos, work hard and play hard. Most important, whenever possible, they want to identify themselves with the values of the now-vanished aristocracy, hence the emphasis on patronizing traditional arts. Fittingly, the author utilizes some of the well-known references to the 11th-century fiction *The Tale of Genji* by Lady Murasaki, such as a spray of blossoms sent as a means of communication between the heroine and her lover or the detached soul of a living person and spirits of the dead floating in the mortuary. In the epilogue, Yuki performs a dance as a tribute to her deceased lover, an artist who had lived in accord with his conscience.

Literary critics may decry the melodramatic extravagance of unusual events turning up one after another in this novel. But *Yukimai* should be viewed as a synthesis of Shibaki's earlier works, some of which were influenced by 19th-century Western women writers, especially the Brontë sisters. The novel is rich in poetic quality, dramatic tension, in-depth knowledge of the field of arts, and Japanese manners and customs.

BIBLIOGRAPHY

Translations

"Dance Entitled Snow." Tr. Michiko Aoki. *Proceedings of the Tenth International Symposium on Asian Studies.* Hong Kong: Asian Research Service, 1988.

"Dance Entitled Snow, Part II." Tr. Michiko Aoki. "The Role of Geisha in Japanese Society," in Shibaki Yoshiko's *Dance Entitled Snow* (Yukimai), *Proceedings of the Eleventh International Symposium on Asian Studies.* Hong Kong: Asian Research Service, 1989.

Critical Works

Aoki, Michiko. "Three Generations of Tokyoites as Depicted in Shibaki Yoshiko's Stories: *Seika no Ichi, Yuba, Sumidagawa,* and *Marunouchi Hachigokan.*" *Proceedings of the Ninth International Symposium on Asian Studies.* Hong Kong: Asian Research Service, 1987.

Michiko AOKI

SHIRAISHI Kazuko (1931–), poet, essayist, translator.

Life: Shiraishi was born the eldest daughter of a Japanese businessman residing in Vancouver, Canada. According to her biographical essay, *Shiraishi Kazuko no arubamu, 1, 2,* and *3* ((Shiraishi Kazuko's Album, 1, 2, 3), she was remarkably healthy in her infancy, and at school in Canada, she was extremely popular among her peers in spite of World War II. Returning to Japan at age seven, she spent her teens in Tokyo, attending theaters, bars, and various gatherings of artists. She joined a group called VOU, an heir to the avant-garde art movement of the prewar days. Under the tutelage of Kitazono Katsue (1902–78), a surrealist poet, Shiraishi published her poems in magazines. Her first collection, *Tamago no furu machi* (A Town Where Eggs Fall), came out in 1951, when she was a freshman at Waseda University.

Japan was still under the Allied occupation at the time, and in Tokyo's bars and theaters there were always Americans who played jazz expertly. Shiraishi patronized a bar called Kiyo in particular, a mecca for such musicians and the vanguards of modern act. There, she wrote poems to music, and the music inspired her creative urge. She polished these poems on her way home from Kiyo, riding the night trains that circled Tokyo. However, she was not able to published them until 1960, due to her marriage, childbearing, and other events that occurred in the last half of the 1950s. Her husband was Shinoda Masahirr (b. 1931), whom Shiraishi had met at Waseda as a classmate. He went on to become a controversial movie director pursuing the theme of eroticism coupled with death, perhaps best-known in the West for his 1972 film based on Chikamatsu Monzaemon's (1653–1724) puppet play *Shinjū ten no Amijima* (Love

Suicide at Amijima, or Double Suicide), starring Iwashita Shima, who was to be his second wife.

By the time her *Tora no yūgi* (Games Tigers Play, 1960) came out, Shiraishi had been divorced and found herself in financial straits. She began "violently composing poems like an animal in heat" (Album 2). Many of her friends then were American. She "loved" John Coltrane and wrote poems in praise of him. When she met a bass player named Gene Taylor, she "lost" a ring she was wearing (Album 3). In Japan, memories of the war and the country's defeat were still being felt, and her free life-style was frowned upon by many. Her life was unsettled, but she felt "something new" had formed within her and was "trying to gush out of her throat" (Album 3).

Career: Shiraishi proved herself a prolific poet. Unlike most Japanese poets, she can serve as a modern troubadour, both in Japan and abroad. She unifies not only words with music but words with action, even words with social trends and fads. She has been known to wear a colorful kimono loosely like a geisha, sit cross-legged on a stool on stage, and read her poems. She helped make the contemporary audience aware that poetry was not only for reading but also for hearing and seeing and that it could provide an exhilarating experience.

The third collection, *Mō sore ijō osoku yatte kitewa ikenai* (You Should Not Come Any Later Than That), appeared in 1963, and her fourth, *Konban wa aremoyō* (It Seems to Be Stormy Tonight), in 1965. Her fifth book, *Seinaru inja no kisetsu* (Seasons of Sacred Lust, 1970; tr., 1975) consists of seven chapters spanning three cycles of the four seasons in which men and women meet, love, and part. It won the coveted award in poetry, the Mr. H's Prize. Next came *Kōyōsuru honoo no 15-nin no kyōdai Nihon retto ni kyūsoku sureba* (As the Fifteen Brothers like Tree Leaves Aflame Rest on the Japanese Archipelago, 1975). Then *Issō no kanū, mirai e modoru* (A Single Canoe Returns to the Future, 1978) received a Mugen Prize, the second major poetry award for Shiraishi. She followed up the productive 1970s with *Sunazoku* (The Sand Tribe, 1982), a collection on the theme of sand, to win the Rekitei Prize. On its heels came such works as *Dōbutsu shishū* (Collection of Animal Poems, 1985), *Fūkei ga utau* (Scenery Sings, 1986), and *Moeru meisō* (Burning Meditation, 1986).

Shiraishi rejects the kind of poetry that adheres to established stylistic and thematic patterns, comparing it with "cooking that is only seasoned with soy sauce" (Mieru [Visible]). She dislikes the poems that are lean in word and singular in imagery and encourages "stealing" the ideas, methods, and feelings from other arts such as music, painting, drama, and film. "A mixed marriage with other arts," she claims, is the most effective way to enrich poetry (Mieru). What she "stole from jazz" was the blues—the mood, the variable tempo, and the harmonic, melodic, and rhythmic elements reminiscent of distant Africa that filtered through in the hoarse voice and the direct, earthy lyrics from America's deep South. For Shiraishi, modern jazz was "like thunderstorms" that supplied her heart with nourishing moisture (Album 3). Nina Simone, Keith Silber, Miles Davis, and Cecil Taylor soaked her heart with inexplicable melancholy and

sensation that melted her in rapture. Critic Kagiya Yukinobu says in his intro-
duction on Shiraishi in *A Play of Mirrors* (1986) that only Dylan Thomas,
Kenneth Rexroth, Allen Ginsberg, Henry Miller, Nishiwaki Junzaburo, and
Yoshioka Minoru share the resonance of Shiraishi's spirit.

As she could not abide by short, structured poems (Mieru), she began to write
longer poems. Some of her contemporaries in Japan were also doing the same,
as though they had concluded that they had exhausted every linguistic and thematic possibility of short poetic forms. Some consciously tried to create epics,
which Japanese poetic traditions had lacked. Shiraishi's long poems born of the
"mixed marriage" with jazz, nevertheless, are not like the tightly structured
Greek epic; rather, they are more like John Coltrane's improvised saxophone
passages.

Shiraishi compares herself with a long-distance runner: once she starts to run
(write), by the time the road conditions, atmospheric pressure, and her heartbeat
undergo changes, she has already covered some distance, accumulating several
hundred lines of verse (Chōhenshi ni idomu [Challenging the Long Verse
Form]). Yet, Shiraishi's long poems leave no discernible tracks on which the
poet ran. Instead, they exhibit her breathing and pauses, so to speak, as well as
improvisational repetitions in lines, imagery, and rhythm, on their way to inconclusive endings. They may be reflections of the fragmentary vision of life
she has had since her modernist days. The long poem is for her a marathon, by
which she enters a new world, an unexplored field of creation that she evidently
believes to exist beyond time and space.

Shiraishi's poems are generally free from the "wet" autumnal feel typical of
Japanese lyrical tradition. Many contain English sentences; some have English
titles. They are crisp, unsentimental. Critics attribute these characteristics to the
influences of the VOU group, including Kitazono Katsue's cubist visions, their
sense of universal time and space, and their economy of words.

Major Works: Tamago no furu machi (A Town Where Eggs Fall, 1951).
Showing Shiraishi's surrealist visions and techniques, the title poem of this
collection goes:

　　　As I rest on the ridge of green lettuce
　　　Eggs come falling
　　　Cheap   expensive   hard   even soft eggs
　　　Babies too come falling
　　　Even little boys come falling
　　　Rats, heroes, monkeys, and grasshoppers
　　　Fall in town on the churches and playgrounds
　　　I had extended both my arms
　　　But all slipped by me as swiftly as sorrow
　　　And the funny top hats
　　　Made the skyscrapers look dramatic
　　　While eggs fall into the cold blood-vessels of vegetables

What for?
<I don't know   don't know   don't know>
This is an editorial in this small-town paper

The spirit of political revolt, which earlier drove some artists to modernism, is seldom present in Shiraishi's poetry. Devoid of ideological messages or metaphoric embellishments, this is a stoically clean poem.

Tora no yūgi (Games Tigers Play, 1960). Here stylistic stoicism and cleanliness are diminished somewhat, and the poet's weariness in life seems to surface. She is also more concerned with modernist techniques. Poet-critic Takahashi Mutsuo in his ''Kazuko-shi shiron'' (Critique on Ms. Kazuko's poetry) points out a dark shadow, probably a reflection of her unhappy marriage, in this phase of Shiraishi's career. A short piece in this collection called ''Sangatsu'' (March) is structurally fragmentary but modernist and melancholy:

March was
opposite to me   rambling

though within earshot

my voice was eaten by a dog
and on the soundless waves
I am a mere light   gliding

March was
on my shoulder about to fall if I looked back
but   at that moment   I could not see
my eyes fell like that dog   into the dark gorge
and the distant sea
swells like a paved road
washing my shoulder   and recedes

It is possible that the poet passed her March here, and entered the summer of her life.

Konban wa aremoyō (It Seems to Be Stormy Tonight, 1965). This fourth collection contains a poem, ''Dankon'' (Male Root), that made Shiraishi instantly famous. Because of this bold poem and of the rumors regarding her personal life-style, she was tagged *dankon shijin*, or the *dankon* poet. The two characters *dan* (male) and *kon* (root) in combination make a neutral euphemism for penis, with an unmistakable association with *daikon* (big root). Daikon means the long, white, and juicy Japanese turnip, which is perhaps *the* most popular vegetable in the traditional Japanese diet. Its color and shape have made it a familiar metaphor for female legs, since young girls began to wear Western-style skirts that exposed their lower limbs. Shiraishi makes use of the vegetable imagery here but turns it into a male symbol.

Unabashed as she is, Shiraishi does not treat *dankon* merely as a sexual organ.

In her poem it is a universal root of humankind or a god. If anything, she is against contemporary abuses of sex and is critical of traditional moralists as much as of current immoralists. As the poem develops, the male organ transforms into the human will to persist, and the poet wishes to get it for a friend named Sumiko; hence the subtitle, ''Sumiko no tanjobi no tameni 2'' (For Sumiko's Birthday). In excerpt, it goes:

God isn't here   yet he is
so humorous
that he resembles a certain man

Today
he is here   with a gigantic dankon
above my dream's horizon
to join the picnic
when
I regret
that I didn't give Sumiko anything for her birthday
I wish I could transmit
a seed of the dankon   that God brought
to Sumiko   the distant lovely voice
at the other end of the line

Forgive   Sumiko
the dankon grew   day by day
until it stood   in the heart of the cosmos
as stubborn as a broken bus
so that
if you want to see
the beautiful night sky   where stars shine
or another man
who speeds down the highway with a hot woman
you ought to
thrust yourself through the bus's window
and look really hard
Should the dankon
move to the side of the cosmos
you will have a splendid view   But then
Sumiko
you will be imbued
with the loneliness   of the starry night
and the coldness   of the mid-day light
to the core of your body
and everything will become visible   when we
cannot help going mad

Such a dankon has no name   nor character
nor is it dated   so

only when someone carries it
like a portable shrine
it is known
from the atmospheric noise
whose household it belongs to

Also from the noise
the hollow voices of abuse
the premature revolt of the seeds
that are yet to be controlled by God
can be heard   only occasionally

God isn't here   as usual
He is gone   it seems
leaving debts   and the dankon

So it's that dankon   forgotten by God
coming   this way
youthful and gay
full of confidence   It's like
casting the shadow of the experienced grain

Dankon grows all over
infinitely it seems   moving this way
but in fact it is singular   solitary
from whichever horizon you view it
without a face   nor a word
I would like to give you, Sumiko
something like that for your birthday
to completely wrap your existence   when
you will not see   your self
and you may become   the very will of dankon
until you endlessly begin   drifting
softly   I want to embrace it

Kōyō suru honoo no 15-nin no kyōdai nihon retto ni kyūsoku sureba (As the Fifteen Brothers like Tree Leaves Aflame Rest on the Japanese Archipelago, 1975). Here the poems may be considered a parody on the popular Japanese translations of Jules Verne's adventure stories for children. The fifteen men in the title poem, stocky as they are, represent ignorance and other undesirable traits of mankind. The first-person narrator seems to confront them, but they all resemble phantoms floating in an amorphous, shifting world of the past and the present. The Japanese archipelago is something that could be any real or imagined place in the universe. Shiraishi probes the periphery of the realm she envisions. When read aloud by the poet, these poems have incantational effects.

''Chikyū e no chinkonka'' (A Requiem to the Earth, 1978). More banal than liturgic, this poem, referring to jazz, has been relegated to the unpublished poems section of one of her collections:

. . . .
land   still full of green
air   polluted but still sweet
incomplete poem   not yet died
ear of a twenty-year-old sailor going to sea

on it   perches Black Sounds
voice   of the blind
Stevie   sweating   rainbow
to each of these
before they leave the earth
I must salute
and offer them a requiem
the amulet for the anniversary of my death

rising from the coffin
my girlfriend's spirit asks
"Have I been dead? I didn't know."
for such a spirit
I play Mary Wells' record
but for the soul on this shore of the living
I play
EARTH, WIND & FIRE
for the living
death has started
and we make peace   fight   loathe
with death which has started
loving
we move toward the last shore. . . .

Translated Works: Sei naru inja no kisetsu (Seasons of Sacred Lust, 1970).
This award-winning collection of longer verse contains lines indicating that her
"human will to persist" is breached, perhaps by the Buddhist belief that lust is
emptiness and emptiness is lust. Noting that Shiraishi turned to Eastern spirituality, while retaining a Western sensibility, critic Kagiya in *A Play of Mirrors*
claims that she is comparable to Allen Ginsberg. Shiraishi may have realized
that all things eventually turn to nothing, but her thoughts along this line are
hackneyed and thin at times.

Sunazoku (The Sand Tribe, 1982). Translated partially and included in *A Play
of Mirrors,* this is a collection of separately published poems on sand, the object
that can be found in Tokyo just as easily as in Cairo, where Shiraishi visited
on her travel through the Middle East. The first-person narrator explores the
territories of sand tribes, passing through Palm Beach, California, and Egypt.
The narrator meets the sun god Ra, Lawrence of Arabia, and many others from
various times and spaces, all of whom belong to the Sand Tribe. This book is
full of history and legends, Shiraishi's dimension, in which both man and land
are arid.

BIBLIOGRAPHY

Translations

The Burning Heart. New York: Sunbury Press, 1977.

"The House of Madame Juju." In *Contemporary Japanese Literature,* ed. Howard Hibbett. Rutland, VT: Charles E. Tuttle, 1978.

Japanese Poetry Today. New York: Schocken Books, 1972.

"Little Planet." Tr. Allen Ginsberg. *Review of Japanese Culture and Society-Josai University* 4 (December 1991): 79.

Modern Japanese Poetry. Tr. James Kirkup. University of Queensland Press, 1978.

New Writing in Japan. Harmondsworth: Penguin Books, 1972.

A Play of Mirrors. Rochester, MI: Katydid Books, 1986.

The Poetry of Postwar Japan. Iowa City: University of Iowa Press, 1975.

Quadrant (November–December 1970).

Seasons of Sacred Lust: The Selected Poems of Kazuko Shiraishi. New York: New Directions, 1975.

Ten Japanese Poets. Hanover, NH: Granite Publications, 1973.

Three Contemporary Japanese Poets. London: Magazine Editions, 1972.

"Town Under a Rainfall of Eggs" and "Bird," tr. James Kirkup; "The Orient in Me," tr. Ikuko Atsumi and Graeham Wilson. In *Longman Anthology of World Literature by Women: 1875–1975,* ed. Marian Arkin and Barbara Schollar. New York: Longman, 1989.

Critical Works

Lyons, Phyllis. "Shiraishi Kazuko." In *Longman Anthology of World Literature by Women: 1875–1975,* ed. Marian Arkin and Barbara Schollar. New York: Longman, 1989.

James R. MORITA

SONO Ayako (1931–), novelist, essayist, social critic. Real name: Miura Chizuko; (Mrs. Miura Shumon); née Machida Chizuko.

Life: In 1931 Sono Ayako was born in Tokyo to Machida Eijirō, an executive of a rubber manufacturing company, and his wife, Kiwa. Named Chizuko by her parents, Sono was raised as an only child after her elder sister died. Sono received all her education, including college, at the prestigious Seishin Joshigakuin (Sacred Heart School for Girls), where many courses are taught in Western languages by foreign nuns. In 1945 her education was interrupted by the war, and her family was evacuated from Tokyo to Kanazawa, a town on the coast of the Sea of Japan. Sono resumed her education at Seishin the following year. She became a Catholic in 1948, and Catholicism has had a strong impact on her writings.

In 1949 she joined Ra Mancha, a literary coterie that had writer Nakagawa Yoichi (1897–1982) as its central figure and assumed the pen name Sono Ayako. In 1951, when the critic Usui Yoshimi (1905–87) introduced her to another literary group, the Shin Shichō, she met the novelist Miura Shumon (b. 1926). They married in 1953, and she graduated from college in 1954. Their son, Tarō, was born in 1955, and he inspired Sono's fictional work *Tarō monoqatari* (The Story of Tarō), published in two parts in 1972 and 1975.

Career: In 1954, a month after her graduation from college, Sono published the short story "Enrai no kyakutachi" (The Guests from Afar) in the literary journal *Mita Bunqaku.* This well-received story was nominated for the thirty-first Akutagawa Literary Award. Although the prize was given instead to Yoshiyuki Jun'nosuke's "Shūu" (Sudden Rain), the nomination singled out Sono as a competent writer and launched her literary career. The critic Okuno Takeo (1926–) dubbed Sono "the first young woman writer to appear in the literary world (*bundan*) after the war."

In 1955 Sono serialized her autobiographical novel *Reimei* (Daybreak) in the journal *Bungakukai.* Her short story "Tamayura" (Flickering) appeared in the journal *Gunzō* in 1959. Sono ventured abroad in 1960, visiting the United States, the Amazon area, and the Dominican Republic. Her novel *Rio gurande* (The Rio Grande, 1961) was based on her trip to the Dominican Republic.

Sono Ayako suffered from insomnia for many years but began to recover in 1965, the year she published *Satōgashi no kowareru toki* (When a Sugar Cookie Crumbles), a novel centering around an insomniac heroine whose experiences are modeled after those of Marilyn Monroe. In 1966 she traveled to Thailand and visited the road construction site of a Japanese company, eventually drawing upon this experience to write the novel *Mumeihi* (Unnamed Monument, 1969). She produced *Ikenie no shima* (The Sacrificial Island) based on reports she collected in Okinawa during 1967 and 1968 from the survivors of the fatal battle that took place at the end of the war. This documentary was serialized in the weekly magazine *Shūkan Gendai* in 1969. Her collection of essays *Dare no tame ni aisuruka* (For Whom Do We Love?) sold over a million copies in 1970. *Kiritorareta jikan* (Time That Was Cut Out), a fictional work based on her research in Okinawa, appeared a year later.

Sono has traveled extensively. Her 1971 visit to Poland furnished the material used in *Kiseki* (Miracle, 1972), and the trip to the Japan Leprosy Center in India in that same year provided background for her work *Ningen no wana* (Human Trap). Sono's eyesight deteriorated until a cataract operation in 1981 restored her vision. This experience was described in *Okurareta me no kiroku* (The Record of Eyes Which Were Given, 1982). In 1979 one of her most ambitious novels, *Kami no yogoreta te* (The Left Hand of God), was completed. One of her most recent sojourns abroad, crossing the Sahara Desert, yielded an essay-document, *Sabaku: kono kami no tochi* (Desert: This Land of God, 1985).

Sono has served on several public committees. Among them are the United States-Japan Foundation Committee and the Ad Hoc Educational Council Committee of the Japanese Ministry of Education. The awards she has received include the Cross "Pro Eculesia et Pontifice" from the Vatican and the Father Damien Award from the Korea Catholic Leprosy Workers' Association.

Major Works: "Enrai no kyakutachi" (The Guests from Afar, 1954), short story. This work marked Sono's debut as a promising young writer. The story is told from the viewpoint of an eighteen-year-old girl, a spunky and witty interpreter working at a resort occupied by the American armed forces. Her keen observations of foreign "guests" and of those compelled to accommodate them lead her to boldly declare to a soldier: "America has an obligation, a secret obligation. The war wrought havoc upon the Japanese. Therefore, as the victors, you have an obligation to help the Japanese in some way." Many critics and readers alike were shaken by this remark because they knew all too well the feeling of utter impotence that came with the devastating experience of defeat in World War II. The heroine's insight provided relief from the humiliation and pain of being an underdog and from the trauma caused by the onslaught of American culture with its display of wealth. The same theme was dealt with by Kojima Nobuo (1915–) in "The American School" (1954) and by Nosaka Aki-yuki (1930–) in "American Hijiki" (1967), but Sono's characteristic, well-wrought structure, engaging character sketch, uncluttered syntax, lucid and carefully chosen vocabulary, and unsentimental style, is already discernible in "The Guests from Afar." Ever since its publication, Sono has been ranked among the *saijo* (talented women), along with her contemporary Ariyoshi Sa-wako (1931–85).

Reimei (Daybreak, 1955–56), novel. The heroine is also a perceptive young girl but is now endowed with a vulnerable sensitivity. This semiautobiographical work is based on Sono's own betrothal at the age of twelve and subsequent cancellation of that engagement. The novel captures the author's tumultuous relationship with her autocratic father and close alliance with her mother, and it also covers her wartime evacuation to Kanazawa on the coast of the Sea of Japan, along with observations on the impact of the war on people around her. Many of the personalities who seem to grow out of her life experience reappear in different forms in her later works: a sadistic individual who preys on the weak, a helpless victim who tries to survive adversity, a compassionate being who supports and sympathizes with the weak and handicapped, a compulsive individual whose life is strictly regulated by a motto, and effusive persons who smother others with blind and selfish goodwill.

"Tamayura" (Flickering, 1959), short story. Considered one of her early mas-terpieces, this work depicts the enigmatic, amorphous impressions that humans have of one another. Sono portrays five women involved with Yoshioka Kiyo-hiko, a character reminiscent of Prince Genji, the amorous protagonist of the 11th-century romance *The Tale of Genji*. Each woman that Kiyohiko becomes associated with feels that she knows him well, yet his total image is elusive. He leaves for Brazil on an assignment, promising to marry one of them, Zushi Keiko, upon return, but he then disappears without a trace. Learning that she and the other women in Kiyohiko's life each has a different image of Kiyohiko, Keiko feels that all of them, including herself, have merely toyed with their own illusory idols. She shudders at the realization that she could have wasted her time immersed in a fragile, misconceived image of someone, utterly lost in a boundless delusion. Why Kiyohiko avoids committing himself to anyone is left unexplained, and the novel leaves the impression that it is futile to ever attempt to establish secure relationships.

Satōgashi no kowareru toki (When a Sugar Cookie Crumbles, 1965), novel. In 1962, while Sono was in Paris with her husband, she learned of Marilyn Monroe's death and became intrigued by the actress, who reputedly died from an overdose of sleeping pills. Sono was at that time suffering from insomnia and was dependent on sleeping pills. She collected material about Marilyn for the work portraying the life of a young Japanese actress whose experiences parallel those of the American star. Sono portrays the heroine Kyōko as a physically attractive but emotionally insecure woman who constantly needs care and protection. People take advantage of her, and she seems to misuse others, yet the actress secretly cries out in her heart: "I like sincerity. This word touches me more deeply than any other word." Her belief in sincerity, however, is apparently contradicted by her actions: although she is sorry that she hurts others, she cannot apologize to those who suffer from her misconduct. No one suspects that Kyōko remains taciturn because the anguish she feels for causing inconvenience is too painful to express in words. In "Flickering" the hero is presented through a series of impressions that others have of him, but in *When a Sugar Cookie Crumbles,* Sono uses a different technique—she delineates the heroine by untangling her psychological webs. This novel was not as well received as her other works, but the story skillfully discloses the throes of a woman who cannot balance what her physical beauty brings with her inner needs.

Mumeihi (Unnamed Monument, 1969), novel. This novel, one of Sono's most ambitious works, was begun in 1968, when she was in Iowa with her husband, who was attending the writers' workshop at Iowa University, and was completed the following year. The focus is on Mikumo Ryūki, a construction engineer, and two women whose lives are entwined with his. The women present a contrast: Yōko is prim, tense, and fair and reminds Ryūki of snow, while Yoshie seems to him like the open sea—relaxed, friendly, and dark. An orphan living on Miura Peninsula with her aunt, Yoshie proposes to him, confident that he would be happy with her. Ryūki values Yoshie's empathy, but he is also attracted to Yōko, a student at Kanazawa University. Ryūki's interest in Yōko derives partially from his own childhood experience: when Ryūki was eight, his mother was driven out by her husband, because she had slept once with her cousin. Ryūki's father could not forgive his wife for this one misbehavior, and this caused Ryūki to resent his father for banishing his mother from his life. When Ryūki found that Yōko had been rejected by a man she met at an arranged date because she confessed a past affair, he felt as though:

[he] was standing at a crossroads. In front of him sat a "pitiful" girl who was the most intense woman he had ever met, and whose heart was full of scars. This pitifulness was related to the memory of his deceased mother. He felt that Yōko roused neither a sense

of misery nor scorn in him. Yōko represented for him the ultimate proof of womanhood. For him the meeting with Yōko was immensely endearing.

He chooses Yōko, convinced that he is the only one who can accept and love her. Their married life begins at a dam site that is materially deprived but emotionally rich. When their only daughter dies in a heart operation and Yōko becomes so distraught that she undergoes treatment at a mental hospital, their happiness shatters. The couple can still draw comfort from each other. Ryūki, however, is then given a road construction assignment in Thailand.

All the dams and highways he helped to build in Japan were constructed exactly according to plan, but in Thailand unexpected troubles continually mar the progress. Frustration with the work even affects the usually competent engineers, and Ryūki watches his colleagues change into undisciplined opportunists. After Yōko joins him in Thailand, her nervous breakdown intensifies, and eventually she stabs him to death.

Sono Ayako says that this novel, inspired by the Old Testament story of Job, is one of her religious novels. In her essay entitled ''Kono kontontaru sekai'' (This Chaotic World, 1973), Sono describes her joy at discovering the meaning of Job's life. When she learned that in the original biblical story Job's suffering was unabated and that the happy ending of Job's story was interpolation, she wrote:

I had never read a piece of literature which described such a heroic death and a destiny so common yet great and frightful. I felt [then] that I would be able to accept the absurdity of this world and I would be allowed to keep straying. Truth is not something completely attainable in this world. . . . Since we are not to know the answers or expect fair judgment, we are forced to use all our mental resources in wondering and worrying. This must be God's plan.

Just as Job lost everything, so does Ryūki. He loses his mother, daughter, his wife's companionship, joy in his work, and finally his own life. Although he has deliberately chosen Yōko and tries to stand by her, he dies in vain, without receiving any reward for sacrifices. He seems to be dying in utter chaos, yet the image of Ryūki fatally wounded yet still trying to embrace his deranged wife represents complete acceptance of his choice. Ryūki spent his entire life building dams and highways based on grand blueprints, although he did not know how these blueprints were originally conceived. The only thing Ryūki knew for certain is that all the engineering projects, including the one in Thailand, would someday be completed. These construction projects serve as a parable for an earthly master plan in which each individual struggles to perform small tasks with great physical and emotional difficulties. An unnamed memorial commemorates each of these ''Jobs'' who carries out part of the eternal plan without ever understanding the total scheme of life.

Kizutsuita ashi (A Bruised Reed, 1970) novel. "A bruised reed," a term from the Book of Isaiah, symbolizes an unenlightened believer who will find true faith through a leader. Sono's story depicts a parish priest at a small Catholic church in the Shōnan area and the people around him. Father Mitsumori tries to fulfill all the ecclesiastic tasks assigned to him and at the same time to satisfy his own daily needs and petty comforts. Saying mass is as routine for him as garbage collection or the laundryman's weekly visit. He does not want to disturb his status quo. Although he feels envious of a young priest who has the courage to leave the priesthood, marry a girl impregnated by another man, and become a father to the child, Father Mitsumori avoids conflict as much as possible. Nothing dramatic ever happens to him. He recognizes his minor stature as a human, but when he discovers the extent of his congregation's trust in his guidance, he also comes to the same understanding of the meaning of Job's trial. As a humble carrier of God's will, Father Mitsumori will never comprehend God's ultimate intentions, but he finds his mission in sharing people's wounds. Sono's intention to "write about people who work silently somewhere and die quietly" is carried out in the characterization of Father Mitsumori, who is portrayed not as a lofty personage but as one of the bruised reeds with modest hopes, joys, disappointments, and progress.

Kiritorareta jikan (Time That Was Cut Out, 1971), novel. This work focuses on the inner lives of three people who witnessed mass suicide on an Okinawan island in 1945: "the angler," a former soldier who was stationed on the island during the war; "the woman," a survivor of the tragedy that occurred when American forces landed on the island; and the "priest." The angler and the woman together take a psychological and emotional journey back to the fatal day a quarter of a century ago. Through the woman, the angler meets a priest who also witnessed the mass suicide. The priest is still burdened with survivor's guilt and feels that he missed the opportunity to bear witness to his humanness, by taking an action such as protesting to God at the risk of his own life or soiling his hands in some way. The angler, the woman, and the priest all share this journey to the past, reliving moments violently cut out from the present flow of time. Ultimately, however, they share nothing more than the act of probing. Their actions in the past leave each with a unique cross to bear. Through these three nameless souls, the novel poses the question: what does it mean to be a human in a time of crisis? Sono appears to imply that there is no easy answer.

Translated Works: "Fuji" (Fuji, 1975), short story. The work captures in a few pages the alienation between a housewife and her ambitious, knowledge-craving husband. It is a rather common phenomenon in Japan for male white-collar workers to form small cliques and only rarely to include their wives in social outings with their coworkers. Housewives have scanty knowledge of their husbands' work except for occasional gossip alluded to by their husbands. Being married to a "salaryman" (male office worker on company payroll) is considered an easy "lifetime employment," which is sweetened further if it comes "with a house, a car, and without a mother-in-law." The housewife's comfortable security is threatened in Sono's story when the husband decides to study at a company-sponsored school located at the foot of Mt. Fuji. In return for receiving this schooling, the "salaryman" is no doubt expected to be eternally grateful and indebted to his company. The story, written from the wife's viewpoint, succinctly portrays her initial uneasiness at being left by her husband to go to school and her later frustration at being mentally and psychologically left behind. Completely happy in her narrow world, she impatiently waited to graduate from high school and did not want any further education. As if to compensate for this intellectual lethargy, she gained weight after marriage, and her breast provide more than enough milk for her son. Her husband comes home once a month and eagerly enjoys her bodily comfort and her traditional pickles. She becomes a provider of his physical needs, and their verbal communication declines. Mt. Fuji, which used to be regarded as a sacred mountain where normally only males were allowed to climb, now appears as a mechanism that has changed her husband into an incomprehensible being. There once were replicas of the mountain for women to tread on to quell their desire for religious experience, but the housewife's resentful and tearful cry, "What is this damn Fuji anyway," reveals that she has neither the capacity nor intention to transform herself. The predicament is insoluble.

"Love" (Ai, 1970), short story. The story describes the psychological reactions of a newly divorced, middle-aged woman when she unexpectedly encounters her old boyfriend. He is now a married man operating a moving company, and he helps her relocate to her new apartment. The rapport that she believes still lingers between them is not expressed through words but is manifested by the act of driving on the same road to her new lodging in two separate cars: she leads the way, he and his wife, who is his assistant, in his truck. The divorcée believes that his truck follows closely no matter how she drives and that it protects her from other vehicles.

Ten years ago she preferred her husband, who was from a good family and was culturally sophisticated, to this boyfriend, who had "nothing but a healthy body and wholesome faithfulness" to offer. Now she realizes that he should have been her choice, since her husband turned out to be a feeble-willed philanderer. Just as she chose her husband, she now chooses to take the initiative and to get a divorce. She is not the type of woman who merely obeys what circumstances dictate. Yet her rekindled "love" is tenuous. The life course once set by her is irreversible, and their driving together is only a temporal detour that enables her to taste what might have been. The story ends with her full consciousness of lost "love." It is an ironic title.

Kami no yogoreta te (The Left Hand of God, 1979), a novel. This story of an obstetrician-gynecologist, Nobeji Sadaharu, who is in charge of a private clinic in Yokosuka, describes his interactions with his patients, wife, daughter, and friends. The physician's clinical cases are presented in detail and are solidly documented. The central theme evolves around the doctor's quest for understanding: he wonders if there is an entity larger than man and if so, how his own personal role fits into the larger plan. His questions arise out of his daily encounters with patients and are not always theologically consistent. His situational ethics leads him to perform an occasional abortion, for example, but whenever his treatments turn out contrary to his prognosis, he suspects that an invisible mocking or compassionate hand is steering the course of human actions. He questions whether he is merely acting as God's left hand (lit. the Japanese title means "God's soiled hand"). This gynecologist echoing the author's worldview expressed in *For Whom Do We Love?* (1970):

The earth is moving with a force which is quite independent of individual will. . . . The world continues in its grand course, impelled by a complex logic full of contradictions, in which human endeavors, good will, and justice are all ignored. I am immensely impressed by such a mystic process. Noah's ark did not reach Mt. Ararat because Noah wanted it to. Noah happened to be taken there. Our fate is no different from that of Noah.

The gynecologist confesses to his Catholic priest friend that he believes "only a small and impotent mind would consider it unscientific to pray. That viewpoint comes from human arrogance. After we have done as much as we can, there is nothing left but prayer."

The collection of letters exchanged between Sono Ayako and Father Shirieda Masayuki, a Roman Catholic priest, was published under the title of *Wakare no hi made* (Until the Day When We Part) in 1983. In a letter Sono comments that one of her important concerns is to understand how each individual's speciality is used by God and to accept the use as a part of his total plan for humanity. The gynecologist hero, then, embodies the author's view of the purpose of life. He, however, is not free from responsibility for his daily actions: his hands are soiled with blood, and he must stand by his decisions. The novel ends with the protagonist standing by himself on a hill where he feels he is "commanded to be beaten by the rough wind." Like many of Sono's other positive heroes and heroines, the doctor, a lonely being, faces his choice (and God) alone. The idea of the "soiled hand" repeated in *Time That Was Cut Out* stands as human worth, which is determined only when using one's own judgment in a concrete human situation.

The Supreme Being in Sono Ayako's works appears as an enigmatic entity from which all human strengths and foibles emanate but which never acts as an identifiable guiding force. Sono's characters keep struggling and groping for the light, relying on their own resources and subjective judgment. Sono focuses on their efforts rather than on end results. These vulnerable, sincere characters contribute to the widespread popularity of Sono Ayako's works, especially among those readers who are modern "doubting Thomases," forever in search of incontrovertible evidence.

extent to which Takasue's Daughter had access to her aunt's writings is not clear.

However, her access to fictional *monogatari* (prose narratives) and poetry collections is unusually well documented within her memoir itself. In addition to the approximately fifty chapters of *Genji monogatari* (The Tale of Genji, early 11th c.) and *Ise monogatari* (Tales of Ise, extant from the early 10th c.), other literary works mentioned in her memoir include a copybook in the hand of the daughter (d. 1021) of the renowned calligrapher Fujiwara Yukinari and a copy of the Chinese poet Po Chu-i's "Song of Everlasting Sorrow," rewritten as a *monogatari,* as well as a number of other specifically named *monogatari* that survive now only as titles of lost works.

Equally well documented within the memoir is her ambivalence about the possibly pernicious effects of such literature on its readers. Professor Hosono Tetsuo suggests that the memoirist's notorious preoccupation with the spiritual dangers of secular fiction and poetry may have been fed in part by the professional concerns of the men in her traditionally literary family (*"Sarashina nikki shoko: sono bungeikan no haikei ni tsuite,"* *Kokugo to kokubungaku* [February 1953]: 29–36). As Professor Hosono notes, during the Chōgen era (1028–36), her brother Sadayoshi was a prominent member of the Society for the Advancement of Learning (Kangakue), which conducted Buddhist rites for the absolution of literary scholars from the sin of composing or indulging in the readership of nonreligious literature, that is, informal poetry and fiction in Chinese and Japanese. The rites conducted by the Kangakue underscore the ambiguity of Heian beliefs regarding the religious value of literary fictions. On one hand, it was generally believed that writers and readers of fiction risked committing one or more of the four sins of language (*kugō*) proscribed by the sutras. On the other hand, the Kangakue ceremonies themselves made prominent use of poetry whose theme was the possibility that secular literature might function as an expedient means (*hōben*) of leading the nonenlightened to an apprehension of the illusory nature of existence. Whatever the source of the memoirist's ambivalence about her readerly appetites, it seems her work was calculated to address a general atmosphere of debate concerning the relationship between fictional literature and religious truth.

Born in the capital, Takasue's Daughter accompanied her father and stepmother (dates unknown; the daughter of Takashina Shigeyuki) to the distant eastern province of Kazusa in 1017, where she spent some four years of her girlhood. At the end of Takasue's term as governor in 1020, the family returned to the capital, where the memoirist would spend the rest of her life, except for occasional pilgrimages to outlying temples and shrines and a trip to Izumi province around 1050, when her brother was posted as governor there.

Despite her cloistered life, the idea that Takasue's Daughter was a strictly reclusive, otherworldly dreamer is something of a distortion. It has been argued that the carefully crafted girlishness of her persona as memoirist was intended to mask what may have been a far more practical personality. It is now becoming commonplace among biographical critics to seek some balance between the familiar image of her as a dreamer and other circumstances in her life and times. Her elder sister died in childbirth in 1024, leaving two daughters, whom Takasue's Daughter seems to have helped raise, though she herself, unlike many women of her class, remained unmarried and childless until she was in her thirties. Her memoir also suggests she was in charge of her parents' household from the time her mother took lay religious orders not long after Takasue's return from his term as assistant governor of Hitachi in 1036. It is likely that her lack of success at court and her apparent indifference to her late marriage was the result not simply of her own want of ambition but of her father's less than stellar career and lack of politically useful connections. In fact, passages in the memoir may be interpreted as indications of her own keen interest in a career in court service.

Beginning in 1039, when she was about thirty-one years old, Takasue's Daughter served a number of brief terms of attendance at the Takakura Detached Palace, then the residence of Princess Yushi (1038–1105), the young daughter of Emperor GoSuzaku (1009–45; r. 1036–45) and Empress Genshi (1016–39; r. 1037–39). Empress Genshi had just died earlier that same year, shortly after giving birth to Yushi's sister, Princess Baishi (1039–96). The current scholarly consensus is that the marriage of Takasue's Daughter to Tachibana Toshimichi (1002?–58) took place in 1040 and interrupted her attendance on Yushi only temporarily. Her husband, Toshimichi, was, like her father, a member of the provincial governor class, and when he was posted as governor to Shimotsuke province the following year, Takasue's Daughter remained in the capital and continued her attendance on the princess off and on during the four years of his absence. Professor Tsumoto Nobuhiro speculates that she bore her son Nakatoshi (b. 1041?) during the first year of her marriage to Toshimichi and the early years of the princesses' lives (*Sarashina nikki no kenkyū* [Waseda Daigaku shuppanbu, 1982]: 93–95). Perhaps, as Professor Tsumoto suggests, it was the timely birth of her son that gave rise to the ambitions her memoir implies she harbored at this period in her life: to "become an Imperial wet nurse (*onmenoto*), serve at the Imperial palace, and be able to gain the favor of the Emperor and the Empress" (Akiyama Ken, ed., *Sarashina nikki,* Shinchō Nihon koten shūsei 39: 108; all translations in this entry by Edith Sarra). The role of wet nurse traditionally involved more status than that accorded ordinary ladies-in-waiting, as well as the possibility of benefits for any of the nurse's children who became "breast siblings" (*menotogo*) of the upper-class nurslings. Raised together with their mother's charges, *menotogo* often went on to become intimate companions and attendants of their foster siblings for life (Saigō Nobutsuna, *Genji monogatari o yomu tame ni* [Heibonsha, 1983]: 70–71). Ultimately, however, Takasue's Daughter does not seem to have made any great success at court for herself or her children, though it seems likely that she contributed to, and was in turn stimulated by, the literary activities surrounding the princesses she served.

Both Princesses Yushi and Baishi were the wards of the regent Fujiwara

Yorimichi (992–1074), the eldest son and heir of the powerful regent Fujiwara Michinaga. Yorimichi's long period of regency is noted, as was his father's, for the brilliance of its literary salons. Yorimichi himself seems to have been quite consciously involved in promoting the practice of literature, particularly among the women in service in his household and the households of his various offspring. The households of Yushi and Baishi sponsored more than twenty-five poetry competitions *(utaawase)* altogether, beginning with the decade of the 1040s. Baishi was an especially active promoter of poetry during her tenure as High Priestess of the Kamo Shrine (1046–58), sponsoring more than twenty contests herself, including in 1055 a rare and important contest matching poems taken from *monogatari (monogatari utaawase)*. Yushi's household, with which Takasue's Daughter was directly connected, was less active than Baishi's, but it is worth noting that two of the six contests known to have been sponsored by Yushi centered on poems involving poetic toponyms *(uta makura)* associated with sites famous in poetic tradition *(meisho)*, tropes that deeply interested Takasue's Daughter, as even the most cursory glance at her memoir reveals. The first of these *meisho utaawase* took place in 1041, during the memoirist's period of service with Yushi, but it is impossible to know whether Takasue's Daughter participated in this or any of the other six contests since a proper text exist for only one of them. If she did participate, she makes no mention of it in her memoir, the later pages of which are almost wholly given over to accounts of the various religious pilgrimages she made during her late middle age.

Major Works: Takasue's Daughter is remembered for her memoir, *Sarashina nikki* (The Sarashina Memoir, completed ca. 1058–65). But her wholly posthumous fame was late in coming. After her death, her memoir was kept in the closely guarded possession of the Sugawara family and not circulated until the early part of the Kamakura period. In addition to the excellence of the memoir itself, the literary survival of Takasue's Daughter owes much to the influence of Fujiwara Teika (1162–1241). He was the poetic arbiter of his day, having achieved the unprecedented honor of serving as compiler for two imperially commissioned poetic anthologies, *Shinkokinshū* (1201–6) and *Shinchokusenshū* (ca. 1234). In his later years Teika devoted much time and energy to collecting and copying manuscripts of Heian literary texts, and in 1230 he first mentions *The Sarashina Memoir* in his diary in Chinese, *Meigetsuski* (Record of the Clear Moon, 1180–1235). All of the surviving texts of the memoir seem to be related to Teika's copy; no text originating from a different textual line has been discovered. Later premodern readers, the great Edo period philologist Motoori Norinaga (1730–1801) among them, read a scrambled version of the text, which was finally reconstructed in the 1920s by the scholar Tamai Kōsuke. The memoir currently enjoys the status of a minor classic; passages from it are required reading for high school students of classical Japanese.

Waka (thirty-one-syllable court poems) by Takasue's Daughter made their first appearance in the imperially commissioned anthologies during Teika's time, with about fifteen of them included over the following century and a half, beginning with *Shinkokinshū* and ending with *Shinshūishū* (1364). Except for the two *waka* included in *Shokukokinshū* (1265), all of the anthologized poems also appear in *The Sarashina Memoir.*

Teika's colophon to *The Sarashina Memoir* gives tacit authority to the tradition that Takasue's Daughter was also the author of four fictional *monogatari,* of which two, *Hamamatsu chūnagon monogatari* (The Tale of the Hamamatsu Middle Counsellor, no earlier than 1064) and *Yoha no nezame* (The Tale of Nezame, last quarter of 11th c.) still survive in part and have been translated into English (see bibliography). The other two works mentioned (*Mizukara kuyuru* and *Asakura*) have been lost. Her authorship of these tales—indeed, the whole notion of single-handed authorship of *monogatari* in general—is under debate and will probably remain so.

Translated Work: For the general reader, *The Sarashina Memoir* is best remembered for its portraits of the narrator-heroine as a young reader, bent over her beloved volumes behind a screen. The image has exercised a similar fascination over generations of scholars as well, who have cited it repeatedly as a standard illustration of what reading *monogatari* meant to the young, cloistered women of the Heian aristocracy. But while much of the memoir evokes the image of an almost incredibly naive reader, it is no naïf who narrates the account, but an artful confessional persona who commemorates her own former naïveté, as well as an ongoing preoccupation with literary fictions, religious truth, and the enigma of her own destiny. The initial two-thirds of the memoir circulate around the story of the narrator-heroine's inordinate desire for *monogatari,* a genre censured in some 11th-century circles as inseparably associated with women and their foolish and morally reprehensible interest in fictions. These early sections of the memoir build upon one of the great character types of earlier Heian tales and memoirs: a young, naive woman of less than ideal family background who whiles away the tedium of her confined existence by reading *monogatari.* Just what were *monogatari* to such women? Many scholars believe they played a crucial role in the early literary training and socialization of upper-class and upwardly mobile Heian girls. Professor Mitsuno Yōichi has gone so far as to postulate three distinct stages in the education of young Heian ladies, all of which involved varying degrees of *monogatari* reading and composition practice, in training for the adult business of *waka* composition and poetic correspondence with men and other people beyond the confines of their own households (''Uta manabi to uta monogatari,'' *Kokugo to kokubungaku* 712 [May 1983]: 28–39). For the woman whose options in life were a priori limited by both gender and class, *monogatari* provided exciting glimpses of multiple worlds. Life offered her only a very limited range of possibilities, chief among these being (at least by fiction's standards) romantic alliance with a handsome and sensitive upper-class man. *Monogatari* are thus thought to have provided both solace for the emptiness of the female reader's sedentary existence and training for the courtships that would shape her married life and (if she was the daughter of ambitious parents) the political career of her fathers or brothers.

The training they imparted would have been not only in the practical matter of teaching the reader what sort of poems are appropriate to specific types of occasions but also an ideological indoctrination, illustration (and romanticizing) the passive role young women were supposed to play in their relations with fathers, lovers, husbands, and children.

Given this more sophisticated understanding of the part played by *monogatari* in the education of Heian ladies, biographical scholars have begun to reassess the nature and meaning of the *Sarashina* memoirist's obsession with fictional tales. Earlier commentators assumed that her infamous fascination with them sprang from her desire to escape reality. Tada Kazuomi has recently argued that it signifies, on the contrary, her awakening interest in the "real world" the courtly tales were supposed to resemble and the possibility of participating in that world ("Sugawara Takasue no musume," in *Ōchō bungakushi,* ed. Akiyama Ken [Tokyo Daigaku Shuppankai, 1984]: 350). According to his reading, the heroine's initial infatuation with tale literature suggests not negative escapism, but active desire. Indeed, the word used throughout the memoir to describe her interest in tales is *yukashisa,* a longing to hear or see something, the state of being intrigued by something. In this respect, the image of the *Sarashina* narrator-heroine resembles other Heian women (both fictional and historical) who read *monogatari* because they offered models they presumed were usable for making sense of the course of their own lives. Tada's argument builds on the suggestions of other Japanese scholars who have pointed out the memoirist's apparent preference for *Genji* heroines who occupy socioeconomic positions similar to her own. Inukai Kiyoshi has argued that the *Sarashina* heroine's affinity for the two *Genji* heroines Yūgao and Ukifune might be linked to the fact that these two characters most closely corresponded to herself in terms of social rank and hence potentially similar careers ("Takasue no musume ni kansuru shiron: shu toshite sono chūnenki o megutte," in *Heianchō nikki,* 2 [Yūseidō, 1975]: 164). But Tada's argument also assumes a more or less unreflective mode of reading on the part of Heian women in general and the *Sarashina* memoirist in particular. Taken literally, it does appear that the *Sarashina* narrator-heroine approaches fiction with the kind of literal-mindedness that resembles that of, say, the young heroine Tamakazura in *The Tale of Genji.* But such an interpretation fails to come to terms with the ironic use of the naive reader as a rhetorical figure throughout the memoir. If one follows Tada's reading, tales should figure in this memoir only as a means of access to a world the girl has not experienced or cannot experience for herself. But in fact, as I can only briefly suggest here, the case is far more complicated. Consider only the opening passage of the memoir:

A person raised in a province even more remote than the one at the end of the Eastern Road—how utterly outlandish I must have been. What started me thinking about them, I don't recall, but hearing there were in the world these things called tales, I fell to wondering how I might see them for myself. On idle afternoons and evenings I would listen to my sister, and my stepmother and the others telling snatches from this or that tale—the kind of things that were written about in the Shining Genji—but their talk just made me long to find out more. With only memory to rely upon, how could they tell the tales in a way that would satisfy me? In my restlessness, I had a Yakushi Buddha made to my own size. Cleansing my hands, when no one was around I would go to it in secret and kneel down, touching my head to the ground to pray, "Grant that I may soon go to the capital where there are so many tales, and there let me read all the tales there are." The year I turned twelve we left our house in preparation for the journey up to the capital. It was the third day of the ninth month: we moved to a place called Imatachi (Shinchō Nihon koten shūsei 39, 13–14).

By her own account, her first conscious thoughts concern not so much the real world of the capital but rather the marvelous "things called tales" that the city was said to contain. Her first desire, the one that catalyzes her initial wanderings and indeed the very course of the narrative, is the longing to see these tales for herself. Yet way out in the eastern provinces, at the outset of the memoir and its heroine's readerly pilgrimages, it is precisely the tales themselves that are impossible to procure. The heroine is yet only a would-be reader of the fabulous stories she has heard in tantalizing bits and pieces from older women in the household. Fiction, not the world it is supposed to resemble, constitutes the initial object of her desire. So from the very beginning, fiction—and all the desires and fantasies it licenses—becomes for her an end in itself. Before she reaches the point in her narrative where she confesses an anxious disillusionment with tales, she presents fictional literature as creating a kind of tertiary realm intervening between herself and the unglamorous realities beyond the confines of her father's house. As the narrative unfolds, the more subversive idea of fiction as a means of shaping and controlling (rather than simply reflecting) one's own destiny rises to the surface of the story again and again. Nor does her ostensible disillusionment with tales in midlife spell the end of her dreams of self-importance, dreams born of, and nurtured by, the years she has spent immersed in *monogatari*. The hectic pilgrimages that comprise the last third of the memoir suggest not a repression of readerly desire but rather a displacement of it onto the plots and texts of religious myth. To the very end of the memoir, the *Sarashina* heroine continues the role of a resisting reader, rewriting and reinterpreting the texts of her religious dreams according to the exigencies of her own eccentric desire.

If not all Heian females began and ended as literalists, neither were all the tales they read simply vehicles for their indoctrination as proper wives and daughters. While the depiction of romantic love across class boundaries persisted as a staple of the *monogatari* repertoire throughout its history, by the year 1020, when Takasue and his family began their journey up to the capital from the eastern provinces, the genre had begun to realize its potential as a medium for subtle critiques of social realities, particularly the kinds of risks and pressures women (especially women of the Heian "middle classes": orphans, unrecognized daughters of the nobility, provincial governors' daughters) encountered in their relations with politically powerful men in court society. The great exemplar of this new direction in the genre of prose fiction was, of course, the *Tale of Genji,* which Takasue's Daughter avidly read and deeply admired. Whatever she might have gleaned from the tales regarding life and love in court circles, it is apparent that the portrayal she gives of her abiding interest in them has much to do with general problems of fictional literature and its relationship to questions of truth and (feminine) desire. The early sections of the memoir can be read as a sustained meditation, in narrative form, on the potentially subversive role of *monogatari* in young women's lives. The *Sarashina* heroine spends most of her teens and twenties shut up behind her screens, reading whatever fiction she can get her hands on. This portrait extends and exaggerates the image of certain socially marginalized heroines of *monogatari* (Suetsumuhana, Tamakazura, and Ukifune, to name only three from the *Tale of Genji* alone). What is especially interesting about her reinscription of this character type, however, is the way she uses it to dramatize the Heian ambivalence about fictionality. This ambivalence surfaces elsewhere in Japanese court literature but was perhaps most memorably staged in the famous dialogue between Genji and Tamakazura in the "Fireflies" chapter of the *Tale of Genji.*

As in the *Tale of Genji,* the issue of gender differences complicates the preoccupation with fiction, truth, and reading in the *Sarashina* memoir. If Genji and Tamakazura can be said to voice conventionally masculine and feminine perspectives in an argument about the nature and value of fictional tales, the *Sarashina* narrator-heroine portrays her own life as an arena for the acting out of dialectic tensions between masculine authority and feminine resistance, religious dogma, and literary fictions. Gendered attitudes toward fiction riddle *The Sarashina Memoir.* They become most vividly apparent in the accounts of the heroine's obsessive search for books and the guilty dreams and prayers her search inspires. While the heroine's fears about the spiritual evils of fiction find form and voice in censorious male authority figures (the various admonitory priests who figure in the early dreams she records), her female relatives and acquaintances license her illicit desires for fiction and abet her in her passionate acquisition and readership of them. She presents the arrival of her first bundle of books as the result of a lengthy series of cross-class and cross-generational exchanges between various female intercessors. The heroine begs tales of her mother, who in turn begs tales of her mother, who in turn begs them on her behalf from a certain Emon no myōbu, a female relative in service at the neighboring Sanjō Palace, then the residence of Princess Shūshi (996–1049). The texts finally sent her had been themselves a gift from the princess to Emon no myōbu, who in turn gives them to the heroine. In these episodes, female figures emerge clearly (and conventionally) on the side of fantasy and indulgence in fictional literature. The relationship of women and fiction to religious salvation and power, however, remains tantalizingly ambiguous, as other episodes in the memoir suggest.

The story of the heroine's acquisition of her own copy of the *Tale of Genji* raises (but leaves unresolved) the possibility of women and fiction as vehicles for the transmission of religious enlightenment. Biographical scholars date the episode to 1021 and speculate this copy of *Genji* may have come ultimately from Murasaki Shikibu's daughter, Daini no Sammi (999–?), to whom the memoirist's stepmother was related by marriage. By this time her stepmother, having separated from Takasue, was again moving in court circles as a lady-in-waiting to Emperor GoIchijō's Empress Ishi (999–1036; r. 1016–36). But true to her persona as an outsider to court society (outdoing even Ukifune and Yūgao, the *Genji* heroines she most admired as a girl) the *Sarashina* narrator frames the transaction far more romantically. She reports that the tales came to her as a gift from an aunt (*oba naru hito*) who had just returned from the provinces. But the sequence of events leading up to the visit suggests the ultimate provenance of the tales was even more miraculous than books from an aunt in the provinces. In the passage immediately preceding the account of the visit with the aunt, the narrator describes a religious retreat she made with her mother to a temple at Uzumasa, where, obsessed with her desire for more tales, the one thing she prays for is that she may be "shown the entire *Tale of Genji* from the first chapter on" (Shinchō Nihon Koten Shūsei 39: 34). She confesses that she was bitterly disappointed when her prayer was not immediately answered upon her return from Uzumasa, but this is somewhat misleading since the next event she records is the momentous visit soon thereafter with the aunt who gives her, as though in answer to her prayer, "the fifty-odd chapters of the *Tale of Genji*" (Shinchō Nihon Koten Shūsei 39: 35). At this point, as at other key junctures in the memoir, the sequence of events in the narrative subtly implicates a Buddhist figure as the apparent benefactor in the tale of the heroine's acquisition of presumably bad books. In fact, Buddhist icons haunt the narrative, like signs the narrator-heroine cannot quite (or does not wish to) decipher explicitly. She leaves her readers to draw their own conclusions.

One conclusion we might draw is that *The Sarashina Memoir* expresses a profound ambivalence about the conventional terms by which Heian women were expected to accommodate themselves to existing standards of behavior and religious belief. Despite the narrator's ultimate denunciation of *monogatari,* her narrative subtly and repeatedly suggests that the alternatives to these tales—at least for her—were worse and just as unlikely to offer a realizable blueprint for her own destiny. Consider, for example, the dream the narrator recalls having during the height of her immersion in the *Tale of Genji.* A handsome priest who disapproves of her preferred reading material appears before her and orders her to learn the fifth chapter of the Lotus Sutra immediately. The chapter the dream priest recommends contains the tale of the Dragon King's daughter and her miraculous transformation into a Buddha (complete with a male body) upon attaining enlightenment. The text was important to revisionist developments in contemporary and later medieval Mahayana Buddhist thought because it provided a scriptural basis for the argument that even women might be capable of attaining religious enlightenment—though significantly not without transcending their female bodies first. It is likely that the memoirist, recounting the dream as part of the memoir she carefully crafts in her later years, was well aware of the content of the fifth chapter of the Lotus Sutra. But here, as in so many other passages in the memoir, these matters will not be spelled out. What she commemorates instead are the apparent blindness and passion of her girlhood. What is the girl's response to the dream? She will read only what she wishes to read. This sign—both the man in the dream and the sacred text he recommends— will go unheeded and unread. Displaced before it can fully emerge, the image of the Dragon King's wise but ultimately (disappointingly?) transsexual daughter pales before the autoerotic, feminine figures the heroine prefers aspiring to. She confesses:

I told no one of the dream, nor had I any intention of learning the sutra. I cared only for tales. I may not be much to look at these days, but when I come into full flower, I will be as lovely as any, and my hair will get so long. In my heart I imagined that I would be just like Shining Genji's Lady Yūgao, or the Uji Captain's love Ukifune—and now, before all else, it is this memory that I find so very vain and appalling (Shinchō Nihon Koten Shūsei 39: 35–36).

In a rare aside, the narrating voice disclaims the folly of her youthful heedlessness ("before all else it is this memory"). But one suspects her regret is not wholehearted, that she is not fully convinced of the spiritual worthlessness of her chosen reading matter. Nostalgically evoking the euphoric spaces of *monogatari,* her memoir implicitly underscores the impoverished alternatives that await the Heian lady in other spheres: a peripheral position in court service and an arranged, polygynous marriage, and, if she is spiritually inclined, she can contemplate the unsatisfactory subtext in the tale of the Dragon King's daughter (the only woman worth imitating is a woman who relinquishes womanhood entirely and becomes more like a man).

The fluid, simple style of this memoir belies its rhetorical and intellectual sophistication. I have tried to suggest here some of the ramifications of its concern with the theme of court fiction and female readership. Readers have also long noted the beauty of its travel narratives and its innovative play with the rhetorical device of *uta makura.* The work has much to recommend it, both as a classic of Heian literature and as a rich, enigmatic meditation on that literature and its contexts.

BIBLIOGRAPHY

Translations

As I Crossed a Bridge of Dreams: Recollections of a Woman in Eleventh Century Japan. Ivan Morris, trans. London: Oxford University Press, 1971.
The Tale of Nezame: Part Three of "Yowa no Nezame Monogatari." Carol Hochstedler, trans. Ithaca, NY: Cornell China-Japan Program, 1979.

A Tale of Eleventh-Century Japan: Hamamatsu Chūnagon Monogatari. Thomas H. Roh-
    lich, trans. Princeton, NJ: Princeton University Press, 1983.

Critical Works

Keene, Donald. "The Sarashina Diary." In *Travelers of A Hundred Ages.* New York:
    Henry Holt, 1989.
Richard, Kenneth L. "Developments in Late Heian Prose Fiction: *The Tale of Nezame.*"
    Ph.D. diss., University of Washington, 1973.
Sarra, Edith. "*Sarashina nikki:* The Destiny of a Reader." In "The Art of Remembrance,
    the Poetics of Destiny: Self-Writings by Three Women of Heian Japan." Ph.D.
    diss., Harvard University, 1988.

Edith Lorraine SARRA

T ─────────────────────────────────────

TAMURA Toshiko (1884–1945), novelist, actress. Née Satō Toshi (Mrs. Tamura Shōgyo); other pen name: Satō Roei; stage name: Hanabusa Tsuyuko.

Life: Toshiko was born on April 15, 1884, as the eldest daughter of a rice merchant in Asakusa, Tokyo. Her father had married into the Sato family as an adopted heir. Toshiko's mother, the only child of a venerable wholesale house harking back to the feudal times, never loved the husband chosen for her. By the time Toshiko was in her low teens, her father was no longer living with them. Her flamboyant mother soon spent the family fortune on Kabuki actors and made a living as teacher of traditional music such as *nagauta* songs and *gidayū* chanting. Toshiko grew up in the atmosphere of the "lower-town (*shitamachi*)," steeped in the cultural heritage from the Edo period (1600–1868).

Toshiko's interest in literature began at a very young age, and she wrote her first romantic story for girls when she was thirteen years old. She also read Western novels translated into Japanese as well as many Japanese novels. In 1901, she entered the newly founded Nihon Women's College to study Japanese literature. As a student in the first class of Japan's first institution of higher learning for women, she would have become one of the most educated and intellectual women in the Meiji period (1868–1912). Unfortunately, she left school in the second semester because of a heart condition. But this short college life made her realize that writing was her life's work.

Among a number of novelists prominent in Meiji Japan, she chose Kōda Rohan (1867–1947) as her mentor. Well known for his dislike of taking on private students, Rohan nonetheless admired Toshiko's talent and allowed her to be his only female disciple. Under the pen name of Satō Roei, given by Rohan, some of her short stories began to be published in 1903, launching her on a professional career. However, Rohan's emphasis on the classics as sole literary models conflicted with her desire to depict a new type of woman with strong character. Gradually Rohan's guidance became a heavy burden to her and made her reluctant to follow him. In 1906 she gave up writing and diverted her energy toward acting. From 1906 till 1908 she played some roles in costume plays on stage, but without great success.

In 1909 she married Tamura Shōgyo upon his return from a five-year stay in America. Also Rohan's student, he had already established himself as a promising novelist. But after their marriage, none of his novels sold as well as expected so that the couple was always poverty-stricken. Furthermore, Toshiko had no sense of economy: she poured what money Shōgyo earned into clothes and jewelry, and consequently, the couple owed more debts to all of their friends and relatives than they could possibly repay. Gradually the tension caused by poverty mounted between them, and quarrels took place day and night. Weary of marriage, Toshiko engaged herself in acting again. This time she became an actress of modern drama and in 1910 played the heroine in *Nami* (Waves). Her performance won applause and was favorably received by critics. But shortly afterward the company she joined went bankrupt and put an end to her attempt at acting.

Now Toshiko realized that she had no choice but to write if she was to fulfill her need to express herself. Again she began to spend most of her time in writing and finished a novel, *Akirame* (Resignation), in 1911. Urged on by her husband, she entered it in the fiction contest sponsored by the *Osaka Asahi* newspaper and won the top prize, which established her as a new star in the literary circle of the early Taishō period (1912–26). For the next three or four years, she energetically published her stories one after another, her name appearing almost every month in various magazines, including *Chūō kōron* and *Shinchō,* the two most authoritative magazines in Japan. Toshiko became known throughout the country as the first professional woman novelist.

Ironically, the popularity she enjoyed made the downward slide of her husband, Shōgyo's, literary fortune look all the more pronounced. He reached a point where he had to depend on Toshiko as a provider, even as gossips concerning her love affairs irked him. Her sociable nature and her intelligence led Toshiko to enjoy friendships with men, and regardless of her true feelings toward them, Shōgyo viewed such relationships as scandalous. In 1916, the couple agreed to separate.

Toshiko fell in love with Suzuki Etsu, a youthful journalist and Shōgyo's friend, who had been a frequent visitor at their house. It was not a love to be openly celebrated because Suzuki too had been married with two children. The love triangle among Toshiko, Suzuki, and Shōgyo was a good target for the mass media, which sensationalized it. To help cool the scandal, Suzuki went to Canada in 1918 in the hope of starting a new business abroad, and one year later Toshiko divorced Shōgyo and joined Suzuki in Canada. They married and settled down in Vancouver, where they made their home for the next eighteen years.

Suzuki was keenly aware of the adverse condition of Japanese workers in

Canada, and, in order to improve their lot, he devoted himself to establishing a labor union. Toshiko helped him publish a weekly newspaper in Japanese language and promote Japanese women's welfare in many ways, including teaching them birth control. Novelist Setouchi Harumi (b. 1922) in her award-winning "biographical novel" *Tamura Toshiko* (1961) notes that Suzuki wanted Toshiko to serve him as his assistant and did not encourage her to write for herself and that this partly accounts for her unproductiveness as a novelist in those years. Whatever the reason, it is true that Toshiko produced nothing substantial during her stay in Canada. In 1932 Suzuki returned to Japan, intending to go back to Canada before long, but he died of appendicitis in his hometown in 1933.

Three years later Toshiko moved back to Japan and tried to make a literary comeback. But she had difficulty in adjusting herself to Japanese life after the eighteen-year absence and recapturing the popularity she had won from Japanese readers. In 1938, after publishing "Yamamichi" (Mountain Path), a story based on her love affair with Kubokawa Tsurujirō, a leftist social critic nineteen years her junior who was the husband of her friend and proletarian novelist Sata Ineko (b. 1904), she left Japan again, this time for China, on the *Chūō kōron* magazine's assignment as a special correspondent. She visited Beijing and settled in Shanghai to work as a nonregular member of the Japanese embassy. In 1940 she was entrusted with the task of publishing *Josei* (Women's Voice), a monthly magazine in Chinese language, sponsored by the Japanese military, to enlighten Chinese women. In spite of the war and the inflation caused by it, she edited and published this magazine regularly until 1945, when she fell down on a Shanghai street in a fit of apoplexy and died in a hospital nearby three days later, on April 13.

In 1961, sixteen years after her death, the Tamura Toshiko Prize was established in her honor to be awarded to talented women writers. The first winner was Setouchi Harumi for her *Tamura Toshiko*.

Career: Toshiko's first major work produced under Kōda Rohan's guidance, *Tsuyuwakegoromo* (Dew Drenched Robe, 1903), is written in the pseudo-Higuchi Ichiyō style, that is, a classical style that was no longer very popular in her own time. The plot is also old-fashioned. Okimi, an orphan who has long suffered from tuberculosis, lives with her elder brother Shōji and his wife. Since Shōji loves an actress and very often spends nights with her, Okimi feels very sorry for her sister-in-law, who kindly takes care of her. One cold, rainy day, despite her illness, she visits her brother at his mistress's house and implores him to return to his wife. Moved by her earnest entreaty, Shōji promises her to come home. The ending finds her brother and his wife shedding thankful tears by the bed on which Okimi lies dying. This is a kind of traditional *ninjōbanashi* (human interest story), which emphasizes patience, devotion, and self-sacrifice of women. Okimi is very different from the women with strong character that Toshiko was to create in her later fiction. Understandably, she was not satisfied with this work and agonized for the next few years whether or not she should remain a disciple of Rohan. Finally she parted ways with him in 1906.

In 1911 with *Akirame* (Resignation) she established her own style and found the theme she would pursue throughout her career—a woman's search for independence. The heroine, an orphan, Tomie, is put in the care of her elder sister, Tsumako, and her husband, Ryokushi. One day Tomie learns from Tsumako that Ryokushi is carrying on with their younger sister, Kie, who has been left in the care of a woman running a small restaurant in Tokyo's "lower-town." Tsumako cries her heart out and, in her desire to find her husband faithful to her, makes herself believe that her sister is the only one to blame. But Tomie notices that Ryokushi deceives Tsumako in collusion with Kie and that both enjoy their secret trysts.

Tomie observes her sisters critically. She finds her elder sister's married life grossly degrading, since she shuts her eyes to her husband's adultery. Tomie is also pained by the realization that her younger sister's lustful nature and lack of self-control make her fit only to be men's mistress. To Tomie, her two sisters seem the examples of weak women relying on men. For her part, Tomie keeps her distance from a friend of hers, Someko, to whom she is the only object of affection. In fact, Someko's growing love toward Tomie contributes to her physical breakdown, and at last Someko becomes so weak that she can only lie in bed, feverish and unable to eat. Though Tomie cares for Someko, she finds her love burdensome, because this girl clings to Tomie and does not have a will to live an independent life of her own. In contrast with her sisters and Someko, Tomie is spirited and intelligent. She decides to live without the help of others, and in order to support herself she writes a drama and succeeds in getting it performed on stage. She recognizes the importance of being independent, and this awareness makes her a new type of heroine in Japanese fiction of the day.

Tamura Toshiko is very good at delving into women's sexuality. Particularly, scenes such as Tsumako's suffering from jealousy, Kie's seduction of Ryokushi, the lesbian love between Tomie and Someko, and Tomie's friend Miwa taking a bath evoke a strongly sensual, erotic atmosphere that makes these women extremely real and even endearing. *Akirame* is memorable for the candid way it deals with women's sexuality exactly as seen by women's eyes. Conflicts between husband and wife as well as the spiritual independence and passion of women are the main themes on which Toshiko repeatedly put the utmost emphasis. Seiko, the heroine of "Seigen" (An Oath, 1912), fights her husband's attempt to crush her individuality, asking herself: "Even if there is something in my character my husband does not like, is it my duty to change it so that he may like it? . . . Even if my attitude is offending to everyone, my attitude is my own. Even if many people hate and ostracize me because of my character, it is still a character all my own."

A similar declaration of spiritual independence can be heard from Tatsuko in "Hōraku no kei" (Capital Punishment by Fire, 1914). She goes out with a young man but refuses to apologize to her husband for it. She excuses herself by presenting the following logic: it is true that she loves the young man, but love is beyond reason so that nobody can control how she feels toward a particular person; even her husband has no right to restrict her spiritual freedom; since she will always love her husband more than the young man, she need not feel guilty. Rather than apologize to her husband for her affair, she is willing to accept even an extreme sentence, be it death by burning.

In their protest against male domination, Toshiko's heroines seem very much abreast of the contemporary feminist movement that swept Japan in the Taishō period. Toshiko had been a member of Seitō (Bluestocking Society), a feminist organization established in 1911: "Ikichi" (lit., Living Blood) published in their journal's inaugural issue marks the first appearance of Toshiko's central theme—the male-female dichotomy—but this time a relationship revolving around "a man who sucks a living woman's blood," or a victimizing male and a victimized female. Nonetheless, Toshiko did not speak for women as a group but rather presented her heroines as special cases. Both Seiko of "Seigen" and Tatsuko of "Hōraku no kei" are too strong to be ordinary women of their time, and their totally uncompromising character tends to go to extremes. In this sense, Toshiko's fiction does not constitute a forum or a platform from which feminists can speak out on women's behalf, calling for social reform.

Toshiko, moreover, differs from contemporary feminists in that she draws much attention to the difficulty of gaining independence. In her fiction, there is always an ironic twist when the heroine can no longer ignore the limitation upon her freedom. Minoru in *Miira no kuchibeni* (A Mummy's Lipstick, 1913) and the anonymous heroine of "Onnasakusha" (A Woman Writer, 1913) are afraid to get divorced, for they know that it is impossible for women to live by themselves in the society of their day. With great reluctance these heroines persuade themselves to endure the unsuccessful marriage as long as they cannot transcend the material circumstances.

Significantly, the problem of the heroines mirrors the one that the author suffered in her real life. Small wonder Toshiko could find no solution for her heroine's dilemma over dependence and independence, mark no new development in their lives, and go no further in her novels. Accordingly, the insoluble dilemma leads to the heroines' breakdown but also, more important, to Toshiko's own impasse. Even more tragic, after finishing a number of stories about this frustrating female situation, Toshiko looked for a new subject matter but found almost nothing left for her to write about. In an effort to find a way out of their artistic dead end, Toshiko wrote *jōwa bungaku,* a genre of decadent, erotic love stories, but they did less well than her previous works. Toshiko's golden age proved very short. By 1916, when she left Shōgyo, the number of works she produced had sharply decreased. Although she continued to write, some of her stories were turned down by literary magazines. It seems as if her creativity had already dried up.

Toshiko might have hoped to escape from this disappointing situation by leaving Japan. But most critics have taken a negative view of her stay abroad. Novelist Sata Ineko notes that her running away from Japan constituted a victory for her love toward Suzuki Etsu but a defeat for her literature (Postscript to

Tamura Toshiko's story collection, *Akirame, Miira no kuchibeni,* Iwanami Bunko, 1952). An award-winning nonfiction writer, Kudō Miyoko, agrees with Sata's view: "She lost her stage for creative activity that was as important to her as life itself, when she left Japan" (Kudō Miyoko, *Tabibitotachi no Bankūbā,* Chikuma Shobō, 1982). Yet, Toshiko never gave up writing. Before she left for China, for example, she published some novellas and stories, including "Chiisaki Ayumi" (Small Steps, 1936) about the Japanese society in China. But none of them were good enough to overturn the critical consensus that her artistic life was over when she left for Canada.

A recent study calls attention to the significance of *Josei.* Professor Watanabe Sumiko holds that although this magazine was published under the auspices of the military, it did not carry on propaganda for militarism and that it was devoted entirely to enlightening Chinese women who suffered ill treatment both from their family and society: Toshiko meant it to be "of the women, by the women, and for the women" ("Tamura Toshiko no Josei ni tsuite," *Bungaku* 56, [March 1988]). To be fair, Toshiko lived such a dramatic life, spanning foreign language zones over two continents, that it is still difficult to draw a complete portrait of this pioneering professional woman writer. Some periods of her career have been illuminated, but the rest has been unjustly neglected so far. The complete works of Tamura Toshi, including her letters to Suzuki Etsu, came out for the first time in 1988.

Major Works: Miira no kuchibeni (A Mummy's Lipstick, 1913), novel. Minoru is a writer living with her husband, Yoshio, who is also an out-of-luck novelist. Every day he visits publishers to peddle his manuscripts, but all in vain. Since there is no way to make a living out of their literary endeavors, the couple frequent the pawnshop, taking their humble possessions in a bag. One day Yoshio is very disappointed to find a magazine review referring to him as an old-fashioned and dull writer. Honest in her critical opinion, Minoru agrees with the critic, making Yoshio furious. As usual the irreconcilability of the two artists leads to violence: he kocks her down to the floor, and she fights back, beating his face and body again and again. Thinking that he can no longer support his unsympathetic wife, he asks for separation. Also feeling the need to be away from him, Minoru frankly admits that they live together not because they love each other but merely out of financial necessity. Yet, she can think of no way to survive other than staying with her husband.

Yoshio orders her to enter a fiction contest so that she might help ease the economic pressure on them. Working distractedly under his stern eyes, Minoru somehow finishes a novel she has long been working on. Luckily she wins the top prize, and the couple rejoice over their good fortune. But after the one thousand-yen prize money has been spent, the gap between them widens: Minoru begins to work independently, and Yoshio sadly notices that she needs his advice and guidance no more. Toward the end, Minoru has a dream about two mummies in tight embrace. The female mummy has rouge on her lips, and its glaring color makes a strange contrast with her darkly dried body. Intrigued by the meaning of such a dream, Minoru tells Yoshio about it, but he shows no interest at all.

Toshiko's best-known novel, *Miira no kuchibeni* is directly based on her actual experiences around 1910. In divulging a part of her own life, especially her relationship with her husband, she elaborates her examination of female consciousness into a central theme. Like Toshiko's other heroines, Minoru is impressive in her self-assertion. She is direct and to-the-point in criticizing her husband. There is no flattery or compliment in the description of this heroine. She sees her husband as a comrade or, more often, as a rival in the same profession. Their quarrels are, therefore, conflicts between two equal individuals rather than between a tyrannical man and his acquiescent wife. The husband, Yoshio, is a progressive man because he makes her write and does not allow her to be just a housewife. In fact, sometimes he abuses her, but this can be taken as one of his ways to encourage rather than deny her talent. He is exceptional in that he proposes a more flexible and personalized relationship than an ordinary marriage.

The cause of the tragedy lies, therefore, on the heroine's side. She cannot love Yoshio but fears living alone. One of the novel's most painful ironies is the way in which her desire for independence is undercut by her own lack of confidence. Economic pressure pushes her back to the married life, and the rebellious woman reduces herself to an unsatisfied wife in order to safeguard her welfare. Along with the economic need, Minoru's fear of sexual loneliness stops her from leaving Yoshio. She is aware of her "heavy body filled with wanton blood" and would not know how to deal with it if she loses a sexual partner. The female mummy of her dream is very much suggestive of the heroine herself. Her rouged lips reveal her sexuality, and her embrace symbolizes her need for a man to satisfy her sexual urges. Through this figure, the author implies that no matter how attractive the word *independence* may sound, the way to it for women is long and full of difficulties.

Translated Works: "Onnasakusha" (A Woman Writer; original title, *Yūjo* [Courtesan], 1913), short story. At the outset, a woman writer, who remains nameless throughout, is suffering in an attempt to write a novel. She has long been in a slump: every day she sits at the desk from morning till night having no idea at all to put into words. Almost neurotic, she at last breaks down and cries in front of her husband, who looks at her quite indifferently. Suddenly, driven by impulse, she beats him down and pinches his cheeks and lips, but her husband, who is used to her violence, puts up no resistance. She grows moody when she remembers a friend who paid her a visit several days ago and reported that she got married but was living separately, since she regarded a free union without sex as a radical alternative to conventional marriage. But the nonsexual relation seems no more than an expression of optimism to the woman writer, whose sexuality is the decisive element forcing her to stay with her husband. To her it seems unrealistic to think that any male-female relationship could exist apart from sexuality.

The woman writer wishes to be independent but also knows her limitations. For years she has dreamed of independence, but this dream has never come true, because she fears loneliness. She now turns her critical eye inward and censures herself for being weak and miserable: "No woman is so lacking in self-will as I am. Pulled from right, I lean right, and pulled from left, I lean left. What a slothful woman I am!" She is ashamed of depending on her husband both sexually and financially, but there is no way for her to make it on her own. Trapped in this frustrating position, she is overwhelmed by despair.

"Onnasakusha" is one of Toshiko's representative works, showing her keen interest in the inner self of a heroine easily identifiable with herself. This autobiographical short story shares the same theme with *Miira no kuchibeni.* The author focuses on the painful process of writing, the heroine's longing for independence, her disappointment with her inability to become independent, and her awareness of sexual obsession. There is a repeated pattern of the confrontation between her inner ideals and reality. The woman writer is, like Minoru in *Miira no kuchibeni,* a commentator on women's precarious situation as well as female psychology torn between dependence and independence.

"Eiga" (Glory, 1913), short story. Komatsu is a young, beautiful widow. Since the death of her husband she has had many love affairs and spent all the money left for her. Now she is in love with Koisaburō, a good-looking Kabuki actor, but he is already bored with her. Hoping to keep his interest, she has raised money by selling everything she possessed and borrowing from everyone around her. Still, it is evident that he is much less affectionate to her than he used to be. She cannot possibly forget the glorious days in the past. Before she became penniless, numerous men admired and wooed her, a wealthy, charming widow. It was the brightest period of her life. Now that she is poor and lonely, Koisaburō is the only person who reminds her of her past glory. As long as she is with him, she can forget the present predicament.

Today she has come to an inn to meet Koisaburō, but he failed to come, pleading illness. Even so, she waits for him for hours in vain. Even the maids at the inn seem to neglect her, as if treating her with the disdain that they think her present humble position deserves. Unable to stand their scornful attitude, she at last decides to leave the inn. On her way home, still wanting to see Koisaburō, Komatsu phones him, but he coldly refuses to meet her. This call finally forces her to recognize that their relationship is over and to make up her mind to give him up. Exhausted and in a state of shock, she totters toward home, where her little daughter is asleep, waiting for her return.

Komatsu is quite different from Toshiko's typical heroine. She indulges herself in love affairs with no desire to be independent. This prodigal widow seems much less intellectual than Minoru and the woman writer, both of whom are artists and beyond the ordinary as such. Yet Komatsu faces the same problem that plagues Minoru and the woman writer. Frustrated with her life, she seeks an outlet for all her passion and energy. In this context, her love affairs should be seen as something that makes her forget the frustration. Knowing that love is a disruptive force, she tries but cannot master the only thing that kindles her passion. When she loves men, she can take refuge in a fantasy world away from reality, where she feels herself totally alienated. But the affair with Koisaburō brings her nothing but a momentary respite; living as she is in the actual world, the tragedy is that reality keeps intruding upon her. When he abandons her, she realizes that her glory is gone forever and that she must confront the hostile reality once again.

By no means an idealized heroine, Komatsu nonetheless leaves a strong impression, largely due to her seriousness in love affairs. Miserable as she may have ended up, she never regrets her love, even taking fierce pride in her past affairs and regarding them as her glory. She blames no one for her present adverse circumstances and expects no pity from others. She has dignity and charm even as she is being destroyed by her own passion. Reflected in this unforgettable heroine are Toshiko's own mother and Toshiko herself, both of whom were quite honest with their emotions, be it love, hatred, or jealousy: neither feared to live a life of her own as her passion led her.

BIBLIOGRAPHY

Translations

"Glory." In *To Live and To Write: Selections by Japanese Women Writers, 1913–1938,* ed. Yukiko Tanaka. Seattle: Seal Press, 1987, 19–38.
"A Woman Writer." In *To Live and To Write: Selections by Japanese Women Writers 1913–1938,* ed. Yukiko Tanaka. Seattle: Seal Press, 1987, 11–18.

Critical Works

Kudō, Miyoko and Susan Phillips. *Bankuba no Ai: Tamura Toshiko to Suzuki Etsu* (Love in Vancouver: Tamura Toshiko and Suzuki Etsu). Tokyo: Domesu Shuppan, 1982. (An English version is in preparation.)
Tanaka, Yukiko. "Tamura Toshiko." In *To Live and To Write: Selections by Japanese Women Writers 1913–1938.* Seattle: Seal Press, 1987, 5–10.

                                                      Kyoko NAGAMATSU

TANABE Seiko (1928–), novelist, essayist. Real name: Kawano Seiko (Mrs. Kawano Sumio); née Tanabe Seiko.

Life: Seiko, the oldest daughter of photograph studio owner Tanabe Kan'ichi and his wife, Katsuyo, was born in Osaka. Her house was burned down in an air raid two months before the end of World War II in 1945. She lost her father in the same year. Graduating from a girls' high school, she entered Shōin Joshi Senmon Gakkō (Shōin Womens' Technical School) and received a degree from the Department of Japanese Literature in 1947. After clerking in a retail kitchen utensil store in Osaka for seven years, she joined Osaka Bungaku Gakkō (Osaka Literary Art School) to practice and polish her writing skills. She married a private practice physician and divorcé, Kawano Sumio, in 1966. They maintained separate residences for over a year in order to preserve their established work patterns. Upon his father's death, she moved into Kawano's house in Kōbe. There she engaged in the double life-style of a writer and housekeeper of his large household, including his mother and stepchildren. When all the children became independent, Seiko and her husband moved to an apartment in Itani city in 1976. Her trips abroad included those to Southeast Asia, Taiwan, Europe, and America.

Career: Since entering Osaka Bungaku Gakkō, Tanabe wrote rigorously, and her novel *Hanagari* (Flower Gathering) was nominated at a competition for fiction sponsored by a women's magazine in 1957. In addition to fiction, she wrote several plays for radio broadcasting. Tanabe's fame as a skillful, humorous fiction writer came when she won the fiftieth Akutagawa Award in 1964 for her short story, "Senchimentaru jānī" (Sentimental Journey).

Tanabe Seiko is a very prolific writer, and her voluminous works span several categories. Many of her contemporary stories are set in Osaka, as effectively and successfully as in "Sentimental Journey" and *Watashi no Osaka Hakkei* (Eight Scenes from My Osaka, 1965). New renditions of Japanese classical literature include *Shin Genji Monogatari* (New Tale of Genji, 1974–78), and *Mukashi Akebono* (Long Time Ago at Dawn, 1979) based on Sei Shonagon's late 10th-century essay collection, *Makura no sōshi* (Pillow Book). Tanabe's novels with historical themes are often dramatized, as in the case of *Hayabusawake Ōji no hanran* (Prince Hayabusawake's Rebellion, 1975), which was later staged by Takarazuka Women's Revue Company. Popular biographies include *Sensuji no kurokami* (Thousand Strands of Black Hair, 1972) on Meiji poetess Yosano Akiko, and *Hanagoromo nuguya matsuwaru* (Upon Disrobing Flowery Kimono, 1987) on another poetess Sugita Hisajo, which won the twenty-sixth *Joryū Bungakushō* (Women Writers' Award). Tanabe's essays on classical literary works and historical figures are poignant, as shown in *Fuguruma nikki* (Book-Cart Diary, 1973–74). Her satiric social commentaries are highly popular among male readers who avidly read her long-continuing columns in national newspapers and weekly magazines. They feature Kamoka no Occhan (Uncle Kamoka), who seems to be vaguely modeled on her husband, as Tanabe's chatting and drinking companion whose humorous Osaka dialect counterbalances her point of view with his male voice. For her many works vividly and lovingly capturing and popularizing the idiosyncracies of her native region, she was honored with the Osaka Geijutsu-shō (Osaka Art Award) in 1976.

Major Works: "Senchimentaru jānī" (Sentimental Journey, 1964), short story. When this work was chosen as winner of the Akutagawa Award, some judges, impressed by the author's prose-writing skill but uncomfortable with the work's humorous touch, criticized the theme as too frivolous for the prestigeous award. One of the judges, Ishikawa Tatsuzō (1905–85), however, defended the frivolousness, comparing it with jarring sounds of modern jazz music being appropriate for expressing new urban life. The story, the title of which is taken from a very popular Doris Day song, is a young radio scriptwriter's narration about his interlude with his senior, but rather naive, female writer. The lively delineation of the activities of scriptwriters, whose hectic lives are constantly segmented by the pressure of time, found its source in Tanabe's own experience. The senior writer, energetic in career and sexual adventures, falls in love with a muscular railroad worker, who dumps her promptly in spite of her earnest but futile efforts to understand his commitment to communist ideology. After the falling-out, the boy sleeps with her, and both promise to take a journey together soon, which they know will not take place. After the one-night stand, the female character mutters: "Do you honestly think there is love? Haven't we mistaken small parts of life, such as sexual drive, attraction to nice faces, common interest . . . calculation for old age . . . for love? Have these things taken over the throne of love?" The boy does not know the answer either.

The story is a vivacious portrayal of urbanites' almost blind search for love and their countless failures produced by mismatched expectations. The story also depicts the tenderness, even if momentary, that is shared between these urbanites. Though the pair's night was a "sentimental" one, they were able to take a short jaunt to touch each other, perhaps the best and most that they could hope for.

This early work already shows promise of Tanabe Seiko's enormous future popularity, which comes from the reader's empathy toward her characters as well as her tactfully wrought plots and vivacious dialogues. Her characters range from teenagers to the elderly, both males and females, and all of them are brimming with curiosity and vitality for life. In her autobiographical novel, *Shinkozaiku no saru ya kiji* (Cookie Monkeys and Cookie Pheasants, 1977–78), Tanabe confides that she aims to be a novelist in the mode of an *ukiyo-e* artisan. As in *ukiyo-e* prints, the popular Edo period wood-block genre prints, Tanabe's characters are common people whose particular traits and actions are vividly and colorfully carved out. In contrast to some later *ukiyo-e* prints, however, such as those made by Keisai Eisen (1790–1848) or Tsukioka Yoshitoshi (1839–1892), where vice and grotesquerie expose the dark side of human nature, Tanabe's main characters are equipped with a healthy balance between self-fulfillment and self-discipline and a proper equilibrium between their private and public selves. Peculiarities of her characters bring unexpected smiles to the readers but never threaten their understanding.

Tanabe's works on modern themes are placed here and now; even her deity is endowed with human qualities, largely reflecting the common Japanese world-view. In her short story "Yama nukete sanga ari" (The Mountain Collapses But Hills and Rivers Remain, 1977), Tanabe says, "Since I was little, I have envisioned Fortune as a persona—a prankster." Her Fortune constantly plays trick on people and contradicts their expectations. People's only recourse in dealing with the whims of Fortune is to stay resilient and resourceful. The most important topic for Tanabe in her totally humanoid world is the interaction between individuals, and she probes into people's efforts, under the taunting hand of Fortune, to seek out each other's worth in an attempt to develop compassionate relationships. Tanabe's definition of humor is rooted in her trust in human understanding. She explains in her essay "Yūmoa ni tsuite" (On Humor, 1975) that, for her, humor stands for gentleness and consideration for others; it is a social skill employed to avoid judgmental conclusions of right and wrong and to preserve each person's "face" intact so that the two can see each other again without feelings of embarrassment. To be humorous is to keep a multilateral view of human traits.

Watashi no Osaka hakkei (Eight Scenes from my Osaka, 1965), novel. Tanabe Seiko is optimistic about life and believes in people's basic good nature. The worst form of vice for her is a war, which interrupts and destroys small people's honest endeavor to live out their natural course of existence. Tanabe admits in *Shinkozaiku no saru ya inu* that she tends to become overly emotional when she deals with an antiwar theme. She describes with tender feeling many now middle-aged and elderly characters who still carry scars from the war. Her antimilitarism stand clearly appears in *Watashi no Osaka hakkei,* which is based on her childhood memory of growing up during the war. The sensitive teenager in the novel first firmly believes in the justificatory claims made by Japan's imperial military force as a rationalization for the war, but the conviction gradually changes into mistrust and disappointment as her beloved cousin dies on the Southeast Asia battlefield, as Osaka, including her house, is bombed flat, and as people barely manage to sustain their lives. The novel is written humorously, but the ending scene, where the Showa emperor, now a symbol of democratic Japan, visits Osaka, is a bitter testimony to the confusion of the citizens, who now suddenly have to reconcile what they trusted and believed in during the war with the king under a new robe. The heroine sees a ghostly illusion of millions of those deceased during the war calling after the emperor's hurriedly departing vehicle, begging him not to leave them behind. Tanabe saw and felt the great loss during the war, and the memory of the disaster adds a melancholic hue to the ordinary people's lives and their tenuous but precious interrelationships, which she cherishes and describes with deep sympathy.

Shin Genji Monogatari (New Tale of Genji, 1974–78), modern translation. In her postscript to this work, Tanabe explains her motive to translate the classic narrative of the 11th century as re-creating for modern readers an engrossing reading while keeping the original flavor. She states that the original is a well-constructed romance of believable characters with consistent personal dispositions, and the psychology of love has not changed much since the Heian period (794–1192), when Lady Murasaki's *Tale of Genji* was written. In order to modernize the story, Tanabe adds her own brush, as needed, to reflect nuances in characters and human relationships. In the original chapter of Yūgao, Lady Rokujō is touched on in passing, but in Tanabe's version, right before Genji encounters the young and unasssuming Yūgao, Tanabe discloses Lady Rokujō's figure darkly gazing into the mirror reflection of her own beautiful but no longer youthful face, while Genji is still asleep: the contrast of the two women, naïveté against self-consciousness, frailty against self-will, is well heightened. As Tanabe digs into the characters' psychology, the readers' intimacy with the narrative figures increases, recapturing an effect akin to the feeling of the author of *Sarashina Diary* (ca. 1060) when she, as a young girl, was completely absorbed in reading the world of *The Tale of Genji.*

Tanabe's curiosity does not stop at Lady Murasaki's characters but extends to the author herself. In the postscript to the work, Tanabe speculates on Lady Murasaki's personal history. She compares the images of children in Sei Shonagon's account, *Makura no Sōshi* (The Pillow Book, ca. 1000) with those in *The Tale of Genji* and detects that, while Sei Shōnagon is delighted and entertained by lovely children, Shōnagon's admiration for the child is limited to its outer form, perhaps a reflection of her never having borne her own. Lady Murasaki's observation of children, on the other hand, underlies the joy and sorrow of motherhood. Tanabe sees that Lady Murasaki's children inevitably grow up and become independent of their parents, thus adding complexity to interrelationships, Lady Murasaki's advantage as a novelist, Tanabe concludes.

Shin Genji Monogatari is a translation with serious intentions, but Tanabe has a hilarious travesty of the original in her *Shihon Genji Monogatari* (Private Tale of Genji, 1980). The hero is a middle-aged servant working under Koremitsu, who is Genji's faithful retainer in the original. Genji is called *Uchi no taishō* (our big honcho) by his servants, and all the characters speak in Osaka dialect. The hero complains of Genji's nocturnal outings, which summon the servants any time of night, and grumbles that this is no life for a middle-aged man. Grumpy as he is, considering the young master's marital problems with his wife, Lady Aoi, the servant sympathizes with Genji, whose high social status makes it impossible for him to divorce his wife. All of Genji's affairs are recounted from this worldly, sagacious man's point of view. Along with the gossipy tones of the narrative, witty conversation and the description of activities of lowly people in the society make the world of Genji ever so open and "reader friendly." *Shin Genji Monogatari* and *Shihon Genji Monogatari* together are the exemplification of Tanabe's versatile and brilliant skill as a fiction writer.

Translated Works: Miyamoto Musashi o kudoku hō (How to Woo Miyamoto Musashi, 1985), collection of short stories. The book is an assemblage of stories where men and women strain their wits and deploy their best tactics to catch the opposite sex. There are alluring categories such as "How to Woo a Female Writer," "How to Woo a Younger Man," and "How to Woo a Female Private Detective," but best of all is the title story, "How to Woo Miyamoto Mushashi," one of the most famous swordsmen in the early Edo period and author of the highly celebrated book on martial art, *Gorin no sho* (The Book of Five Rings). Tanabe's story is a comical takeoff on the famous Yoshikawa Eiji's voluminous *Miyamoto Musashi* (1935–39), in which one of the minor characters, Granny Osugi, pursues Musashi in order to kill him in revenge for the dishonor he brought to her family. In Tanabe's work, the central figure is Osugi, who savors the freedom of traveling all over the country, under the pretense of revenge, following Musashi wherever he goes. To Osugi, Musashi is merely a simple-headed, awkward, but lovable youth, and she has no intention of eliminating this convenient excuse for her traveling. Musashi, greatly popularized and minimized in his stature with his colloquial Osaka dialect, comes to unwittingly depend on the old woman for emotional support. This unusual symbiosis is another representation of Tanabe Seiko's ingenious skill in capturing phases in human life from various angles.

BIBLIOGRAPHY

Translations

"Let's Get Some Things Straight." Trans. Geraldine Harcourt. *PHP Intersect* (July 1985):41.
"The Marriage Game." *PHP Intersect* (July 1988):44–45.
Miyamoto Musashi o kudoku hō (How to Woo Miyamoto Musashi). Trans. Geraldine Harcourt. In press.

Fumiko Y. YAMAMOTO

TANAKA Sumie (1908–), dramatist, novelist, scriptwriter, essayist. Mrs. Tanaka Chikao, née: Tsujimura Sumie.

Life: Tanaka Sumie was born in Tokyo. Her mother was a strong-willed woman, widowed when her child was young. Her mother's matriarchial independence, witnessed even in such formative years, provided an obvious thematic constant for her later works. Tanaka, a precociously self-aware child with a romantic temperament, was recognized as gifted. A number of her *waka* and other poems were published in children's magazines, and she developed special affinities for painting and music. Tanaka studied at Tokyo Women's Normal College, a prestigious training school for teachers. After graduating in 1931, she taught at Sacred Heart Girls' High School. She was deeply influenced by this brief experience of living among women confined to the strictly regulated life of orthodox Catholicism, as is evident in her later works.

In October 1931 she married the rising director and playwright Tanaka Chikao (1905–). A year later, she resigned her teaching position and became involved in a drama work-study group led by the famous playwright and novelist Kikuchi Kan (1888–1948). Tanaka's career as a playwright began at this time. In 1942 she stopped writing to devote herself to family matters. In 1944, Tanaka, her husband, and three children were evacuated from Tokyo to Tottori City, where they remained until the end of the war. In 1947 her eldest son's illness forced Tanaka to move with him to Kyoto, where she became a reporter for *Kyoto Deiri Nyuus* (Kyoto Daily News). Two years later, the family was reunited first in Kyoto, then Tokyo. She took up film scriptwriting to support the family. Tanaka became a Catholic in 1952. Her conversion worked to foster even more strongly the major thematic constant in her works, namely, images of Christian women.

Career: Tanaka's literary career began in her student days at Tokyo Women's

Normal College. Her mentor was Nugata Roppuku (1890–1948), one of the leading dramatists of the time. He was instrumental in the publication of Tanaka's work in the theater magazine *Butai* (Stage). The magazine had been founded by Okamoto Kidō (1872–1939), a dramatist deeply involved in the New Theater Movement. The movement by this time had turned its attention from translations of Western drama to plays by contemporary Japanese writers. Encouraged by this increased interest, a number of dramatists gained recognition. Novelists, too, often tried their hand at stage works. Tanaka's theatrical debut was eased by this climate, but she soon grew restive under the close teacher/ apprentice scrutiny imposed by the editors of *Stage*.

Breaking free of such constraints, Tanaka found an outlet for dramatic writing in the coterie magazine *Iteki* (Barbarians). Her plays in this phase tended toward romanticism—celebrations of the purity of love, as in *Tekona to Koi to* (Tekona and Love, 1930). Reminiscent of the lyricism found in *The Manyōshū* (Collection of Myriad Poems, compiled in the 8th c.) and set in the world of myth, this play explores the plight of a heroine torn between three suitors. Another contribution to *Barbarians* was *Sōmeikyoku Ni-tanchō* (Sonata in D Minor, 1932), in which the ideal of romantic love culminates in the confession of a pianist heroine who shoots herself onstage.

Tanaka's marriage to her director-playwright husband was important in her creative development. So was her association with the play study group led by Kikuchi Kan, who helped publish a number of Tanaka's works in leading literary magazines and in a volume of collected plays. These pieces exhibit some major changes in narrative style and subject matter. Characters from ordinary families replace romantically idealized ones as lyricism yields to realism in plays like *Akiko no Kao* (Akiko's Face, 1936) and *Izoku-tachi* (Survivors, 1937).

Tanaka's first long play, *Haru Aki* (Spring and Autumn, 1939) is based on her brief career at the Sacred Heart Girls' High School. It is an ambitious depiction of the joys and sorrows of the women, both single and married, who live out their workaday lives in the isolated, intensely feminine world of a Catholic girls' school. The sensitivity and pathos of this play established Tanaka as an important playwright of the day.

The difficult, war-torn years 1942–47 were a blank in Tanaka's literary output, though her experiences provided a wealth of material for works to be published in the late 1940s and early 1950s. In addition to newspaper hackwork, Tanaka helped support her family by writing radio and film scripts and a number of plays, mostly of an autobiographical nature. *Akujo to Me to Kabe* (Bad Woman, Eyes and Walls, 1948) vividly re-creates her own disillusionment with life. It concerns a housewife's yearning for freedom in an atmosphere of rigidly repressive traditional in-laws, a husband lacking in family responsibility, and an ailing son. Two other plays, titled *Hotaru no Uta* (Song About Fireflies, 1949) and *Akai Zakuro* (Red Pomegranate, 1950), project the same image of a wife busy with part-time work at home, struggling to support a good-for-nothing husband and three small children.

After her conversion to Catholicism in 1952, Tanaka's plays utilized less autobiographical material, focusing more on larger philosophical concerns. In *Tsuzumi no Onna* (Adultress: The Drum of Waves, 1952) she brings a Christian perspective to the *bunraku* puppet play *Horikawa Nami no Tsuzumi* (The Drum of Waves at Horikawa, 1706) by Chikamatsu Monzaemon (1653–1725). Her heroine does not commit suicide merely as a victim of feudal oppression but does so by following the dictates of an active, decisive conscience. *Garashia Hosokawa-Fujin* (Garacia: Lady Hosokawa Gracia, 1959) offers a new interpretation of a historical figure in the 16th century, the devout Christian wife of a feudal lord, who ends her life by having her retainer stab her. Again, the heroine's death represents atonement for her traitorous father's sin, not defense of her personal honor.

Tanaka's last play for the *shingeki* (the New Theater) stage was *Tori ni wa Tsubasa ga Nai* (A Bird Does Not Have Wings, 1960). Thereafter, she wrote for different theaters, like the Shinpa and the Zenshinza Groups. Her interest in these directions, however, was short-lived and only led her back toward fiction, most of it autobiographical. Between 1967 and 1975 Tanaka wrote a number of short stories imbued with Christian themes. Among them were "Kakitsubata Gunraku" (Villages with Irises, 1972) and "Tubakidani" (Tsubakidani Village, 1973). Written in the first-person narrative, both are noted for their reflective, personal view of the emotional chasm separating characters bound by Catholic doctrine. The single volume of Tanaka's three short stories, also entitled *Kakitsubata Gunraku,* received a Ministry of Education Arts Award for 1973. Always concerned with women's issues, especially women's right to be themselves, Tanaka has devoted considerable time to feminist essays in recent years, among them, *Watakushi no Eranda Onna no Ikikata* (The Woman's Way of Life I Have Chosen, 1981) and *Ai no Kindai Joseishi* (Women In Love: A Modern History, 1984).

In 1984 Tanaka was awarded an Imperial Decoration of the Fourth Grade for her contribution to two literary genres: drama and fiction.

Major Works: Bad Woman, Eyes and Walls (Akujo to Me to Kabe, 1948), drama: two acts, seven scenes. A major thematic constant in Tanaka's work is explored here, namely, a woman's attempt to assert herself in spite of rigid traditional constraints. Set in the last years of World War II, the play concerns the heroine, Miné, in her mid-thirties. She and her husband, Shinkichi, and their son are evacuated to a small rural town to live with her in-laws, who are shabby, genteel, and resolutely hidebound in their devotion to traditional values. The transition from city to country life is difficult enough for Miné, but the sense of constraint is made intolerable by her in-laws. She begins to imagine that the very walls have eyes as the miserly, disapproving parents-in-law watch her every move, demanding absolute loyalty to family values. Miné's rebellion is as limited as her freedom, however. Her husband, an impoverished scholar still subsidized by her parents, offers little consolation. He promises to expedite their return to Tokyo but shares enough of his parents' dismal practicality to make

Miné feel all the more alone and dissatisfied. She unburdens herself on a widowed newspaper reporter. "Where," Miné asks, "is a woman to turn who cannot stand her life with a loving, well-meaning husband?"

Miné is desperate enough to contemplate suicide as the possible escape, but her plight is undercut by a kind of textual irony. Her confessions tend to be melodramatic and overemotional, even a shade pretentious. Her darkest mood is lightened with a certain humor when she says that instead of weeping she will try to laugh—like noodles. These confessions clearly fill a need: Miné is enough of an egotist to enjoy giving vent to her misery and enough of an artist to think of giving her self-assertion a form, however self-indulgent.

Nevertheless, Miné's rebelliousness takes strictly domestic forms. Her in-laws' unconscionable stinginess gives her a weapon of a sort. They would risk malnutrition, not because they are too scrupulous to buy on the black market but because they are misers. When a sparrow flies into the house, they can only think of turning it into teriyaki; Miné sets the bird free. When her mother sends some money, she buys a huge eel for a feast. Miné also starts getting tough with her husband. Even in front of her mother, who comes to visit her, Miné calls him a good-for-nothing, saying that any man who fails to finish his novel after ten years' trying cannot seem very appealing to the wife who has worked like a housemaid all that time. By the end of the play, Miné is prepared to go all the way in her accusations: she tells her husband and father-in-law that women's lives are sacrificed on the Buddhist altar of male egotism.

Outspoken as she is, Miné is reflective too. In fact, she does not have the courage of her convictions after all. Her tendency all along has been to accuse herself of being a "bad" woman. Her son turns out to be losing his sight. Miné sees this as divine punishment for her own lack of affection for the now-deceased father-in-law. She breaks down in front of the family Buddhist altar and begs forgiveness. She asks an astonished husband to beat her for her selfishness. Miné's self-accusations are met with a generosity and broad-mindedness hitherto unsuspected in her husband. He assures her that she is a good woman. In this play Tanaka's ultimate value reference turns out to be family solidarity.

Niji (Rainbow, 1970). Some of the motifs from *Bad Woman, Eyes and Walls* are repeated in this television drama. The circumstances, too, are similar, involving the heroine's traumatic experiences during and after the war in contexts of friction with small-town in-laws, followed by a struggle for independence in a big city. In 1971, *Rainbow* was expanded into a two-volume novel of the same title. The novelistic version fills in the twenty-year gap since the end of the war. Still, the heroine struggles with the desire to assert herself, even as she continues to be frustrated by family obligations and her writing career as well.

Rainbow in Kyoto (Kyoto no Niji, 1952), drama: one act, three scenes. Tanaka said about the autobiographical nature of this play, which is centered around survival in the traumatic postwar period: "I write about myself because my spiritual history interests me. All my plays—this one included—have been called ego-dramas. Yet my aim is not to record my own experience so much as to portray as objectively as possible reactions that happen to be mine to social changes that happen to be taking place.''

Again, this play reworks familiar material. Its heroine, simply identified as a woman, leads the complex life demanded by postwar conditions. She has to deal with stingy, authoritarian in-laws, a feckless husband, and three children. She supports them all as a black marketer and commutes to work in Kyoto. There she seeks release in a platonic, but intense relationship with an old friend living alone away from his family. As in *Bad Woman, Eyes and Walls,* the man serves as a means to an end: a woman's yearning to be free. The play is, in effect, an extended dialogue between a heroine given to emotional outbursts and a man speaking the soft and gentle dialect of Kyoto. Though he is her own age, the heroine asks the man, also presented as anonymous, to take the place of the father she lost as a child. She pours her heart out to him, complaining of her sufferings, living out her dreams. Since he used to be a friend of her brother's, they share memories of happier days before the war. Even as she complains about wifely duties and male domination, this woman behaves like a child, asking her friend to tuck her kimono sleeves so that she can wash her face. She even shares his bed, not in the heat of passion, but for the simple warmth of childlike trust and comfort.

By the end of the play, the heroine reflects on her playacting and sees that the dream of being free must give way to the stark realities of family responsibility. She whispers to her sleeping friend that she is ashamed of the way she has behaved. Yet she returns to her awful life not entirely defeated. She feels energized and determined to shake her husband out of his lethargy.

Adultress: The Drum of Waves (Tsuzumi no Onna, 1958), drama: three acts, five scenes. In 1947, the Japanese government repealed the law that criminalized female adultery. As a result, the subject of a wife's adultery was taken up by a number of serious novelists, such as Ōoka Shōhei (1909–), whose popular novel *Musashi no Fujin* (The Lady of Musashino, 1953) became a best-seller. Tanaka treats this new topic from a Christian moral perspective. Her source is Chikamatsu's puppet play *The Drum of the Waves at Horikawa.* The original feudal piece places the issue of the heroine's adultery squarely within the neo-Confucian social structure, which values social obligation (*giri*) over personal inclination (*ninjō*). Chikamatsu's heroine, Tane, a samurai's wife, is a victim of circumstance. During her husband's long absence, she is threatened by a former samurai suitor. Unless she gives herself to him, he will force her into a double suicide. Not knowing what to do, she temporizes, making a false promise to let him visit her later. The drum teacher Miyaji overhears, and to guarantee his silence, Tane offers herself to him—a commoner.

Chikamatsu invites the audience to consider whether Tane is motivated by *giri* (protecting family respectability) or by *ninjō* (lustfulness). She is depicted as a woman who has been drinking and whose lust might well have been sharpened by her husband's long absence. Yet one thing is clear: *giri* and *ninjō* are incompatible in feudal life. The feudal family is united by the demands of honor and respectability. Though Tane's husband, Hikokurō, wants to spare her life, *giri* dictates to him to assent to the family's demand that the erring wife pay the ultimate price. Tane, too, accepts this judgment and stabs herself with scarcely any hesitation between *giri* and *ninjō*.

The modern playwright Tanaka gives Tane's adultery somewhat different circumstances. Her would-be seducer is not a former suitor but a man who was rejected by Tane and underwent a psychological transformation to become a pederast interested in Tane's younger brother. Money is also an issue. In order to preserve a tenuous hold on respectability, Tane sees to it that her younger brother (her husband's adopted son) is well placed in society. She is reduced to seeking the good offices of a lowly drum teacher with good connections. Along with her materialistic motive, Tanaka's Tane, like her feudal counterpart, is portrayed as a woman who drinks too much in the presence of the man with whom she commits adultery. Tanaka, however, is not concerned with *giri/ninjō* conflicts. She concentrates on the results of this adultery. Once she breaks her marriage vows, Tane goes to extremes; she begs the drum teacher to run away with her. She even confesses to him that devotion to parents and husband is a sham, that a woman's life is fulfilled through pursuit of passion, self-destructive as it may be. The drum teacher, astonished, declares that he is, after all, a married man. The resolution of Tane's dilemma is given a rebellious modern twist as well. Wanting at all costs to preserve the façade of respectability, her husband tries to hush the matter up. Tane calls him a patronizing hypocrite and announces that she is pregnant with the drum teacher's child. She even dares the husband to kill her. When he hesitates, she goes to another room and commits suicide.

While Tanaka by no means condones Tane's adultery, whatever its causes, she still concludes her play with an indictment of male egotism. Whereas Chikamatsu's drum teacher is unattached, his modern counterpart has married twice. Relaxing with his second wife, the teacher says that a wife is like a drum—the newer the better. His new wife refers to her predecessor as the old drum now discarded. When confronted by Tane's husband bent on revenge, the drum teacher pretends not to have known her at all.

BIBLIOGRAPHY
Goodman, David. *Japanese Drama and Culture in the 1960s: The Return of the Gods.* Armonk, NY: London: M. E. Sharpe, 1988.
Rimer, J. Thomas. *Toward a Modern Japanese Theater: Kishida Kunio.* Princeton, NJ: Princeton University Press, 1974.

Keiko McDONALD

TOMIOKA Taeko (1935–), novelist, poet, essayist, scenarist, playwright, biographer.

Life: Tomioka Taeko was born in Osaka on July 28, 1935. Her father, a merchant engaged in recycling used iron products, deserted his family when

Taeko was about ten. For a few years, she served as the liaison between her father and mother, especially in matters of family finance.

In her teens, Taeko was introduced to traditional theater, such as Kabuki and Bunraku (puppet plays) and to the semimodern popular drama of Shinkokugeki and Shimpa troupes. She was able to frequent Minami-za in Kyoto, where her uncle was the head stage carpenter. This exposure proved important to the later development of her interest in theater. In 1958, upon graduation from the Osaka Municipal College for Women with a major in English literature, she won the Mr. H. Prize for a collection of poems. Her father had financed the publication of this collection. In the same year, she accepted a position as an English teacher at a high school, which she held for a little more than a year. At the age of twenty-six, Taeko moved to Tokyo and published the second book of poetry from a vanity press, which earned her the Murō Saisei shō, another prestigious prize. She began to expand her writing to screenplays, essays, short stories, and novels. She married in 1969.

Since 1965, Tomioka has traveled worldwide: five times to the United States, including a ten-month stay in New York City, and three times to Europe. She has also visited the Soviet Union, China, Korea, Malaysia, Singapore, and Australia.

Career: By 1990, Tomioka Taeko published six collections of poems, seven novels, twelve books of short stories, fourteen collections of essays, and three biographies. She has also authored or coauthored six scenarios for the movie director Shinoda Masahiro. She has written a handful of plays, some of which were staged by major theatrical groups. She has won many literary prizes, including major ones, such as the Tamura Toshiko Prize in 1974 for *Shokubutsu-sai* (Feast of Vegetation), the Women Writers Prize in 1974 for *Meido no Kazoku* (Family in Hell), and the Kawabata Yasunari Prize in 1977 for a short story, "Tachigire" (Quitting).

Even though the range of her creative activities clearly indicates an unusual versatility of her talents, her readers were amazed in 1977 when she recorded on an LP album her singing of her own poems to music composed by Sakamoto Ryūichi (b. 1952; actor in *Merry Christmas, Mr. Lawrence,* 1983, and winner of the Oscar for music for *The Last Emperor,* 1987). To promote its sale, she made her debut as a singer in a concert. She has made no more records.

Tomioka Taeko's poetry is primarily of everyday life, often involving two people either in or out of love. Her images include trees, mountains, and dogs. There is usually a subtle development, in common language, of a quasi-story that has a beginning, middle, and ending. She is concerned with human relationships. For example, the title poem of her first publication, "Henrei" (Courtesy in Return, 1958), seems to tell us about a young couple who fall in and out of love, eventually get married, and have children. At the end of this fairly long poem, a faint stomachache visits them (or one of them; it is not clear), as if their mundane life were paying them a "courtesy call in return."

She almost always talks about love, but it is love with absolutely no passion or sensuality. She examines human relations that are created because of love and talks about them in intimate terms of her own private life, but with a studied "detachment." Quintessential in Tomioka's writing, this quality makes her works elusive, and, in turn, that elusiveness creates a greater latitude for interpretation.

In writing fiction, Tomioka Taeko's attitude remains basically unchanged. Her style is sensitive to the natural Japanese syntax. It is often flavored by her native Osaka dialect and probably influenced by Bunraku performances, especially those by Chikamatsu Monzaemon (1653–1725), with lifelong admiration for whom she wrote *Chikamatsu Jōruri shiko* (Private Observations on the Chikamatsu Bunraku Plays, 1977). Her settings are by and large realistic; her treatment of characters is naturalistic; and the plots are discernible. Her earlier stories, such as *Oka ni mukatte hito wa narabu* (People Line Up Toward the Hills, 1971), are obviously based on experiences with her family. Some segments in her novels often resemble episodes she includes in fragmentary essays as her own life experiences. This approach smacks of *shishōsetsu,* or the "I-novel," the first-person narrative, in which emotionality matters most. Unlike the "I-novel," however, Tomioka's fiction is characterized by a strange absence of emotions.

Another conspicuous feature about her fiction is that her characters are more or less devoid of the power of mental faculties. They are often mentally retarded, mute, and sexually promiscuous. Some are compulsive gamblers and lunatics. Yet other characters usually and easily succumb to physical desires and lead dissolute lives. Human weaknesses are intentionally magnified. This magnification is effective in presenting the author's major assumption that humans are vulnerable by nature. It also works well as a means of "defamiliarization," which serves the "purpose of art" as defined by Victor Shklovsky, a Russian formalist critic, "to impart the sensation of things as they are perceived and not as they are known" (*Russian Formalist Criticism: Four Essays,* tr. Lee T. Lemon and Marian J. Reis, Lincoln: University of Nebraska Press, 1965, 12). Tomioka Taeko's characters are typically difficult to perceive as holistic human beings. Yet, they cannot be anything but humans because of the very negative attributes the author focuses on. She deals with her characters with an air of matter-of-factness. She does not pass judgment: from time to time, the reader senses a kind of warm forgiveness by the author. Her victimized characters never hold any grudge either. The middle-aged heroine in "Tōi sora" (A Faraway Sky, 1982), for example, even sympathizes with a young man who murdered an old woman after an attempted rape. This world of feeble-minded people embraced by the author's Buddha-like forgiveness clearly betrays Tomioka Taeko's interest in Buddhistic redemption of sins and the final salvation of all human beings. The "Meido" (Hell) in her novella's title, *Meido no kazoku,* is the underground world in the Buddhist cosmology where the dead live.

Tomioka touches upon her interest in legends and folklore in an essay, "Shiseikatsu to Shishōsetsu" (Private Life and the "I-Novel") in *Hyōgen no*

Fūkei (Landscape of Expressions, 1985). She posits that the novel is something between the ''I-novel'' and legend/folklore. When combined with an author's experience, the elements of legend/folklore can make the novel more universal.

A Buddhist legend of ''Mu-lien Rescuing His Mother from the Underworld'' is an important clue to the true appreciation of Tomioka's fiction. ''Mother'' is often a central figure, and there is usually a son who is searching for his mother. Mu-lien (Mu-lien in Chinese; Mokuren in Japanese; Maudgalayāyana in Sanskrit), whose childhood name was Turnip, left his mother for a business trip after pleading with her to lead a virtuous life. As soon as he left, however, she committed all sorts of sins and, as a result, fell into the bottom of all the hells. After mourning for three years, Mu-lien went through the underground, visiting one hell after another. He found the mother at long last and redeemed her sins by being tortured many times and getting himself killed. In this process, the mother repeatedly pledged to reform, but to no avail. In the end, the mother was saved by the virtue of Buddha and returned to this world.

This legend, recounted in *Tun-huang Popular Narratives* by Victor H. Mair (Cambridge: Cambridge University Press, 1983, 87–121), emphasizes the filial piety of Mu-lien, but his childhood name, Turnip, is a phallic symbol. Mu-lien's attachment to his mother, therefore, is oedipal, which suggests a natural cycle of death and rebirth. The mother's sinfulness in food and sex is a necessary condition for the preservation of life and reproduction of it. When told that a monk whose name as a child was Turnip wanted to see her, the mother exclaims, ''He is the precious darling of this sinful body.'' This presents not only the impossible dilemma that human life can perpetuate itself only when the Buddhist commandments are broken but the notion that turnips grow in Mother Earth as well.

Mother Earth is a crucial element in Tomioka Taeko's literary world. In many of her stories and novels, her characters go through the natural cycle of life as though they were manipulated by nature. They are born from the earth and will return to the earth after they die. In that sense, they are like vegetation. This plant imagery is linked to the evocation of primordial memories in Tomioka's fiction, as female fecundity is the central force in the ancient agricultural society. Michael Czaja elucidates the development of feasts of vegetation and the notion of Mother Earth in his *Gods of Myth and Stone: Phallicism in Japanese Folk Religion* (Tokyo: Weatherhill, 1974):

Following the introduction of rice cultivation in Yayoi times, . . . agricultural techniques became highly specialized, . . . The performance of the sequence of work also became so specialized that in itself it became ritualistic. . . . Women performed a key role in agriculture, not only as members of the labor force but also in the rituals dedicated to it. . . . The mystical connection between the fertility of the soil and the creative force of woman is one of the basic institutions of what one may call the agricultural mentality. The earth is commonly regarded as female: it has the capacity to bear fruit as if it were a mother and so it is called Mother Earth (165).

For Tomioka Taeko, sex is the driving force in the eternal cycle of death and rebirth and the source of human miseries at the same time. Completely stripped of romantic or erotic connotation, her description is not anatomical either. There is no human psychological ramification. In her, sex is a concept of fate that humans cannot escape. In order to present this literary theme, Tomioka's characters are deprived of mental abilities. They are manipulated by sexual desire implanted in them as part of nature's scheme. They do not even realize that they are victimized by sex. Miseries and predicaments from this fate constitute the purgatory that the characters accept with a sense of resignation.

Recognizing that sexual union leads into familial union, Tomioka investigates the human relationships within a social unit called "family" founded on sex. Later on, complicated blood relations will be built on that foundation. As more sexual relations intermesh, the family grows into a superstructure of human relations.

In more recent works, such as *Sunadokei no yōni* (Like an Hourglass, 1985), and *Byakkō* (White Light, 1988), Tomioka Taeko experiments with a new type of family. In both, a sterilized man plays an important role, which suggests the ultimate failure of sex as a means of life extension from generation to generation.

Major Works: Tomioka Taeko gendaishi bunko 15 (Tomioka Taeko Modern Poetry Library, Vol. 15, 1968). This contains fifty-six poems selected from four books, two new pieces, three essays on poetry, and a short autobiography. Two essays by other poets about her are appended. One conspicuous feature of Tomioka's poetry is her extensive use of the personal pronouns *watashi* (I), *anata* (you), and *watashitachi* (we), usually omitted in Japanese. This is attributable to the fact that Tomioka is influenced by English poetry, her major field of study as an undergraduate. The pronouns are quite effective: even though the poet is emotionally detached, the use of personal pronouns eliminates the distance between the poet and the poem and creates a kind of immediacy that draws in the reader. Her main interest here is in exploring human relations. Her language is sensitive and witty, but her vocabulary is commonplace, leaving the exact point of the poem elusive.

Shokubutsu-sai (Feast of Vegetation, 1973), novel. Her first full-length novel is about a dissolute young man who commits incest with his sister and then goes off to seek out their dead mother. It harks back to a major Japanese myth deriving from the description of the early Japanese political federation of the Yamatai kingdom that appears in the Chinese chronicle "History of the Kingdom of Wei," ca. 297 (*Sources of Japanese Tradition,* ed. William Theodore De Bary, 1958). According to the Wei Chih Chronicle, it was ruled by Queen Himiko (or Pimiko), a shamaness, served by one thousand female slaves. A younger brother, who was also her mate, assisted her in ruling the federation.

Himiko to yuu onna (The Woman Called Himiko, 1974), screenplay, was written before she started to work on *Feasts of Vegetation,* even though their publication dates indicate the opposite. Curiously, these two pieces, one set in the 3d century and the other in contemporary Japan, share a similar plot pattern.

In the screenplay, Tomioka Taeko creates her own version of the Himiko legend: here Himiko and Takehiko are only half-sister and brother. They do mate, but Takehiko's real lover is another woman, Adahime. Himiko is the head of the country of heavenly gods (Amatsu-kami no kuni), and Adahime is the daughter of a high official in the country of earthly gods (Kunitsu-kami no kuni). In a war between these two countries, Himiko is killed by farmers, and her country is defeated. This outcome points to the author's interest in "earth." Her novella with the same title, appended in the same volume, presents yet another version: Takehiko, after a brief life with Himiko, takes off to the country of darkness searching for his mother. In this novella, the author introduces another brother, named Nakatsuhiko. The name of the hero in *Feasts of Vegetation* is Naka Natsuki, an obvious derivative of Nakatsuhiko. Here, Tomioka Taeko creates a similar plot with characters that clearly parallel those in her versions of the Himiko legend. Naka Natsuki also sets out on a journey in search of his dead mother.

"Sūku" (Straw Dogs, 1980), short story. This piece consists of four short episodes, each telling of a casual sexual encounter by the same heroine-narrator. The four men are observed objectively in their physical movements and psychological behavior by the "I" narrator. The narrator, however, is not interested in these men as human beings, considers rituals before sex unnecessary, and is concerned only with the moment "the part of this stranger's body comes into her." Tomioka endeavors to isolate sex from the human factors so as to define sexuality in its simplest form. The title, "Sūku," is a Chinese term meaning straw dogs used in rituals in medieval China. These dogs were discarded when they were once used.

"Tōi sora" (A Faraway Sky, 1982), short story. The theme of sexuality is further developed here with a fifty-five-year-old woman who has three sons as the narrator-heroine. From nowhere a young deaf-mute comes along and asks her to have intercourse with him. He is interested only in sex. The narrator reacts compassionately and grants him his request. The man stays for a few days at a time and then disappears for a few months, returning only in spring and fall. The fact that the man is deaf and mute lessens the possibilities of human ties between the man and woman, reducing sexuality in its simplest form to that of animals. The woman, however, gets tired of this practice and tries in vain to avoid him. When she finally hides herself, the man climbs a nearby mountain and kills a sixty-nine-year-old woman who was picking herbs. He violates the corpse, and the police apprehend him. Good riddance, the woman thinks, but at the same time she feels anger toward the victim for not obliging him. In spite of her consternation upon finding another man at her door, she eventually goes to bed with him not as much from her own desire as out of pity.

"Ibara no moeru oto" (The Burning Sound of Thorns, 1971), short story. This concerns two family situations involving their adopted children. In one, a son becomes a hoodlum, and another becomes the victim of his own sexual desire, which leads him to murder and then his own suicide. In the other, harmony prevails when the adopted son marries the woman the mother has found for him and lives with the mother. This work was the first to introduce Tomioka's notion of forming a family not by sex but by adoption.

Sunadokei no yō ni (Like an Hourglass, 1985), novel. The plot centers around two sisters. One sister is unmarried, but the other sister's husband is involved with a mistress. The two sisters become interested in a divorced and sterilized man who rejects them for a mysterious and pregnant young girl. He considers adopting the baby, but she resolves the matter by abortion. The author's interest here is in families not built around procreation. This notion presupposes the termination of time at the end of one's life just as time runs out in an hourglass.

Byakkō (White Light, 1988), novel. This is a story about a family at Tamaki House in the mountains. Its members are not related by blood but have chosen to live together. Tamaki, a middle-aged woman responsible for the house, has adopted a boy. The narrator is an old girlfriend of Tamaki visiting the house. It is Tamaki's hope that the people she invites will live together to form a new kind of family. The basic philosophy here is to eliminate sex and to break down the endless cycle of death and rebirth. Tomioka Taeko created Morita, a sterilized male character, to experiment with this idea. He says, "It doesn't matter if the human race discontinues." Tamaki House goes through several crises. First, Tamaki's son wants to go to Tokyo so that he can get a job, making her lament: "Nobody can say it's bad, because he wants to go to Tokyo to work. Alas! People cannot stand inactivity. I was hoping at least my son could live without doing anything—without having a family, without having children, without having possessions." Then Morita's father, who does not subscribe to Tamaki's progressive concept, shows up and takes his son away. Finally, the narrator has sex with a young boy who wants to become her son. The oedipal urge motivates rebirth in this novel. Tamaki House dissolves itself, and Tomioka's experiment collapses with it.

Translated Works: See You Soon: Poems of Taeko Tomioka (original title in English: See You Soon, 1968) poetry collection. Some of these fifty-seven verses have been published previously in English-language journals. When translated into English, Tomioka's poetry seems less elusive than in original Japanese, partly because it has been filtered through the translator's interpretation. The poet's interest predominantly lies in human relations. "Just the Two of Us," for example, explores the understanding that "you" and "I" reach over the passage of time, but ultimately only after one of them has buried the other in the garden. Daily routine sets the stage where such mundane actions as having tea and toast can surely bury life. In the event one of them dies, however, the poet makes no mention of funeral arrangement. In their private life, the one left behind must face up to what has been lost in their relationship. This work is typical of Tomioka's poetry telling a story along the passage of time.

"Dumb Question, Dumb Answer" is in three stanzas. The logic here is almost syllogistic. The question and answer in the first stanza are obviously rhetorical, concerning whether or not "I" feels happy about being born, alive, Japanese, poor, and female. This poem is an example showing how Tomioka starts out in a small, mundane topic and then pushes it into a larger, universal context. It is clear here that the poet cannot stay in the realm of poetry any longer with this kind of weighty, fundamental human problem to ponder.

Facing the Hills They Stand (Oka ni mukatte hito wa narabu, 1971), novella. This first work of fiction by Tomioka presents two of her most essential themes: human life as the result of sins and the eventual return to the earth for rebirth. The story is set in a mythical situation: a nameless man from Yamato (the old name for Japan) comes to a nameless place. The man marries and starts a family. Knowing the husband may have a venereal disease from his visits to brothels while single, the couple agrees to throw their first baby away into the river at night if the baby is abnormal, as did the ancestral divine couple with the first born in *Kojiki*. Ironically, their firstborn, a girl, is normal, but the other six children are abnormal, either outrightly crazy or totally lacking in mental capacity. The father leaves the family for a woman. One of the crazy daughters is constantly pregnant by somebody in the village. Their salvationless life is described for two generations. The story has no conclusion. Tomioka's seemingly flowing narrative combined with her matter-of-factness suggests that time flows only toward death.

Family in Hell (Meido no kazoku, 1974) novella. This is a study of relationships in the familial setting, especially that of the mother and son and of the mother and daughter. An unmarried girl, the heroine, lives with a married man whose wife will not grant him a divorce. The girl becomes pregnant. The girl's mother is a no-nonsense, sharp-tongued realist who accuses the heroine of being nothing but a gullible baby. In contrast, the man's mother is happy-go-lucky, unable to make any important decision, and keeps saying, "Things will work out before long."

The work also illustrates how difficult it is for a human being to understand another. The heroine often does not know who the man really is. She attempts to find out what the man is thinking, but she always bumps into his mother's image before she gets a good grip on him; the man is the exact replica of his mother.

The man is described as "an out-and-out good-for-nothing," just like all other characters in Tomioka's works. He is a product of the endless cycle of death and rebirth, generated by desires. The women's groans sound like "recitation of sutra." The heroine escapes that trap because of a miscarriage. When the man leaves her for yet another woman, she finally starts to think, "Things will work out before long."

This story is not so much detached from the author's emotions as in her other works; the third-person narrative takes the heroine's point of view, and the author's voice expresses the heroine's emotions, enabling the reader to emphasize with the heroine's frustrations.

BIBLIOGRAPHY

Translations

"Facing the Hills They Stand." Tr. Kyoko Selden. In *Stories by Contemporary Japanese Women Writers,* ed. Noriko Mizuta Lippit and Kyoko Iriye Selden. Armonk, NY: M. E. Sharpe, 1982, 120–52.

"Family in Hell." Tr. Susan D. Videen. In *This Kind of Woman: Ten Short Stories by Japanese Women Writers 1960–1976,* ed. Yukiko Tanaka and Elizabeth Hanson. Stanford, CA: Stanford University Press, 1982, 141–77.

See You Soon: Poems of Taeko Tomioka. Tr. Hiroaki Sato. Chicago: Chicago Review Press, 1979.

"Still Life," "Girlfriend," and "who's afraid of t. s. eliot." Tr. Hiroaki Sato. In *Longman Anthology of World Literature by Women: 1875–1975,* ed. Marian Arkin and Barbara Schollar. New York: Longman, 1989, 888–89.

Critical Works

Lyons, Phyllis. "Tomioka Taeko." In *Longman Anthology of World Literature by Women 1875–1975,* ed. Marian Arkin and Barbara Schollar. New York: Longman, 1989, 887–88.

Tanaka, Yukiko. "Introduction." In *This Kind of Woman: Ten Stories by Japanese Women Writers 1960–1976,* ed. Yukiko Tanaka and Elizabeth Hanson. New York: Perigee Books, 1984, ix–xxv.

Sanroku YOSHIDA

TSUBOI Sakae (1899–1967), novelist, essayist, television dramatist, children's story writer, (Mrs. Tsuboi Shigeji); née Iwai Sakae.

Life: Tsuboi Sakae was born in a small village on Shodo Island in the Inland Sea. There were twelve children (two adopted) in this family, which sank into grinding poverty when the father's cooperage business failed. Tsuboi was forced to work part-time, but she managed to graduate from high school, becoming a clerk in a local post office. Her interest in literature developed early, thanks in part to various literary and children's magazines passed on to her by older brothers. She also became acquainted with the work of writers from her own area such as Kuroshima Denji (1898–1943) and her future husband, Tsuboi Shigeji (1897–1975). Her own writing would draw heavily on difficult formative years of experience with poverty, family solidarity, and closeness to nature.

In February 1922, a year after the great earthquake in the Tokyo area, Tsuboi went to the capital. She was twenty-three years old, anxious to move in literary circles and ready to find a husband. Before long she married Tsuboi Shigeji, known then as a proletarian writer. Her circle of acquaintances gradually widened to include poets of "anarchism" and working-class women writers such as her neighbors Hirabayashi Taiko (1905–72) and Hayashi Fumiko (1903–51). Those two helped turn Tsuboi's thoughts to the critique of the social system, which put women at such a cruel disadvantage. Tsuboi also came of intellectual age in a turbulent phase of Japanese politics. The so-called Taisho democracy, which had taken shape around 1910, was being swept away by a rising tide of Japanese militarism. This political shift brought government persecution of proletarian magazines like *Senki* (Battle Flag). Tsuboi's husband became an active member of a Marxist group called Nappu (NAPF) after its Esperanto name, Nippon Artista Proleta Federatiot (the All Japan Proletarian Art League). Their home became the headquarters of this organization, whose membership included a number of college students, among them the future leading novelist-poets Takami Jun (1907–65) and Miyoshi Jūrō (1908–58).

In this tense political climate, Tsuboi published her first work, "Purobunshi no tsuma no nikki" (Diary of a Proletarian Writer's Wife, 1928). Though written for money, this work heralded a long and prolific career. By the mid-1950s Tsuboi was recognized as one of Japan's leading female novelists. She had no children herself but adopted her motherless niece in 1925 and her orphaned nephew in 1945. After some years of declining health, Tsuboi died from asthmatic complications at the age of sixty-six.

Career: In 1932, Tsuboi's activist husband was jailed for six months. This incident brought her into closer contact with the wives of other political prisoners. The most prominent of these were Miyamoto Yuriko (1889–1951), already an established "proletarian" novelist, and Sata Ineko (1904–), editor of the magazine *Hataraku Fujin* (Working Women), published by Proretaria Bunka Renmei (Proletarian Arts League). Sata asked Tsuboi to join the editorial staff and nurtured her protegée's talent by stressing the virtues of a simple, colloquial style. By 1935, Tsuboi had published a short piece, "Gekkyūbi" (Payday) in the prestigious *Fujin Bungei* (Women's Literary Magazine, edited by Kamichika Ichiko (1888–1981), herself a feminist and, after World War II, a socialist politician.

Despite her close association with the proletarian movement, Tsuboi was not strongly committed to it. She tended rather to take an objective, analytical view of its politics and personalities. Her best writing of this sort appeared only after the war. *Tsuma no za* (The Position of the Wife), serialized from 1942 to 1949 in the proletraian journal *Shin Nihon Bungaku* (New Japanese Literature), is an autobiographical account of her younger sister's marriage to the proletarian writer Tokunaga Sunao (1899–1958). Tsuboi offers a harshly realistic view of the husband's cruelty and egotism, which she saw as the darker side of a self-proclaimed, cultured intelligentsia supposedly sympathetic to the plight of women in prewar Japan. A four-part novel, *Kaze* (The Wind, 1949), also draws directly on her contact with the "anarchist" poets and her husband's involvement with the proletarian movement, serving as a case study of writers confronting social trends unfavorable to them.

By the time she was thirty-five, Tsuboi began to take herself seriously as a writer, though she was reluctant to continue where she had already succeeded, namely, in an autobiographical vein and in opposition to the prevailing political climate. Then, she was introduced by Sata to a novel depicting the world of children, *Kaze no naka no kodomotachi* (Children in the Wind) by Tsubota Jōji (1890–1982). This book inspired her to use her own regional experiences in a children's story. The result was one of her masterpieces, the short story "Daikon no ha" (Radish Leaves, 1938), the success of which led to similar publications in quick succession. Her autobiographical first novel, *Koyomi* (Calendar, 1940), won the *Shinchō* magazine Literary Award.

By 1941 Tsuboi was well established and writing busily, even as Japan became steadily more involved in the spreading calamity of World War II. Her adult writing was chiefly directed at women. Her children's stories appealed to both boys and girls. Unlike many of her contemporaries, Tsuboi recognized that juvenile literature should not be considered a separate and inferior category. In 1942, one of her stories was chosen by the literary giant Shimazaki Tōson (1892–1943) for inclusion in *Shinsaku Shōnen Bungakusen* (A New Selection of Literature for Boys). During the summer of 1943 Tsuboi escaped the horrors of war-torn Tokyo to spend two months at a hot spring resort where she finished "Kaki no ki no aru le" (The House with a Persimmon Tree). In 1951, this short story was given the first Postwar Award for Children's Literature by the Japanese government. The following year she earned the prestigious Minister of Education Award in Literature for *Haha no nai ko to ko no nai haha* (Motherless Child and Childless Mother, 1951) and *Sakamichi* (Slope, 1951).

The climax of her career came with *Nijūshi no hitomi* (Twenty-Four Eyes, 1952). The novel itself was not immediately successful, though it became a sentimental best-seller after the release of the 1954 film version directed by Kinoshita Keisuke (1912–). The same year, *Motherless Child and Childless Mother* was also filmed to fit the cinema industry's highly successful *hahamono* or tear-jerker mother genre. These films created something of a "Tsuboi boom," which in turn brought her a stream of requests from magazine editors and book publishers and even from the broadcasting industry. Her serialized drama, *Dokoka de nanika* (Something Happened Somewhere, 1959), was aired in 1959 by the national television network NHK. Its success led to another NHK production, the television drama *Ashita no kaze* (Tomorrow's Wind, 1962). Ill as she often was, Tsuboi remained productive, issuing her last work, *Haha to ko to* (Mother and Daughter), in 1965.

Major Works: "Daikon no ha" (Radish Leaves, 1938), short story. Regionalism and maternalism are the keynotes of Tsuboi Sakae's writing. Early in her career, many critics pictured her as a housewife popping out of the kitchen, drying her hands on her apron. There is some truth in this image, since Tsuboi's stories tend to evoke the warmth and affection associated with working-class motherhood. Her characters often live close to nature, especially those from Tsuboi's own home island in the idyllic Inland Sea.

"Radish Leaves" is notable for its success in conveying a child's own view of family hardship. Poverty, temporary separation from parents, and a little sister's blindness all demand adjustment from five-year-old Ken. Since farming alone cannot provide a livelihood on Shodo Island, his father must work in

Tokyo. The mother's household routine is complicated by frequent trips to Kobe, where a doctor tries to save her baby daughter's eyesight. Left behind with the grandmother and an uncle's family, Ken rebels with all a child's anger and anguish. The story traces his gradual understanding of his mother's suffering.

This story also treats family solidarity as a force for survival. The uncle treats Ken like one of his own children during his stay with them. Ken's close relationship with his grandmother is revealed through trivial incidents like feeding the pigs together. The story is saved from lapsing into sentimentality partly by the homely and humorous Shikoku rural dialect used throughout.

The maternal theme runs strong throughout as well. Ken's mother must serve as head of the household during her husband's absence. Tsuboi's thematic constant of female self-reliance is seen in this woman's determination to save her daughter's sight, as she says: "My conscience won't be clear unless I do everything possible. I will work till I drop to pay for an operation, even if there is no guarantee of success!"

As the story ends, Ken and his mother walk homeward along a country road. The pungent smell of young radish leaves hangs in the air—a fit symbol of commonplace survival, since the poor feed their livestock on these greens, which they also pickle and eat themselves. Tsuboi celebrates the moral strength of the mother-son bond in this quiet moment of simple shared delight.

Koyomi (Calendar, 1940), novel. The image of woman challenging her environment through moral fortitude and maternal affection is also the mainspring of this autobiographical fiction. As with Tsuboi's own large family on Shodo Island, the absence of a commanding male presence has led to the formation of a powerful and resourceful matriarchy. *Calendar*, in fact, studies the dissolution of such a matriarchy. The story begins at the end, with the family reduced to the two youngest daughters still living together at home. The younger, Mie, plays housewife while her sister, Kuniko, teaches school as she has done for the past ten years. These two sisters represent different attitudes to the position of women. Kuniko is for independence, believing that no woman should marry in order to be supported by a man. Engaged to be married, Mie expects to find happiness with her engineer husband.

The opening chapter foreshadows the final stage of family dissolution, since Kuniko will soon be the only person left at home. The succeeding chapters, all but the last, unfold a twenty-year history of disintegration. It begins with collapse of the family cooperage business, reducing grandmother, parents, and twelve children to extreme poverty. Tsuboi studies the relations among these individuals as they face new hardships and react to burdens that the family adversity places on each member.

The theme of female sacrifice begins with the mother, Ine. Her own mother had tried to spare Ine the horrors of a "good" match with the patriarchal gentry by wedding her to the gentle, but socially undistinguishable, Jūkichi. Unfortunately, escape from patriarchal oppression led to the unforeseen horrors of poverty. Tsuboi presents this woman as haunted by images of death and separation, and indeed Ine nearly dies in childbirth. By the time Ine is in her mid-forties, at last ready to see her own eldest son and daughter marry, she is worn out by thirty years of childbearing and hard labor. Significantly, Ine derives strength from these afflictions. Her husband has gone to sea, so Ine quite literally is left at the helm at home. Not even a partially paralyzing stroke prevents her from carrying on as matriarch. Yet before the age of sixty Ine is on her deathbed, "an old hag defeated by age, her hair completely white," a powerful symbol of the individual woman sacrificed to that abstract entity: family.

Ine's children react to family obligation in various ways. The eldest son, Shota, goes to law school at night in Tokyo. As future head of the family, he imagines that money will be the answer. Paradoxically, his very desire to succeed in the world contributes to the disintegration of his family. Having to work and study and support his own wife and son, he cracks under the strain and returns to the family home to die. All but the two younger sisters choose dependence over independence, marrying into the bondage of patriarchal families.

At last, Mie, the youngest of all, is ready to follow in the footsteps of all these silent sufferers by choosing a man from the same village. Kuniko is the only one who steadfastly refuses to sell herself into the slavery of marriage. Her security must come from her profession as a teacher. Moreover, now that the sole male heir is gone, Kuniko is courageous enough to assume responsibility for the family name. In Kuniko the familiar theme of matriarchy returns.

A family reunion brings the five surviving sisters together. This occasion only confirms Kuniko in her belief in independence. Alone among all her sisters, she seems ready to take that risk at the end of this powerful saga of Japanese women's lives in the 1920s—in a society then still very much male-dominated.

Uchikake (The Wedding Gown, 1955), novel. This chronicle of another matriarchy encompasses five generations spread over almost a century (1860–1948) in which Japan moved from a feudal to a modern society and experienced the traumatic wars. This time, the family is a distinguished one. It survives the momentous changes by trading its feudal social preeminence as village head on Shodo Island for the preeminently modern functions of a landlord/moneylender.

The Wedding Gown concerns women torn between conformity and rebellion as they face the absolute feudal entity called "family" and participate in its survival and change into modern times. As each of the five women takes her place as head of the family, she rebels; then gradually she yields to preemptive family values. The difference is that each generation does become progressively more assertive.

The story begins in the mid-19th century, when the Fukumoto family is forced to adopt a male heir to marry their only daughter, Suzu. This girl is determined to marry the man she loves but is foiled by pressures of respectability. All she can do is show her spouse that she will not endure the male double standard uncomplainingly. Yet her rebellious nature goes hand in hand with a sense of wifely duty. When her sister, her husband's paramour, dies in childbirth, Suzu raises the child, Tatsu, as her own and makes her heiress of the family estate.

Suzu's husband dies, so the family must again adopt a male to carry on its name. The wife perforce this time is Tatsu. She rebels by refusing to sleep with her husband, seducing one of the family's poor tenants, and becoming pregnant by him. Yet she too gives in to family code, acting the part of the wife in order to raise her illegitimate daughter, Koume.

Suzu and Tatsu had local husbands. When Koume's turn comes, her rebellious choice signifies a geographical strain put on notions of family solidarity. Her mate is an outsider and, worse, a roving seafarer.

Social changes also play a part in this family history. As modern Japan embarks on its imperialist quest in the world, Koume's daughter, Kotoji, fourth heiress in the family, chooses to become a medical doctor. This choice signals more than just the arrival of modern professional independence for women. It is a sign of greater mobility as well. Whereas Koume's independence was realized through frequent visits to her husband aboard ship in port cities, her medical student daughter lives on her own in Tokyo. Kotoji's rebellion against the family takes the form of channeling her extravagant allowance into student antiwar movements. Arrested by the police and labeled a traitor by her colleagues, she is rescued by the family. Now she has no choice but to return home, to the sanctity of an unwanted marriage.

Kotoji's rebelliousness is nonetheless channeled into the daughter she has named Sayaka; literally translated, her name means "bright" or "true." Kotoji hopes that this child will be true to herself, not to the rigid, outmoded family structure that has kept so many generations of women in bondage. The spirit of female independence asserts itself when Sayaka declares herself determined to go to a women's college in Tokyo, even if it means working her way through school with a part-time job.

The powerful image of matriarchy is evoked when Tatsu, Koume, and Kotoji mount a challenge to the feudal family structure that has bound them all. They join forces to do all they can to support Sayaka in her quest for education.

The wedding gown serves throughout as a controlling metaphor in this saga. Each woman's response to this silk garment offer clues to the shifting influence the family system has on her. Specially ordered from Kyoto, it was the first-generation Suzu's gown. It is at once a symbol of wished-for happiness and the family pride that limits personal freedom. When Tatsu is forced into marriage at the age of seventeen, she is "made to wear Suzu's wedding gown." Even the third-generation Koume is willing to wear Suzu's wedding gown to marry the man of her own choosing. Its heaviness conveys a sense of family prestige and burden as well. She is pleased to see her own daughter, Kotoji, choosing the old gown over a new one suggested for her wedding. Kotoji's resignation to her fate dictates this choice. She says: "That old gown has been used to bind our women to the family. That's why I want to wear it." Fifth-generation Sayaka, however, treats the gown lightly. Trying it on, she imitates an actress and declares that the gown is "a symbol of the family system." One of the sleeves catches on her watchband, tearing the silk. The symbolic importance of this is obvious. Yet Sayaka waits for great-grandmother Tatsu's response to this accident—the old lady's "last farewell to the wedding gown."

Translated Works: Twenty-Four Eyes (Nijūshi no Hitomi, 1954), novel. Regionalism, maternal affection, and women's issues are all crystallized in this life story of the elementary school teacher Ōishi. Set on Shodo Island in the years between 1929 and 1946, the chronicle covers her assignment to a small school with twelve pupils; thus her relationship with the children spans the tumultuous period of Japan's imperialist expansion marked by the China incident of 1937, the Tripatrite Pact of 1940, and finally World War II. The chronicle ends when Ōishi returns to teaching after losing her husband and youngest child. She holds a reunion with the surviving members of the original twelve.

Twenty-Four Eyes is perhaps the best example of Tsuboi's emotional or melodramatic novels and is the best known of her works. It makes effective use of mood shifts signaled by children's songs and their guileless perspectives on adult life and social forces generally. Tsuboi is a master of sentimental indulgence kept within bounds by careful narrative control. She takes pains in setting her scene, making use of clues to the sociopolitical milieu these children inhabit. She also balances points of view, taking us in and out of complex interactions between children's and adult's (Ōishi's) sense of the world and human relationships.

The opening section describes the age-old pattern of an outsider coming into a conservative village, creating a stir, and finally winning acceptance. Ōishi, a young woman in Western dress riding a bicycle, is too modern for the old-fashioned locals. Her democratic approach to teaching also goes against the conservative grain of the villagers. Her students, however, soon grow to love this teacher, who cycles four miles a day to teach them. This sense of teacher-pupil solidarity is expressed in things as simple as the children's song "Awate Dokoya" (A Hasty Barber) and in an episode that clinches the matter for the villagers as well.

The second section takes place four years after Ōishi's arrival. Though the country's jingoistic mood affects even this village, a happy mood predominates as the children grow and change. The depression, however, changes the lives of children like Matsue. Tsuboi uses an example as simple as a metal lunch box with a lily pattern to show how a child's happiness can be destroyed by forces far beyond her control. Matsue is ashamed of her old wicker lunch box—sign of her family's desperate poverty. When her mother dies in childbirth, Matsue must stay home to care for the baby. When Ōishi visits, bringing a new lunch box—symbol of their bond—Matsue is incapable of showing joy or thanks.

The third section explores the effects of the war on the islanders. Ōishi's husband is drafted into the army. One of her colleagues is arrested on suspicion of leftist activism. Some of her former pupils join the military. The mood of otherwise utter despondency is lightened by Ōishi's maternalism, which takes on a new dimension now: her challenge to the prevailing mania for patriotic self-sacrifice.

The fourth section brings the theme of solidarity—dissolution—solidarity full circle. Ōishi is shown as a victim of uncontrollable social forces. The author uses this section to express her antiwar sentiments and anger that militarism destroyed so many lives. The widowed Ōishi observes that men had the bad luck to be killed while women survived them with lives in ruins. Ōishi's attitude is softened, however, by the sentimental celebration of reunion pervading this section. The past is relived as she meets her former pupils, some of them bringing their children for her to teach. A touch of melodrama creeps in, of course. The earlier image of the lunch box symbolic of teacher-pupil solidarity returns. This time, her former students have bought Ōishi a new bicycle. This symbolic return to her youth and zest for education reminds us of the drastic changes that affect individual lives. A former pupil sings, "Kōjō no Tsuki" (The Moon over the Ruined Castle). This famous children's song evokes keen nostalgia and reminds the reader powerfully of the law of mutability, always at work in human life.

"Umbrella on a Moonlit Night" (Tsukiyo no Kasa, 1953), short story. Set in the changing world of postwar recovery, this first-person narrative deals with the plight of women in a male-dominated society. The narrator is a housewife and mother of three, married to a self-centered husband. The story begins with a statement of self-awareness defining the narrator and her friends: "We were housewives who for some twenty years had relied solely on our husbands' pocketbooks. We were . . . faithful wives who took comfort in being ordinary mothers." The hectic pace of modernization in postwar Japan opens up two alternatives for these women: rigid adherence to traditional roles or a breakaway transformation. The narrator and her friends pursue the latter, though painfully aware of the limits set by their age on any attempt to recapture "what little rebelliousness" they once had. Nevertheless, these four housewives follow the national trend toward democratization by forming a club. Self-assertion does not come easily, as is subtly shown through a rivalry with a similar club formed by younger women in the neighborhood. Eagerness to break out of the housewife mold leads to a fuss about the name of the club. It cannot have an old-fashioned ring, but it must convey a sense of women clubbing together to "dominate" their husbands, once in a while at least.

Progress in the club's affairs depicts a gradual transformation in these women. They move from mere chitchat to discussion of popular books and even political issues. Their treasurer's report reflects dramatic increases in the club dues collected. Clearly, these good housewives are getting better at managing the money their husbands give them for keeping the household running. The narrator's sense of freedom is expressed in her pride in this deft management of her household budget. Like her friends, she feels entitled to this money in a new and inspiriting way. Emboldened by their bit of financial independence, the women get beyond meeting in one another's homes: they splurge by going out to eat.

Tsuboi does not simplify the psychological consequences of this bid for freedom. She follows the progress of the narrator's ambivalence, which makes her feel guilty about leaving the house and tempts her to resign from the club. Tsuboi ends her story, nevertheless, on a note of quiet celebration in honor of the virtues of patience, flexibility, and caring. Even in a society so rapidly democratizing itself, the narrator reaffirms her point about balance in marriage and family as she reflects on the joy these have brought her and her husband. He is the unyielding one, so any move toward reconciliation must come from her. She goes to meet him at the train station. Without even noticing her, he opens an umbrella under a cloudless sky and heads home. The narrator follows quietly "behind this strange figure holding an umbrella in the moonlight." Tsuboi's humor comes to the fore in this wife's acceptance of her husband as he is— and of herself as wife and mother these twenty years.

"Under the Persimmon Tree" (Kaki No Ki no Au le, 1958), children's story. This piece exhibits two "auteuristic" constants in Tsuboi's novels: motherly warmth, affection, and concern for the working class and deep love of nature. Set in Tsuboi's hometown on Shodo Island in the Inland Sea, the story concerns a little boy's maturing in a short space of time. Told chiefly through Yoichi's childlike perspective, his experience of birth, separation, and death offers insights into the lives of a tightly knit, three-generation family living close to the soil.

Yoichi's uncle and aunt are farmers. The beauty of life lived close to nature is symbolized by the natural abundance surrounding their house—the grapes and chestnut trees and orchard of pears and peaches. Similarly, Yoichi's parents are nature-bound: the father is away at sea. The mother, though a seamstress, tends a small vegetable garden. A huge persimmon tree in the backyard is the focus for this family's closeness to nature. The children pass it many times a day and learn to love its comforting seasonal changes. They also come to have a sense of its place in family history. When their parents were small, a little brown sugar served on "a shiny persimmon leaf" was considered a marvelous treat. Yoichi's uncle cut down a large old tree after his only child died of eating too much of its fruit. In little Yoichi's mind the persimmon tree becomes almost a sacred object to be venerated and cared for. This is a feeling he shares with Grandfather, who says this tree has "protected the family like a god" for so many long years.

The silent communication between old man and ancient tree is beautifully conveyed as Yoichi witnesses family history unfolding with poignantly sad results. One autumn the tree fails to bear fruit because villagers digging a well nearby piled large stones on its roots. Grandfather is so accustomed to treating the tree like a human presence that he says it "must have had a hard life." Seeking to unburden its roots by moving the stones, the old man works too hard and dies. Yoichi and Fumie are brought closer to their grandfather as they learn about death this way. Their bond is expressed in an offering of persimmon flowers they place on the old man's tomb.

When Yoichi's mother gives birth to twins, his world is given a rough shake.

Uncle, it is decided, will adopt one of the babies. Yoichi is unwilling to part with one of his brothers. Yet a sudden transformation occurs in the shade of the old persimmon tree. Yoichi and Uncle are standing there when Uncle asks for a branch to graft onto a tree for his family. Yoichi gives him one and agrees to the adoption too. The moral of sharing as a means of strengthening the family bond comes directly from Tsuboi, whose characteristic authorial voice conveys an affectionate maternal message: "The baby who is now sleeping in a cradle will soon awake. Held in Aunt's arms, and accompanied by a goat and a persimmon branch, it will leave Yoichi's house." Tsuboi also uses personification to create deep and abiding sympathy between this simple, rural family and the land that sustains them: the old persimmon keeps watch over these humane events spanning three generations, sometimes "smiling," sometimes "chuckling."

BIBLIOGRAPHY

Translations

Twenty-Four Eyes. Tr. Akira Miura. Tokyo: Kenkyusha, 1957.
"Umbrella on a Moon Night." Tr. Chris Hefrel. In *The Mother of Dreams and Other Short Stories: Portrayals of Women in Modern Japanese Fiction,* ed. Makoto Ueda. Tokyo: Kodansha International, 1986.
"Under the Persimmon Tree." Tr. Kiyonobu Uno. *The Reeds* 10 (1965): 49–63.

Critical Works

Desser, David. "Twenty-Four Eyes." In *Childhood and Education in Japan.* New York: Japan Society, 1990, 30–34. The third teaching module in *The Japanese Society Through Film* series. The film on video, *Twenty-Four Eyes,* is included in this module.
McDonald, Keiko. "Kinoshita and the Gift of Tears: Twenty-Four Eyes." *Cinema East: A Critical Study of Major Japanese Films.* London: Fairleigh Dickinson University Press, 1983, 231–54.

Keiko McDONALD

TSUMURA Setsuko (1928–), novelist, essayist. Real name: Yoshimura Setsuko (Mrs. Yoshimura Akira); née Kitahara Setsuko.

Life: Tsumura Setsuko was born on June 5, 1928, second daughter of a silk merchant in the city of Fukui, the climate of which, Setsuko writes, was gloomy, especially during winter. After she lost her mother at the age of nine, the father moved his remaining family to Tokyo in 1939, hoping that the brighter climate of Tokyo would improve Setsuko's rather frail disposition. Her father, however, died suddenly of heart failure in 1944; fortunately he left enough money for Setsuko, her two sisters, and their grandmother to live on.

In 1945, the year the war ended, Setsuko graduated from a middle school. In 1947 she enrolled at a dressmaking school in Tokyo. Knowing that numerous young men who could have been candidates as her husband had been killed in the war, she wished to have some means of livelihood for herself. After finishing her training, she opened up a dressmaking store in 1948. Even though she was very successful in her business, she closed the store in two years. In 1951 she became a student of the two-year junior college of Gakushūin University, majoring in Japanese literature. Setsuko started writing stories for students' magazines and sold some of her stories to teenage girls' magazines. Upon graduation in 1953, she married Yoshimura Akira (1927–), who was the editor of a students' magazine at that time and who now is a very active writer himself. They have remained married since then, but their literary tendencies are far apart from each other: Setsuko concentrates on the study of human psychology, and her husband is an adept writer dealing with documentary and historical novels. As of 1988, Yoshimura Akira won eight major prizes, including the Mainichi Arts Prize, the Yomiuri Literature Prize, the Education Ministry Prize (1985), and the Japan Academy of Arts Prize (1987).

Tsumura Setsuko took a trip to Greece in 1979, to Korea in 1980, and to Okinawa in 1981, all to collect materials for her writing. She lives in Mitaka, Tokyo, with her husband and their two children.

Career: Tsumura Setsuko began writing short stories and novels in 1956 for various *dōjin zasshi* (literary coterie magazine), including the prestigious *Bungakusha* (Writers) edited by the celebrated novelist Niwa Fumio (1904–). In 1959 and 1963, three of her short stories were nominated for the Naoki Prize, the most important prize in the category of ''popular'' literature in Japan. Her story ''Saihate'' (To the End of the Land), which had been published in a dōjin-zasshi, was reprinted in 1964 in the leading literary magazine *Shinchō* and awarded the Shinchō Dōjin Zasshi Prize. This same piece was nominated in the spring of the following year for the Akutagawa Prize, the prestigious award for ''serious'' literature. Her next story, however, ''Gangu'' (The Toy), won her this coveted prize in the fall of the same year.

As of 1988, Tsumura Setsuko has written about thirty novels, some 160 short stories, and numerous essays. Most of her works usually appear in various monthly literary magazines first and then as collection or single novels in hard cover published by a wide range of publishers, including such prestigious houses as Shinchōsha, Kōdansha, Chuōkōronsha, and Bungeishunjū. Most of her pieces are reprinted in *bunkobon* (pocket-size, paperback edition) in multiple printings.

Tsumura Setsuko's novels mostly deal with women who find themselves in a dilemma; whether to marry and be happy as wife and mother or to pursue their professional careers. Whether a jewelry designer (*Umi no seiza* [Stars in the Sea, 1984]) or a traditional potter (*Honoo no mai* (Dancing of the Flame, 1974]), the heroines oscillate between marriage and career during romantic involvements with various men. In the case of the jewelry designer, she gets both a husband and a brilliant future career; the potter turns down an ardent proposal and decides to stay single so that she can work without the yoke of a family.

Some of Tsumura Setsuko's heroines are tortured by the difficulty of getting pregnant, by having a miscarriage, or by the death of their child, as in ''Tanjōbi''

(The Birthday, 1977), the heroine of which is crazed by the death of her baby born after long and arduous efforts to overcome her sterility. Tsumura has written quite a number of stories dealing with female sterility with all of its psychological ramifications, focusing especially on the effects of family pressures. Tsumura's heroines, who attempt to remedy their sterility, resort to all sorts of methods, medical and nonmedical, to the extent that they are often emotionally and financially exhausted. When they finally become pregnant and eventually have a baby, they are almost always desperately and expressly obsessed with the child's upbringing and education, or else they are annoyed by their child so much that they try to get rid of it.

In essence, the most conspicuous element in Tsumura Setsuko's writing is her inventive skill. Especially in the genre of the short story, she is an accomplished storyteller: her stories are tightly knit, each word carefully chosen. They sometimes remind the reader of the classic examples of Guy de Maupassant or Edgar Allan Poe, even though Tsumura's themes are much more modern. In her full-length novels, however, what seems to be the perfect plot structure for the chosen theme often turns out faulty. For example, the plot may be dependent on a rather convenient coincidental meeting of the heroine with the hero, which takes place in more than one novel. Her short stories and novels are highly entertaining, but most of the novels fall a little short of the criteria of serious literature. They lack the ambiguity, for one thing, that makes more than one interpretation possible. No extensive or systematic use of symbols or images can be seen in her novels, whereas some of her short stories show her masterful use of these literary techniques.

Major Works: Saihate (To the End of the Land, 1972), short story collection. This volume comprises five linked stories: "Haru tōku" (Spring Is Still Far Away, 1965), "Kazabana" (Wind Flowers, 1967), "To the End of the Land," "The Toy," and "Aoi mesu" (The Blue Surgical Knife, 1971). One unique device employed is the shifting narrative viewpoint: in the first three stories the narrator is the first-person "I," whereas the last two stories are told by an omniscient narrator whose viewpoint is strictly focused on the heroine. The five stories are linked in that they share the same main characters and that the stories are chronologically arranged.

This volume owes its success to Tsumura's effective use of counterpoint, as if in a musical composition, to create an uneasy tragicomic atmosphere. One element in this counterpoint is the heroine's husband who is always obsessed by something and behaves erratically; the other is the innocent and naive wife who is being victimized by her husband's erratic behaviors.

The first three stories deal with the trips taken by a newly wed couple into the northeastern part of Honshu, then all the way to the northern island of Hokkaido. The husband, who miraculously survived the usually fatal disease of tuberculosis, is now obsessed by his failing clothing business. The purpose of their trip is to sell, at each town where happen to stop, a huge quantity of clothing sent by the manufacturers. The husband is also preoccupied with his dream of becoming a professional writer.

The seemingly endless supply of items that have to be sold, crate after crate, measures the passage of time in the never-ending and trying journey in the mind of the heroine. The husband's unpredictable behavior and the gloomy wintry landscape of the northern Japan seem to underscore their unstable future. When they finally reach Nemuro at the northernmost tip of Hokkaido, which is literally at the end of Japanese soil, the heroine is relieved to think it is the end of their journey and that they will now go home directly to Tokyo. Ironically, they are to turn around and continue to peddle their way home, since they haven't come to the end of their time, which is represented by their merchandise. The wife's innocence, sympathy for her husband, and trust in their marriage counterbalance the story's pessimistic overtone and at times generate a very subtle comical atmosphere.

The fourth story, "The Toy," deals with the husband's obsession with small animals, such as mice and goldfish, and eerie objects like human bones. As a counterpoint, the pregnant wife grows increasingly sensitive in her morning sickness and develops a strong aversion to these objects. She shows an incredible ability to analyze her husband's behavior and to understand his personality; she even tries to manipulate him, but only in her innocent, uncalculating way. As a result, she invites even more insensitive behavior by her husband. When she is finally taken to the hospital for delivery, however, the husband suddenly changes his attitude and becomes like a helpless child who is being left by his mother. The images of the small animals and goldfish that the husband obsessively admires overlap with that of the baby growing in the heroine's womb, to create an eerie atmosphere. But, again, the element of irony makes this story tragicomic. The heroine tries very hard to please her husband, but, ironically, her good intention is actually the very cause of the husband's annoying behavior. The husband bought the goldfish, for example, when they were taking a walk; she had come along only because he wanted her to. Another ironic effect is seen in the ending: the heroine, after being victimized by her husband's obsession, makes her mind up while in labor on the hospital bed to be obsessed by one little animal—her own baby.

"The Blue Surgical Knife," which concludes the volume, is thematically an extention of "The Toy," in which Tsumura Setsuko experiments with the power of suggestiveness, through the scene of live frogs being dissected. A fifteen-year-old girl who likes to kill a frog by cutting open its belly and the husband seem to develop an affinity for each other. As their affinity grows, the heroine, Haruko, feels more and more estranged from her husband. The baby who was born in the previous story died within an hour, and Haruko is pregnant again in this story. As usual, the heroine suffers a great deal from the husband's erratic and often inconsiderate behavior; for example, on the very day when Haruko had the baby with only the help of a midwife in their small apartment room, he brings his friend home late and starts a drunken party beside the newborn. The author builds up an incredible, almost Hitchcockian dramatic tension when the young girl shows up asking for Haruko's permission to look at the baby. Haruko, with her usual innocence, is not aware of the girl's possible intention. The ending is ironic in spite of the threatening shadow of death: Haruko thinks the baby is dead and cold, but it is only because of her own high fever. This tragicomic effect is a very rare quality in Japanese serious literature.

"Futari dake no tabi" (The Journey for Two Only, 1970), short story. The creeping shadow of death is the subject matter in this story, but it is told in such a way that the reader will not be aware of its theme until the very end. The narrative technique is Maupassant-like. It also deals with the serious problem of how to maintain oneself in old age. It is interesting that the heroines (two old sisters) measure the last segment of their time by sewing children's clothes that are to be donated to a nearby orphanage.

"Yuuenchi" (The Amusement Park, 1980), short story. The plot centers around a family dispute over the husband's lover; the victim of the shadow of death is the little girl of the family. The reader, however, never knows if the girl is killed or not. This ambiguous ending adds to the story's disturbing effect.

"Usagi no mimi" (The Rabbit's Ear, 1980), short story. This is a representative piece of Tsumura's motherhood category. During her pregnancy, the heroine takes every possible care to nurse the baby in her womb as she receives warm blessings from everybody in the family, especially from the parents-in-law. The baby, however, was born with one ear conspicuously shorter than the other. Now the heroine obsessively pulls the short ear as she feeds it in her arms in the midst of silent accusations from the family.

"Mino mushi" (The Bag Worm, 1980), short story. The title not only suggest the physical resemblance of an insect to a child who hangs himself but seems to be a metaphor as well of a child deprived of freedom by an overprotective mother. The mother invents a theory that the child's death may have been an accident. This, however, does not save her from her difficulty and painful position; now, she is accused of not being watchful enough. The chilling irony here is twofold: the mother's careful consideration for her cherished child—for its health and education—actually drove the child to death, and at the end of the story, the mother does not seem to understand why he killed himself.

"Mishiranu machi" (An Unfamiliar Town, 1976), short story. The heroine is a young impoverished divorcée who has abandoned her baby at a railway station and gets enraged with the woman who picks up the baby and takes it back to her apartment as if the baby were her own. The scene where the heroine verbally accuses the other woman of stealing the baby, forgetting her own crime of abandoning it, is highly comical.

Hisae [the heroine] started to feel extremely uneasy. The woman was apparently not going to the police today. It's inexcusable, Hisae thought angrily, not to report to the police when one picked up a baby. . . . Hisae knocked on the woman's door. . .

"Who are you?" the woman said accusingly.

"You picked up a baby at the station, didn't you?" Hisae said, trying to be low-keyed. . .

"That's my baby. You sound as if I stole it. Mind what you say!"

"But the baby was sleeping on the bench—and you just picked. . . ''

"That doesn't mean the baby was somebody else's. I left it on the bench while I went to the washroom.''

Hisae lost her temper at the woman's nerve.

How very presumptuous! That baby is mine—I nurtured it for nine months in my womb. . .

"That child. . . '' Anger made Hisae's mouth dry. "That child is mine. I gave birth to it!''

The woman glared at her. Hisae winced a little as if she were hit in the face.

"Are you saying you abandoned your child?''

Hisae was at a loss what to answer.

"Go away. Or I call the police,'' the woman said forcefully and banged the door shut.

Thief! *I'*ll call the police!

Hisae had to swallow these words.

The ironic element is the diametric opposition between the two women—one wants to get rid of a baby; the other cannot bear her own—and between the heroine's initial intention and her hidden strong attachment to the baby. This irony turns the tragedy of the helpless heroine into a comedy.

"Haha no heya'' (The Mother's Room, 1980), short story. Through the eye of a six-year-old girl, the somewhat decadent life of her mother is described. The mother is obsessed by the dream of becoming a professional writer and ignores all aspects of her life as a mother and wife. Here Tsumura utilizes the same technique of counterpoint as in *To the End of the Land:* the mother is obsessed and erratic in her behavior; the girl does not fully understand why she is always shut out of the mother's apartment. The mother's total indifference to the girl's needs and feelings is appalling, and yet, the story does not seem to be sentimental as this kind of story tends to be, because it is told through the innocent eye of the girl. The narrator's voice presents the mother's behavior as interpreted and filtered through the girl's limited experiences. The girl is naive and tries to win the mother's love and attention in an innocent way. The reader, on the other hand, is made well aware of the grave significance of the effect of the mother's unfeeling attitude on the child's mind.

Omoi saigetsu (Weighty Years, 1980), novel. Although Tsumura Setsuko often takes up materials for her stories from her own life, this is the only work that is strictly autobiographical. This piece depicts the economically trying and emotionally difficult life of a woman writer with her husband, who is also struggling to become a professional writer. The novel ends when the heroine, Akiko, is finally recognized as a writer upon receiving the Akutagawa Prize. It is obvious the novel is based on her own life, and most of the details of the heroine's life overlap what actually happened in the author's life. Yet, the overall impression is somewhat different from that of a so-called "I-novel'', which many of contemporary Japanese writers resort to as a major technical device. The difference is in the distance the author puts between the heroine and herself. The distance objectifies even emotionality and enables the author to weave the facts into fiction. As a result, Tsumura Setsuko's style is far removed from the traditional confessional style of the "I-novel."

Fuyu ginga (The Milky Way in Winter, 1982), novel. This work should be of considerable interest from the sociological point of view; it treats all sorts of social problems that Japan faces today: *tanshin funin* (a worker transferred to a faraway region where the family cannot accompany him), a husband's unfaithfulness during the *tanshin funin* tour of duty, a wife's overzealous concern for her children's education, and the children's suicides under the tremendous pressures of competition in the educational system.

Tsumura Setsuko's narrative is straightforward, even though she frequently resorts to the flashback technique. Her use of language is standard and exemplary, except when she intentionally utilizes a particular dialect in some of her works. Other than that, her stories are linguistically easy to understand, suitable reading materials for advanced students of Japanese.

Translated Work: "Luminous Watch" (Yakōdokei, 1969), short story. Of Tsumura's many works, this is the only one that has been translated into English (another two have appeared in Chinese) and is undoubtedly one of her best stories in that it shows Tsumura's artfulness in the craft of storytelling. The heroine is a young woman with a little child. She manages to produce a meager income to support the child and herself by hand-washing many *tabi* (kimono socks) for the barmaids and prostitutes living nearby. The gnawing loneliness, since her husband left them, has become a major problem; she comes to know a stranger—a middle-aged man who spends every day simply sitting on a park bench. Loneliness, which looked so perpetual, seems to cease for a while, as the seemingly endless rain in the story stops for some time. One night, however, this man commits suicide, leaving his luminous watch to her as a memento.

The incessant rain represents the heroine's loneliness; the numerous damp *tabi* hung in the small apartment room—the rain keeps her from drying them outside—symbolize the languid passage of time and the lack of prospect in the future as well as the wretched, downtrodden lot of the poor and lonely. (Tsumura uses the same technique in the first three stories in *To the End of the Land.*) The man's watch ticked the time away on his wrist in vain; he was laid off and spent all of his time sitting on the bench doing nothing. The watch, luminous in the dark when everybody is asleep, also points to futility or wasted effort, just like the man's life. When the heroine puts the man's watch on her wrist, she decides to live this time, no matter how futile it is now. The widow, however, comes and takes the watch away from her.

BIBLIOGRAPHY

Translation

"Luminous Watch." In *This Kind of Woman: Ten Stories by Japanese Women Writers, 1960–1976,* ed. Yukiko Tanaka. Stanford, CA: Standford University Press, 1982. 115–140.

Critical Work

Tanaka, Yukiko. ''Introduction.'' In *This Kind of Woman: Ten Stories by Japanese Women Writers 1960–1976,* ed. Yukiko Tanaka and Elizabeth Hanson. New York: Perigee Books, 1984, ix–xxv.

Sanroku YOSHIDA

U/W

UI Einjeru (1948–), novelist, artist. Née Senda Uiko (formerly Mrs. Monkman).

Life: Born in Nagano prefecture, Ui graduated from high school in Tokyo. After receiving some art education, Ui worked at various jobs, including planning art exhibitions and television reporting. In 1969 she left Japan for New York, and in 1971 she took up residence in London, which was to be her home for the next ten years. After returning to Japan in 1981, she turned to writing. Little else is known of Ui's personal background except that she is divorced from a British musician.

Career: The publication of *Pureryūdo* (Prelude) in the December 1982 issue of the monthly literary magazine *Gunzō* marked Ui's debut. She won a prestigious award for this novel, set in London and depicting the unhappiness of a Japanese woman artist living with her British rock musician husband. In citing the reasons for selecting this work for the Fifth *Gunzō* New Writer Award, the selection committee mentioned the force of Ui's language and the fact that her story is representative of a growing trend among younger Japanese writers to employ experiences in a foreign country as material for their fiction. *Pureryūdo* is notable for the appearance of a new type of Japanese heroine, undaunted by Western culture, determined to cultivate the self, and equipped with a tremendous energy born of the rage she feels toward her "laid-back," egoistic husband.

Her second novel, *Kiseki* (The Miracle, 1984) chronicles the physical as well as spiritual odyssey in England of a Japanese heroine named Ushio, who has escaped from a degrading life under the thumb of her prostitute mother. The real "miracle" of the novel is the first affirmation of her self, which Ushio experiences in London. It occurs in her love-friendship with a Jewish youth, Asher, who claims to be a Messenger from Beyond. The novel is significant in that it encompasses Ui's romanticism and begins a trail of what might be called the "fables of trust and love," which all of Ui's stories are, though they portray relations in different phases of aspiration and bitter disappointment.

The third novel, *Himeko in London* (1987), falls between *Kiseki* and *Purer-yūdo* in the saga of Ui's London tales: here the naïveté that characterized the heroine of *Kiseki* is implanted in a wealthy young man called Simon, an Englishman destined to be educated in life and into sense by Himeko, the fiery proprietress of a Japanese restaurant in London. By using this young man as narrator, Ui gains something of the advantage Gertrude Stein achieved in *The Autobiography of Alice B. Toklas:* the ultimate praise of Simon's adulation is turned on Himeko and her wisdom. Simon suffers through the various events in the novel not knowing whether to trust or love Himeko, in much the same way that the heroine, Ushio, of *Kiseki* suffered from the ambiguity surrounding the person of Asher. When Simon decides to affirm their love, it is too late, for Himeko has disappeared from England just as Asher did in the earlier novel, leaving the narrator to contemplate the lesson he has learned.

Ui's short stories, mostly published in *Gunzō,* deal chiefly with an "Ui-type heroine" as well, someone who is living or has lived abroad and who brings the brunt of her abrasive ego to bear on conflicts arising in her own relationships or on the relationships of people around her. Ui's London novels represent, in some sense, various stages of reaction to the experience of living in a culture not one's own. *Kiseki* describes the second birth and the romance of "the Promise of the Unknown" that a foreign culture accords an individual, a benevolent culture that allows an affirmation denied in his or her native culture. In many ways, her stories resemble accounts of the lives of Puritan settlers in the New World or Dante's in *Vita Nuova:* the old self is worthless, compared to the self that experiences this new life; the misery of the old life is all the more wonderful for the transformation it undergoes with the new love, the fiery flake falling that will bring beauty and significance to the self and to the earth.

Ui's novels delineate various modes and stages of disillusionment with the foreign culture. Ari, the Japanese wife of rock star Daniel in *Pureryūdo,* is found in a no-exit situation at the outset: she despises her husband for his egotism, but in this novel the protagonist's frustration seems to be more on an individual level than on a cultural level. There is a foreshadowing of the romanticism to come in *Kiseki:* Ari falls in love with her husband's manager, Charlie, and the conclusion of the novel finds them planning a new life in America away from their current spouses. Simon of *Himeko in London,* a potter who believes his own karma is intimately linked with things Japanese, does not delight Himeko with his interest; rather, his facile understanding is a source of great irritation to her, and a good deal of her energy is spent in an effort to set Simon straight. Himeko's frustration with British ways is all too evident, and in her London there is no sign of the magic landscape Ushio stumbled through in *Kiseki.* An Oriental waiter in Himeko's restaurant is Simon's rival and foil to some extent, and Simon is found wanting at the end of the novel.

A 1986 short story, "Hōmonsha (The Visitor), describes the aftermath of a foreign experience. The heroine is living in Tokyo alone, divorced from her British husband and mourning the death of Maya, their daughter. She realizes that Maya was a victim not only of a traffic accident in Tokyo but also of her parents' insoluble war of egos. The grieving mother and ex-wife finds herself placed in the position of counselor to a friend's marriage problems.

Ui's heroine patrols the boundaries of her hard-won self-identity, turning violently upon those who come trespassing in search of a repository for their own egos. The marital relationship is a battleground over which two egos struggle against each other, unconsciously in the case of the male antagonist, and consciously in the case of the female protagonist. Yet the sheer misery of such an infernal state is obvious to the heroine, who thirsts after some tinge of the tremendous significance that the original discovery and affirmation of her own self afforded her. Male characters carry with them a false beacon, an empty promise of growth in relationships beyond what is possible at each stage. None of Ui's heroines find happiness in a domestic setup with a man, for such a relationship is too static, too bereft of the *process of becoming.*

The romanticism in Ui's novels is profound: it requires that life provide for people who have themselves stopped struggling and who have the wisdom, emotional breadth, and psychological depth to educate others. Rebirth in another culture can provide the luxury of a second childhood, in which learning is again one's main activity and in which the people around one are full of a yet-to-be-discovered significance. But when the mist of incomprehension has cleared, the landscape is all too familiar, and the individual is faced with the quite ordinary task of getting on with life. The logical conclusion to Ui's brand of romanticism is a modern Ulysses-type heroine, who sails forever into the setting sun, endlessly renewing the illusion of rebirth.

Ui's novels are interesting and important for many reasons, not the least of which is a new type of Japanese heroine, neither prostitute nor mother figure. They are important also because they are modern in a sense that few Japanese novels are: they confront the dilemma of the coexistence of naked egos colliding with each other, devoid of any altruistic excuse to coexist. Ui's works may very well mark a new stage in the Japanese consciousness of what it means to be Japanese and how that fact is reconcilable with one's status as citizen of a larger world. One hundred years after the opening of Japan to the West, the Japanese have the same type of self-consciousness about their nationality that the characters of Henry James carried around with them in Europe one hundred years after the birth of America. Ui's characters, desperate to be reborn, are less consciously Japanese than most characters set in international context in other Japanese novels—what is important to Ui's people is personal growth.

Major Works: Pureryūdo (or *Zensōkyoku;* Prelude, 1982), novel. Love and change are possible for Ui only in characters who are undergoing an education at another's hand; for those who have graduated from this process, life is a cold game of ego conflict; the only way to love again is to find another teacher. That is exactly what happens in this prizewinning first novel. Ari, the heroine, is not a "pure" Japanese: her father, who runs a gay bar in Tokyo, is half American. As the novel begins, Ari is at the end of her rope with her English husband because he has not the least bit of curiosity about her past. Other people are like flowers and weeds growing together in the garden surrounding his ego: he does nothing to control them. Ari is seeking a confessional release from the past, but she cannot get it from Daniel because of his chronic lack of concern for others, including his wife. Ari is months into her pregnancy, and still Daniel has not noticed.

Approaching motherhood prompts Ari's determination to make herself famous, for she fears her self will drown if her identity has nothing stronger than the social label, or the status of, ''mother'' to prop it up. At first she decides to make use of her husband's fame as a rock artist to launch her own career as a singer. She buys a Julie tape and practices singing in the bath. Her efforts come to nothing. Daniel dismisses her performance of a Japanese song, saying that Japanese pop music, like the Italian, can approach rock only from the romantic angle. The absurdity of her idea does not seem to occur to Ari, who is struggling for her identity.

Then, at a party, she meets Daniel's manager, Charlie, and they retire to the bathroom, where they share an intimate time. Although Ari is abusive and hard in her attitude toward her husband, toward Charlie she has some romantic feeling. The two relationships bring out both the Himeko-side and the Ushio-side in her. Charlie is destined to become Ari's teacher, and the lesson he teaches her is to free herself of the jealousy she feels about Daniel's fame. As do Asher and Himeko in later novels, Charlie subjects Ari to deceptive scenes that fill her with jealousy and desperation, but at the end, he stands revealed as the great manipulator whose tricks are all for the purpose of Ari's growth as a person: Charlie asks her to accompany him on his promotional trip to New York, playfully choking her until she agrees.

Kiseki (The Miracle, 1984), novel. Though not the first in order of publication, this work makes up the first part of the Ui canon of London tales. The heroine, Ushio, is cast as the ''author'' of this epistolary novel, consisting of a long letter, a testament of love addressed to Asher, the young man who has disappeared from London and gone out of Ushio's life. The first section unfolds the story of Ushio's escape from her hometown of Hamamatsu before fleeing to England. She dropped out of high school, unable to bear the constant humiliation of being taunted because of her looks: she is grossly overweight, a condition she worked at to make herself less attractive to her mother's clients, who try to seduce her when her prostitute mother is out. Her mother smacks of Cinderella's stepmother: not a single kind word comes Ushio's way. The misery of the situation and the human relationships is hardly typical of modern Japanese fiction. The graphic scenes of sexual exploitation and the frank, abusive language are other elements that mark Ui's writing as unusual.

After an incident in which Ushio is raped by her employer, the owner of a coffee shop, she reaches a point where she has to flee or perish. This sexual experience is degrading, for the man wants sex with her not because he is attracted to her but because he is a sort of "sexual gourmet" out to collect experiences with freaks. The realization makes Ushio stop struggling:

He kept at it for a long time. The first thing he did was to turn the naked enormity of my body this way and that, drinking in every detail. His bright, cold eyes were devoid of all expression. Then, he came at me repeatedly from every angle. . . . Halfway through, I stopped resisting him and resigned myself to it. But it wasn't any sort of masochistic pleasure that I was resigning myself to; it was more like a struggle with the self to find the outer limits of humiliation.

Shortly after this incident Ushio determines to steal half her mother's considerable savings and flee to London, where a friend has been living for some time. Within the space of eighteen pages, Ushio leaves her Japanese past behind and stands on Kensington High Street in London, full of anticipation.

Ushio's initiation into the magic world of Asher and his friends is a significant accident of the sort one encounters in Herman Hesse: going along a street that seems to be part of the familiar landscape of a dream, one finds a narrow door in the wall and knows that one must enter, for significance and fate wait beyond it. Wearing high heels for the first time, Ushio runs after a bus, misses her footing, and falls onto the road. A van stops short, and out jumps Jonathan, a kindly young British hippie who helps Ushio up, offers to drive her home, and brings her to meet his mate, Asher. The two of them tell Ushio that the meeting was preordained and that Ushio had shared a previous existence with Asher. She cringes but cannot ignore the fact that at last someone is being kind to her.

What follows is the story of the self that Ushio brings to fruition with the nourishment of this nonsexual, loving relationship with Asher even as she struggles with the apparent absurdity of Asher's claim that he is a visitor from outer space, here only to help mankind avert the catastrophes that await them. He is angry that Ushio cannot remember their previous existence, but all his weirdness hardly matters to her, for she has found a new life in which she is free to choose to love Asher. She herself shares a sort of mystical experience with him on a winter's night on a hill in Hamstead Hearth. Snow is falling, transforming the park, when Ushio arrives with Jonathan. Asher is already there with a good number of people from his "community." As Ushio approaches, the crowd begins to chant her name. She goes to join Asher and is recognized as his partner by the group, who seem to expect something from her. Asher tells her that they are there to await the imminent coming of some extraterrestrial beings, and, with her usual good humor, she says nothing and waits with him.

Just when the cold is becoming unbearable, the miracle happens: mixed with the snow, glowing, crystal-like particles begin to fall. Then Asher warns Ushio that the extraterrestrial "object" is approaching and that she should concentrate and call out to it to come. There is a moment of unintentional comedy when Ushio ponders whether the object would respond to a call in Japanese. She settles for English and shouts, "Come here!" What happens next is ambiguous: she *thinks* she sees an object appear but later realizes that she saw it not with her eyes but with her consciousness. In the end, Asher borrows money from his community, from Ushio, and from others, ostensibly to build a site that can serve as a base for space landings. He then disappears with the funds, confirming the reader's suspicions about him but leaving Ushio quite a different character from the abject fat girl who fell off the bus at the beginning of the novel. As in Greene's *Brighton Rock* and Golding's *Free Fall,* what is apparent here is that the miracle of the transformation of the self does not require "valid ingredients" to take place. Even in seamy surroundings, with sleazy, untrustworthy characters, the furnace that forges the new self can be found. Asher's deceit is incidental to the true miracle of the novel, the birth of Ushio's self in her adopted country.

While Asher may have "put one over" on Ushio, no male character in Ui's other London tales can take advantage of the heroines by psychologically dominating them; rather, they teach and manipulate the men around them. The dichotomy between sexual and spiritual love in *Kiseki* is natural enough, given Ushio's early sexual experiences in Japan. Her friend and roommate in London, Aiko, argues with Ushio that the love between man and woman must be sexual or it is not love. Working at a club for Japanese businessmen in London, Aiko is a sort of prostitute. Her abrasive, filthy language closely resembles that of Ushio's mother. Ushio herself plays a polite, almost masochistic role that sharply contrasts with Aiko's vulgar sadism, but she comes to confront Aiko as her sense of self grows stronger. Paradoxically, Aiko is closer in her attitude toward sexuality to the other Ui heroines, the abrasive types who do not mince their words and whose maintenance of the self seems to require them to abuse those around them. Sexuality is a vital tool in the relations between male and female characters, and that relation itself is seen increasingly as a "game" that must be played out in Ui's novels.

Himeko in London (1987), novel. This story takes up, vaguely, where *Kiseki* leaves off. The very name of the heroine, Himeko (lit., Ms. Princess), has an echo of Himiko (commonly known in the West as Queen Pimiko), the early shamaness ruler of Yamataikoku in 3d-century Japan. This novel's title gives a hint of what the flavor of the story is to be. Himeko is placed in London, not to study Western culture but rather to knock some sense into the heads of the hopeless British, whose country, it seems, is falling apart. The very concept is an interesting, refreshing change from the scholarly Japanese approach to Europe with a neurosis-inducing reverence, as evidenced in the works by prominent male novelists from Natsume Soseki (1867–1917) to Endo Shusaku (b. 1923). In this sense, Ui bears a striking resemblance to Kimura Akebono (1872–90), a young girl who authored the newspaper serial novel *Fujo no kagami* (A Mirror for Womanhood, 1889): in it "Akebono . . . vicariously fulfills her [own] thwarted ambitions through the international activities of a young superwoman [a Japanese who has studied at Cambridge]" (Margaret Mitsutani, Introduction to her translation in *The Magazine* [May 1988]).

Ui opens *Himeko in London* with the narrator Simon's confession that he believes he was Japanese in some previous existence. Like many of the other characters, Simon is "in touch" with things Japanese. He is a potter who makes Japanese-type ware; he has read the philosophy of the 18th-century swordsman Miyamoto Musashi, and he cannot forget the image of the actress Michiko Kyo in Kurosawa Akira's film *Rashomon.* The first time Simon goes to the Japanese health food restaurant Himeko runs, she is about to physically expel a down-and-out poet who cannot pay his bill. The air is blue with the abuse they are heaping on each other. She catches sight of Simon halfway up the stairs and shouts down: "And what the hell do you think you're doing down there? If you're coming in, get up here. If you're not, let's see the back of you."

Himeko has her hair dyed fiery orange and wears strange clothes; she is full of creativity and quite free of any bondage to tradition. She subjects Simon to various trials, including a consuming jealousy over her apparently sexual relationship with one of her waiters, to "educate" him out of the protected, unexamined life he has led to the present. She criticizes his work as being purely imitative; she makes him see to what extent his ideas about Japan are stereotyped. Simon grows more and more dependent upon this font of educative vitality. He brings Himeko to meet his aristocratic mother, the force that has dominated his life so far. He introduces Himeko to Elizabeth, the blond, shapely member of his own class whom his mother intends for him to marry. Himeko is undaunted; she takes on every comer on her own terms. While Simon is open and free of prejudice, his mother and Elizabeth are not. Elizabeth, who is employed at the Korean embassy in London, has been sadistically abused and abandoned by Himeko's mysterious waiter, Ryo; she has also been verbally abused and humiliated by Himeko and gives Simon the full benefit of her prejudice:

Who the hell do they think they are, those bastards, coming to a country not their own, thinking they can have things their own way with an attitude like that! Impudent horrors, forgetting their own place! Ugly monkeys! Let them perish from the face of the earth. ... Please, Simon, put an end to living with that woman. There's no way things will work out with an Oriental.

Simon vacillates between his love for Himeko and the voices in him that make him doubt her. Resolution finally comes via a deus ex machina, in the form of the immigration authorities, who catch Himeko on her reentry to England from Spain, where she and Simon vacationed: Himeko had been working in England on a tourist visa. Simon thinks he can fix things up with the Immigration Office, but Himeko has had enough. She returns to Japan and sends Simon a tape saying good-bye and explaining that, had they married, life would have ceased being a game that kept one fresh and full of vitality.

I'm afraid I didn't like your country. No matter what I did, I couldn't get people to react. God, the lack of energy! England is dead. Then why, you may ask, did I live there? Because it was the country that presented the greatest challenge to me.

For Simon, their relation has not been a ''game'': he was, and still is, in love with Himeko. No way to respond to her now, he goes out on the balcony and stretches his arms out to the East and declares his love, explaining:

It is true that there are many stages in love. And, as you said, a large part of what people call love is simply self-deceit. My love for you was like that at one stage. But you can't deny the fact that my love has changed and developed.

Simon has undergone growth and change, while Himeko has remained largely a static force. She has freed Simon from the confines of his unexamined class attitudes and assumptions and taught him to penetrate beyond the surface of things. In this novel, the male character Simon is put in much the same position as the heroine, Ushio, was at the end of *Kiseki*.

BIBLIOGRAPHY

Mulhern, Chieko. ''Japan.'' In *Longman Anthology of World Literature by Women: 1875–1975*, ed. Marian Arkin and Barbara Schollar. New York: Longman, 1989, 1152–62.

Paul McGRATH

UNO Chiyo (1897–), novelist, magazine publisher and editor, kimono designer. (Mrs. Kitahara Takeo); other published name, Fujimura Chiyo.

Life: Uno Chiyo was born in Iwakuni, Yamaguchi prefecture, as the first child of Uno Toshitsugu, the son of a prosperous and socially prominent sake-brewing family. Her father had been in line to inherit the family business but shunned the responsibility and wandered about the country squandering his money before marrying Doi Tomo and finally settling in Iwakuni at the age of forty-two. He never held a job and depended on his family for financial support, which he used to pay for his own personal pleasures, often at the expense of his wife and children. Chiyo, therefore, though born to wealth and high social status, was raised in poverty. Little is known of her mother, who died of tuberculosis when Chiyo was two. Toshitsugu soon remarried, and though his second wife eventually bore him five children, she treated Chiyo with loving respect. Toshitsugu was not as kind. A volatile, often abusive man, he was generally cold to Chiyo and the rest of the family. He died of consumption in 1912, freeing the family from his tyranny but fettering them financially, as the Uno family discontinued support.

Upon graduation from the Iwakuni High School for Girls in 1914, Uno took a job as a teacher's assistant in an elementary school. After little more than a year she was dismissed over an affair she was having with a fellow teacher. Chiyo fled to Korea to escape the town censure but returned after six months, and in 1916 she accompanied her maternal cousin Fujimura Tadashi to Tokyo, where he entered Tokyo University. Chiyo was to cook and clean for him, but, as funds from his home were insufficient, she was compelled to take several part-time jobs. She worked as a maid, a baby-sitter, and a model. But her most lucrative job was at the Enrakuken, a fashionable café across from Tokyo University patronized by such literary men as Akutagawa Ryūnosuke (1892–1927), Kikuchi Kan (1888–1948), and the editor of the intellectual literary journal *Chūō Kōron,* Takita Choin (1882–1925). Despite the financial and intellectual rewards, Chiyo did not stay long at the Enrakuken. In 1919 she married Tadashi and moved with him to Hokkaido.

She began to write to dispel the boredom of the long winter nights. Her story "Shifun no Kao" (Painted Face, 1921), about an impoverished waitress who agrees to become a foreigner's mistress, won first prize in a short-story contest run by the newspaper *Jiji Shimpō,* netting her a sizable amount of money. Encouraged by the prospects of earning money, Chiyo wrote a novel, *Haka o Abaku* (Opening the Grave, 1922), and sent it to Takita Choin, who she remembered had generously tipped her at the Enrakuken. Too impatient to await his reply, she traveled to Tokyo and discovered that her work had been published in the *Chūō Kōron* under her married name, Fujimura Chiyo. She decided to stay on in Tokyo temporarily to develop her career as a writer.

Before long, she met the handsome young novelist Ozaki Shirō (1898–1964) and began to live with him in Magome Village, on the outskirts of Tokyo. In 1924 Uno divorced Tadashi and married Ozaki. Jazz and Western-style dancing soon infiltrated Magome, and in 1927 Uno bobbed her hair, becoming one of Japan's first "flappers." Ozaki was not pleased with Uno's new image. He was jealous of her literary success and of the lovers she was rumored to have. In late 1927 he began living with another woman, and in 1930 he and Uno divorced.

Uno soon became involved with Tōgō Seiji (1897–1978), a Western-style painter who had recently made headlines over his love suicide attempt with Nishizaki Mitsuko, the daughter of an admiral in the imperial navy. Uno and Tōgō built an exotic, Westernized house in a fashionable section of Tokyo's Setagaya Ward, where they entertained their bohemian friends with wild parties. Soon, however, they found themselves pressed with debts, and by 1934 their relationship had soured. Tōgō resumed his romance with Nishizaki, and Uno moved to an apartment in Yotsuya, where, in 1936, she founded *Style,* Japan's first fashion magazine.

In 1939 she married Kitahara Takeo (1907–73), a literary critic and newspaper reporter ten years her junior, who had just made his debut as a novelist the year before. They worked together on *Style* until 1941, when Kitahara was dispatched to Southeast Asia as a war correspondent. Uno continued her work with the magazine until January 1944, when government pressure forced it to close. After the war Uno and Kitahara revived *Style,* but in the early 1950s the company was charged with tax evasion and subsequently went bankrupt. Uno and Kitahara could not endure the strain. They divorced in 1964, and Uno did not marry again.

Career: Most critics consider *Opening the Grave* the work that launched

Uno's career. In this long, ambitious work Uno describes the humiliations and injustices a young schoolteacher endures in her small village where she witnesses, among other horrors, the mistreatment of a deaf boy, an outcast girl, and a Korean. Uno very skillfully evokes the feel of the rural community and the mood of pride and despair that grips the people there. However, when she tries to portray the plight of the outcasts or the Koreans, her descriptions seem forced, as if she were purposely imitating the socialist-inspired works in vogue at the time. Uno admits that as she wrote *Opening the Grave,* she dreamed of becoming another Miyamoto Yuriko (1889–1951), a woman writer who had recently published her maiden work, ''Mazushiki hitobito no mure'' (The Mass of Impoverished, 1916) in the *Chūō Kōron.* Regardless of its flaws, however, Uno's work is important for two reasons. First, it is an indication of Uno's sensitivity to local dialect and color, and second, it is an example of the direction her writing might have taken had she been so inclined. Uno could have written social criticism, for she certainly had the material for it. But, lacking the temperament, she never attempted another work like *Opening the Grave.*

Shortly after Uno's debut, her stories were published in a variety of well-respected literary journals. By 1925 she had five collections in print. Her success was stunning. She had leaped into the literary world without a mentor, without a supporting coterie, and without even much effort. Perhaps the primary reason for Uno's meteoric rise was the fact that her works brought a spontaneity and sensuousness to a literary scene long dominated by the ponderous pessimism of the naturalists and socialists. Her early works, almost all *watakushi-shōsetsu* (autobiographical fiction, or, the ''I-novel''), reveal a personality that is capricious and bold. Set in either her hometown Iwakuni or the back alleys of Tokyo, these stories describe with candor and sensitivity a young woman who struggles to explore her own sexuality and individualism regardless of the cost to herself and others.

Further fueling public interest in Uno's works were the successive relationships she had with several well-known men. Uno did not hesitate to expose and explore her various marriages and liaisons in her writing. ''No one is as fortunate as a woman writer!'' she was to exclaim in a 1972 essay. ''As soon as she breaks up with a man she can write about it all without the slightest sense of shame.'' Uno's brief marriage to Ozaki netted her more than a few works of autobiographical fiction, and her five-year affair with Tōgō Seiji, in particular, provided her with rich source material. Shortly after her separation from Tōgō she wrote about their life together in ''Wakare mo Tanoshi'' (Parting Pleasure, 1935) and ''Miren'' (Lingering Affection, 1936); and in 1935 she wrote her first important *kikigaki,* or ''hear-write tale,'' *Irozange* (Love Confessions), which describes the series of affairs Tōgō had before meeting Uno. So fecund was her period with Tōgō that he later suggested she stayed with him only to gather inspiration for her works. Uno's twenty-five-year marriage to, and subsequent divorce from, Kitahara Takeo were also important influences, yielding such outstanding works as *Sasu* (To Stab, 1966), ''Kōfuku'' (Happiness, 1970), for which she received her second Japanese Women Writers' Award, and *Ame no oto* (The Sound of Rain, 1974). Because of the sensational life she led and portrayed in her works, Uno was soon dubbed "a writer of illicit love," a label that stuck with her long after her works grew more serious.

The war had a tremendous, though indirect, role in tempering Uno's art and bringing a depth to her writing. Many of her contemporaries, including her husband Kitahara Takeo, gave themselves over to the war effort, traveling to China and Southeast Asia as correspondents. But Uno stayed behind and, in a world stripped of garish modern colors, discovered the simple beauty of old Japan. Her discovery came in the form of a puppet, the kind used in the classical puppet theater. Intrigued by the silent beauty in the puppet's face, she rushed off to Shikoku to meet the man who had made it. Uno's "hear-write tale" entitled "Ningyōshi Tenguya Kyūkichi" (The Puppet-Maker Tenguya Kyūkichi, 1946) culminated from the meeting. But more than that, through Kyūkichi, Uno came to appreciate the importance and resilience of the traditional arts. She was deeply moved by the old man's dedication to his art—he had done the same work for over sixty years. For the restless Uno, barely able to stay in the same house or with the same man for more than five years, this was a revelation, which perhaps contributed to the subsequent production of her finest works. Among them are *Ohan* (1957), for which she received the Noma Prize for Literature and the Japanese Women Writers Award, *Kaze no oto* (The Sound of the Wind, 1967), *Aru hitori no onna no hanashi* (Story of a Certain Woman Alone, 1971), *Usuzumi no sakura* (The Grey Cherry Tree, 1974), and *Suisei shoin no musume* (The Daughter of Westshore Hall, 1977).

After 1977 Uno stopped writing fiction and began concentrating on essays depicting her past experiences and present observations. Reader response to her optimistic view of life was so positive that she was asked by the *Mainichi* newspaper to carry an advice column. Her collection of memoirs, *Ikite yuku Watashi* (I Go On Living), serialized in the newspaper, became a best-seller when issued in book form in 1983 and was later made into a television series as well as a stage play. In addition, Uno maintained an ongoing column in a popular woman's magazine. In December 1987, at age eighty-nine, she published her first short story in nearly a decade, "Ippen ni harukaze ga fuitekita" (Suddenly a Spring Wind), a charming story about a young couple in rural Japan who are happy despite their poverty.

The majority of Uno's works fall into the "I-novel" category, yet Uno has been called the least "I-novel"-like writer of all women writers. In the first place, her "I-novels" stand apart from others in the way she is able to treat her alter ego with extreme detachment. She exposes even her least admirable traits with the objectivity of a stranger, often tempering her self-portraits with gently condescending humor. What is remarkable is not simply that she makes compelling fiction out of her own life but that she is able to do so without resorting to the self-pity or self-justification so often the bane of the genre. She does not revel in her flaws or reveal them out of any desire to "confess." Uno has nothing to confess. She is not ashamed of her life. She simply presents the good with the bad, because they are both a part of herself. Second, Uno's finest works are not ''I-novels'' at all but ''hear-write tales'' in which she creates a narrator other than herself who tells forthright his or her own tale. For an ''I''-novelist to efface herself from the narrative and write from a perspective outside her own is indeed significant, even ''revolutionary,'' and in these narratives Uno's art excels.

Major Works: Aru hitori no onna no hanashi (Story of a Certain Woman Alone, 1971), novella. Here Uno creates a third-person narrator for herself, Kazue, to gaze back objectively on her childhood and her relationship with her father and the several men she has known. The subject is not a new one for Uno. She has written of her past many times before, but in consonant narration, as if the narrator were still embroiled in the emotions of the past. However, the seventy-year-old Kazue in this dissonant narration is so distanced from the events she describes that her voice is clear and unencumbered by emotional rhetoric. She describes her father's death, her rape by the village headman's son, and her first divorce in the same quiet monotone she uses when she counts off the names and ages of her brothers and sisters. All are equal threads in the fabric of her life.

Ame no oto (The Sound of Rain, 1974), novella. This work is a veritable collection of memoirs covering the entire spectrum of Uno's life, past to present, but with a dominant focus on her relationship with her third and last husband, Kitahara Takeo (named Yoshimura in the story). Perhaps the loveliest and most lyrical of all Uno's autobiographical works, this volume has very little form. Rather, it is said to follow the ''natural mental process,'' progressing as a pastiche of memory—one episode leading to another as the author weaves past and present in a tapestry of time. Because of the quiet, almost mournful tone of the story—induced by the sound of the rain—some critics have called this novella a ''requiem.''

Translated Works: To Sting (Sasu, 1966), novella. This story in five parts (only the third of which is translated) describes the collapse of Uno's magazine as it parallels both the end of her marriage to Kitahara and the final onset of old age. The title derives from a parable about a scorpion who asks a turtle to ferry it out to sea. When they are in deep water the scorpion stings the turtle, dooming them both, but as they are drowning the scorpion cries: ''I cannot help but sting. Please forgive me!'' The first-person narrator realizes that she, too, has stung and has been stung. It is sad, but it is the nature of things. She does not resist her fate but waits for her husband to administer his sting.

As the story begins, the narrator and her husband are struggling to revive their magazine business after the war. The woman soon comes to realize that her husband has taken several young lovers. Rather than confront him with the truth, she fights to deny it and to deny the fact that she is old. In a frantic attempt to bind him to her, she launches a satellite magazine, a venture so reckless that it eventually destroys the entire company.

In the final sections the focus shifts from the magazine business to the woman and the way she adjusts to her imminent divorce. The story takes on a quietness that is beautifully lyric and tinged with an undercurrent of sorrow. Yet despite this gentle melancholy, the narration reflects the resolution of a woman determined to survive no matter what the cost. As the story ends, the husband prepares to leave while the woman busily, almost gaily, helps him pack. She sees him to the door and watches him disappear into the evening shadows, knowing he will not come back.

Uno's intense yet extraordinarily delicate portrayal of her protagonist's emotions is impressive. Moreover, the degree of emotional control that Uno was able to exercise in *To Sting,* despite the obvious proximity of the subject matter to her own life, earned her high critical acclaim.

"Happiness" (Kōfuku, 1970), short story. Uno's only "I-novel" to be translated in its entirety, this work, too, is marked by her characteristic objectivity. The tone of "Happiness," however, unlike that of her other works, is imbued with an ironic humor—as if the author is amused that such a character as herself exists. This is an optimistic work, rare in Japanese serious fiction, and the third-person narrator, Kazue, is a very likable character. Unlike the protagonist of *To Sting,* Kazue is very comfortable with her old age. She truly seems to love life and herself as well. No matter how many hardships she has had to face, she does not let them dampen her resolve to participate actively and lustfully in life. Kazue's happy-go-lucky attitude allows for a tone of gentle self-mockery. Few Japanese authors are capable of caricaturing themselves for the amusement of others. Tanizaki Jun'ichiro did so in *Diary of a Mad Old Man* (1962), and in many ways Uno's Kazue is like his mad old man. Both are able to laugh at themselves because both have finally come to accept and understand themselves. In the opening scene, Kazue steps out of the bath and admires her body in the mirror. Because of the steam and her failing eyesight, she is able to convince herself that she looks like Botticellli's Venus. This is one of her happinesses. This story leaves the impression that, despite the swirling steam and vision problems, Kazue is better able to see herself than did all her own younger counterparts.

Confessions of Love (Irozange, 1935), novel. As Uno's first important "hear-write tale," this work is of significance to the development of her narrative style. Ostensibly based on the story Tōgō Seiji told Uno about the series of affairs he had with several upper-class women upon his return from a seven-year stay in France, the account is narrated in the first person from the perspective of Yuasa Jōji (Tōgō's fictional counterpart). He is a Western-style painter who, though married, becomes involved with three young women in a succession of complicated affairs that are both humorous and poignant. The setting clearly reflects the mood of the 1920s in its heady excitement and decadence. *Confessions of Love* was extremely popular when it appeared in 1935 with its showcase of adventure, suspense, and romance. No doubt the sexual promiscuity presented in this work was shocking. But despite all its salient modernity, it is deeply rooted in the classical tradition—a modern variation, as it were, on the classical theme of love suicide, though this time it is a suicide gone awry and rendered humorous by the rationalizations of a modern man.

"The Puppet-Maker" (Ningyōshi Tenguya Kyūkichi, 1942), short story. Uno continued her experiments with narrative voice by employing two narrators: an interviewer and Kyūkichi, the eighty-six-year-old puppet maker. The interviewer opens the story with an explanatory preface, and then Kyūkichi takes over, telling the tale of his life and art. His anecdotes and his descriptions of times gone by are at once delightful and touching. This brief work, barely fifty pages, marks an important turning point in Uno's narrative technique in that she minimizes "plot" and concentrates on "the telling." Kyūkichi speaks entirely in the rustic Tokushima dialect (of Shikoku Island), which enhances his character, adding depth and vibrancy to his utterances and making the readers feel he were sitting before them. The dialect also adds a sorrow not conveyable through crisp standard Japanese. This melancholy beauty, deepened by both the quaintness of Kyūkichi's language and the simple profundity of his words, draws the reader into his world and renders this work a brilliant achievement.

Ohan (1957), novella. Barely one hundred pages that took her ten years to write, this is nonetheless Uno's masterpiece. She based *Ohan* on a story she heard from the owner of a secondhand shop she visited while in Shikoku interviewing Kyūkichi. A man describes to an unseen interlocutor how he left his demure, gentle wife, Ohan, to live with the brazen, domineering geisha Okayo. The story is simple, but the very simplicity enhances the beauty and mastery of the work—for in *Ohan* it is not the story alone that is important but the way it is told. Through careful characterization, keen attention to mood, and skillfully crafted narration, Uno has created what critic Kobayashi Hideo (1902–83) called "a storybook world of fantasy, rare among contemporary novels."

The setting is a castle town very much like Uno's Iwakuni at the end of the Meiji period (1868–1912). But, as the story progresses, time and place become suspended, and the reader is transported back to the feudal world of the old puppet theater. Here can be found the tiny white face of a timid wife glowing palely among the shadows of the deep-eaved wooden house. In a flurry of vibrant silks the geisha emerges, her gorgeous face barely visible beneath her rich coiffure. Interspersed here and there are the sound of *geta* (wooden clogs), the click of flint stones, and the twang of the three-stringed samisen—all woven into a musical brocade worthy of the master playwright of the puppet theater, Chikamatsu Monzaemon (1653–1724).

The narrative style Uno employs furthers the association with the old plays. The narrator often addresses his interlocutor directly, but since the interlocutor is never given a voice in the tale, the effect is as if the man were addressing the readers personally, pulling them into an intimate relationship with him, one that parallels the relationship between the dramatic chanter in a puppet play and the audience.

Of greatest significance to the character and mood of *Ohan* is the language.

Uno uses dialect as in "The Puppet-Maker," except here she creates her own by combining the regionalisms of Tokushima and Iwakuni and polishing them with the soft elegance of Kyoto speech. It is an artificial language, but one endowed with the color and nuance of an old ballad. The beauty of the language informs the characters with life and credibility.

The Sound of the Wind (Kaze no oto, 1967), novella. Unlike her other "hear-write tales," this one is not taken from a specific story told her by a specific individual. Uno states that she based the tale on the lives of her parents, and many of the incidents described in the work seem to parallel her father's life and character. But rather than a concrete biography, *The Sound of the Wind* is a collage of memories from Uno's childhood, not so much memories of actual events as memories of the moods and feelings that colored the past. In language, setting, and story line the work is similar to *Ohan,* again set in Iwakuni at some indefinite period in the past and featuring a timid wife, a brazen mistress, and a wayward husband. But unlike the earlier tale, the narrator here is a woman, the neglected wife, Osen. She recounts how her husband brings Oyuki, the town harlot, home to live with them and then kills a man in a fight over her. Never once does Osen allow herself to complain or to rebuke her husband. If emotion creeps into the narration, it usually betrays itself as a boastful respect for this swaggering man or as an awed envy for Oyuki's headstrong capriciousness. As in *Ohan,* the language is an important element of her characterization: Osen's Iwakuni dialect imparts an artlessness and gentle rusticity to her utterances, rendering them not only credible but rich with understated sorrow.

BIBLIOGRAPHY

Translations

Confessions of Love (Irozange). Tr. Phyllis Birnbaum. Honolulu: University of Hawaii Press, 1989.

"A Genius at Imitation" (mohō no tenshi, with analytical introduction). In *To Live and to Write: Selections by Japanese Women Writers 1913–1938,* ed. Yukiko Tanaka. Seattle: Seal Press, 1987, 183–96.

"Happiness" (Kōfuku). Tr. Phyllis Birnbaum. In *Rabbits, Crabs, Etc.* Honolulu: University of Hawaii Press, 1982, 134–47.

"Ohan." Tr. Donald Keene. In *The Old Woman, the Wife and the Archer.* New York: Viking Press, 1961, 51–118.

"The Puppet Maker" (Ningyōshi Tenguya Kyūkichi). Tr. Rebecca Copeland. In *New Leaves: Studies and Translations of Japanese Literature in Honor of Edward Seidensticker,* ed. Aileen Gatten and Anthony Hood Chambers. Ann Arbor: Center for Japanese Studies, University of Michigan, 1993, 185–222.

"The Puppet Maker" (Ningyōshi Tenguya Kyūkichi), "The Sound of the Wind" (Kaze no oto), and "This Powder Box" (Kono oshiroiie). Tr. Rebecca Copeland. In *The Sound of the Wind: The Life and Works of Uno Chiyo.* Honolulu: University of Hawaii Press, 1992, 105–236.

"Shopgirl" (Garasu no naka no musume). Tr. Mitsugi Teshigawara. In *Young Forever and Five Other Novelettes.* Tokyo: Hokuseido, 1941, 122–39.

"Sting" (A synopsis of "Sasu" with brief biography). *The Japan PEN News,* 19 (June 1966): 7–10.
A Story of a Single Woman (Aru hitori no onna no hanashi). Tr. Rebecca Copeland. London: Peter Owen, 1992.
"Suddenly a Spring Wind" (Ippen ni harukaze ga fuitekita). Tr. Rebecca Copeland. In *Winds* (December 1989): 43–48.
"To Stab" (Sasu). Tr. Kyoko iriye Selden. In *Stories by Contemporary Japanese Women Writers,* ed. Noriko Lippit and Kyoko Iriye Selden. New York: M. E. Sharpe, 1982, 92–104.

Critical Works

Birnbaum, Phyllis. "Profiles." *The New Yorker* (October 31, 1988): 39–59.
Carpenter, Juliet Winters. "Uno Chiyo: Writer and Femme Fatale." *Japan Quarterly* (October–December 1992): 502–505.
Chapman, Christine. "First and Last of the Red Hot Literary Ladies." *Winds* (December 1989): 30–40.
Copeland, Rebecca. "Between Wife and Prostitute: A Search for Place in the Works of Uno Chiyo." *Humanities: Christianity and Culture* 22 (December 1988): 61–78.
———. *The Sound of the Wind: The Life and Works of Uno Chiyo.* Honolulu: University of Hawaii Press, 1992.
———. "Uno Chiyo: Not Just a 'Writer of Illicit Love.' " *Japan Quarterly* (April–June 1988): 176–82.
Keene, Donald. "The Revival of Writing by Women." In *Dawn to the West Japanese Literature of the Modern Era.* New York: Holt, Rinehart and Winston, 1984, 1113–1167.

Rebecca L. COPELAND

WADA Natsuto (or Natto, 1920–83), film scriptwriter, columnist. Real name: Ichikawa Yumiko (Mrs. Ichikawa Kon), née Wada Yumiko.

Life: The eldest daughter of a ship's captain, Wada attended Tokyo Women's College, majoring in English. After graduating in 1946, she went to work for the Fujimoto Cinema Production Co. formed during the Allied occupation. There she met Ichikawa Kon (1915–), a struggling assistant director who would later become one of Japan's leading filmmakers. They were married in 1949. Wada's talent was discovered by her husband, who helped launch her scriptwriting career in the almost exclusively male-dominated Japanese cinema industry. From 1951 to 1965 Wada wrote scripts on her own as well as with her husband for his films. In the late 1960s, she began writing an advice column, "Personal Life Consultation," in the *Asahi* newspaper. She died of breast cancer at the age of sixty-two.

Career: Wada's accomplishments cannot be discussed without reference to her husband-mentor Ichikawa Kon. After a troubled beginning (due, in part, to the occupation censorship), he made a successful directorial debut with the New Tōhō Company in 1947. As often was the case in Japanese cinema, Ichikawa's career came to be based on a close collaboration with a single scriptwriter—his wife. Many famous directors have relied on this form of artistic partnership.

Mizoguchi Kenji (1898–1956) and Yoda Yoshikata (1910–) formed such a team; Ozu Yasujirō (1903–63) and Noda Kōgo (1893–1968) another. Kinoshita Keisuke (1912–) wrote scripts for most of his own films, while Kurosawa Akira (1910–) worked closely with the scenarist Oguni Hideo (1906–) and Hashimoto Shinobu (1918–).

Ichikawa's choice of his wife as collaborator was a significant departure from the traditional male chauvinism of the industry. Even in the so-called golden age of Japanese cinema in the 1950s, only a handful of female scenarists broke the gender barrier, Mizuki Yoko (1910–) among them. Wada's first film with her husband was *Koibito* (The Lover, 1951). Their last joint effort was *Tokyo Orinpikku* (Tokyo Olympiad, 1965). In between, they wrote scripts for thirty Ichikawa films. In addition, Wada herself worked on nine for her husband. The couple experimented with many genres, comedy, satire, and melodrama among them. In the late 1950s especially, they turned their attention to the adaptation of serious works of literature. Thus, the Wada-Ichikawa collaboration produced works of notable versatility in which the director relied heavily on the talents of his wife. As one critic has noted: ''Willing pupil of Disney, he [Ichikawa] is at the same time drawn to the dark matter of *Enjō* and *Bonchi*. Maker of official documentaries, he is also drawn to the most intimate psychological revelations. A humanist, he is, almost consequently, drawn to death and destruction.'' While Ichikawa's wide range of genres and subject matter undoubtedly represent a certain amount of compromise with studio policies, his involvement in scripting gave him a measure of leverage and artistic freedom.

Most of the Ichikawa-Wada screenplays were derived from other media— radio dramas, serialized newspaper stories, even comic strips. Their weightier frames of reference, however, derive from serious works of literature, novels especially. Their typical script is timely and direct, relevant to contemporary life. Avoiding complexity of dialogue and narrative, their scripts free Ichikawa to make the most of the camera's expressive power. His films, in fact, are noted for the virtuosity of composition and camera movement and for their visually beautiful style. Difficult as it is to assess the contribution of either partner in a close collaboration, many critics agree in giving Wada credit for important strengths in her husband's films. Moreover, some of Ichikawa's finest works were scripted by his wife alone. In 1963, the Asia Cinema Festival recognized Wada's contribution with a Distinguished Scriptwriter Award.

Major Works: Koibito (The Lover, 1951), script/film. This first Wada-Ichikawa collaboration, based on a novel by Umezaki Haruo (1915–65), is typical of the light-hearted romantic genre marketed by the Tōhō Company at the time. It displays the humorous touch that would become an Ichikawa hallmark, culminating much later in a vein of black humor. The subject is an ancient one, given a contemporary setting: expectations and anxieties on the night before the wedding. Here, the tearfully nervous bride-to-be of melodrama is replaced by a heroine prepared to enjoy one last fling as a single girl. Kyoko asks a young boy from her childhood to share a night out on the town in Tokyo's Ginza district. While the two enjoy themselves at a movie, an ice-skating rink, and a dance hall, Kyoto's parents fret at home. But she bounces in early in the morning safe and sound, cheerfully ready to get married that very day.

Puu-san (Mr. Pu, 1953), script/film. The story represents a conflation of two enormously popular serial comic strips by Yokoyama Taizo (1917–): *Puu-san* (Mr. Pu) and *Ganko* (Miss Ganko). Set in postwar Japan, the plot centers round the good-natured, third-rate prep school teacher Noro (''dimwit''), a classical fall guy. In the crowded Ginza, he is the one hit by a car; he is given the brush-off by his landlady's daughter; and when he asks a student for a simple favor, he is made to pay. The simple comic portrayal of this luckless hero takes on depth and sharpness, thanks to the satirical thrust that Wada and Ichikawa bring to it. Noro's misfortunes are contrasted with the cunning manipulations of the politician Ozu. Arrested for rigging his own election, Ozu turns his disgrace into a major best-selling book. His type of cynical, aggressive opportunist is clearly seen as the man of the hour in the fast-paced, materialistic Japan of the postwar economic miracle. As might be expected, Wada and Ichikawa pursue this savage satire to the bitter end: Noro's misadventures gradually transform him into a capable opportunist.

Shokei no Heya (Punishment Room, 1956), script/film. Cowritten by Wada and Hasebe Keiji, this exploration of the dark side of Japanese life is adapted from a novel by Ishihara Shintarō (1935–; future politician and author of *Japan That Can Say No,* 1989). The film, like the book, studies Japan's ''lost generation'' of the mid-1950s that sought satisfaction in sex and violence. The script takes its cue from an enormously popular literary genre—the so-called Sun-tribe genre—that focuses on a contemporary phenomenon: rebellious youngsters' responses to a materialistic society defined in terms of fast cars and motor boats.

Nihonbashi (Nihonbashi, 1956), script/film. As a woman struggling to succeed in a male-dominated profession, Wada was keenly aware of the struggle of her sex to survive oppression. Her concern shows clearly in her adaption of a 1914 melodrama by the novelist Izumi Kyoka (1873–1939). A young doctor's search for his elder sister takes him to Nihonbashi, a famous geisha district, where he meets two women in professional rivalry. Wada uses his relationship with two geisha to elucidate the tragic plight of women in a male-dominated, money-oriented society. The resulting melodrama is rich in scenes of unrequited love, insanity, murder, and suicide, going beyond the scope of the Shinpa (new-style) theater that specialized in tear-jerker treatment of such stuff.

Kuroi Jūnin no Onna (Ten Dark Women, 1961), script/film. This original script is a mystery comedy whose plot concerns women who turn to murder, since their lover cannot be possessed by any one of them. Irony is Wada's forte here. The macho philanderer-hero is actually a helpless weakling when his life is at stake. He turns to his neglected wife for help, and the wife takes the day with wit and energy. Two kinds of characters are satirized in this film: the male egotist caught in his own double-standard trap; and the kind of woman whose manipulation of men makes her a victim.

Hakai (Broken Commandment, 1961), script/film. This work brings Wada's altruistic philosophy to the fore in her humanistic treatment of the novel by Shimazaki Tōson (1872–1943) of the same title. Published in 1906, the book was heralded as the first work of Japanese naturalism in its treatment of a taboo subject: discrimination against Japan's outcast minority. Shimazaki's novel is more than a study of social determinism. The confessions of the outcast protagonist Ushimatsu reveal details of his inner life and project the author's thoughts and feelings as well. Wada's script also centers on the inner torment of Ushimatsu, a schoolteacher in a small, conservative country town in central Japan. Having kept his outcast origins secret, he is thrown into turmoil by his mentor, Inoko, who fights social prejudice by acknowledging his lowly ancestry. In the end, stirred by Inoko's death, Ushimatsu follows his conscience; he kneels in front of his pupils and begs forgiveness for having concealed his true identity.

The film radically differs from the original novel characterization of Inoko's wife, not herself an outcast. While her fictional counterpart is not fully developed, the heroine in the film represents a type of courageous humanist. Wada's script strengthens her character even more toward the end of the film. After Ushimatsu's public confession, they meet. For the first time, this woman speaks out and with forceful eloquence. She claims the constitutional equality of human rights and advises Ushimatsu to ignore prejudice. She also speaks about the future of mankind as well, with obvious authorial intent, when she renounces the idea that ''history is not made by the masses, but by a charismatic individual.'' The film concludes with the scene of reconciliation, which also clearly addresses Wada's humanistic concerns. While the fictional hero leaves for Texas to seek freedom, Ushimatsu in the film opts for confrontation. Determined to devote the rest of his life to eliminating caste discrimination, he leaves for Tokyo with Inoko's wife. They are given a tearful farewell by some unprejudiced souls in the town: his pupils and Oshio, a woman of the samurai stock who loves him. A final straightforward subtitle reinforces the contemporaneity of this film: ''Ushimatsu left Iiyama in December, 1905—one year after the outbreak of the Russo-Japanese War.'' Clearly, the audience is invited to consider how far Japanese society has or has not progressed in the elimination of discrimination since the Meiji era.

Translated Works: No printed translations of Wada's scripts per se are available in English to date. Many of Ichikawa's best films, however, are in circulation with English subtitles, offering insights into Wada's skill as a scenarist and testifying to the way in which Ichikawa's thematic concerns were strengthed by his wife's collaborations. Listed below are some of their well-known films readily available in the West.

Harp of Burma (Biruma no Tategoto, 1956), film. Wada worked alone on this script, which closely follows the novel by Takeyama Michio (1903–). Published in 1946, the original deals with Japanese soldiers facing their country's defeat in war-torn Burma. The purpose of the book is frankly didactic: to inspire youth with hope for the future, even as their country undergoes traumatic social change after the war. Takeyama's point of reference is the traditional Japanese value system based on the Buddhist ideal of compassion. The hero of his novel, Private Mizushima, remains behind in Burma in order to hold services for his fallen comrades.

Shifting the emphasis forward a decade, the film stresses individual response to defeat in war. The three value systems at work are highlighted and contrasted more dramatically than in Takeyama's novel. In order to accomplish this aim, Wada's script offers three character types to personify value systems in more dynamic conflict. As in the novel, Mizushima is a heroic altruist. The new type of soldier—a group of his comrades led by a captain fresh from a music academy—represents individualism. The old type of soldier, led by another tenacious captain intent on dying in honor, is motivated by collectivism. Wada tightens the thematic structure of the film by omitting or alternating some episodes. In the novel, for example, Mizushima is captured by cannibals and fattened for a feast. The alternative is marriage to the chief's daughter, but she obligingly helps him escape. A monk's robe becomes part of his fugitive disguise. To dramatize the hero's psychological transformation more effectively, Wada substitutes a deft transition, using a simple costume change: Mizushima's uniform is stolen while he is bathing, so he is given the robe of a Buddhist monk.

Supported by a script concise and well focused, Ichikawa succeeds in weaving a complex psychological drama heightened by moments of lyrical beauty. Three levels of revelation are involved: the first deals with various stages of perception Mizushima experiences on the way to a final epiphany; another concerns his comrades' search for an ultimate sense of mission; and finally, the audience is carried forward by degrees to a revelation of a tragedy of cosmic proportion.

Undoubtedly the director's cinematic rubric, particularly his use of tightly organized cross-cutting, flashbacks, and frequent close-ups, contributes to the psychological dimensions of the film. In one scene, Mizushima, dressed as a monk, takes refuge in a Buddhist monastery, where he sees a group of British nurses holding a memorial service for unknown soldiers. A medium shot of the nurse's faces is quickly transformed into a close-up of Mizushima's face expressing awe and consternation. This transition deftly registers Mizushima's moment of epiphany, his recognition that altruism is universal, common to East and West alike. This scene is succeeded by a rapid sweep of flashbacks to two previous confrontations with death. In the first, Mizushima sees dead soldiers around him when he regains consciousness on the battlefield. In the second, he comes face-to-face with a mummified corpse leaning against a tree, surrounded by more corpses littering the riverbank. The leitmotif music, "Oh Sacred Head Now Wounded," returns to signal Mizushima's awakening—and to foreshadow his determination to dedicate his life to Buddhist altruism.

The expressive power of the film is such that the purely linguistic contribution of the script is overshadowed. Yet Wada's skill as a scenarist is evident in the dramatization of conflicting values, providing a sharply focused narrative in collaboration with the dynamic of the film's expressive mode.

Conflagration (Enjō, 1959), film. Based on *The Temple of the Golden Pavil-ion* (Kinkakuji, 1956) by Mishima Yukiko (1925–70), this is an excellent ex-ample of the scriptwriter's contribution to the communicative power of a film. Here, Wada, together with her collaborator Hasebe Kenji, achieves simplicity and immediacy through her use of narrative style, thematic constants, and tex-ture. Wada dispenses with the novel's standard confessional mode and in its place puts the dramatically arresting opening sequence of police interrogation of the arsonist-hero, Mizoguchi. Thus at the outset, the film is given a more realistic and pragmatic texture in accordance with its contemporary subject. Mi-zoguchi's life at the temple is then explained in a series of flashbacks that Wada has arranged, transposing key incidents from the novel.

In the original, Mishima's probing into his protagonist's obsession with the temple—the thematic substance of the book—is extremely complex. The temple is seen as the focus of the young acolyte's aesthetic sensibility, as well as a projection of his alter ego. Unable to make contact with the external world, Mizoguchi invests his sense of self in the temple. Ironically, the temple takes charge of the young man's life, frustrating his attempts to socialize himself. It stands in the way even of the powerful drive of libido. Eventually, Mizoguchi feels compelled to free his ego by destroying this artifice of eternity. Only after he sets fire to it in the end does he feel he wants to live.

Wada eliminates such complex psychological motives. Her arsonist simply wants to protect the purity of the pavilion from contamination by the vulgar. The film's interest lies in a contemporary treatment of the traditional-versus-modern dichotomy. Among those violating the temple (as Mizoguchi sees it) are his own surrogate father, Reverend Tayama, who has got his geisha pregnant, and an American GI who visits the temple with his pregnant Japanese girlfriend. The film, more dynamically than the novel, indicts the values of a postwar secular culture seen as vulgarizing and destroying the traditions of which the Japanese have long been proud. This is obvious in the scene where Mizoguchi pushes the GI's girlfriend out of the temple door, lest she defile it.

Mishima's novel is rich in complex symbols serving the psychological content of his story. A stone image corresponds to the rigidity of Mizoguchi's ego, his inability to communicate with the world outside himself. Recurrent images of hands (his father's especially) suggest a note of fatherly protection shielding him from the gross and carnal pleasures of life all around him. Wada and Ichi-kawa dispense with such symbols in order to concentrate on direct thematic exploration of Mizoguchi's attempts to save the temple from defilement. Wada and Ichikawa also alter the ending of the original story. For them, death, not arson, must be Mizoguchi's way to freedom. In the final sequence policemen escort the young man, now a prisoner, to a train. Voices off-screen tell us that he is to serve a seven-year sentence and that his mother has committed suicide. Mizoguchi is seen wrestling with one of his guards and then leaping from the moving train. A cut to his dead body shows investigators approaching. Wada and Ichikawa have created a different sort of hero. Whereas Mishima made his an object of complex psychological interest, the film's protagonist is more accessible, with human strengths and weaknesses that appeal to our sympathy.

Odd Obsession (Kagi, 1959), film. Based on a controversial novel by Tanizaki Juncihiro (1886–1965), the script is a collaboration of Wada, her husband, and Hasebe Keiji (1914–). Japanese readers were shocked by the overt treatment of sex when the book was published in 1953. It takes the form of diaries kept by a respectable married couple in contemporary Japan. Both are determined to rejuvenate themselves through sex rather than resign themselves to dignified old age in the traditional Japanese manner. Since they are aware that each is reading the other's diary, the resulting intimate jottings take on a complex rhetoric as the writers seek to manipulate one another to achieve their aims. The reader is expected to play the knowing spectator in this game, comparing diary entries, noting ironies of deceit and self-deception, always on the lookout for motives that are real among so much elaborate shamming. The novel is sharply satirical as it mocks the respectable couple's desperate attempt to reverse the flux of time.

The filmscript takes its cue from the element of satire and works to show what happens to a respectable, middle-aged couple engaged in a dangerous game of sex. The detachment required by satire is achieved in several interesting ways. First, in order to communicate more directly with the film audience, the confessional diary format is put aside in favor of direct narration by one of the characters: the young doctor Kimura. Like his fictional counterpart, he is a party to a ménage à trois, as the fiancé of the daughter of the house and lover of the mother. The ironic mode of the film is established immediately: Kimura appears, and after describing the physical symptoms of aging, points a finger directly at the audience, saying in a mocking tone: "No one can escape growing old—not even you out there."

In the novel, irony arises largely out of discrepancies between what characters say in their diaries and what they really mean and do. The film translates this into visual irony, adding a vein of black humor missing in the book. For example, the aging protagoanist Kenmotsu is not Tanizaki's university professor, but a connoisseur of antiques! When the daughter, Toshiko, and her fiancé, Kimura, make love in a cheap hotel, the scene is cross-cut with a view of trains coupling. The ending of the film is radically different from that of the novel. The blackest notes of humor come to the fore when the elderly, myopic housemaid becomes the agent of poetic justice. She has seen through all the elaborate role playing in the house and has witnessed the consequences. The wife has hastened her husband's death by manipulating his desire to stay young through feats of sexual prowess. Playing by her own set of rules, the daughter has helped destroy her parents' marriage. In the end, mother and daughter begin a new life with their shared lover, Kimura. Then the elderly maid poisons all three. A voice-over of the expiring Kimura wonders at this strange fate. The film ends with a blackly humorous footnote. The maid confesses her crime to policemen, who can only conclude that she suffers from senile dementia. The police report insists on a stolidly conventional explanation for the event: mother and daughter, left in poverty, committed suicide; the young intern, Kikura, joined them in sympathy. Case closed.

Fires on the Plain (Nobi, 1959), film. In this film, based on a war novel of 1952 by Ōoka Shōhei (1909–), Wada adapts a highly complex psychological novel to suit the mass entertainment demands of the film studio. This entails considerable simplifications of thematic material and narrative device. Ōoka's theme is the conflict between man's idealism and the beast within. In the final stage of World War II, Private Tamura is on Leyte Island. Separated from his unit and suffering from malaria, he wanders behind enemy lines. His struggle to survive brings him face-to-face with a choice as extreme as cannibalism versus starvation. Ōoka invests this cruel dilemma with a wealth of Christian imagery, giving a biblical dimension to Tamura's ethical conflict. For example, a soldier who offers his thin body to his comrades for food is treated as a Christ-like martyr. The Bible is quoted directly in the scene where Tamura experiences a sense of the divine. Images of nature, too, are used to provide objective cor-relatives and enhance the psychological dimensions of Tamura's inner conflict.

Wada's scenario leaves such complexities aside in favor of clear-cut issues of moral choice and physical survival. Tamura must decide whether or not he will do the abhorrent thing—eat human flesh to live (as another soldier does) or risk dying of starvation. Similarly, subtle symbols and nature imagery are sacrificed to simpler issues. Nature becomes a hostile environment battle-weary soldiers must fight. The novel's narrative mode is simplified in the film as well. Ōoka's first-person narrator speaks mainly of the past, reliving his ordeal in a confessional mood that exposes his innermost sense of himself. The horrible story he has to tell becomes the backdrop for wide-ranging reflections on phil-osophical and religious issues as they relate to complex human responses to life on the battlefield. The novelist leads the reader through an intricate series of rhetorical stance, shifting back and forth between empathic identification (inside view) and objective detachment (outside view). The two come together only at the end, in an epilogue entitled ''A Dead Man's Writing.'' Since the dead man turns out to be an inmate of a lunatic asylum, the reader is left to ponder the validity of Tamura's ordeal—and to wonder if perhaps the whole of the book should be read from ''outside'' after all, as if by an observer as detached, say, as a staff psychiatrist.

Such is not the case with Wada's filmscript. The first-person narration gives way to frequent point-of-view shots seen from Tamura's perspective. The issue is clearly set in realistic terms of the horrors of war and this soldier's struggle to survive them. The novel's epilogue is omitted entirely. Tamura is accepted at face value, becoming a victim of war, a casualty of human decency forced to choose under cruel and unusual circumstances. Clearly, the scenarist seeks first and foremost to deepen audience empathy. The film ends with Tamura's return to humanity. Ōoka's fire imagery survives to serve as an index of human life. In the final sequence, Tamura is ready to give himself up to the enemy after the long, solitary struggle. As he walks toward the fires on the plain, he says to himself, ''I know it's dangerous, but I want to see people who are leading normal lives.'' Villagers emerge from the smoke. The film concludes with a shot of Tamura staggering toward them and falling. Thus, scriptwriter and director have joined forces to give this story a more conciliatory ending than provided by Ōoka's darkly doubting epilogue.

BIBLIOGRAPHY

Allyn, John. *Kon Ichikawa: A Guide to References and Resources.* Boston: G. K. Hall & Co. 1985.

Wada's scripts appear in subtitles for the following films available in the United States through Films Inc. All these films were directed by her husband, Ichikawa Kon.

The Harp of Burma (Biruma no Tategoto, 1956).

Conflagration (Enjō, 1958). Script collaborated by Hasebe Keiji.

Odd Obsession (Kagi, 1959). Script collaborated by Hasebe Keiji and Kon Ichikawa.

The Fires on the Plain (Nobi, 1959).

Actor's Revenge (Yukinojō Henge, 1963). Script collaborated by directors Daisuke Ito and Teinosuke Kinugasa.

Tokyo Olympiad (Tokyo Orinpikku, 1965).

Keiko McDONALD

Y ————————————————————————————

YAMADA Eimi (1959–), novelist, cartoonist, songwriter. Real name: Yamada Futaba.

Life: Yamada was born in Tokyo but moved frequently as her father's work demanded, until she settled in Utsunomiya and enrolled in Tochigi Prefectural Shikanuma High School. Enjoying the intellectual atmosphere of her middle-class family, she became an avid reader during her high school years, particularly of works of François Sagan and James Baldwin. At the same time, she became convinced of her own special talent for "perceiving what others seemed unable to see" and decided to pursue a career as either a painter or a writer. She entered Meiji University's Japanese Literature Department in 1978 and joined the school's Cartoon Study Club, which encouraged her to synthesize her interests in drawing and writing. During this period she became fascinated by jazz music, and Afro-Americans who were "wonderfully free and direct in expressing themselves." She withdrew from the university in her junior year and concentrated on writing the so-called *Shōjo manga* (Girls' Comics), narrative cartoons dealing primarily with the intricate and often fantastic and romantic relationships among high school students. She was successful in her endeavor and published her first comics, *Shugā bā* (A Sugar Bar) in 1981 under her real name.

Yamada was nonetheless frustrated by the low status of comics as a form of popular literature. She consequently decided to try her hand at fiction writing. Her strategy was "writing by experiencing," for "nothing held much meaning to me unless I could see, feel, and hear it." Thus began the life of adventures that transformed her into a bar hostess and a nude model. In the fall of 1984, she met an Afro-American soldier, Cavin Wilson, a divorced father of an eleven-year-old son. She moved into their apartment outside a U.S. military base near Tokyo and stopped working altogether. Her relationship with Wilson was precarious from the start, and she soon decided to leave him. Having no means of supporting herself, however, she remained with him for another month and began writing fiction in order to earn a living. The short story that she wrote during this difficult time turned out to be a masterpiece that launched her on a writing career. This literary success also calmed her stormy relationship with her soldier lover, with whom she continued to share her life. She subsequently returned to "experiencing real life" by working as "the Queen" of a "sado-masochists' club." Her daring strategy and unconventional life-style, coupled with the arrest in 1987 of Wilson for allegedly assaulting a neighborhood house-wife, constantly made her the choice target of the mass media for ridicule and criticism. The sensationalism deeply disturbed her, but she has won with her mature disposition inspiring enthusiasm of supportive editors and readers and has continued to produce works of consistently high quality. She also ventured to Bali and New York and wrote a novel and short stories based on the trips.

Career: Although she had been a successful writer of "girls' comics," her novella, *Beddotaimu aizu* (The Bedtime Eyes, 1985), written during her one-month moratorium with Wilson, earned her public recognition. Her debut im-mediately stirred up a great commotion rare in the history of contemporary Japanese literature. First, the story excited critics and readers alike with its little-known setting (a U.S. military base on the edge of Tokyo); highly unusual characters (a young Japanese woman living with an Afro-American, a quiet rebel who deserted the military with classified documents tucked under his arm, and their striptease-dancer friend); bold diction (orthodox Japanese words spiced with a large dosage of American slang); and explicit, but never pornographic, sex scenes. Second, the quality of this work impressed seasoned critics, who hailed her as "a truly new writer with a rare literary talent" and acknowledged her with the coveted *Bungei* Award and a nomination for the even more pres-tigious Akutagawa Award. The work stimulated the imagination of filmmakers as well, who eagerly tackled the linguistic difficulty of this story and produced a fine film adaptation. Third, her "scandalous" life-style shocked the public and placed her on the center stage of gossip journalism. Thus an "anomaly" from the very start, Yamada continued to write and produced in the following year another Akutagawa Award nominee, "Jesshi no sebone" (Jessie's Spine), and followed it up with "Yubi no tawamure" (Finger Play); "Onion puresu" (On-ion Press); "What's Going On?"; "Me and Mrs. Jones"; "Precious, Precious"; "Kuroi yoru" (A Black Night); and "Mama Used to Say," all in 1986.

These early works are representative of Yamada's opus. First, they often por-tray attractive young Japanese women with too much time and money on hand but little sense of purpose in life, and their Afro-American lovers. Second, the majority of the characters are thrill-seekers, who mutually communicate their intricate and often sadomasochistic emotions and needs through the five senses. Sex, music, dancing, and drinking, consequently, are indispensable elements bonding their precarious relationships. Third, as seen in the suggestive titles, Yamada freely incorporates English words, primarily slang and profanities, in order to evoke vivid, dynamic images. These images, often appearing in protagonists' recollections of their lost love affairs, contribute to creating intense passion and deep pathos akin to the motifs and rhythm of jazz music.

"Finger Play," for instance, depicts a highly promiscuous Japanese woman who reigns over black soldiers enslaved to her. One of the men in particular, she recalls, had become spellbound under her sexual power, but she had callously rejected him after a short-lived affair and married another black man. Tormented, the first soldier left for the United States. Two years later, she learns that he has returned to Japan, this time as a dazzlingly successful jazz pianist. The power he exerts over his female admirers transforms him into a slave driver who manipulates the heroine in their renewed relationship as though she were "the keyboard of his beloved piano." At once resisting and craving the playful touch of his powerful fingers, she begs him never to leave her. He is unyielding, however, and she "accidentally" kills him in the midst of their sadomasochistic intercourse. The police pronounce her act to have been in self-defense against a rapist, enabling her to reclaim her power over her deceased lover.

Yamada proved just as prolific in 1987 with short stories—"Groove Tonight"; "Feel the Fire"; "Otoko ga onna o aisuru toki" (When a Man Loves a Woman); "You Know Who"; "Boku no aji" (The Taste of Me); "Boku wa bīto" (I'm Beat); "Bad Mama Jama"; and "Kuroi kinu" (Black Silk)—and novels—*Hāremu wārudo* (Harlem World); *Nettai anraku isu* (An Easy Chair in the Tropics), set in Bali; and *Chōcho no tensoku* (Foot-Binding a Butterfly), later nominated for the Akutagawa Award. The first exciting moment in her career came during the same year when her *Sōru myūjikku rabāzu onrī* (For Soul-Music Lovers Only), a collection of eight previously published short stories, won the prestigious Naoki Award for popular literature. She again stirred up much commotion when she appeared at the formal ceremony accompanied by a horde of Afro-American friends and nonchalantly asked in her acceptance speech: "Isn't this some kind of a mistake? I thought these [literary] awards were given only to old writers." She was nonetheless enormously pleased by this turn of events and immediately embarked on writing an autobiographical fiction, *Hizamazuite ashi o oname* (Kneel Down and Lick My Feet, 1987–88).

In 1988, Yamada contributed short stories to various magazines: "Seijinmuki mōfu" (Blankets for Adults; translated as X-Rated Blanket); "Boku no ai was in o fumu" (My Love Rhymes); "Daburu jointo" (Double Joints); "Kurōzetto furīku" (A Closet Freak); "Tanjōbi" (A Birthday); "Green"; "Boku wa bīto" (I Am Beat); "Kogitsune kon" (A Little Fox); and "Fūsō no kyōshitsu" (Burying Them in the Wind). She published in 1989 "Gas" and *Furīku shō* (A Freak Show).

Major Works: Beddotaimu aizu (Bedtime Eyes, 1985), novella. Portrayed is a young Japanese woman, Kim, a nightclub singer, who frequents a bar on an American military base patronized by black soldiers. Her lover, Spoon—so called because of his "obscene" habit of fondling in his pants pocket a silver spoon that he carries as a good-luck charm—is a "cool" client of the club who deserts the military and moves in with her. As she later laments, however, Spoon is "terrific at loving me, that is to say, loving my body, but not my soul." Similarly, she "can let Spoon hold me, but can't really embrace him, no matter how often I tried." They, in other words, are bound together only through the immediate and momentary pleasure of senses and consequently remain strangers to each other. If not busy with lovemaking or babbling "dark lyrics in the cheerful rhythm of a rap" while drinking or taking drugs, Spoon simply drifts in and out of the woman's apartment carrying a briefcase. Neither the content of his treasured possession nor the nature of his activities outside the home is of any concern to Kim, however. She is simply drawn to this "mentor of carnal love" by his "hands and tongue" and "body odor . . . the odor familiar to me from a far-off past . . . the sweet-and-sour smell of stale cocoa butter" that "is never unpleasant, no, not really never, but is the kind of a decaying smell that makes me realize my own purity whenever it assails me."

The only character capable of genuine love is Maria *nēsan,* or Big Sister Maria, a striptease dancer who secretly loves Kim. Intensely jealous of her preoccupation with Spoon, however, Maria seduces him and confesses her love to Kim. This incident and Maria's subsequent denunciation of Spoon as "an ordinary man with nothing special to offer" make Kim realize that she is little different from her lover and from Maria, whom she has worshiped. This self-discovery enables her to "communicate with Spoon for the first time in my life, not through my body alone but also through words." They are consequently able to develop their love for each other. This happy development comes too late, however: Spoon is arrested for stealing classified military documents that he has carried in his briefcase with the intention to sell them, and Kim is left only with "memories" that "used to be just a dumb word I had no use for."

Drawn largely from the author's personal experiences, the characters in this story are invariably fully developed and convincing. Particularly noteworthy is the heroine's transformation from a narcissistic thrill-seeker to a woman unsure of herself and eventually to a fully mature woman who has tasted both the sweetness and the bitterness of tragic love. The role of Maria is equally significant: she is a classic Madonna-prostitute figure responsible for the heroine's sublimation. Yamada's empathic, yet realistic, eyes coupled with her exceptional sensitivity for both Japanese and English words, however, appear to be the key factor that enabled her to confront the reality of affluent and stagnant contemporary Japan and capture in this work of subtle tenderness the pathos of marginalized people caught in a vacuum.

"Jesshi no sebone" (Jessie's Spine, 1986), short story. The heroine is a Japanese woman (this time given a Japanese name, Koko) who boasts of knowing "practically everything there is to know about men." The story focuses on her difficult relationship with her black lover's eleven-year-old son, Jessie, and her eventual understanding of the boy's complex emotions. Koko's interest in the recently divorced, near-alcoholic American soldier is aroused in large part by her curiosity about Jessie, of whom he speaks fondly. Meeting this part-Japanese boy, however, she immediately becomes dismayed by the "little devil" with "the face of a monkey, a half of it obviously Oriental" and singles him out as the only source of misery in her otherwise happy relationship with her lover. Similarly, Jessie, who is still strongly attached to his mother, resents Koko's intrusion into his life and tries everything in his power to destroy her relationship with his father. She nonetheless sympathizes with him for the ten years of neglect and hatred he must have suffered before his parents' divorce. She even offers her service as a surrogate mother while his father is away in the United States for two weeks. Feeling rejected by his mother and missing his father as well, Jessie takes his anger out on Koko, defying her openly and harassing her friends who come to visit her. The situation helps her realize the depth of his pain and loneliness and the complexity of his emotions toward his parents. She also discovers the importance of verbal communication for smoothing out her relationship with him. Jessie gradually begins to respond to Koko's efforts and even tries to play the role of his father to her. He becomes jealous of her male friend, for instance, and physically attacks her while she is talking on the telephone. When his father finally returns, however, Jessie constantly follows him, ignoring Koko altogether. What is more, he tries to win over his mother's sympathy by claiming that Koko neglects his needs. Yet, when his mother invites him to live with her, he rejects the offer by telling her, "I'll stay here, for the time being." Jessie, in short, is an unhappy child tormented by his own love, jealousy, resentment, and mistrust. What eventually helps him untangle his complex and confusing emotions are his father's verbal reprimands that force him to confront his mixed emotions toward the three adults around him and verbalize them to his father and Koko. Witnessing Jessie's transformation to a more mature, happier boy, Koko concludes that his spine is made not of love and hate, as she had thought earlier, but of "discs just like any ordinary human being's."

Despite the superficiality of Jessie's overnight transformation, Yamada convincingly depicts the intricate emotions of a young boy in growing pains. Like her 1986 short story, "Me and Mrs. Jones," which captures a teenager's tender love for a glamorous married woman much older that he, and *An Easy Chair in the Tropics,* which portrays the quiet love of a deaf-mute Indonesian boy toward a young woman visitor from Japan, "Jessie's Spine" illuminates the best quality in this author—her sensitive and empathic insight into the psychology of youth vulnerable to their own puppy love and its painful consequences. While *The Bedtime Eyes* exudes subtle tenderness, "Jessie's Spine" enhances supreme tenderness with a pleasing aesthetic quality.

Chōcho no tensoku (A Foot-Bound Butterfly, 1987), novel. Rare among Yamada's fiction, this story is narrated by the first-person protagonist, who reminisces on her life from early childhood through high school years. It shares a common ground with "Girls' Comics" in that the intricate love-hate relationships among high school students triggered by their adolescent anxieties over approaching adulthood are a predominant theme. One young girl, Hitomi, willingly subjugates herself to a narcissistic, domineering Eriko living next door. Soon Hitomi begins to resent Eriko's popularity among boys and teachers. Seeing herself as a "foot-bound butterfly" deprived by this "friend" of freedom to grow on her own, Hitomi at age sixteen throws herself into adult activities such as drinking, smoking, and sex and enjoys for the first time the sense of superiority over "socially naive" Eriko. Yet, Hitomi realizes that she has "no feet of my own to stand on" and laments:

I was driven by my own mad desire to return to my childhood, to those years filled with the sweet taste of honey, and happiness tinged only by a bit of anxiety. If only I could remain a child, I would have been able to stay innocent, like a butterfly fluttering among flowers. But those days are gone forever, and I am now a butterfly unable to enjoy the sweet nectar of flowers.

The nostalgia and the romantic images explicit in these passages, too, are characteristics of "Girls' Comics." If the story lacks depth because of an insufficient probing of adolescent psychology, the clear images, like illustrations in comics, compensate for the shortcoming and make this work pleasant reading, particularly for young adults.

Sōru myūjikku rabāzu onrī (For Soul-Music Lovers Only, 1987), a collection of short stories. Comprising eight tales titled after popular soul-music numbers, this Naoki Award-winner introduces Yamada's "favorite" people, namely, young Afro-American men and women who are "slovenly, feeling-oriented, caring and self-conscious, and have insatiable appetite for love." The stereotypical view of Afro-Americans aside, the stories illuminate the author's imagination to capture the people in vivid, dynamic images. Many of the stories are set in black ghettos in the United States, but, unlike the majority of contemporary Japanese fiction set in the West, racism and economic oppression are never the issues in Yamada's writings. Instead, she focuses her attention on the black characters' spontaneous actions and works that reveal their deep feelings, particularly passion and sorrow. Her use of blues motifs is explicit. Take, for instance, the opening paragraphs of "Mama Used to Say," depicting the homecoming of its protagonist, Bruce, a basketball scholarship student at "a college in the East":

It's *God damn crowded* as usual, Bruce muttered choking on cigarette smoke as he pushed his way into Yobo's pub.
"Bruce! How've you been?" A prostitute he has known for some time cried out. Immediately hands reached out to him through the stagnant air. Slapping them noisily, he greeted the people.
"*Hey, guys,* how you doing?"
"Hey, *what's up?*"
"You askin' me? *You got it,* right?"
Men threw the words at him while the prostitutes showered him with kisses. Unable to move, Bruce clicked his tongue irritably but realized, too, how much he had missed this atmosphere he grew up in. His body, away from it all for so long, didn't know how

to react. But it didn't take long for the warmth of it to seep into his body, and he began to smile against his will.

"Hey, Yobo. Hey, Dan, your son's back."

"It's O.K. Hey, stop it," begged Bruce.

Dad must be washing dishes, his eyes cast down intently on them, or he may be shaking his shaker, with his head turned the other way. His shyness and anger must be making his dark black face even darker, while the white of his eyes are turning reddish with excitement. Bruce knew his father well. But he was more anxious to know how the woman who must be working alongside his father was doing. Bruce wanted to run up to the counter to see her but instead stood around and talked to his not-so-close friends.

In the original Japanese text, the italicized parts are written in Japanese but are accompanied on their side by the English words transcribed in Japanese phonetic *kana* script and the name Yobo is spelled out in English letters. This visual scheme, too, contributes to the vividness of images and dynamic style.

"The woman who must be working alongside his father" is Bruce's step-mother, the only "straight" woman with whom he had an affair. The rest of the story is his recollection of their first meeting, the jealousy he had felt toward her over his father's affection, his illicit love affair with her that began "accidentally" but developed into true love, and his guilt, which eventually led him to a decision to leave his home.

Other stories compiled in this book follow similar story lines. The heroine of "What's Going On?" is a married woman whose chance encounter with her former lover triggers in her mind the sweet and sad memories of her bygone days with him. Similarly, "Feel the Fire" portrays a woman who is devastated by her husband's death but, helped by the quiet love of his best friend, gradually regains strength to face life anew. Revealing the lives of ordinary black people about whom the majority of Japanese are curious but still unfamiliar and capitalizing on the fundamental human emotions that enable readers to identify themselves with the black people, those stories of uniquely high quality pack an enormous appeal to a wide range of Japanese readership.

Hizamazuite ashi o oname (Kneel Down and Lick My Feet, 1987–88), semi-autobiographical novel. Unlike the traditional *watakushi-shōsetsu,* or the auto-biographical "I-novel," in which there is little emotional distance between the author and the protagonist, this work is an objective account of Yamada's adult life, narrated by a friend. The narrator, Shinobu, and the heroine, Chika, share some common ground as coworkers, first, as striptease dancers and, later, as "the Queens" of a "sado-masochist club" in a obscure back alley of Tokyo. More important, however, they enjoy their mutual respect and are drawn to-gether through their empathy for marginal people—for instance, customers at the "club" and striptease dancers illegally brought to Japan from developing countries in Southeast Asia. The two women, however, are the antithesis of each other. First, while Shinobu is married to an ordinary Japanese man quietly sup-portive of her, Chika lives with a divorced black American who causes her much dismay by allegedly assaulting a neighbor and her daughter. Second, much older and tradition-bound, Shinobu is critical, although sympathetic of Chika's life-style. Third, contrary to Shinobu, who prefers status quo, Chika aspires to become a fiction writer and succeeds in winning a Naoki Award. This setup, with the two women representing at once a parallel and a dichotomy, and the frequent use of flashbacks and seriously personal dialogues reveal Yamada's exceptional literary talent as well as her honest, sensitive personality.

BIBLIOGRAPHY
After School Keynotes. Tr. Sonya Johnson. Tokyo: Kodansha International, 1992.
Trash. Tr. Sonya Johnson, Tokyo: Kodansha International, 1995.
''X-Rated Blanket.'' In *New Japanese Voices: The Best Contemporary Fiction from Japan* ed. Helen Mitsios. New York: Atlantic Monthly Press, 1991, 50–54.
                                                           Yoshiko Yokochi SAMUEL

YAMAMOTO Michiko (1936–), novelist, short story writer, essayist. Real name: Furuya Michiko (Mrs. Furuya Kazuyoshi); née Yamamoto Michiko.

Life: Yamamoto was born into an upper-middle-class family in Tokyo on December 4, 1936, the eldest daughter of Yamamoto Heihachi and Mihoko. Other siblings include one older brother and two younger brothers. Yamamoto's family was well established in Tokushima prefecture in Shikoku, and her grandfather was known throughout the region as an eccentric. She later wrote that many of her unpleasant memories regarding ''adults'' stemmed from this eccentricity. Her mother was the oldest daughter of a physician, and her father was employed by a Tokyo elevator manufacturer. In 1943 as World War II worsened, the father evacuated the family to Tokushima to escape the bombing of Tokyo; in 1946 they moved back to the city, where Yamamoto resumed her schooling as a fifth grader. Her father, by then an independent businessman, founded his own elevator company. While she was a literature student at Atomiseki Junior College, her story ''Mitsubachi'' (Honeybee), which she submitted to the Students Short Story Contest, sponsored by a major publisher, Kawade Shobō, won a place in the semifinals of the contest. She was also invited to work on the staff of a prestigious literary magazine, *Rekitei,* and several of her poems appeared there and in other literary journals. Collections of her poetry followed: *Tsubo no naka* (Inside a Jar, 1959), *Midori-iro no hitsujitachi* (Green Lambs, 1960), *Kago* (A Basket, 1961), and *Kazaru* (To Decorate, 1962). In 1962, she lost her mother to cancer, which had lasted for two years: Mihoko was only forty-nine, Yamamoto twenty-six. They had enjoyed a warm, intimate relationship, and Mihoko's death was a tragic blow to the young fledgling writer. ''If I have a grudge against my country, mine would be a very personal one, the bereavement of my mother,'' she said in a *taidan* (an informal interview) with a contemporary novelist Ōba Minako (1930–). ''Apart from the confusing situation of the post-war days which as a nine-year-old I remember like a dream, my mother's death was the greatest single unhappy event of my life.'' For the next two years Yamamoto suffered from hallucinations, seeing Mihoko's ghost or hearing her voice. It took her eleven years before she could write about Mihoko's death at all. The result was the 1973 story "Wagamama na yūrei" (A Selfish Ghost).

In 1965 she married Furuya Kazuyoshi, a poet friend's younger brother, because, in her words, "he had absolutely no knowledge of literature," and there would be no chance of building up a competitive atmosphere where they could hurt each other's feelings. In 1966 a baby girl, Rui, was born, and the following year her husband, who worked for the Japan Fisheries Company, was transferred to Darwin, Australia, where the Yamamotos lived till 1971.

Career: During her stay in the inhumanly hot, dry "boondocks" in Australia, Yamamoto gave birth to another baby girl, Amiko, and wrote a short story, "Mahō" (Powers, 1971), a winner of the *Shinchō* New Writers' Prize. Back in Japan, feeling the pressure to produce, yet burdened with domestic obligations, she went through a writer's slump. Encouraged by the moral support of a *Shinchō* editor and the kind words of novelist Minakami Tsutomu (1919–), this relatively unknown writer set to work on a project that became the short story "Betty-san no niwa" (Betty-san's Garden, 1973). It won the Akutagawa Prize, the highest a writer can receive in Japan. This event made quite a stir and gave rise to the coinage *shufu-sakka* (a housewife writer). Like Ōba Minako, Yamamoto was a "middle-aged housewife/mother" when she won the prize, and Japanese opinion makers feel obligated to distinguish such writers from their unmarried counterparts, who are simply called *joryū sakka* (women writers). Although Yamamoto is a far cry from a militant feminist, she was clearly uncomfortable with how she had been categorized. Her reply to a group of journalists at a news conference took her audience by surprise: "If you call us *shufu sakka,* why not call the men *teishu sakka* [husband writers]?" On another occasion, she went one step further with her comment on the sexual injustice of the society: "Those male writers do their writing while their wives serve them hand and foot from morning till night. I envy them." Between 1974 and 1977 her professional life was in full gear with the publication of three collections of short stories, *Razō* (Nudes, 1974), *Umi to satōkibi* (The Sea and Sugarcanes, 1975), and *Shōnen no koe* (A Boy's Voice, 1977); numerous essays; and *Yamamoto Michiko Shishū* (A Collection of Yamamoto Michiko's Poetry, 1976). In the hurly-burly of this period she also managed to take a European tour in July 1976. However, two years later Yamamoto had to adjust herself to another disruption of her domestic life: this time, her husband was transferred to Seattle. She accompanied him with the same dutiful reluctance she had shown when he was sent to Darwin, Australia. The homesickness and loneliness of that early sojourn plagued her during the family's four years in Seattle. She often categorizes herself as "someone who is incapable of living abroad, away from the homeland." However, what she calls *yamuoenai gaikoku-gurashi* (no-choice situation of living abroad) has been the driving force of frantic literary activities, because "the act of writing and her own being became one" when she was in an alien land, whereas at home she deals with writing as a job. Her 1985 novel, *Hito no ki* (Human Trees), received the Women's Literature Prize.

Major Works: Tenshi yo umi ni mae (Dance, Angels, High upon the Sea, 1981), novel. Yamamoto's first full-length fiction poses questions about conventional marriage, family, sex, and morality, issues for the most part still unchallenged by the majority of Japanese, including the younger generation. The author intentionally draws upon what she saw, heard, thought, and experienced in her four years in the United States. The protagonists, Tani Takashi and Yoshiko, are a typical newly wed couple, who have recently moved to Seattle, where Takashi is a *shōsha man* (employee of a shōsha, major trading company). While he shuttles back and forth between home and company, which, as far as he is concerned, is a rather uncomplicated extension of his Japanese life, Yoshiko finds herself abandoned and purposeless in a strange land. She has too much time on her hands yet has very little desire to mingle with other *shōshamen's* wives. The honeymoon atmosphere quickly evaporates; the marriage and life abroad that Yoshiko believed would renew their intense premarital sexual relationship fall well short of her expectations.

This condition of loneliness is a narrative raison d'être of the story: Yoshiko chooses to do the only thing she feels she can do under the circumstances, to get out of the house and wander. She encounters several outrageously eccentric people. The narrative discourse of this novel is made up of several questions that reveal different levels of Yoshiko's emotional state of mind. The first has something to do with her piano, which she had shipped all the way from Japan: "Why did I bring it to the States?" We are told that she is a graduate of a music conservatory, but she never touches the piano after the marriage. This question leads to a more personal one: "Why did I come here at all?" In turn, "Why did I marry Takashi?" When she becomes acquainted with Lowe, a typical, "uncomplicated, country folk" who immediately opens himself up to her, she asks herself typically Japanese questions: "Why does Lowe want to show me his house when he hardly knows me? Why does he want to invite me to this and that all the time? Why do Americans wave at total strangers?" Her unvoiced inquiries demand no answers. Instead of finding reasons for the cultural differences that are upsetting her, she simply assumes, fantasizes, and is often critical of "American ways." However, the ultimate question, "What am I going to do with my life?" or "What do I want in life?" is triggered by two external factors, one originating in her home country, the other in the United States. Her older sister, Maoko, who had a brief affair with Takashi prior to his marriage, begins to write to him regularly. When her letters elicit no response, she comes to the United States to try to repossess Takashi. At the same time, a friend's unwanted son, Ken, helps Yoshiko refocus her life: she changes from someone who pities the child to someone who takes an active interest in his welfare. With the help of a neighbor, Lowe, Yoshiko finally finds answers to the questions that have been hounding her: she takes a plunge into the role of mother by adopting Ken; she accepts Lowe's kindness for what it really is, and the two agree to take care of Ken together; she ends her marriage with Takashi.

Yamamoto's portrayal of Japanese who live abroad not by choice but by necessity explores two opposing camps: those who temporarily shed their native shell to "enjoy life" and create a microcommunity with their fellow countrymen; and those who can do neither, retreating farther into their shells to taste the bitter sense of loneliness. Yoshiko belongs to the latter, and the *shoshamen's* wives belong to the former. Unlike Ōba Minako, whose female characters take off on their own to integrate themselves into an alien culture, the third category of Japanese abroad, represented by Ken's mother, Shii, is clearly not a focal point of Yamamoto's literary world. This has a lot to do with domestic circumstances that left her no choice but to accompany her husband abroad twice, three years the first time, four the second. In other words, Yamamoto as artist and person speaks for the great majority of ordinary Japanese who are perfectly happy to stay where they are, the secure maternal shelter called Japan. However, the remarkable thing about *Dance, Angels, High upon the Sea* is that the author consciously provides a way out for the female protagonist, not by causing her return to Japan but by letting her start an entirely new kind of life in the United States. The novel is one of the very few bildungsroman in Japanese literature: the protagonist undergoes a painful rite of passage and actually emerges as a different person. The reader actually witnesses the emotional, psychological growth of Yoshiko toward the end of the novel. This, indeed, is a welcome departure from the conventional character development of the protagonists in many well-known Japanese masterpieces, such as Sensei in *Kokoro,* Shimamura in *Snow Country,* and Kaname in *Some Prefer Nettles.*

Hito no ki (Human Trees, 1985), novel. The winner of the Women's Literature Prize explores the intricate workings of the human psyche that can produce hallucinations and agoraphobia, other points of fascination for Yamamoto. The story covers two years in the life of a middle-aged, agoraphobic housewife, Horikoshi Mayuko, married to an accountant, Yusaku, who leads a double life. How she finds out her husband's secret and the strange way the couple dances around the subject once the secret is out are the gist of Yamamoto's third novel.

Even though the plot has the ring of a real domestic squabble with a twist of melodrama, the story moves in an unexpected direction, far removed from the context of everyday life. First of all, Yamamoto begins the novel with a short discourse on the habitat, characteristics, and magical power of *tengu,* a folkloric long-nosed tricksterlike goblin: "When a *tengu* wants to talk with humans—he takes up residence in the grove that belongs to a village shrine, he stands watch on the branch of a two-thousand-year-old zelkova tree, gazes down at the world below and waits patiently for some passersby who might be willing to listen to him. They say he is originally made up of the spirit flowing in the mist of the deep forest." Second, the Chinese character *mayu* that Yamamoto applies to the name of her female protagonist who ponders the existence of *tengu* literally means a "cocoon." Third, her residence is a condominium located on the tenth floor with gauzy sheer curtains over the living room windows. Mayuko's routine consists of occasional grocery shopping and watering the fifty-some houseplants she has collected. In other words, the condominium provides her self-sufficiency in a self-contained cocoon; her outside world is seen only through the sheer, translucent walls of the cocoon.

Yamamoto continues to build up this hallucinatory, surrealistic atmosphere: Mayuko receives anonymous phone calls from a woman. The caller becomes a *tengu* in Mayuko's mind, and she begins hallucinating that the voice on the phone is "my own deranged voice." Since no personal relationship develops between the protagonist and the anonymous caller, and no dialogue of any consequence is exchanged between the wife and husband, the narrative discourse carries on only inside Mayuko's head, leaving reality as it is: nothing out in the open, no outbursts, no complaints, no accusations. The temporary paralysis of her legs and the death of some of the houseplants are the only outward manifestations of her emotional stress. Even after Mayuko learns the name of the anonymous caller, Maki Otoko (lit., a "real tree-sound"), and sees her briefly in the distance at a wedding, one regards the other as a ghostlike figure. To Mayuko, Yusaku is also a ghost king who lives with a princess and their two children in a dream castle in a strange town. To Otoko, Mayuko is someone unreal who stays shut up in a condominium, with no children to take care of, no apparent illness to deal with, so carefree, cut off from the outside world, and apparently perfectly "serene and unperturbed." In the end Otoko is drawn to Mayuko. In Yusaku's mind's eye, the two women are two sides of the same woman; it is in his best interests to keep the double life going as long as possible. Like Yoshiko in *Dance, Angels, High upon the Sea,* Yamamoto's female protagonists in the end take the initiative and become independent with a new direction in their life, while male characters remain essentially the same.

Yamamoto's other major works include *Birejji ni ame* (Rain over the Village, 1982) and *Hitori kasokeki* (Alone in the Dark, 1987).

Translated Works: Betty-san (Betty-san no Niwa, 1972), novella. It appeared in the November issue of *Shinchō* and caught the immediate attention of the literary world. When the new year came around, Yamamoto was an overnight celebrity, the winner of the Akutagawa Prize. The story tells of a petite Japanese war bride, Betty-san, married to an antisocial, snobbish Australian, Mike, and their three sons. Yamamoto's unhappy, frustrating life in Darwin echoes on every page. From the start Betty-san is plagued with disadvantages: she did not speak a word of English before she met Mike; she did not get along with her family, and her marriage to a foreigner dooms any chance of reconciliation; Mike is an eccentric and probably would not have found any Australian woman to marry him; Betty-san does not know how to drive, a fatal disadvantage in Australia; she has low self-esteem and very little self-confidence. The combinations of personal circumstances are so overwhelming that the reader quickly realizes Betty-san's plight is largely brought on by herself; that is, if she had had a Japanese husband and lived in Australia, her personal problems would not have been much different.

Betty-san shares one common trait with many of Yamamoto's female characters: a morbid fear of being in open, public places—agoraphobia. Her self-

image is a degrading one, as pitiful as that of novelist Natsume Sōseki (1867–
1916) in London, where he suffered from a severe case of inferiority complex
among "English gentlemen." What he saw in his own reflection in a shop
window was a "dwarf," a "lost dog," and a "yellow monkey." Seventy years
later, Betty-san in a foreign country, noticing the "peculiar woman in the mirror," reacts in exactly the same manner as the intellectual Sōseki: "Though she
stopped a little short of the Aborigines, she was burned black by the sun. . . .
The lips, sharply outlined in orange lipstick, appeared positively angry. . . . She
studied the reflection of one hand. . . . How ugly it was." To be outside is to
be compared with self-assured foreigners. "As long as I'm at home I'm perfectly
safe. . . . And when I'm home there's no need to be driven—after all this time—
by the thought that this is a foreign country." Yamamoto's identification with
Betty-san runs deep because this ill-adjusted war bride speaks for her own fear
of living abroad, as well as the basic Japanese fear of living "uprooted" in a
foreign land. However, this is as far as the similarities between author and
protagonist extend, because Betty-san feels inferior even to a fellow country-
woman, the first Japanese she sees since having left Japan.

Closely connected with Betty-san's agoraphobia is an uncontrollable urge to
run away from her shelter, her self-made womb, and ultimately from Japan. She
transfers all her needs—the kind of security and *amae* (self-indulgent "dependence") she failed to get as a child—from her parents and her homeland to
Mike. Again, Yamamoto creates a situation in which no dialogue exists between
husband and wife; Betty-san and Mike do not even quarrel. After the three sons
are born, the only domestic function left to her husband is providing her with
transportation. Her house becomes a prison as well as a sanctuary. Japan, for
which she yearns so much, also caged her in; Mike, a quiet, gentle man who
never raises his voice, who always comes "at the appropriate moment" to find
the wandering Betty-san, hides an "arm" that "would seem to stretch out of
the car—long, like a chain—and wind itself around her with a gentle finality."
Tossed back and forth between the two extreme emotions and in the end losing
Mike's love, Betty-san still has her three children, always at her service. A
Japanese living abroad who feels equal to the "white men" and comfortable
with his or her sense of self is still a rarity in Japanese literature.

"The Man Who Cut the Grass" (Kusa o karu otoko, 1975), short story. An
almost plotless story, it simply provides a glimpse into someone's *nichijō seikatsu* (daily life) that reveals her hallucination that she once drove a man to
suicide. In this regard it is a very difficult work to relate to, because the author's
focus is unclear and shifts according to the kind of flotsom that might be thrown
about in the protagonist's obsessive mind. Mayo, a young housewife with nothing to do but kill time watching the world go by, begins to fantasize a murder.
Frightened by the man with a glinting sickle who has cut the grass, she super-
imposes him on another man who hanged himself fifteen years ago. The story
is so private, so personal that in a sense it has no message, no audience to
communicate with. One gets the feeling that the reader must become the voyeur,

simply following the incomprehensible, purposeless conduct of Mayo, whose mind wanders, and who is almost on the verge of madness. However, another interpretation could show that someone placed in a humdrum, eventless, everyday life, that is, a typical Japanese housewife, is, in fact, the possessor of a tremendous imaginative and creative energy on the verge of release.

"Father Goose" (Rōjin no kamo, 1972), short story. Yamamoto's obsession with finding meaning in daily life is also the topic of this work. Tomoko, seven months' pregnant, alone in the condominium while her husband is abroad on business, starts chatting with the plumber who came to repair the water heater. This eleven-page story, again plotless, could be retitled as "A Day in the Uneventful Life of a Housewife." The plumber, a stout old man, tells Tomoko about the ducks he says he has been feeding for the past ten years. The reader is not sure whether the plumber is making up the duck story, while Tomoko on a whim tells him that he should catch one and eat it. Another day has passed for her; at the end of the story Tomoko recognizes herself as completely housebound. Yamamoto employs in "Father Goose" the "narrative present" tense, which reinforces the voyeuristic sense of things happening now. Her early stories are evidence of Yamamoto's portrayal of a stereotypical Japanese woman who abandoned whatever intellectual interests or job she might have had in her premarital life, believing marriage and eventually motherhood compensate for all the loss. However, the reality of daily life betrays her.

"Chair in the Rain" (Ame no isu, 1972), short story. Nakako in this story, like Mayo and Tomoko of previous stories, represents a typical case of a woman in a double bind. An ex-copy writer for an advertising agency, a *shōhaman's* wife in Australia, she makes a total commitment to her husband's life abroad. The following passage from the story sums up what Yamamoto really feels about the ambiguity of women's position:

She was sure she had come unencumbered, bringing nothing from her niche in that little world. Her efforts to maintain that niche for herself had suddenly lost meaning. . . . That job. . . . Those things had made life worth living. . . . Nakako thought of her husband. Living with him was simply a fortuitous arrangement. A man and a woman had merely conspired in acquiring the convenient title "Mr. And Mrs." because it looked better; it conferred on them the status "not single," and that was all. Had they really had a home [*katei*]? She was jolted by her own question.

Yamamoto contrasts this stereotypical Japanese housewife with her spouse. The difference is total; one renounces everything, the other keeps himself intact intellectually as well as emotionally: "Ryūji had been sent out by a joint mining venture. A Japanese company man first and last, he'd transported everything with him—his life and work—to be reassembled in this foreign land. He had lost nothing. Whereas Nakako had stripped herself of everything." Underneath the thinly veiled resentment Yamamoto's female characters feel about the injustice of their situation lies a sense of ambivalence: if not marriage and motherhood, then back to square one, life as "a single." What then? Is there anything in between? Any alternative? Yamamoto's early female characters do not yet seem ready to explore uncharted seas.

BIBLIOGRAPHY

Translations

"Betty-san," "Father Goose," "Powers," "Chair in the Rain." In *Betty-san.* Tr. Geraldine Harcourt. New York: Kodansha International, 1983.

"The Man Who Cut the Grass." Ed. and Tr. Yukiko Tanaka and Elizabeth Hanson. In *This Kind of Women.* Stanford, CA: Stanford University Press, 1982, 176–196.

Michiko N. WILSON

YAMAZAKI Toyoko (1924–), novelist. Née Yamasaki Toyoko (Mrs. Sugimoto Kikuo).

Life: Yamazaki Toyoko was born in the Semba district of Osaka into a well-established merchant family dealing in the kelp business. Upon graduating from the Faculty of Japanese Literature of Kyoto Joshi Senmon Gakkō (today's Kyoto Women's College), she joined the Mainichi Newspaper Company in Osaka and worked as a reporter under the future novelist Inoue Yasushi (1907–91) in the department of arts and sciences. She resigned in 1958 to devote herself full-time to a literary career, following up on her successful debut with *Noren* (Shop Banner, 1957). She traveled to Europe in 1961 and, at a chapel attached to the British embassy in Paris, married Sugimoto Kikuo (1921–92), a Mainichi newspaper arts editor and later a painter. On her way back to Japan later that year, she extended her trip to see the United States. Since then, she has undertaken several other trips to Europe and China to collect research materials for her novels.

Career: Yamazaki's first novel, *Noren,* derives its material from her merchant family background. In 1958 she serialized her *Hana noren* (Flower Banner) in the literary magazine *Chūō Kōron* and earned the thirty-ninth Naoki Literary Prize. Early works that followed depicted the lives of Osaka families, especially traditional Semba merchants, and include the full-length novels *Bonchi* (Young Master, 1959), about a young son growing up in a wealthy *tabi* (split-toe kimono socks) merchant household, and *Nyokei kazoku* (The Matriarchal Family, 1962), which describes the infighting over money among the fifth-generation women in a matriarchal clan engaged in the cotton thread business.

Next, Yamazaki turned her attention to social issues. *Shiroi kyotō* (The Great White Tower), a novel serialized in two parts, in 1963 and 1967, in a weekly newsmagazine, *The Sunday Mainichi,* probes the ambitions and corruptions in the Japanese health care field through the dubious activities of a prominent surgeon professor at a national medical university. *Kareinaru ichizoku* (The Magnificent Family, 1973) depicts a power game played by financiers and high-echelon bureaucrats, featuring a ruthless banker and his polygamous household.

Her *Fumō chitai* (The Barren Zone, 1973–78) traces progress and conflicts in Japan's international business arena after World War II. Her ambitious novel *Futatsu no sokoku* (Two Home Countries, 1980) recaptures the traumatic experiences of Japanese Americans during World War II (1941–45) and its immediate aftermath. Recently Yamazaki wrote *Daichi no ko* (Child of the Great Earth, 1987–91), a novel tracing the fate of Japanese children who were separated from their parents during the war and left behind in China, as well as the difficulties Japanese companies faced in their efforts to establish themselves in modern China. These recent works, based on meticulous investigation and data collection, won her acclaim as one of the *shakaiha* (social issues-oriented) novelists, a title rarely accorded a woman writer.

Yamazaki has been accused on several occasions of plagiarism. The first case was triggered by *Kaen* (Flower Party, 1968), when a passage was found to be identical with one in a Japanese translation of Remarque's *Arch of Triumph* describing the scenery around the Arch. The mishap, for which Yamasaki apologized, had occurred partially due to her reliance on her research assistants for collecting the vast amount of data she uses for her writing and partially due to her training as a newspaper writer, whose aim is to report an integrated picture out of amassed data. Her experience as a reporter may also be observable in her preference for employing the omniscient point of view in her fiction. Yamasaki's characters are often obsessed with a single motive for success. Many of her recent long novels portray men who show prowess in maneuvering their socio-economic and political milieu. Along with the dynamic depiction of spectacular social successes and failures in Japan's global age, Yamazaki's broad social perspective and critical insight on the evils of the modern world have placed her in a prominent position among contemporary Japanese writers.

Major Works: Noren (Shop Banner, 1957), novel. Marking Yamazaki's debut as a writer with an insider view of the business world in Osaka, this novel traces two generations of kelp merchants. The first part resembles bildungsroman in a mercantile setting. In 1896, Hatta Gohei, from Awaji Island, finds work at Naniwaya, dealing in edible seaweeds. Small but stout and determined to succeed, he toils for thirteen years, starting from servant boy and, through hard physical labor and constant attentiveness, gradually rising to the rank of head clerk. Eventually he is allowed to open his own kelp shop with the same name, Naniwaya. His business begins to fail during World War II, when kelp, along with other foodstuffs, was put under the control of the government. The extreme shortage of goods in postwar Japan has made black marketing lucrative, and Gohei can no longer keep up with the fast-paced marketplace where shrewd tactics and quick profits have replaced business ethics. Gohei's second son, Kohei, is repatriated from Rabaul and makes his entry into the business by using his quick wit and physical strength to worm his way into the black market. Joining the committee established by the city government for distribution of kelp, Kohei acquires the ability to discern quality kelp, to understand kelp trading, and to develop personal connections in the Osaka business world. He opens his own shop and soon even secures sales counters in newly built department stores in Osaka and Tokyo. The novel ends with Kohei's preparing himself to reestablish the past commercial glory that belonged to Osaka before it was snatched away by Tokyo after the war.

In Yamazaki's own words, *Noren* portrays "ideal Osaka merchants . . . who are endowed with a seemingly archaic but strangely new rationality . . . and with a philosophy and knack for business." Her protagonists are the Semba merchants, who represent the essence of the trade spirit. The Semba district, bordered by four rivers, developed as the center of commerce when the warlord-turned-chancellor, Toyotomi Hideyoshi (1536–98), relocated merchants from the port city Sakai to this area in the late 16th century. Since then, the inhabitants in this small section came to embody a high sense of honor and a strict business code. The symbol that stands for their dignity and pride in business is a *noren,* a short curtain designating the store's identity hung sideways at the shop's entrance during business hours. Everyone who works for the store, including the owner, is expected to pass through the *noren* with a slight bow. The *noren* is handed down from one generation to the next, and when an employee who has completed long years of apprenticeship becomes independent, he is permitted to use a replica of the *noren* of the main house. When the time comes for "dividing the *noren,*" as it is commonly called, the main house endows "the *noren* fee" as a partial starting fund for the new shop, establishing a strong bond between the main house and branch stores.

In a literal sense, a *noren* is worth as much as the store's capital. Once Gohei successfully convinces a banker to lend him money with his *noren* as collateral, his son uses the same *noren* to claim his business lineage and also to re-create an ambience of the once-shattered elegance. His "knack for business" tells him that his return to tradition would please both the established customers who used to frequent the old shop and the new customers who seek an authentic flavor now that the goods are available in abundance ten years after the end of the war. Kohei's calculation foreshadows present-day Japan's "brand orientation" (*burando shikō*), exhibited by Japanese tourists whirling through the exclusive shops in Paris or London. In *Noren,* both old and new generations of Osaka merchants are contrasted and finally approved. Their driving desire for better business knows no end. The merchants are comparable to soldiers in the battlefield, fighting on with little time or care for romance or sentimentality. Their children count as combat members of the store to strive under the *noren* banner, which Yamasaki lovingly calls "the flag of the commoners."

Hana noren (Flower Banner, 1958), novel. This Naoki Prize winner depicts the life course of a woman entrepreneur named Kawashima Taka from the turn of the century through the end of World War II. She emerges as the creator of a new business insignia and the master of her own life. The story follows Taka's career evolution from her initial efforts at running the *yose* (theater for storytellers) in place of her weak-willed husband, who proved himself a total failure in business; building an empire with twenty-seven theaters in her prime; desperately struggling to keep them open during the war under government censorship with only a few undrafted entertainers left; all the way to her death shortly after the war, with the business at a complete halt in the rubble of bombed-out cities.

The ethos of the Osaka merchant is carried on by this heroine, who married into a Semba family, perhaps reflecting the author's belief that it is possible for the business tradition to germinate in an ingenious individual at any time. As the title suggests, the novel is almost a female version of her first work, *Noren*, tracing a businesswoman's growth from a complete novice to a full-fledged entrepreneur. In addition to the courage, hard work, and attentiveness to detail that are characteristics of Semba merchants, Taki uses her (dis)advantages as a woman to take daring actions that a normal male merchant would consider too humiliating. Casting pride aside, Taki stoops to wash a petty moneylender woman's back at a public bath every day to gain her trust; she stations herself at a corner of a public toilet, rank in scorching midsummer heat but close to a rival theater, to keep watch on the comings and goings of entertainers so that she can dash out and throw a tip into their sleeves to win them over. The details of her trade strategy and the ingenuity of her ideas make for very engaging reading. The lively portrayal of the enterprising woman, the fascinating backstage scenes of the entertainment world, and tales of the colorful entertainers all add special flavor to the story. Perhaps the most outrageous of the episodes is that of a storyteller (*hanashika*) who pawns his best story to get money to spend on a woman. *Hana noren* is a fact-based story modeled on the life of a woman owner of the famous Yoshimoto Amusement Enterprise in Osaka. Many entertainers appearing in the novel are real people, but the plausibility of Taka's personality and the colorful antics of the notable entertainers owe much to Yamasaki's artistry in weaving fiction out of facts.

The *noren* that Taka designs for her business shows the name of her establishment, Hanabishitei (Flower Diamond House), and flowers of the four seasons in white against the indigo background. The flowers in the *noren* represent one of the very few touches of feminine gaiety in Taka's personal life. Her husband dies at his mistress's house, Taka never consummates her love with a man she adores, and her only son develops an attachment to his nurse rather than to his own mother. Taka is not a new, modern type of businesswoman who is capable of juggling many roles of life, and her self-expression consists of making personal sacrifices for business success. The white flowers in the *noren* parallel the only other bright symbol for her, a white mourning kimono that she wears at her husband's funeral. Rather than the customary black, Taka unconsciously somehow chooses the white mourning garb, which traditionally indicates a widow's determination not to marry again. The funeral is the first and only occasion when Taka publicly plays the central role in family affairs. The impact of the excitement of being the focus of attention and the awareness of her own initially unconscious choice of the kimono start molding her life course. The widow's determination, symbolized by the color white, translates into her commitment to business success. Fittingly, the last image she sees of herself on her deathbed is of a woman walking in a white kimono under the falling petals of cherry blossoms—all alone. She sets the stage and holds it to the end.

Translated Works: Bonchi (Young Master, 1959), novel. The title suggests that the central figure is a man named Kikuji, but the story also presents a rich mandala of many women around him. The protagonist plays the pivot of a fan, as the women interact with one another through him. Handsome, wealthy, and generous, Kikuji echoes the Shining Prince Genji, the hero of the 11th-century narrative by Lady Murasaki Shikibu, *The Tale of Genji*. Kikuji seeks out women of his liking, visits them when he wishes, and financially supports them. As Prince Genji had little luck with his legal first wife, Kikuji has little success with his short-lived marriage; and as Genji lost his mother while in his early childhood, Kikuji experiences little love from his aloof mother, or from his grandmother. Prince Genji at least enjoyed life with his foremost love, young Murasaki, but his modern counterpart is not so blessed. Kikuji's desires and yearnings for the opposite sex are met by different types of females. Ponta is a vivacious plaything; Ikuko, a modest pseudowife; Ofuku, a drinking companion and also a surrogate wet nurse. Korin is a verdant girl who gives Kikuji a chance to deflower a pure maiden. Hisako, a bar hostess, stimulates Kikuji by providing him a glimpse of the world outside his own milieu. What Kikuji lacks in his search for women is the instinct to cultivate a lasting relationship with a woman who would bear his children and share responsibilities in nurturing their growth. Each woman knows exactly where she stands with him and fulfills his needs with silent understanding. Very little confrontation takes place in the dialogues.

All but one of his women are from the geisha profession. Kikuji's life is rigidly ruled by the customs of the Semba merchants, and the geishas' lives are no less controlled by their own traditional codes of behavior, which coordinate with, and are subservient to, the ways of the merchants' world. As long as the prescribed rules are observed, there are harmony and a balance of give-and-take. The scale is tipped, or worse, becomes nullified, when outside forces crush the framework. The matriarch grandmother chooses to kill herself rather than live to see the total ruin of her family fortune due to the war, and Kikuji's mother turns into a frail shadow. Those women who sustained themselves by their inheritance and other people's labor perish, but those who earned their living, once freed from the fabric of group mores, survive to live as they wish. The last scene, where the women are frolicking together in a bath at a temple to which they have been evacuated, is symbolic: they begin to see one another and themselves without reference to the pivotal male figure. As Kikuji tries to venture out, with his ingenuity as the basic weapon, into the new business world devoid of tradition, the women are on the verge of cutting their own niches in the new era. Perhaps Kikuji's life and the lives of the women were, after all, not closely intertwined but happened to run along smoothly only in the protective pretext of the conventional formula.

Fumō chitai (The Barren Zone, 1973–78), novel. This voluminous work consists of four parts, the first of which has been translated into English. Parts 1 and 2 cover the white, arid zone of Siberia, where the hero serves in a prisoner-of-war (POW) labor camp, and the last two take place in the red, unfertile zone of the Middle East, where he engages in oil rigging for a Japanese company. The color demarcation notwithstanding, the focus is on the image of the national and international business world as a barren zone, where the welfare of the corporate body, be it a private company or a nation, is pursued at the expense of individual members. This novel is an exposé of the business world, consisting of enterprises trying to outdo each other in the manipulation of political, financial, and human resources and connections. The fictional veneer is thin, and the reader can get a good inside view as well as behind-the-scenes pictures of real-life political and business incidents, the insidious effects of which persist in Japanese society even today, as evidenced by the Lockheed bribery case, which toppled the Tanaka Cabinet in 1974.

The barren zone is a battlefield where businessmen's survival skills are put to the test. Japanese "salarymen" have been compared with the samurai or soldiers. Iki Tadashi, the protagonist of *The Barren Zone,* is their legitimate representative—a former staff member of the Japanese imperial army's General Headquarters. The similarities between business and war tactics are amply illustrated in the novel. Iki is recruited by a powerful company president, who expects Iki to contribute his military acumen in assessing business deals, to utilize tactical insights in mapping out a plan of action, to make swift decisions in choosing the appropriate course to take, and to organize, deploy, and move manpower effectively. Iki satisfies all these expectations in his executive role: he proves himself an elite among elitist leaders in business wars, as he was in army operations.

The analogy of businessman as samurai and soldier is an ironic one, since traditionally both premodern samurai and modern soldiers were expected to shun the idea of money as their personal reward. Obviously, however, the samurai-soldier-businessman is not a *rōnin* (masterless samurai) or a draftee. As is the case with most of Yamazaki's heroes and heroines who are driven by an aspiration for accomplishment, the businessmen in *The Barren Zone* have chosen their careers and committed their lives to the advancement of their companies, and, in this spirit of total dedication, they are akin to warriors serving their lord, willing to sacrifice their private lives for their work. The difference between Iki and other men is that his ideal for accomplishment does not stop at the company level but aims at the benefit of the nation. Iki's concept of nation is not clearly defined, but it seems to point to the concept of *Kokutai,* or national polity, which was hailed as the political and ideological identity for the Japanese people until their defeat in World War II. This high goal gives Iki a personal aura, though the other characters in the novel seem to remain unaffected by it, and he even assumes a heroic dimension at the very end of the novel when, after the successful oil drilling in Iran, he resigns from the exalted post of vice president to devote himself to caring for his fellow ex-POWs and their families. His loyalty to hierarchical systems transforms into a sense of responsibility for those who suffered with him under these systems. Thus he escapes becoming a total victim of the barren zone.

It has been estimated that there were about six hundred thousand Japanese POWs in the Soviet territories, with more than sixty thousand of them losing their lives there. The names of many of those who died are yet to be revealed by the former Soviet government, and search for the whereabouts of the POW grave sites is a persistent concern for their relatives in Japan. In this regard, *The Barren Zone,* a novel Yamazaki Toyoko completed over a decade ago, besides tracing the aggressive advancement of the postwar Japanese economy, poses unresolved political, social, and personal questions that will remain current issues for many years to come.

Futatsu no sokoku (Two Home Countries, 1980), novel. The story follows the fate of the Amoh family and the ordeal of over 110,000 Japanese Americans who were suddenly relocated after Japan attacked Pearl Harbor in 1941, placed in internment camps, and forced to start from scratch after the war. Amoh Otoshichi and Teru, the *issei* (lit., ''first-generation'' immigrants) couple, come to the United States from Kagoshima and work at a farm under severe conditions. Later they run a popular laundry shop in ''Little Tokyo'' in Los Angeles and raise four children. When the war breaks out, not only do they see what they have built taken away, but they also agonize over the division within their own family. Their children are products of the different soils of their two countries, and their sense of identification and loyalty is tested in a conflict as their two homelands fight on. The protagonist of the novel is Kenji, the oldest son, who spent his youthful, formative years in Japan but came back before the outbreak of the war. The next son, Tadashi, still studying in Japan, is drafted into the Japanese army, even though he is under constant suspicion simply because he is American-born. The two younger children, a son, Isamu, and a daughter, Haruko, know only America. Isamu volunteers for the army from the relocation camp in order to prove that he is a citizen of the United States as brave and loyal as any other American. He enters the famous 442 Nisei Regiment and dies in action in Europe. The parents, who still strongly identify with their native land, see their son lose his life for the country that has deprived them of their property and placed them behind barbed wire.

Kenji, with his notable bilingual competence, is recruited in the relocation camp to serve as an instructor at the Camp Savage language institute for American army officers in Minnesota. He accepts the assignment in spite of his parents' objections, in the belief that he can contribute to ending the war quickly. While assisting in decoding Japanese messages at the camp, he translates one reporting on the development of a new type of American bomb, which turns out to be the atomic bomb. Later he is encouraged to join the American armed forces and is eventually sent to the Philippines, where Japanese soldiers are waging their final battle. Yamazaki Toyoko often uses ironic turns in people's lives to heighten dramatic tension in her fiction: she sets the stage for an encounter between the two Amoh brothers, who are on opposite sides. Kenji shoots his brother in the leg, mistaking him for one of his brother's commanding officers.

Posted in Japan after the war, Kenji serves as a chief interpreter for the International Military Tribunal trying Japanese war criminals. Motivated by his desire and hope to be of service to Japan, he does his best to transmit the messages correctly and justly between prosecutors and the accused. Yamazaki uses ample documentation to follow the daily procedures of the tribunal and, through Kenji's eyes, brings out the immediacy of scenes fraught with suppressed emotions in the real-life drama of humans judging other humans. While participating in these trials, Kenji begins to feel that they are one-sided interrogations of the defeated by the victors. His sympathetic attitude toward the defendants results in his surveillance by the Central Intelligence Agency, and after the Tokyo trial he is barred from holding any responsible position in the armed forces. Realizing with despair that he has been only a pawn in an international power game, Kenji shoots himself in an empty monitor booth a few days after the execution of those who were judged guilty and whose death sentences he was required to translate and announce.

With meticulous care, Yamazaki describes the upheavals during and following World War II in the political and social arenas, both national and international, that engulfed Japanese Americans. She delineates with merciless exactness the living conditions in the relocation centers and the psychological turmoil of those who were thrown into detention. The point she makes is that they not only lost their fortunes but also began to question their identity and lose faith in citizenship. The predicament of having to choose between two countries was epitomized by the infamous questionnaire containing items no. 27 and 28, which asked all the Japanese Americans if they would serve in the American armed forces and if they would abandon their loyalty to the Japanese emperor and pledge it to the United States. Young men who answered "no" to each question were labeled "no-no-boy," a name that became the title for a poignant novel in English by a *nisei* writer, John Okada (1923–70). Yamazaki illustrates the absurdity of the questionnaire that the American authorities required of the internees by showing there was no response correct for all the Amoh family members: the parents, who answered "no, no," were sent to the Tule Lake camp for the incorrigibles; the younger son, who answered "yes, yes," died for the United States; and the hero, who answered "yes, no," confessed before he took his life that he could not tell which was his own country. The true tragedy of the Japanese Americans is that no matter what identity and loyalty they chose and expressed, they were not completely trusted by either country and were left to agonize in an endless limbo. Yamazaki Toyoko's novel universalizes the fate of hapless persons who get caught in an immense international political drama in which the integrity of the individual is manipulated, ignored, and eventually destroyed.

BIBLIOGRAPHY

Translations

The Barren Zone. Tr. James T. Araki. Honolulu: University of Hawaii Press, 1985.
Bonchi: A Novel by Toyoko Yamasaki. Tr. Harue and Travis Summersgille. Honolulu: University of Hawaii Press, 1982.
Two Home Countries. Tr. in progress.

Critical Works

Befu, Harumi. "Power in *The Great White Tower:* Contribution to Social Exchange Theory." In *The Anthropology of Power,* ed. Raymond D. Fogelson and Richard N. Adams. New York: Academic Press, 1977, 77–87.
Mulhern, Chieko. "The Japanese Business Fiction." In Arai Shinya's novel, *Shoshaman: A Tale of Corporate Japan.* Tr. Chieko Mulhern. Berkeley, CA: University of California Press, 1991, vii–xxv.

Fumiko YAMAMOTO

YOSANO Akiko (1878–1942), poet, essayist, critic, children's story writer. Real name: Yosano Shō (Mrs. Yosano Hiroshi); née Hō Shō.

Life: Akiko was born into a family in the confectionery business in the port city of Sakai, south of the large commercial city Osaka. Besides two older stepsisters, she had an elder brother (later an engineering professor at Tokyo University), a younger brother (who would carry on the family business), and a younger sister. As was customary with daughters of merchants, Akiko was given private lessons in traditional Japanese musical instruments early in life and put to work in her early teens, keeping account books and attending customers during the day and packaging sweets and sewing servants' work wear at night. But throughout her childhood and youth, she read Japanese classics in her father's book collection. In 1892, she graduated from Sakai Women's School, finishing a junior high school education, quite advanced for women of the times.

Thereafter, Akiko's life course and career evolution began their dramatic spiral, with personal and public aspects inseparably entwined. Akiko's earliest published work was a *tanka* (short poem consisting of thirty-one Japanese syllables) appearing in a small anthology produced by a group of local poets in 1896. In 1899, she became a member of Kansai Seinen Bungakukai (Osaka-region Youth Literature Society), a more prominent literary coterie that included professional writers in the area, and she contributed her *tanka* and free verse to its organ journal. Dreamy, yet far from shy, she actively developed friendships with a few male members of the group by frequently writing to them, an action women did not usually take in those days. Akiko also read contemporary *tanka* published in Tokyo. She wrote a letter to a Tokyo poet, Yosano Tekkan (real name: Yosano Hiroshi, 1873–1935), who in turn invited her to contribute her works to *Myōjō* (Morning Star), a literary magazine that Tekkan had just started in Tokyo in April 1900.

Both the development of Akiko's relationship with Tekkan and her rise to stardom in *Myōjō* were quick. Not only did Tekkan publish eight of Akiko's *tanka* in the second issue of *Myōjō*, but he also introduced in his article two others that she had published in Osaka. *Myōjō*'s third, fourth, and fifth issues continued to carry her *tanka*. In August, Akiko met Tekkan when he traveled to the Osaka area. Before long, she fell in love with him, but Tekkan already had a wife, his second, who had just borne him a child. He published two verse collections of his own, even as he unsuccessfully fought a libel suit against a Tokyo publishing house that had disclosed his affairs with Akiko and others.

In June 1901, Akiko left home for Tokyo to live with Tekkan, and in August she published what was to become her most renowned work, *Midaregami* (Tangled Hair), the first of her many *tanka* collections. Akiko and Tekkan were married that same year after his second wife left him.

From then on, Akiko published her poems, novels, and essays almost continually. She gave birth to a son in 1902, another in 1904, and two daughters in 1907. She served as a lecturer of classical Japanese literature and *tanka* composition at the seminars of Keishu Bungakukai (Literature for Women Society). She would bring her students and friends home to poetry gatherings, at which she herself would produce as many as one hundred *tanka* in sequence and encouraged the participants to compete in composition. Poet Ishikawa Takuboku (Ishikawa Hajime, 1886–1912), who was Yosano's houseguest at the time, was one of the fastest in composing *tanka* on the spot.

Myōjō, long a major publication medium for Akiko and many other romantic poets, developed certain internal problems; with the withdrawal of some key members, it ceased publication in 1908. Thereafter, Akiko contributed her *tanka* to *Subaru* (Pleiades), launched by Takuboku, and other journals and newspapers. In 1909, she gave a series of lectures on *The Tale of Genji* at her house, which yielded a request to translate this 11th-century masterpiece into modern vernacular. This new venture would prove to augument her finances quite well. In 1911, following the popular practice of writers at the time, Tekkan planned to travel abroad. Akiko raised money for him by selling her calligraphy. In 1912, while he was in Europe, the first version of ''Akiko Genji'' came out, and she crossed Siberia to join Tekkan in Paris, where they visited artists of the day, including Gustav Rodin and Emile Verheren. She returned to Japan in October of the same year, followed by Tekkan a few months later. In April 1913, Akiko gave birth to her fourth son and shortly afterward began serializing a novel, *Akarumi e* (Toward the Light), in a Tokyo newspaper.

In addition to *tanka* and *shi* verse, she wrote essays on *tanka,* on social issues, and on political problems. In 1914 alone she produced a poetry collection, a travelogue, a collection of children's stories, and a modern translation in serial form of *Eiga monogatari* (Tale of Glory), a long medieval historical tale attributed to Lady Akazome Emon. In the following year, she published a commentary on the poems of Izumi Shikibu (ca. 970–1030) jointly with Tekkan, her own book of verse, two selections of her *tanka,* an essay collection, a book of children's stories, and a guide to *tanka* composition, in addition to editing a collection of works by women writers. To top it all off that year, Akiko gave birth to another daughter, helped her husband run, though ultimately unsuccessfully, for a seat in the House of Representatives, and moved to another house. This busy life-style continued as she went on to give birth to their fifth son and lose their sixth two days after his birth. She participated in a public discussion on the issue of governmental protection of pregnant women's health. Akiko's sixth daughter was born in good health in 1919, the year Tekkan became a professor at Keiō University, and Akiko published two collections of essays on social issues, one book on *tanka* composition, and one collection of *tanka,* along with her first complete collection of *tanka* in three volumes.

Women's education had long been her concern, and in 1921 she joined forces with her friends in establishing Bunka Gakuin, a junior high school for girls, with an initial enrollment of thirty-three students. While teaching classical Japanese there, she assisted Tekkan in managing the journal *Myōjō,* which had just resumed publication that year. By then, radical political thoughts had pervaded Japan's intellectural world to eclipse purely literary concerns. Akiko's publishing activity began noticeably to slow down. She frequently traveled to resorts outside Tokyo. As leftist writers increased their influence, the women's liberation movement gathered momentum, and Akiko was asked to take part in various functions.

In 1928, accepting an invitation from the Southern Manchurian Railway Company, a government subsidiary to develop Manchuria, Akiko made an inspection trip of sorts through Manchuria and Mongolia. Upon her return, she launched a *tanka* magazine called *Tōhaku* (Cameria-Camellia), became a dean at Bunka Gakuin, and vacationed Hokkaido and Kyushu. She also made leisurely trips to Shikoku, the Japan Sea coast, and the mountain regions all over the country, as reflected in her poems. Meanwhile, in America, Shiho Sakanishi (1896–1976) was preparing to publish her English translation of Akiko's poems.

In 1935, Tekkan died suddenly. Akiko mourned him in an article titled "Otto no hatsubyō yori rinjū made" (From the Outbreak of My Husband's Illness till His Death) in her journal, *Tōhaku.* In 1937, at the request of Kaizosha Publishing House, she participated in the compilation of *Shin Manyōshū* (New Manyoshu), which eventually included fifty of her *tanka.* In 1940 Akiko suffered a cerebral hemorrhage, the year she was reportedly baptized. The right half of her body was paralyzed, but she continued to produce poetry until her death on May 29, 1942. Of her eleven surviving children, a number of them went on to become prominent in the intellectual sphere.

Career: Akiko was mostly self-taught. Already in her school days, she had read several major Japanese classical works—not an easy task in the face of the intrinsic difficulty due to their archaic styles and the sheer volume of the texts. Akiko must have read some contemporary works by the new poets of the romantic school, including Shimazaki Tōson (1872–1943), for she wrote *shintaishi* (new-form poetry), free verse in a form similar to that of Tōson's.

Undoubtedly, Akiko learned much from Tekkan, her husband and a superior poet himself, who had earlier rallied against the mainstream of *tanka* in what he considered elegant, effeminate, meager, moralistic styles. Tekkan criticized the highly technical and conformist *tanka* selected into the imperial anthologies and favored simpler, less decorative, more straightforward styles exemplified in the 8th-century poetry collection *Manyōshū*. In her youth in the city of Sakai, Akiko belonged to a poetry coterie of the old court school, but after she came under the influence of Tekkan's poetics, she began immediately to produce *tanka* embodying Tekkan's teachings and expressing honest feelings, her love for him. The passionate *tanka* of her early days are notable in the use of the bold style that endorsed Tekkan's rejection of imitativeness, timidness, and dead language. Pretenseless as she was, Akiko demonstrated that *tanka* should be based on her own "actual feeling," not an artificial one assumed to fit set topics, such as assigned at poetry meetings back in Sakai. Thus, she nurtured an awareness of individuality, or her self-identity.

The impact of honest feeling was mutual: inspired by Akiko, Tekkan began producing a kind of masculine love poems he had not written before. Akiko and Tekkan edited and published *Myōjō*, as virtual spokespersons of the members of Shinshi-sha (New Poetry Society). Shinshi-sha upheld an ideal resembling the art-for-art's sake belief, emphasizing originality in feeling, thinking, and expression. They strove to create a national literature as worthy of the new era as *Manyōshū* was of ancient Japan. Their movement represented one reaction against pervasive criticism on the *tanka* form on the ground that it was too brief a medium to deal with human spirits of the modern times. Many progressive literary critics and poets of the late 19th century, including Tsubouchi Shōyō (1859–1935) and Yuasa Hangetsu (1858–1943), had written negatively about *tanka*. With their ardent romanticism and unconventional style, however, the Shinshi-sha members captured the field blazed open by such innovative poets as Masaoka Shiki (1867–1902) and Tekkan and dominated it to restore *tanka* as a regnant genre.

The popularity of Shinshi-sha and its *Myōjō* owed in part to the support of some influential men of letters, such as novelist Mori Ōgai (1862–1922) and translator-scholar Ueda Bin (1874–1916). Both Ōgai and Bin served as godparents of sorts for Akiko's children and sponsored Akiko's books by writing introductions. Associates of such prominent literary figures contributed their works to *Myōjō*, attended Akiko's *tanka* parties, and expressed their support of Shinshi-sha in writings of their own. Not only writers but also talented modernist painters gathered at Shinshi-sha. The romantic fever did not last very long, however. Realists looked at the darker side of life and wrote critically about it. Some of them found modern spoken Japanese, instead of the traditional written language, to be a more appropriate means to depict contemporary scenes of the world. Naturalism provided a fitting milieu for them. Some chose to write in the longer verse form of *shi,* feeling that they could demonstrate their talent more freely in it, and created Western-style, truly modern poetry in Japanese. In *tanka,* the young Takuboku raised a distinctly pronounced voice in social and political protests and devised innovative techniques such as the use of modern punctuation marks in classical language. With his collections of such *tanka, Ichiaku no suna* (Handful of Sand, 1910) and *Kanashiki gangu* (Sad Toy, 1912), Takuboku swept the popularity polls in the field.

As many of Takuboku's best-loved poems indicate, the times did not allow poets to make a decent living. Tōson, in the process of transforming himself from a poet to a novelist, lost two of his daughters to malnutrition. The poet Shiki died from tuberculosis in similar economic adversity. Woman poet-novelist Higuchi Ichiyō (1872–96) struggled to support her mother and sister by writing, only to die of consumption. Ironically, the Sino-Japanese War (1894–95) and the Russo-Japanese War (1904–5), both of which Japan won, brought considerable economic prosperity to the country as a whole. Most publishing firms expanded their business, but it was only in the 1930s, after bitter labor disputes had shaken some sectors of Japanese industry, that authors like Akiko and Tekkan began to benefit financially from their publications.

As more and more writers sold novels, skepticism about the future of *tanka* grew, too. Onoe Saishū (Onoe Hachiro, 1876–1958) in his article ''Tanka metsubō shiron'' (The Fall of Tanka—A Personal View, 1911) denounced *tanka* as a genre in favor of fiction. Akiko tried to promote *tanka* by writing a few beginners' guides and advocating that *tanka* was a means to cultivate man and that it was a part of life's curricula. In *Uta no tsukuriyō* (How to Compose Tanka, 1915), she relied heavily on her own experience and presented the concept of ''real feeling'' (*jikkan*), her belief that *tanka* must be born from the poet's spontaneous reaction to genuine emotion aroused by a particular subject, with language to follow it. Elsewhere, she criticized the popular Araragi (Hollyhock) school of *tanka,* which upheld Masaoka Shiki's objectivism in sketching nature and the use of certain archaic words. Nevertheless, *tanka* was already on the decline, overshadowed by *shi* free verse and fiction. Among the Shinshi-sha members, artist Takamura Kōtarō (1883–1956) and poet Hagiwara Sakutarō (1986–1942) published *shi* collections, establishing themselves as leaders in the field.

Akiko's return from her European trip coincided with the surge in Japan of the so-called Taisho democracy—political and social movements, including the women's liberation movement and attempts to democratize the country during the Taishō period (1912–26). Akiko's *tanka* leaned more and more toward subdued *jikkan* and subtle tone, and her essays on contemporary issues increased in number. Her social criticism was not echoing imported ideologies but was solidly based on her observations and experiences in Europe, Japan, and her family life. Her concerns were humanistic and practical, free from any political creed. In 1917, for example, Akiko demanded that Tokyo's Kōjimachi Ward Office issue ''rice coupons'' to needy people like her family. She supported women's suffrage but showed little interest in the power struggle within the Fusen Kakutoku Dōmei (Women's Suffrage League). She complied with the league's request to write a fight song, but her actual involvement with the organization was minimal. Dismissing organized activities, she kept her distance from both the fashionable women activists and the government authorities to maintain her intellectual independence. When Akiko traveled to China on the Southern Manchurian Railway, she questioned little about what imperial Japan was doing on the Asian continent.

As the government censorship on literary publications intensified, some leftist writers were imprisoned, others went underground, and many radicals were forced to change their political stand. While the proletarian literature was suppressed, popular literature took over the market. Literacy was up, and inexpensive books poured out of large publishing houses.

Akiko spent much of her last years translating the *Tale of Genji* into modern Japanese for the third time. She produced no book of verse after 1928. Her last collection contains fifteen hundred *tanka* composed during her travels and is aptly entitled *Kokoro no enkei* (A Distant View of the Heart). Her very frequent travels perhaps represented creative efforts to renew her capacity to feel things at heart so that, hopefully, real emotions would go into full combustion to energize her poetry. In 1930, she launched the journal *Tōhaku,* hoping to recapture the glory of *Myōjō.* Some old Shinshi-sha members returned to join, but Takamura Kotaro and Hagiwara Sakutaro did not.

Yosano Tekkan encapsulated Akiko's art in his *Complete Works* in 1932: "The richness of her idea, the freedom of her expression, and her mythical intellect all struck at the divine speed of lightning." By 1933, when Akiko's *zenshū* (complete works) came out, she had written seven hundred *shi* free verse and ten thousand *tanka.* Her lifetime output of *tanka* probably amounted to fifty thousand.

Major Works: 1. Poetics. *Uta no tsukuriyō* (How to Compose Poetry, 1915), *Tanka 300 kō* (Commentary on 300 Tanka, 1916), *Akiko kawa* (Akiko's Talk on Tanka, 1919). These writings on poetic methodology emphasize unbridled expression of emotions. She elucidates that "emotions" mean unique, individualistic feelings, rather than previously acquired knowledge or common sense, for only a unique, individualistic feeling could achieve spiritual elation, which is poetry. Against such techniques as *shasei* (sketches from nature), controlled or limited use of the language, and allusive or indirect depiction of the experiencing heart, she advocates *jikkan,* or the fresh, impulsive real feeling in the poet's honest-reacting, innermost heart, which would eventually combust to form poetry. Conveniently, she puts her messages in the *shi* form of free verse, as in "Shi ni tsuite no negai" (My Wish on Poetry):

> Poetry is a sculpture of real feeling;
> Between lines, and between stanzas
> Lies a shadow.

Enwrapping details
The shadow is the depth,
According to which
A part of its immanent body
Clearly
Should rise above the lines. . .

"Uta wa dōshite tsukuru" (How to Write Poetry) is even more instructional:

How do I write poetry?
Quietly observing
Quietly loving
And quietly embracing.
But what?
"The truth."

Where is "the truth"?
Close to me.
Always with me.
Near what I observe.
By what I love.
In both my hands. . . .

2. Poems. *Akiko shihen zenshū* (Complete Collection of Akiko's Free Verse, 1929). By the time this volume, containing 421 *shi* came out, the *shi* genre itself had undergone a considerable transfiguration through exposure to the influences of symbolism and various experimental techniques. Akiko's preface reiterates that these serious revelations of the poet's heart over the years since 1900 are purely personal and self-styled, shunning universality with a hope that they will be read some day by her children as records of her life.

Kokoro no enkei (A Distant View of the Heart, 1928), her last collection of *tanka,* contains serene pieces quite different from the powerful poems in her earlier ones. Aged Akiko is looking backward. What *jikkan* there is seems mature, well-wrought, intellectual, but merely metaphoric rather than symbolic.

What I count on
is a white birch
that stands
where no human language
is ever heard.

Waga yoru ha
subete jingo no
kikoenu
tokoro ni tateru
shirakaba ni shite

White birch is
never deflied
by the daytime mist.
The likes of larch
have long since succumbed.

Shirakaba ha
hirufuru kiri ni
okasarezu
Karamatsu nado ha
atokata mo nashi.

Yesterdays	Kinou oba
people seem to have	hito wa tashika ni
without fail.	motsu gotoshi
More evanescent than the fog	moya yori awashi
are my yesterdays.	ware no kinou wa.
What I can see	Waga miru ha
is limited	koshikata nomi ni
to the way I have come.	kagirareru
No dream this is,	yume ni mo arazu
the season for forgetting.	wasurenaru koro

3. Social Commentaries. ''Sozorogoto'' (A Rambling Talk, 1911), a poem marking her first involvement with political issues:

> ''This is the day mountains shake,''
> I announce it but no one believes.
> The mountains were just asleep.
> In olden days
> All those mountains were aflame, shaking.
> That, you don't have to believe,
> But you must believe
> That all women who were asleep are now awake, shaking.

This *shi* appeared in the inaugural issue of *Seitō* (Bluestocking), a women's magazine launched by Hiratsuka Raichō (Okumura Haru, 1886–1971), a pioneer of the women's liberation movement.

''Bosei henjū o haisu'' (In Opposition to Overprotection of Motherhood, 1916), an essay, is Akiko's answer to Raichō's criticism of Akiko's comment against Ellen Kay's opinion on love and marriage. For Akiko, government aid for women's health problems would not be necessary, if women could achieve financial independence from their husbands. Raichō's position was that women, by nature, required a certain security or protection to enable them to go through pregnancy, delivery, and raising of children. Akiko's stance was based on personal *jikkan,* so to speak, deriving from her own experience of many childbirths. *Hiratsuka, Yamakawa, Yamada no san-joshi ni kotau* (My Answer to the Three Women, Hiratsuka, Yamakawa [Kikuel], and Yamada, 1918) presents Akiko's repeated argument for women's financial independence and against government financial protection. *Warera nani o motomuru ka* (What Do We Demand?, 1917) likens the Japanese women to ''weeds floating aimlessly on the water of material civilization'' and urges them to be educated, to be aware and thinking, and to be financially and spiritually independent.

Zakkichō (Miscellaneous Notes, 1915), *Hito oyobi onna to shite* (As a Human Being and Woman, 1916), *Ai, risei oyobi yūki* (Love, Intellect, and Courage, 1917), *Wakai tomo e* (To Young Friends, 1918), *Shintō zassō* (Weeds Growing on My Head, 1919), *Nyonin sōzō* (Creation of the Woman, 1920), and *Ningen raihai* (Worshiping Human Beings, 1921). These essay collections, nearly contemporary to World War I, all preceded or paralleled such epoch-making events as the publication ban on *Seitō* as the result of a controversy over the abortion issue; the launching of a women's intellectual journal, *Fujin kōron* (Women's Public Forum); the establishment of Shin Fujin Kyōkai (New Women's Association); and the start of Fusen Kakutoku Dōmei. Written in clearly spoken vernacular, these essays were logical, easy to understand, and persuasive for general readers.

Japanese intellectuals, the larger percentage of whom were men at the time, were groaning under the burden of the Confucian-bound, traditional family responsibilities. The influential naturalist novelists were good examples of the kind, as attested to by the dominant themes of their major works. In *Katei ni tsuite no hansei* (Reflections on the Family, 1917), Akiko proposes a viable alternative in family structure:

> In this type of family there is neither a head nor any impossible, absolute authority who exercises unreasonable, despotic power. What there is is a cooperative unit consisting of two people—a man and a woman bonded by love, i.e., a husband and a wife. In this unit everything is decided by mutual agreement. The husband is not the family head; likewise, the wife is not a subordinate to serve him. This is what scholars call the family of equality.

Akiko goes on to attack the traditional concept of "good wife, wise mother," remarking that a "good wife" was comparable to a concubine and a "wise mother" to an unthinking mother.

Shuppei to fujin no kōsatsu (Deployment of the Military and Women's Thoughts, 1918) presented one of the most powerful prose messages to women:

> From my standpoint that arms are only for self-defense, the present state of armament in our country, especially of the Army, is far in excess. So much extraordinary expansion of armament was made recently that the only country to match Japan in the whole world is Germany. Since the last war, the United States of America has also hurried to expand her arms. However, is it not shameful for the so-called benevolent country in the Eastern Seas to be equipped with this much horrible weaponry expending most of the national revenues and neglecting all the urgent cultural needs?

Toward the end of this essay, Akiko appealed to women:

> I want you housewives to listen to my humble opinion so you can give me your thoughts on the issue of whether we should send our army to Siberia.

When the war ended, Akiko wrote in 1919:

I have realized after the war that men initiate war and engage in it, any war. But those who suffer are not limited to men; they include women. War is always started by smart men. And men expose the ugliest, cruelest, most barbaric parts of their nature in war.

Men's intellect seems parallel to their education, surpassing women's. However, men's love is less pure and passionate than women's so that their intellect is used less for good and more for bad. In fact, there has been no example in history like the last war, which made the maximum use of science and caused such insane disaster to mankind.

The war Akiko was denouncing was World War I. The subsequent history of Japan proved to be a negative print of the picture that she so accurately depicted in her foretelling essay, in which she also defended women.

The war, the violence that men perform by forming cliques and wielding weapons, does not match any of the crimes that women have personally committed since the beginning of our history, even the most serious cases.

How women have toiled and raised so many human beings since the olden days! How men, on the contrary, have injured or killed so many people by the wars they themselves caused!

Akiko's participation in the founding of Bunka Gakuin in 1921 was a necessary development in the course of her life. Her philosophy of women's education had been amply expressed: "I think that just too many of the daughters in the middle-to upper-class families in Japan simply want to become brides" and "If the women elevate themselves from the present status of high-class prostitutes, high-class nurses, or high-class maids to a new awareness of womanhood where they use their ability for both spiritual and material work in order to enjoy a cooperative life with men, then those new women deserve rights equal to men's" (Miscellaneous Notes). Akiko wanted the school's graduates to be able to "speak out in public what they believed in."

4. Modern Translations of Classics. Though sometimes criticized as being marred by some incorrect interpretations, omissions, and so forth, Akiko's endeavors were instrumental in popularizing the otherwise difficult-to-read classics. "Akiko Genji," for example, is still in print today, with prominent contemporary novelists such as Tanizaki Junichirō, Enchi Fumiko, and Tanabe Seiko to follow suit in producing their own modern versions of *Genji* to immense popularity.

Translated Works: Midaregami (Tangled Hair, 1901), *tanka* collection. In *tanka,* Akiko succeeded best in crystallizing her real feeling in poetic form, giving impetus to the Romantic movement and reigning in the field.

So I may chastise	Tsumi oki
Men steeped in sin,	otoko korase to
Was I created	hada kiyoku
Fair of skin and	kurokami nagaku
Abundant of black hair.	tsukurareshi ware

Twenty she is,	Sono ko hatachi
Black hair flowing	kushi ni nagareru
Through the comb	kurokami no
Glorious	ogori no haru no
In the height of her spring.	utsukushiki kana

All too short is the spring.	Haru mijikashi
What matters	nani ni fumetsu no
If we are immortal,	inochi zo to
Said I, letting him palm	chikara aru chi o
My full-blooded breast.	te ni sagurasenu

Breaking the long-held conventions with her ardor and poetic genius, she created *tanka* possessed of curious beauty, enwrapping awkward expressions or even grammatical errors in a sensuous veil of mysticism.

Under the soft skin,	Yawahada no
The blood is hot.	atsuki chishio ni
Never trying even to feel it,	fure mo mide
Aren't you missing something,	sabishikarazu ya
Master, who teaches the Way?	michi o toku kimi

Bracing my breasts,	Chibusa osae
I undid the curtain of mystery	shinbi no tobari
With a flick of my toes.	so to kerinu
Deep is the crimson	koko naru hana no
Of the blossom within.	kurenai zo koki

Midaregami created enthusiastic women followers, liberating them from the yoke of feudal morality that had long bound them. Akiko's poetry made women aware of their own mind and body, and taught them self-assurance. It gave *tanka* a renewed life and a solid footing in modern Japanese literature. More than thirty years after the sensational debut of *Modaregami,* Akiko wrote in her complete *tanka* collection:

My poems have no relation to the contemporary *tanka* conventions. Some critics say that my *tanka* are romantic. I think that they are just guessing; they probably have not read all of my *tanka.* My poems are expressions of my blood and sweat *jikkan* that I gained from complex experiences in real life.

Kimi shinitamau koto nakare (Die Not, My Brother, 1904), *shi.* Akiko's free verse tended to be rather prosaic presentation of opinions that she "really felt (*jikkan-shita*)." When she was in a somber mood about her *jikkan,* she chose the *shi* form, often rendering it in modern vernacular, the language she did not use in her *tanka.* That was the case even with this most renowned of her *shi,* exhorting a soldier not to waste his life on the battlefield for the emperor, "who is a benevolent man,'' and reminding the young man of his family tradition and merchant ethics. Akiko published this bold poem in *Myōjō* during the Russo-Japanese War (1904–05), addressing it to her younger brother, who had been conscripted and sent to the front. She was censured as being unpatriotic and even treasonous by such literary critics as Ōmachi Keigetsu (1869–1925) and Hirotsu Ryūrō (1861–1928). Her explanation was that her poem had nothing to do with antiwar ideology or socialism; what she found truly dangerous was the general trend to make light of death in the names of patriotism and the Imperial Rescript on Education, basically a Confucian tract that the government propagated as the absolute code of ethics. The initial value of this verse was that the poet asserted her opinion truthfully and without fear. Hindsight proved its historical significance.

BIBLIOGRAPHY

Translations

''My Brother, You Must Not Die,'' ''First Labor Pains.'' Tr. Laurel Rasplica Rodd. In *Longman Anthology of World Literature by Women, 1875–1975.* New York: Longman, 1989, 189–90.
The Poetry of Yosano Akiko. Tr. Heihachiro H. Honda. Tokyo: Hokuseido Press, 1957.
''The Poetry of Yosano Akiko.'' Tr. Ikuko Atsumi and Graeme Wilson. *Japan Quarterly,* 21, 2.
Tangled Hair. Tr. Shiho Sakanishi. Boston: Marshall Jones, 1935.
Tangled Hair. Tr. Seishi Shinoda and Sanford Goldstein. Lafayette, IN: Purdue University Press, 1971.
''Thirty-nine *Tanka.*'' Tr. Hiroaki Sato. In *From the Country of Eight Island.* New York: Doubleday, 1981.

Critical Works

Beichman, Janine. ''Yosano Akiko: The Early Years.'' *The Japan Quarterly.* (January–March 1990) and ''Yosano Akiko: Return to the Female.'' (April–June 1990).
Cranston, Edwin A. ''Young Akiko: The Literary Debut of Yosano Akiko (1878–1942).'' *Literature East and West* 19-1.
Journal of Association of Teachers of Japanese 25-1 (April 1991). A special issue on Yosano Akiko.
Keene, Donald. ''Tekkan, Akiko, and the *Myōjō* Poets.'' In *Dawn to the West: Poetry, Drama, Criticism.* New York; Holt, Rinehart and Winston, 1984.
Lyons, Phyllis. ''Yosano Akiko.'' In *Longman Anthology of World Literature by Women, 1857–1975.* New York: Longman, 1989, 187.
Rodd, Lauren Rasplica. ''Yosano Akiko and the Taisho Debate over the 'New Woman'.'' In *Recreating Japanese Women, 1600–1945,* ed. Gail Lee Bernstein. Berkeley: University of California Press, 1991.
Ueda, Makoto. ''Yosano Akiko.'' In *Modern Japanese Poets and the Nature of Literature.* Stanford: Stanford University Press, 1983.

James R. MORITA

YOSHIDA Tomoko (1934–), novelist, essayist. Real name: Kira Tomoko (Mrs. Kira Jin'ichi); née Kanie Tomoko.

Life: Yoshida Tomoko, born February 6, 1934, in Hamamatsu, is the eldest daughter of a career military man. Between 1940 and 1945, as an elementary school pupil, she attended six different schools, one of which was in Manchuria and another in Sakhalin, as her father moved from one military base to another. When the war ended in 1945, Yoshida and her family were in Toyohara (present-day Yuzhno Sakhalinsk), Sakhalin. Her father was taken away by the Soviet troops, and what became of him is still unknown. In 1947, the mother took the family back to her parents' home in Shizuoka prefecture.

In 1952 Yoshida became a student of Nagoya Municipal Two-Year Junior College for Women in economics. She spent most of her time, however, participating in the activities of the drama club, inaugurating a drama journal and writing plays. Upon graduation in 1954, giving up the plan to go on to Aichi University due to financial difficulties, Yoshida looked in vain for a position in local journalism. With no other prospect, she took a teaching job at a high school in the city of Hamamatsu. Two years later, she married. In 1959 she won the prize of Y50,000 (equivalent to an average monthly salary of working women at the time) for a drama she wrote for a local radio station. She then quit teaching in order to concentrate on writing.

Yoshida traveled to Sakhalin in 1972, Soviet Russia in 1974 as a member of the Writers' Delegation, Korea in 1978, and Singapore and Taipei in 1979. She now lives in Hamamatsu with her husband.

Career: Yoshida Tomoko won prizes for a story and for a play she entered in a contest sponsored by the Shizuoka prefectural government in 1961. Two years later, she established a *dōjin zasshi* (literary coterie magazine), *Gomu* (Gum), with her husband, Kira Jinichi (b. 1926), and a friend, and started writing stories for it. In 1966 and 1968, two of her pieces were reprinted in the leading literary magazines, *Shinchō* and *Bungakukai,* and awarded the Dōjin Zasshi Prizes. She was asked to publish several stories in these magazines as a professional writer. In the spring of 1970 *Mumyō chōya* (The Long Night of Illusion), a novella, was awarded the Akutagawa Prize, the most prestigious prize for young writers of serious fiction.

Yoshida has written more than seventy short stories, some fifty essays, and seven novellas and novels. One novella, *Manshū wa shiranai* (I Don't Care About Manchuria, 1983), won the 1983 Prize for Women Writers.

There are two major themes in Yoshida's works. The first, confrontation with the past, investigates what actually happened in Manchuria and China during the Japanese invasion between 1931 and 1945. The stories are based on the fading memory of her own experiences as a little girl. The constant effort to delve into the dubious past, by the narrator-heroine of such works as "Chichi no haka" (Father's Grave, 1975) and *I Don't Care About Manchuria,* stems from the author's personal desire to know the past. The image of her father is blurred since she was separated from him at a young age. She suffers from the negative image of his career as a military man in Manchuria, which is created, by and large, by the hearsay from the survivors of the war. At the same time, however, his disappearance in Sakhalin accounts for the warm, compassionate feeling invoked toward the composite figure she calls "father."

While the author's personal interest fuels that confrontation with the past, the reader comes to realize that Yoshida is recounting her wartime experiences for all the Japanese people. The confrontation with the past is of vital importance. As shown in her works, the future can be built only after the past is confronted, evaluated, and interpreted. The narrator-heroine in Yoshida's works survives the confrontation and looks toward the future at the end of the story.

The second major theme in Yoshida's literature is an identity crisis. It seems to derive from the feeling that one is somehow at the wrong place at the wrong time. It may take the form of disorientation or alienation. Again it is possible to trace this literary tendency back to Tomoko's personal experience in Manchuria. In addition to about one million soldiers, a large number of civilian Japanese emigrated there after the Manchurian incident in 1931. Some were associated with government-supported industries; others were simple-minded, impoverished farmers who dreamed of the instant success suggested by the government's publicity. Manchuria perished at the end of World War II. With some incredible hardship the survivors of the Soviet takeover made their way back to Japan. *Manshū-gaeri* (returnees from Manchuria) refers to the social misfits who have somewhat suspicious pasts in Manchuria. Again and again, Yoshida incorporates such characters in stories.

This sense of estrangement and alienation points to madness. Some bizarre notions are expounded, often in a self-contained dream world. For example, human existence is unreal until it is turned into a form of material. Like the "temple" in *The Long Night of Illusion,* a thing becomes the symbol of real human existence. Murder turns a human being into a material existence. Murder is more like a dream, without a sense of reality and, therefore, without a sense of committing a crime.

The narrative form in many of her works is "synchronic." The incidents or episodes are not arranged according to the natural flow of time, but they are told in an order synchronous to the nature of incidents or thoughts or even to a place. In this kind of narrative, the time sequence between episodes is totally ignored, and it is extremely difficult to pin down what happened in what order. Yoshida's works require active participation on the side of the reader.

The Long Night of Illusion, for example, owes its success to her skillful use of synchronic narration. The author accumulates the maddening experiences of a peculiarly introverted young woman who is obsessed by the idea of turning a human being into a material object. The synchronic treatment minimizes the element of time. Unlike the diachronic arrangement, in the synchronic narrative there is very little element of casuality resulting from the passage of time. The author, however, successfully combines the timeless synchronism with a dramatic climax, a form of casuality, as in the dreamlike description of the burning of the temple.

In his posthumously published critique, *Shōsetsu towa nanika?* (What Is the Novel? Shinchōsha, 1972, 113–14), novelist Mishima Yukio (1925–70) comments on this work. He says that even though a novel must have a plot structure inevitable for the theme, one dealing with madness might as well do without a dramatic climax because madness has no structural inevitability. Yoshida's burning of the temple is, therefore, an unnatural dramatic climax, which the novel would be better off without.

Unlike the similar lending of Mishima's *Kinkakuji* (The Temple of the Golden Pavilion, 1956), however, the burning of the temple in Yoshida's story is only a scene envisioned by the crazed mind of the heroine. There is no clear causality, concerning the plot, as Mishima interprets, but it is causality necessary for accelerating the heroine's desperation.

Another area of Yoshida's modernist experiment in narrative technique is the combination of shifting of viewpoints and blending of time sequences. In "Kazoku danran" (Happiness of a Family Life, 1984), the past incidents in Manchuria are told by the husband, and the episodes in the narrative present are presented through the wife's eyes. With this technique, the story is remarkably well written.

Even though not as prolific as most Japanese writers, Yoshida Tomoko is clearly one of the few modernist women writers in contemporary Japanese literature. In the works associated with her Manchurian experience, she examines and interprets the meanings of the Japanese war there and explores the relevancy of those experiences to the present and future of people's life in Asia. In another category, she continues to deal with madness caused by estrangement, alienation, and anxiety of old age. Here Yoshida resorts extensively to the synchronic narration in order to create a bizarre and disturbing atmosphere.

Major Works: "Chichi no haka" (Father's Grave, 1975), short story. The narrator's father was taken away by Soviet troops when the war ended, and he has been declared dead by the Japanese government. The narrator comes to realize that most of what she thinks are fond memories are actually the result of her romanticizing his image, not as a real person but as somebody called "father." Gradually, the reality of the past emerges out of the mist of time. As she relentlessly scrutinizes what she remembers, she not only sees a fat and arrogant middle-aged man, but also recognizes that she has inherited many of his undesirable idiosyncracies. At a gathering of returnees from northern Manchuria, she is told how mean and unfeeling the father was.

The narrator's understanding of the past comes very close to what it actually was; but she still feels pity for her father, who probably died miserably, and does not want to accept the fact of his death. On the other hand, the mother erects a grave for the family, which the narrator thought indicates her acceptance of his death. Later, however, the mother obstinately refuses to have a monk perform a service for the husband, saying that the grave is for herself and not for the husband. The twist is the narrator's misunderstanding of the mother, who looked as if she did not care about her missing husband at all. Actually she would not recognize the past and, therefore, would not accept her husband's death.

"Nōten *huai la*" (The Crushed Brains, 1977), short story. This piece is unusual for a female author. Its main characters, two males, Mokuhei and Nakase, spent a good many years together in Manchuria, looking askance at each other, cheating each other, and double-crossing each other. After they returned to Japan separately, there have been only sporadic contacts. When Mokuhei hears a rumor that Nakase is dying of cancer, he starts to recall all the atrocities they committed together during the war, for which he has no guilt feelings. Mokuhei's value judgment is so narrowly focused on his queasy relationship with Nakase that the only thing he has in mind is to get even with the dying Nakase for the sake of his self-image. Mokuhei has nothing but the past and sees Nakase as the reflection of his own existence. The author created Mokuhei in order to examine the past shared by so many Japanese but now fading in memory, as represented by the dying Nakase.

"Kikoku" (Homecoming, 1982), short story. This is a powerful story about a so-called Japanese orphan brought back from China after nearly forty years and the farm family that has accepted her. In 1978, the People's Republic of China and Japan signed the Chino-Japanese Friendship Peace Treaty. Under this treaty, both governments worked together in the ensuing years to locate Japanese "orphans" in China and send them back to Japan. Japanese orphans were the children left in China by their parents on their extremely difficult and chaotic exodus right after Japan's surrender in 1945. When the governments started to look for them, they were already middle-aged, acculturated into Chinese society, and had completely forgotten their mother tongue. Often such items as old discolored pictures of Japanese families they found in their wallets made them believe that their parents were Japanese. Invited by the Japanese government, they have come to Japan in several groups of one hundred to two hundred over the last ten years. Television and newspapers are instrumental in disseminating information nationwide concerning individual cases. There have been many happy reunions.

In Yoshida's "Homecoming," however, the reunion is very uncomfortable, to say the least, and the story ends in the returnee's death. The entire village makes much commotion at the news that the long-lost Tsuneko is coming back to her Aunt Nobu. Tsuneko turns out to be a stout, unfriendly woman who looks like a man. She does not understand a single word of Japanese, and communication becomes a major problem immediately after the translator left her. Tsuneko herself, it seems, does not understand why she is staying with this Japanese family. In spite of the efforts on the part of Nobu and her family to make her feel at home, Tsuneko disappears from the house, probably frightened by the sound of a helicopter spraying herbicide over the field, and is found dead in an old well.

What is represented by Tsuneko is the unreasonable, ugly scar made by the war; Tsuneko's experience in wartime is reenacted in this peaceful Japanese village. Her raison d'être is not established either in China then or in Japan now; she cannot make herself understood; cultural differences stand between society and herself; and the helicopter reminds her of an airplane that attacked the refugees in China. Also, the hard feeling created by the fact that her parents abandoned her cannot be easily forgotten, even though the parents themselves are now long dead. An old man of the village blurts out, "Tsuneko would have been better off, perhaps, if she had not come back to Japan." Then, what does it mean to be Japanese or, for that matter, to be a citizen of any country? The story, albeit short, asks many questions.

Manshū wa shiranai (I Don't Care About Manchuria, 1983), novella. This same theme is more extensively treated in this novella. The heroine, Shizuka, is married and has a daughter. In spite of her seemingly tranquil life, she suffers from several gnawing obsessions. All stem from the bitter experiences in the past, especially from the fact that she was taken back to Japan from Manchuria by an unknown woman and that she was raised by her aunt. The author explores all sorts of psychological ramifications of being a returnee from Manchuria, not having any verifiable family history. Her husband is indifferent to her past and insensitive enough to say, "Your parents must have sold you to a Manchu." To locate someone who can verify her existence, she goes to see one of the "orphans" who, by looking at his picture in a newspaper, could be her brother, even though she does not know whether she had one. She is in a terrible dilemma: she wants to know the past very much, but at the same time, she is afraid of knowing it.

The key to the past is the woman who took the little Shizuka back to Japan. After a toilsome search, the heroine finally locates the woman, but only to find her too old to talk. She could not remember anything; she was delirious in a nursing home. The last scene, where Yoshida blends the past and present so skillfully, creates a kind of timeless sphere. Manchuria does not matter any more: the confrontation with the past makes the heroine realize what is more important in life.

"Kazoku danran" (Happiness of a Family Life, 1984), short story. The setting is somewhat similar to that of "Homecoming," but this is a happy-ending story. A Japanese woman, left in Manchuria as a child, is now back in Japan, with her Chinese husband and four children. She relates how difficult it is to readjust herself into Japanese society and to support her family as the sole breadwinner. The husband, nostalgic about his old way of life in China, is humiliated by the fact that the family's finances are partially supported by the wife's lover. The husband also tells of what happened in China. The narrative viewpoint alternates between the husband and wife, and the story gradually reveals the entire picture of the family life, with its present difficult situation and its miserable past. Yoshida's synchronic narrative and the shifting viewpoints are especially effective in portraying almost inhumane, atrocious incidents involving the family during the war in China and in the seemingly peaceful present-day Japan as well. No matter what, the author seems to say, life has to continue.

"Umibe no ie" (The House on the Beach, 1974), short story. This is in the category of "madness." A lonely, middle-aged woman receives an oblong package about a foot long. Its sponginess suggests it contains a severed part of a human body. The heroine may or may not know what it is but is afraid of this package and would not open it. She tries to get rid of it without being watched by others. As a final resort, she purchases a small refrigerator and keeps the package in it. A young boy, grandson of the old couple who are the owners of the house and live downstairs, watches her every move. The gray sands of the beach, the grumpy old couple, and the weird young boy all underscore the lonely, hopeless lot of this woman. Perhaps the package symbolizes life the woman does not know what to do with.

"Hito sute" (Dumping People, 1976), short story. Various kinds of human relationships, especially those between family members, are examined in terms of their psychological impacts after the relationships cease. The author's treatment can be best explained by the theory of Sartrean psychoanalysis: "Our self-consciousness exists only because it exists for another person. Thus self-consciousness is basically 'acknowledgement' by another person; and our being-for-others is a necessary condition for the development of our self-consciousness, our being-for-ourselves" (A. Stern, *Sartre: His Philosophy and Existential Psychoanalysis*). The heroine, for example, who verifies her existence by being watched by her husband, further develops an intriguing theory that people must have someone they can desert, in order to prove they are human. In other words, if you have no one you can abandon, that is, if you have no relationship, you cannot say you are human.

When the husband leaves the heroine for another woman, the husband turns into a dead bird in the heroine's mind, so that she does not have to wait for her husband any longer. Waiting for the husband who would not return makes her realize that she is "dumped." In her psyche, however, the husband and his father, who died long ago, keep coming back. To her, they are needed in order to acknowledge her raison d'être in her self-consciousness.

Gokurakusen no hitobito (The Passengers on the *Paradise*, 1984), novel. Each of the ten chapters, except for the first and last, is told by a passenger on this mysterious boat. It seems like a luxurious cruise boat, but its destination is unknown. In the first chapter the "I" narrator is getting on board with other passengers and tells of her experience with her roommates on the boat. From there on, however, major parts are stories told by various passengers about their past or stories of how they have ended up on board. Most are elderly people, and their stories center around the difficulties of old age. The last chapter seems to be the author's attempt to justify the novel, that is, to make its incidents plausible in a realistic sense.

The novel reminds one of Chaucer's *Canterbury Tales,* in which different individuals tell stories, each of which is not intrinsically linked to one another. The stories told on the *Paradise* are sometimes realistic but other times surrealistic: for example, one man believes he is feces moving around in somebody's bowels. A woman confesses that she killed her mother because the mother's vagina was prettier than hers. A man who thinks he was a rhinoceros in his previous incarnation reminisces about his old days. As time passes, food on board is getting scarce, and the symptoms of madness become prominent among the passengers. Some commit suicide by throwing themselves into the sea. One topic by a passenger is cannibalism, and then people find a man, who says he ate human flesh, caged in the bottom part of the boat. In the final stage, the passengers in extreme hunger see paradise in their illusion and end up in a grand orchestration of madness and mass suicides.

The "paradise" in the title is, of course, only rhetoric; in fact, it is "hell." Madness, however, reverses cognition, which in turn questions the ontological meanings of paradise or happiness. In the final analysis, this is a seaborne version of the old tradition of *obasute-yama* (the mountain where the old and useless were discarded), a tradition not practiced per se any longer. One can draw any number of metaphors and analogies concerning the ontological observations of human existence from these episodes told by the mostly old, useless, crazed narrators.

Meiō-sei (Pluto, 1978), novella. The heroine-narrator of this piece is a typical female character for Yoshida Tomoko: a lonely orphan at a marriageable age, raised by an unfeeling aunt, always victimized by the self-consciousness that she is at a place where she is not supposed to be. The incident central to the heroine's mental landscape is the police allegation of a murder charge against her. The heroine, Tatsuko, as a nurse at a mentally retarded children's institution, pushed a severely handicapped little girl off the precipice behind the institution and left her to die. The incident itself is described in such a dreamlike manner that the reader is not quite sure what actually happened or did not happen.

Since the nurse is very popular among the children, a citizens' group is organized to protect her from the police allegation. Tatsuko, extremely introverted, tries to refuse the offer of protection. It is too late, however, since the issue has already become a public matter. The allegation, together with the citizens' involvement, estranges the heroine even more from the administration of the institution and from the society it represents.

Tatsuko's haven seems to be the world of the retarded. She is comfortable in this closed haven because nobody here accuses her of anything. Besides, all the retarded children are alienated by their parents who put them in the institution, and then by society by the fact that they are institutionalized. A retarded mind, however, often closes, just as an insane mind does, as if it wishes to become a nonhuman entity. Since there is no human communication, there seems to be no possibility of any human relationship. To some extent, however, the heroine succeeds in communicating by writing down everything she wants to say to a seemingly deaf-mute youth who volunteers to work at the institution. At this point, the story takes a highly surrealistic turn. The young man starts to say that he is the reincarnation of the heroine's older sister, who died young. In spite of the heroine's desperate search, she could not verify the fact that she had a sister.

In many of the dreams the heroine has about her mother, a severely retarded girl begins to appear as her sister. In one of the dreams, Tatsuko kills this sister because she could not stand seeing her in a totally hopeless physical condition.

This incident, which probably never occurred, overlaps the alleged murder she is charged with, and in the heroine's mind, the two segments of time, the past and the narrative present, both dreamlike, are fused into a sort of timeless, shapeless world. Thus the crazed heroine is unable to verify her past or present.

Translated Works: Mumyō Chōya, (The Long Night of Illusion, 1970), novella. This Akutagawa Prize-winning story is probably prototypical of *Pluto* in its search for the true meaning of human existence. The ''I'' narrator, a divorcée about thirty, refers to the Buddhist temple ''Gohonzan'' as something immobile and solid, a thing of unalterable reality. She thinks to herself: ''All things are like a box of new crayons—they are packed neatly and orderly and can be grasped firmly in one hand. . . . For example, *time* was like that—also'' (59: All the quotations are from the translation by James Kirkup and Harvey Eiko; see *Bibliography*). A young acolyte, an extension of the temple, symbolizes such a neat and orderly existence for a while, but he becomes disqualified quickly when the heroine starts to have romantic dreams about him.

Right before an epileptic attack, Tamaye, the narrator's one and only girl-friend, displays a moment of ''immobile, solid, absolute reality'' on her face. When the heroine discovers this, she dodges, probably unconsciously trying to prolong that moment, Tamaye's falling body and lets her hit her face on the corner of the desk. This leaves a permanent scar on her forehead.

The theory that Yoshida Tomoko's characters often adhere to is that a dead body represents human existence more adequately because it is ''immobile, solid [for a while, at least], and unalterable.'' The obvious fallacy here is that the moment the body is dead, it is not human any longer. Overlooking this fallacy is, however, the very core of madness Yoshida deals with in this story. The final murder scene is so dreamlike it is difficult to determine whether it is supposed to be real or hallucinatory, but one thing clear is that it is the necessary step to make an unstable human being stable, that is, to turn a human being into a material object.

The heroine here is again estranged in the family and in society, having a strong feeling that she is at a wrong place. Her ex-husband had been missing for some time before she left his house in order to live with her mother. Later on he turns up in an insane asylum, while, at his mother's house, his old mad dog is lying half-dead, unable to die. The sense of desperation seems to derive from the fact that one is an unstable being at a wrong place and that, because of this very premise, one cannot make oneself a solid being. In other words, because one is not really living, one cannot die. The narrator confesses: ''I had always believed that I would never die—that I was not worthy to die. It would be impossible for me to do a natural thing like that. I was simply marking time with this temporary life'' (67).

The Gohonzan temple attracts the heroine as something immobile and solid, but its gate refuses her. To be exact, the color red with which the gate is painted refuses her. For that matter, anything red, even such a thing as a red flower or a bonfire, excites her, assails her by an unpleasant, indescribable feeling, as though she were dragging something behind that she cannot cope with. The heroine identifies herself with this: *"Something that could not be coped with was really myself and the long uncertain road ahead of me"* (63). The dream in which the temple and naked men and women are set ablaze resembles a picture of the Buddhistic inferno. The author seems to suggest that only madness, since death does not avail, makes it possible to cope with the salvationless existence: *Mumyō chōya* (lit., unenlightened long night), used as the original title, is the Buddhistic term for ''Limbo.''

BIBLIOGRAPHY

''The Long Night of Illusion.'' Trans. James Kirkup and Harvey Eiko. *Japan Quarterly* 24.1 (1977): 57–95.

Sanroku YOSHIDA

CHRONOLOGY

NARA Period   710–94 (under imperial rule through the centralized government based in Japan's first permanent capital in Nara. Major literary works are imperial histories and *Manyōshū*, a poetry collection.)

HEIAN Period   794–1192 (ruled by court nobles under the Fujiwara regents)

ONO no Komachi	fl. 800s
ISE	ca. 875–no earlier than 938
FUJIWARA Michitsuna's Mother	ca. 936–95
SEI Shōnagon	965?–?
IZUMI SHIKIBU	ca. 974–1030?
MURASAKI Shikibu	ca. 978–ca. 1016
SUGAWARA Takasue's Daughter	ca. 1008–after 1059
SANUKI NO SUKE	1079?–after 1119
FUJIWARA Shunzei's Daughter	1171?–1252

KAMAKURA Period   1192–1333 (under warrior rule by the Kamakura shogunate through the Hōjō regents)

BEN NO NAISHI	1220?–1270?
ABUTSU-NI (Nun Abutsu)	1222?–1283
NAKATSUKASA no Naishi	fl. ca. 1250–92
JŪNII Tameko (Kyōgoku/Fujiwara Tameko)	ca. 1250–after 1315
GO-FUKAKUSA'IN Nijō (Lady Nijō)	after 1258?–1306
EIFUKU MON'IN (Dowager Empress Eifuku)	1271–1342

MUROMACHI Period   1336–1573 (ruled by warrior nobles under the Ashikaga shogunate based in Muromachi. Literary output consisted of plays for the male-only Noh theater, Chinese poems by Zen monks, and anonymous popular short stories known as *otogizōshi*.)

EDO Period   1600–1868 (in the feudal system centralized under the Tokugawa shogunate based in Edo—today's Tokyo. Commercial publishing flourished for the first time, but few literary works attributable to women exist.)

MEIJI Period   1868–1912 (the first modern period in Emperor Meiji's reign)

HIGUCHI Ichiyō	1872–96
YOSANO Akiko	1878–1942
TAMURA Toshiko	1884–1945
NOGAMI Yaeko	1885–1985
HIRATSUKA Raichō	1886–1971
OKAMOTO Kanoko	1889–1939
UNO Chiyo	1897–
MIYAMOTO Yuriko	1899–1951
TSUBOI Sakae	1899–1967
MORI Michiyo	1901–77
HAYASHI Fumiko	1903–51
ŌTA Yōko	1903–63
KŌDA Aya	1904–90
HIRABAYASHI Taiko	1905–72
ENCHI Fumiko	1905–86
TANAKA Sumie	1908–

TAISHŌ Period   1912–26 (in the reign of Emperor Taishō)

SHIBAKI Yoshiko	1914–91
WADA Natsuto (Natto)	1920–83
MIURA Ayako	1922–
SETOUCHI Harumi	1922–
YAMAZAKI Toyoko	1924–
HASHIDA Sugako	1925–

SHŌWA Period   1926–89 (in the reign of Emperor Shōwa—Hirohito)

HARADA Yasuko	1928–
MORI Reiko	1928–
TANABE Seiko	1928–
TSUMURA Setsuko	1928–
MUKŌDA Kuniko	1929–81

SAEGUSA Kazuko	1929–
HAYASHI Kyōko	1930–
KOMETANI Fumiko	1930–
ŌBA Minako	1930–
ARIYOSHI Sawako	1931–84
SHIRAISHI Kazuko	1931–
SONO Ayako	1931–
YOSHIDA Tomoko	1934–
KURAHASHI Yumiko	1935–
TOMIOKA Taeko	1935–
YAMAMOTO Michiko	1936–
MEIŌ Masako	1939–
MORI Yōko	1940–93
KANAI Mieko	1947–
UI Einjeru	1948–
YAMADA Eimi	1959–

HEISEI Period   1989– (in the reign of the current emperor)

BIBLIOGRAPHY

BIBLIOGRAPHICAL REFERENCES

Asian Literature in English, A Guide to Information Sources, comp. and ed. G. L. Anderson. Detroit: Gale Research, 1981.

Bibliography of Asian Studies, comp. and ed. Estrella Bryant, et al. New Haven, CT: Association of Asian Studies. Annual.

Contemporary Authors, ed. Anne Evory. Detroit: Gale Research, 1981.

Encyclopedia of World Literature in the Twentieth Century. 1982.

Hisamatsu, Sen'ichi, ed. *Biographical Dictionary of Japanese Literature.* Tokyo: International Society of Educational Information, 1973; reprint, New York: Kodansha International, 1982.

Japanese Women Writers in English Translation: An Annotated Bibliography. New York: Garland, 1989.

Kodansha Encyclopedia of Japan. Tokyo and New York: Kodansha International, 1985.

MLA International Bibliography of Books and Articles on the Modern Languages and Literatures. New York: MLA of America. Annual.

Modern Japanese Literature in Translation, A Bibliography, comp. International House of Japan Library. New York: Kodansha International, 1979.

Modern Japanese Literature in Western Translation, A Bibliography, comp. Fujino Yukio. Tokyo: International House of Japan, 1972.

Schierbeck, Sachiko Shibata. *Postwar Japanese Women Writers,* ed. Soren Egerod. Copenhagen: East Asian Institute, University of Copenhagen, 1989.

BACKGROUND

Aoki, Michiko Y., and Margaret B. Dardess. *As the Japanese See It: Past and Present.* Honolulu: University of Hawaii Press, 1981.

Bernstein, Gail Lee, ed. *Recreating Japanese Women, 1600–1945.* Berkeley: University of California Press, 1991.

Blacker, Carmen. *The Catalpa Bow*. London: George Allen and Unwin, 1975.

Hall, John Whitney. *Japan: From Prehistory to Modern Times*. Tokyo and Rutland, VT: Charles E. Tuttle, 1973.

Kuwahara, Takeo. *Japan and Western Civilization,* trans. Tsutomu Kano and Patricia Murray. Tokyo: University of Tokyo Press, 1983.

Libra, Takie Sugiyama. *Japanese Women*. Honolulu: University of Hawaii Press, 1984.

McDonald, Keiko. *Cinema East: A Critical Study of Major Japanese Films*. London and East Brunswick, NJ: Fairleigh Dickinson University Press, 1983.

Morris, Ivan. *The Nobility of Failure*. New York: Holt, Rinehart and Winston, 1975.

———. *The World of the Shining Prince*. New York: Alfred A. Knopf, 1964.

Mulhern, Chieko. *Heroic with Grace: Legendary Women of Japan*. Armonk, NY: M. E. Sharpe, 1991.

Plath, David W., ed. *Work in Lifecourse in Japan*. Albany: State University of New York Press, 1973.

Powell, Irena. *Writers and Society in Modern Japan*. New York: Kodansha International, 1983.

Reischauer, Edwin O. *Japan: The Story of a Nation*. Tokyo: Rutland, VT; Charles E. Tuttle, 1981.

Reischauer, Edwin O., and Albert Craig. *Japan: Tradition and Transformation*. Tokyo and Rutland, VT: Charles E. Tuttle, 1978.

Sansom, George. *The Western World and Japan*. Tokyo and Rutland, VT: Charles E. Tuttle, 1950.

LITERARY ANTHOLOGIES AND CRITICISMS

Algrin, Joanne P., ed. *Japanese Folk Literature*. New York: R. R. Bowker, 1982.

Aston, W. G. *A History of Japanese Literature*. Tokyo and Rutland, VT: Charles E. Tuttle, 1972.

Bownas, Geoffrey, and Anthony Thwaite. *The Penguin Book of Japanese Verse*. London: Penguin Books, 1964.

Brower, Robert, and Earl Miner. *Japanese Court Poetry*. Stanford, CA: Stanford University Press, 1961.

Carter, Steven D. *Traditional Japanese Poetry: An Anthology*. Stanford, CA: Stanford University Press, 1991.

Honda, H. H., trans. *The Shin Kokinshu*. Tokyo: Hokuseido Press, 1970.

Introduction to Classical Japanese Literature. Tokyo: Society for International Cultural Relations, 1948.

Introduction to Contemporary Japanese Literature 1902–1935, vols, 1 and 2. Tokyo: Society for International Cultural Relations, 1939.

Introduction to Contemporary Japanese Literature. Tokyo: Japan Cultural Society, 1972.

Introduction to Contemporary Japanese Literature: Synopses of Major Works 1956–1970. Tokyo: University of Tokyo Press, 1972.

Kato, Shuichi. *A History of Japanese Literature,* vol. 1 [The First Thousand Years], trans. David Chibbett. Tokyo and New York: Kodansha International, 1979.

———. *A History of Japanese Literature,* vol. 2 [The Years of Isolation], trans. Don Sanderson. Tokyo and New York: Kodansha International, 1983.

———. *A History of Japanese Literature,* vol. 3 [The Modern Years], trans. Don Sanderson. Tokyo and New York: Kodansha International, 1983.

Keene, Donald. *Dawn to the West: Japanese Literature of the Modern Era,* vol. 1 [fiction] and vol. 2 [poetry, drama, and criticism]. New York: Holt, Reinhart, and Winston, 1984.

———. *Japanese Literature: An Introduction for Western Readers.* Tokyo and Rutland, VT: Charles E. Tuttle, 1955.

———. *Landscapes and Portraits: Appreciation of Japanese Culture.* Tokyo and New York: Kodansha International, 1971.

———. *Modern Japanese Literature: An Anthology.* Tokyo and Rutland, VT: Charles E. Tuttle, 1957.

———. *Travelers of a Hundred Ages.* New York: Henry Holt, 1989.

———. *World Within Walls: Japanese Literature of the Pre-Modern Era, 1600–1867.* London: Secker Warburg, 1976.

Konishi, Jin'ichi. *A History of Japanese Literature,* vol. 1 [The Archaic and Ancient Ages], trans. Aileen Gatten and Nicholas Teele, ed. Earl Miner. Princeton, NJ: Princeton University Press, 1984.

———. *A History of Japanese Literature,* vol. 2. [The Early Middle Ages], trans. Aileen Gatten, ed. Earl Miner. Princeton, NJ: Princeton University Press, 1986.

———. *A History of Japanese Literature,* vol. 3 [The High Middle Ages], trans. Aileen Gatten and Mark Harbison, ed. Earl Miner. Princeton, NJ: Princeton University Press, 1991.

Lippit, Noriko. *Reality and Fiction in Modern Japanese Literature.* London: Macmillan Press, 1980.

McCullough, Helen. *Brocade by Night.* Stanford, CA: Stanford University Press, 1985.

———. *Classical Japanese Prose: An Anthology.* Stanford, CA: Stanford University Press, 1990.

———. *Kokin Wakashu: The First Imperial Anthology of Japanese Poetry.* Stanford, CA: Stanford University Press, 1985.

Marra, Michele. *The Aesthetics of Discontent: Politics and Reclusion in Medieval Japanese Literature.* Honolulu: University of Hawaii Press, 1991.

Minor, Earl. *An Introduction to Japanese Court Poetry.* Stanford, CA: Stanford University Press, 1968.

———. *Japanese Poetic Diaries.* Berkeley: University of California Press, 1969.

Minor, Earl, Hiroko Odagiri, and Robert E. Morrell. *The Princeton Companion to Classical Japanese Literature.* Princeton, NJ: Princeton University Press, 1985.

Miyoshi, Masao. *Accomplices of Silence.* Berkeley: University of California Press, 1974.

Okada, Richard. *Figures of Resistance: Language, Poetry and Narrating in ''The Tale of Genji'' and Other Mid-Heian Texts.* Durham, NC: Duke University Press, 1991.

Putzar, Edward. *Japanese Literature: A Historical Outline.* Tuscon: University of Arizona Press, 1973.

Rexroth, Kenneth. *One Hundred Poems from the Japanese.* New York: New Directions, 1964.

Rodd, Rasplica Laurel, with Mary Catherine Henkenius. *Kokinshu: Collection of Poems Ancient and Modern.* Princeton, NJ: Princeton University Press, 1984.

Saeki, Shoichi, ed. *The Shadow of Sunrise.* Tokyo: Kodansha International, 1966.

Sato, Hiroaki, and Burton Watson. *From the Country of Eight Islands.* New York: Anchor Books, 1981.

Swann, Thomas, and Kinya Tsuruta, eds. *Approaches to the Modern Japanese Short Stories.* Tokyo: Waseda University Press, 1982.

Synopses of Contemporary Japanese Literature. Tokyo: Society for International Cultural Relations, 1970.

Takeda, Katsuhiko, ed. *Essays on Japanese Literature.* Tokyo: Waseda University Press, 1977.

Ueda, Makoto. *Modern Japanese Poets and the Nature of Literature.* Stanford, CA: Stanford University Press, 1983.

LITERARY WORKS BY JAPANESE WOMEN IN COLLECTIONS

Birnbaum, Phyllis, trans. and ed. *Rabbits, Crabs, Etc.: Stories By Japanese Women.* Honolulu: University of Hawaii Press, 1983.

Gessel, Van C., and Tomone Matsumoto, eds. *The Showa Anthology: Modern Japanese Short Stories,* vol. 1 [1929–61] and vol. 2 [1961–84]. Tokyo and New York: Kodansha International, 1985.

Hibbett, Howard, ed. *Contemporary Japanese Literature.* Tokyo and Rutland, VT: Charles E. Tuttle, 1978.

Keene, Donald, ed. *An Anthology of Japanese Literature.* Tokyo and Rutland, VT: Charles E. Tuttle, 1957.

Lippit, Noriko, and Kyoko Selden, eds. *Stories by Contemporary Japanese Women.* Armonk, NY and London: M. E. Sharpe, 1983.

Longman Anthology of World Literature by Women, 1875–1975, ed. Marian Arkin and Barbara Schollar. New York and London: Longman, 1989.

Morris, Ivan, ed. *Modern Japanese Stories.* Tokyo and Rutland, VT: Charles E. Tuttle, 1962.

Rexroth, Kenneth, and Ikuko Atsumi, trans. *The Burning Heart: Women Poets of Japan.* New York: Seabury Press, 1977.

Tanaka, Yukiko, ed. *To Live and To Write: Selections by Japanese Women Writers 1913–1938.* Seattle: Seal Press, 1987.

————. *Unmapped Territories: New Women's Fictions from Japan.* Seattle: Women in Translation, 1991.

Tanaka, Yukiko, and Elizabeth Hanson, eds. *This Kind of Woman: Ten Stories by Japanese Women Writers, 1960–1976.* Stanford, CA: Stanford University Press, 1982.

Ueda, Makoto, ed. *The Mother of Dreams and Other Short Stories: Portrayals of Women in Modern Japanese Fiction.* Tokyo and New York: Kodansha International, 1986.

Vernon, Victoria V. *Daughters of the Moon: Wish, Will, and Social Constraint in Fiction by Modern Japanese Women.* Berkeley: Institute of East Asian Studies, University of California, 1988.

INDEX

Page numbers in **bold** indicate main entries

CONTRIBUTORS

MICHIKO AOKI, Assistant Professor of Japanese Language and History at Clark University, is author of *Izumo Fudoki* (1971), *Ancient Myths and Early History of Japan: A Cultural Foundation* (1974), and coeditor of *As the Japanese See It: A Sourcebook for the Study of Japanese Society* (1981). Her other published works include two chapters, "Empress Jingū: The Shamaness Ruler" and "Jitō Tennō: The Female Sovereign," in *Heroic with Grace: Legandary Women of Japan* (1991); three articles on Shibaki Yoshiko (1988–90); and three on Manyō poets (1978–90).

REBECCA L. COPELAND, Assistant Professor of Japanese Literature at Washington University, was born in Fukuoka, Japan, and reared in North Carolina. Her doctoral dissertation at Columbia University was on Uno Chiyo. Her recent publications include *The Sound of the Wind: The Life and Works of Uno Chiyo* (1991) and *The Story of a Single Woman,* a translation. Currently she is preparing a study of prewar Japanese women writers.

FELICE FISCHER, Curator of Japanese Art and Acting Curator of East Asian Art at the Philadelphia Museum of Art, wrote her doctoral dissertation at Columbia University on Ono no Komachi. Of her numerous publications, the latest include "Murasaki Shikibu: Court Lady" in *Heroic with Grace: Legendary Women of Japan* (1991) and *Meiji Painting* (1992). On a research fellowship from the Japan Society for the promotion of science study at the Tokyo National Museum, she organized exhibits of contemporary Japanese designs.

S. YUMIKO HULVEY, Assistant Professor of Japanese Language and Literature at the University of Florida, specializes in premodern Japanese women's literature of the Heian (794–1185) and Kamakura (1185–1333) periods. Relevant publications include her 1989 doctoral dissertation at the University of California-Berkeley on the study and partial translation of Ben no Naishi's 13th-century poetic memoir, ''The Nocturnal Muse: *Ben no Naishi Nikki*'' (1989); and ''Intertextuality and Narrative Subversion in the Works of Enchi Fumiko'' in *Japan in Traditional and Postmodern Perspectives* (forthcoming).

KEIKO McDONALD, Professor of Japanese Literature and Cinema at the University of Pittsburgh, is author of *Cinema East: A Critical Study of Major Japanese Films* (1983), *Mizoguchi* (1990), and *Japanese Classical Theater in Films* (forthcoming); and editor of *Ugetsu* (1991). She is currently writing a book on modern Japanese novels made into films.

PAUL McGRATH, Professor of English at Nagoya Gakuin University in Japan, published articles on myth and irony in the fiction of Mukherjee (1991), Atwood (1992), and the works of the American feminist philosopher Madonna Kolbenschlag (1993). His publications in comparative literature include articles on Ōoka Shōhei and William Golding and on women in the fiction of Endō Shūsaku. He is currently researching metaphor, culture, and freedom in Doris Lessing's works.

LIVIA MONNET, Associate Professor of Japanese and Comparative Literature at the University of Montreal, has taught at the University of Heidelberg, Germany, and at the University of Minnesota. Her 1989 translation of Ishimure Michiko's ''nonfiction novel'' *Paradise in the Sea of Sorrow* won a German Culture Center's Award. Her 1993 publications include ''The Politics of Miscegenation: Reading/Theorizing Fantasy in Tsushima Yūko's Story 'Fusehime''' and ''Connaissance Dé licieuse or the Science of Jealousy: Tsushima Yūko's Story 'Kikumushi.''' She is studying the intersections of gender and sexuality and the narratives of nationalism/national culture in contemporary Japanese fiction.

JAMES R. MORITA, Professor of Japanese Literature at Ohio State University, has published numerous works on Japanese and comparative literature both in Japan and the United States, including *Kaneko Mitsuharu* (1980) and articles on the writer Ōtsuka Kusuoko as a model in Natsume Sōseki's English poems.

CHIEKO I. MULHERN, Professor of Japanese and Comparative Literature at the University of Illinois until 1992, is currently teaching in Japan as Professor of Japanese Studies at Fukuoka Jogakuin College. Author of two historical novels (1985, 1992) and three books on comparative culture in Japanese as well as many scholarly works in English, she has recently published ''Japanese Harlequin Romances as Transcultural Woman's Fiction'' (1989), translated Arai Shinya's business novel, *Shoshaman: A Tale of Corporate Japan* (1991), and edited *Heroic with Grace: Legendary Women of Japan* (1991).

KYOKO NAGAMATSU, Assistant Professor of English at the Faculty of Policy Studies, Chūō University in Tokyo, has done graduate study in English literature at the University of Illinois. She has published five articles on Thomas

Hardy, including "*A Group of Noble Dames* as a Metafiction" (1988) and "'The Romantic Adventures of a Milkmaid' as an Anti-Romantic Novel" (1992), in addition to a joint translation (1991) of Robert Scholes's *The Protocols of Reading.* Following her 1992 article, "Fiction and Reality in *The Collector,*" she continues to study John Fowles.

H. RICHARD OKADA, Associate Professor of Japanese Literature at Princeton University, authored *Figures of Resistance: Language, Poetry and Narrating in the Tale of Genji and Other Mid-Heian Texts* (1991) in addition to many articles and literary critiques. He is currently working on the modern institutionalization of literature studies in Japan and on issues of gender and sexuality related to Heian texts and contemporary Japanese culture.

JOSEPH D. PARKER, Assistant Professor of Asian Studies at Pitzer College of the Claremont Colleges, has specialized in late Kamakura and early Muromachi religion, literature, and aesthetics, culminating in his 1989 doctoral dissertation at Harvard University, *Playful Nonduality: Japanese Zen Interpretations of Landscape Paintings from the Ōei Era (1394–1428).* Forthcoming are "The Hermit at Court: Reclusion in Early Fifteenth-Century Japanese Zen Buddhism" and papers on Nijō Yoshimoto's linked verse theory and Kyōgoku school women poets.

YOSHIKO YOKOCHI SAMUEL, Associate Professor of Japanese at Wesleyan University, has coedited *Literary Review: Japanese Writing, 1974–1984* (1987), which contains works by Kōno Taeko, Nogami Yaeko, Shinakawa Kazue, Shiraishi Kazuko, and Tsushima Yūko. She has presented papers on the images of Westerners in works by women writers (1986), as well as on the culture shock theme of Kometani Fumiko (1987), and organized a panel, "Modern Japanese Women Writers as Social Critics" (1991). Having launched courses on Japanese womanhood and women writers, she is researching Japanese writers dealing with minority issues, such as the award-winning woman novelist Sumii Sue (b. 1902).

EDITH LORRAINE SARRA, Assistant Professor of Japanese and Adjunct Assistant Professor of Women's Studies at Indiana University, has been applying modern Western critical theories in analyzing premodern Japanese literature, from her 1988 doctoral dissertation at Harvard University, "The Art of Remembrance, The Poetics of Destiny: Self-Writings by Three Women of Heian Japan," to a monograph she is writing on Heian court women's writings.

ANN SHERIF, Assistant Professor of Japanese Literature at Case Western Reserve University, has published articles on Kōda Aya as well as a translation and studies of Yoshimoto Banana's fiction, in addition to her 1990 doctoral dissertation at the University of Michigan, *A Dealer in Memories: The Works of Kōda Aya.*

NOBUKO TSUKUI, Professor of English at Kansai University of Foreign Studies, was Associate Professor of Literature at George Mason University till 1992.

Her numerous publications include a translation of Japanese contemporary stories, articles on tragic heroines of Chikamatsu plays, and works on atomic bomb literature. Forthcoming is her translation of Hotta Yoshie's novel *Judgment,* featuring the Enola Gay's crew and Hiroshima.

MICHIKO N. WILSON, Associate Professor of Japanese Literature and the Director of the Japanese Language Program at the University of Virginia, is author of *The Marginal World of Ōe Kenzaburō: A Study in Themes and Techniques* (1989), as well as entries on Ōe in *World Authors 1980–1985* and *Dictionary of Literary Biography: Modern Japanese Novelists II,* and is translator of Ōe's novel *The Pinchrunner Memorandum* (1995). In addition to publishing articles, "The Artist as Critic as Mishima" and "Three Portraits of Women in Mishima's Novels," she serves as a regular reviewer for *Choice* and wrote a review with gender study perspectives of *The Vision of Desire: Tanizaki's Fictional World* for the *Journal of Japanese Studies* (1993). She published a translation of Ōba Minako's *Birds Singing* in *Chicago Review* (1993), and is currently working on a book analyzing Ōba's narratives.

FUMIKO Y. YAMAMOTO, Associate Professor of East Asian Studies at the University of Kansas, has published on the fantastic elements and recurring images in Japanese literature, art, and culture. Her cross-disciplinary works include "Metamorphosis in Abe Kōbō's Works," "Two and a Half Worlds: Humans, Animals, and In-Between," "A Study of the Image of the Sun in Japanese Culture," and a collaborative book, *A Haiku Menagerie: Living Creatures in Poems and Prints* (1993).

SANROKU YOSHIDA, Professor of Comparative Literature and Culture at Kansai University of Foreign Studies in Japan, was Professor of Japanese at Miami University until 1993. With research interests ranging from traditional values in contemporary Japan to postwar Japanese literature, he has published extensively in both American and Japanese leading academic journals, such as *The Journal of Intercultural Studies, Nihon Bungaku,* and *Critique: Studies in Modern Fiction.* Particularly notable are his critique of Ōe Kenzaburō's fiction in *Comparative Literature Studies* (1988) and his dialogue with Ōe in *World Literature Today* (1989). The topics of numerous papers he presented encompass Kanai Mieko's novelistic techniques and the heroines of Chikamatsu plays.

ISBN 0-313-25486-9

EAN

9 780313 254864

HARDCOVER BAR CODE